Advances in Shipping Data Analysis and Modeling

Shipping flows – maritime 'footprints' – remain underexplored in the existing literature despite the crucial importance of freight transport for global trade and economic development. Additionally, decision-makers lack a comprehensive view on how shipping flows can be measured, analyzed, and mapped in order to support their policies and strategies. This interdisciplinary volume, drawing on an international cast-list of experts, explores a number of crucial issues in shipping data estimation, construction, collection, mining, analysis, visualization, and mapping.

Advances in Shipping Data Analysis and Modeling delivers several key messages. First, that in a world of just-in-time delivery and rapid freight transit, it is important to bear in mind the long-term roots of current trends as well as foreseeable future developments because shipping patterns exhibit recurrent, if not cyclical and path-dependent, dynamics. Second, shipping flows are currently often understood at the micro-level of intra-urban logistics delivery and at the national level using commodity flow analyses, but this volume emphasizes the need to expand the scale of analysis by offering new evidence on the changing distribution of global and international shipping flows based on actual data. Third, this multidisciplinary approach to shipping flows can shed important light on crucial issues that go beyond shipping itself including climate change, urban development, technological change, commodity specialization, digital humanities, navigation patterns, international trade, and regional growth.

Edited by experts in their field, this volume is of the upmost importance to those who study industrial economics, shipping industries, and economic and transport geography.

César Ducruet is the Research Director at the French National Centre for Scientific Research (CNRS) & UMR 8504 Géographie-cités laboratory, Paris, France. His work focuses on transport geography and network science with applications in Europe and Asia.

Routledge Studies in Transport Analysis

For a complete list of titles in this series, please visit www.routledge.com/Routledge-Studies-in-Transport-Analysis/book-series/RSTA

Advances in Shipping Data Analysis and Modeling

Tracking and Mapping Maritime
Flows in the Age of Big Data

**Edited by
César Ducruet**

LONDON AND NEW YORK

European Research Council
Established by the European Commission

First published 2018
by Routledge

2 Park Square, Milton Park, Abingdon, Oxfordshire OX14 4RN
52 Vanderbilt Avenue, New York, NY 10017

Routledge is an imprint of the Taylor & Francis Group, an informa business

First issued in paperback 2019

British Library Cataloguing-in-Publication Data
A catalogue record for this book is available from the British Library

Library of Congress Cataloging-in-Publication Data
Names: Ducruet, Cesar, editor.
Title: Advances in shipping data analysis and modeling : tracking and
    mapping maritime flows in the age of big data / edited by Cesar Ducruet.
Description: Abingdon, Oxon ; New York, NY : Routledge, 2018. |
    Includes index.
Identifiers: LCCN 2017033013 | ISBN 9781138280939 (hardback) |
    ISBN 9781315271446 (ebook)
Subjects: LCSH: Shipping. | Shipping—Mathematical models. |
    Shipping—Data processing.
Classification: LCC HE571 .A366 2018 | DDC 387.5—dc23
LC record available at https://lccn.loc.gov/2017033013

ISBN: 978-1-138-28093-9 (hbk)
ISBN: 978-0-367-88628-8 (pbk)

Typeset in Times New Roman
by Apex CoVantage, LLC

To Léonard, Hong, Tempête et Tonnerre

Contents

Figures

Tables

Contributors

César Ducruet, geographer, is the Research Director at the French National Centre for Scientific Research (CNRS) & UMR 8504 Géographie-cités laboratory, Paris, France. His work focuses on transport geography and network science with applications in Europe and Asia. Working as an expert for various organizations (OECD, World Bank, Korea Maritime Institute, JETRO), he is currently the Principal Investigator of the Word Seastems research project funded by the European Research Council (2013–2019).

Pablo Achurra-Gonzalez is a PhD researcher at the Port Operations Research and Technology Centre (PORTeC) within the Centre for Transport Studies, Imperial College London. His research focuses on the development of mathematical models for container cargo routing and resilience assessment of maritime shipping networks.

Alfredo Alessandrini is a Researcher at the Joint Research Centre (JRC – Ispra), where he has been since 2012. He is currently working as a Geographical Data Scientist in the Demography, Migration and Governance Unit, a European Commission Centre of expertise created to support EU policies related to migration and demography. Between 2012 and 2015, he was a postdoctoral researcher at the JRC Maritime Unit to support the implementation and monitoring of EU Maritime policies mainly through the application of data mining, statistics, and geospatial analysis techniques. Between 2011 and 2012, he was a postdoctoral researcher at the EMMAH INRA Unit (Avignon, France), where he was using remote-sensing techniques and field experimental surveys to model the functioning of the Mediterranean forest ecosystem. He holds a degree in forestry and environmental management from the University of Tuscia (2005) and received a PhD in forestry management in 2008.

Panagiotis Angeloudis is a Senior Lecturer in Transport Systems and Logistics in the Department of Civil & Environmental Engineering at Imperial College London. His research spans the areas of network optimisation, resilience, logistics, and maritime transport.

Pascal Arnaud is a Professor of Roman History at Lyon II University, with a specialization in philology, geography, and archaeology, following successive studies at the Ecole Normale Supérieure, Ecole Française de Rome, Sorbonne University; fellowships at the Institut Universitaire de France, Cincinnati (Tytus), and Berlin (Topoï); and professional experiences at Bordeaux and Nice universities. His research interests include the Roman and Parthian Near East, ancient geographical knowledge, mapping and sea-based descriptions (periploi), ancient seafaring, travel, and trade, and he has published ten books and 150 articles.

Jean-François Arvis is a Senior Transport Economist with the World Bank Group Trade and Competitiveness Global Practice, where he is in charge of the knowledge activities in the area of trade logistics. Prior to joining the Bank, he worked in various positions with the French Ministry of Economy and Industry (regulation, trade, finance and development aid). He is a graduate of the École Normale Supérieure in Paris and École Nationale Supérieure des Mines, and holds doctorate degrees in physics.

Françoise Bahoken, Geographer and Cartographer, is a Research Fellow (UMR 8504 Géographie-cités and IFSTTAR – AME – SPLOTT, Paris). Her research topic is the quantitative analysis of spatial mobilities by means of cartographic representations of origin/destination flow matrices.

David Barriopedro is a Senior Scientist at the Instituto de Geociencias (CSIC-UCM) in Madrid. He is interested in analyzing extremes from different perspectives, including their long-term variability and the forcing induced by the stratosphere-troposphere coupling. Currently, he is co-IP of the PALEOSTRAT project ((PALEOmodelization from a STRATospheric prespective).

Mia Bennett is a PhD candidate and National Science Foundation Graduate Research Fellow in the Department of Geography at UCLA. Her research examines critical and material practices of Arctic infrastructure and natural resource development by integrating fieldwork and remotely sensed data. Bennett received an MPhil in Polar Studies from the University of Cambridge, where she was a Gates Scholar.

Leah Beveridge is a Doctoral Student in the Interdisciplinary PhD Program at Dalhousie University, studying multi-stakeholder and cross-cultural governance for Arctic marine spaces in Canada, with a particular interest in marine navigation and vessel management and finding collaborative processes that support the environment and way of life in the North. She has a BSc in Biology and Aquatic Resources from St. Francis Xavier University, and a Master's in Marine Management from Dalhousie University.

Charles Bouveyron is a Professor of Statistics and head of the Department of Statistics at Université Paris Descartes, Paris, France. He received, in 2006, a PhD degree from Université Grenoble 1 (France) for his work on high-dimensional classification. From 2006–2007, he was a postdoctoral researcher in the Department of Mathematics and Statistics of Acadia University in Canada, where he worked on a statistical analysis of networks. Then, he was

Assistant Professor (2007–2012) and Associate Professor (2012–2013) at Université Paris 1 Panthéon-Sorbonne. His research interests include the classification of high-dimensional data, classification under uncertainty and weak supervision, adaptive and online learning, as well as network analysis. He has become a recognized expert in model-based classification (EM algorithm, latent variable, etc.) and analysis of high-dimensional data (latent subspaces, variable selection, intrinsic dimension estimation, etc.). In this context, he has developed several innovative clustering and classification methods and applied them with success in medical imaging, mass spectrometry, and chemometrics.

David Brosset is an Assistant Professor of computer science at the Naval Academy Research Institute in France. He holds a PhD degree in computer science from Arts et Métiers. His research is composed of two main topics. The first one deals with real problems containing spatial and temporal data. The second topic relies on cyber security, particularly of naval systems.

Mattia Bunel is a PhD student (IGN COGIT). He integrated the ERC World Seastems project as an Engineer in Humanities and Social Sciences in 2016. He is the lead developer of GeoSeastems, a website for interactive visualization of Lloyd's data.

Daniel Castillo is a postdoc researcher at the University of Las Palmas de Gran Canaria, Spain. He has published widely on West African seaport development, especially on patterns of long-term evolution of regional port systems and port communities and how seaborne trade influenced the economic development process in Africa.

Marcelo do Vale Cunha is a Professor at the IFBA (Federal Institute of Education, Science and Technology of Bahia). His research interests include complex systems, instrumentation in physics, social and complex networks, semantic networks, and time-variable graphs.

Sylvain Cuyala, Postdoctoral Research Fellow (CNRS, UMR 8504 Géographie-cités), received his PhD degree in Geography in 2014 from University of Paris 1. In the World Seastems project, he was in charge of data processing and analysis of interdependencies between urban development and the maritime network.

Ali El Hosni obtained his master's degree (2015) at Paris 4 Sorbonne University on port-city relationships. He was a team member of the ERC World Seastems project and is currently preparing a PhD project about city logistics.

Laurent Etienne is an Assistant Professor at University Francois Rabelais, Tours, France. He holds a PhD in Geomatics from the University of Brest (France) and an MSc in Computer Science from the University of Rennes (France). His main research interests include spatial data mining and knowledge discovery from moving objects databases, spatio-temporal patterns of mobile objects, outlier detection, and maritime geographic information systems (GIS).

Tim Evans is a Senior Lecturer at Imperial College London, where he is part of the Theoretical Physics research group but also a member of the cross-disciplinary Centre for Complexity Science and the Social and Cultural Analytics Lab.

Virginia Fernandez Arguedas received BS and MS degrees in Telecommunication Engineering from Universidad Autonoma de Madrid in 2008 and a Ph.D. in Electronic Engineering from Queen Mary University of London (QMUL) in 2012. From 2008 to 2013, she was a Researcher with QMUL, working on image processing techniques for surveillance applications. From 2013 to 2016, she was a Scientific/Technical Project Officer with the European Commission, Joint Research Centre, where she was involved in maritime awareness through the analysis of satellite imagery and self-reporting positioning data. She is currently a Senior Image Processing Engineer with the Deimos-Elecnor Group. Her current research is focused on image processing, machine learning, and data mining for security applications. Furthermore, she has participated in several European projects and collaborations with the private sector related with multimedia data analysis and representation.

Claudio Ferrari is a Full Professor of Applied Economics at the University of Genoa, Italy. His scientific research is focused on transport economics, transport planning, and regional economics, namely with regard to ports and transport infrastructures. He is the author of several contributions published in academic journals and books.

Mélanie Fournier holds a PhD in Geography from Montpellier III University. Her research mainly focused on maritime surveillance and illegal trafficking. She is currently an Associate with NEXUS Coastal Resource Management Ltd., a Canada-based company.

María Jesús Freire-Seoane is an Economist at the Institute of Maritime Studies (University of A Coruña, Galicia, Spain), with a PhD in Economic Sciences. She works currently as a Professor of Applied Economics in the University of A Coruña. She has a wide path in maritime transportation research, with relevant contributions to the analysis of a port's foreland and hinterland. Since 2010, she has also been the co-director of the Spanish Government's MSc programme on Port Management and Multimodal Logistics.

David Gallego is an Associate Professor of Atmospheric Physics at the Universidad Pablo de Olavide in Seville (Spain). His research background focuses on understanding climate variability at different time scales. Currently, he is the PI of the project INCITE ('INstrumental Climatic Indexes. Application to the study of the monsoon-Mediterranean Teleconnection').

Ricardo García-Herrera is a Full Professor of Atmospheric Physics at the Universidad Complutense de Madrid and the Instituto de Geociencias (CSIC-UCM). His current research interests vary from the analysis of weather and climate research, to the use of documentary sources to characterize climate variability in the las 500 years. He is the author of more than 140 research papers.

Fernando I. González-Laxe is an Economist at the Institute of Maritime Studies (University of A Coruña, Galicia, Spain), PhD in Economic Sciences, and a professor and researcher of Applied Economics. He has been designated for many governance positions and institutions (president of the regional government, Spanish fisheries policies representative in the European Union, and director of Spanish Ports State Entity, among others). He's performed and published many studies related with port efficiency, port sustainability, and foreland-hinterland interactions.

Daniel J. Graham is a Professor of Statistical Modelling in the Department of Civil & Environmental Engineering at Imperial College London. His research includes work on various aspects of transport modelling and spatial statistical analysis.

Kateryna Grushevska is a Marine Insurance Broker at Proteus Risk Solutions based in Antwerp (Belgium), where she provides insurance and risk management services to ship owners and managers, port and terminal operators, multimodal operators, and other parties involved in shipping activities. Dr Grushevska acquired her doctoral degree at the University of Antwerp in 2016. She holds an MSc in Transport and Maritime Economics from ITMMA, as well as an MBA from Antwerp Management School. Her academic interests particularly focus on ports and logistics in the Black Sea region.

Carlos Guedes Soares is a Professor of Naval Architecture and Marine Engineering and is heading CENTEC, the Centre for Marine Technology and Ocean Engineering, of Instituto Superior Tecnico, University of Lisbon, which is recognized and funded by the Portuguese Foundation for Science and Technology. He received his MS degree from the Massachusetts Institute of Technology, USA, in 1976; a PhD from the Norwegian Institute of Science and Technology, University of Trondheim, Norway, in 1984; and a Doctor of Science degree from the Technical University of Lisbon, Lisbon, Portugal, in 1991.

David Guerrero is a Researcher on the freight transportation team (Ame-Splott) of the French Institute of Science and Technology for Transport, Development and Networks (Ifsttar). He received a PhD in economic geography in 2010 at the University Paris 7. His field of interest is the geography of freight transport, especially topics pertaining to ports, maritime transport, and global supply chains.

Jan Hoffmann is Chief of UNCTAD's Trade Logistics Branch and responsible for UNCTAD's research, teaching, and technical assistance programmes in international transport and trade facilitation. Publications of the branch include the "Review of Maritime Transport", "Maritime Country Profiles", and the "Liner Shipping Connectivity Index". Previously, he worked for ECLAC (1997–2003), IMO (1995–1996) and a family shipping company. He is president of the International Association of Maritime Economists; he has studied in Germany, the UK, and Spain and holds a PhD in Economics from the University of Hamburg.

Yan Hong obtained her MSc from the School of Urban & Regional Science, East China Normal University, China. She was a visiting student at the French National Centre for Scientific Research (CNRS), Paris, France.

Hidekazu Itoh is a Professor of Marketing with the School of Business Administration and an Adjunct Professor of Technology Management, Institute of Business and Accounting (IBA), Professional Graduate School, Kwansei Gakuin University, Japan.

Atiya Habeeb Kidwai is a Geographer and Regional Planner. She has served as a Professor at Jawaharlal Nehru University and at the School of Planning and Architecture, New Delhi. Her research interests are urban history and maritime studies.

Carl Knappett teaches in the Department of the History of Art at the University of Toronto, where he holds the Walter Graham/Homer Thompson Chair in Aegean Prehistory. He works on the societies of the Bronze Age Aegean, focusing in particular on questions of urbanism, artistic expression, and interaction, for which he employs network concepts. Recent publications include *Human Mobility and Technological Transfer in the Prehistoric Mediterranean*, coedited with Evangelia Kiriatzi, and the edited volume *Network Analysis in Archaeology: New Approaches to Regional Interaction*.

Claire Lagesse has been an Associate Professor (UMR 6049 ThéMa, CNRS / University of Burgundy – Franche-Comté) since 2016, after a post-doctoral fellowship in the World Seastems project. She holds a PhD degree in Physics (University Paris-Diderot, Sorbonne Paris-Cité), and an Engineering degree in Geomatics (from ENSG, French National Higher School of Geomatics). Her research work deals with the analysis of complex networks embedded in space, providing methodologies to characterize spatial graphs, with applications to road and maritime networks.

Pierre Latouche is an Associate Professor in Applied Mathematics, SAMM Laboratory, Université Paris 1 Panthéon-Sorbonne, France.

Damien Le Guyader is a Coastal and Marine Geographer specializing in spatial data analysis and computing. Based at Terra Maris, his research interests include human activities interaction, human impact mapping, and movement analysis in the context of Marine Spatial Planning.

Sung-Woo Lee is the Director General at Port & Logistics Div., Korea Maritime Institute. His research fields are multi-logistics in Northeast Asia and Arctic shipping.

Yushan Lin is a Postgraduate Student at the School of Urban & Regional Science, East China Normal University, China, and she is interested in port geography.

Bruno Marnot is a Professor in Modern History at the University of La Rochelle, a member of the Center for Research in International and Atlantic History, and an assistant director of the Interest Scientific Group in Maritime History and Sciences.

Javier Mellado is a PhD student at the Instituto Dom Luiz, Universidade de Lisboa. His research is focused on the use of logbooks to characterize climate variability in the last centuries in the Euro Atlantic area.

Eric Mermet is a CNRS Research Engineer appointed to Social Mathematic Analysis Centres and the Institute of Complex Systems. He works at the EHESS GIS Platform, where he has been developing organization components. He also manages several projects in interaction with 60 researchers, as well as technical components by implementing different tools (software, plugins, WebGIS, websites). He was trained as a science engineer and focused his interest on robotics and intelligent systems. He earned a PhD in computer science and geomatics for the structural analysis of transport networks.

Amin Mobasheri is a research scientist in the field of GIScience. He received his BSc in computer software engineering and MSc in geo-informatics. Currently he is a doctoral candidate at GIScience research group of Heidelberg University. His research interests include GIS and spatial planning, geospatial data quality and analysis, and open geospatial data and services.

Ali Niknejad is a Research Associate in the Department of Civil & Environmental Engineering at Imperial College London. His research involves maritime transport, network optimisation, risk management, and relevant decision support tools.

Theo Notteboom is a Professor in Port and Maritime Economics and Management. His work is widely cited. He is a Chair Professor at Ghent University in Belgium and a Research Professor at the China Institute of FTZ Supply Chain of Shanghai Maritime University. He also is a part-time Professor at the University of Antwerp and the Antwerp Maritime Academy in Belgium. He is co-director of www.porteconomics.eu, a knowledge dissemination platform on port studies. He is an immediate Past President (2010–2014) and Council Member of International Association of Maritime Economists (IAME).

Carlos Pais Montes is a Mathematician at the Institute of Maritime Studies (University of A Coruña, Galicia, Spain), with a PhD in maritime transport, and is working currently as a database programmer and researcher in the mentioned university. He received an MSc in Port Management, and since 2010, he's developed multidisciplinary approaches in different fields of applied economics.

Ronald Pelot is a Professor in the Department of Industrial Engineering at Dalhousie University. In 1997, he founded the Maritime Activity and Risk Investigation Network (MARIN) at Dalhousie. Since then, his team has developed new software tools and analysis methods applied to maritime safety (accidents), marine spills risks, and emergency response planning.

Hernane Borges de Barros Pereira is currently a Professor at the State University of Bahia and at the University Center SENAI CIMATEC. Professor Pereira's main interests in the fields of science, information technology, and innovation lie in the areas of network theory through computer modeling techniques.

Séléna Petit, Geomatic Engineer, holds a Master's degree in Cartography (University of Paris 1). She worked on the development of an online platform for the visualization and analysis of maritime networks.

Cyril Ray is an Associate Professor in Computer Sciences, MOTIM Group, Ecole Navale, Brest, France.

Ray Rivers is an Emeritus Professor and Distinguished Research Fellow in Theoretical Physics and a member of the Centre for Complexity Science at Imperial College London. His interests include non-equilibrium behaviour of quantum systems and of social networks, particularly proto-historic maritime networks and city-state formation.

Stanislas Roussin is the Director of SERIC in South Korea, graduated with a degree in geo-economy, and is a Senior Researcher at ASEM Institute for International Relations, Seoul, South Korea.

Carlos César Ribeiro Santos is an Assistant Professor and coordinator of graduate and postgraduate courses at the University Center SENAI CIMATEC. His research interests include complex systems, social and complex networks, logistics, maritime networks, time-variable graphs, and production management.

Tiago A. Santos graduated with a degree in Naval Architecture and Marine Engineering in 1995 from Instituto Superior Técnico (IST), University of Lisbon, Portugal, and obtained a PhD degree in 2007 at IST. Currently, he is an assistant professor at IST and a researcher at the Centre for Marine Technology and Ocean Engineering (CENTEC) in the field of Maritime Transportation, Ports, and Logistics.

Guoqiang Shen is a Full Professor of Regional and City Planning at the University of Oklahoma, USA. He is interested in urban, regional, and global freight transportation models and logistics management.

Brian Slack is Distinguished Professor Emeritus at Concordia University, Montreal. He holds degrees from the London School of Economics and McGill University, as well as an honorary doctorate from the University of Le Havre. In a career spanning more than 40 years his research has focused on ports, shipping and intermodal transport. In recent years his work has dealt with a range of issues related to scale, from small ports, family firms in container shipping, mega ships, and the need to consider individual terminals rather than the port as a whole. He continues to be engaged in extensive consultancies.

Mark Stoddard is a PhD student in the Department of Industrial Engineering at Dalhousie University. As a member of the Maritime Activity and Risk Investigation Network (MARIN) at Dalhousie, his research has focused on the development of new computational methods and analytical processes to support Arctic maritime risk assessment.

Alessio Tei is a Lecturer in Maritime Economics at Newcastle University, United Kingdom. His scientific research is focused on port economics, shipping regulation, transport planning, and regional development. He is the author of several contributions published in academic journals and books and a member of the editorial board of the *International Journal of Transport Economics*.

Kenmei Tsubota is a Research Fellow at the Institute of Developing Economies, JETRO. His main research field is regional integration. His works have appeared in *Economic Modelling*, the *Journal of Economic Geography*, and others.

Michele Vespe is a Scientific Officer at the European Commission – Joint Research Centre (JRC), where he coordinates the activities of a research team in the fields of data analytics, big data, and knowledge discovery. Between 2011 and 2013, he was a Senior Scientist with the NATO Centre for Maritime Research and Experimentation, where he was involved in maritime data mining and anomaly detection. Prior to this, he was a Senior Engineer in the private sector and a Postdoctoral Researcher at the JRC. He holds a degree in telecommunications engineering from the University of Florence (2003) and a PhD in signal processing from University College London (2006).

Lie-Hui Wang is an Associate Professor at the School of Urban and Regional Science and a fellow at the Center for Modern Chinese City Studies of East China Normal University in Shanghai, China. He got a PhD degree in historical geography from Fudan University in 2008 and after that did a two-year postdoctoral research study about urban geography at East China Normal University. From September 2013 to 2014, he was a visiting scholar at ITMMA, University of Antwerp. He published a book (*Forming the New Hub: Geographical Study on the Relationship between Shanghai and Ningbo Ports, 1843–1941*) and more than 20 papers. Now he is taking charge of a project about the maritime network of East Asian container ports from 1996 to 2016 supported by the National Natural Science Foundation of China (NSFC).

Haoxiang Xia is a Professor of Management Science and Engineering in the Faculty of Management and Economics at Dalian University of Technology, China. In recent years, he has focused on the structure and dynamics of complex systems, including complex networks of road transportation and maritime shipping.

Mengqiao Xu is a Postdoctoral Research Fellow on the Faculty of Management and Economics at Dalian University of Technology, China. Her work focuses specifically on the structure of maritime transport and its impact on international trade and the wider economy.

Konstantinos Zavitsas is a Research Associate in Operations Research and Transport in the Centre for Transport Studies of Imperial College London. His research interests lie in efficient transport systems operations, management, and maintenance.

Alexander Zipf is Chair of GIScience (Geoinformatics) at Heidelberg University (Department of Geography) since late 2009. He is member of the Centre for Scientific Computing (IWR), the Heidelberg Center for Cultural Heritage and PI at the Heidelberg graduate school MathComp. He is also a founding member of the Heidelberg Center for the Environment (HCE).

Rawya Zreik is a Research Fellow in Applied Mathematics, SAMM Laboratory, Université Paris 1 Panthéon-Sorbonne, France.

Acknowledgements

The editor would like to thank Ms. Laura Johnson and Mr. Andy Humphries for their kind support, as well as Mrs. Penelope Eades for her revision of the language. The research leading to these results has received funding from the European Research Council under the European Union's Seventh Framework Programme (FP/2007–2013) / ERC Grant Agreement n. [313847] "World Seastems".

Foreword

Since antiquity, shipping networks have been consubstantial to international trade and the prosperity of nations. The position on global shipping networks influences integration in trade and value chains. Connectivity is a growing concern of developing countries. Policy makers look at investment and other means to increase their global connectivity.

The World Bank, among others, is called to support or advise interventions by developing economies. Obviously, not every country can become a global shipping hub. Most countries have few options to influence networks beyond their borders and shape their connectivity outcome. Assessing the economic value for the money invested is methodologically challenging and very contextual. Understanding the structure and evolution of shipping networks matters for decisions today.

This volume is a remarkable contribution to the yet-limited policy knowledge on global connectivity. The research looks how shipping networks evolve and support economic development. Insights come from case studies of many regions of the world at different time periods. The book builds on critical advances in the descriptions of connectivity and global economic networks. Automation and tracking technologies make available detailed data on shipping routes and ports: massive records of individual movements. Forensic data from old logs are also increasingly available. Techniques from the young science of complex networks bring qualitative and quantitative insights. An otherwise overwhelming trove of information becomes practical for decision making.

Network-based models of global networks have not only a strong explanatory power, but also make up a natural framework to develop cross-country indicators and assess the relationship between network connectivity and economic development. The World Bank and other organizations, such as the OECD and the UNCTAD, are adopting them in their data and advisory contributions. Applications targeted aviation, shipping, and trade networks. They are driven by the liaison with the academic community, which, including in this book, has been piloting new concepts.

The book should appeal not only to researchers, but also to professionals and decision makers. It will stimulate further ground-breaking research in this field of practical relevance.

Jean-François Arvis
Lead Economist
Trade Practice
The World Bank

1 Introduction

Taking the pulse of world trade and movement

César Ducruet

Water, water, everywhere, nor any drop to drink.
Samuel Taylor Coleridge (1798) *The Rime of the Ancient Mariner*

How many maps of worldwide maritime flows have been printed during the last century based on actual shipping data? The response is extraordinarily ridiculous: less than a dozen. This is particularly surprising, given that in the past and still nowadays, about 90% of global trade volumes travel via maritime transport, so being aware of the precise nature, volume, and distribution of shipping flows in the past, present, and future should be crucial for both researchers and practitioners. Like many other research fields, the digital revolution of the late 1990s and early 2000s had the effect of exponentially increasing our knowledge on all sorts of shipping flows, from the real-time position of individual ships to the macroscopic pattern of global maritime routes (Ducruet, 2016; Hoffmann et al., 2017).

Yet, maritime research is characterized by a number of weaknesses that the current book wishes to address. First, it remains a much fragmented area due to its strong disciplinary focus and limited dialogue among the different perspectives. There is an urgent need to explore and reveal existing and potential bridges between dispersed works on shipping, the backbone of the world economy (Lau et al., 2017). Second, shipping itself still occupies a relatively peripheral place in mainstream research, as it is often seen (and also advertised) as a technical, specialized subdiscipline of either history, economics, geography, management, or engineering (Ng et al., 2014). Links with wider themes and issues are underexplored to such an extent that huge efforts are needed to enhance the recognition of shipping in the academic and professional sphere. Third, and related with the former, the richness, diversity, and explanatory power of shipping data are underestimated – if not unknown – to a large audience, as well as the concepts, tools, and methods dedicated to analyze such information.

This volume proposes to tackle these three lacunae head on. The methodological entry based on shipping data is the common ground of all contributions, while those also question the nature of shipping itself as an industry but also as a vector and imprint of economic, cultural, and political interactions. How are shipping flows distributed and evolving across space and time? What do they tell us about the maritime and port sector and about the rest of the economy and society? This chapter aims to provide a comprehensive review of shipping data analyses and introduce the book's contents. The next section is a tentative categorization of existing works distinguishing amongst two sets of approaches, where shipping-specific issues are central or peripheral, depending on the research angle. Finally, we present the perspectives and structure of the book.

Shipping data as a source for shipping and non-shipping research

Shipping information serves industry-specific purposes for a better understanding of the port and maritime sector itself. This is the case of traffic engineering, operations research (Windeck, 2013; Teodorovic, 2015), transport economics and management (Stopford, 2009; Song and Panayides, 2015; Cullinane and Lee, 2015; Luo and Yip, 2017), but also transport geography, through its focus on shipping line strategies and port competition (Rodrigue et al., 2017). Shipping data are thus vital to improve our understanding of the maritime and ports sector and therefore can be regarded as a support to decision-making. From such a perspective and beyond the increasing capacity to measure and analyze vast amounts of information, shipping data help in quantifying performance and cost issues in the operation of ports and ocean carriers. The main question here is how shipping is physically organized and can make supply and value chains more efficient. Nevertheless, shipping information remains costly and mainly used within the shipping world for commercial or operational purposes. Despite the abundance of scholarly works on ports and maritime transport in social sciences, the immense majority are essentially qualitative or bypass the lack of data by applying different sorts of techniques based on aggregated figures, estimates, and simulation models without any data. Many maps that appear in handbooks about maritime geography, economics, and history are drawn by hand in a very unprecise manner.

Interestingly, early cartographies of actual shipping data were explicitly motivated by providing accurate pictures of the world economy, shipping being less considered as an industry than as a footprint of wider human interactions across the Earth, at a time when maritime transport overwhelmingly dominated human and cargo mobilities. The first-ever example was provided by the French geographer André Siegfried (1940) when mapping the exact position of British merchant vessels on the globe in the late 1930s. Soon after, the American geographer, Edward Ullman (1949), mapped US seaborne trade routes with the objective to "*take the pulse of world trade and movement*". Later on, another French geographer, Jacques Bertin (1973), mapped wheat maritime flows in medieval Europe, while the *Massachussets Transportation Systems Center* (McKenzie, 1975) proposed a density map of global vessel movements. During the next three decades, however, such analyses literally disappeared from academic and professional literature. Only a few examples could be found in other dark corners of the transport literature until the 2000s, mainly focusing on specific shipping companies or geographic areas (see Ducruet, 2016 for a review).

In line with the aforementioned digital revolution, an increasing volume of shipping data and variety of analytical tools emerged overtime. For instance, the online calculation of inter-port shipping distances and the visualization of these routes replaced the tedious reading of large printed tables (e.g., the *Lloyd's Maritime Atlas* since 1951), such as *Sea-distances* and *Searates*. Other systems even made it possible to measure the cost and impact of intermodal shipping (e.g., the *Geospatial Intermodal Freight Transportation* or GIFT model)[1] at present time or in antiquity.[2] In terms of shipping data visualization, one may mention an online route-planning algorithm to model maritime paths between harbors (Poncet-Montanges, 2013); a *European Atlas of the Seas*[3]; and the *OpenSeaMap*[4] and *Google Oceans*[5] projects and applications. The most common online products consist of so-called *heatmaps* of shipping data based on radar (Automated Identification System, AIS) or satellite information. A variety of those maps are freely accessible online: ship emissions in the Baltic Sea (Johansson and Jalkanen, 2016), cargo and tanker ship distribution (Nelson, 2011), and a cartography of the Anthropocene (Globaïa, 2016). Major providers of shipping data, such as *MarineTraffic* and *ExactEarth,* show the real-time position of individual ships or through density maps. *FleetMon Satellite AIS* and *FleetMon Explorer* propose dynamic visualizations seen from space,[6] while other projects visualize real-time ship trajectories to estimate carbon emissions[7] and shipping patterns in the Bering Sea.[8] Beyond sole visualization, shipping data analyses addressed various issues such as climate change, marine bioinvasions, anthropogenic noise monitoring and management, the diffusion of infectious diseases and terrorist attacks, environmental and health impacts, global urban accessibility, world regionalization, urban and regional dynamics, and the location of maritime advanced producer services, to name but a few (Ducruet, 2016).

A number of existing contributions adopted network analysis with the double objective and outcome to underline the mechanisms at stake behind the distribution of shipping flows and increase the visibility of maritime research in network science (Ducruet, 2015). In recent years, maritime network analysis kept growing apace with additional studies on network topology (Kang and Woo, 2017), robustness (Wang et al., 2016; Viljoen and Joubert, 2016), multiplexity and dynamics (Ducruet, 2017), and relationship with trade networks (Calatayud et al., 2017; Medda et al., 2017). In the field of digital humanities, several research projects excavated diverse historical records, such as *Navigocorpus* (1700–1821) (Marzagalli, 2015), the *Venice Atlas* (1283–1453) (Fournier, 2015), the *Climatological Database for the World's Oceans* (1750–1850),[9] the *Trans-Atlantic Slave Trade Database* (1500–1900),[10] the *Sound Toll Registers* (1497–1857),[11] the *Old Weather* project (Rogers, 2012), and the *World Seastems* project (1880–2009).[12] Other immense historical corpuses remain unexploited to date, such as the Suez Canal Archives[13] reviewing origin-destination ship flows since 1869, the archives of the *East Indian Trading Corporation* containing 25 million shipping records (1595–1795),[14] and North Atlantic migration flows (1815–1914).[15]

Measuring and visualizing shipping flows in the age of big data is thus everything but outdated, despite the recurrent belief that nowadays, our world only functions through virtual and digital flows (see also Antonopoulos, 2016). Immaterial connectivity is, of course, a huge challenge that goes along with physical, material movement as seen with the growing impact of e-commerce on global logistics and shipping (Wang, 2014). Our book is thus another push recalling the necessity not to ignore the material dimension of mobility and development as well as the particularity of actors and places (Hall and Hesse, 2012; Rodrigue et al., 2013; Urry et al., 2015; Laloë, 2016; Schwanen, 2016). The World Seastems project No. 313847, funded by the European Research Council (ERC) over the period 2013–2019, organized its second international workshop in April 2016 at the Paris Institute for Complex Systems (ISC-PIF). This event gathered no less than 72 participants coming from 14 different countries to offer a multidisciplinary perspective about the current theories, concepts, and data used to study shipping-related issues in the past and present, with a strong methodological focus. This book offers a vast array of models and methods borrowed from econometrics, computer science, engineering, spatial analysis, cartography, geomatics, statistics, mathematics, physics, geography, history, archaeology, and regional science. It also gathers, perhaps for the first time, studies of all kinds of shipping data, such as archaeological records, ancient texts, papyrus, and records, ship logbooks, vessel movements, customs data, liner shipping schedules, and AIS or radar data.

Perspectives and structure of the book

The remainder of the book is organized into three parts, each of them corresponding to a particular approach or type of shipping data analysis, namely connectivity analyses, geospatial analyses, and vulnerability analyses. The opening three chapters of Part 2 on connectivity all deal with winds but in very different ways. Ray Rivers et al. (Chapter 2) examine the likely effect of winds on shipping in ancient Greece to refine their spatial, inter-island network model nicely balanced between archaeological expertise and spatial analysis. Pascal Arnaud (Chapter 3), while acknowledging the influence of weather conditions on the design of Roman Empire shipping routes, provides a much-needed update on their underestimated geographic extent and economic importance, thereby questioning natural determinism and continental dominance. Part and parcel of dealing with shipping in ancient times is the lack of information on actual flows and routes, thus motivating the effort put into the reconstitution of these flows. In Chapter 4, Ricardo Garcia-Herrera et al. do the opposite: they improve our knowledge of past climatic conditions by providing us with a wealth of shipping data. Long years of tedious extraction of weather reports from no less than hundreds of thousands of *ship logbooks*, through international cooperation, provide the basis for the analysis, starting in the year 1662 cf. the CLIWOC project. Such efforts provide the missing link to better understanding climatic evolution up to the present day and into the future, while their shipping database could be useful for other scholarly purposes in maritime studies.

Another set of chapters addresses connectivity more contemporarily, with a strong emphasis on graph theory and complex networks. These contributions range from intra-national to transnational level in various regions of the world. The distribution of coastal shipping flows in Brazil in Chapter 7 (Carlos César Ribeiro Santos et al.) and the maritime forelands of Portuguese ports in Chapter 6 (Tiago Santos and Carlos Guedes-Soares) both address port selection, concentration, and competition dynamics on the dividing line between national policies and private interests. Geopolitical considerations as well as regional integration issues are discussed in the case of cross-strait shipping flows between China and Taiwan in Chapter 5 (Liehui Wang et al.), internal and external linkages of Black Sea ports in Chapter 8 (Kateryna Gruchevska et al.), and freight/people mobility across the vast Artic in Chapter 9 (Bennett), with a subtle mix between quantitative and qualitative elements.

Part 3 on geospatial analyses gives the utmost importance to state-of-the-art methodologies serving to map and analyze shipping data across space. Another goal is to shed new light on the influence of local factors (socio-economic, morphological) on the distribution of shipping flows. Guoqiang Shen (Chapter 10), through data mining and GIS methods, provides new 2D and 3D visualizations of U.S. maritime trade flows around the globe based on customs data as well as critical discussions about the vital link with China and the role of specific commodities, regions, cities, and ports. A common feature with Chapter 12 (Bunel et al.) involves assigning shipping flows to a virtual maritime grid, but for a fundamentally different purpose: the analysis of the transition from sail to steam shipping in the late 19th and early 20th centuries based on Lloyd's vessel movements. The main results provide the first-ever maps of global maritime trade at the time, a new tool for shipping data visualization and help underscoring the chapter's contribution to an important debate in maritime history about the diffusion pace and geography of steam navigation. Other chapters can be classified into two groups. One of these focuses on spatial patterns taking place in the ocean space. Based on their mastering of AIS data, Damien Le Guyader et al. (Chapter 15) delineate fishing zones in France, while Alfredo Alessandrini et al. (Chapter 11) determine clusters of ports and shipping spatial structures in the Mediterranean region. Another example by Amin Mobasheri et al. (Chapter 16), based on *Lloyd's List* magazines, visualizes ship-to-ship interaction in the mid-19th-century Atlantic Ocean to identify hot spots of legal, illegal, or unknown encounters. The second group of chapters is more concerned with the sea-land interface, namely how coastal or continental factors influence the nature, volume, and intensity of shipping flows. Besides descriptive statistical tools exploring the influence of numerous regional socio-economic indicators, spatial interaction models test the role (or friction) of distance. This distance is continental for David Guerrero et al. (Chapter 13) in their study of European hinterlands, and maritime for Ducruet et al. (Chapter 14) when analyzing interregional shipping flows among 40 countries of the developed and developing world. The first-ever analysis of the global system of cities through shipping data across the last 120 years is the major innovation of César Ducruet et al. (Chapter 17). Despite a fading overlap between port and urban hierarchies over time, the largest cities, in particular, inland urban areas with distant maritime access, continue to be the most dominant nodes due to their cargo traffic volume, value, and diversity and to their stronger centrality in the worldwide shipping network.

The last section, Part 4, mainly focuses on the concept of vulnerability, which is understood here as the risk of disruption for a given transport system and its capacity to absorb or resorb the given shock. A corollary to this would be to question the ability of shipping flows to follow or transgress geophysical, technical, geopolitical, and economical obstacles and opportunities to continue prospering and connecting the world. In turn, shipping data are often the only information capable of documenting wider changes outside the industry, such as the impact of territorial change. Chapter 18 by Pablo Achurra-Gonzalez et al. and Chapter 22 by Laurent Etienne et al. both address how the shipping industry may overcome or adapt to natural or economic constraints, using drastically different methodologies, such as GIS and econometrics. In Chapter 20, presented by Mengqiao Xu and Haoxiang Xia, the focus is more on the vulnerability of ports themselves, through the identification of China's largest external nodes. Chapters 19, 21, 23, and 24 deal with the impact of borders and political change on the evolution of shipping flows. Rawya Zreik et al. use network analysis and applied mathematics to detect how the USSR ego network was functionally and spatially organized before, during, and after the 1991 collapse. With different methods but still using vessel movement data, Daniel Castillo and César Ducruet focus on Northwest Africa and Tsubota et al. on the Indian Subcontinent to document the influence of decolonization on the evolution of port hierarchies and shipping patterns. The extreme example of North Korea provided by Ducruet et al. shows to what extent shipping data can make the world's most isolated country speak, insisting on the effects of a deepening crisis on the nature, volume, and spatial distribution of shipping flows. In all cases, shipping flows may reflect political evolutions, but the latter never fully determine the former. Economic and technological factors may take precedence over political structures and events, given their specific operational requirements and financial imperatives.

The likely conclusion of this book is that shipping data analysis and modeling might be an apparent drop in the current academic and business oceans; it has the potential to become a snag in the machine that could change our increasingly virtual vision of the world. As one of the few truly global footprints of human activity on Earth, shipping data have, more than for any other transport and communication mode, the unique potential to see the invisible, ephemeral, but long-standing maritime "*arteries delivering life just like large avenues feeding urban centers with diverse activities*" (Vigarié, 1968).

Acknowledgements

The research leading to these results has received funding from the European Research Council under the European Union's Seventh Framework Programme (FP/2007–2013) / ERC Grant Agreement n. [313847] "World Seastems".

Notes

1 www.rit.edu/gccis/lecdm/gift2.php
2 http://orbis.stanford.edu/orbis2012/
3 http://ec.europa.eu/maritimeaffairs/atlas/index_en.htm
4 http://openseamap.org/
5 www.youtube.com/watch?v=6ATw1f_qcEg
6 www.youtube.com/watch?v=gtffmxJmehs
7 www.shipmap.org/
8 www.gagecarto.com/#!portfolio-item/bearing-sea-shipping-routes-wildlife-conservation-society/
9 http://pendientedemigracion.ucm.es/info/cliwoc/
10 www.slavevoyages.org/
11 www.soundtoll.nl/index.php/en/over-het-project/str-online
12 www.world-seastems.cnrs.fr
13 www.youtube.com/watch?v=s5eKkEo5m88
14 www.monetdb.org/Downloads/VOC/background
15 www.business-of-migration.com/data/migration-flow-statistics/north-atlantic-1815–1914/

References

Antonopoulos, C.N. (2016) Why the new maritime geographies matter. *Geography Compass*, 10(8): 346–359.

Bertin, J. (1973) *Sémiologie Graphique*. Paris: Mouton-Gauthier-Villars.

Calatayud, A., Mangan, J., Palacin, R. (2017) Connectivity to international markets: A multi-layered network approach. *Journal of Transport Geography*, 61: 61–71.

Cullinane, K., Lee, P.T.W. (2015) *Dynamic Shipping and Port Development in the Globalized Economy: Applying Theory to Practice in Maritime Logistics*. New York: Palgrave Macmillan.

Ducruet, C. (2015) *Maritime Networks: Spatial Structures and Time Dynamics*. London and New York: Routledge Studies in Transport Analysis.

Ducruet, C. (2016) *The Spatiality of Maritime Networks: Maritime Contributions to the Analysis of Networks in Geography*. Paris: University of Paris I Panthéon-Sorbonne (in French).

Ducruet, C. (2017) Multilayer dynamics of complex spatial networks: The case of global maritime flows (1977–2008). *Journal of Transport Geography*, 60: 47–58.

Fournier, M. (2015) Venetian supremacy through time. A visualization experiment. In: Ducruet, C. (Ed.), *Maritime Networks: Spatial Structures and Time Dynamics*. London and New York: Routledge Studies in Transport Analysis, pp. 77–91.

Globaïa. (2016) *A Cartography of the Anthropocene*. Available at: http://globaia.org/portfolio/cartography-of-the-anthropocene/

Hall P.V., Hesse M. (2012) *Cities, Regions and Flows*. London & New York: Routledge.

Hoffmann, J., Wilmsmeier, G., Lun, Y.H.V. (2017) Connecting the world through global shipping networks. *Journal of Shipping and Trade*, 2(2). doi:10.1186/s41072-017-0020-z

Johansson, L., Jalkanen, J.P. (2016) *Baltic Sea Environment Fact Sheet 2016*. Available at: http://helcom.fi/baltic-sea-trends/environment-fact-sheets/maritime-activities/emissions-from-baltic-sea-shipping/

Kang, D.J., Woo, S.H. (2017) Liner shipping networks, port characteristics and the impact on port performance. *Maritime Economics and Logistics*, 19(2): 274–295.

Laloë, A.F. (2016) *The Geography of the Ocean: Knowing the Ocean as a Space*. London: Routledge.

Lau, Y.Y., Ducruet, C., Ng, A.K.Y., Fu, X. (2017) Across the waves: A bibliometric analysis of container shipping research since the 1960s. *Maritime Policy and Management*, 44(6): 667–684.

Luo, M., Yip, T.L. (2017) *The Economics of Maritime Transportation*. London & New York: Routledge .

Marzagalli, S. (2015) Navigocorpus database and eighteenth-century French world maritime networks. In: Ducruet, C. (Ed.), *Maritime Networks: Spatial Structures and Time Dynamics*. London and New York: Routledge Studies in Transport Analysis, pp. 92–111.

McKenzie, F.D. (1975) *Maritime Dynamic Traffic Generator. Volume III: Density Data on World Maps*. Working Paper No. AD-A012 498, Transportation Systems Center, Cambridge, MA.

Medda, F.R., Caravelli, F., Caschili, S., Wilson, A. (2017) Scenario analysis of shipping networks: Consolidation. In: Medda, F.R., Caravelli, F., Caschili, S., Wilson, A. (Eds.), *Collaborative Approach to Trade*. Basel, Switzerland : Springer, pp. 65–82.

Nelson, J. (2011) Shipping mix. IDV solutions. *UX.BLOG*. Available at: http://uxblog. idvsolutions.com/2011/10/shipping-mix.html

Ng, A.K.Y., Ducruet, C., Jacobs, W., Monios, J., Notteboom, T.E., Rodrigue, J.P., Slack, B., Tam, K.C., Wilmsmeier, G. (2014) Port geography at the crossroads with human geography: Between flows and spaces. *Journal of Transport Geography*, 41: 84–96.

Poncet-Montanges, A. (2013) *Final Report*, May 15. Available at: https://mappingeurope annavy.wordpress.com/2013/05/15/final-report/

Rodrigue, J.P., Comtois, C., Slack, B. (2017) *The Geography of Transport Systems*. New York: Routledge.

Rodrigue, J.P., Notteboom, T.E., Shaw, J. (2013) *The SAGE Handbook of Transport Studies*. London, UK: SAGE Publications.

Rogers, S. (2012) Britain's Royal Navy in the First World War – Animated. *The Guardian*, October 1. Available at: www.theguardian.com/news/datablog/interactive/2012/oct/01/ first-world-war-royal-navy-ships-mapped

Schwanen, T. (2016) Geographies of transport II: Reconciling the general and the particular. *Progress in Human Geography*, 41(3): 355–364.

Siegfried, A. (1940) *Suez, Panama et les Routes Maritimes Mondiales*. Paris: Armand Colin.

Song, D.W., Panayides, P. (2015) *Maritime Logistics: A Guide to Contemporary Shipping and Port Management*. London: Kogan Page.

Stopford, M. (2009) *Maritime Economics*. London: Routledge.

Teodorovic, D. (2015) *The Routledge Handbook of Transportation*. New York: Routledge.

Ullman, E.L. (1949) Mapping the world's ocean trade: A research proposal. *The Professional Geographer*, 1(2): 19–22.

Urry, J., Savitzky, S., Birtchnell, T. (2015) *Cargomobilities: Moving Materials in a Global Age*. London: Routledge.

Vigarié, A. (1968) *Géographie de la Circulation*. Paris: Genin.

Viljoen, N.M., Joubert, J.W. (2016) The vulnerability of the global container shipping network to targeted link disruption. *Physica A*, 462: 396–409.

Wang, J.J. (2014) Recent development of e-tailing and its logistics in China. In: Waters D., Rinsler S. (Eds.), *Global Logistics: New Directions in Supply Chain Management*, pp. 419–431, London, UK: Kogan Page.

Wang, N., Wu, N., Dong, L.L., Yan, H.K., Wu, D. (2016) A study of the temporal robustness of the growing global container-shipping network. *Nature Scientific Reports*, 6: 34217.

Windeck, V. (2013) *A Liner Shipping Network Design*. Basel, Switzerland: Springer.

Part I
Connectivity analyses

2 Winds and maritime linkages in ancient Greece

Ray Rivers, Tim Evans and Carl Knappett

For most of recorded history, the sail has been a major component in sea-borne propulsion, permitting the existence of large-scale maritime exchange. To create such connectivity is not plain sailing. Sailing vessels require usable winds, but winds show seasonal behaviour which restricts the periods in which safe journeys can be made. Furthermore, although the weather may permit safe travel, there can be regional patterns in which the prevailing winds are predominantly in the wrong direction. Even then, when the winds are congenial, they are often intermittent, restricting journeys.

In this chapter, we shall discuss ways in which wind can be incorporated into the modelling of sail-based maritime networks. Our motivation derives from our interest in a set of processes observed in the Aegean Middle Bronze Age and the early years of the Late Bronze Age (MBA–LBA) whereby the cultural, and perhaps the political influence of the Aegean's largest island to the south, Crete, is seen to spread quite widely across the islands of the Cyclades and Dodecanese, to coastal Anatolia and the Greek mainland. This phenomenon has been called 'Minoanisation', as Cretan culture in the Bronze Age is often referred to as 'Minoan' (see Broodbank, 2004; Knappett and Nikolakopoulou, 2005; Gorogianni et al., 2016). The significance of wind here is that Minoanisation was presumably sustained by a powerful exchange from south to north, whereas the winds predominantly blow from north to south in the summer sailing season with only intermittent relief (Lambrou-Phillipson, 1991). We would like to understand what effect, if any, these non-congenial winds have on the formation of links between Crete and the rest of the Aegean to its north. For example, one possibility is that adverse winds encourage short hops rather than longer journeys which, in turn, could lead to routes along the mainlands of the Peloponnese and the Dodecanese having advantages over more central and perhaps exposed travel.

Much has been written on the data modelling of maritime travel, particularly in the Mediterranean: for example, see Leidwanger (2013) and references within (see also Chapter 3 on Roman antiquity shipping routes). However, given the poverty of sailing data for Minoan networks, we are obliged to adopt theoretical network methods in which as a substitute for detailed datawe attempt to impute 'agency' to the function of the network. The implications of this agency can then be tested against the broad patterns of data that we possess (e.g., site ranking). In this, we are building upon our earlier modelling of the maritime Aegean (Knappett et al., 2008; Evans et al., 2009) in which wind direction was ignored. We are not alone in the theoretical modelling of maritime networks (e.g., see Hage and Harary, 1991; Terrell, 1986; Broodbank, 2000), but there is no theory modelling that addresses wind directly, and this chapter represents a first step in this direction. The methods that we shall adopt, of constrained entropy/gravity models, have greater generality than their use here (Wilson, 1967).

In practice, the inclusion of wind in the determination of maritime networks, even for as small a region as the South Aegean, is a huge programme and as proof of principle of our approach we have narrowed the problem to that of examining the effects of intermittent winds for a much reduced and highly idealised Aegean 'network', a simple archipelago within the Eastern Aegean (see Figure 2.1) running from Rhodes to Ikaria (adjacent to Samos). This was not chosen for its historical importance but because the sites, forming an evenly spaced chain, permit algebraic analytic solutions under simple assumptions regarding exchange which give us more insight than numerical simulations alone.

Experimental archaeology

A direct way to try to estimate the effects of varying winds on historic maritime travel has been to build replica vessels, insofar as that is possible, and sail them. The most relevant contemporary demonstrations of uncongenial Aegean winds have been seen in the voyages of the *Minoa* (2004) and *Kyrenia II* (1986/7). *Minoa*, a replica of a Minoan MBA galley sailed up the Western coasts from Crete to Athens for the 2004 Olympics. Even against low winds it took many days (Simandiraki, 2005); travelling only by day and close to the coast along the westerly route given in Figure 2.1, only ten sailing days were recorded in a four-week May/June period for a journey of 400 km. The crew experienced winds up to 3 Beaufort (7–10 knots or 13–20 km/hr). It was often necessary to supplement sails with oars. Average speeds were: oars 2.4 knots, oars and sail 3.2 knots. The open sea legs in particular were the most difficult. In a second northerly journey *Kyrenia II*, a replica of a fourth-century BC Hellenic merchant ship, sailed from Cyprus to Piraeus in April '87 (Katzev and Katzev, 1989). We have not shown that part of its westerly journey within the S Aegean from Rhodes along the E. Coast (along the first few steps of the sites highlighted in Figure 2.1 in the archipelago) before continuing NE towards Athens. The reason is that storm damage and long periods when the ship was becalmed made it unrepresentative in the context of our modelling. Of the 12 days in transit from Rhodes to Piraeus, seven days were available for sailing, but for 40% of that time, the Kyrenia was towed. For the total journey beginning from Cyprus, the average speed under sail was 2.85 knots.

What do we learn from these experiments? Certainly, they confirm that exchange from S to N is hampered by adverse winds, but some caution is needed. There is an inevitable discrepancy between ancient competency in maritime skills and the skills of contemporary mariners adjusting to earlier technology. This can be compensated for in part if current sailing practices are related to their historic predecessors, as demonstrated in the Polynesian journeys by Ben Finney in the *Nalehia* (Finney, 2004), but this is not the case in the Aegean. Of greater importance to our discussion is that these exercises are costly to organise and as a result travelling is limited. In the case of the Minoa, the single journey of Figure 2.1 is its only large-scale Aegean journey, and for the Kyrenia, there was only a round trip from Piraeus to Cyprus and back. However, let us suppose that we had crisscrossed the S Aegean in such replicas until the principal sea lanes between the main sites had been explored (as exemplified by our idealised route in the E. Aegean of Figure 2.1). If we were to enter all these routes on the Figure 2.1 map, it would look as if we had constructed an exchange network that takes wind into account. This would be misleading. A set of solo journeys does not constitute a network, except in the most trivial sense. If we were to change one route (e.g., whether to include the route of *Kyrenia II,* or not), there would be no need to adjust any of the other routes. As far as this 'network' of imaginary journeys is concerned, we have an aggregation of trips whose whole is no more than the sum of the parts. Since the characteristics of networks are such that we expect something new to

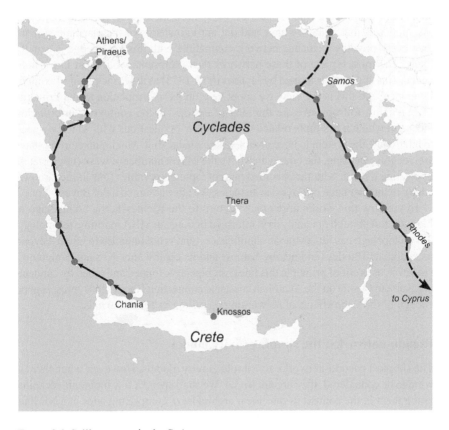

Figure 2.1 Sailing routes in the S. Aegean

come from putting sites and links together, what we would have here is a 'non-networking' pseudo-network.

This could give a distorted picture of the effects of wind. More simply, in such a modern pseudo-network replica, ships' captains are in control of their own travel and, to a large extent, can choose when to sail. Even when not, for exogenous reasons such as avoiding contemporary shipping or satisfying sponsors, erasing a single journey still has no effect on other putative journeys. However, if exchange is genuinely networked, captains have to abide by other, often endogenous, constraints.

Not that it is any easier to sail into the wind if you are free or contracted. However, these constraints, which are the basis of networking, might force owners/captains to sail in adverse conditions more than otherwise. For example, Lavrion (see Figure 2.1) was an important source of metallic ores and metals, which would have been in demand from MBA Crete, and journeys very like those of the Minoa would have taken place irrespective of the difficulty of travelling. Although there is no way that sailing vessels can achieve the timetabled regularity of contemporary container shipping, this suggests that networking can mitigate the consequences of adverse weather.

To see how this might be we attempt to quantify the question 'given what we know about sailing and wind what is the most likely network to have occurred?' The key assumption is that, once we have laid out our knowledge of the maritime system, then every possible exchange network compatible with this knowledge is equally likely. The most typical of these networks then represents what most likely happened. This approach is termed by Jaynes (1957, 1973) as the Principle of Maximum Ignorance, and this is the view we adopt here, in its reformulation as the Principle of Maximum Entropy. We are thinking of entropy in the context of information theory, in which it is simply related to the number of questions with which we need to interrogate the system to have complete knowledge of it. Maximum entropy states are, roughly speaking, the ones which have the largest number of ways (microstates) of creating a result with the specified macroscopic observables (our limited knowledge). In the language of Bayesian statistics, we have assumed a flat Bayesian prior.

To see how this works in practice we turn to the Rhodes-Ikaria archipelago in Figure 2.1. Although our analysis is informed by Aegean MBA maritime technology, this archipelago has little Minoan significance, (and is not intended to have), beyond its endpoints Rhodes (and nearby Samos) and its central sites Kos and Kalymnos. However, as proof of principle this linear archipelago, topped and tailed by connecting Ikaria to Çesme on the Anatolian coast and connecting Rhodes to Cyprus, is good enough to show the effects of networking on sailing in adverse winds.

Pseudo-networks: the simple gravity model

The simplest pseudo-networks are simple gravity models. However, when there is wind to be considered, they are not trivial. We shall spend a few moments recapitulating them in the context of our linear archipelago, comprising sites in a NE line. There is one site on each island which, for computational simplicity, we take to be *equally spaced* with separation d. In this Bayesian spirit, in the absence of further information we have taken the sites to be equal and that, in appropriate units, exchange between sites on different islands requires a 'cost'/effort that is related to the distance over which it occurs, equal for adjacent islands.

Although our archipelago has been chosen for proof of principle, its orientation fits in with our earlier statement that the prevailing winds are from top to bottom (Leidwanger, 2013). (To simplify terminology, we use N-S for the archipelago to mean NE-SW.) If this were a more realistic analysis, we would separate winds into those that help us go south or go north, that do neither or are non-existent. However, we will assume just two winds, the aforementioned dominant northerly and an intermittent southerly blowing from bottom to top. For the moment, we are ignoring the southern Cyprus connection and the northern Çesme connection. We are also ignoring currents.

Let us begin by assuming that winds are favourable and available, (i.e. there is no preferential direction up or down the archipelago). We begin by assuming that the *total* cost/effort that can be expended on exchange between all the islands is capped. This is natural, given that any society has limited resources. In reality, Bronze Age exchange took many forms; trade goods, barter, elite exchange, slaves, etc. For simplicity, hoping at best to capture something of the intensity of exchange, let F denote the flow between *adjacent* islands, flattened to a *single* number whose magnitude reflects this intensity, small when the exchange is weak, large when it is strong. Assuming nothing more, then making the best use of this limited knowledge (maximising the Shannon entropy of the exchange flows subject to this capping) gives the most likely value of F as proportional to $f = exp(-\beta c) < 1$ (Wilson, 1967), where c is the cost/effort of making one inter-island crossing, and β is a coefficient for converting cost/effort into distance. We take larger distances to require larger effort/cost.

It is this result – that exchange falls off with distance – which makes this a gravity model, in analogy with Newtonian gravity, whose force falls off with distance. What is particular to entropy maximisation is that exchange flow falls off *exponentially* with cost. We make the simple choice that cost/effort is proportional to the distance over which exchange occurs: $\beta c = d/D$, where d is the distance travelled, determined by geography, and D is related to the distance scale that can be achieved in a reasonable voyage, related to the available marine technology (e.g., oar, sail, rigging, anchors). We can think of f as proportional to the likelihood of making a single journey. For example, if, for the archipelago of Figure 2.1 we consider MBA vessels travelling effective typical inter-island separations of $d \approx 35km$ for an estimated $D \approx 50km$, then $f \approx 1/2$.

We shall only quote results here. For discussions of how to implement entropy maximisation, see Wilson (1967) and a recent article by us (Evans and Rivers, 2017), particularly its appendices for a discussion of D. Looking for the most likely outcome, the general result is that up to a common coefficient of proportionality the flow between nearest neighbours is f, to next-to-nearest neighbours f^2, to next-to-next to nearest f^3 and so on. That is, the flow F_p for P island hops (or a hop of P islands) is $F_p = Af^P$, *independent* of the position of the starting site on the line. This is very much like Renfrew's 'down-the-line' transmission (Renfrew, 1972: 466).

Including other links in the Aegean would not affect these results: we only have a pseudo-network.

Let us now introduce wind in as simple a way as possible, taking the exponential fall-off with cost into account. Sailing into an opposing wind introduces a frictional coefficient $\mu > 1$, replacing D by D/μ, whereby the flow from one island to the next *into* the wind is now proportional to $n = exp(-\mu d/D) < f$. We note that strong winds preventing sailing contribute towards this high frictional value. Similarly, sailing with a supporting wind introduces a coefficient $v < 1$, replacing D by D/v whereby the flow from one island to the next into the wind is proportional to $s = exp(-vd/D) > f$. We further assume that travelling south, running with the dominant northerly wind is no different from sailing north with one of the intermittent southerly winds.

Consider island-hopping north. Suppose intermittent helpful southerly winds occur with a frequency κ. (The choice $\kappa = \frac{1}{2}$ is equivalent to ignoring the effects of wind.) Then, the northern island-hopping flow (i.e. from an island to its nearest NE neighbour) is, with coefficient of proportionality A,

$$F_N = A f_N; \quad f_N = \kappa s + (1-\kappa)n.$$

Similarly, the single-hop southern flow is:

$$F_S = A f_S; \quad f_S = (1-\kappa)s + \kappa n.$$

These results are independent of the sites' positions, and we have not labelled them. This has not changed the simple gravity nature of the model. Deleting this island chain would not affect any other network flows that we might be considering. We see that, as κ increases, the ratio F_N/F_S increases also. The critical frequency of favourable winds κ_C needed for these intermittent beneficial winds to match the difficulty of sailing into adverse winds is small, satisfying

$$\kappa_C/(1-\kappa_C) = n/s.$$

We should stress that n/s is not the ratio of frictions into and against the wind (which occur in their exponents) but the ratio of likelihoods of making single journeys into and against the wind. Reasonable values of friction are $\mu \approx 2$, $v \approx \frac{1}{2}$ (Leidwanger, 2013) whereupon, for exemplary purposes, n and s are $n = \frac{1}{4}$, $s = \frac{3}{4}$, for which $\kappa_C = \frac{1}{4}$. Note that effects are exacerbated by longer sailing distances. This is already sufficient to show that, if favourable winds are infrequent (for example, one day a week) then northern sailing is island-hopping, whereas in southern sailing, the ships run with the wind on longer journeys, as we would expect.

Networking: generalised PPA with wind

An early example of network modelling in the Aegean was given by Broodbank (2000: 175–200) for the Early Bronze Age Cyclades using Proximal Point

Analysis (PPA). PPA assumes that any site only has the capacity to interact strongly with a (given) limited number of nearest neighbor sites and that those further away are ignored. This is equivalent to fixing the outflows of each site to a common value. There are many further examples of PPA in archaeological literature (for example, see Terrell, 1977, 1986), since it can be a ruler and compass exercise which, qualitatively, shows how important sites (as measured by inflows) are determined by their close neighbours. PPA differs from simple gravity models in that removing sites changes the behaviour of other sites by forcing them to interact with new neighbors. In that regard, it reflects a key attribute of trading communities.

We shall adopt the same local assumption that individual site outflows are fixed (and equal for equal sites), in addition to our global assumption that total cost/effort is fixed. Since we have a linear archipelago in which the direct exchange to sites that are not close is very small, this model is a generalisation of (directed) PPA in the presence of wind. Again, this can be couched in the language of maximum entropy. Northern and southern island-hops now have flows

$$F_N = A_N f_N; \quad F_S = A_S f_S$$

respectively, where f_N and f_S are as before, but A_N and A_S now depend on direction and on the *position* of the site along the chain.

For sites near the middle of the chain, where edge effects are small, we find, approximately, that $A_N \approx A_S \approx A$. That is, the north and south flows are as before. Our simple networking has no effect. The reason is straightforward. When summing over outflows from a central site so as to constrain them, the north-south symmetry means that, for each northern flow, there is a mirror southern flow related to it by the substitution $\kappa \leftrightarrow (1 - \kappa)$. The addition of these terms gives a κ-independent total, whence the result follows.

However, for Rhodes and Ikaria and their near neighbours at the end of the chain, for which there is no N-S symmetry in the flows about them, the networking does have an effect: in fact, two effects. Firstly, even in the absence of wind, networking increases the flow from the periphery to the centre and hence the northern flow from the south of the archipelago. Secondly, when there is wind the effects of favourable winds are enhanced. Our interest is in the latter. Thus, for our choices of $n = \frac{1}{4}$, $s = \frac{3}{4}$ simple algebra shows that the enhancement factor for northern travel from Rhodes by one hop due to networking (in comparison to a single northern hop in the centre of the archipelago) varies from an order of magnitude (approximately $s/[n(1-s)] \approx 10$ for the values above) to a significant multiple $1/s \approx 4$ as κ increases from zero to a value $1/s \approx 4$ at κ_c. Although half the enhancement is due to networking *per se*, half is due to beneficial winds, still a distinct advantage for a ship-owner. The enhancement for the second leg north (to Tilos) is less, but still noticeable. In Figure 2.1 we have not taken Rhodes and Ikaria as terminals, but as way-stations on a longer route from the E Mediterranean to Anatolia. However, the legs connecting this ten-island archipelago to the rest of the Aegean are long legs, of the sort that the *Minoa* found difficult and the lack of N-S symmetry in each case means that the contributions of these far-flung sites can be approximately ignored.

Simple as these results are, they have important implications. As we said, it is not that it is easier to sail into the wind if you are part of a trading network than it is for a solitary traveller. Rather, if there are constraints (in the case above: fixed resources to operate the network and fixed local outflows), then the most likely outcome is that you will adopt increased island hopping against the prevailing winds, even though superficially it looks like a costly way to proceed. In a technical sense of counting microstates (the networks of flows), the effect of imposing constraints gives rise to more network possibilities with flows against the wind than if those constraints were absent.

Networking the S. Aegean

The conclusion from this idealised network model that closer northern than southern neighbours to a site can lead to enhanced northerly travel with intermittent southerly winds is a plausible one. Besides, it suggests that the effects due to intermittent wind are even greater if sailing into the wind is more difficult because of longer journeys. This is particularly relevant to Minoan influence, where it is necessary to go north from Crete to the Cyclades. In Figure 2.1 we have shown Knossos, a major Minoan centre for trade and influence, and Thera, an important hub for its connectivity to the Cyclades.

Favourable winds from N Crete to Thera are infrequent (see Dorsey, 1990 for the man-powered flight of Daedalus 88 from Heraklion/Knossos to Santorini/Thera, more a case of experimental myth than archaeology). This approximately 100-km stretch would be a taxing journey for MBA sailing vessels, even with favourable winds. From our previous analysis, we would expect that the lack of N-S symmetry for N Cretan sites (i.e. E-W rather than southern links) means that Knossos could have stronger direct northern links to Thera in comparison to the more circuitous E-W island-hopping than anticipated. Also with a strong N-S imbalance, Thera could well have stronger links into the Cyclades. Unfortunately, the data are not good enough to confirm this, and this is a major problem. The situation could not be further removed from the extensive contemporary shipping data discussed elsewhere in this volume.

To do better requires a reanalysis both of the data and of the relevant models. Let us consider the data first. Specifically, our previous analysis shows that we cannot consider the Knossos-Thera link in isolation. Although we know enough about Aegean exchange to identify some significant sites and some strong linkages into the Cyclades (Knappett et al., 2008; Evans et al., 2009), our knowledge is very partial. Ideally, we would set up similarity measures for material culture (typically pottery) between sites and complement this with some understanding of the different roles of sites as producers and consumers. In very simple terms, one might well imagine that Cretan sites had greater agricultural potential than Cycladic sites, and that therefore Cretan sites could have exported grain, olive oil and/or wine to the Cyclades. This would seem to fit the qualitative evidence, which does seem very directional from Crete to the Cyclades in transport and storage jars, such as amphorae and pithoi. However, the Anatolian mainland would also presumably have had great agricultural potential, and yet we do not see quantities of such jars sourced there and making their way to the Cyclades or elsewhere. At best, the data show a heterogeneous resource environment – certainly for mineral resources and agricultural goods whose production and distribution is crucial to this period. That is enough to suggest that the seasonal nature of the latter means that there is a necessity for timely distribution.

Might the networking necessary to implement such distribution mitigate in part the unfavourable northerly winds in the sailing season? To see if this could be the case, we look for models whose coarse-grained exchange, again flattened to a single variable, is a fair match to the coarse-grained data that we do possess that reflects this exchange (e.g., that plays down the role of the Anatolian mainland) if we ignore wind. This requires us to go beyond the simply constrained outputs of our previous example of the linear archipelago to more sophisticated modelling which can incorporate winds specific to the Aegean MBA/early LBA. We have seen (Rivers et al., 2015) that a partial answer lies in the ease with which the marine technology of the time enables the necessary journeys to be made, as reflected in the ratio d/D. For our idealised archipelago, for which $d/D < 1$, our previous model is appropriate. However, for the S Aegean at large, this is not so. The 100-km separation between the Cretan and Theran coasts is replicated between the Cyclades and the two mainlands. The creation of a thriving maritime network arises once sailing vessels involved in substantial trade and exchange can travel that distance in a single journey (i.e. $d/D \approx 1$). Changing our perspective, rather than looking for the most likely outcome of constrained entropy, we look for the 'best' outcome, which enables us to incorporate this balance between 'geography' and 'technology' more transparently. At the moment, it is difficult to take this further. Our earlier model of stochastic 'rational choice' for MBA/early LBA Aegean exchange which implemented this balance, termed *ariadne* (Knappett et al., 2008; Evans et al., 2009), and which ignored wind, is already complicated, and the inclusion of even further wind-related parameters makes it difficult to reach robust conclusions. In particular, with so much E-W travel necessary, just a N-S separation of wind is too simple.

Rather, we believe that we should begin modestly, and the best way to proceed is through more idealised networks in which we can both test a different agency, including *ariadne,* as discussed in Rivers et al. (2015) and different wind modelling. This is under way. Although this exploration of agency seems at variance with our initial Bayesian entropic approach, there is, in many cases, an epistemic/ontic duality that enables us to replace statements about 'likelihood' with descriptions in terms of 'actors' which we shall not pursue here. For example, see Wilson (1970).

These idealisations should provide a more solid platform upon which to build a S Aegean–wide maritime network. Only then can we determine whether N winds had an effect on Minoanisation.

References

Broodbank, C. (2000) *An Island Archaeology of the Early Cyclades*. Cambridge: Cambridge University Press.

Broodbank, C. (2004) Minoanisation. *Proceedings of the Cambridge Philological Society*, 50(1): 46–91.

Dorsey, G. (1990) *The Fullness of Wings: The Making of a New Daedalus*. New York: Viking Press.

Evans, T., Knappett, C., Rivers, R. (2009) Using statistical physics to understand relational space: A case study from Mediterranean Prehistory. In: Lane, D., Pumain, D., van der Leeuw, S., West, G. (Eds.), *Complexity Perspectives in Innovation and Social Change*. Berlin: Springer Methodos Series, pp. 451–479.

Evans, T., Rivers, R. (2017, forthcoming) Was Thebes necessary? Contingency in spatial modelling. *Frontiers in Digital Humanities*. Available at: http://arxiv.org/abs/1611.07839

Finney, B. (2004) *Sailing in the Wake of the Ancestors: Reviving Polynesian Voyaging*. Honolulu, HI: Bishop Museum Press.

Gorogianni, E., Pavúk, P., Girella, L. (2016) *Beyond Thalassocracies: Understanding Processes of Minoanisation and Mycenaeanisation in the Aegean*. Oxford: Oxbow Books.

Hage, P., Harary, F. (1991) *Exchange in Oceania: A Graph Theoretic Analysis*. Oxford, UK: Clarendon Press.

Jaynes, E.T. (1957) Information theory and statistical mechanics. *Physical Review*, 106(4): 620–630.

Jaynes, E.T. (1973) The well-posed problem. *Foundations of Physics*, 3: 477–493.

Katzev, M., Katzev, S.W. (1989) Voyage of Kyrenia II. *INA Newsletter*, 16(1): 4–10.

Knappett, C., Evans, T., Rivers, R. (2008) Modelling maritime interaction in the Aegean Bronze Age. *Antiquity*, 82: 1009–1024.

Knappett, C., Nikolakopoulou, I. (2005) Exchange and affiliation networks in the MBA southern Aegean: Crete, Akrotiri and Miletus. In: Laffineur, R., Greco, E. (Eds.), *Emporia: Aegeans in East and West Mediterranean*. Liège: Aegaeum 25, pp. 175–184.

Lambrou-Phillipson, C. (1991) Seafaring in the Bronze Age Mediterranean: The parameters involved in maritime travel. In Laffineur R. and Basch L. (Eds.), *THALASSA: L'Egée préhistorique et la mer. Actes de la troisième Rencontre égéenne internationale de l'Université de Liège*. Liège: Aegaeum 7, pp. 11–20.

Leidwanger, J. (2013) Modeling distance with time in ancient Mediterranean seafaring: A GIS application for the interpretation of maritime connectivity. *Journal of Archaelogical Science*, 40: 3302–3308.

Renfrew, C. (1972) *The Emergence of Civilisation: The Cyclades and the Aegean in the Third Millennium BC*. London: Methuen and Co. Ltd.

Rivers, R., Evans, T., Knappett, C. (2015) From oar to sail: The role of technology and geography in the evolution of Bronze Age Mediterranean networks. In: Ducruet, C. (Ed.), *Maritime Networks: Spatial Structures and Time Dynamics*. London and New York: Routledge, pp. 63–76.

Simandiraki, A. (2005) Minoan archaeology in the Athens 2004 Olympic Games. *European Journal of Archaeology*, 8: 157–181.

Terrell, J. (1977) Language and material culture on the Sepik Coast of Papua New Guinea: Using social network analysis to simulate, graph, identify, and analyze social and cultural boundaries between communities. *The Journal of Island and Coastal Archaeology*, 5: 3–32.

Terrell, J. (1986) *Prehistory in the Pacific Islands*. Cambridge: Cambridge University Press.

Wilson, A. (1967) Statistical theory of spatial distribution models. *Transport Research*, 1(3): 253–269.

Wilson, A. (1970) *Entropy in Urban and Regional Modelling*. London: Pion.

3 Reconstituting the maritime routes of the Roman Empire

Pascal Arnaud

In a book published in 2005, I was able to propose the reconstruction of about 130 sea-routes of the Ancient Mediterranean (Figure 3.1). Such reconstructions are made possible thanks to what remains of ancient sailing directions, either preserved or quoted by early geographers, who used those directions as their main source for mapping (Rougé, 1952; Duncan-Jones, 1974, 1996; Morton, 2001; Arnaud, 2011a; Beresford, 2013; De Romanis, 2014). Combined with evidence from inscriptions on stone, papyri and archaeological remains, these data provide us with a bit more than a broad footage of the Ancient Sea Routes of the Mediterranean. This chapter is a valuable opportunity to discuss some of the conclusions derived from that work and to focus on a larger area including the Atlantic and the Indian Ocean. Contrary to the *communis opinio*, in fact, sailing the oceans was not terrifying to Roman sailors and merchants.

Routes and ports of the Mediterranean and the Black Sea

The figure that can be drawn is summarized in Figures 3.1 and 3.2. Since I started drawing these maps, the number of routes has increased significantly thanks to the huge amount of data gathered by Marinus of Tyre and used by Ptolemy in the second century CE, but the overall image does not change basically. It fits in perfectly with the prevailing winds and underlines the main patterns of ancient sea-routes in general and of Roman imperial sea-routes in particular. Neither sailors nor traders have ever liked sailing against the wind. Maritime trade is not a regatta. Where prevailing winds are sufficiently sustainable, they always become trade winds. This is especially the case in the Southwestern and Eastern Mediterranean in summer.

The first point to underline is the importance of deep-sea sailing (Cunchillos, 1998; Arnaud, 2011b). Modern scholarship has tended to restrict ancient sailing to coasting. This was absolutely not the case. As early as the rise of Greek civilization, Homer describes how Ulysses learns from Calypso how to build a new kind of boat, and how to sail offshore, day and night, following the stars, far away from any visible coast. Almost three centuries before the reign of the first Roman emperor, Eratosthenes, librarian at the Library of Alexandria, considered coasting an outdated way of seagoing. In a 'small' sea like the Mediterranean, most journeys

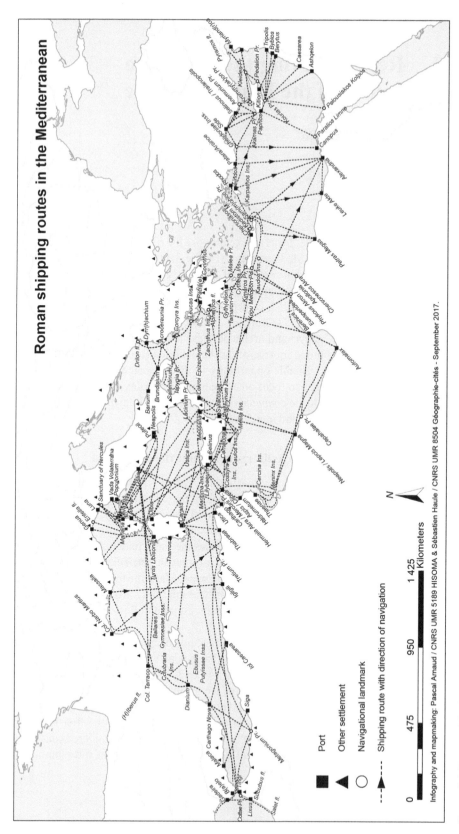

Figure 3.1 Roman shipping routes in the Mediterranean

Infography and mapmaking: Pascal Arnaud / CNRS UMR 5189 HISOMA & Sébastien Haule / CNRS UMR 8504 Géographie-cités - September 2017.

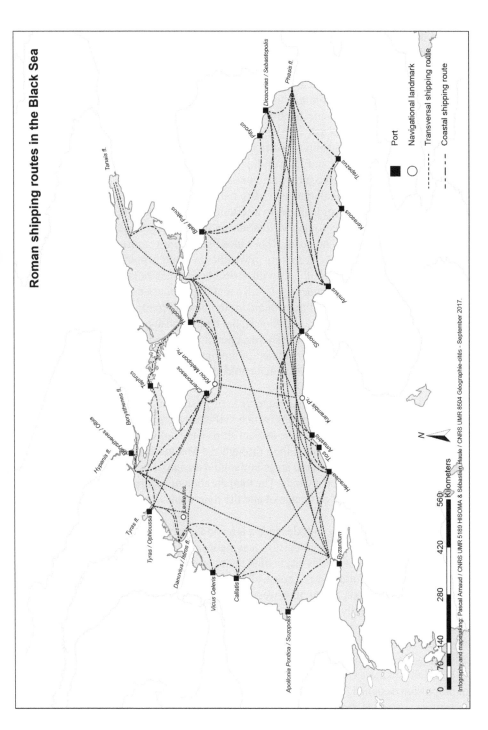

Figure 3.2 Roman shipping routes in the Black Sea

started and finished with some coasting, but coasting was not a constraint unless prevailing summer winds prevented a more direct route. It was normal to sail several days and nights out of sight of land: direct journeys of four or five days and nights were quite normal (between Gaul and Africa, Crete and Africa, Rhodes and Alexandria). A one-week return journey between the straits of Messina and Alexandria following the wind in a direct route was considered an amazing speed.

Prevailing winds, always more sustainable in summer, make sailing easier in one direction, but they become an obstacle for those sailing in the opposite direction (see also Chapter 2 for a discussion on the influence of winds on Greek antiquity shipping routes). They imposed different routes between A and B, on account of the direction of sailing and the conditions of wind and swell, and created a serious asymmetry of distances between the same points.

A second point is the importance of seasonality. Maritime trade followed seasonal routes and the cycle of journeys to a certain destination and back was widely framed by seasonality. The Roman Mediterranean was sailed in all seasons, though at different speeds, risks and costs. The 'closed sea' (*mare clausum*) was just a period of reduced traffic. The instability of weather in winter would lead to the use of smaller boats, galleys or sailboats with spritsails or lateen sails (whose use for commerce before the fifth century CE is still a matter of discussion), sailing at their own risk. The more stable conditions found in summer and coastal thermic breezes placed the peak of traffic in July and August, but spring and autumn offered a wide range of different predictable wind patterns, opening some routes and closing others every month. The 'big' merchantmen of the time, with a carrying capacity of 350 metric tons or more (up to 700 tons) could sail the Mediterranean, alongside thousands of smaller ships.

The main characteristic of sailing routes is their segmentation. This has been the case of almost all the periods during which sail and oars prevailed in maritime trade. Because they had no staysails, ancient ships were not very efficient against the wind. A common feature of sailing through the Mediterranean was therefore the necessity of stops in sheltered areas at the intersection of two meteorological systems, waiting for favorable winds. The total duration of a journey was therefore the sum of the segments it was made of and the time spent waiting at the junction of two segments.

The route between Rome and Alexandria is a good illustration of these variables. In July and August, the larger grain ships leaving Rome could follow a direct route once they left the straits of Messina behind them; on their way to Rome, the same grain ships usually followed the coast of Africa to Cyrenaica in spring, and in autumn the coast of Asia Minor; they were mainly exposed to the contrary Meltem in summer and generally had to winter en route. In the more favorable conditions (including any delays arising from corrupt officialdom or bureaucratic concerns), it was possible to make the round trip or part of the way over two winters by cleverly using seasonal characteristics to their advantage.

In addition to these considerations, different kinds of ships using different modes of propulsion designed for different sailing programs would follow different routes in various seasons at variable costs (Table 3.1). Before the first century BCE, the

Table 3.1 Transport costs by mode during the Roman antiquity

Mean	Ratio
Land (chariot)	42.3
Land (camel or donkey)	33.84
River-borne (upstream)	7.7
Laguna	5.7
River-borne (downstream)	3.84
Seaborne (Alexandria to Rome)	1

big ships of reference throughout the Mediterranean were thin, long merchant galleys (ratio 1:7) of poor stability and resistance in swell. Under the Roman Empire, the normal big merchantman was rather a 'round' sail ship (ratio: 1:3 or 1:4) with more ability on the open sea, more draft and less maneuverability close to the coast. Coasters and other ships that had to face poor wind conditions and make several shorter round trips along the same itinerary would often be small merchant galleys; these are almost all the ships entering a port on the Nile Delta in mid-August in a port register of the late second century CE (Papyrus Bingen 77).

One of the questions that may have arisen was: when routes were segmented, where was it economically more interesting to transship than to continue? A small number of entrepots seem to have organized most of the trade routes in an economic context where tramping seems to have been marginal with respect to the routine of sustainable relations between linked trade-places (Arnaud, 1992; Nieto-Prieto, 1997).

For a good understanding of the economic importance of sea-routes, both at long and short ranges, it is necessary to bear in mind the costs of seaborne transportation with respect to river-borne and road transportation. Although worthy of further detailed discussion, the table that can be drawn with the data gathered from Diocletian's price's edict shows the following figures,[1] giving us at least a broad idea of the ratio between the costs of all types of transportation.

This table illustrates the gap that existed between the costs of land- and water-borne transportation. Some cheaper sea-routes would even increase this gap. It also illustrates that sailing rivers upstream would be almost eight times more expensive than sailing the same distance at sea. This represents a strong incentive to revisiting the importance of the sea routes of the Atlantic, especially with respect to the Rhone-Saone, whose economic role is indeed indisputable, but may have been somewhat exaggerated.

The Atlantic: the Canaries to the Rhine

Modern scholarship is slowly revisiting the importance of the trade routes of the Atlantic (Uertega Artigas and Noain Maura, 2005; Schäfer, 2016). Yet, the ancient Romans themselves stressed the high level of maritime activity of this ocean, that was no longer the old mythic and frightening Okeanos, but the 'Outer Sea', accessible to a great deal of merchantmen.[2] To the southwest, clear traces of sustainable commerce with the Mediterranean area are known as far as the Canaries and Madeira (Figure 3.3). To the northwest, it reached the British Isles and the Rhine. Archaeology is constantly revealing the importance of ancient ports on the Atlantic, even before the Roman conquest. Nevertheless, a majority of scholars, while admitting a coastal trade, are still reluctant at the idea of deep-sea sailing in the Atlantic (Cobo and Martin, 1996; Alvarez and Gaspar, 2001; Arce, 2005; Fernández Ochoa and Morillo Cerdán, 2009, 2010, 2013; Hugot and Tranoy, 2010; Mantas, 2003, 2010; Rodriguez A lmeida, 2008; Rippon, 2008).

The most important port in the 'Mediterranean Far West' was actually not in the Mediterranean, but in the Atlantic. This was Cadiz, the ancient *Gades*. The Guadalquivir valley and the Atlantic coasts of Morocco, Spain and Portugal used to be essential places for the industrial production of oil and salted fish. Gibraltar was not a barrier for the Mediterranean merchants. Items produced within the Mediterranean were exported there and re-exported from there to other areas of the

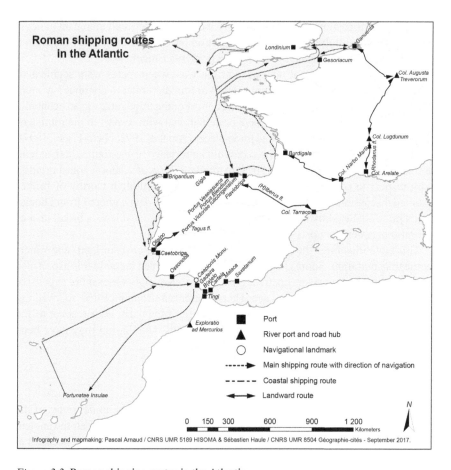

Figure 3.3 Roman shipping routes in the Atlantic

Mediterranean. Cadiz, Seville and to a lesser extent the neighboring Baelo Claudia were Mediterranean ports. But they were ports of the Atlantic, too. Some of the trade routes from and to these ports extended far beyond Cape S. Vincent.

The routes between Spain, Britain and Ireland are mentioned by several authors and were reviewed between 17 and 50 CE by a certain Philemon according to reports by merchants. The existence of a sustainable trade route between Spain, Britain and the Lower Rhine is also demonstrated by the distribution of artifacts (Carreras and Rui, 2012). These show that their trade pattern was entirely different from the Rhone route. It clearly followed an Atlantic route whose main elements can be reconstructed. From the Guadalquivir area, the cargo either followed the river to its mouth, or was brought directly to one of the port-cities at the mouth of the Sado river (Caetobriga [Troia], Salacia [Alacer do Sal]) or to Olisipo (Lisbon). This unusual concentration of significant urban centers likely echoes their role as prominent port-hubs between the Atlantic and rivers. Salacia is the Latin name of one of the wives of Neptune, and underlines the maritime status of the city, and both Salacia and Olisipo bore the title of *municipium*. Exports of salted fish from this area to the Mediterranean reached a high volume during the empire.

Here again, the segmentation of sailing and trade routes was organized by natural conditions and most probably also by seasonality.

The so-called Portuguese Trades blow all year from the north along the whole Lusitanian coast, up to Cape Finisterre. They are stronger in summer. These make sailing southwards easier and sailing northwards significantly more difficult, although not impossible. Ships sailing northwards would either tack far West, which is unlikely given the lack of instruments, or follow the coast using thermic breezes in spring and autumn and stop every night. The numerous estuaries of that coast, all described by ancient periplographic literature would have provided the required sheltered areas to stop at. They are never more distant than 30 miles from one another, which is more or less the distance a ship could sail between sunrise and sunset, according to ancient writers (Arnaud, 2005).

The Bay of Corunna marked the limit between the Portuguese Trades and the system of the Bay of Biscay. Emperor Augustus built one of the most important lighthouses of the Roman Empire there, immediately after the conquest of Cantabria. This was not only a symbol. Trade with Britain was important even before the conquest of the island by Claudius. In the early fifth century, Orosius (1.2.71) considered this lighthouse 'a lookout post for Britain' and Ptolemy's data illustrate direct routes thence to Ireland and Britain (the latter making Cape Finisterre, in Brittany). These were actually much safer than sailing along the leeward coast of the Bay of Biscay. Two major ports emerged in that area: Corunna (Brigantium) and the *Portus (Victoriae) Iuliobrigensium* at Santander. These too are emphasized in Ptolemy's maps. There is epigraphic evidence of people involved in customs at Corunna and an inscription mentions the guild of ship-owners whose activity was based at the *portus Iuliobrigensium*,[3] an important hub between the Atlantic and the Mediterranean through the Ebro valley. These two ports were likely transshipment ports.

The major routes were directed to Cape Finisterre and thence to the British or Irish ports. Among the former, the 'Great Port', between Portsmouth and Chichester, the 'New Port', at Brighton, and to the Thames area. London, the provincial capital was also its largest port of trade, connected with Spain and Gaul as well. A large amount of evidence illustrates the importance of trade between Britain and Lower Germany too. 'Those who trade with Britain' are mentioned in several ex-votos from the sanctuaries of the *Nehalenniae* Goddesses at Domburg and Colijnsplaat at the mouth of the Rhine, as are the traders from the Upper Rhine. Also found there was one 'trading with Kent and Boulogne-sur-mer' and one who specialized in ceramics trading with Britain. In addition to the large amount of olive oil imported into the area to satisfy the needs of the legion, the supply of grain to the legions in Lower Germany came from Britain (Ammianus Marcellinus 18.2.3). The main entrepot of Roman Britain was its capital.

The ports of the Bay of Biscay, especially those close to the main estuaries, were apparently active ones. The choice to place the capital of the Roman province of Aquitania at Bordeaux (Burdigala), whose economic links with Lyon on the Rhone river, are well established through the 'isthme gaulois', is probably a clue to the importance of the Atlantic ports. Bordeaux (Burdigala), a major port, was preferred to Mediolanum Santonum (Saintes) whose port (Barzan), once a major one, was becoming silted. Coastal connections between ports of lesser importance obviously also existed.

The 'Erythraean Sea' (the Red Sea, the Persian Gulf and the Indian Ocean)

At the opposite corner of the known world as the Romans imagined it, the Roman Empire had a significant maritime outlet in the so-called 'Erythraean Sea' (Figure 3.4). In ancient cartography, this was the name given to the Indian Ocean, the Red Sea and the Persian Gulf. Whoever questioned whether it was possible to sail long distances across the oceans would be convinced it was, if they looked to the East (Hirth, 1885; Casson, 1989; Tomber, 2008; Seland, 2013; Cooper and Zazzaro, 2014; McLaughlin, 2014; Arnaud, 2015).

Ancient commerce within the Indian Ocean is slowly being unveiled, although a large amount of archaeological evidence is still needed in order to have precise footage of the routes and ports of the 'Erythraean Sea' during the first half-millennium of the Christian era. A large part of our knowledge relies on a complex text, the *Periplus of the Erythraean Sea*, which is probably a compilation of data covering a period that extends from 40 to 120 CE or so (Arnaud, 2012). It provides the reader with information about ports and markets situated in the area around Zanzibar. Long thought to be a prefiguration of modern colonial trade, based on the technological, economic and political predominance of Rome, Red Sea trade appears to have been a wide-open system where the Arabs and the Tamils were very active and had large diasporas (the Nabateans had a common house at the port of Puteoli, near Naples). India was a gateway between the Far Chinese East, Africa, Iran, Arabia and the Roman Mediterranean. Unlike the routes of the

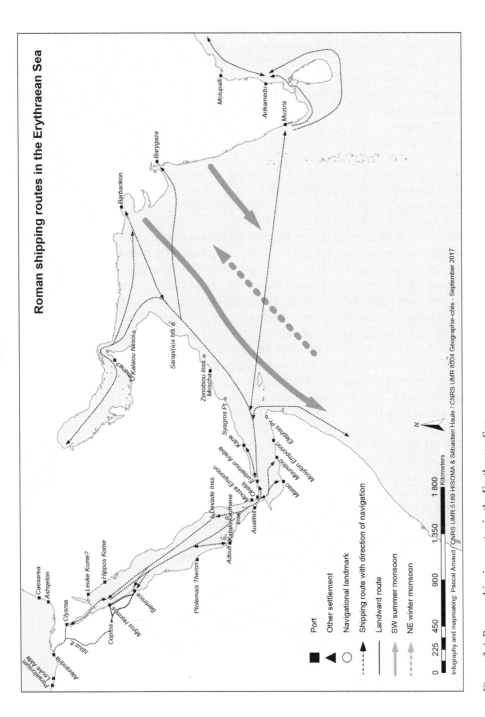

Figure 3.4 Roman shipping routes in the Erythraean Sea

Infography and mapmaking: Pascal Arnaud / CNRS UMR 5189 HISOMA & Sébastien Haule / CNRS UMR 8504 Géographie-cités - September 2017

Roman shipping routes in the Erythraean Sea

Port
Other settlement
Navigational landmark
Shipping route with direction of navigation
Landward route
SW summer monsoon
NE winter monsoon

0   225   450   900   1,350   1,800
Kilometers

Motupalli
Arikamedu
Muziris
Barygaza
Barbarikon
Zeueidia
Kalaiou Nesoia
Sarapi(a)s Ins.
Zenobiou Inss.
Moschia
Syagros Pt.
Kane
Moundou
Mosylon Emporion
Malao
Elephas Pt.
Eudaimon Arabia
Okelis
Mouza
Aualites
Adouli
Katakekaumene Inss.
Devade Inss.
Ptolemais Theron
Hippos Kome
Leuke Kome?
Clysma
Myos Hormos
Coptos
Nilus fl.
Berenice
Caesarea
Ashqelon
Alexandria
Paraetonium
Leuke Akte
N

Atlantic Ocean that connected countries mostly subject to the Roman rule, the trade routes of the Indian Ocean involved performers from various origins and legal trade-places under the authority of a number of states and rulers.

The routes between the Mediterranean and India on the one hand, and Zanzibar on the other hand, included several meteorological systems. The monsoons ruled the main streams of ships. The NE winter monsoon blows from mid-November in the North of the basin (late November to mid-December in Southern India and Sri Lanka) to March (or April in Southern India and Sri-Lanka). It is characterized by smooth breezes that rarely exceed 15 kn. The summer SW monsoon blows from June to September. It is much stronger and harsher than the winter one and weakens in August and September, as its direction becomes more variable. The Red Sea is mainly exposed to north winds. Only during the summer monsoon do southern winds blow up to a latitude comprised between 18 and 20° N during the peak of the monsoon. The same wind system allowed for sailing the Nile upstream from early July and February.

Evidence of direct relationships between Alexandria and the coast of Malabar is provided by a famous papyrus (*SB* 18. 13167), dated about the mid-second century CE. The entire voyage by sea was made on a single ship. This trade route and the patterns it was based on was so common that it gave its name to a special kind of bottomry loan contract (De Romanis, 2014). The timetable for a journey from Alexandria to India and back was rather familiar to ancient writers of the first century.

This was indeed a complex multimodal journey. According to Pliny the Elder (*Nat. Hist.* 6. 101–106), the best time for departure to India from Egypt (Alexandria) would be in early July, at the beginning of the flood. Ideally, it took 12 days to sail the Nile upstream from Alexandria using the etesian winds, to Coptos, and an additional 12 days by road onwards to the port of Berenike. It would then take one month from Berenike to reach Ocelis, from where, after a possible watering-stop, in normal sailing conditions, it would take about 40 days to Muziris (Pattanam) on the coast of Malabar, following the summer monsoon. This route of 2,000 nm was a 'direct one', for the entire area between Southern Gujarat and Muziris was pirate-infested. The figures for both sailing journeys to Ocelis (1.1 kn.) and from Ocelis to Muziris (2 kn.) are well below the average sailing speed of 3.5 kn. or more following the wind, (Arnaud, 2005) and would rather apply to the return journey. East Cape Komari, Palk Strait, between India and Sri-Lanka, was accessible only to catamarans, and the passage from the coast of Malabar needed transshipment. During the first century, the Romans had little knowledge of Sri-Lanka and of the ports beyond Pondicherry. During the second century, they had acquired quite precise information about the sequence of ports to Cattigara, usually situated near Hanoi that would have been first reached by a merchant named Alexander, most likely in the late first century. These routes were probably more familiar to Tamil traders.

According to the length of the journeys recorded by Pliny, arrival at Muziris would then take place in mid- to late September, leaving two months for selling the ingoing cargo and buying the return cargo, but the arrival date was probably significantly earlier. Then, leaving in early December, and 'not later than January

15th', it was possible in theory to be back in Alexandria sometime between late February and mid-April. The cycle would then have taken less than one year, as Pliny argues.

Pliny's affirmation seems quite positive. The 'etesian winds', necessary for sailing northwards against the flood, start blowing about July 20th and would impose a departure from Berenike in late August and an arrival about mid-October in a cyclonic period. It contradicts the idea of cargoes leaving from Berenike in July. We must consider the journey from Alexandria to Berenike as an entirely distinct segment that necessarily took place before the drop in water-levels (February to late June).

As for the journey back, leaving in early December would mean an arrival in the Bab-el-Mandeb at some time between mid- and late January, when SE winds are still blowing on the southernmost part of the Red Sea, up to a latitude of 18° to 20°N, which is roughly that of Ptolemais Thêrôn. An early departure would then greatly facilitate sailing northwards, always against the winds above 20° N and more difficult for big ships designed for sailing on the quarter. The more ports were situated at the south of the Red Sea, the better was their connectivity for ships sailing northwards. Berenike seems to have been a compromise. Myos Hormos, situated further north, had shorter road connections with Coptos and the Nile. It would have been a better port of departure, but was more difficult to reach on the way back. The opening of a canal between the Delta and Klysma, in the northernmost recess of the Red Sea, made the Red Sea more accessible in all seasons (Aubert, 2015), but it was more difficult to reach for those sailing northwards. There was no easy choice (Cooper, 2011).

An alternative pattern may have been to transship cargoes somewhere in the southern Red Sea, although there is no explicit evidence to support the claim. However, the existence of a Roman garrison on the island of Farasan ties in with this idea.

It was also possible to deal with ports of trade under the control of foreign states situated in the southern part of the Red Sea or in the Horn of Africa. Such was Adulis, the trade-port of the Aksumite kingdom, to which items from Africa (ivory, rhinoceros horn), Arabia (frankincense), India (cotton, pepper) and the Roman Empire (wine, olive oil, coral) converged and from where they were re-exported. Such was Aden (Eudaïmôn), the trading port of the Kingdom of Saba.

Routes from and to Northwestern India would follow two itineraries: one reached the Euphrates and the Persian Gulf through Palmyra and brought Chinese silk to India, as well as wine, coral, glass and oil along the silk-road to Iran. Return cargoes were spices and precious woods. The other route followed the Arabian coast and was mainly concerned with shipping frankincense to India as well as to the Roman area. Ports like Kanè (Qana) and Moscha, situated on this route, were very active. Ships on their way from the Red Sea to Gujarat could sell part of their cargo en route and load items to be sold at destination. The Arabs had taken control of African routes down as far as Dar es-Salaam (Rhapta), south of Zanzibar, and some of their main ports and were selling mixed cargoes from their ports of trade on the Red Sea, like Muza.

Along with the Roman ports, the legal places of trade (*emporia*) and the related ports of the area of the Bab-el-Mandeb, especially Adulis, the main trading port of the Aksumite kingdom, were clearly a crossroads of commercial routes where items from the Mediterranean, Arabia, Central and Western Africa and India converged and were reloaded to further destinations. The fragmentation of trade routes into two shorter circuits made it easier for many a merchant to buy and sell here, albeit with less profit. Adulis was the northernmost place that could be reached with favorable winds. As had been once the case of Aden (Arabia Eudaïmon, cf. *PME* 40), it was a perfect transshipment zone onto ships with greater ability to sail against the wind than the Greco-Roman merchantmen and oriental junks sailing the Indian Ocean (Cooper, 2011).

Despite the existence of connections between China and the West – The Romans were as found of Chinese Silk as the Chinese were of African rhinoceros horn and Roman coral and glass – there is no clear evidence to support the existence sustainable direct intercourse. Silk trade was mainly a terrestrial one and was under the control of the Parthian Empire (*An-hsi* of the Chinese) and thence reached Palmyra (whose people, subject to Rome, were not only involved in caravan trade through the desert. They were also in charge of the police along the Euphrates river, sailors and maritime traders in the Indian Ocean.

The image Chinese sources[4] had of the 'Great Sea' (this is, aside from 'Red Sea', the Roman name for the Indian Ocean) and of the route to *Ta-Ts'in* (a name that encompasses both Syria and, by extension, the Roman Mediterranean) was a terrifying and dreary one: the *Hou-han-shu* , partly written in the fifth century AD and embracing events that took place 25 to 220 AD, and the *San-kuo-chih*, compiled before 429 AD and relating to the period between 220 and 264 AD, describe a heartbreaking voyage by sea that could take years between the mouths of the Indus and the Red Sea, but had a good direct knowledge of the maritime outlets of the *An-hsi*, that well may have extended to the mouths of the Indus and to Muziris. Both works know perfectly the average duration of sea travel (likely to Alexandria, first mentioned as *Ch'ih-san* by the *San-kuo-chih*): two months, but up to two years (if winds, likely in the Red Sea, were not favorable). But this is clearly second-hand knowledge

Later texts, like the *Liang-Shu*, referring to the first half of the sixth century AD, show sailors from the West reaching Tongking, Annam and Cochin China. This fits rather well with the location usually assigned to Cattigara. It seems that the development of direct maritime relationship between the West and Vietnam was the result of a slow process, that had its origin in the West and never led to direct trade-connections. An embassy was first sent by Rome to China in 166. It has been widely reported by Chinese sources. The *San-kuo-chih* illustrates the development of maritime streams of goods to China, as the number of items imported listed in Chinese sources increases through time. But this text also makes it clear that the Chinese had established direct intercourse with the ports of the Yunan only and that these were a place for the transshipment of ships from and to the West. This is likely a consequence of the raise of the Sassanid kings, who defeated and replaced the Arsacid dynasty in Iran in 226, opening the way to a centuries-long state of war with the Roman Empire, and closing the terrestrial road to China. The same text points out the importance of Buddhism on the development of maritime trade (Sen, 2017). To summarize, notwithstanding the growing need for luxury items from the West and a real interest for direct trade, for many reasons, including cultural ones, the Chinese had little interest in becoming the agents of overseas trade.

This short footage of ancient sailing-routes during the first half-millennium of the Christian era clearly illustrates that, despite the lack of maps and instruments, sailing long distances offshore and complex multi-modal routes were not unusual at all. This network of routes supposed a complex network of hubs, entrepôts and transshipment areas. It also reveals a high level of specialization of ships and shipmasters in some routes, and a high degree of routine. The economy of the old world relied as early as the Roman Empire, and in many cases significantly before, on the close association of river-borne and seaborne transport, and on the conjunction of direct connectivity between distant entrepôts and redistribution on a more abbreviated scale.

Acknowledgements

The author would like to thank César Ducruet and Sébastien Haule for their support on cartography. The research for this project has received funding from the European Research Council under the European Union's Seventh Framework Programme (FP/2007–2013) / ERC Grant Agreement no. [339123] "Portus Limen".

Notes

1 After Duncan-Jones (1974), re-calculated using the value of 'bushel of the camps' established by Duncan-Jones (1996).
2 Strabo, *Geographia*, 3.5.3; Seneca, *Quaestiones Naturales* 4.2.24; Aelius Aristides, *Aegyptiakos* 9.
3 *CIL* II, *242 = *ERCantab*, n°*2. This lost inscription is usually considered as a modern forgery. This is unlikely (Cunchillos, 1998).
4 All of the Chinese texts relating to the topics have been translated into English by Hirth (1885).

References

Alvarez, M.E.C., Gaspar, A.T. (2001) Los discutidos hallazgos subacuáticos de anforas romanas de las Islas Canarias. *SPAL: Revista de prehistoria y arqueología de la Universidad de Sevilla*, 10: 311–325.
Arce, J. (2005) Hispania y el Atlántico en los siglos III-V d.C. In: *Mar Exterior, el occidente atlantico en epoca romana*, Actas del Congreso International Pisa, Santa Croce in Fossabanda, November 6–9, 2003, pp. 53–60.
Arnaud, P. (1992) Les relations maritimes dans le Pont-Euxin d'après les données numériques des géographes anciens (pseudo-Scylax, Strabon, Pomponius Mela, Pline, Arrien, Anonyme de 500, Marcien d'Héraclée). *Revue des Etudes Anciennes*, 94(1): 57–77.
Arnaud, P. (2005) *Les Routes de la Navigation Antique. Itinéraires en Méditerranée*. Paris: Errance.

Arnaud, P. (2011a) La mer dans la construction de l'image grecque du monde. In: Santos Yanguas, Juan, Diaz Arino, Borja (Eds.), *Los Griegos Y El Mar, Revisiones de Historia Antigua 6*. Universidad del Pas Vasco: Vitoria-Gasteiz, pp. 129–153.

Arnaud, P. (2011b) Ancient sailing routes and trade patterns: The impact of human factors. In: Robinson, D., Wilson, A. (Eds.), *Maritime Archaeology and Ancient Trade in the Mediterranean*. Oxford: OCMA, pp. 61–80.

Arnaud, P. (2012) Le Periplus Maris Erythraei: une œuvre de compilation aux intentions géographiques. In: Boussac, M.F., Salles, J.F., Yon, J.B. (Eds.), *Autour du Périple de la Mer Erythrée (Topoï, Supplt n°11)*. Maison de l'Orient et de la Méditerranée: Lyon, pp. 27–61.

Arnaud, P. (2015) Navires et navigation commerciale sur la mer et sur le 'Grand fleuve' à l'époque des Ptolémées. *Nehet – Revue Numérique d'Egyptologie*, 3. Leiden and Boston: Brill, pp. 105–122.

Aubert, J.J. (2015) Trajan's Canal: River Navigation from the Nile to the Red Sea. In: De Romanis, F., Maiuro, M. (Eds.), *Across the Ocean: Nine Essays on Indo-Mediterranean Trade*. Leiden and Boston, pp. 33–42.

Beresford, J. (2013) *The Ancient Sailing Season*. Leiden and Boston (Mnemosyne, Supplt. 358).

Carreras, C., Rui, M. (2012) The Atlantic Roman trade during the Principate: New evidence from the Western façade. *Oxford Journal of Archaeology*, 31(4): 419–441.

Casson, L. (1989) *The Periplus Maris Erythraei: Text With Introduction, Translation, and Commentary*. Princeton: Princeton University Press.

Cobo, G.E., Martín, A.M. (1996) ¿Ánforas romanas en las Islas Canarias? Revisión de un aparente espejismo histórico. *Tabona*, 9: 75.

Cooper, J.P. (2011) No easy option: The Nile versus the Red Sea in ancient and medieval North-South navigation. In: Harris, W., Lara, K. (Eds.), *Maritime Technology in the Ancient Economy*. Journal of Roman Archaeology Supplements 84, Portsmouth Rhode Island, pp. 189–210.

Cooper, J.P., Zazzaro, C. (2014) The Farasan Islands, Saudi Arabia: Towards a chronology of settlement. *Arabian Archaeology and Epigraphy*, 25(2): 147–174.

Cunchillos, M.C. (1998) Santoña y los puertos de la Cantabria romana: un estado de la cuestión. *Monte Buciero*, 2: 137–150.

De Romanis, F. (2014) Time to repay a maritime loan: A note on SB III 7169 and SB XVIII 13167 Recto. *Sileno*, 40(1–2): 73–89.

Duncan-Jones, R. (1974) Diocletian's Price Edict and the cost of transport. In: Duncan-Jones, R. (Ed.), *The Economy of the Roman Empire: Quantitative Studies*, New York: Cambridge University Press, pp. 366–369.

Duncan-Jones, R. (1996) The size of the Modius Kastrensis. *ZPE*, 21: 53–62.

Fernández Ochoa, C., Morillo Cerdán, A. (2009) Faros y navigacion en el Cantabrico y el Atlantico Norte. *Brigantium. Boletín do Museo Arqueolóxico e Histórico da Coruña*, 20: 115–135.

Fernández Ochoa, C., Morillo Cerdán, A. (2010) Roman lighthouses on the Atlantic coast. In: Carreras Monfort, C., Morais, R. (Eds.), *The Western Roman Atlantic Façade: A Study of the Economy and Trade in the Mar Exterior From the Republic to the Principate*. Oxford: Archaeopress, pp. 109–118.

Fernández Ochoa, C., Morillo Cerdán, A. (2013) Oceanus Hispanus: Navegación y comercio a orillas del Atlántico en época romana. In: Morais, R., Granja, H., Morillo Cerdán, A. (Eds.), *O irado mar atlántico: o naufragio bético augustano de Esposende (Norte de Portugal)*. Braga: D. Diogo de Sousa, Museu de Arqueologia, pp. 57–97.

Hirth, F. (1885) *China and the Roman Orient.* Shanghaï and Hong-Kong [reprint Chicago: Ares Press, 1975].

Hugot, L., Tranoy, L. (2010) *Les Structures Portuaires de l'Arc Atlantique dans l'Antiquité.* Supplement 18. Bordeaux: Aquitania.

Mantas, V.G. (2003) O porto romano de Lisboa. In: Berlanga, G.P., Ballester, J.P. (Eds.), *Puertos Fluviales Antiguos: Ciudad, Desarrollo y Infraestructuras.* València: Universität de València, pp. 13–29.

Mantas, V.G. (2010) Atlântico e Mediterrâneo nos portos romanos do Sado. *Revista Portuguesa de História,* 41: 195–221.

McLaughlin, R. (2014) *The Roman Empire and the Indian Ocean: The Ancient World Economy and the Kingdoms of Africa, Arabia and India.* Barnsley: Pen and Sword.

Morton, J. (2001) *The Role of the Physical Environment in Ancient Greek Seafaring.* Leyde: Brill Academic Publishers.

Nieto-Prieto, J. (1997) Le commerce de cabotage et de redistribution. In: Pomey, P. (Ed.), *La Navigation dans l'Antiquité.* Aix-en-Provence: Edisud, pp. 146–159.

Rippon, S. (2008) Coastal trade in Roman Britain: The investigation of Crandon Bridge, Somerset, a Romano-British transshipment port beside the Severn Estuary. *Britannia,* 39: 85–144.

Rodriguez Almeida, E. (2006) Ad speculum Britanniae: la boa ideale del periplo ipercantabrico. In: *Atti del Convegno "Mare Exterior", El Occidente atlántico en época romana.* Pisa: Gipuzkoako, pp. 13–19.

Rougé, J. (1952) La navigation hivernale sous l'Empire romain. *Revue des Études Anciennes,* 54: 316–325.

Schäfer, C. (2016) Oil for Germany. Some thoughts on Roman long-distance trade. In: Schäfer, C. (Ed.), *Connecting the Ancient World: Mediterranean Shipping, Maritime Networks and their Impact.* Rahden: Verlag Marie Leidorf GmbH, pp. 211–248.

Seland, E.H. (2013) Networks and social cohesion in ancient Indian Ocean trade: Geography, ethnicity, religion. *Journal of Global History,* 8(3): 373–390.

Sen, T. (2017) Early China and the Indian ocean Networks. In: Arnaud, P., de Souza, P. (Eds.), *The Sea in History, Vol. 1., The Ancient World.* Woodbridge: Boydell & Brewer, pp. 536–547.

Tomber, R. (2008) *Indo-Roman Trade: From Pots to Pepper.* London: Duckworth.

Uertega Artigas, M., Noain Maura, M.J. (2005) *Mar Exterior. El occidente Atlántico en época Romana.* Actas del congresso Internacional, Pisa, Santa Croce in Fossabanda, 6–9 November 2003, Rome: Escuola Española de Historia y Arqueolgía a Roma.

4 Ship logbooks help to understand climate variability

Ricardo García-Herrera, David Gallego,
David Barriopedro and Javier Mellado

Climate has been defined as the "typical weather" of a particular location quantified by the average values of certain variables such as temperature, precipitation or wind, among many others. This simple definition is nowadays considered incomplete because it does not explicitly consider changes in climate, due to either internal variability or changes in the external forcings. It is clear that a significant part of the recent change has an anthropogenic origin. As stated in the IPCC Fifth Assessment Report, "*Anthropogenic greenhouse gas emissions have increased since the pre-industrial era [. . .] Their effects, [. . .] are extremely likely to have been the dominant cause of the observed warming since the mid-twentieth century*" (IPCC, 2014). This human-induced change is superposed on that arising from changes in external forcings of natural origin (volcanic eruptions, solar activity, orbital forcing) and from internal processes (e.g., the El Niño-Southern Oscillation) as revealed by reconstructed records of past climate. Due to the complexity of the interaction among the different phenomena, external forcings and scales, our ability to accurately forecast future changes and to determine human impact on climate not only depends on the evaluation of the effects of the increasing concentration of human-produced greenhouse gases, but on the precise understanding of the underlying variability of the climate system.

This chapter is intended to give some insight on how the meteorological observations contained in old ships' logbooks can help to improve our knowledge of the climate and to better quantify the ranges of natural variability of the climate system (see also Chapters 2 and 3 on winds and shipping in the antiquity).

The historical record of the climate

Climate proxies

The earth's climate has experienced variations in time scales ranging from years to thousands of years. To characterise climate fluctuations at decadal and longer time scales, which are relevant for decadal predictions and future climate projections, researchers need climate series to be as long as possible. Ideally, these series should be constructed from direct measurements of atmospheric variables such as temperature, precipitation or wind using specific meteorological instrumentation. Climate series of this kind constitute the "instrumental record" of climate. Throughout the twentieth century, a world-wide network of meteorological observatories has been developed, and by the 1950s, this network was dense enough to characterise the climate of a large part of the continental areas with reasonable spatial and temporal resolution. With the advent of meteorological satellites in the 1970s, it has been possible to observe and monitor on a regular basis the oceans and other land areas that were poorly sampled. Consequently, the diagnosis of the occurrence of climate changes since the mid-twentieth century is nowadays quite precise. For some specific locations, mostly European cities, a limited number of instrumental records of temperature and precipitation cover more than a century and have provided an accurate representation of the local climate. Unfortunately, these series are quite scarce and much of what is known about climate variability prior to the twentieth century does not rely on these old instrumental series but on "climate proxies". These can be defined as indirect variables whose changes over time depend to some extent on the local climatic conditions. Good examples are the annual variations in tree-ring width and density (Fritss, 1971), the accumulation of snowfall in the polar ice caps and sheets (Lüthi et al., 2008) or the changes in composition of the layers of lake and marine sediments. These indicators have long been recognised as an important source of chronological and climate information and have provided a valuable record of the past climate for the last two millennia (PAGES 2k Consortium, 2013). However, the relationship between proxies and the actual climate has significant uncertainties and a number of "a priori" assumptions need to be made.

Documentary sources: ships' logbooks

"Documentary records", based on written accounts of old weather by contemporary eyewitnesses, are currently considered an important source of meteorological data. They are particularly useful, as they deal with all year-round, short-term climatic fluctuations, usually not resolved by proxies. In addition, historical sources typically contain detailed information of extreme events such as floods, severe droughts, hurricane occurrence etc.

Here we are focusing on the documentary legacy of navigation during the sailing era (cf. 1650 to present). It must be emphasised that climate was the main factor determining routes and navigation season. Thus, for example, the ships from Europe to the Americas could not sail against the mid-latitude westerlies prevailing over the Atlantic between 30°N and 60°N. Consequently, they had to sail south until they reached the subtropical easterly trade winds. Similarly, the time span for voyages from Europe to India was conditioned by the Indian summer monsoon. If the ships did not reach the Indian Ocean in time (between late May and late September), they had to remain anchored on the East African coast for almost a year, until the new monsoon brought favourable south-westerly winds. On the other hand, meteorology determined the actual duration of voyages. Natural variability of weather systems such as anticyclones, fronts or storms, resulted in changes of winds and currents, which partly explain the range of sailing times recorded in the main oceanic routes of that time.

The Manila Galleon, the commercial route which connected Manila and Acapulco during the longest period in history (1565–1815) is a good example of the mixed influences of climate and weather on sailing (García et al., 2001). The merchandise in the Galleon came from Guangdong and, thus, the sailing dates were a compromise between the onset of the East Asian monsoon, which allowed the Chinese merchants to deliver their merchandise in Manila, and the start of the peak typhoon season, which could impede the eastward route from Manila to Acapulco. Changes in meteorology altered the navigation schedule. We have explicit references to some of these changes. A letter to the Spanish king, written after 1656 by an unknown correspondent (AGI, Philippines 935) reads: "H. M. has also ordered that the ships not wait until April [to sail from Acapulco]; this time was formerly held to be safe, but because of the changes in the monsoons and the great lengthening of the voyages it seems appropriate that navigation should commence earlier. It is considered a good voyage from the Philippines to Acapulco one that does not exceed seven months, so in order to be able to return in time they should not wait until July to leave [Manila]". Most of the main incidences along the early part of this route were associated with tropical cyclones (García et al., 2001), similar to what happened in the Caribbean. Thus, logbook records such as changes in frequency or route tracking have helped to characterise the variability of the East Asian monsoon and different features of Atlantic hurricanes (García-Herrera et al., 2005a, 2007, Mock et al., 2010).

Fortunately, records of the weather conditions along the routes have survived in ships' logbooks (Wheeler and Garcia-Herrera, 2008), which enabled the compilation of long and continuous series of climatic information for specific areas with sufficient data coverage. Logbooks served two important functions: firstly, as an official account of how the vessel was managed and furthermore they were navigational tools in which the ship's course and estimated location was annotated. Importantly, the crew recorded the main meteorological events. Probably the first use of logbooks information was done by the famous astronomer E. Halley, who used wind records to draw a map of tropical wind circulations (Wheeler and García-Herrera, 2008). In general, the weather information contained in logbooks was split into four main categories: wind force, wind direction, state of the sea and the general state of the weather. Notes on the weather usually contain data on rain, fog or thunderstorm occurrence and have been used to investigate interesting case-studies (e.g., the weather influence on marine battles, Wheeler, 1995), but they are not an adequate source of homogeneous and continuous records of a single variable, since they were not necessarily taken in a systematic form. On the other hand, wind measurements were of primary importance for navigation and hence they were routinely taken, potentially providing the best set of figures for long-term climatic indices. The conversion of the terms used for wind force into their modern equivalent can be done (Prieto et al., 2005), but has an uncertainty which can be difficult to quantify (Gallego et al., 2007). This was one of the main objectives of the EU-funded CLIWOC project (García-Herrera et al., 2005b), which was the first exercise involving massive abstraction of early meteorological data from logbooks prior to the instrumental era. This project also showed that wind direction was recorded on a 16- or a 32-point compass, similar to present-day standards. Thus, early measurements of the wind direction can be regarded as equivalent to high-quality current instrumental observations. The only possible source of non-climatic signal could be the changes in the north reference, but wind direction was recorded with respect to the magnetic north and the magnetic variation can be easily corrected. Apart from this, logbook information is useful for a number of different disciplines, such as the history of navigation, commerce and conflicts, environmental history and ports activity (see Wilkinson, 2005). However, to the best of our knowledge, these possible applications have not been developed so far, possibly because they require a multidisciplinary approach which includes research communities with little tradition of common ventures. Figure 4.1 shows two pages of the logbook from the Spanish brig *S Francisco Javier (La Suerte)* sailing from Cadiz to Cartagena de Indias in Colombia. The setting is quite typical, with bihourly observations of the ship's course, wind direction and leeway (columns 3–5). In other cases, the records were taken hourly and the observations included wind force. The date is recorded in the second row on the right. The main text accounts for changes in weather conditions or relevant issues of daily life on board, while the computations of latitude and position are included in the final rows.

Currently, there are large datasets of digitised historical wind direction measurements. During the last three decades, a number of international projects have aimed

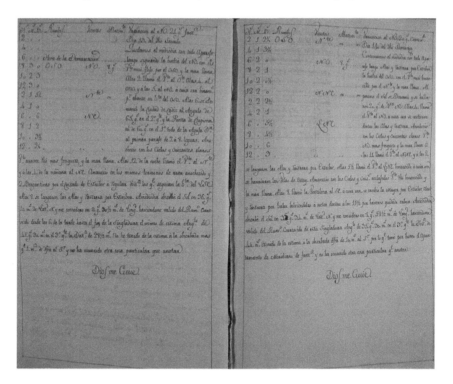

Figure 4.1 Pages of the Spanish brig *S Francisco Javier* (La Suerte)

at the search, abstraction and digitation of historical ships' logbooks contained in several archives. Most of their output is included in the International Comprehensive Ocean-Atmosphere Data Set (ICOADS), which provides the most complete source of surface marine data spanning the past three and a half centuries. This dataset started as a US project (COADS) in 1981, with the aim of providing global surface marine data from the late seventeenth century. The project is supported by NOAA (National Oceanic and Atmospheric Administration), but a new name, International COADS (ICOADS), was agreed on in 2002 to recognise the multinational input to the project. Currently, it is supported by institutions from the United States, United Kingdom and Germany. The last release of the database (version 3.0) starts in 1662 and contains over 455 million individual marine reports. Up to the end of the nineteenth century, ICOADS was composed essentially of observations and metadata reported from sailing ships and retrieved from logbooks. After that date, ICOADS also contains data from buoys, coastal platforms and oceanographic instruments from different collections and countries (see Freeman et al., 2016 for details). We will now present some examples to illustrate the importance of long wind direction records in understanding the variability of some climatic systems.

Historical reconstructions of the monsoonal circulation

One of the key systems of the global climate is the monsoonal circulation. Monsoons are usually defined as a seasonal reversal of the wind driven by changes in land-sea thermal contrast and accompanied by large changes in precipitation. Due to its influence on agriculture and food production, the arrival (onset), retreat (withdrawal) and intensity of monsoons have an impact on hundreds of millions of people. As described above, they were a key element for navigation in the sailing era.

On a world-wide scale, the major monsoon systems are the West African Monsoon and the Indo-Asian monsoon. Rainfall over large areas of West Africa from Senegal to Chad is linked to the first one, while the Indo-Asian monsoon drives changes in precipitation over almost all the Indian Subcontinent. The wind signature of the monsoonal circulations is illustrated in Figure 4.2, which shows the average winds during August, the month when the African and Indian monsoons are fully developed. These monsoons are characterised by a strong south-westerly component in the wind (see black rectangles), which transports moist oceanic air over continental areas, generating the seasonal rainfall.

The most prominent wind signature of the monsoonal circulation is found over oceanic areas. As the majority of direct meteorological observations are taken inland, the oceanic branch of monsoons has often been under-sampled, especially in the past. Figure 4.3 shows the total number of wind observations from ICOADS for 1662–2013 over the Atlantic and Indian oceans. The darker areas indicate the main shipping routes over the years. It is worth noticing that monsoonal areas are located over some of the oldest and busiest shipping routes from Europe to South America and to Asia circumnavigating the African continent. Thus, monsoons can

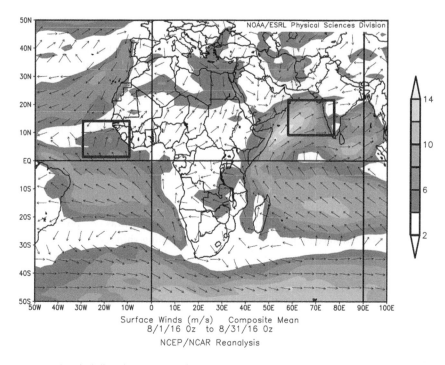

Figure 4.2 Wind direction (arrows) for August 2016

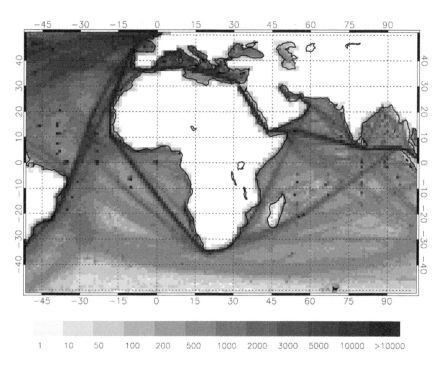

Figure 4.3 Density or raw wind direction measurements for the months between July and September in a 1°x1° grid in the ICOADS database (1662–2013)

be characterised by constructing climatic indices based on the seasonal wind reversals reported by ships' logbooks.

The case of the West African monsoon

The area between 29°W and 17°W and from 7°N to 13°N is especially sensitive to the West African monsoon, which emerges as a sudden increase in the southwesterly winds there, triggering moisture advection and determining the start of the rainfall season. Since the early nineteenth century, this area was regularly crossed by British and Dutch ships travelling to the Far East. In the twentieth century, ships from other nationalities also travelled frequently across this region, mainly from Germany, France and later on from Russia (former USSR) and the United States, among others. In consequence, a large number of individual wind observations are available for this area.

To quantify the strength of the African monsoon, indices are often designed according to the magnitude of the increase in the wind speed. Alternatively, as a measure of the African monsoon intensity, an index relying solely on wind direction can be defined by quantifying the percentage of days within a month with prevailing winds blowing from the southwest quadrant (between 180° and 270° from the true north) inside the indicated area (Gallego et al., 2015). The so-called ASWI (African South Westerly Index) measures the persistence of the southwesterly wind component in the oceanic sector most affected by the African monsoon. Figure 4.3 shows the close relation of this index to the wind speed – and consequently to the monsoon strength – for a period (1948–2013) when wind speed measurements became highly reliable. By late May or early June, the frequency of the south-westerly winds starts to increase, marking the climatological start of the African monsoon (see the continuous line in Figure 4.4). The frequency of the south-westerly winds rapidly increases in June and July, peaks in August and decreases until October. Interestingly, when the wind speed is also displayed (dotted line in Figure 4.4), its seasonal evolution closely mimics that of the

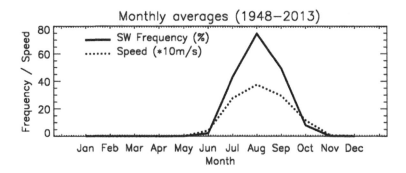

Figure 4.4 Monthly percentage of wind blowing from the south-westerly direction in the West African monsoon area (continuous line) and corresponding wind speed (dashed line)

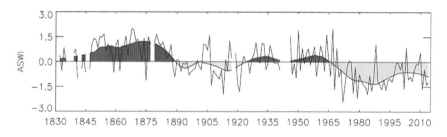

Figure 4.5 Standardised ASWI index between 1830 and 2014

south-westerly wind frequency. This indicates that the monthly persistence of the south-westerly winds in the subtropical North Atlantic provides a direct measure of the West African monsoon strength.

During the past four decades, the West African Monsoon has received much attention due to the long period of severe drought that has experienced the Sahel's region since the 1970s. In a temporal context, the relevance of this unusual dry period has been limited to the twentieth century, because instrumental indices of the West African monsoon precipitation only extend back to 1900 (see Janowiak, 1988), when the first precipitation gauges started to be operative in West Africa. Figure 4.5 shows the seasonal (July to September) mean series of the ASWI index computed from ICOADS data for the period with enough wind observations over the West African monsoon region (1830–2014). Positive/negative values indicate a stronger/weaker monsoon (and precipitation) compared to the climatological mean. The recent drought is clearly shown as a persistent period of negative ASWI values, in good agreement with early precipitation series. However, wind data observations from historical ships' logbooks have resulted in a notorious increase of the length of the series, which now tracks monsoon strength as early as 1830. The new series indicates that the second half of the nineteenth century was indeed characterised by a persistently strong monsoon in West Africa and above-normal precipitation in the Sahel. This finding can be considered as the first instrumental evidence of the severity of the recent drought in this region and its unprecedented occurrence in the last 170 years.

The Indian monsoon onset as seen by logbook data

One of the main advantages of historical meteorological records taken aboard ships is their high temporal resolution. Frequently, logbooks offer daily and even sub-daily meteorological observations, which can be used to characterise atmospheric circulation at a temporal resolution that cannot be attained with climate proxies. One of the best examples is the determination of the start of the monsoonal rains. The summer monsoon onset in India is one of the most expected meteorological events worldwide. It determines the start of the rainy season, and small changes in its precise date affect food production of highly vulnerable regions with a population of around one billion people (Wang et al., 2009). The study of long-term changes in the onset of the Indian monsoon (ISM hereafter) is, therefore, quite relevant.

The IMS is evidenced as a relatively fast and sustained increase in rainfall beginning in southern India. It occurs typically in late May or early June. The rains then progress northwards covering the whole of India by late June. Traditionally, the official date of the IMS has been considered as the date of the Monsoon Onset over the city of Kerala (MOK hereafter), located on the southern tip of the Indian peninsula. The India Meteorological Department officially announces the MOK when a sudden increase in the precipitation is observed in Kerala, along with changes in wind speed and atmospheric moisture content coherent with a monsoonal circulation (Joseph et al., 1994). Historically, the MOK has been declared without using precise thresholds, and hence, the historical MOK series is considered subjective. Several alternative definitions have been proposed in order to achieve an objective determination, and to this end the India Meteorological Department adopted objective criteria in 2006. Unfortunately, all these new definitions require the use of data that were unavailable during the first half of the twentieth century, such as satellite-based long-wave radiation measurements. Obviously, this impedes the generation of homogeneous MOK series before the satellite era.

Fortunately, Kerala is placed just eastwards of a main shipping route with a large number of wind observations (see Figure 4.3), from which a MOK series can be derived. To compute the MOK series from ICOADS data, the area between 60°E–80°E and 7°N–11°N was selected (Ordóñez et al., 2016). When the Indian monsoon is fully developed, the winds over this area are characterised by a persistent westerly south-westerly component (WSW). Thus, the daily percentage of observations with this wind component was computed and smoothed with a 21-day temporal window to eliminate transient variability. Figure 4.6 shows the mean annual cycle of this index (continuous line). The

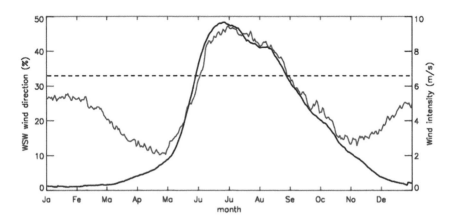

Figure 4.6 Climatological (1948–2013) mean annual cycle of westerly south-westerly wind observations in the [60°E–80°E, 7°N to 11°N] region

frequency of WSW winds starts to increase sharply in April and exceeds 40% by June. The maximum value is reached at the end of June and the index progressively declines up to December. The largest WSW frequency values occur between the end of May and the beginning of September, marking the peak of the monsoon season.

It must be stressed that the frequency of WSW winds in the selected area is strongly related to the wind speed therein and, in consequence, to the monsoon strength, as evidenced in Figure 4.6 (fluctuating line). Two wind speed maxima are found in January and July. The first is related to the northeasterly flow associated with the winter monsoon and the second and stronger one reflects the summer monsoon. Interestingly, from mid-February to late April, the wind speed slowly decreases to reach the annual minimum in the first days of May. The wind speed then experiences a very fast increase, marking the transition between late winter conditions and the full summer monsoon regime. The annual maximum is reached in late June, and it is during this period when the monsoon onset occurs. Wang et al. (2009) used this fast increase in wind speed to define a dynamical monsoon onset, and their index proved to be in very good agreement with onset dates derived from precipitation measurements. According to the results shown in Figure 4.6, a similar definition can be established by using the frequency of the WSW winds (black line), which only requires wind direction measurements. A calibration procedure between the frequency of the WSW winds and the onset dates published by the Indian Meteorological Department showed that the onset date occurs when the frequency of the WSW winds within the selected area reaches 33% (horizontal dashed line in Figure 4.6). By determining the date of this threshold exceedance for each year, it has been possible to build a new historical MOK series starting in 1885 (see Figure 4.5) (Ordóñez et al., 2016).

The results indicate that the MOK date oscillates in a wide range of 46 days between the earliest monsoon in 1956 (11 May) and the latest one in 1915 (25 June), 28 May being the climatological mean, with a standard deviation of 7.3 days. The 15-year moving average of the MOK series (curve in Figure 4.7) shows interdecadal IMS fluctuations. In general, the first and the last third of the

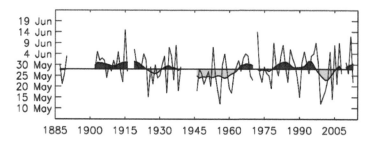

Figure 4.7 Historical series of the Indian monsoon onset dates based on ICOADS data for the period 1885–2013

twentieth century were characterised by later onsets while the period between 1940 and 1965 was mostly dominated by earlier monsoons. Unfortunately, the ICOADS database still has insufficient data coverage for the period prior to 1900. The periods 1917–1918 (end of World War I), 1939–1943 (World War II) and the years around 1971 (Indo-Pakistani War) also have some gaps in the MOK series. However, this index can be extended further back in time as new data become available from logbooks that have not been digitised yet.

Reconstruction of the atmospheric circulation in the North Atlantic back to 1685

The applicability of logbook data to the development of instrumental climatic indices is not restricted to monsoonal latitudes. One of the most important modes of climate variability in the Northern Hemisphere is the North Atlantic Oscillation (NAO, Hurrell, 1995), a seesaw of atmospheric mass between the high pressure system in the subtropical North Atlantic and the extratropical low pressure belt. Changes in these coupled pressure systems modulate the dominant westerly winds arriving to Europe. Some years these winds are stronger than the long-term average (the so-called positive NAO phases) and the increased oceanic influence originates warmer temperatures in Europe, a significant increase in the precipitation of Central and Northern Europe and a decrease in the precipitation of Southern Europe (Trigo et al., 2002). Opposite responses occur during years of weak westerlies (negative NAO phases). The characterisation of the long-term variability of the westerlies in this area is extremely important as it has huge impacts on the temperature and precipitation of large areas of Europe and hence on derived magnitudes, such as energy consumption and hydroelectric power availability (Vicente-Serrano and Trigo, 2011).

Traditionally, the NAO index is computed by subtracting the sea level pressure of two single locations that are representative of the pressure centres, usually the Azores and Iceland (Jones et al., 1999). This gives a direct measure of the latitudinal pressure gradient in the North Atlantic which is related to the intensity of the zonal wind component. These particular locations have been selected because they have long records of sea level pressure observations, giving rise to a reliable instrumental index back to 1821 (Jones et al., 1999). However, the lack of earlier pressure measurements prevents us from extending this index further back in time. By contrast, there are plenty of wind direction measurements in areas highly affected by the North Atlantic westerlies such as the English Channel, an extremely busy area from a nautical point of view since very early times. Wheeler et al. (2009) showed that wind direction changes in the English Channel also reflect the atmospheric circulation over the North Atlantic. Consequently, they constructed an index (the Westerly Index, WI hereafter) between 1685 and 1750 based on logbooks by computing the percentage of days in a month with prevalent wind blowing from the west in the English Channel. Later, Barriopedro et al. (2014) assembled data from logbooks stored at The National Archives in London and merged them with data from the ICOADS database to derive the WI index for the

DJF prec   JJA prec

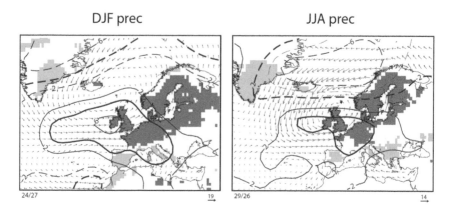

Figure 4.8 (Left) Winter (December-January-February) and (right) summer (June-July-August) composite differences between high (>0.75 standard deviation, SD) and low (<-0.75 SD) WI phases of storm tracks (contours), land precipitation (shading) and 1000–500 hPa vertically integrated moisture transport (arrows) for the period 1901–2008

entire 1685–2013 period at seasonal scale. Currently, the WI series is the longest instrumental climatic record of Atlantic atmospheric circulation to date.

Figure 4.8 shows an example of the strong signal of the WI index in the European climate. Changes in the frequency of the westerlies are strongly related to precipitation anomalies over large areas of Europe. The WI signature in the precipitation field is observed through the entire year (see the winter and summer responses in Figure 4.6) and displays a tripolar structure (shaded areas). Persistent westerlies are associated with above-normal precipitation in central and northern Europe and drier conditions in some areas of southern Europe, northern Mediterranean and south-eastern Greenland. The opposite is found for years with a low frequency of westerlies. These anomalies in precipitation are due to changes in synoptic activity (extratropical storms), with high WI values reflecting an enhanced activity over the eastern part of the North Atlantic and northern Europe (contour lines) resulting in significant changes in the transport of atmospheric moisture. The WI is also an excellent indicator of hydrological conditions in central and northern Europe, with an increased (reduced) frequency of westerlies denoting surplus (deficits) in the water-balance (Vicente-Serrano et al., 2016). Thus, logbooks have now enabled the tracking of changes in North Atlantic wind circulation back to 1685. Contrary to the traditional NAO indices, which are mostly representative of the winter season, the WI is able to characterise the precipitation and temperature variability in Europe during the entire year. Furthermore, its tight link with hydrological anomalies in central and northern Europe opens up the possibility of characterising past extreme events (e.g., droughts) by placing their recent changes in a long temporal framework.

Conclusion

In this chapter, the potential of logbook data in climate reconstruction for periods and areas poorly covered by other instrumental meteorological measurements has been discussed. The examples cited stem mostly from logbook records already digitised and included in the ICOADS database. With these records, it has been possible to build reliable instrumental indices of the strength of the West African Monsoon, the date of the Indian monsoon onset and the strength of the atmospheric circulation in the North Atlantic. In all cases, a good agreement between new and traditional indices has been found, showing that the information of wind direction contained in historical ship's logbooks is extremely reliable and useful.

It must be stressed that logbook-like historical meteorological data can be found not only over the oceans, but also on land at facilities ruled by the Navy such as watchtowers, offering an additional source of data and an invaluable opportunity to calibrate logbook-derived climatologies against direct meteorological measurements at a fixed location (Gallego et al., 2007). In fact, during the last decade logbooks have become a significant contributor to global-scale climate reconstructions. By merging logbook data from the CLIWOC project with early instrumental and proxy records of temperature and precipitation over land, Küttel et al. (2010) produced a gridded sea level pressure field over the entire North Atlantic as far back as 1750, significantly improving the reliability of previous reconstructions based on land data alone. These new products help to better understand the long-term variability of wind-derived sub-products of unquestionable applicability such as storm severity at coasts (Santo et al., 2016) or wave power variability in the North Sea (Santo et al., 2015). As mentioned in the introduction, the future development of forecasting capabilities of variables of this nature crucially depends on the correct understanding of their long-term variability, particularly for periods before the twentieth century.

Finally, it is worth mentioning that these methodologies still have a large margin for improvement as new data from logbooks become available from new research projects (Compo at el., 2011). In this sense, according to Wheeler and Garcia-Herrera (2008), there are thousands of logbooks in several archives that have not been digitised, with data probably going back to the end of the seventeenth century. It is also possible that data for war periods are still classified and not yet made public. Any effort to disclose and digitise these data would help to better understand the climate of the past.

Acknowledgements

Most of the research shown in this chapter was funded by the Spanish *Ministerio de Economía y Competitividad* through the projects CGL2013-44530-P and CGL2014-51721-REDT and by the Portuguese FCT under grant PD/BD/106028/2014.

References

Barriopedro, D., Gallego, D., Álvarez-Castro, M.C., García-Herrera, R., Wheeler, D., Peña-Ortiz, C., Barbosa, S.M. (2014) Witnessing North Atlantic westerlies variability from ship's logbooks (1685–2008). *Climate Dynamics*, 43: 939–955.

Compo, G.P., Whitaker, J.S., Sardeshmukh, P.D., Matsui, N., Allan, R.J., Yin, X., Gleason, R.E., Vose, R.S., Rutledge, G., Bessemoulin, P., Brönnimann, S., Brunet, M., Crouthamel, R.I., Grant, A.N., Groisman, P.Y., Jones, P.D., Kruk, M.C., Kruger, A.C., Marshall, G.J., Maugeri, M., Mok, H.Y., Nordli, O., Ross, T.F., Trigo, R.M., Wang, X.L., Woodruff, S.D., Worley, S.J. (2011) The twentieth century reanalysis project. *Quarterly Journal of the Royal Meteorological Society*, 137(654): 1–28.

Freeman, E., Woodruff, S.D., Worley, S.J., Lubker, S.J., Kent, E.C., Angel, W.E., Berry, D.I., Brohan, P., Eastman, R., Gates, L., Gloeden, W., Ji, Z., Lawrimore, J., Rayner, N.A., Rosenhagen, G., Smith, S.R. (2016) ICOADS Release 3.0: A major update to the historical marine climate record. *International Journal of Climatology*, 37(5): 2211–2232.

Fritss, H.C. (1971) Dendroclimatology and dendroecology. *Quaternary Research*, 1: 419–449.

Gallego, D., Garcia-Herrera, R., Calvo, N., Ribera, P. (2007) A new meteorological record for Cádiz (Spain) 1806–1854. Implications for climatic reconstructions. *Journal of Geophysical Research*, 112: D12108.

Gallego, D., Ordoñez, P., Ribera, P., Peña-Ortiz, C., Garcia-Herrera, R. (2015) An instrumental index of the West African Monsoon back to the nineteenth century. *Quarterly Journal of the Royal Meteorological Society*, 141: 3166–3176.

García, R.R., Diaz, H.F., García-Herrera, R., Eischeid, J., Prieto, M.R., Hernández, E., Gimeno, L., Rubio-Durán, F., Bascary, A.M. (2001) Atmospheric circulation changes in the Tropical Pacific inferred from the voyages of the Manila Galleons in the sixteenth-eighteenth centuries. *Bulletin of the American Meteorological Society*, 78: 2435–2455.

García-Herrera, R., Gimeno, L., Ribera, P., Hernández, E. (2005a) New records of Atlantic hurricanes from Spanish documentary sources. *Journal of Geophysical Research*, 110: 1–7.

García-Herrera, R., Gimeno, L., Ribera, P., Hernández, E., González, E., Fernández, G. (2007) Identification of Caribbean basin hurricanes from Spanish documentary sources. *Climatic Change*, 88: 55–85.

García-Herrera, R., Können, G., Wheeler, D., Prieto, M.R., Jones, P., Koek, F. (2005b) A climatological database for the world's oceans 1750–1854. *Climatic Change*, 73: 1–12.

Hurrell, J.W. (1995) Decadal trends in the North Atlantic oscillation: Regional temperatures and precipitation. *Science*, 269: 676–679.

IPCC. (2014) Climate change 2014: Synthesis report. In: *Contribution of Working Groups I, II and III to the Fifth Assessment Report of the Intergovernmental Panel on Climate Change*, Geneva, Switzerland.

Janowiak, J.E. (1988) An investigation of interannual rainfall variability in Africa. *Journal of Climate*, 1: 240–255.

Jones, P.D., Davies, T.D., Lister, D.H., Slonosky, V., Jonsson, T., Bärring, L., Jönsson, P., Maheras, P., Kolyva-Machera, F., Barriendos, M., Martín-Vide, J., Rodríguez, R., Alcoforado, M.J., Wanner, H., Pfister, C., Luterbacher, J., Rickli, R., Schuepbach, E., Kaas, E., Schmith, T., Jacobeit, J., Beck, C. (1999) Monthly mean pressure reconstructions for Europe for the 1780–1995 period. *International Journal of Climatology*, 19: 347–364.

Joseph, P.V., Eisheid, J., Pyle, R.J. (1994) Interannual variability of the onset of the Indian summer monsoon and its association with atmospheric features, El Niño, and sea surface temperature anomalies. *Journal of Climate*, 7: 81–105.

Küttel, M., Xoplaki, E., Gallego, D., Luterbacher, J., García-Herrera, R., Allan, R., Barriendos, M., Jones, P.D., Wheeler, D., Wanner, H. (2010) The importance of ship log data: Reconstructing North Atlantic, European and Mediterranean sea level pressure fields back to 1750. *Climate Dynamics*, 34: 1115.

Lüthi, D., Le Floch, M., Bereiter, B., Blunier, T., Barnola, J.M., Siegenthaler, U., Raynaud, D., Jouzel, J., Fischer, H., Kawamura, K., Stocker, T.F. (2008) High-resolution carbon dioxide concentration record 650,000–800,000 years before present. *Nature*, 453: 379–382.

Mock, C.J., Chenoweth, M., Altamirano, I., Rodgers, M.D., García-Herrera, R. (2010) The great Louisiana Hurricane of August 1812. *Bulletin of the American Meteorological Society*, 91: 1653–1663.

Ordóñez, P., Gallego, D., Ribera, P., Peña-Ortiz, C., Garcia-Herrera, R. (2016) Tracking the Indian summer monsoon onset back to the pre-instrumental period. *Journal of Climate*, 29: 8115–8127.

PAGES 2k Consortium. (2013) Continental-scale temperature variability during the past two millennia. *Nature Geoscience*, 6: 339–346.

Prieto, M.R., Gallego, D., García-Herrera, R., Calvo, N. (2005) Deriving wind force terms from nautical reports through content analysis. The Spanish and French cases. *Climate Change*, 73: 37–55.

Santo, H., Taylor, P.H., Gibson, R. (2016) Decadal variability of extreme wave height representing storm severity in the northeast Atlantic and North Sea since the foundation of the Royal Society. *Proceedings of the Royal Society A*, 472(2193). Available at: http://rspa.royalsocietypublishing.org/content/472/2193/20160376

Santo, H., Taylor, P.H., Woollings, T., Poulson, S. (2015) Decadal wave power variability in the North-East Atlantic and North Sea. *Geophysical Research Letters*, 42: 4956–4963.

Trigo, R.M., Osborn, T.J., Corte-Real, J.M. (2002) The North Atlantic Oscillation influence on Europe: Climate impacts and associated physical mechanisms. *Climate Research*, 20: 9–17.

Vicente-Serrano, S.M., García-Herrera, R., Barriopedro, D., Azorin-Molina, C., López-Moreno, J.I., Martín-Hernández, N., Tomás-Burguera, M., Gimeno, L., Nieto, R. (2016) The Westerly Index as complementary indicator of the North Atlantic oscillation in explaining drought variability across Europe. *Climate Dynamics*, 47: 845–863.

Vicente-Serrano, S.M., Trigo, R.M. (2011) *Hydrological, Socioeconomic and Ecological Impacts of the North Atlantic Oscillation in the Mediterranean Region*. Advances in Global Change Research 46, Springer Science+Business Media.

Wang, B., Ding, Q., Joseph, P.V. (2009) Objective definition of the Indian summer monsoon onset. *Journal of Climate*, 22: 3303–3316.

Wheeler, D. (1995) A climatic reconstruction of the Battle of Quiberon Bay, 20 November 1759. *Weather*, 50: 230–239.

Wheeler, D., García-Herrera, R. (2008) Ships' logbooks in climatological research. *Annals of the New York Academy of Science*, 1146: 1–15.

Wheeler, D., García-Herrera, R., Wilkinson, C.W., Ward, C. (2009) Atmospheric circulation and storminess derived from Royal Navy logbooks: 1685 to 1750. *Climate Change*, 101: 257–280.

Wilkinson, C. (2005) The non-climatic research potential of ships' logbooks and journals. *Climatic Change*, 73: 155.

5 Complex network analysis of cross-strait container flows

Lie-Hui Wang, Yan Hong and Yushan Lin

The spatial structure of port systems mainly refers to the combination of spatial or functional relations between ports. In the port system, there are many ports, and the ports' spatial distribution is adjacent (Yang et al., 2012; Wang, 2012). Its evolution is the result of the interaction between the different port groups or different ports within the port group in the region. The evolution of the port system is characterized by dynamics, periodicity and so on (Bird, 1971; Cao, 1999).

Since the 1970s, the development of maritime container transport has gradually attracted the attention of domestic and international scholars who have produced explorations on the evolution mechanism and the container port system model. A five-stage model of the evolution in the container port system in the United States is proposed by Hayuth (1981, 1988), while Airriess (1989), Kuby and Reid (1992), Hoyle and Charlier (1995) and other scholars generally proved that the model can be used to describe port evolution in Southeast Asia and East Africa, and described the obvious centralization development process of the American container port system. Like Marcadon (1999), several scholars provided evolutionary perspectives of container port system decentralization in Europe, Japan, Korea and other regions. Wang (1998) emphasized that with a changing regional environment, the developed path of the ports would change at the same time. Some studies looked at the political factors influencing maritime network patterns (Ducruet et al., 2009). Rimmer and Comtois (2005) have discussed the role of specific shipping lines and in particular across the Taiwan Strait (Comtois and Wang, 2003).

Since the1990s, many Chinese scholars, utilizing the relevant research experience of the international container port system, have carried out substantial research into the formation and evolution mechanism, as well as the spatial structure and competition pattern of the Chinese container port system (see also Chapter 20 on China's shipping networks). Cao (1999) recorded scientific evidence on the formation and evolution mechanism and the spatial structure of the Chinese container port system in the Yangtze River and Chinese coastal area (Cao et al., 2003, 2004). Based on the container network and shipping enterprises, Wang (2008) concerned himself with discussing and summarizing the evolution and spatial organization of global container ports. More recent research has mainly focused on new phenomena in port development and demonstrated the evolution and process of container ports in different areas (Jian et al., 2012; Yang et al., 2014; Wu et al., 2013).

In general, research projects on the spatial structure of the container port system mainly consisted of two aspects: 1. the qualitative study of the formation mechanism in the spatial structure of port systems; based on spatial distribution, this study discussed port functions and the evolution between the hub ports and the feeder ports in the system; and 2. the quantitative study of the evolution model whereby the basic law of the evolution of the container port system is deduced in the system, and the evolution characteristics of the port system are analyzed by means of an evaluation index, such as the Hirshman-Herfindahl index, the Gini coefficient, offset-sharing and so on.

These studies noted the importance of the theory and model of the formation and evolution of the port systemand have been verified and amended in many countries and regions. However, less attention was paid to the institutional factors. Most of the research concentrated on the evolution of the concentration and decentralization of the port in terms of traffic volume, and neglected to evaluate the realistic implications on the spatial structure of ports, their functional characteristics and evolution law in terms of the network connection between ports and container flows.

At present, research on the complex network of container shipping is mostly confined to the analysis of the topology characteristics and route optimization of the shipping network from the perspective of the design of the liner routes and the discussion with regard to the evolution rules and spatial structure of regional port systems are still at an initial stage (Mo et al., 2008).

Researchers such as Kaluza et al. (2010), Deng et al. (2009) and other scholars constructed the container shipping network structure in global or regional terms, using the complex network method to describe the topological structure and physical properties of the network and prove that it had a small and scale-free world; Ducruet and Notteboom (2012) systematically described the dynamic process of the evolution of the development of the container port system in the world, and used the related indicators of network centrality to analyze the spatial structure of global container port systems, measure the port system's properties and classify the ports' level in the system; González-Laxe et al. (2012) used the complex network characteristics analysis index, such as degree, centrality and vulnerability et al., to explore the changing pattern of global container shipping network structure before and after the global financial crisis (see also Part 3 of this book on vulnerability studies and political factors affecting shipping flows). The complex network method can directly reveal the connections between ports and the status of the port in the network, and it provides a new perspective for the identification of the shipping network system structure.

Trade volume between Taiwan and the Chinese mainland has steadily increased. Direct shipping greatly enhanced the efficiency and the demand for port cargo transportation and brought new opportunities to ports on both sides and their hinterlands (Li et al., 2011; Tai, 2012; Xie et al., 2012; Zhang and Zhai, 2009; Cao and Shou, 2014; Wang et al., 2011; Huang et al., 2003). With the development and improvement of port operations and route settings across the Taiwan Straits, certain scholars began to study the transfer function, competition and development model of container hub ports in Taiwan, Hong Kong and the Chinese mainland.

Others focused on analyzing the structural evolution between Fujian and Taiwan as well as the influential factors and principal effects on the development of ports in Taiwan since the opening of direct sailing routes (Wang and Zhen, 2009; Huang and Tai, 2008; Chen et al., 2012).

In terms of content, the above literature mainly focused on the influences of direct shipping on regional ports or the interaction of main hub ports. There has been scant in-depth research on the evolution model and dynamic mechanism of the container port system between Taiwan and the Chinese mainland (for other analyses of transnational port systems, see Chapters 8, 9, 11, 19, 23 and 24 on the Black Sea, Arctic, Mediterranean, USSR, Northwest Africa, and Indian subcontinent, respectively). The methodology used by most research projects was that of centralized measurement or classification based on port throughput. The identification of the complexity of the spatial structure of the container port system is still insufficient. There is qualitative knowledge about the changing situation, but it lacks a comprehensive, quantitative assessment, which this chapter provides.

The geographical location of ports on either side of the strait between China and Taiwan is similar: with the situation constantly changing, cross-strait relationships are both competitive and collaborative. This research, based on the perspective of complex networks, tries to describe in depth the evolution of the spatial structure of the container port system against the background of direct sailing routes, thereby revealing spatial mechanisms, which include social institutions, market economy and other factors.

Cross-strait navigation history

The situation of cross-strait relations has been changing since 1949, from tension and isolation to relaxation and intercommunication. In 1991, the trade value between mainland China and Taiwan was 4,234 million dollars. It reached 198,283 million dollars in 2014 (Figure 5.1). The degree of dependence between the

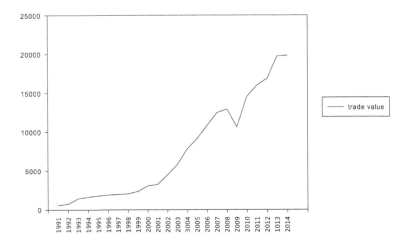

Figure 5.1 Trade value between mainland China and Taiwan (1991–2014)

mainland and Taiwan is greatly increased by the complementary nature of their respective economies. Marine navigation has experienced three stages displaying different characteristics as follows: "transshipment via a third port"; "indirect container liner shipping" and "direct shipping-links".

Transshipment via a third port (1984–1997)

The Standing Committee of the National People's Congress published a "Message to Compatriots in Taiwan" in 1979, which put forward the suggestion of achieving cross-strait intercommunication in trade, shipping and mail. However, this was rejected by the Taiwanese authorities. Until 1984, Taiwan allowed goods to be shipped to both sides via a third port. This meant that goods had to be first transported to a third port. Once approval documents were obtained, the goods could then be transported to their destination.

Indirect container shipping (1997–2008)

The Ministry of Communications of the People's Republic of China released documents that strengthened the management of cross-strait container liner transportation in April, 1997 (Ministry of Communication, 1997). 1. Indirect shipping: the Taiwanese authorities decided to open up indirect container liner shipping business between ports on the mainland and in Taiwan. Indirect container liner shipping ports included Fuzhou, Xiamen and Kaohsiung, Keelung and Taichung etc. However, participating ships needed to first go to Ishigaki in Japan or to Hong Kong. Once they had customs clearance, they were able to enter Taiwan. So the shipping mode for container ships during this period was indirect navigation. 2. Direct shipping: Fuzhou and Xiamen became pilot direct ports and Kaohsiung the "offshore shipping center". Direct shipping routes were opened between Fuzhou and Kaohsiung as well as Xiamen and Kaohsiung. However, bilateral trade goods could not be directly transported.

Direct shipping links (2008–)

The "cross-strait maritime agreement" was signed in 2008 (Association for Relations Across the Taiwan Strait, 2008). It meant that direct shipping had opened officially 11 ports in Taiwan and 63 on the mainland as the first cross-strait direct ports. With the improvement of cross-strait policies and measures, the number of participating seaports and shipping companies increased. Until 2013, there were 72 ports on the mainland, 11 ports in Taiwan and 40 ships participating. The ships that joined this program could transport goods corresponding to direct and indirect trade across the strait. But goods shipped by foreign enterprises, foreign business organizations or foreign individuals were forbidden.

Data and method

Data

The National Ministry of Transportation issued a "Shipping Capacity List of Indirect Container Lines on both sides of the Taiwan Strait" and a "List of Direct Shipping Lines and Ships of the Taiwan Strait", as well as other policies and documents relating to the cross-strait shipping operation. It also made detailed descriptions of the cross-strait container shipping routes, which included the ship operating company, the container liner name, operating routes and other specific content of cross-strait container line shipping, together with a detailed description of the shipping routes and their anchored ports (Ministry of Communication, 2004, 2009, 2013). These showed the development structure of the cross-strait container port system. Therefore, this study has chosen the above-mentioned three-stage container shipping routes as the data for the study of the cross-strait port system. We used Gephi8.0.2 software as the platform and conducted a directed weighted network of cross-strait container transport in 2004, 2009 and 2013.

Research method

Degree is an important index to describe the complex network node, as the degree of node is defined as the number of other nodes connected to the node; the greater the degree of a node, the more closely the node is connected with other nodes in the network and the greater the influence in the network. In a maritime network, the degree of a node is the number of ports connected to the port.

In a regional maritime network, there can often be more than one route connecting the two ports, and the connection between one port and another port contains a weight relationship on the number of routes. Node degree can represent the importance of the node in the unweighted network, which reflects the close relationship between a port and other ports in the port system, and there is a certain limitation in the frequency of port-to-port connection, which cannot accurately express the strength of the node connection in the weighted network. Therefore, this study introduces the strength of the midpoint in weighted network analysis, defined below (Barrat et al., 2004):

$$s_i = \sum_{j \in N} w_{ij} \tag{1}$$

In Gephi software, also known as the Weighted Degree, the sum of the edge between nodes and all other nodes connected in the network, including Weighted In-Degree and Weighted Out-Degree:

$$S_i = S_i^{in} + S_i^{out} = \sum_{j=1}(w_{ij} + w_{ji}) \tag{2}$$

In network topology, the clustering coefficient of a node is a parameter used to measure the local clustering of a network node. The clustering coefficient C_i of a node *i* refers to the number of edges that actually exists between all adjacent nodes and node *i*. The mathematical expression is defined below (Wang et al., 2006):

$$C_i = \frac{2E_i}{k_{i\bullet}(k_i-1)} \tag{3}$$

In the equation: k_i is the degree of the node *i* and is the actual number of edges between node *i* and adjacent nodes. From the geometric characteristics, the range of the aggregation coefficient is $0 \leq C_i \leq 1$. In the container liner shipping network, the agglomeration coefficient of the port node measures the degree of freight traffic between the neighboring ports. The higher the clustering coefficient of nodes is, the higher the degree of closeness of neighboring nodes is and the more likely a cluster comes into being between the node and the sub networks constituted by the peripheral nodes. The clustering coefficient of the network is defined as (Wang et al., 2006):

$$C = \frac{1}{n}\sum_n C_i \tag{4}$$

The bigger *C* is, the greater the degree of short-distance connection between the points in the whole network; therefore, the connection of each node in the container liner shipping network has a significant agglomeration effect.

Betweenness centrality mainly reflects the influence of the nodes in the network; it is an important parameter of network centrality and is used to represent the strength of the indirect link between nodes. In general, all kinds of transportation hubs are examples of large betweenness centrality of the node. Betweenness centrality of a node refers to all the shortest paths in the network, after the number of nodes of the proportion of the number of shortest paths, the node of the interface of the mathematical expression for (Xiong, 2009):

$$C_{Bi} = \sum_{k,j} \frac{\sum\limits_{l \in S_{kj}} \delta_l^i}{|S_{kj}|} \tag{5}$$

In the equation: S_{kj} is the shortest path combination between *k* and *i*, $\sum\limits_{l \in S_{kj}} \delta_l^i$ is the sum of the shortest path through the node *i*. In the container shipping network, the greater the centrality of the port, the stronger the hub of the port, and the more powerful the accessibility of other ports in relation to this port.

Assuming a connected network, Closeness Centrality (CC) can be defined as below (Crucitti et al., 2006):

$$C_i^C = \frac{N-1}{\sum\limits_{j=1; j \neq i}^{N} d_{ij}} \tag{6}$$

In this equation: d_{ij} is shortest distance between node *i* and *j*, while *N* is the number of nodes in this network. According to the formula, if a node is closer to a network of significant node density, there will be a shorter network path distance from this node to more nodes. Therefore, a node in a dense network, or one which is closely connected to or near other network nodes, will have a higher neighborhood centrality. In a complex network, proximity centrality can be perceived as a measure of the speed of the information transfer from a given node to other reachable nodes in the network. The greater the neighborhood centrality of the port node in a port system, the more convenient the port is to other ports; in other words, the transshipment function is stronger.

The evolution of maritime networks

The evolution pattern of the spatial connection of cross-strait ports

This study takes the network degree and the weighted degree of the cross-strait container ports in 2004, 2009 and 2013 as the port contact areas and the index of connection strength evolution, using ArcGIS to visualize the relationship index among the ports in the port system with a fuzzy clustering method (Figures 5.2 and 5.3). On the basis of the direct development mode and special policy system, it divides the evolution pattern of the ports' spatial connection of cross-strait containers into two important stages: "embryonic–development period" (2004–2008) and "development–maturity period" (2008–2013).

(1) 2004–2008: cross-strait shipping is still in the period of indirect container liner transportation, the main features of which are: ① the two ports of Xiamen and Fuzhou on mainland China can be directly related to the port of Kaohsiung; ② except for Xiamen and Fuzhou, the container liner requires transshipping via the third port of Hong Kong or Ishigaki. Therefore, the port system at this time covers a small number of ports, in addition to the anchored foreign ports, including only a total of 14, and the space connection between the two ports is weak. However, with the third port transfer function, the third port has a wide contact range and intensity concentration of spatial characteristics; the connection range of the ports of Ishigaki and Hong Kong reach 14 and 11, respectively, and the contact strengths are 53 and 54. The two ports had an important influence in the port system; Kaohsiung has the highest connection intensity in the port system, with a weighted degree of 57. Kaohsiung's contact range is second to Ishigaki. Of the mainland ports, Shanghai's connection range and intensity are the highest.

(2) 2009–2013: cross-strait containers did not need to transfer via a third port at this time. The direct port system gradually increased with the overall development of the port system. The characteristics of the port space contact pattern evolved mainly as follows: ① In general, the scope and intensity of the port space was gradually expanded and strengthened. In 2009, there were only three ports whose connection space was more than ten, and most of the links were concentrated in Kaohsiung, while by 2013, the connection degree above ten had increased to six ports: Keelung, Kaohsiung, Shanghai, Xiamen, Taichung and Hong Kong. ② The status of secondary ports was highlighted, with connections between ports becoming increasingly networked and less hierarchical. This can be clearly seen from the evolution of the scope and intensity of the shipping network. In 2009, the overall

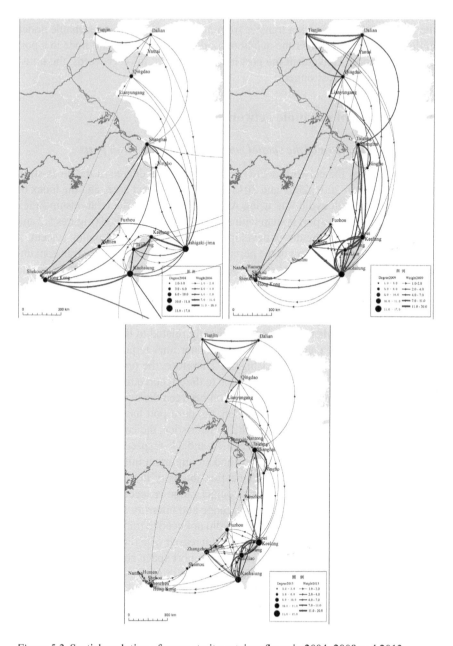

Figure 5.2 Spatial evolution of cross-strait container flows in 2004, 2008 and 2013

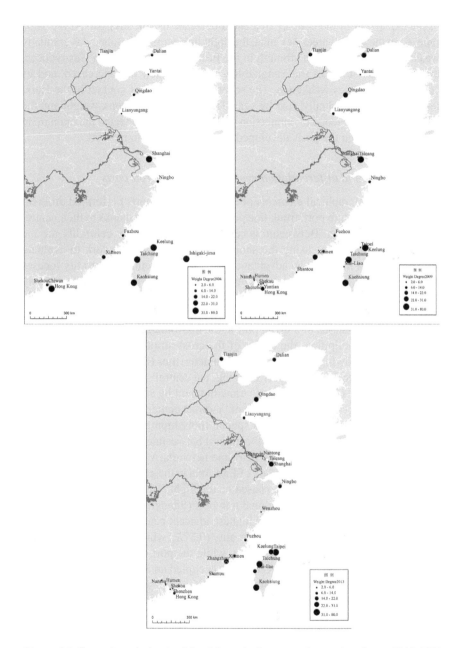

Figure 5.3 Strength evolution (weighted degree) of cross-strait container flows, 2004, 2008 and 2013

links between the two sides of the line were smaller, but the main trunk weight was large, while in 2013, the increase in routes and ports reflected the characteristics of the expansion of the contact area and a decrease in link strength. At the same time, from the coastal areas of China, the flight link across the Bohai was gradually weakened, and the contact strength in the Pearl River Delta region was reduced, but the contact scope of the Yangtze River Delta region was increased, and its contact strength was weakened. The scope and intensity of contact in the Haixi region increased gradually year by year. The weakening of trunk weight and the enlargement of the scope of connection of the port system reflected the main trend as the link between the ports developed from hierarchical to network.

The central spatial differentiation evolution of cross-strait ports

As the basic geographical elements of the port system, ports performed different functions, such as hub port, trunk line port and regional port thanks to their central spatial differentiation. Betweenness centrality and proximity centrality are the modes of measurement using the shortest distance in the network to evaluate whether the port node has an advantage in space. Betweenness centrality focuses on the convenience of the other port nodes in the system to a port node (namely accessibility). Proximity centrality emphasizes the difficulty of access to the node of a certain port in relation to other port nodes (namely, the transfer function), reflecting the hub status of a given port in the maritime network. Against a background of direct shipping, the center of the cross-strait container ports mainly presented the following space evolution characteristics (Figure 5.4).

At the commencement of direct shipping, the central spatial distribution of the port presented the characteristics of "transshipment by specific ports". Under the influence of the special shipping mode of "indirect container liner transportation", the port center was centralized in a special transshipment port (Ishigaki, Hong Kong), with the former occupying the highest betweenness centrality (0.387) and proximity centrality (0.409) in the maritime network. At the same time, through the impact of the status enhancement of East Asia in the global skill network, capital elements of the flow were also based on the flight route to form the hub center "cluster" in an important international hub port (Shanghai, Kaohsiung). On both sides of the Strait, Shanghai had the highest adjacent center (0.443), while Kaohsiung had the highest betweenness centrality (0.373), which indicated that Shanghai's port transport function was strong, while the port of Kaohsiung was more easily accessible. Shanghai and Kaohsiung occupied an important hub function.

For the ongoing development of direct shipping, the spatial distribution of the centrality function showed a trend from "concentration" toward "decentralization". This is the stage when the cross-strait port system was formed and developed gradually. The evolution of its port system was not influenced by specific transshipment ports. In 2009, the centrality of the cross-strait port system was mainly concentrated in Hong Kong, Shanghai, Kaohsiung and other ports. Among them, the betweenness centrality (0.400) and adjacent centrality (0.541) of Kaohsiung were the strongest. The hub function of Hong Kong was weakened by comparison with the embryonic stage of direct shipping, but it also maintained a high degree of accessibility within the port system, and the port of Shanghai still held onto a strong transport function. In 2013, with the increase of direct ports in the coastal areas of China, the central transport function was no longer

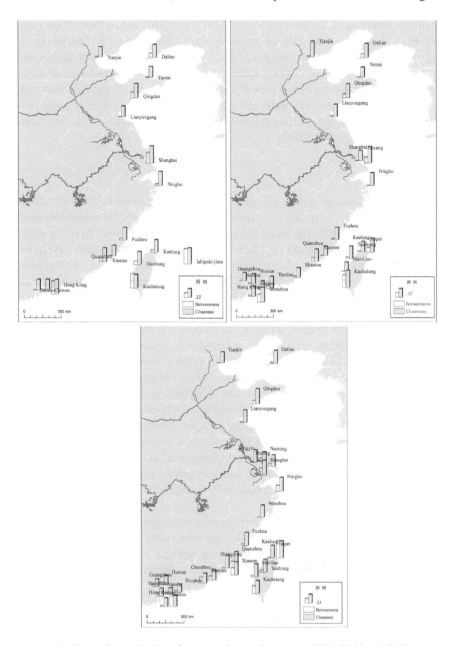

Figure 5.4 Centrality evolution of cross-strait container ports, 2004, 2008 and 2013

concentrated in the three regional hub ports. The ports around the hubs began to strengthen gradually to share or even replace the accessibility and transport function of the original hubs in the cross-strait port system. Kaohsiung's transport function and accessibility decreased significantly, and Keelung became the port with greater ease of access with an important transport function in the region. The transfer function of the port of Shanghai fell to 0.397, below that of Qingdao (0.403). Hong Kong became increasingly accessible (0.363). Furthermore, the accessibility of Xiamen also improved greatly compared with the past, and moved into second place only after Hong Kong. In general, the spatial centrality distribution for the port system in this period was characterized by the gradual reduction of the centrality of original hubs and the gradual improvement of original sub-harbors. Therefore, the spatial evolution of port centrality also moved from "concentration" to "decentralization".

Conclusion

From the "indirect container shipping" policy implemented in 1997 to "direct maturity" in 2013, the spatial structure of the container maritime network on both sides of Taiwan Straits has demonstrated the tendency to move from "specific transport port concentration" to "hub port concentration", and then developed towards a "regional network". In the first stage, under the influence of special direct shipping mechanisms, the port system with its spatial connection patterns and central functionality of a third port-Ishigaki and Hong Kong- had a strong agglomeration effect, and Kaohsiung became the most powerful link, with a pivotal role in the port system, while the links between the cross-strait ports were weak. In the second stage, in parallel to the construction of cross-strait shipping networks and the initial formation of the port system, Shanghai, Kaohsiung, Hong Kong and other international hub ports enjoyed advantages in the initial period and acted as a self-strengthening mechanism, determining the characteristics of the port space contact area and the strength and development of the central accessibility of the port; overall the port system presents the spatial characteristics of a hierarchical structure. In the third stage, under the influence of what could be called the "periphery challenge effect", shipping companies began to choose routes concentrated on regional trunk ports and some small peripheral port areas, thus creating a decentralized development of the maritime network, and the regional development of peripheral ports.

The spatial evolution mechanism of the cross-strait port system is influenced by the cross-strait special navigation mode, "core-periphery" competition in the port regions, regional economic development and strategic planning and other social system environment and market economy factors. Among them, the policy effect is the main driving force on evolution and development in the cross-strait container port system. In general, the development of the cross-strait container port system is affected by special policies. From the perspective of the social institution environment, both the specific navigation mode of continuous evolution and the general promotion of ECFA have made it possible to save shipping costs and improve time efficiency and to open up the new supply market of cross-strait industry. In addition, the choice of location for Taiwanese investment also to some extent affected the route configuration and shipping links with the main ports in the four major economic zones along the coast of China.

After 2013, the cooperation of ports on the mainland of China – Shanghai, Tianjin, Dalian, Qingdao, Xiamen, Ningbo, Quanzhou, Zhoushan, Taizhou and Humen – has led to the establishment of strategic partnerships with Kaohsiung, Keelung, Taichuang and Hualian. But in the wake of the international economic downturn, the economic slowdown in China and the new government in power in Taiwan, the development of the cross-strait ports is slowing down.

References

Airriess, C.A. (1989) The spatial spread of container transport in a developing regional economy. *Transportation Research Part A*, 23(6): 453–461.

Association for Relations Across the Taiwan Strait. (2008) *Explanation Concerning the Cross-Strait Sea Transport Agreement*, November 4.

Barrat, A., Barthélemy, M., Pastor-Satorras, R., Vespignani, A. (2004) The architecture of complex weighted networks. *Proceedings of the National Academic Sciences USA*, 101(11): 3747–3752.

Bird, J. (1971) *Seaports and Seaport Terminals*. London: Hutchinson.

Cao, T., Shou, J. (2014) The analysis of the driving effect on Taiwanese port. *Special Zone Economy*, 2: 70–71.

Cao, Y. (1999) On the evolution model of the container port system – A case study of the lower Changjiang River container port system. *Scientia Geographica Sinica*, 19(6): 485–490.

Cao, Y., Cao, W., Jin, S. (2003) The evolution mechanism of the coastal container port system of China. *Acta Geographica Sinica*, 58(3): 424–432.

Cao, Y., Li, H., Chen, W. (2004) The spatial structure and the competition pattern of the container port system of China. *Acta Geographica Sinica*, 59(6): 1020–1027.

Chen, C., Yang, Q., Zhu, J. (2012) A study of the issues and response strategies for container ports in Taiwan after the commencement of Cross-Strait direct shipping. *Transportation Planning Journal*, 41(1): 55–79.

Comtois, C., Wang, J.J. (2003) Géopolitique et transports: nouvelles perspectives stratégiques dans le détroit de Taiwan. *Etudes Stratégiques*, 34(2): 213–227.

Crucitti, P., Latora, V., Porta, S. (2006) Centrality in networks of urban streets. *Chaos*, 16(1): 1–9.

Deng, W.B., Long, G., Wei, L., Xu, C. (2009) Worldwide marine transportation network: Efficiency and container throughput. *Chinese Physics Letters*, 26(11): 118901.

Ducruet, C., Notteboom, T.E. (2012) The worldwide maritime network of container shipping: Spatial structure and regional dynamics. *Global Networks*, 12(3): 395–423.

Ducruet, C., Roussin, S., Jo, J.C. (2009) Political and economic factors in the evolution of North Korea's maritime connections. *Journal of International Logistics and Trade*, 7(1): 1–23.

González-Laxe, F., Freire Seoane, M.J., Pais Montes, C. (2012) Maritime degree, centrality and vulnerability: Port hierarchies and emerging areas in containerized transport (2008–2010). *Journal of Transport Geography*, 24: 33–44.

Hayuth, Y. (1981) Containerization and the load center concept. *Economic Geography*, 57(2): 160–176.

Hayuth, Y. (1988) Rationalization and concentration of the U.S. container port system. *The Professional Geographer*, 40(3): 279–288.

Hoyle, B.S., Charlier, J. (1995) Inter-port competition in developing countries. *Journal of Transport Geography*, 3(2): 87–103.

Huang, C., Tai, H. (2008) Analysis of relative competitiveness among major hub-ports across Taiwan Strait. *Journal of the Chinese Institute of Transportation*, 20(1): 1–38.

Huang, M., Li, W., Wu, P. (2003) Study on the status of small three links in the both sides of the Taiwan Strait and prospect on direct voyage between Fujian & Taiwan. *Economic Geography*, 23(4): 495–498.

Jian, L., Li, D., Liu, L. (2012) Research on the evolution law of China container port system. *Economic Geography*, 32(12): 91–96.

Kaluza, P., Kölzsch, A., Gastner, M.T., Blasius, B. (2010) The complex network of global cargo ship movements. *Journal of the Royal Society Interface*, 7(48): 1093–1103.

Kuby, M., Reid, N. (1992) Technological change and the concentration of U.S. general cargo port system: 1970–1988. *Economic Geography*, 68(3): 272–289.

Le, Y., Ieda, H. (2010) Evolution dynamics of container port systems with a Geo-Economic concentration index: A comparison of Japan, China and Korea. *Asian Transport Studies*, 1(1): 46–61.

Li, L., Liu, J., Li, C. (2011) Analysis of dynamic efficiency of main ports in mainland China, Hongkong, and Taiwan – Based on DEA-Malmquist productivity index. *Soft Science*, 25(5): 80–84.

Marcadon, J. (1999) Containerization in the ports of Northern and Western Europe. *Geojournal*, 48: 15–20.

Ministry of Communication. (1997) *The Announcement on Strengthening the Taiwan Strait Indirect Container Liner Transportation Management*, April 11.

Ministry of Communication. (2004) *The Announcement on Strengthening the Taiwan Strait Container Liner Transportation Management*, June 24.

Ministry of Communication. (2009) *The Shipping Companies and List of Working on Direct-Sailing Across Taiwan Strait*, March 5.

Ministry of Communication. (2013) *The Container Liner Transportation Companies and List of Direct-Sailing Across Taiwan Strait*, March 5.

Mo, H., Wang, J., Jin, F. (2008) Complexity perspective on transportation network. *Progress in Geography*, 27(6): 112–120.

Notteboom, T.E. (1997) Concentration and load centre development in the European container port system. *Journal of Transport Geography*, 5(2): 99–115.

Rimmer, P.J., Comtois, C. (2005) China's extra- and intra-Asian liner shipping connections, 1990–2000. *Journal of International Logistics and Trade*, 3: 75–97.

Tai, H. (2012) The influence on transshipment function of Kaohsiung port by the trunk-route deployments in the East Aisa and Cross-Strait direct shipping. *Transportation Planning Journal*, 41(4): 435–464.

Wang, C. (2008) Spatial organization networks of world marine container transportation. *Geographical Research*, 27(3): 636–648.

Wang, C. (2012) *The Evolutionary and Developmental Mechanism of Container Port Network*. Beijing: Science Press.

Wang, J.J. (1998) A container load center with a developing hinterland: A case study of Hong Kong. *Journal of Transport Geography*, 6(3): 187–201.

Wang, L., Zhen, H. (2009) Study on the development patterns of Xiamen & Kaohsiung double hub-ports in the context of direct-sailing. *Shipping Management*, 31(7): 21–25.

Wang, Q., Wu, S., Xu, L. (2011) Structural evolution and spatial matching of port system in the context of the three direct links between Fujian and Taiwan, China. *Scientia Geographica Sinica*, 31(5): 513–519.

Wang, X., Li, X., Chen, G. (2006) *The Theory and Application of Complex Network*. Beijing: Tsinghua University Press.

Wu, Q., Zhang, H., Ye, Y., Chen, J. (2013) Port system evolution model in Pearl River delta. *Tropical Geography*, 33(2): 171–177.

Xie, Y., Zhu, J., Wang, K. (2012) *The Influence of Taiwanese Port Operation on Deployment of Fleet and Routes for Container Shipping Companies After Direct-sailing Across Taiwan-strait*. Taibei: Institute of Transportation.

Xiong, W. (2009) *The Research of Structural Characteristics and Dynamic Behavior in World Marine Network*. Doctoral Dissertation, Qingdao University, Qingdao.

Yang, J., Luo, M., Wu, X. (2012) Research on the evolution process of U.S. container port system. *Economic Geography*, 32(2): 94–100.

Yang, J., Wu, X., Luo, M. (2014) Regional economy, transport infrastructure and container port system evolution process: A comparative study of China and the U.S. in 1979–2010. *Economic Geography*, 34(2): 80–85.

Zhang, M., Zhai, Z. (2009) The brief talk of direct-sailing container transportation across Taiwan-strait. *Container Transport*, 20(11): 12–14.

6 Liner shipping forelands of Portugal's main ports

Tiago A. Santos and Carlos Guedes Soares

Globalization has led to a large increase in trade between countries, most of which is carried out by sea. In order to meet the increasing demand for maritime transport, particularly in the case of manufactured goods, a large and complex network of liner services has been developed, linking the major economic regions of the world. At the same time, recent years have seen major changes in the economic importance of different regions of the world, namely a shift in the economic center of gravity towards the Asia-Pacific region, perhaps the most recent stage of the Westline theory described in Stopford (2009).

Liner shipping connectivity has become a major issue for modern economies due to the highly integrated nature of the modern globalized world. This holds especially true for small open economies of maritime countries that are highly dependent on exports for economic growth, such as Portugal. For these countries, the number and type of the liner services calling at its ports are determinants for the competitiveness of its exports.

Liner services relate mostly to containerized cargo, whose volume has continuously expanded since the 1960s, with special relevance since the beginning of the twenty-first century. This growth has been also largely achieved at the expense of general cargo. Apart from general cargo, other liner trades exist, for example for roll-on roll-off cargo, but their relative magnitude is much less significant. In particular, ports in Portugal receive a regular service using ConRo ships, implying that some additional container capacity exists in these services, but the geographical scope is the same as the pure container services, which are the only ones considered in this study. Likewise, domestic containership lines have not been included here.

Liner services have evolved from the traditional pattern, typical of the general cargo era, to the contemporary hub and spoke pattern. In this new pattern, liner services directly link fewer ports, calling rather on large hub ports, which can be gateways to major economic regions or transshipment hubs. In both cases, the hubs are connected to a rather large number of smaller ports, the spokes, via feeder services. Transshipment hubs also provide the possibility of acting as relays, allowing the transfer of cargo between different deep sea services. Examining the network of liner services offered by major shipping companies provides insight into the typical services offered to the different types of trade. This study examines data relating liner services to types of trade for the Atlantic Ocean routes and their connections with Northern Europe and the Mediterranean Sea.

Portugal is located in a strategic location, in the vicinity of these two connections, and a substantial number of liner services pass along the Portuguese coast. It is therefore of interest to examine this particular network of liner services, especially those that call in ports of the so-called 'Portuguese Range'. In this range, the most important ports are Leixões, Lisbon, Setúbal and Sines, and all except Setúbal (which now shares a common management with Lisbon) are EU core network ports. Leixões and Sines are located near oil refineries, and, as a result, the cargo throughput is much larger than in the other ports. Lisbon is important for dry bulk cargos (agrobulks) due to industry which consumes these cargos. Sines is also a major coal import port thanks to two coal-fired power plants located nearby. For the purposes of the main focus of this chapter – containerized cargo – the principal ports are Sines, Leixões and Lisbon.

The main issue for the Portuguese range has long been the attraction of cargo from Spain, especially containerized cargo. The focus is therefore on the enlargement of the ports' hinterland to landlocked regions of Spain, as detailed in Santos and Guedes Soares (2015). This objective depends on improvements in rail corridors between both countries, which are now under the scope of EU freight rail corridor Nº4. The Portuguese government is actively seeking EU funding for rail-related projects and private investment in ports, namely the expansion of existing container terminals and the construction of new ones. It is therefore of interest to study in detail the existing liner services in Portuguese ports and identify which types of services are needed or may be attracted for transshipment purposes.

Since 2004, the Portuguese range integrates a major transshipment hub in Sines, which competes directly with other hubs in the Strait of Gibraltar region. The first step in the development of these hubs came in 2000 when a large expansion of the existing Maersk container terminal in Algeciras was inaugurated. Four years later, in 2004, the Sines container terminal (named Terminal XXI) in Portugal started operations as a public service concession granted to the Port of Singapore Authority (PSA). Years later, in 2008, the Morocco-based Tangier container terminals (APMT and Eurogate) opened to traffic. Finally, in 2010, the South Korean shipping company Hanjin opened a new terminal in Algeciras. Taking into consideration the prominence that these two ports have achieved in transshipment in the Strait of Gibraltar, this study aims at assessing also their connectivity with Portuguese ports and the relative importance of these hubs in comparison with traditional hubs, such as Rotterdam and Antwerp.

This study also allows the classification of ports in the 'Portuguese Range' according to the types of services calling at them and the identification of the foreign ports to which these services provide connection. These services are compared with the types of services typical of the global network that pass near the Portuguese coast to identify overlaps and missed opportunities. In order to carry out this study, a database of liner services in Portuguese ports (effective in the spring of 2015) was created using information from port administrations and shipping companies.

The chapter is organized as follows: first, a brief literature review is given for liner shipping network analysis, followed by a general description of Portuguese ports and of a database of liner services that serve these ports. The database results are then used to identify the major types of liner services that call at Portuguese ports. The number of services, type of services, regions served, frequency and capacity are discussed. A comparison is made with the typical container trades that pass near the Portuguese coast. The matter is then analyzed from the perspective of which ports are most often connected to Portugal, how numerous the services are and what their geographical dispersion is. This analysis is carried out for direct-call ports only, with no consideration given to ports that can be reached only by means of transshipment.

Literature review

The study of liner shipping networks is relatively recent. Different approaches have been used, from graph theory applied to transport networks, (see Ducruet et al., 2010), to functional analysis or individual and group practices while using transport networks (studies on shipping companies' own liner networks, such as Frémont (2007, 2015) and Rimmer and Comtois (2005)). One major problem in these studies is the quantification of the transport flows, which involves substantial amounts of data, frequently not publicly available. This problem is generally overcome by studying the physical layout of the network itself, rather than the cargo flows. It is implicitly assumed that the network layout will result, to a certain extent, from the relative magnitude of the cargo flows.

Apart from network analysis, authors such as Wilmsmeier et al. (2006) and Márquez-Ramos et al. (2005) have examined the relationship between port connectivity and international maritime transport costs (expressed by freight rates). These studies do not focus on the quantitative assessment of the port connectivity of different countries, a topic considered by Hoffman (2005) in the development of the Liner Shipping Connectivity Index (LSCI). This index has subsequently been published annually by UNCTAD (2016), covering a significant number of maritime countries and helping public decision-makers to promote maritime transportation. However, this index does not consider ports or liner services individually, a topic considered by relatively few authors, most notably Low et al. (2009). Jiang et al. (2015) adopt yet another perspective: that of global liner shipping companies mainly interested in the impact in transportation time and capacity of individual liner services and each of its links.

Despite being limited by statistical data, network analysis has allowed improved knowledge of maritime networks in general and of trading patterns of specific shipping companies (for example, those serving the Atlantic Ocean, see Slack (1999) and Ducruet et al. (2010)), and it has enabled the identification of different categories of port regions or port systems. Major ports in Northern Europe, for example, form a gateway into that geographical region (direct-call ports), while the Caribbean is a typical hub port region. Interestingly, the ports in the Portuguese coast now include a hub port, which may be considered as part of the hub port region of the Strait of Gibraltar (Algeciras, Tangier, Sines but also Las Palmas), but consist primarily of medium-sized ports engaged primarily in short sea shipping. These ports form a gateway to Portugal, but currently not so much to Spain, as shown in Santos and Guedes Soares (2015) and Santos et al. (2015). Within the scope of regional studies, it is also worth mentioning Tovar et al. (2015), which presents a comprehensive review of network analysis studies, including the most common connectivity indicators and applies these to the specific case of the Canary Islands (Spain) ports (for other analyses of the external linkages of national port systems, see Chapters 10, 20 and 21 on USA, China and North Korea, respectively).

This study presents research focused on the examination of each port's connectivity using metrics such as number of liner services, vessel capacity and frequency of service. Preferential attachments of ports are also explored, especially taking into consideration that new hub ports came into operation in Portugal and in the Strait of Gibraltar (Sines, Tangier, new terminal in Algeciras) and that, as recognized by De Langen et al. (2002), liner shipping networks evolve over time and so does the hierarchy of ports.

Liner services in Portuguese ports

Characteristics of the Portuguese range

The commercial ports that constitute the Portuguese range are divided into two groups: the northern group, with Leixões and Aveiro; and the southern group, with Lisbon, Setúbal and Sines. More commercial ports exist along this coast, but their throughput is smaller, and they are not engaged in containerized cargo. Figure 6.1 shows the location of the Portuguese range on the west coast of the Iberian Peninsula, centered on the three core European network ports: Leixões, Lisbon and Sines. The same figure shows that a total of five port authorities exist in Portugal, each one managing two (in one case, only one) geographically close ports. This management structure is relatively new in Portugal and is still undergoing a phase of testing and monitoring.

Out of the ports shown in Figure 6.1, the ports called on by liner services (containerized cargo) are Leixões in the north and Lisbon, Setúbal and Sines in the south, and these are the ones that will be considered in this study. The maximum dimensions of the allowable ships in the different ports are shown in Table 6.1, demonstrating that Sines is the port capable of receiving the largest ships.

Table 6.2 shows the characteristics of the container terminals in the port mentioned above. Leixões possesses the main container terminal in the north (TCL), which serves mainly the north and center of Portugal and is engaged primarily in SSS. Lisbon possesses three container terminals (Liscont, Sotagus, TML), which, together with the Sadoport container terminal in Setúbal, serve the Lisbon metropolitan area and the southern part of the country, and are engaged primarily in SSS.

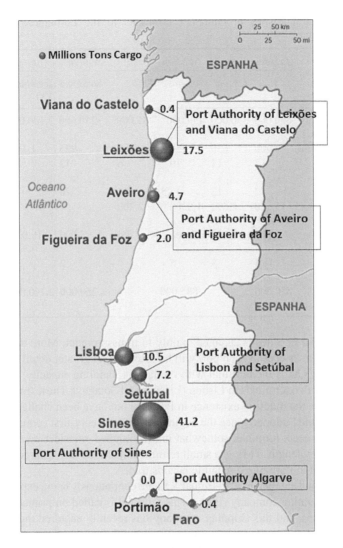

Figure 6.1 The Portuguese range, port cargo throughput and governance structure in 2015

Table 6.1 Maximum capacity of containerships allowable in Portuguese ports

Port	Maximum capacity of ship (TEU)	Maximum length for port (m)	Maximum draught for port (m)
Leixões	4,000	220	12
Lisbon	6,000	240-WL	16.5
Setubal	5,000	WL	12.5
Sines	18,000	400	17.5

Table 6.2 Characteristics of container terminals in the Portuguese range (own elaboration)

Characteristic	Leixões	Lisbon			Setúbal	Sines	Total
	TCL	Liscont	Sotagus	TML	Sadoport	Terminal XXI	
Handling capacity (TEU)	850,000	350,000	450,000	~85,000	~250,000	2,100,000	3,305,000
Quay length (m)	900	630	750	480	725	1,146	4,631
Quay water depth (m)	12	14	10	6	12	17	–
Area (ha)	22	12	16.5	4.8	20	39	114
Yard capacity (TEU)	13,150	8,592	1,0300	2,300	–	–	–
Maximum size of ships (TEU)	4,000	6,000	2,000	~700	5,000	18,000	–
Quay gantries (units)	5	3	5	–	2	9	24
Total capacity per port (TEU)	850,000		885,000		250,000	2,100,000	3,305,000

Terminal XXI in Sines is engaged mainly in transshipment. More details on the existing liner services in each port will be discussed in greater detail below.

Terminal XXI is the terminal with the largest handling capacity, followed by TCL and by two terminals in Lisbon (Liscont and Sotagus). These three container terminals are the oldest in existence in Portugal but have been challenged by Terminal XXI and Sadoport since the beginning of the twenty-first century. Sadoport is the most recent terminal, somewhat underequipped, considering the available area and quay length. TML is a small terminal, operating only geared feeder vessels engaged in Portuguese Atlantic islands trade.

The area and equipment of Terminal XXI are continuously being expanded by the terminal operating company (PSA). This terminal is called on primarily by MSC containerships, and this shipping company has recently acquired the Portuguese state-owned freight railway operator and is currently running this service between various intermodal terminals (some owned by MSC logistics) and Sines. The latest significant development is the acquisition of the TCL, Liscont and Sotagus terminals (and other terminals for different types of cargo) by Yildirim Port Holdings, another global terminal operator company. Further details on these developments and on long-standing port regionalization objectives (primarily directed to the Spanish hinterland) may be found in Santos and Guedes Soares (2015) and Santos et al. (2015).

Figure 6.2 shows the evolution of container throughput (in TEU) in the four ports between 2001 and 2015. The most significant ports, according to their TEU throughput, are Sines and Leixões. At the same time, these are the ports where throughput has grown significantly. Setúbal also grew considerably last year, by approximately 18%, although throughput remains low. Although Sines is by far the most important port, it is necessary to take into account that in 2015 around 78% of its throughput consisted of transshipped containers. The remaining 22%

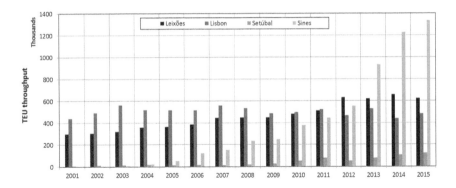

Figure 6.2 Container throughput in Portuguese ports (all types of containers)

are domestic containers, distributed mainly by rail, while a small fraction corresponds to containers bound for/from Spain.

Database of liner services

Considering the ports of Lisbon, Leixões, Setúbal and Sines, a liner services database has been compiled using the information reported and freely available in the spring of 2015. This information comes mainly from the Portuguese port authorities (see, for example, Lisbon Port Authority (2015)), shipping companies' websites, annual reports and network and service reports (see, for example, Hamburg-Süd (2014) and Hapag-Lloyd (2015)). Several ports in the Portuguese islands in the Atlantic Ocean (the Azores and Madeira) are also handling containers, but these come exclusively from the liner services connecting with the Portuguese mainland, so these ports have not been considered in the present study, which adopts an international perspective. It is also important to bear in mind that liner services are continuously being updated by shipping companies through schedule and port rotation changes. However, the overall picture that emerges from the study of these data sources is largely stable in the medium term, with the previously mentioned minor changes in the short term and major changes, at the port level, only occurring in the long term.

Overall, these four ports are called at by 79 liner services, but if the domestic services and the repeated services (same service calling at several ports) are removed, only 44 services call at Portuguese ports. For each of these liner services, a number of important parameters have been recorded, including the following: commercial designation, shipping company, full port sequence, Portuguese ports called at, capacity of ships currently deployed and frequency of service. In order to categorize the different services, it is first necessary to define the meaning of deep sea services, short sea services and feeder services in the context of the analysis carried out in this study:

* Deep sea services are regular services carried out between different continents or between very distant regions of the same continent. These include east-west services and north-south services.

- Short sea services are defined by the EU as regular services carried out between ports of the EU and ports outside the EU of countries along the Mediterranean, Black Sea, Baltic Sea, Norway and Iceland, including national and international traffic along the coast and up to islands, rivers and lakes in those countries.
- Feeder services are those intended to carry containers to and from hub ports, and may be or not short sea shipping services. For the purpose of this study, feeder services have been considered to be those calling at Tangier Med, Algeciras and Sines. Calls at other hubs in the region, such as Valencia and Barcelona, have not been considered as sufficient to categorize the service as a feeder service, since transshipment volumes in these ports are typically lower than in the above ports.
- Domestic services are those between ports of the same country in the EU and they fall within the scope of short sea shipping services. In the Portuguese case, these consist of the services bound to the Portuguese islands in the Atlantic Ocean: Madeira and the Azores.

Table 6.3 shows the number of liner services in Portuguese ports. The two ports with the most services are Lisbon and Leixões, followed by Sines. However, seven of the services calling at Lisbon and Leixões are bound for the Portuguese islands (domestic services). Neither of the other two ports have services dedicated to these domestic trades. Also shown is the number of coincident services in each port, that is, the number of services in each port which also call at another Portuguese port. This is very significant in Lisbon, Leixões and Setúbal and derives from the fact that these are the main ports on the western coast of the Peninsula, serving two important metropolitan areas with a high number of manufacturing industries. The vast majority of the services calling at Sines do not call at other Portuguese ports.

Table 6.3 also shows the number of domestic, feeder, SSS and deep sea services in Portuguese ports. Sines has the largest number of pure deep sea services, which

Table 6.3 Characteristics of liner services in Portuguese ports

	Leixões	Lisbon	Setúbal	Sines
Number of services	26	31	6	10
Number of coincident services	25	22	4	2
Types-Domestic	7	7	0	0
Types-Feeder	9	13	1	4
Types-SSS	5	2	5	0
Types-Deep Sea	5	9	0	12
Weekly	18	21	4	15
Bi-weekly	1	0	1	1
Two weeks	4	6	1	0
Three weeks	1	1	0	0
Monthly	2	3	0	0

in some cases call at more distant transshipment hubs. No deep sea service is present in Setúbal. A substantial number of feeder services are present in Lisbon and Leixões, indicating a substantial number of connections with Algeciras and Tangier-Med. Sines is called at by four feeder services. Setúbal, but also Leixões, are substantially engaged in SSS services, mainly for Northern Europe. Regarding the frequency of the liner services, most services are weekly, followed by a few calling every two weeks and in rare cases once a month. Services calling twice a week or every three weeks are residual. These results are in line with what is now common in the liner industry worldwide, given the preference of shippers for weekly services.

Geographical coverage of liner services

Figure 6.3 shows the regions served by liner services calling at each different port. It may be seen that Sines has the widest reach, connecting Portugal with every continent and fully integrated in the major east-west trade lanes. Setúbal is restricted to short sea shipping (Europe and North Africa). Lisbon and Leixões are also engaged primarily in short sea shipping and domestic services, but Leixões features some deep sea lines to West Africa and southern Africa, while Lisbon is additionally connected to the Americas (North and South), implying some integration in the major east-west trade lanes. In general, Portuguese ports provide comprehensive direct connections with most of the world, although several regions outside Europe and Africa are poorly connected. The main regions not directly connected with Portugal are Japan/Korea, the west coast of South America and the Black Sea. The East Coast of the US and East Mediterranean are served only by services calling in Sines, a situation shared with all regions east of the Suez Canal. This situation represents a large dependence on the success of Sines as a transshipment hub.

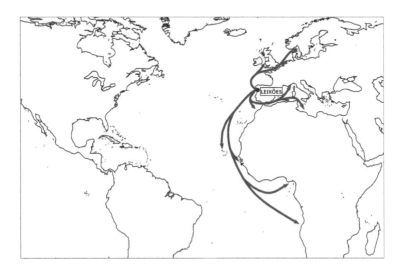

Figure 6.3 Maritime forelands of selected main ports

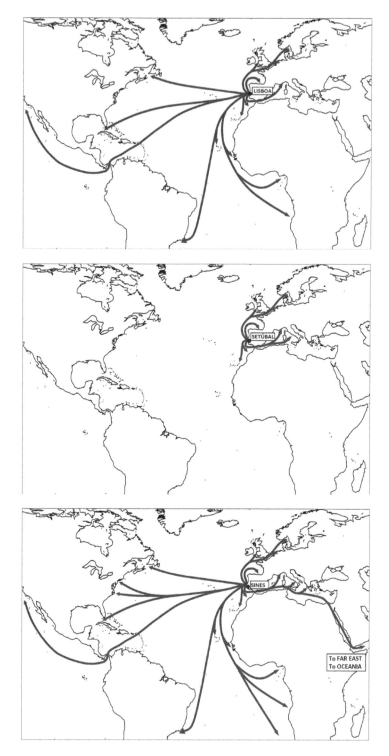

Figure 6.3 (Continued)

Insertion in global liner services patterns

In order to identify the global liner services patterns relevant for the Portuguese coast, the reports or websites of major shipping companies as CMA-CGM, MSC, Maersk, Hamburg-Sud and Hapag-Lloyd have been analyzed. The major types of liner services which pass close to the Portuguese coast as identified in those reports and websites (see, for example, Hamburg-Süd (2014) and Hapag-Lloyd (2015)) and its typical variants were identified. Table 6.4 shows the number of variants which pass near the Portuguese coast and those that call at least one Portuguese port. The conclusion is that only a few services from Northern Europe and West Mediterranean to regions around the Atlantic call at Portuguese ports. Overall, since most major shipping companies operate several services in each variant and generally only one service of each variant calls in Portuguese ports, the conclusion is that Portuguese ports are not very important to most of these trades. The exceptions are the short sea trades and trades to Africa.

Capacity of liner services

Figure 6.4 shows the capacity of the ships currently deployed in services calling at the different ports. In Sines, one service uses ships in the 13,000 TEU capacity range and three other services use ships in the 7,000–9,000 TEU range. Another five services use ships with capacities above 4,000 TEU, (i.e. postpanamax ships). It is also worth noting that the ships deployed in feeder services are all below 1,000 TEU capacity. For Setúbal, the largest ship has a capacity of 1,200 TEU.

In Lisbon, the maximum capacity of calling ships is 6,000 TEU. There is also a service deploying ships of 4,000 TEU and five others use ships of around 2,000 TEU. All of these services are either deep sea or feeder services (to Algeciras or Tangier-Med). Domestic services and other feeder services use ships predominantly below 1000 TEU capacity. Regarding Leixões, three services use ships slightly larger than 2,000 TEU capacity and two other use ships 1,500–2,000 TEU capacity. All the other services use ships below 1,000 TEU capacity.

Figure 6.5 shows a comparison of the maximum size of ships deployed in liner services calling at a given port and the maximum sizes of ships that the ports can handle. This port capacity may be dictated by the harbor entrance or by the

Table 6.4 Variants calling in Portuguese ports for each type of liner service

Type of liner service	Number of variants passing close to coast	Number of variants calling in Portuguese ports
Asia-Northern Europe and USA	2	2
Northern Europe-Atlantic	11	4
West Mediterranean-Atlantic	8	3
Short Sea Shipping and West Africa	9	9

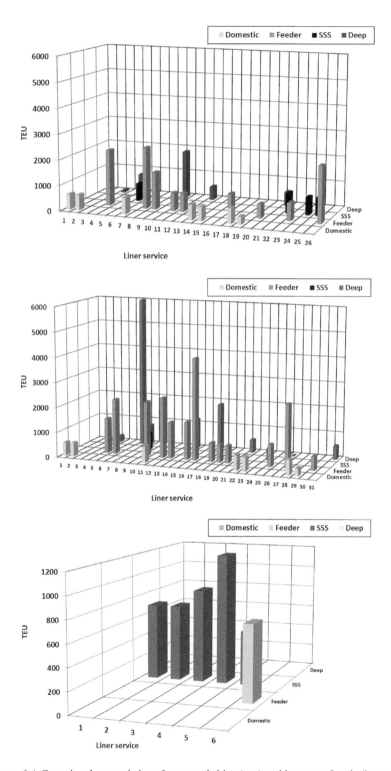

Figure 6.4 Capacity characteristics of ports and ships (top) and by type of trade (bottom)

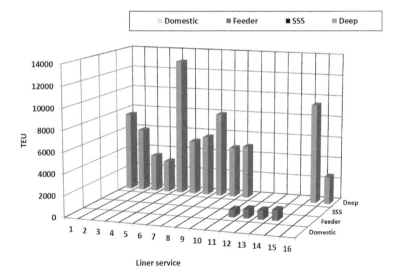

Figure 6.4 (Continued)

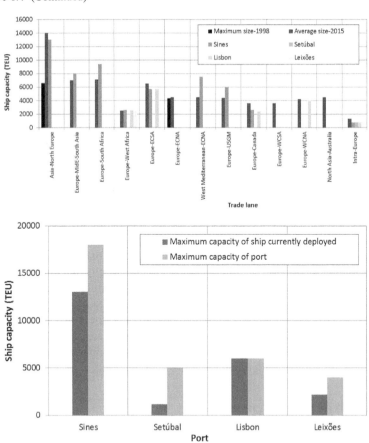

Figure 6.5 Capacity characteristics of ports and ships (left) and by type of trade (right)

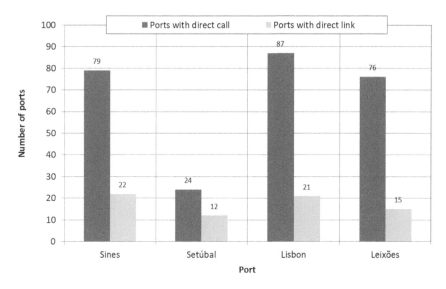

Figure 6.6 Number of ports with direct call and with direct link to Portuguese ports

terminal quay limitations, considering fully loaded ships. It may be seen that Lisbon is already receiving ships of maximum possible size, but this corresponds to the Brazil service and is an exception rather than the rule. This port also receives another service in which ships of 4,000 TEU are deployed, but otherwise the ships are in the range of less than 2,000 TEU. This is approximately the same range of capacity of ships calling at Leixões. Sines is able to receive ships of 18,000 TEU and currently receives ships of 13,000 TEU or, in a few cases even larger, deployed in the Far East trade. The largest ship received currently in Setúbal has a capacity for 1,200 TEUs but the port can receive much larger ships. Bearing these considerations in mind, Leixões and Lisbon appear to be the more restricted ports in terms of maximum ship size.

Figure 6.6 shows the average and maximum capacity of ships deployed in different trade lanes in 1998 and 2015 compared to the capacity of the ships currently deployed in liner services in the same lanes that call at Portuguese ports. The figure is based on the results of the database and on results from Slack (1999) and Sharma (2015). It can be seen that for services calling in Sines, the actual capacity of the ships is often higher than average. For Lisbon, the ships are generally at the average size or slightly below. In the intra-Europe trades, ships calling at any of the Portuguese ports are smaller than the average in such trades.

Connectivity of Portuguese ports

Figure 6.7 shows the number of ports throughout the world served by liner services calling in each Portuguese port (direct calls). The same figure also shows the number of ports with a direct link to each Portuguese port. The first indicator is

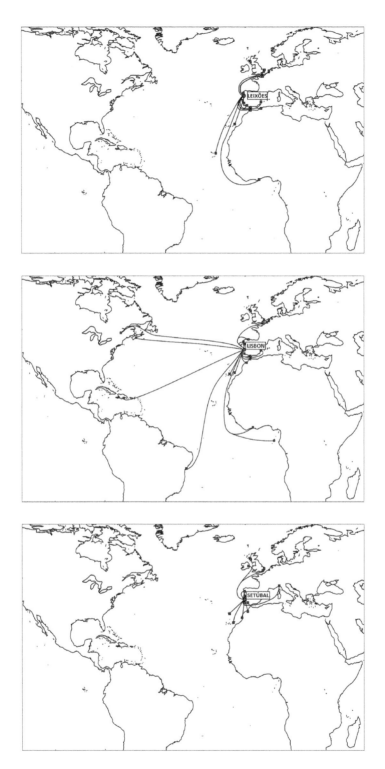

Figure 6.7 Ports with direct link to main Portuguese ports

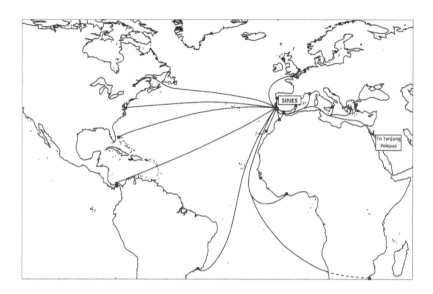

Figure 6.7 (Continued)

analogous to the 'all linkages' mentioned in Ducruet and Notteboom (2012a), and the second indicator is analogous to the 'direct linkages' mentioned in the same study. Sines, Lisbon and Leixões all have more than 70 direct port connections each along the various liner services (not necessarily being the following port). Lisbon takes the lead in the total number of ports. Setúbal has about one-third of the connections to ports. When considering only the ports directly linked to each Portuguese port (being the next or previous port of call in a given service), Sines and Lisbon have the most direct links (22 and 21, respectively), while Leixões and Setúbal have fewer direct links (15 and 12, respectively). For this indicator, however, the difference between the four ports is smaller than that for direct calls, with Setúbal having almost as many direct links as Leixões.

It also shows the ports with direct links to Portuguese ports (the immediately previous or subsequent call to each Portuguese port). Setúbal has direct links with ports in Europe or in countries close to Europe; it is therefore a typical short sea shipping port. Leixões adds a few direct links with ports in Africa. Lisbon adds direct links to the American continent. Sines has direct links to all these regions, the Eastern Mediterranean and Asia. Leixões, Lisbon and Sines may be considered deep sea ports, although with varying degrees of connectivity.

Figure 6.8 shows the total weekly capacity of the ships calling in the different ports and calling also in each Portuguese port. These are the aggregated sums of the ship's maximum capacities (nominal) and only a fraction of these will be available when actually calling in Portuguese ports. It is possible to see that the major ports connected with Sines are Valencia and Gioia Tauro, MSC's preferred ports of call. Other important ports are Rotterdam, Antwerp, Hamburg, Bremen and

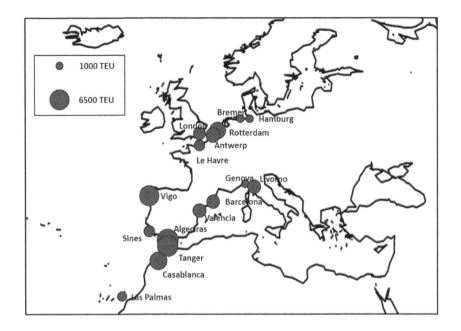

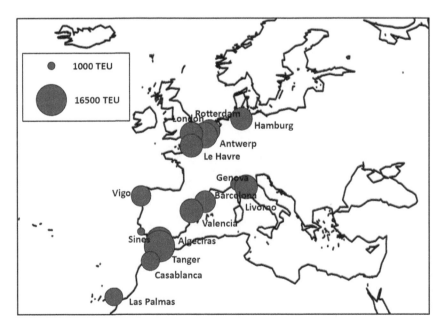

Figure 6.8 Aggregated TEU capacity per weekly services connecting major Portuguese and other European ports

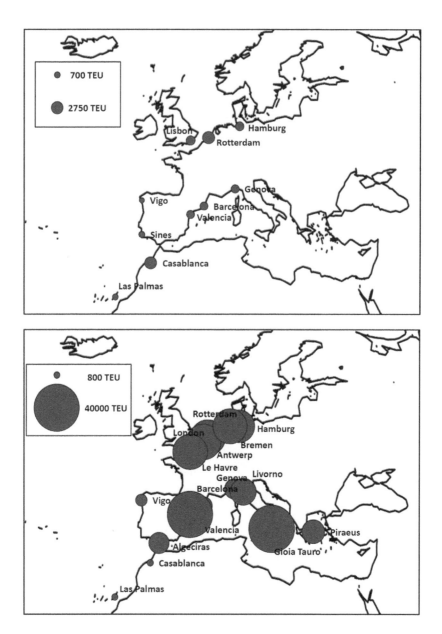

Figure 6.8 (Continued)

Havre, that is, the hubs in Northern Europe. Algeciras and Tangier, other transshipment hubs in the Strait, are not significantly connected with Sines. They are mainly its competitors. The most important ports for Setúbal are Casablanca, Rotterdam and, to a lesser extent, Hamburg and London. Leixões and, more especially, Lisbon

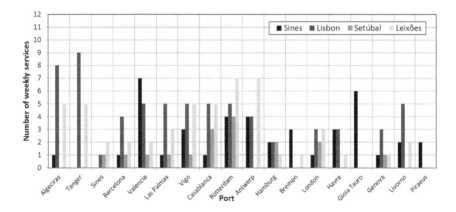

Figure 6.9 Number of weekly services from each Portuguese port to the most connected ports

have a significant number of services connecting with Algeciras and Tangier-Med, but they are also well connected with Spanish and Northern European ports.

Figure 6.9 shows the number of connections per week between each Portuguese port and the most connected ports. As may be seen, these are ports in Europe and Northern Africa, and the situation is more evenly balanced between Leixões, Lisbon and Sines than was the case for the aggregated capacity of the services. This observation results from the fact that the average ships calling in Sines are much larger than those calling in the other ports. Lisbon is the port with the most balanced split of ports between Northern Europe, the Western Mediterranean and North Africa. Sines is more focused on Northern Europe and two hubs in the Mediterranean: Valencia and Gioia Tauro. Of the four ports, Setúbal is the port with the fewest calls.

Conclusion

The study presented in this chapter demonstrates how other sources of information apart from AIS ship movement databases may be used to characterize the profiles of ports with regard to the number and type of liner services. The information used in this study is freely available, derived mainly from shipping companies, port authorities and shipping agents, but it has been found that a significant effort is required to ensure its completeness and robustness. This approach is deemed to be feasible when studying regional networks in detail or fragments of wider networks.

It has been shown that the database developed from this information may be used to assess the geographical coverage of liner services calling in a number of ports. In the case of this study, the ports are located in the Portuguese range, and the examination of the database enabled the identification of the regions and ports connected to Portugal, including also an evaluation of capacity offered by the ships. World coverage has been found to be fairly complete but some regions are connected to Portugal through only one liner service. Significant connectivity with the transshipment hubs in the Strait of Gibraltar was also identified, which comes as a partial surprise, since Portuguese ports had been heretofore much more dependent on major Northern European hubs like Rotterdam and Antwerp. However, the very significant development of ports in the Strait in recent years has allowed for this evolution, which, in addition, makes sense from an economical point of view.

This case study has also revealed the extent of Portuguese dependence in 2015 on the deep sea services calling in Sines. In fact, only the port of Lisbon features some transcontinental deep sea services for the American continent. All remaining services are SSS, feeder services or services bound for the African continent. This situation has developed slowly from 2004 onwards, with the progressive development of the connectivity of Sines through the continuous increase in the number and importance of liner services in that port. One of the important outcomes of this study has been the quantification of this development and its comparison with the number and characteristics of the liner services calling in other ports of the Portuguese range. A significant gap was found between Sines and Lisbon and Leixões. A still larger gap was found between these three ports and Setúbal.

The Portuguese authorities certainly need to take into account this dependence (for the longest liner services) of the Portuguese range on a single port, Sines, when developing investment policies, probably through increasing the capabilities (ability to receive somewhat larger ships) and competitiveness of Lisbon as a backup to Sines, but without hindering the development of the latter as a major transshipment hub, a role for which it is more suited than Lisbon. The port is also restricted in terms of land space available and hinterland accesses to container terminals and both of these issues need to be addressed by the Portuguese authorities. In any case, the two ports are EU core network ports, eligible for EU funding and located at the western extreme of EU rail freight corridor N°4, a situation which facilitates the financing of port development projects.

The services in Portuguese ports have also been compared with the many different types of services currently passing near the Portuguese coast, which is characterized by dense shipping lanes, and it has been found that many are not actually calling at ports along this coast. It thus appears that Portuguese ports are relatively unimportant for many trades, but the development of hinterland connections to Spain and possibly to Northern Europe (EU rail freight corridor N°4) may assist in making them more attractive as a gateway to Europe rather than only for transshipment. As the situation stands in 2015, the country is not taking full advantage of its geographical location when it comes to making Portuguese ports attractive for international shipping.

Acknowledgements

This work was performed within the scope of the Strategic Research Plan of the Centre for Marine Technology and Ocean Engineering (CENTEC), which is financed by the Portuguese Foundation for Science and Technology (Fundação para a Ciência e Tecnologia – FCT). The authors would also like to acknowledge the work carried out by Pedro Martins, who collected the data required to build the database on which this study is based.

References

De Langen, P.W., Van der Lugt, L., Eenhuizen, J. (2002) A stylized container port hierarchy: A theoretical and empirical exploration. In: Paper presented at the *International Association of Maritime Economists Conference*, Panama, November 13–15.

Ducruet, C., Notteboom, T.E. (2012) Developing liner service networks in container shipping. In: Song, D.W., Panayides, P. (Eds.), *Maritime Logistics: A Complete Guide to Effective Shipping and Port Management*. London: Kogan Page, pp. 77–100.

Ducruet, C., Rozenblat, C., Zaidi, F. (2010) Ports in multi-level maritime networks: Evidence from the Atlantic (1996–2006). *Journal of Transport Geography*, 18(4): 508–518.

Frémont, A. (2007) Global maritime networks: The case of Maersk. *Journal of Transport Geography*, 15(6): 431–442.

Frémont, A. (2015) A geo-history of maritime networks since 1945. The case of the Compagnie Générale Transatlantique's transformation into CMA-CGM. In: Ducruet, C. (Ed.), *Maritime Networks: Spatial Structures and Time Dynamics*. London and New York: Routledge Studies in Transport Analysis, pp. 37–49.

Hamburg-Süd. (2014) *Product and Service Guide*. Available at: https://www.hamburgsud-line.com/liner/en/liner_services/index.html Accessed on December 2014.

Hapag-Lloyd. (2015) *Service Overview – Hapag-Lloyd and CSAV*. Available at: Shipping Company Website. https://www.hapag-lloyd.com/en/news-insights/news/2014/12/hapag-lloyd-csav-service-overview_37426.html Accessed on February 2015.

Hoffmann, J. (2005) Liner shipping connectivity. *UNCTAD Transport Newsletter*, 27(1): 4–12.

Jiang, J., Lee, L.H., Chew, E.P., Gan, C.C. (2015) Port connectivity study: An analysis framework from a global container liner shipping network perspective. *Transportation Research Part E*, 73: 47–64.

Lisbon Port Authority. (2015) *Navigation Regular Lines*. Available at: www.portodelisboa.pt/. Accessed on February 2015.

Low, J.M.W., Lam, S.W., Tang, L.C. (2009) Assessment of hub status among Asian ports from a network perspective. *Transportation Research Part A*, 43(6): 593–606.

Márquez-Ramos, L., Martínez-Zarzoso, I., Pérez-Garcia, E., Wilmsmeier, G. (2005) Determinants of maritime transport costs. Importance of connectivity measures. In: *Proceedings of the International Trade and Logistics, Corporate Strategies and the Global Economy Congress*, Le Havre, September 28–29.

Rimmer, P.J., Comtois, C. (2005) China's extra- and intra-Asian liner shipping connections, 1990–2000. *Journal of International Logistics and Trade*, 3: 75–97.

Santos, T.A., Guedes Soares, C. (2015) Port regionalization in the Portuguese range. In: *Proceedings of the European Conference on Shipping, Intermodalism & Ports* (ECONSHIP 2015), Chios, Greece, June 24–27.

Santos, T.A., Santos, A.M.P., Guedes Soares, C. (2015) Competition dynamics of ports in the Portuguese range. In: Guedes Soares, C., Dejhalla, R., Pavletic, D. (Eds.), *Towards Green Marine Technology and Transport*. London: Taylor & Francis, pp. 705–716.

Sharma D. (2015) Global dynamics changing the landscape of cargo flows. Paper presented at the Marine Terminal Finance and Investment Summit, New York, NY, May 5–6.

Slack, B. (1999) Across the pond: Container shipping on the North Atlantic in the era of globalization. *Geojournal*, 48: 9–14.

Stopford, M. (2009) *Maritime Economics*. New York: Routledge.

Tovar B., Hernandez R., Rodriguez-Deniz H. (2015) Container port competitiveness and connectivity: the Canary Islands main ports case. *Transport Policy*, 38: 40–51.

UNCTAD. (2016) *Liner Shipping Connectivity Index*. Available at: unctadstat.unctad.org

Wilmsmeier, G., Hoffmann, J., Sanchez, R.J. (2006) The impact of port characteristics on international maritime transport costs. *Research in Transportation Economics*, 16(1): 117–140.

7   The complex network of coastal shipping in Brazil

Carlos César Ribeiro Santos, Marcelo do Vale Cunha and Hernane Borges De Barros Pereira

In the last two decades, the need for deconcentration and balance in Brazil's logistics network has become a priority of the federal government due to the growth of commodities and basic product exports, increased industrial production and the need for an efficient outflow of agricultural production, reduced logistics costs and greater safety in the transportation of Brazilian citizens. Thus, endeavors such as the Growth Acceleration Program, the National Logistics and Transportation Plan, the emergence of the Brazilian Logistics Company and the recent Logistics Investment Program brokered by the Ministry of Transportation have already brought about important results in terms of strengthening the country's transportation infrastructure. Incentives for the privatization of railways and airports, as well as the concession of ports and airports, have guided public policies in the country in an effort to integrate its logistics network, which remains overly focused on road transportation.

Many studies have analyzed this road hypertrophy syndrome and rail and waterway anemia. According to COPPEAD-UFRJ (2012), road transportation accounts for approximately 60% of all transport in the country, while in countries with equivalent territorial dimensions to Brazil, such as the United States and Russia, these percentages are 35% and 19%, respectively. Brazil's efforts have already produced positive results in the search for balance in the logistics network, thus addressing the importance of the growth and valuation of the waterway transportation mode.

Brazil is a country with a navigable coastline extending for almost 7,500 km, a high population density along the coast, with 80% of the population living in coastal regions, several public and private ports and 75% of international trade conducted by sea. It is therefore indispensable for the country to have a structured waterway transportation network capable of meeting all the demands of the states and their producers, according to the records of the National Agency of Waterway Transportation (ANTAQ, 2014).

Brazil currently has 22,037 km of navigable waterway networks including sea (maritime), river (fluvial) and lake (lacustrine), with three types of navigation: cabotage, inland and long-range. The waterway mode is efficient for large loads and large volumes over long distances, but logistics management is highly complex, which is added to by the long transit time. Worth emphasizing here is the importance of cabotage in comparison with the other two types of waterway transportation, due to its lower freight costs, larger cargo storage, greater control over cargo communication/information, lower level of breakdowns, improved reliability of delivery times and increased cargo safety.

These characteristics significantly strengthen the importance of the use of cabotage in Brazil, as well as the obvious need for scientific studies and the contribution of technology to promote the countrywide expansion of cabotage. Accordingly, this chapter presents the use of network theory as a technological tool to provide cabotage and sea transportation in general with strategic information to assist logistics managers in making more assertive decisions. Hence, the main objective was to analyze Brazilian cabotage between 2010 and 2015 with the support of network theory (on national port systems and connectivity see also Chapters 6, 10, 20 and 21 on Portugal, USA, China and North Korea, respectively).

To achieve the proposed objective, we used a database from the Statistical Monitoring System of the Brazilian National Agency of Waterway Transportation (*Agência Nacional de Transportes Aquaviários do Brasil* – ANTAQ) concerning cargo movement between Brazilian ports via cabotage for 2010 to 2015. After collecting the data for the construction of networks, we established the Brazilian ports as the vertices and the routes of ships from one port to another as the edges. The programs Pajek and Gephi 0.9.1 were used for the construction and analysis of the waterways network data. We then performed a strategic analysis of cabotage in Brazil based on the features and particularities obtained from the network theory.

Theoretical framework

Cabotage

As defined in Brazilian law n. 9.432/97, cabotage navigation takes place between ports or points of the Brazilian territory using sea and inland waterways. Transportation between two river ports is not included, however, but instead falls under the concept of inland navigation. When analyzing seaports as connection elements of logistics chains, the complexity of the activity and the form of organization must be considered.

Ports offer different levels of activities and promote the outflow of products, thus contributing to converting a country's wealth into currency. In this sense, ports have significant representation in world trade, where more than 80% of the traded volume is transported by sea, according to World Bank data. In Brazil, the extensive coastline, the concentration of production sectors and the consumer market along the coast are some of the development-friendly aspects of cabotage. The total Brazilian cabotage fleet comprises156 vessels belonging to 31 companies, with an average age of 17.4 years.

In 2015, according to ANTAQ, cabotage in Brazil transported 32,290,334 tons of goods including liquid and gas bulk, containers, dry bulk and general cargo. In Brazil, cabotage regulation is drafted by ANTAQ, which supervises and oversees maritime activities in Brazilian territory.

Network theory

Network theory has been prominent in research seeking to understand the structure and dynamics of systems that contain connected elements. Within this context, a network is the abstraction of these elements, called vertices, and their mutual relationships, called edges or arcs. Technological networks, biological networks, social networks, organizational networks and information networks are examples of real systems modeled in the form of networks. A network can be represented mathematically by a graph $G = \{V, E\}$, where V is the set of vertices containing n elements, and E, with m elements, is the set of edges (i.e., pairs of vertices related through some pre-established criteria).

Despite the possibility of using other sets within G, (for example, sets with information on the evolution of the network over time), in this work, we will study the maritime network from a static perspective and with directed edges, which represent relationships directed from one vertex to another. This analysis is sufficient to reveal the structure of the network and highlight high-prestige vertices, according to some of the main network indicators. They are as follows: number of vertices (n); number of edges (m); average minimal path length ($\langle l \rangle$) diameter (D); density (Δ); average clustering coefficient ($\langle C \rangle$); in-degree $\left(k_i^{in} \right)$; out-degree $\left(k_i^{out} \right)$; degree (k_i); betweenness centrality ($\boldsymbol{B'}$); average degree ($\langle k \rangle$) and degree distribution ($P(k)$).

If weighted or multiple edges are considered in the network, the in-degree and out-degree will change according to the weights of the edges or the number of repeated edges. Consequently, all measures that depend on the in- and out-degrees will undergo the same adjustment.

Depending on the values of its indices, a network may be considered as a complex network. We can classify a network according to its classical topologies. In this sense, a network can be classified as follows (Carneiro et al., 2016: 95):

- Regular, if all vertices have the same number of connections;
- Random, if its degree distribution follows a normal distribution;
- Small-world network, if the connections between the vertices favor short distances between any two vertices in the network, making the network more efficient in terms of information transmission. (Milgram, 1967; Watts and Strogatz, 1998);
- Scale-free network, if its degree distribution follows a power law, (i.e., $P(k) \sim k^{gama}$), favoring the existence of hubs, which are vertices that concentrate many connections. In the theoretical model, the growth of the network is based on the preferential adhesion of vertices (Barabási and Albert, 1999).

Maritime networks

Clark et al.'s study (2004) on the geography of the world economy points to the constant reduction of trade barriers around the world, resulting in a general reduction in transportation costs. In this sense, there is greater opportunity to use the various types of transportation modes. Glaeser and Kohlhase (2004) stated that the world market exists in a new context, in which political, economic and technological transformations have promoted the globalization and regionalization of market processes. In this new market setting, the use of sea transportation becomes a competitive approach for modern organizations.

Bird (1984) noted that in this new competitive global environment, organizations have come to value and scientifically analyze the routes and seaports around the world in search of competitive advantages. This led to the emergence of the Global Maritime Network as an object of study for scientists, looking at its evolving structure, the position of ports as nodes, among other aspects (Ducruet, 2015). Despite the importance of maritime networks for increased competitiveness, they have not received as much attention as land transportation networks. Ducruet (2015) highlighted a lack of technical and scientific studies on the subject of maritime networks. In his view, the use of maritime structures by modern organizations of a country, city or region is one of the main avenues for achieving business objectives in competitive terms.

In spite of a notable lack of research on maritime networks, sea transport in Brazil has already attracted the attention of researchers, due to the current economic situation that demands logistics innovation in terms of competitiveness, combined with a rapid response to the current Brazilian crisis. Thus, some studies have focused on the relevance of Brazil's ports to the country's maritime competitiveness. Haddad et al. (2010) presented an integrated computational modeling of a transport network system that simulates the impacts of increased port efficiency in Brazil, highlighting the role of the main ports of entry and exit of goods. The work also emphasizes the importance of analyzing the cost of the port operation, as well as the different efficiency indicators for Brazilian ports.

Cabral and de Sousa Ramos (2014) compared the efficiency of 17 Brazilian port terminals in terms of competitiveness, establishing criteria for comparison between ports, namely: number of containers handled, berth length, terminal fees and berth depth, among others. Wanke et al. (2011) studied the efficiency of 25 port terminals in Brazil through Data Envelopment Analysis (DEA) and SFA (Stochastic Frontier Analysis) methods. The results showed the low operational capacity of Brazilian ports to receive exported goods, due to a lack of investment in ports.

For Ducruet (2015), maritime networks are among the most ancient forms of spatial interaction. The so-called port hierarchies and the already established spatial pattern of sea routes can be considered examples of the regionalization and globalization of trade patterns and business cycles between organizations, cities, regions and countries.

It is in this competitive environment of maritime networks that the present study is set. It is generally accepted that a waterway system is divided according to the geographical features of the navigable pathways. River transportation uses navigable rivers and maritime transportation encompasses movement across seas and oceans. Given these two different systems, our analysis of maritime transportation in this chapter is restricted to cabotage, in view of the facts highlighted in the introductory section of this chapter.

Method

For the proposed analysis of maritime cabotage in Brazil based on network theory, we depended on exact data collection. It is worth mentioning here how difficult it is to find, in Brazil and worldwide, precise indicators related to maritime

Table 7.1 Sample of cabotage cargo movements, January 2015

Origin city	Destination city	Origin state	Destination state	Port/PUT	Tonnage
Fortaleza	Itaguaí	CE	Rio de Janeiro	Itaguaí	533
Fortaleza	Itajaí	Ceará	Santa Catarina	Itajaí	265
Fortaleza	Rio Grande	Ceará	Rio Grande do Sul	Rio Grande	1,563
Fortaleza	Salvador	Ceará	Bahia	Salvador	445
Fortaleza	São Francisco do Sul	Ceará	Santa Catarina	São Francisco do Sul	1,794
Fortaleza	Vitória	Ceará	Espírito Santo	Vitória	328
Imbituba	Salvador	Santa Catarina	Bahia	Salvador	6,282

Source: Organized by the authors based on data from ANTAQ

movement, either due to lack of scientific research in the area or to the high prices charged by institutes or research firms.

By contrast, public institutions (e.g., ANTAQ) were willing to provide access and the data that enabled the proposed study to be accomplished objectively and responsibly. Thus, we were granted access to ANTAQ's Waterways Statistical System, from which it was possible to obtain the following information:

- all types of cargo moved via cabotage yearly or monthly from 2010 to 2015;
- the cargo's city and state of origin and destination;
- the cargo's maritime installation of origin and destination (port or private use terminal-PUT); and
- the total value of the cargo transported via cabotage from 2010 to 2015.

Once in possession of this data, we organized the Origin-Destination Table, which contains information on cabotage for each trip. A sample of this table is shown in Table 7.1.

Following this organizational procedure, it was possible to model the system in the form of a network, where:

- V: {Set of Ports/PUTs}.
- ε: {Trips between Ports/PUTs of v, from 2010 to 2015}.

Next, considering the major network indices, some vertices were investigated, as well as the network as a whole. The next section presents the main results of this analysis.

Data analysis

We conducted two analyses of Brazilian maritime cabotage networks from 2010 to 2015. Analysis 1 uses all data from the system that represent the network, called the General Maritime Network. Analysis 2 uses data from the maritime network without multiple edges and loops, called Maritime Network with simple edges.

Analysis of the general maritime network

For analysis of the General Maritime Network, we considered a total of 118 vertices (ports) and 16,273 edges (trips from one port to another) concerning cargo movement via cabotage in Brazil, between 2010 and 2015. Figure 7.1 is the graphical representation of this network.

The analysis of this network (Figure 7.1) highlights the existence of two main hubs in green. The hubs are the Port of Santos in the state of São Paulo and the Port of Suape in the state of Pernambuco. It is important to highlight the growth in cargo movement of the ports of Vitória in Espírito Santo, Rio de Janeiro and Salvador in Bahia. These ports may in the future play a role as important as the ports of Santos and Suape if they receive infrastructure investments such as increased bottom clearance, terminal enlargement for cargo loading and unloading and the construction of logistics platforms that would facilitate multimodal transportation.

Based on the network in Figure 7.1, Santos and Suape are the main spheres of port influence in Brazil and can thus be called hinterland ports. This is the name used to describe ports with high cargo movement, given the intermodality and quality, communication and automation of their processes.

From a logistics perspective, this analysis should consider the possible existence of a concentration and, consequently, an excess of moved cargo in these ports. This factor would certainly make a company avoid an overstay of its cargo at the port so as to circumvent generating unwanted demurrage.

Figure 7.2 shows the indices of networks for ports that stand out in this analysis. For the Port of Santos-SP (*P*40) 1,402 incoming and 1,660 outgoing trips are

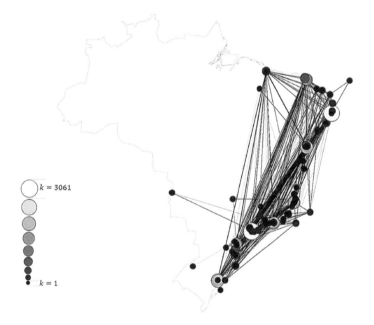

Figure 7.1 Brazilian maritime cabotage network, 2010–2015

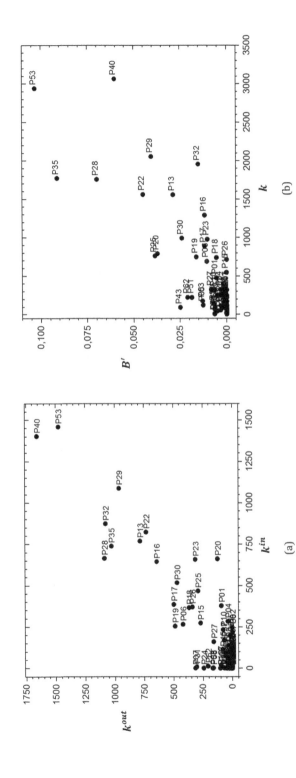

Figure 7.2 Vertex centrality in the general Brazilian maritime network

observed, while for the Port of Suape-PE (*P53*) there are 1,459 incoming trips and 1,478 outgoing trips. Furthermore, Vitória-ES (*P35*) is the port with the fifth highest number of trips (k_{P35} = 1769), but it stands second in relation to betweenness (B'_{P35} = 0.091), (i.e., it is more present in paths between two other ports than Santos (B'_{P40} = 0.060), which has the largest number of trips (k_{P40} = 3062)).

Table 7.2 shows the general network indices. As for degree distribution, no characteristic curve is observed, which clearly indicates a particular network behavior. In the next section (Analysis 2), with the simple edge plot, the degree distribution determined a characteristic behavior for the network.

We built a graphical representation of the in- and out-degree distributions of this network's hubs (ports of Santos-SP (*P40*) and Suape-PE Rio (*P53*)) to provide a better understanding of the functioning of the cabotage system in Brazil. Figures 7.3 and 7.4 represent the distribution of cargo movement for cabotage in the ports of Santos and Suape between 2010 to 2015 and their respective analyses.

Table 7.2 Indices for the General Maritime Network

n	m	$\langle k \rangle$	D	$\langle \ell \rangle$	(%)Largest component
118	16,273	137.91	5	2.46	100%

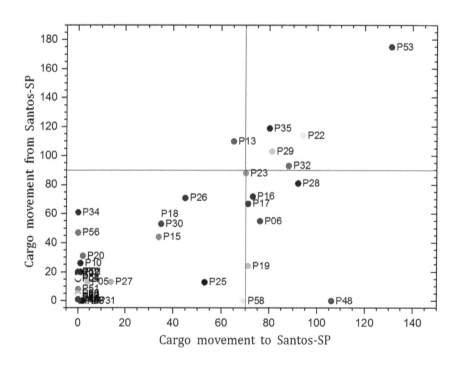

Figure 7.3 Incoming and outgoing traffic distribution of Santos port

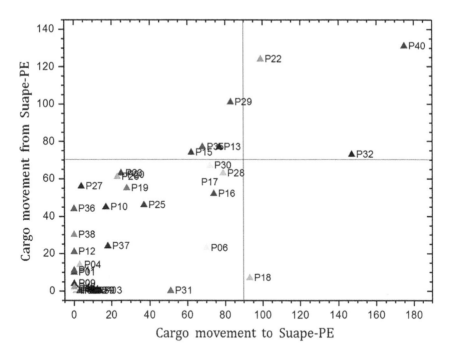

Figure 7.4 Incoming and outgoing traffic distribution of Suape port

Figure 7.3 represents the cargo movement to and from the port of Santos. The **x** axis represents the number of cabotage cargo movement trips received by the Port of Santos over a six-year period. The **y** axis represents the number of cabotage cargo movement trips out of the Port of Santos, also over six years. These trips represent the movement of all types of cargo: general, container and liquid or dry bulk.

The plot of the Port of Santos-SP is split by the **x** and **y** axes into four quadrants counterclockwise from the (0,0) point, for the economic, commercial and logistics analysis of the relationship and the importance of this hub to the other Brazilian ports. The points on the plot with the letter **P** followed by a number represent the individual ports and their relationship with the Port of Santos-SP.

In the first quadrant of Figure 7.3, there is a weak commercial relationship between the Port of Santos-SP and ports such as Terminal de Tubarão-ES (*P*34), Alumar-MA (*P*56), Itaqui-MA (*P*18), São Francisco do Sul-SC (*P*30) and Imbituba-SC (*P*15). These ports in the first quadrant send and receive little cargo from Santos-SP. We also highlight the port of Areia Branca-RN (*P*58) that only forwards cargo to the Port of Santos. Logistically speaking, the situations presented in the first quadrant correspond to potential areas to be analyzed and explored by the Brazilian government for the development of cabotage because maritime movement has increasingly become a low-cost logistics solution for cargo transportation in Brazil.

The second quadrant of Figure 7.3 is interesting, particularly for port *P*48. This port is one of those recorded by the ANTAQ system as unidentified. The Agency claims that in its database there are often operations of cargo movements with unidentified origin due to non-compliance by the logistics operator in providing this information. Port *P*48 only sends cargo to the Port of Santos-SP, with no complete commercial interaction between them. The other ports of the second quadrant, such as, for example, Rio de Janeiro-RJ(*P*28) and Aratu-BA (*P*06), have a moderate business relationship with Santos-SP, as they send and receive a relatively moderate amount of cargo.

The third quadrant is characterized by strong commercial relations between Santos-SP and the ports located there. The Port of Suape-PE (*P*53) is the one with the highest movement of received and sent cargo to the Port of Santos-SP. These findings again indicate the importance of these ports for the transportation of goods in Brazil.

The fourth quadrant contains only the port of Fortaleza-CE (*P*13) in northeastern Brazil. Santos-SP forwards more cargo to the Port of Fortaleza-CE than it receives. Thus, there is an opportunity for possible logistics negotiations to further trade relations in cargo movement between these two ports.

Figure 7.4 shows the list of arrival and departure of cargo, taking as a base the second hub of the General Maritime Network, namely the Port of Suape-PE.

The first quadrant contains a concentration of ports that share a weak commercial relationship with the Port of Suape-PE because they receive from and send to it a small amount of cargo in tons. Ports such as Maceió-AL (*P*19) in the state of Alagoas and Ilha Redonda-RJ (*P*36) in Rio de Janeiro have few cargo movements via cabotage, again indicating the need and opportunity for logistics investments in these locations.

The second quadrant shows that the Port of Itaqui-MA (*P*18), in the state of Maranhão, sends a reasonable amount of cargo to Suape but receives almost nothing from this port. Knowing the importance of Suape-PE as a network hub, we can infer that the Port *P*18 has little relevance to cargo movement in Brazil, either because of its local production and the difficulty of selling it elsewhere, or of structural or economic constraints.

The third quadrant reveals a feature similar to that shown in Figure 7.3: the strong commercial relationship between the network's hubs. Here, Santos appears with the highest movement of cargo received from and sent to the Port of Suape-PE, indicating again the strong relationship and the commercial dependence between these two ports in cargo movement through cabotage.

The fourth and last quadrant shows the ports of Rio Grande-RS (*P*29), Vitória-ES (*P*35), Fortaleza-CE (*P*13) and Imbituba-SC (*P*15). These ports forward and receive goods via cabotage from Suape-PE in an almost uniform way, which suggests that these ports have a good commercial relationship with Suape-PE and a reasonable economic production.

Both figures indicate that Brazil has many ports with very low cargo movement, both incoming and outgoing, due to a lack of appropriate infrastructure and technology, leading logistics operators to an excessive concentration of their cargos at the country's main hubs. Moreover, the Brazilian government needs to consider the fact that the excessive concentration of cabotage cargo movement in Santos-SP and Suape-PE could, in the future, compromise the entire national maritime system.

Topological analysis of the maritime network

To perform a topological analysis of the network, it was necessary to eliminate the directions of the edges; to remove all multiple edges and loops, (i.e., trips between the same pair of ports and from one port to itself, which sometimes occurs as a logistics strategy); and, finally, to disregard the weights of the edges (amount of transported cargo). The indices were recalculated for this new setting (Table 7.3). Figure 7.5 shows the network in this new condition.

Table 7.3 Network indices for the maritime network and its corresponding random network

Network/Indices	n	m	$\langle k \rangle$	D	Δ	$\langle \ell \rangle$	$\langle C \rangle$	(%)Largest component
Maritime network	118	682	11.56	6	0.099	2.45	0.59	100
Equivalent random network	118	699	11.85	4	0.101	2.17	0.09	100

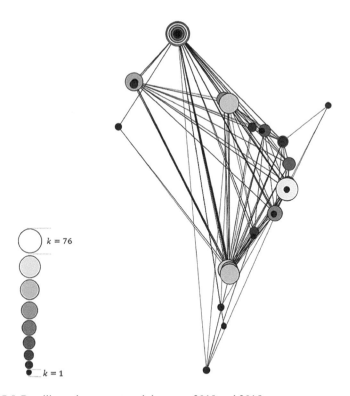

$k = 76$

$k = 1$

Figure 7.5 Brazilian cabotage network between 2010 and 2015

Topological analysis requires two research avenues. First, the network's vertex degree distribution needs to be checked; in other words, how the routes (defined by the trips) are distributed among the ports. This distribution indicates whether the network fits into one of the three theoretical models (regular, scale-free or random). Second, to check if the network displays the small-world phenomenon requires comparing the indices of the network under analysis with the indices of an equivalent random network (i.e., with the same number of vertices and connection probability between them so as to generate the same mean degree value, or very close to it). Table 7.3 shows the properties of the Brazilian cabotage network and of the equivalent random network, and Figure 7.6 shows the network's degree distribution and, for information purposes only, the degree distribution of the equivalent random network.

Although the distributions in Figure 7.6 are far from representing theoretical models, mainly because of the small amount of system elements (vertices), the depicted regression curves help to understand the difference between them.

Figure 7.6 and Table 7.3 allow us to conclude that the network does not fit the theoretical model of a regular network, because the vertices have different numbers of connections. This network would not be random either because its distribution, shown in Figure 7.6a, does not follow or even resemble a normal distribution, as shown in Figure 7.6b. Despite the existence of hubs, considering Barabási and Albert (1999), this network would not match the scale-free category either, because the number of vertices is small, reflecting the lower value of γ.

Only one theoretical model conforms to the network topology: the small-world model. This result is clear when comparing the network indices with their random network equivalent. According to Watts and Strogatz (1998), a non-directed network, which has more than 50% of its vertices connected (largest component), will be small-world if the mean clustering of its vertices is much larger than the equivalent random network's vertex clustering, with its vertices mean minimum path close to that of the random network's equivalent.

This observation shows that this network is efficient because the maritime routes between ports are, on average, short. In this sense, we can compare the highest port

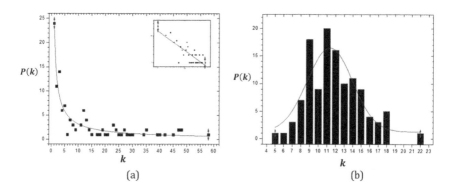

Figure 7.6 Degree distribution of the Brazilian cabotage network

Table 7.4 Degree centrality k and betweenness centrality B' of vertices in the simple network

Rank	Port name (State) – P##	k	Rank	Port name (State) – P##	B'
1	Vitória (ES) – P35	58	1	Vitória (ES) – P35	0.215
2	Rio de Janeiro (RJ) – P28	48	2	Rio de Janeiro (RJ) – P28	0.106
3	Santos (SP) – P40	48	3	Suape (PE) – P53	0.085
4	Suape (PE) – P53	47	4	Madre de Deus (BA) – P20	0.068
5	Rio Grande (RS) – P29	47	5	Usiminas (SP) – P43	0.063
6	Madre de Deus (BA) – P20	45	6	Santos (SP) – P40	0.062
7	Paranaguá (PR) – P22	42	7	Rio Grande (RS) – P29	0.059
8	Porto Itapoá (SC) – P25	21	8	Terminal Marítmo Dow (SP) – P61	0.053
9	Salvador (BA) – P32	40	9	Porto Itapoá (SC) – P25	0.052
10	Fortaleza (CE) – P13	39	10	Paranaguá (PR) – P22	0.045

centralities. Table 7.4 reveals that Vitória (ES) is the port with the most connections to other ports, in addition to being the one that most mediates paths between pairs of ports. Moreover, the Port of Suape, which previously held the rank of largest mediator in the general network, if one disregards repeated, directed and weighted trips, becomes the third largest intermediating port, behind Rio de Janeiro (RJ) and Vitória (ES).

The indicators of Table 7.4 can be interpreted as (a) *(k)* degree: communication activity between ports, that is the number of possible routes that a given port has, and (b) *B'* betweenness: route control, that is, the higher the betweenness of a port, the more likely this port is to become an intermediary between two other ports and become useful for fuel and cargo supply.

Conclusion

This chapter presents the main fundamentals of network theory and its applications to logistics using the waterway transportation mode. We highlight the movement of cargo through cabotage as a type of maritime transportation that uses the country's coast as the main waterway to transport goods by virtue of its current growth and investment trends from institutions such as the Brazilian Ministry of Transportation.

The relationships presented in the maritime network based on the cabotage cargo movement in Brazil from 2010 to 2015 clearly show the ports of Santos and Suape as hubs and hinterlands because the in- and out-degrees of cargo of both ports are superior to all other ports in the country. This information is strategically relevant for the main actors of Brazil's waterway transportation mode, as decisions can increasingly be made with less risk. Thus, the analysis presented here provides the port authorities with a vision of the future in relation to the following decisions:

•   **Intensification of cost control by logistics operators:** This tendency is a global trend in cargo movement. Reducing costs and seeking efficiency and quality has been the goal of the main ports worldwide.

- **Increased investment in planning:** Port authorities need to plan the future of their ports strategically. Thus, the use of network theory in maritime transportation is a powerful analytical tool because it allows the identification of ports with growth potential in a given country.
- **Uncertainty and volatility of the cargo transportation market:** The uncertainty caused by the global unpredictability of the world economy makes all markets susceptible to ruptures and rapid changes. Thus, monitoring and applying network theory to waterway cargo transportation allows those responsible to make timely decisions and identify future scenarios, reducing risks in decision-making, which is critical to the success of any port operator.
- **Container challenge:** There is substantial worldwide growth of cargo transportation using containers on ships. Therefore, at present, one of the great challenges in port management is to increase the amount of cargo moved using containers. It is generally accepted that many containers still travel long distances without being completely full, thus incurring significant financial losses for stakeholders in cargo transportation in Brazil and worldwide.
- **Connectivity and betweenness:** The use of network theory allows the actors in maritime transportation to identify ports with a high degree of connectivity and/or betweenness. This allows port authorities to make various strategic decisions, such as which ports would provide returns on investment in the medium term.

With an extensive coastline, Brazil needs public policies and investments that target the development of these ports and increase the deconcentration of cargo movement. This move will strengthen the national economy and place Brazil among the largest competitors in world maritime navigation.

Acknowledgements

This work was partially supported by the Human Resources Training Program of ANP-PRH 55.

References

Agencia Nacional de Transportes Aquaviarios. (2014) *Technical Reports of Port Performance 2008–2014*. Brasília. Available at: www.antaq.gov.br. Accessed on 29 October 2016.

Barabási, A.L., Albert, R. (1999) Emergence of scaling in random networks. *Science*, 286: 509–512.

Bird, J. (1984) Seaport development: Some questions of scale. In: Hoyle, B.S., Hilling, D. (Eds.), *Seaport Systems and Spatial Change*. Wiley: Chichester, pp. 21–41.

Cabral, A.M.R., de Sousa Ramos, F. (2014) Cluster analysis of the competitiveness of container ports in Brazil. *Transportation Research Part A*, 69: 423–431.

Carneiro, T.K.G, Rios, J.A., Souza, C.R.B. (2016) *Tecnologias Aplicadas à Saúde*. Salvador: Edifba, pp. 89–115.

Clark, X., Dollar, D., Micco, A. (2004) Port efficiency, maritime transport costs, and bilateral trade. *Journal of Development Economics*, 75(2): 417–450.

Ducruet, C., Notteboom, T.E. (2012) The worldwide maritime network of container shipping: Spatial structure and regional dynamics. *Global Networks*, 12(3): 395–423

Ducruet, C. (2015) Maritime flows and networks in a multidisciplinary perspective. In: Ducruet, C. (Ed.), *Maritime Networks: Spatial Structures and Time Dynamics*. London and New York: Routledge Studies in Transport Analysis, pp. 3–26.

Glaeser, E.L., Kohlhase, J.E. (2004) Cities, regions and the decline of transport costs. *Papers in Regional Science*, 83(1): 197–228.

Haddad, E.A., Hewings, G.J.D., Perobelli, F.S., Santos, R.A.C. (2010) Regional effects of port infrastructure: A spatial CGE application to Brazil. *International Regional Science Review*, 33(3): 239–263.

Milgram, S. (1967) The small world problem. *Psychology Today*, 2(1): 60–67.

Wanke, P.F., Barbastefano, R.G., Hijjar, M.F. (2011) Determinants of efficiency at major Brazilian port terminals. *Transport Reviews*, 31(5): 653–677.

Watts, D.J., Strogatz, S.H. (1998) Collective dynamics of small-world networks. *Nature*, 393(4): 440–442.

8 Intra- vs. extra-regional connectivity of the Black Sea port system

*Kateryna Gruchevska, Theo Notteboom
and César Ducruet*

The Black Sea port system is generally considered as a secondary port system in the European port scene. Though located next to the East Med ports, it is not situated along the main east-west shipping routes, due to the existence of the Bosporus Strait, which forms a nautical link between the two seas. The region's economic position is being affected by a range of developments of a more global nature such as (i) nearshoring, (ii) the shift of EDC development from West to Central and Eastern Europe, (iii) SECA regulations in the North and Baltic Seas, (iv) the growth of East Med ports, (v) the Silk Road project revitalization, (vi) Suez Canal expansion etc. However, the political and economic instability of the Black Sea states (mainly Russia and Ukraine) could counterwork global trends and prevent the region from potential dynamic development. The aforementioned global and regional circumstances can significantly affect the configuration of shipping patterns to/from Europe and thus alter the position of Black Sea ports in the global shipping network.

Several empirical studies on maritime network analysis can be found in the extant literature. However, Ducruet et al. (2010) argue that these studies are scarce and quite fragmented. Moreover, shipping connectivity literature shows an absence of a systematized comprehensive analysis of the maritime network of the Black Sea. This chapter addresses shipping dynamics in the Black Sea with a specific focus on internal and external connectivity dynamics, with reference to the wider field of network analysis. Our central research question is whether the foreland regionalization and globalization of Black Sea shipping networks also depends on a certain degree of intra-regional connectivity. In transport geography, intermediacy and centrality (Fleming and Hayuth, 1994) well describe the spatial qualities that enhance the traffic levels of transportation hubs and hence indicate which places are favorably located within transport systems. Centrality focuses on the port vicinity being a point of origin and destination of traffic to/from adjacent areas. At the same time, intermediacy focuses on the port being a point of transit between different systems of circulation. Intermediate ports/airports as defined by Fleming and Hayuth (1994) are the en-route intermediate locations between important origins and destinations chosen as way stops, route conjunctions, break-in-bulk points, gateways etc.

Yet, this chapter wishes to introduce another network-related concept, namely vulnerability, which better describes how certain port nodes grow at the expense of others, the latter becoming peripheral (Fraser et al., 2016) or dependent upon external hubs (Ducruet et al., 2010). While the centralization (or concentration) level of port systems is a classic approach in transport studies (Notteboom, 2006), it had been only recently applied to shipping networks in particular regions (see a comparative perspective in Mareï and Ducruet, 2015) or at the global scale. This chapter goes one step further by relating the internal organization of a given regional network, here the Black Sea, taking into account the external dynamics taking place in the vicinity and in the rest of the world. Nevertheless, it goes beyond the analysis of the maritime forelands of individual ports (Wang and Ng, 2011). We complement this quantitative analysis of shipping data with qualitative information about past and current projects on a local or national scale and compare our results with other data sources (for other analyses of transnational port systems, see Chapters 5, 9, 11, 19, 23 and 24 on Taiwan Strait, the Arctic, the Mediterranean, the USSR, Northwest Africa and the Indian subcontinent, respectively).

First, we will set the scene of the Black Sea container port system by assembling and synthesizing complementary data and knowledge about Black Sea ports and shipping routes, such as by using the liner shipping connectivity and logistics performance index developed by UNCTAD. Then, we will perform a network analysis of the Black Sea region looking at traffic shifts and topological dynamics from the late 1970s up to the present day. Finally, we conclude with the main findings of the chapter and outline the possible future research avenues.

General profile of the Black Sea container port system

Notwithstanding the fact that the Black Sea region accounts for only 2.5% of global seaborne trade (while the leading European trade region – the North Sea – accounts for about 17%), it is an important area of development due to its geographical size and resource/consumption base. The Black Sea container port system is among the world's fastest-growing markets, with a cargo growth rate in 2014 of 6% p.a. and a CAGR (1998–2014) of 14%. In the same period, the global CAGR amounted to 9%, South Asia 11%, Africa 11% and Western Europe 5% (UNCTAD). The Black Sea container port system consists of 11 ports with annual container traffic of about 2.6 mln. TEU (2014).

What became clear in recent decades is the growing share of container traffic in the Black Sea region (Figure 8.1), which traditionally specializes in bulks, as a heritage of the former Soviet/ socialist period. In the late 1970s, container traffic represented no more than 2.5% of the total, followed by 5.0% one decade later, 13.4% in the late 1990s and 25.7% in 2008. Such a trend mainly occurred at the expense of bulks, with solid bulks and liquid bulks declining from 29.0% and 53.3% in 1977 to 19.4% and 35.9% in 2008, respectively. This reflects a growing diversification of Black Sea ports, as reflected by world trends (Ducruet, 2017), but at the same time, the direct effects of liner shipping strategies and actions performed in the region.

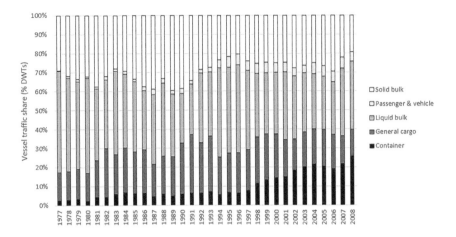

Figure 8.1 Black Sea shipping traffic evolution by main vessel types, 1977–2008

Table 8.1 Top 10 container lines calling Black Sea ports (full containers)

Shipping line	TEU (2013)	TEU (2014)	Share, % (2013)	Share, % (2014)
MSC	446,620	445,133	28%	28%
MAERSK	393,080	359,568	24%	23%
CMA CGM	193,683	170,397	12%	11%
ZIM	166,172	193,159	10%	12%
ARKAS	127,969	136,889	8%	9%
EMC	66,951	62,941	4%	4%
CSAV	61,250	52,929	4%	3%
CSCL	58,583	59,411	4%	4%
HL	50,201	71,481	3%	5%
YML	42,630	32,384	3%	2%
Total	**1,607,139**	**1,584,292**	**100%**	**100%**

Source: Ports of Ukraine

The main container lines serving the Black Sea are MSC, Maersk, Zim, Arkas, Emc, a detailed overview of which is presented in Table 8.1. The peculiarity of the Black Sea is that only few ports are called at directly by shipping lines: Constanta (Romania), Odessa and Illyichevsk (Ukraine) and, since 2011, also Yuzhnyi (Ukraine) and Nororossyisk (Russia). As from 2003, the size of the container vessels entering the Black Sea grew from 2500 TEU up to 10,000 TEU at the present time. A significant restriction on vessel size in the Black Sea is the Bosporus Strait, on account of its physical constraints. Thus, container shipping lines can deploy vessels of up to 10,000 TEU for the Black Sea, while vessels of up to 18,000 TEU are already calling at ports in the Mediterranean. Further-more, shipping economics would not allow for much bigger ship sizes because of the current stagnation in demand –in 2014 and 2015, the total regional container demand dropped by 1–2% per annum. Shipping lines call at the Black Sea basin mainly in a shared calling pattern (Table 8.2). There are only two (out of four previously existing) direct services left between the ports of the Black Sea

Table 8.2 Direct calls to Black Sea ports, January 2016

Shipping company	Liner services	Vessel size (TEU)	Rotation
Caribbean			
Maersk Line	Med-Caribbean-Panama service – String of Ecumed	2800-3200	Algeciras, Marsaxlokk, Izmit Korfezi, Istanbul-Ambarli, Yuzhny, Novorossisk (NCSP), Istanbul-Ambarli, Istanbul-Evyap, Izmir, Marsaxlokk, Algeciras, Caucedo, Manzanillo (Pan) . . . (WCSA) . . . Manzanillo (Pan), Algeciras
Middle East-India			
Maersk Line	Black Sea-East Med-Middle East-India service (ME-3 / Prime 3)	4200-5000 8 x 5 500	Port Said (SCCT), Mersin, Istanbul-Ambarli, Izmit Korfezi, Novorossisk (Nutep), Izmit Korfezi, Istanbul-Ambarli, Izmir, Mersin, Jeddah, Jebel Ali, Pipavav, Hazira, Mumbai-Nhava Sheva, Jebel Ali, Salalah, Port Said (SCCT)
East Asia			
CSCL / K Line / Yang Ming / PIL / Wan Hai Suspended	Asia-Black Sea service (ABX / CBX / SB 1 / SBS) (Zim : ABS)	5500	Piraeus, Istanbul-Ambarli, Ilichevsk, Constantza, Port Kelang, Shanghai, Ningbo, Shekou, Singapore, Port Kelang, Piraeus
2M (Maersk / MSC) Temporarily suspended	Asia-Med Loop 5 (AE-3 / Black Sea / BEX)	8500	Istanbul-Evyap (Izmit), Istanbul-Ambarli, Constantza, Odessa. Ilichevsk, Istanbul, Piraeus, Port Said (SCCT), Singapore, Xiamen, Busan, Qingdao, Shanghai, Ningbo, Yantian, Chiwan, Singapore, Port Kelang, Istanbul-Evyap
O3/YM (CMA CGM / CSCL / UASC / Yang Ming)	Asia-Black Sea service (AE-3 / BEX) (Bosphorus Express)	11 x 8 700 / 9 300 teu (2 sailings skipped)	Port Said, Beirut, Piraeus, Iskenderun, Istanbul-Evyap (Izmit), Istanbul-Ambarli (Avcilar), Constantza, Odessa, Istanbul-Ambarli (Avcilar), Piraeus, Port Kelang, Dalian, Xingang, Kwangyang, Busan, Shanghai, Ningbo, Chiwan, Port Kelang, Port Said

Shipping company	Liner services	Vessel size (TEU)	Rotation
Zim / OOCL	Asia-East Med Express service (EMX) (CSCL : AMX 2)	4250	Ashdod, Haifa, Istanbul-Ambarll, Novorossisk, Odessa, Istanbul-Ambarli, Haifa, Mumbai-Nhava Sheva, Port Kelang, Dachan Bay, Busan, Shanghai, Ningbo, Dachan Bay, Ashdod

Source: Own compilation based on data Alphaliner

and the Far East: the Asia-East Med Express service of Zim/OOCL and the joint Ocean Three/Yang Min service. The changes in the calling patterns accrued during 2015 and 2016 due to the decreased Black Sea demand and low freight rates. Other weekly services are the Ecumed service (Maersk Line, South America, annual capacity of 150,000 TEU) and a Maersk service connecting the Indies and the Middle East to the Black Sea.

These services involve line-bundling operations with calls at three to four Black Sea ports. Roughly, half of the current containers handled in the Black Sea ports are shipped using direct calls, while the other half is feedered from hub ports in the East Med such as Istanbul, Piraeus and, to a lesser extent, Thessaloniki, Gioia Tauro etc. The Mediterranean ports play an increasing role in the Far East-Black Sea trade. As from the mid-1990s, the Mediterranean witnessed an active development of hub-feeder container systems as well as short sea shipping networks driven by the growth of the container volumes serving the southern part of Europe (Notteboom, 2010).

Since 2001, Black Sea ports have attracted global terminal operators. The first entrants were HHLA in Odessa port (2001) and NCC in Novorossiysk port (2002). A second wave of entrants included DPW in Constanta (2004) and NCC in Illichivsk (2005). The last big inflow of global terminal operators included APMT in Poti (2011) and a joint involvement of CMA-CGM in Odessa, together with a local terminal operator (2008). In the coming years two new green field ports in the Black Sea are expected to start operations, namely in Anaklia in Georgia and Taman port in the Russian Federation.

Figure 8.2 provides an overview of container throughput in Black Sea ports. Last year's traffic decline in Black Sea ports is in sharp contrast to the strong growth witnessed by Piraeus and Turkish deep-sea ports near the Sea of Marmara. This demonstrates that shipping lines increasingly prefer a hub-feeder model in the Med to service the Black Sea area instead of direct deep-sea calls in the Black Sea. Constanta's container throughput fell sharply from 1.38 million TEU in 2008 to 0.59m TEU in 2009. The year 2015 witnessed a stabilization in port traffic with limited growth of up to 0.68m TEU. Early on in its

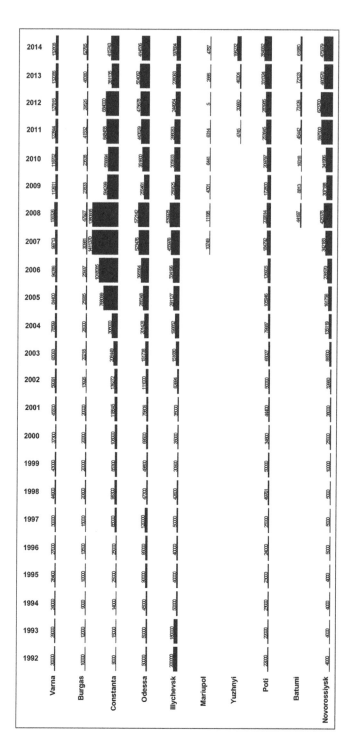

Figure 8.2 Black Sea ports container traffic, TEUs

development, Constanta was very much seen as the transshipment gateway for the Black Sea and registered an incidence of around 75% in 2008. However, the crisis of 2008 hit the regional economies and the shipping lines that likewise motivated the later change in their liner services in search of cost-efficient logistic solutions. A number of direct services from the Far East into the Black Sea region were cancelled, negatively affecting Constanta's transshipment volumes. As a result, by 2012, almost three-quarters of the volumes handled at the port consisted of local import and export containers, with the remaining quarter being transshipment.

The slowdown of Ukrainian port traffic in 2012 was connected to the regulatory changes in customs procedures, while ports lost between 50,000 to 100,000 TEU in favor of Hamburg and Baltic ports and, to a lesser extent, to Romania (Informal BG Black Sea Container Market report, 2014). The Ukrainian economy and container turnover started to stagnate at the end of 2013, due to the political crisis followed by more turbulent times and the annexation of Crimea by the Russian Federation in May 2014, with armed conflict in the East of Ukraine shortly thereafter. As an outcome of these events, the drop in container traffic in 2014 represented about 14.4% p.a. followed by a more drastic fall in 2015 of 29% p.a. Russia showed a negative container growth rate of -0.3% in 2014 in contrast to the growth of 10.1% in 2013, which represents a very drastic change. Romania had a 4.9% growth rate in 2014 compared to 14.34% in 2013. The same dynamic was shown by the Bulgarian ports with a growth rate in 2014 of 8.4% as against 6.5% in 2013 (Informal BG Black Sea Container Market report, 2014).

Connectivity measures at country level using the UNCTAD Liner Shipping Connectivity Index (LSCI) as well as the Logistics Performance Index (LPI) global rankings recent trends among studied countries (Figures 8.3 and 8.4). We applied the LSCI and LPI to the (i) Black Sea countries as well as to (ii) their East Med (Med) neighbors and finally to (iii) North European (NE) countries. The latter show the best performance in Europe based on both indicators. The average LSCI and LPI in the Black Sea is constantly increasing with the average (AVG) growth trend. If Russia is removed from the LSCI analysis, Ukrainian ports are leading, based on the LSCI index, even overtaking Romania as from 2009, since Constanta port has stopped playing a hub role in the Black Sea.

Figure 8.4 on the LPI shows the same general outcome as the LSCI, with the sole difference that Ukraine is no longer a leader in the Black Sea, having been passed out by its Western neighbors Romania and Bulgaria. The LPI leadership of these states can be partially explained by the fact that they joined the EU in 2007 and since then needed to improve and bring their logistics efficiency closer to EU norms (clearance processes, quality of trade and transport infrastructure etc.). Ukraine is the third best performer in the Black Sea based on the LPI index.

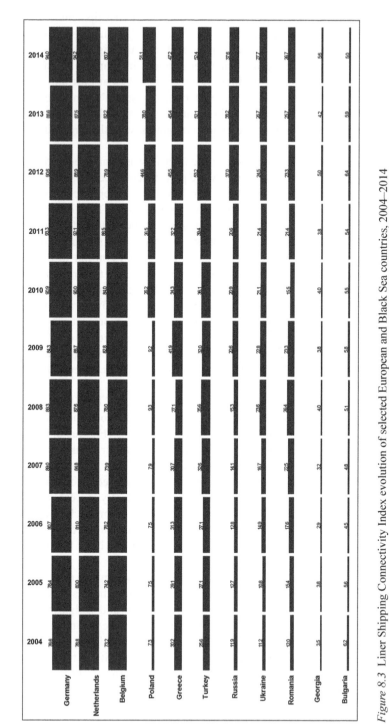

Figure 8.3 Liner Shipping Connectivity Index evolution of selected European and Black Sea countries, 2004–2014

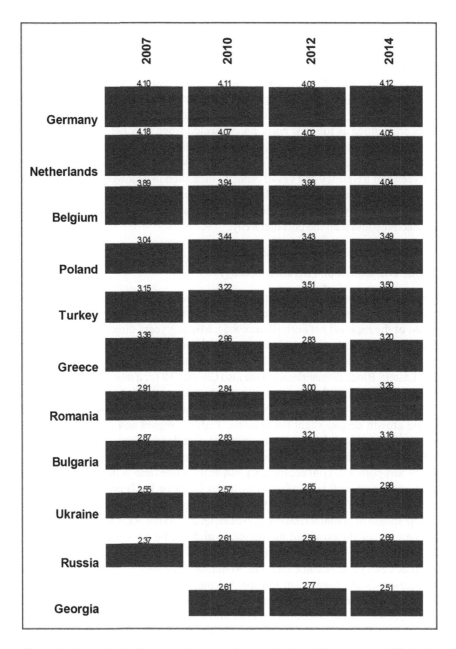

	2007	2010	2012	2014
Germany	4.10	4.11	4.03	4.12
Netherlands	4.18	4.07	4.02	4.05
Belgium	3.89	3.94	3.98	4.04
Poland	3.04	3.44	3.43	3.49
Turkey	3.15	3.22	3.51	3.50
Greece	3.36	2.96	2.83	3.20
Romania	2.91	2.84	3.00	3.26
Bulgaria	2.87	2.83	3.21	3.16
Ukraine	2.55	2.57	2.85	2.98
Russia	2.37	2.61	2.58	2.69
Georgia		2.61	2.77	2.51

Figure 8.4 Logistics Performance Index evolution of selected European and Black Sea countries, 2004–2014

Connectivity shifts of the Black Sea port system

In this section, we use the *Lloyd's List Intelligence* (LLI) database to analyze and map the traffic level and connectivity of Black Sea ports in the last 40 years or so. Such a long period allows us to grasp essential features on how the network had actually evolved across different geopolitical and technological phases, from limited containerization to the era of mega-ships. The daily movements of fully cellular containerships were aggregated each year during the month of June and transformed into global and regional port-to-port adjacency matrices. Inter-port links are defined as follows: ports are connected when they belong to the voyage of the same vessel during the 30 years of circulation. The amount of flows (traffic volume) in such a weighted, but undirected, network corresponds to the product between call frequency and vessel capacity measured in deadweight tons (DWTs). We then apply conventional graph-theoretical measures to the matrix, or graph, in order to extract its topological properties, reveal the geographic distribution of connectivity and map the port hierarchy.

Traffic distribution and network topology

One first step toward understanding past and current dynamics affecting the Black Sea port system is to compare total vessel traffic with the topological size (nodes, links) of the regional network (Figure 8.5). Missing years directly reflect the low containerization rate of the region in the initial period as well as the political instability and transition of the early 1990s due to the collapse of the USSR in 1991 and Eastern Block dismantlement (see also Chapter 19 for a more in-depth analysis of the impact of USSR collapse on related shipping networks). After such a major shock, especially from the mid-1990s onwards, we observe a fast and continuous traffic growth despite slight fluctuations. Traffic volumes and network size grew in parallel with each other, with the gradual containerization of Black Sea ports. This evolution reflects the increasing concentration of shipping traffic among Black Sea ports (cf. Gini coefficient), but at the same time, a decreasing share of the largest ports (cf. Herfindahl-Hirschman index or HHI) probably due to the polycentricism of the system and the emergence of small and medium-sized ports.

The spread of containerization, however, tended to reinforce existing (or to create new) inequalities within the region, which are best visible at country level (Figure 8.6). After a period of minimal traffic (1977–1997), the main players on the Black Sea scene became Ukraine, Romania and Bulgaria, namely the Western sub-region closest to Western Europe. In comparison, and given their relatively shorter coastline and fewer numbers of ports, Russia, Georgia and Turkey remained rather peripheral in the system, in both absolute and relative terms. These ports serve relatively narrow hinterlands and are at a certain remove from the core European markets; therefore, their traffic is limited. One exception is Russia, which rapidly and recently acquired a sizeable portion of the total Black Sea container traffic. Some explanatory factors include transit trade for the Russian Federation itself through third countries, such as Ukraine; port expansion in Russia, such as

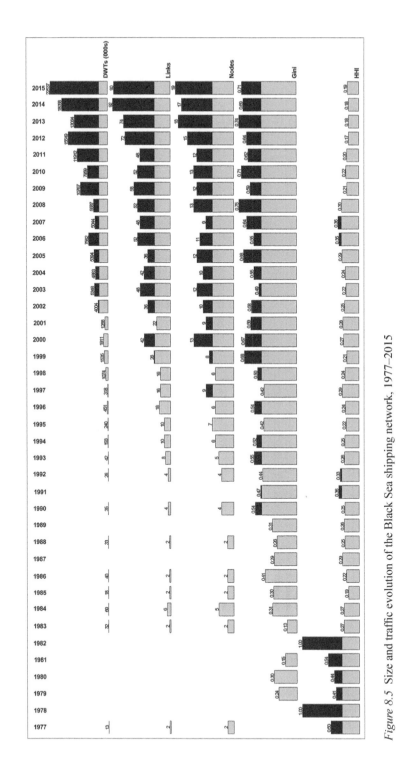

Figure 8.5 Size and traffic evolution of the Black Sea shipping network, 1977–2015

Source: Own realization based on LLI data

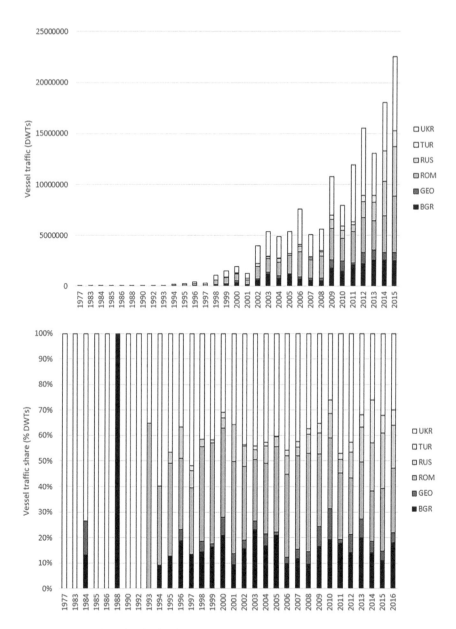

Figure 8.6 Vessel traffic distribution among Black Sea countries, 1977–2015

in Novorossiysk; and conjectural phenomena, such as the Sochi Olympic Games in 2012 fostering traffic growth to build and cater for the new villages. In addition, the somewhat protectionist Russian attitude in terms of trade favored domestic ports over others to serve Russian hinterlands.

Externally, the connectivity of Black Sea ports as a whole went through a similar trend of growth (Figure 8.7, top). Despite some fluctuations, the number of links and nodes connecting the Black Sea with the rest of the world increased somewhat gradually and in parallel until the late 1990s, notwithstanding a noticeable decline in the number of ports after 1990. After 1998, a second phase was marked by rapid growth, despite some gaps in 2001–2003, 2006 and 2013. In the early 2000s, the freshly built Black Sea republics were still in a shaky economic state, namely

Figure 8.7 External connectivity of Black Sea ports, 1977–2015

undergoing rejuvenation after the early 1990s. The case of 2013 is better explained by the delayed impacts of the 2008–2009 global financial crisis in addition to local geopolitical conflicts leading to currency devaluation, high inflation, and less demand for containers. In terms of traffic volume and share (Figure 8.7, bottom), extra-regional vessel tonnage increased in similar ways than connectivity, albeit with an earlier take-off, namely in the mid-1990s. Following the collapse of the USSR, many Black Sea ports in the new republics were forced to diversify their traffic and adopt new technologies (i.e. containerization) to adapt to global standards and compensate the amputation of their formerly vast hinterlands (Thorez, 1998). Each port gateway used to operate separately in the Soviet era, connecting the USSR with the outside world, which explains the very high share of extra-regional traffic in the total Black Sea traffic in the early period, around 90%. For the same reasons cited above, post-Soviet ports strove to develop and multiply their external connections while increasing their mutual links. This resulted in a sharp decline of extra-regional traffic share from around 80% in the late 1990s to about 50% in 2006, the lowest value. During the last decade, however, extra-regional traffic has boomed and reached nearly 70% in 2015. As mentioned earlier, the role of Turkish ports as intermediate nodes ensuring the Black Sea's connectivity is well revealed by Turkey's rapidly growing share in total extra-regional traffic, from around 10% in the mid-1990s to around 60% in 2015.

The geographic distribution of Black Sea ports' maritime forelands brings complementary elements to the understanding of their global and regional connectivity (Figure 8.8). At the level of world regions or continents (left figure), Europe takes the lion's share of total extra-regional traffic with 77.4% on average over the whole period. This share had been relatively stable, except for a decline in the period 2004–2011, with an average of 65.3%. Geographic proximity to Europe, in addition to the fact that Western Europe had long played a crucial role for socialist trade either for transit or real commerce, is the main explanatory factor. The Americas as a whole never played any significant role for Black Sea container shipping, nor did Oceania (zero traffic), so that Europe is only followed by Asia and Africa. Although geographic proximity also explains, at least in part, the heavier weight of West Asia (i.e. Near East, Middle East, Indian subcontinent) compared with East Asia, the latter became more important than the first during the period 2004–2013 despite physical distance. Yet, the recent period was clearly impacted by a fall in demand (i.e. 15% decline in Black Sea–Asia trades) in 2015 and again in 2016 (Gerden, 2015; Ugurlu, 2017). Africa as a whole, despite a relatively low traffic share (3.4% on average), maintained its share in the recent decade (2003–2016) with a 5.6% average, probably due to increased transshipment through Egyptian ports such as Alexandria, Damietta and Port Said. When zooming into Europe (right figure), we see that South Europe in general had always been dominant compared with North Europe, the latter reaching a peak in 1994 (28.1% of Black Sea's total European traffic) but only during the 1984–2001 period. Thus, there has been a shift of Black Sea-related transshipment activities from North to South Europe over time. An important change in regional foreland distribution is the drastic shift from Southwest Europe dominance to East Med dominance.

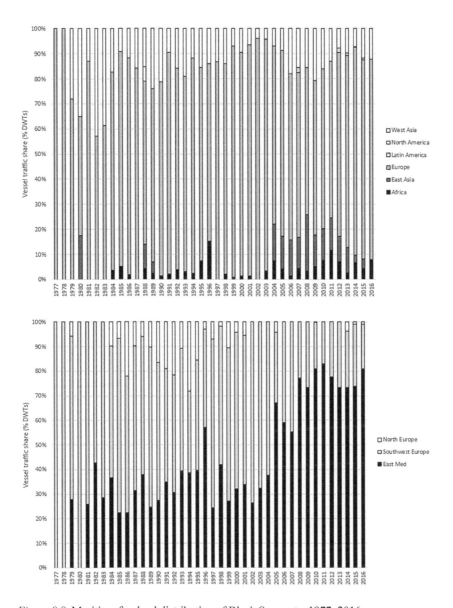

Figure 8.8 Maritime foreland distribution of Black Sea ports, 1977–2016

Southwest Europe accounted for 62.9% on average of the Black Sea's total European traffic in the period 1977–2004, while the East Med reached 72.9% during the rest of the period, with 81.0% in 2016. Such an inversion is directly attributable to the new competitive position and attractiveness of East Med ports for transshipment activities in the Med and the Black Sea. It is also driven by the Turkish effect, as mentioned above.

Multiple linkage analysis

Within any regional port system, it is fundamental to understand the evolution of port hierarchy but also the way in which shipping connectivity spatially spreads among port nodes. To achieve such a goal, we defined eight sub-periods, and, for each of them, we calculated the sum of vessel traffic by port. In addition, we mapped a simplified shipping network made up of the two largest flows of each port in terms of traffic volume. The loss of information is thus counterbalanced by a better view of the network's backbone, with the hypothesis that the multiple linkage analysis can reveal which hubs dominate the port system and the system's degree of centralization (Figure 8.9). The size of nodes corresponds to total vessel traffic including extra-regional traffic.

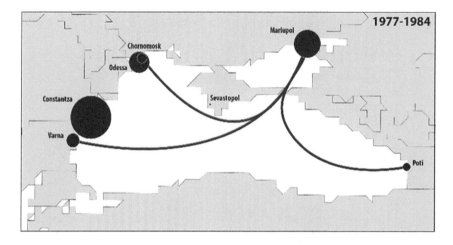

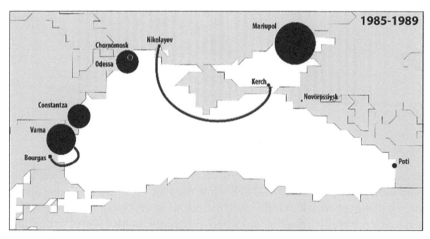

Figure 8.9 Multiple linkage analysis of the Black Sea shipping network, 1977–2016

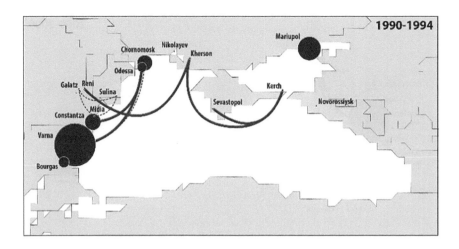

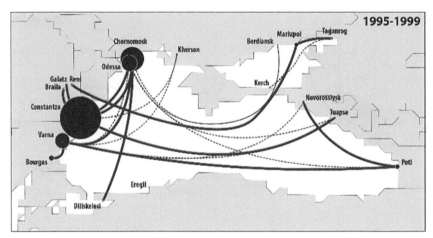

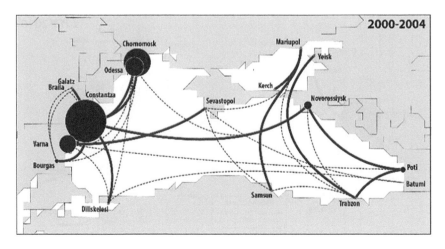

Figure 8.9 (Continued)

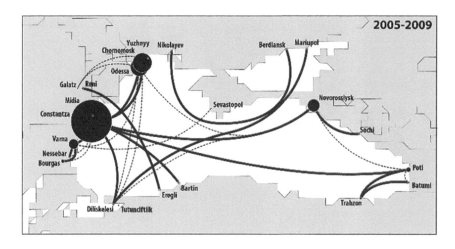

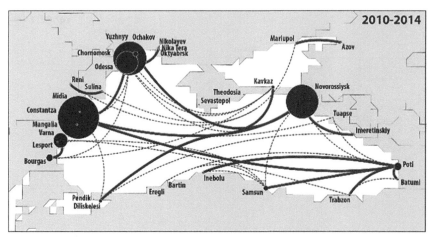

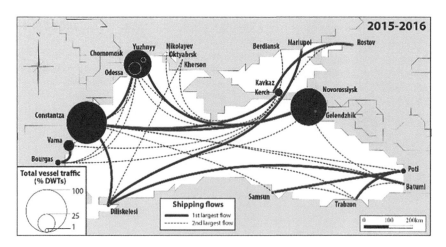

Figure 8.9 (Continued)

Before analyzing the results, it is important to note that over the entire period, we found no evidence of a centralization process in the Black Sea. The gamma index, which corresponds to the proportion of actual links in the total maximum possible number of links among connected ports, did not show any particular trend. The index oscillates around 40% over time, although from 2010 onwards the average index went down to 32–33%. This slight decrease suggests a simplification of the network in recent years, but it remains rather moderate. Such a result indicates that the Black Sea port system might be more externally than internally centralized, due to the absence of a hub-and-spokes configuration in the region. Based on the eight periods under consideration, the constantly connected top five ports (i.e. Constanta, Odessa, Chornomorsk, Varna and Mariupol) exhibit a very high and significant relationship ($R^2 = 0.8945$) between their average traffic size and the standard deviation of their traffic growth rates, thereby depicting a well-integrated region or range (Lemarchand and Joly, 2009).

Apart from providing a clear picture of the port hierarchy, Figure 8.9 sheds more light on the evolution of the dominant shipping linkages within the Black Sea. While Constanta and Odessa are connected only externally in the first period (1977–1984), Mariupol appears as a pivotal port for the other periods. However, Mariupol sustained its activity in the two subsequent periods, but without being connected internally to the region. North-South linkages in the west part of the region then dominate, notwithstanding the emergence of East-West transversals in subsequent periods. Constanta appears as the largest and best connected port, but without centralizing the whole network, as a number of dominant linkages connect Eastern ports, and a number of secondary nodes do not depend on Constanta for their connectivity. Geographic proximity has some visible influence on the sub-regionalization of the Black Sea, between East and West, but remains moderate. As time passes, the network becomes more and more complex and does not exhibit any particular pattern. Perhaps this relates to the absence of a single or twin-hub system internally. It could also reveal, indirectly, the growing dependence of Black Sea ports upon external Med hubs, such as in Turkey.

Conclusion

This chapter investigated the changing internal and external trends affecting the past and current evolution of the Black Sea port system and liner shipping network. Due to a low containerization rate and a peripheral situation from major container shipping routes in the 1970s–1990s, this region exhibited a rather peculiar pattern at the time, characterized by low internal connectivity, extraverted flows, and small traffic and network size. If the gradual and rapid increase of traffic volumes (especially from the mid-1990s) inevitably resulted in growing concentration around a few large ports, network analysis did not confirm the emergence of a centralized system, or hub-and-spokes configuration, within the Black Sea itself. More likely is the growing dependence of these large ports upon external transshipment hubs such as in Turkey, for instance, the latter having absorbed the lion's share of the Black Sea's external connectivity in the past decade or so. Our main findings thus suggest that the Black Sea port system does not have a clear structure, due to the absence of a hub-and-spokes configuration locally and therefore a mismatch between port traffic volume and port centrality, except for Constanta, which took on hub functions for some time until 2008. Thus, contradictory forces characterize the region, between regional integration and network centralization, due to its polycentric structure.

Based on historical analysis and recent developments in the region we conclude that the outlook for Black Sea port connectivity does not seem set to change drastically. Given the fact that (i) the Black Sea remains a remote area, (ii) the economic situation in the region in the near future is expected to gradually grow and (iii) it is hard to estimate the future impact of the new Silk Road development on the Black Sea ports, we forecast a moderate growth-stable scenario. When compared with existing literature on Black Sea ports, this chapter provides mixed evidence, such as the observed growth of direct calls vs. feeder (Gouvernal et al., 2012), which is reflected in the gradual increase of the LSCI index but not in the other analyses. Indirectly, our results at least partially confirm the findings of Notteboom and De Langen (2015) in relation to the fast growth of South European ports, with our chapter bringing new evidence about the regional shift from West Med to East Med as the Black Sea's main external connector. The work by Ducruet and Notteboom (2012) on the global shipping network underlined the emergence of nodal regions around the ports of Constanta, Izmir and Ambarli, the first being also considered in this chapter a major node but not yet the principal hub of the Black Sea, which remains more polycentric. Our findings also support those of Freire Seoane et al. (2013) due to that West-East shift in external connectivity; one explanation for this in recent years being the suspension of two out of four direct Far-East–Black Sea services (2015–2016). These elements might explain why Li et al. (2015) observed a decline in the Black Sea's global shipping centrality despite its overall traffic growth. The absence of traffic concentration internally had been already underlined by Grushevska and Notteboom (2014), with the notable exception of Novorossiysk port, so our study is in line with their work, though adding new evidence from a relational (network) perspective beyond traffic volumes taken in isolation. All in all, this study shows us how important the geographical scale of analysis is when it comes to shipping flows and networks. The Black Sea in itself might not (yet) be a well-organized system; its internal dynamics cannot be understood without taking into account the centralization of its own flows through external hubs. This contribution ties in well with academic literature on the evolution of the vulnerability and hub-dependency of shipping networks (Ducruet, 2008), especially when looking at the impact of both technological and geopolitical factors affecting trade and logistics.

Acknowledgements

The research leading to these results has received funding from the European Research Council under the European Union's Seventh Framework Programme (FP/2007–2013) / ERC Grant Agreement n. [313847] "World Seastems".

References

Ducruet, C. (2008) Hub dependence in constrained economies: The case of North Korea. *Maritime Policy and Management*, 35(4): 374–388.

Ducruet, C. (2017) Multilayer dynamics of complex spatial networks: The case of global maritime flows (1977–2008). *Journal of Transport Geography*, 60: 47–58.

Ducruet, C., Lee, S.W., Ng, A.K.Y. (2010) Centrality and vulnerability in liner shipping networks: Revisiting the Northeast Asian port hierarchy. *Maritime Policy and Management*, 37(1): 17–36.

Ducruet, C., Notteboom, T.E. (2012) The worldwide maritime network of container shipping: Spatial structure and regional dynamics. *Global Networks*, 12(3): 395–423.

Fleming, D.K., Hayuth, Y. (1994) Spatial characteristics of transportation hubs: Centrality and intermediacy. *Journal of Transport Geography*, 2(1): 3–18.

Fraser, D.R., Notteboom, T.E., Ducruet, C. (2016) Peripherality in the global container shipping network: The case of the Southern African container port system. *Geojournal*, 81(1): 139–151.

Freire Seoane M.J., Gonzalez-Laxe F., Montes C.P. (2013) Foreland determination for containership and general cargo ports in Europe (2007–2011). *Journal of Transport Geography*, 30: 56–67.

Gerden, E. (2015) Black Sea port volumes decline deepens. *The Journal of Commerce*, December 4. Available at: www.joc.com/port-news/european-ports/black-sea-port-volumes-still-suffering-russia-slowdown_20151204.html. Accessed on March 2017.

Gouvernal, E., Rodrigue, J.P., Slack, B. (2012) The divergence of regionalization: The challenges of the Mediterranean ports of Europe. In: Paper presented at the *International Association of Maritime Economists (IAME) Conference*, Taipei, Taiwan, September 6–8.

Grushevska, K., Notteboom, T.E. (2014) An economic and institutional analysis of multiport gateway regions in the Black Sea basin. *Journal of International Logistics and Trade*, 12(2): 22–35.

Informall BG Annual Report. (2014) *Black Sea Container Market Review.*Retrieved from http://www.informall.biz/en/archives/1680

Lemarchand, A., Joly, O. (2009) Regional integration and maritime range. In: Notteboom, T.E., Ducruet, C., De Langen, P.W. (Eds.), *Ports in Proximity: Competition and Coordination Among Adjacent Seaports*. Aldershot: Ashgate, pp. 87–99.

Li, Z., Xu, M., Shi, Y. (2015) Centrality in global shipping network basing on worldwide shipping areas. *Geojournal*, 80(1): 47–60.

Mareï, N., Ducruet, C. (2015) The regionalization of maritime networks: Evidence from a comparative analysis of maritime basins. In: Ducruet, C. (Ed.), *Maritime Networks: Spatial Structures and Time Dynamics*. London and New York: Routledge Studies in Transport Analysis, pp. 330–350.

Notteboom, T.E. (2006) Traffic inequality in seaport systems revisited. *Journal of Transport Geography*, 14(2): 95–108.

Notteboom, T.E. (2010) Concentration and the formation of multi-port gateway regions in the European container port system: An update. *Journal of Transport Geography*, 18(4): 567–583.

Notteboom, T.E., de Langen, P.W. (2015) Container port competition in Europe. In: Lee, C.Y., Meng, Q. (Eds.), *Handbook of Ocean Container Transport Logistics*. Basel, Switzerland :Springer International Publishing, pp. 75–95.

Notteboom, T.E., Rodrigue, J.P. (2005) Port regionalization: Towards a new phase in port development. *Maritime Policy and Management*, 32(3): 297–313.

Rodrigue, J.P., Notteboom, T.E. (2010) Foreland-based regionalization: Integrating inter-mediate hubs with port hinterlands. *Research in Transportation Economics*, 27(1): 19–29.

Thorez, P. (1998) La difficile mutation des transports maritimes dans la C.E.I. *Bulletin de l'Association des Géographes Français*, 75(1): 10–29.

Ugurlu, U. (2017) The new Black Sea port. *The Medi Telegraph*, December 4. Available at: www.themeditelegraph.com/en/transport/ports/2017/02/04/the-new-black-sea-port-reportage-eAzWNhvLQaBJlPHbwiCgrI/index.html

Wang, J.J., Ng, A.K.Y. (2011) The geographical connectedness of Chinese seaports with foreland markets: A new trend? *Tijdschrift voor Economische en Sociale Geografie*, 102(2): 188–204.

9 Maritime connections and disconnections in a changing Arctic

Mia Bennett

All maps distort reality (Monmonier, 2014; Wood and Fels, 1992; Stickler, 1990). The three mechanisms through which these distortions appear are scale, projection, and symbolization (de Sousa Santos, 1987). Manipulation of projection is readily apparent in maps of the polar regions, as their landmasses often appear stretched over the top of conventional maps and larger than they are in reality. One of the most well-known distortions as a result of projection is the "Greenland Problem," which results from the use of the Mercator projection. The Arctic island appears larger than Africa despite it actually being one-thirteenth of its size.

Yet there is another set of distortions, or perhaps more precisely, misrepresentations, in maps of the Arctic that have been widely circulated since 2007. That year, sea ice extent reached a record low and a deep-draft passage opened across the Northwest Passage's McClure Strait for the first time in history (Lasserre, 2011). This sparked excitement about the dawn of a new era of Arctic shipping, an industry which involves either transit shipping between Europe, Asia, and North America or destinational shipping (Buixadé Farré et al., 2014). The latter's economic potential lies not so much in supplying Arctic communities but rather in exporting northern natural resources like oil and gas to markets in these three continents. In line with renewed dreams of polar shipping shortcuts, there has been a proliferation of Arctic shipping maps depicting a circumpolar region where ice-free waters have replaced the ice cap. While these maps gesture towards a more interconnected planet, they fail to represent the disruptions occurring for the Arctic's two million residents as a result of climate change and the slowly growing numbers of tankers, barges, and cruise ships in waters covered by less and less ice. Arguably, Arctic shipping maps reify an imagining of the region as a newly opened global space for unrestricted movement, commerce, and natural resource extraction rather than as an inhabited place with existing intra-regional transport networks (for other analyses of transnational regions, see Chapters 5, 8, 11, 19, 23, and 24 on Taiwan Strait, Black Sea, Mediterranean, the USSR, Northwest Africa, and Indian subcontinent flows, respectively).

Arctic shipping maps represent a future form of development that is contingent upon the continued retreat of sea ice. Despite a history of adaptability and resilience among the Arctic's indigenous peoples, this environmental shift may eventually spell the end of their practices and ways of life that rely on the ice. Since the

1970s, Arctic sea ice extent has declined 30% (Stroeve et al., 2007). Anthropogenic forces are responsible for approximately half (47–57%) of its decline (Stroeve et al., 2012). As sea ice continues to melt, a mode of Arctic development marked by inter-regional, open-water transit may come to replace intra-regional, ice-supported transportation networks that have existed in both the pre-industrial and industrial eras. Indigenous peoples like the Inuit, Iñupiat, and Yupik use ice as a conduit for movement (Krupnik et al., 2010). Arctic industrial transportation networks, which supply sites like communities and mines in Canada and Russia and oil platforms on Alaska's North Slope, also rely on ice in the form of winter roads built across frozen rivers and seas. Highlighting the threat to industry posed by climate change since the 1970s, the reduction of Alaska's ice road season from 200 to 100 days on average has significantly raised environmental risks for oil and gas exploration (Hinzman et al., 2005).

Yet for trans-oceanic shipping, the disappearance of ice may finally rid the Arctic of a dangerous maritime obstacle. Ice proved to be the downfall of many European expeditions into the Northwest Passage in present-day Canada, where vessels like Englishman Sir John Franklin's Royal Navy ships, Erebus and Terror, became fatally trapped in ice (Rondeau, 2010). In 1975, to overcome ice from prohibiting free movement in the northern seas, the Soviets launched Arctica, the first in a series of 75,000-hp nuclear-powered icebreakers (Khlopkin and Zotov, 1997). These nuclear icebreakers ensured year-round navigation of the western portion of Russia's Northern Sea Route. Notably, icebreakers are designed to smash through the very material that serves as a foundation for movement for many coastal indigenous peoples in the Arctic. Today, as more ice retreats and thins and if requisite shipping infrastructure is built, five centuries of Western dreams of a clear passage between east and west may be realized while the mobilities of Arctic peoples are jeopardized. At the same time, global economic shifts are rendering intra-Arctic supply networks that deliver much-needed goods to the region's settlements financially unviable while making long-distance extraction of the region's resources more favorable.

The rest of this chapter is structured as follows. The following section describes the two main shipping routes in the Arctic: the Northern Sea Route and the Northwest Passage. Next, we examine the indigenous peoples living along these routes and how their development may impact their ways of life. We then discuss the fragmentation and weakening of industrial intra-Arctic transportation networks due to political and economic shifts. We suggest some alternative ways of mapping the Arctic that might push back against visions of the region's development that are centered on long-distance shipping routes. The last section offers some conclusions.

Commercial pathways across the Arctic: the Northern Sea Route and Northwest Passage

At present and in the foreseeable future, the two main trans-Arctic shipping routes are the Northern Sea Route (NSR), which hugs the north coast of Russia, and the Northwest Passage (NWP), which cuts from north of Alaska through Canada's

Arctic Archipelago to the Davis Strait between Greenland and Canada. In recent years, the navigation seasons for ice-class ships along these routes have expanded. By 2040–2059, conventional open-water ships may be able to transit these passages during peak season in September, when ice cover is lowest (Smith and Stephenson, 2013). By this same period, a shipping route across the North Pole may be viable in peak season for Polar Class 6 vessels (Smith and Stephenson, 2013).

Despite all of the excitement, neither the NSR nor NWP will compete with the Suez Canal anytime soon. The NSR was closed to international navigation under the Soviet Union, and it was not until 1988 that the country began partnering with other nations to explore its economic viability as an international shipping route. Over time, the NSR has become the more developed of the two Arctic shipping routes and could reduce the distance between Europe (London) and Asia (Yokohama) by 4,200 nautical miles (Schøyen and Bråthen, 2011). Yet the number of ships that have transited the entire route is paltry and has decreased in recent years, from 71 in 2013 to 2016 (Northern Sea Route Administration, 2016). Cargo volume statistics, which include cargo that may have only transited a portion of the NSR, tell a slightly different story: given cargo volume in 2015, shipments appear to be headed close to their previous peak in 1987 (see Figure 9.1).

Canada does not officially release NWP cargo volume statistics, but Hedlun (2014) estimates 18 transits in 2013, three between 2013 and 2014, and ten in 2014. For both the NWP and the NSR, 2013 may have been an unusually high year for transits in part because ice cover was significantly reduced, while 2014 was notably colder. The high fees charged by the NSR Administration due to the need for icebreaker service, among other services required, also reduce the route's competitiveness with the Suez Canal. Liu and Kronbak (2010) determine that it costs $979.20 to transport one 20-foot equivalent unit (TEU) along the NSR. In contrast, it costs $56 for the average Panamax containership to transit the Suez Canal (Johns and Associates, 2005). Verny and Grigentin (2009), however, find that NSR fees were only about twice as expensive as those for the Suez Canal.

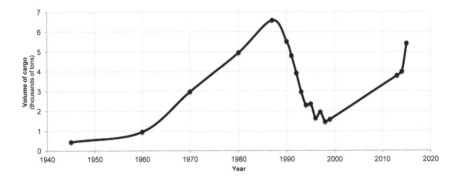

Figure 9.1 Cargo volumes along the Northern Sea Route, 1945–2015

Sources: 1945–1999: Ragner (2000). 2013: Northern Sea Route Administration (2014). 2014–2015: ЕМИСС (2017)

Maps of Arctic shipping routes remain seemingly unaffected by upticks or downturns in cargo volumes. As sea ice continues to retreat, these maps persist in presenting images of routes seamlessly passing through ice-free ocean even when there is little serious support for the industry among private companies for Arctic shipping, as demonstrated in a study of 98 ship owners by Lasserre and Pelletier (2011). Additionally, few concrete investments in infrastructure are being made to support more regularized shipping once the sea ice melts, especially along the NWP. In large part, Arctic shipping maps retain a seductive power because the development of regular polar shipping routes, specifically the NWP, has long been viewed as synonymous with commerce, progress, romance, and nationalism (Krupnik et al., 2010).

Indigenous peoples and pathways along the NSR and NWP

The NSR and NWP cut through areas with varying degrees of local and indigenous maritime activities including subsistence, transportation and recreation. Their development will therefore affect communities living on their shores. Along the western portion of the NSR, inland activities based on the tundra and taiga like reindeer herding tend to be more prevalent than sea-based subsistence. Yet indigenous maritime subsistence activities like whaling, sealing, and fishing increase towards the eastern end of the NSR, where the maritime Chukchi and Koryaks engage in marine mammal hunting (Paulson and Auer, 1964). These activities still carry on despite increased pressure from climate change and industrial development, specifically shipping and oil and gas (Hovelsrud et al., 2008). Along Canada's NWP, the many islands and inlets have given rise to indigenous communities highly reliant on the sea and sea ice (Østreng et al., 2013); yet they, too, are under pressure from increases in cruise tourism and shipping, more so related to mining than oil and gas.

Over time, constant interaction and engagement with the landscape has led Arctic peoples to develop a large spatial-geometric vocabulary (Tuan, 1977). Migrating groups of Inuit, for instance, had a keen sense of location, geography, and astronomy (Hastrup, 2009). This knowledge was shared largely through oral over written traditions, with many northern indigenous communities possessing a "vernacular tradition of terrestrial mapmaking" (Okladnikova, 1998). Historically, knowledge has retained high accuracy as it passes from one generation to the next (Cooke, 1984). The Inuit have disseminated their knowledge outside of their communities, too. Demonstrating how local knowledge of the environment has supported endeavors to open up the Arctic to long-distance shipping routes, the Inuit shared their maps with Europeans trying to navigate the NWP in the nineteenth century (Rundstrom, 1990). Illustrating the precision with which the Inuit interacted with their environment, in the early 1900s, Canadian ethnologist Viljhalmur Stefansson voyaged through Canada's Dolphin and Union Straits and found abandoned Inuit villages of igloos spaced 16 kilometers apart (Riewe, 1991). Seal hunting was typically conducted at a maximum of 8 kilometers away from camp, and once all of the seals in an area had been hunted, the villages would relocate some 16 kilometers away. Revealing the history of the Arctic as an inhabited and intricately connected space, anthropologist Claudio Aporta (2009) shows how in the Western Arctic, moving was a way of living for the nomadic Inuit. He finds, "To Inuit, the Arctic was in fact a network of trails, connecting communities to their distant neighbors, and to fishing lakes and hunting grounds in between" (Aporta, 2009: 132).

In many ways, moving is still a way of living for the Arctic's indigenous peoples even if most are now sedentary. In all five Arctic coastal countries with Arctic indigenous populations, Greenland, Norway, Russia, Canada, and the U.S.,[1] the majority live in permanent settlements planned by governments in the twentieth century. This so-called "infrastructure fix" means that it is now harder for indigenous peoples to adapt, relocate, or change resource use activities. Despite these hardships, to Arctic indigenous peoples, the environment is often still conceived of as a "taskscape that is part of the life-world of people" (Hastrup, 2009: 185) rather than a landscape or surface on top of which people and objects move. For instance, to access food from the sea, which provides a vital source of nutrition due to rampant food insecurity (Wesche and Chan, 2010), people hunt for seals and whales and catch fish. They also move across the sea and ice to visit with friends and family rather than just quickly move across the ocean to reach a destination on the other side of the world, as a container ship might do.

To move about the Arctic, many indigenous peoples use traditional technologies alongside mechanized modes of transportation that they have adapted to suit their needs, like snowmobiles (Pelto, 1987). Indigenous peoples regularly travel long distances using motorized vehicles for activities ranging from hunting to grocery shopping. In the Arctic coastal hamlet of Tuktoyaktuk, Northwest Territories, Canada, some Inuvialuit residents will sail 40 kilometers in a motorboat to hunt beluga whales or drive a pick-up truck 20 hours down a gravel highway to the nearest Wal-Mart for supplies (personal observation, 2016). The adoption of modern technologies, however, has not always been to the most productive ends. The use of Global Positioning Satellite (GPS) technologies in Igloolik, Canada, has been documented as leading to a loss of engagement with the landscape, which can prove perilous for safe navigation and travel (Aporta, 2003).

Changes in the landscape and seascapes are also impacting indigenous abilities to navigate. In the northern Canadian community of Clyde River, elders have expressed disappointment and sadness at not being able to predict the weather or be sure about ice conditions using their traditional knowledge (Gearheard et al., 2006). While indigenous peoples in the Arctic continue to be highly mobile, environmental and economic shifts that are opening up new opportunities for Arctic shipping are profoundly affecting indigenous abilities to reliably navigate based on time-tested knowledge of their surroundings.

Although there are numerous settlements and local ways of moving about in the Arctic, maps of trans-Arctic shipping lanes rarely include more than a handful of settlements, if any. Figure 9.2 presents a representative example of such a map, which may reinforce beliefs that the Arctic is uninhabited. In others maps, a few key commercial ports or urban centers may be included, like Tiksi or Murmansk

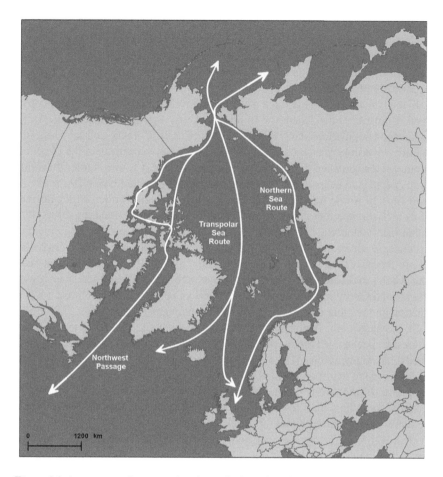

Figure 9.2 A representative example of a typical Arctic shipping map in which potential
shipping routes are depicted against a completely ice-free, unpopulated
background

in Russia and Hammerfest in Norway, but otherwise the Arctic is depicted as a
nearly unpopulated region despite the two million people who live north of the
Arctic Circle, approximately 527,000 of whom are indigenous (Hotez, 2010). The
remainder consists of non-indigenous northerners. In places like Russia, many
non-indigenous northerners were forcibly resettled there to carry out major development projects during the Soviet period, while others both in and outside of the
Russian Arctic have simply been drawn by the allure of the north.

Colonial and Western practices that have sedentarized indigenous peoples in the
Arctic have made them less, not more, able to move around. At the same time,
Western perspectives continue to conflate indigeneity with stagnation, a lack of
development, and immobility while non-indigenous peoples are associated with

"mobility, translocality, and globality" (Cameron, 2012: 104). This divergence in perspectives condones imaginings of indigenous peoples as unaffected by the opening of Arctic shipping routes, when in fact their intimate interactions with the land, sea, and their resources make them vulnerable to external disturbances whether climatic, political, or economic in nature.

Loss of indigenous and industrial intra-Arctic transportation in Canada and Russia

Climate change and dramatic alterations of political and economic systems following the end of the Cold War are weakening indigenous and industrial intra-Arctic transportation networks. When commercial vessels begin to operate in traditional waters, indigenous routes cannot simply just shift over. Even if they did, the traces of commercial passages can spread and linger. For instance, noise from ships can cause animal populations to move away, lengthening the distance a hunter might have to travel. Additionally in winter, ice broken by a ship does not seamlessly stitch itself back together, causing potential obstacles to navigation. The creation of open channels by icebreakers presents yet another hazard for people traveling by snowmobile.

The case of the Mary River iron ore mine on Baffin Island, Nunavut, Canada exemplifies the marginalization of indigenous mobilities in the Arctic for the benefit of the global shipping industry. In some cases, indigenous organizations themselves approve this marginalization. Before the mine's developer, Baffinland Iron Mines Corporation, began operations, it had to apply for permits and licenses from the Nunavut Impact Review Board, the territory's environmental assessment agency tasked with protecting and promoting "the well-being of the Environment and Nunavummiut [people inhabiting Nunavut] through the impact assessment process" (NIRB, 2016). During its review, which accepted comments from community members, one resident of the community of Igloolik (pop. 2,000) wrote in 2007:

> Sea mammals are afraid of noise, back then when we traveled using only sail boats and went walrus hunting. It was easy to find the walrus because we could hear them with the sounds they made. Both female and male that were separated would know by their sounds, they knew which was male and female. We were able to hear them before they came into sight. It is clear there will no longer be walruses if they listen to this constantly all summer and all winter, they will have to hear this noise constantly. It is clear they will move on. Inuit and the dogs will no longer have any more food.
>
> (NIRB, 2008)

Yet in 2012, the Nunavut Impact Review Board gave a positive recommendation of the project to Canada's Minister of Aboriginal Affairs and Northern Development, allowing Baffinland to proceed with its open-pit iron ore mine. The company ships iron ore on bulk carriers from a port near its open pit at Milne Inlet to

Rotterdam and other ports in Europe three to four months a year, with the first delivery being made to Rotterdam in 2015.

Underscoring the increasing potential for conflicts between locally and globally oriented activities in the Arctic, in 2014, Baffinland proposed to expand its shipping season from three to four months to ten months a year (June through March) as a response to the drop in iron ore prices from ~$150 in 2013 to ~$50 in 2016. As the proposal would require winter icebreaking, which could negatively impact ice hunting, some local residents protested. The Nunavut Planning Commission ruled that winter icebreaking would go against the territory's land use plan, which prioritizes indigenous use. Commission chair Hunter Tootoo noted, "In the plan there's essential areas which are harvesting areas and community transportation routes . . . This ice-breaking disrupts that" (CBC News, 2015a). Baffinland applied for a federal exemption, which the minister of the Department of Aboriginal Affairs and Northern Development approved in a break with the Nunavut Planning Commission. In a letter to the body, the minister wrote, "At this point there is no reason to believe that the project cannot be assessed and potentially approved, regulated and carried out in a manner that is consistent with the existing and future well-being of the residents and the communities" (CBC News, 2015b). The matter has now been forwarded to the Nunavut Impact Review Board for its final decision. While not all indigenous peoples or representative bodies oppose industrial activities in the Arctic – indeed, in many places, income and revenue from these industries are what keep communities afloat – it is often difficult for industrial and indigenous activities to coexist in the same waters.

While market pressures threaten indigenous ways of life, they also jeopardize the industrial transport networks within the Arctic that deliver food, fuel, clothing, and other amenities of modern life to numerous settlements. Over the past several decades, in line with the retreat of state services from a region that has become more vulnerable to global economic forces following demilitarization and the end of the Cold War, industrial transport networks in Canada and Russia have fragmented and weakened. In Russia, 1987 marked the peak year for volume of cargo shipped along the NSR; by 2000, there had been a 76% reduction in cargo volumes (Ragner, 2000), although as shown in Figure 9.1, this trend appears to now be reversing. Much of the previous decline consisted of decreases in supplies to the indigenous, industrial, scientific, and military settlements along the country's northern coast, with volume of foreign imports dropping a full 97.5% between 1987 and 1999. Economic contraction following the Soviet Union's dissolution made previous subsidies of the Arctic transport system economically untenable, leading to a general decrease in industrial production, investment, and population in the North.

To reduce its burden of having to provide services to northern communities, the government encouraged outmigration and the resettlement of people from its Arctic regions to more temperate places, which are easier to supply (Heleniak, 1999). At the same time, since the early 1990s, the Russian government has promoted the development of the NSR as a global transportation corridor. With regularized Europe-Asia transit shipping now appearing more unlikely than it did when global excitement peaked in 2007 following the record sea ice minimum, the Russian government has refocused development of the route on the planned export of liquefied natural gas to Europe and Asia from the Yamal Peninsula, situated more or less in the middle of the NSR (Moe, 2014). This exemplifies the government's contemporary strategy of basing Arctic development on international market demands rather than local needs, in which Russia is hardly unique among Arctic states.

In sharp contrast to the shrinking population in the Russian Arctic, the population in the Canadian Arctic grew close to 14% between 2000 and 2010 (Heleniak and Bogoyavlenskiy, 2013) – slightly higher than the global decadal growth rate. A rising population means that more, not fewer, goods and supplies need to be brought to the North. As there are numerous communities not connected by road in the Canadian North (the entire territory of Nunavut has no road connection with the rest of Canada) and air travel is prohibitively expensive, sealift is often the only affordable way for goods to be delivered. But as in Russia, market-based services have replaced state-based services in Canada, leading to more tenuous supply chains whose existence is determined more by corporate balance sheets than local needs.

A prime example is the closure in 2016 of the Port of Churchill in Manitoba by its Denver-based, private operator, Omnitrax, due to a large drop in grain shipments. The company has owned the port and the railway leading up to it from The Pas, Manitoba since 1997, when it purchased the infrastructure from the Canadian state. Churchill is far from the NWP, so its closure does not represent a direct loss of infrastructure for trans-Arctic shipping. It does, however, significantly affect the 1,000 residents of Churchill. Archaeological records show that since at least 1700 B.C., indigenous peoples have made use of the area as a hunting ground. But beginning in 1717, when the Hudson's Bay Company built the first permanent settlement at Churchill – a fur trading post – the town's economy has come to depend on trade with the outside world. In 1927, the Canadian government decided to build a port at Churchill on Hudson Bay in order to ship grain from the Canadian Prairies, where the agricultural frontier had been continuing to expand northward, to Europe (Innis, 1930). Yet exports and imports never fully took off as imagined, in part due to the hindrances of a shipping season that lasted only four months because of ice. $48 million in support for infrastructure upgrades from the federal and provincial governments in 2007 were not enough to halt the port's eventual closure. The Port of Churchill's shuttering has already led to reductions in trains along the railroad, jeopardizing the reliable delivery of supplies to Churchill's residents. In sum, the replacement of state support with privatization has made it possible for a company to write off the port as a loss on a spreadsheet. Had the port either remained in public hands or been situated not on Hudson Bay but rather on the NWP, where state concerns about demonstrating sovereignty, boosting cruise tourism, and attracting transit shipping persist, it may not have been closed.

The Port of Churchill's demise is hardly the only example of the decline of state support for northern intra-regional transportation networks. Additionally in 2016, Northern Transportation Company Limited, which for 80 years provided sealifts that deliver everything from baby formula to pick-up trucks to 12 communities across Canada's Western Arctic, lost court-ordered protection from bankruptcy caused by financial issues (Weber, 2016). Two indigenous-owned corporations had purchased the company from the government in 1985. And in Russia, across the country's Arctic regions, reindeer herding has witnessed cutbacks in state support for everything from helicopters to snowmobiles (Konstantinov, 2002).

While the situations in Russia and Canada highlight the market's role in upsetting intra-regional transport in the Arctic, the state also bears responsibility for promoting this scalar shift in Arctic transport networks. The Russian and Canadian governments claim the NSR and NWP, respectively, as internal waters based on historical presence and use, especially by indigenous peoples in the case of Canada. In 1985, the President of the Makivik Corporation, an Inuit-owned corporation in Quebec, argued, "Canada's claim to the Arctic is more securely founded upon continuing Inuit use and occupation of the area than upon the construction of ice-breakers, the promotion of increased tanker traffic, and investment in military hardware" (as cited in Shadian, 2007: 333). The federal government's ultimate possession of sovereignty over Arctic waterways is what allowed the Department of Aboriginal and Indian Affairs in Canada to permit an exemption for Baffinland to ship ten months of the year despite the Nunavut Planning Commission's recommendations to the contrary. Thus, ironically, the Canadian government leverages a history of Inuit presence and use to bolster its own ability to regulate a space and permit an activity whose operation may jeopardize Inuit abilities to continue practices central to Canada's sovereignty claims.

Towards more comprehensive maps of Arctic shipping

Whether they depict the past, present, or future, all maps have a "tense" (Hadlaw, 2003). In this regard, the Arctic may be somewhat unique among world regions, given its consistent cartographic portrayal as a space of future transit possibilities. Although a somewhat crude example, one of the highest ranking results for a search in Google Images for "Arctic map" is a map published by the Chinese Arctic and Antarctic Administration of an ice-free, blue Arctic Ocean, complete with shipping routes overlaid (SIPRI, 2010). A search for "Europe map," "North America map," or even "Amazon map" did not result in any similar future-oriented transportation route maps. This cursory search suggests that development in the Arctic is often illustrated as contingent and existing in the future more so than the present – even when two million people already inhabit the region and move within it every day.

Future-oriented maps of Arctic shipping routes help promote and legitimize the creation of long-distance networks geared towards extracting the Arctic's natural resources to meet demands in urban centers of consumption to the south. They illustrate the ocean as an ice-free space across which hulking ships and tankers can move, reifying contemporary imaginings of the ocean as a "space of flows" (Steinberg, 2001). The command and control centers of the global economy conceive of the future Arctic Ocean as a planar surface that can be connected into the seamless world of global shipping. Literary theorist Adriana Craciun (2009) offers, "In connecting Asia, North America and Europe, the circumpolar Arctic peripheralizes all of the imperial centers of the northern hemisphere, presenting us with a wholly alien planetary vision" (p. 104). Yet when shipping routes are overlaid on polar-projected maps of the Arctic, it becomes clear that they actually are connecting rather than peripheralizing the three continents. The idea of the Arctic as a shipping shortcut actually becomes less alien the more the public is presented with maps depicting the Arctic as a connective space. Such imaginings transform the region into a space of flows while undermining its distinction as a space of place – a home, in other words – for its residents. Though Arctic shipping may deliver some new jobs, more regular supplies, or even new port infrastructure to coastal communities, they will not benefit from these new trade routes nearly as much urban cores in Asia, North America, and Europe.

While there are no easy solutions to accommodating both intra-Arctic and inter-Arctic shipping, a first step may be to better communicate through maps the complexity of the Arctic as a lived and inhabited space where sea ice still persists, even if it is melting and thinning. Greater acknowledgement of the social fabric and current environmental context of the Arctic would perhaps encourage greater discussion of whether Arctic shipping will really prove to be a tide that lifts all boats.

To that end, Figure 9.3 overlays shipping densities in 2008 with historical indigenous trails and pathways in the Arctic and existing permanent settlements in the region. The indigenous trails are mapped from historical documents meaning that while some might no longer still be in use, many are (Aporta et al., 2014). In addition, a great number of trails have likely been omitted. Arctic coastal settlements (defined as ≤ 20 kilometers from the coast) are mapped based on Natural Earth (2017) data, for which 90% of population estimates are based on LandScan derived population estimates. The map also includes summer sea ice extent in 2008 (NSIDC, 2016), matching the year of the displayed shipping density data. The ship tracks crossing the ice likely represent icebreakers that made the journey towards the North Pole that summer. Figure 9.3 includes historical average sea ice extent to underscore the decline that has occurred (Fetterer et al., 2016), for maps of Arctic shipping in particular are well placed to illustrate and acknowledge dramatic climate change. Finally, rivers and international political boundaries are drawn to better contextualize the Arctic's geography.

In mapping Arctic shipping, more attention should also be paid to the three types of distortions mentioned at the outset of this chapter: scale, projection, and symbolization.

Scale. Arctic shipping should also be shown at finer scales that focus on smaller areas of the Arctic rather than the whole region north of the Arctic Circle at once. These would draw more attention to the potential conflicts between local and global shipping routes that enter into the same place, for at the scale of the region, these local activities are inevitably left out, being too small to render.

Projection. Most Arctic shipping maps use polar projections that are centered on the North Pole. North Pole-centered maps have their benefits in depicting the

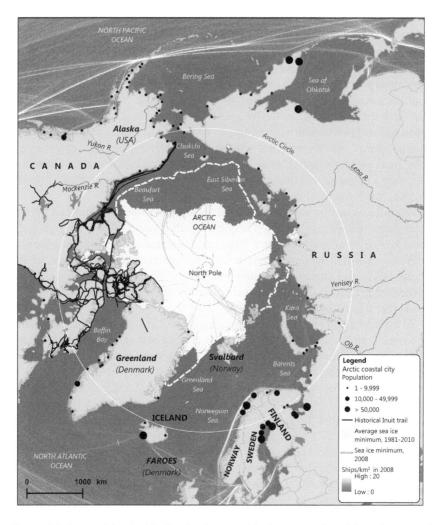

Figure 9.3 A map of Arctic shipping that features shipping routes alongside settlements of
varying sizes in the Arctic, historical Inuit trails in the Canadian Arctic, and
contemporary and recent historical sea ice extent

Arctic, yet they also promote imaginings of the region as a space for connecting
the three continents. Experimentation with non-North Pole centric projections may
be worthwhile in mapping Arctic shipping routes.

Symbolization. When feasible, Arctic communities should be included and
labeled in Arctic shipping maps. Sea ice, too, should be included rather than left
out altogether for as long as it persists in reality, along with at least an indicator of
past sea ice extent to demonstrate how much it has changed so far. Such data is

easily and freely available from the U.S. National Snow and Ice Data Center. Maps of Arctic shipping without sea ice are unrealistic in the short and medium term since sea ice is predicted to persist during winter's low season (March) through 2100 (Stroeve et al., 2012).

Conclusion

Most Arctic shipping maps fail to comment on the potential disappearance of entire ways of life structured around movement on the ice. Trans-Arctic shipping routes are excitedly touted as offering new, faster connections between Asia, North America, and Europe, with barely a moment to reflect on the indigenous and industrial intra-Arctic connections that are disappearing due to climate change and economic and political shifts, including withdrawal of state support. Governments justify expensive outlays for transportation infrastructures that they claim will connect and benefit communities in the Arctic. As a shipping executive in Labrador, Canada, remarked with regard to a potential deep-sea port in Iqaluit, "It will lower the cost of goods. It'll make access much easier; it'll make construction much easier. It will also bring a transportation mode that will help with development in the North and . . . it will also help . . . when it comes to opportunities" (CBC News, 2016). While local shipping routes may make a difference, the majority of Arctic shipping routes being promoted in maps and other narratives are primarily about improving connections between major ports in Europe, Asia, and North America to Arctic natural resources and to each other.

The portrayal of Arctic shipping routes like the NSR and NWP as seamless shortcuts is problematic because it suggests the Arctic is a tabula rasa onto which long-distance shipping routes can be developed without harming anyone's mobility. The ships that are already passing through, however, are negatively affecting indigenous and local peoples who hunt and fish in Arctic waters with their ice-breaking, oil slicks, emissions, and noise. For these reasons, more attention to mapping the Arctic as a space that is presently inhabited and ice-covered would help to counter future-oriented maps that may affect infrastructure decisions and investments in the present. Geographer Deborah Massey (1994) suggests, "If time-space compression can be imagined in that more socially formed, socially evaluative and differentiated way, then there may be the possibility of developing a politics of mobility and access. For it does seem that mobility, and control over mobility, both reflects and reinforces power." (p. 62) If fifteenth-century maps of the Arctic fostered ideas that the region should be a global shortcut, today, perhaps more socially inclusive maps of the Arctic can promote a form of economic development that is more locally centered.

Note

1 Iceland is not traditionally considered an Arctic coastal state, which the country's government has tried to contest (Dodds and Ingimundarson, 2012).

References

Aporta, C. (2003) New ways of mapping: Using GPS mapping software to plot place names and trails in Igloolik (Nunavut). *Arctic*, 56(4): 321–327.

Aporta, C. (2009) The trail as home: Inuit and their pan-Arctic network of routes. *Human Ecology*, 37(2): 131–146.

Aporta, C., Bravo, M., Taylor, F. (2014) *Pan Inuit Trails Atlas*. Available at: http://paninuit-trails.org.

Buixadé Farré, A., Stephenson, S.R., Chen, L., Czub, M., Dai, Y., Demchev, D., Efimov, Y., Graczyk, P., Grythe, H., Keil, K., Kivekäs, N., Kumar, N., Liu, N., Matelenok, I., Myksvoll, M., O'Leary, D., Olsen, J., Pavithran, A.P.S., Petersen, E., Raspotnik, A., Ryzhov, I., Solski, J., Suo, L., Troein, C., Valeeva, V., van Rijckevorsel, J., Wighting, J. (2014) Commercial Arctic shipping through the Northeast Passage: Routes, resources, governance, technology, and infrastructure. *Polar Geography*, 37(4): 298–324.

Cameron, E.S. (2012) Securing indigenous politics: A critique of the vulnerability and adaptation approach to the human dimensions of climate change in the Canadian Arctic. *Global Environmental Change*, 22(1): 103–114.

CBC News. (2015a) Baffinland Iron Mines granted land use plan exemption by federal minister, April 14. Available at: www.cbc.ca/news/canada/north/baffinland-iron-mines-granted-land-use-plan-exemption-by-federal-minister-1.3151834

CBC News. (2015b) Baffinland's icebreaking proposal too disruptive for Nunavut regulator, April 9. Available at: www.cbc.ca/news/canada/north/baffinland-s-icebreaking-proposal-too-disruptive-for-nunavut-regulator-1.3025775

CBC News. (2016) Shipping company says Labrador is a lucrative gateway to the North, May 2. Available at: www.cbc.ca/amp/1.3561418

Cooke, A. (1984) *Historical Evidence of Inuit Use of Sea Ice. Sikumuit: The People Who Use the Sea Ice*. Ottawa: Canadian Arctic Resources Committee, pp. 61–72.

Craciun, A. (2009) The scramble for the Arctic. *Interventions*, 11(1): 103–114.

de Sousa Santos, B. (1987) Law: A map of misreading. Toward a postmodern conception of law. *Journal of Law and Society*, 14(3): 279–302.

Dodds, K., Ingimundarson, V. (2012) Territorial nationalism and Arctic geopolitics: Iceland as an Arctic coastal state. *The Polar Journal*, 2(1): 21–37.

Fetterer, F., Knowles, K., Meier, W., Savoie, M. (2016) *Sea Ice Index, Version 2*. Boulder, CO: National Snow and Ice Data Center (NSIDC). doi:10.7265/N5736NV7

Gearheard, S., Matumeak, W., Angutikjuaq, I., Maslanik, J., Huntington, H.P., Leavitt, J., Kagak, D.M., Tigullaraq, G., Barry, R.G. (2006) 'It's not that simple': A collaborative comparison of sea ice environments, their uses, observed changes, and adaptations in Barrow, Alaska, USA, and Clyde River, Nunavut, Canada. *AMBIO: A Journal of the Human Environment*, 35(4): 203–211.

Hadlaw, J. (2003) The London underground map: Imagining modern time and space. *Design Issues*, 19(1): 25–35.

Hastrup, K. (2009) The Nomadic landscape: People in a changing Arctic environment. *Geografisk Tidsskrift-Danish Journal of Geography*, 109(2): 181–189.

Hedlund, R. (2014) *Transits of the Northwest Passage to End of the 2014 Navigation Season*. Available at: www.americanpolar.org/wp-content/uploads/2014/10/NWP-2014-X-5-layout-for-PDF.pdf

Heleniak, T. (1999) Out-migration and depopulation of the Russian North during the 1990s. *Post-Soviet Geography and Economics*, 40(3): 155–205.

Heleniak, T., Bogoyavlenskiy, D. (2013) *Arctic Human Development Report-II Fact Sheet: Population and Migration*. Available at: https://oaarchive.arctic-council.org/bitstream/handle/11374/1653/MM08_AHDR_FactSheet_Jan_2013.pdf?sequence=1

Hinzman, L.D., Bettez, N.D., Bolton, W.R., Chapin, F.S., Dyurgerov, M.B., Fastie, C.L., Griffith, B., Hollister, R.D., Hope, A., Huntington, H.P., Jensen, A.M. (2005) Evidence and implications of recent climate change in northern Alaska and other arctic regions. *Climatic Change*, 72(3): 251–298.

Hotez, P.J. (2010) Neglected infections of poverty among the indigenous peoples of the Arctic. *PLoS Neglected Tropical Diseases*, 4(1): e606.

Hultgreen, T. (2002) When did the Pomors come to Svalbard? *Acta Borealia*, 19(2): 125–145.

Innis, H.A. (1930) The Hudson Bay railway. *Geographical Review*, 20(1): 1–30.

Jakobson, L. (2010) China prepares for an ice-free Arctic. In: *SIPRI Insights on Peace and Security, 2*. Available at: www.polar-academy.com/Publication/SIPRIInsight1002(2).pdf

Johns, R.K. & Associates. (2005) *Suez Canal Pricing Forecast 2005–2025*. Final Report, The Autoridad Del Canal de Panama, New York, NY.

Khlopkin, N.S., Zotov, A.P. (1997) Merchant marine nuclear-powered vessels. *Nuclear Engineering and Design*, 173(1): 201–205.

Konstantinov, Y. (2002) Soviet and post-Soviet reindeer-herding collectives: Transitional slogans in Murmansk region. In: Kasten, E. (Ed.), *People and the Land: Pathways to Reform in Post-Soviet Siberia*. Berlin: Dietrich Reimer Verlag, pp. 172–187.

Krupnik, I., Aporta, C., Gearheard, S., Laidler, G.J., Holm, L.K. (2010) *Siku: Knowing Our Ice: Documenting Inuit Sea Ice Knowledge and Use*. Basel, Switzerland: Springer Science & Business Media.

Lasserre, F. (2011) Arctic shipping routes: From the Panama myth to reality. *International Journal*, 66(4): 793–808.

Lasserre, F., Pelletier, S. (2011) Polar super seaways? Maritime transport in the Arctic: An analysis of shipowners' intentions. *Journal of Transport Geography*, 19(6): 1465–1473.

Liu, M., Kronbak, J. (2010) The potential economic viability of using the Northern Sea Route (NSR) as an alternative route between Asia and Europe. *Journal of Transport Geography*, 18(3): 434–444.

Massey, D. (1994) *Space, Place and Gender*. Minneapolis: University of Minnesota.

Moe, A. (2014) The Northern Sea Route: Smooth sailing ahead? *Strategic Analysis*, 38(6): 784–802.

Monmonier, M. (2014) *How to Lie With Maps*. Chicago: University of Chicago Press.

National Snow and Ice Data Center (NSIDC). (2016) *Monthly Sea Ice Extent*. Boulder, CO. Available at: https://nsidc.org/data/seaice_index/.

Natural Earth. (2017) *Populated Places*. Available at: www.naturalearthdata.com/downloads/10m-cultural-vectors/10m-populated-places/

Nunavut Impact Review Board. (2008) *Igloolik Comments on Mary River Project (Application 123797)*. Available at: www.nirb.ca/app/dms/script/dms_download.php?fileid=260 093&applicationid=123797&sessionid=jcdene6qo77l0mm1f8b46h5al6

Nunavut Impact Review Board. (2016) *Home Page*. Available at: www.nirb.ca/

Okladnikova, E. (1998) Traditional cartography in Arctic and Subarctic Eurasia. In: Woodward, D., Lewis, G.M. (Eds.), *The History of Cartography*, Volume 2, Book 3: Cartography in Prehistoric, Ancient, and Medieval Europe and the Mediterranean. Chicago: University of Chicago, pp. 329–349.

Østreng, W., Eger, K.M., Fløistad, B., Jørgensen-Dahl, A., Lothe, L., Mejlænder-Larsen, M., Wergeland, T. (2013) *Shipping in Arctic Waters: A Comparison of the Northeast, Northwest and Trans Polar Passages*. Basel, Switzerland: Springer Science & Business Media.

Paulson, I., Auer, N.E. (1964) The animal guardian: A critical and synthetic review. *History of Religions*, 3(2): 202–219.

Pelto, P.J. (1987) *The Snowmobile Revolution: Technology and Social Change in the Arctic*. Long Grove: Waveland Press Inc.

Ragner, C.L. (2000) The Northern Sea Route – Commercial potential, economic significance, and infrastructure requirements. *Post-Soviet Geography and Economics*, 41(8): 541–580.

Riewe, R. (1991) Inuit use of the sea ice. *Arctic and Alpine Research*, 23(1): 3–10.

Rondeau, R.M. (2010) The wrecks of Franklin's ships Erebus and Terror; their likely location and the cause of failure of previous search expeditions. *The Journal of the Hakluyt Society*. Available at: www.hakluyt.com/PDF/Rondeau_Franklin.pdf

Rundstrom, R.A. (1990) A cultural interpretation of Inuit map accuracy. *Geographical Review*, 80(2): 155–168.

Schøyen, H., Bråthen, S. (2011) The Northern Sea Route versus the Suez Canal: Cases from bulk shipping. *Journal of Transport Geography*, 19(4): 977–983.

Shadian, J. (2007) In search of an identity Canada looks north. *American Review of Canadian Studies*, 37(3): 323–353.

Smith, L.C., Stephenson, S.R. (2013) New Trans-Arctic shipping routes navigable by mid-century. *Proceedings of the National Academy of Sciences*, 110(13): E1191–E1195.

Steinberg, P.E. (2001) *The Social Construction of the Ocean*. Cambridge: Cambridge University Press.

Stickler, P.J. (1990) Invisible towns: A case study in the cartography of South Africa. *Geojournal*, 22(3): 329–333.

Stroeve, J.C., Holland, M.M., Meier, W., Scambos, T., Serreze, M. (2007) Arctic sea ice decline: Faster than forecast. *Geophysical Research Letters*, 34(9): L09501.

Stroeve, J.C., Kattsov, V., Barrett, A., Serreze, M., Pavlova, T., Holland, M., Meier, W.N. (2012) Trends in Arctic sea ice extent from CMIP5, CMIP3 and observations. *Geophysical Research Letters*, 39(16): L16502.

Tuan, Y.F. (1977) *Space and Place: The Perspective of Experience*. Minneapolis: University of Minnesota Press.

Verny, J., Grigentin, C. (2009) Container shipping on the northern sea route. *International Journal of Production Economics*, 122(1): 107–117.

Weber, B. (2016) Debt threatens to sink crucial shipping company supplying western Arctic. *The Canadian Press*, September 1. Available at: www.thestar.com/business/2016/09/01/debt-threatens-to-sink-crucial-shipping-company-supplying-western-arctic.html

Wesche, S.D., Chan, H.M. (2010) Adapting to the impacts of climate change on food security among Inuit in the Western Canadian Arctic. *EcoHealth*, 7(3): 361–373.

Wood, D., Fels, J. (1992) *The Power of Maps*. New York: Guilford Press.

Part II

Geospatial analyses

10 GIS-based analysis of US international seaborne trade flows

Guoqiang Shen

International maritime goods are carried by shippers on vessels from origin ports in one country to destination ports in another country. These origin and destination (OD) ports are predominantly coastal seaports engaged in importing and exporting goods. These seaports and the connecting waterways form the global maritime network. Imported, exported, and transitional goods in the maritime network are often measured in value (e.g., $), by weight (e.g., tons), or by container (e.g., 20-foot equivalent unit (TEU)), and classified into different types of commodities (e.g., Harmonized System). Maritime freight is often shipped by container, flat rack, platform, bulk, or tank.

About 90% of international trade in goods is carried by maritime vessels, and about 70% of maritime cargo shipping is carried out by containers (Kite-Powell, 2001). Seaports are critical to maritime transportation, since vessels carrying goods through ocean waterways arrive, depart, or transit at seaports. Globally, there are over 4,000 such ports engaging in international maritime shipment. In the United States, there are over 300 maritime ports engaging in international trade (Maritime Administration, 2012).

This research is on US international seaborne freight flows as proxies for US international trade during the period 1997–2012. The chapter conducts a concise literature review of US maritime freight transportation before introducing several important databases and associated issues. This is followed by a simple framework anchored on DMI, GIS, and OFA for optimal global maritime flows between foreign and US seaports. Important US international trade patterns for top regions, countries, ports and routes are highlighted (see Chapters 6, 20, and 21 on Portugal, China, and North Korea, respectively for other analyses of external linkages of national port systems). Our conclusions and remarks complete this research.

Literature review

On international trade and freight flows

The literature on international trade or freight flows is vast. Rodrigue (2013), Cullinane (2005), and Robinson (2002) studied economic, environmental, safety, technical, and policy issues related to intermodal port and maritime freight. Limão and

Venables (2001), Lyk-Jensen (2011), and Yip (2012) explored spatial, temporal, dynamic, and transport cost effects on trade volumes and patterns for total and commodity-specific international trade using econometric, spatial interaction, or demand forecast models.

Maritime trade flows were studied by Pais Montes et al. (2012) on the evolution of containerized and general cargo maritime routes, by Xu et al. (2003) on the simulation of regional freight and trade in multi-networks; by Frémont (2007) and Ducruet et al. (2010) on multi-level maritime hub-and-spoke strategies; by Ducruet et al. (2010) on maritime network centrality and vulnerability; by Grobar (2008) on the importance of global maritime networks for goods importation, exportation, and transition at seaports. General discussions of maritime freight, including various processes, issues, and policies, can be found in Harker (1985), de Jong et al. (2004), and Frémont (2009).

On DMI, OFA, and GIS

Data mining and integration (DMI) is used to uncover useful information and hidden patterns or knowledge discovery from various databases. DMI commonly involves "clustering", "classification", and "association" for data attributes (Han and Kamber, 2006). Tons of studies on DMI are available. However, specific applications of DMI for international trade and maritime freight are rare, especially when coupled with GIS and optimal flow assignment (OFA). There are some DMI models for spatial information integration and GIS is used as a unifying tool for spatial decision support (Longley et al., 2001). OFA is a linear or non-linear optimization process to assign OD flows to network links or routes (Mapa and da Silva Lima, 2004). An OFA is often solved and visualized in a GIS environment with extensive data processing (Miller and Shaw, 2001; Koncz and Adams, 2002).

Despite these studies on DMI, GIS and OFA, more studies on freight flows for trade patterns at global level are much needed (Guerrero and Rodrigue, 2014). This research explores the US maritime imports and exports as international trade flows with all other countries during the period 1997–2012; it visualizes the movement of goods in the global maritime network in 2D and 3D, and it highlights important US international trade patterns.

Maritime freight databases

Many databases from government agencies and/or private organizations exist for US global maritime freight flows. In general, these databases can be classified into three groups: freight, seaport, and network databases. Maritime freight in this study is primarily related to containerized or non-containerized goods between countries, including their classification, value, tonnage, and TEU attributes. Seaports are essentially ODs for ocean freight vessels to arrive and depart. Networks here refer to the ocean routes and inland waterways that connect seaports for maritime freight.

Freight, seaport, and network databases

Maritime freight databases are mostly about import and export commodity data, such as the Freight Analysis Framework database (FAF) produced by the Federal Highway Administration (2012) and Bureau of Transportation Statistics (2009); the Maritime Administration Database (MAD) of the US Maritime Administration (2012); USA Trade Online (2012) compiled by the Department of Commerce; and the 1997–2012 Navigation Data Center (NDC) database prepared by the US Army Corps of Engineers (2012). These databases contain units, ODs, modes, tons, values, and commodity codes, such as the Standard Classification of Transported Goods (SCTG) initiated by Statistics Canada (2017), the Standard International Trade Classification (SITC) drawn up by the United Nations Statistics Division (2008), or the Harmonized System (HS) of the World Customs Organization (2012) and the Lock Performance Monitoring System (LPMS) drawn up by the US Army Corps of Engineers (2012).

The geographic locations of seaports are imperative. The NDC database contains longitudes/latitudes for all US seaports, all imported/exported goods, but only a few foreign seaports. The World Port Index (WPI) by Landfall Navigation (2005) comprises 4,000+ world seaports with their longitudes/latitudes, including most US seaports.

The NDC database contains some ocean routes near US coasts and US inland waterways, but has almost no global waterways. By contrast, the ORNL (Oak Ridge National Laboratory, 2009) transportation database provides a complete coverage of the global maritime network, which unites the global ocean routes and foreign seaports with US waterways and seaports.

The above maritime freight, seaport and network databases, together with a few other general international trade databases, are summarized in Table 10.1. This research exclusively uses public-sector, free databases. The target database for US maritime trade flows and the contributing freight databases are shown in Figure 10.1.

The modeling framework

The modeling framework is illustrated in Figure 10.2. Here, the boxes are either for data input or output. The round boxes are for data processing – with DMI for selecting data attributes for the target database from various data sources, OFA for optimal flow assignment to routes, and GIS for attribute and network data assembly and visualization.

Data Mining and Integration (DMI)

Databases come with different attributes and formats. Also, the utility of attributes from each database varies with respect to the target database. Therefore, a DMI

Table 10.1 Summary table of common freight databases for US international trade

Database	O-D Level	Commodity Code	Time	Frequency	Unit	Shape file (Y/N)	Free (Y/N)	Mode
ORNL Transportation Networks	None	None	2009	None	None	Y	Y	Highway, Rail, Water, Air
Navigation Data Center (NDC) water networks	U.S port, foreign port	None	1997–2015	Year		Y	Y	Waterway
Maritime Administration	U.S port, foreign port	6 digit, LPMS	1997–2015	Year	Ton, Value	N	Y	Wateway
World Port Index (WPI)	World Port (lon and lat)	None	Up to 2012	None	None	Y	Y	None
U.S. Trade Online	U.S ports, foreign country	10 digit, HS	1992-	Month, Year	Ton, Value, TEU	N	Y	Waterway, Air
Global Insight-Transearch	U.S. state, county, BEA, Foreign country	2 digit, STCC	1995–2030	Month, Year	Ton, Value	Y	N	Highway, Rail, Water, Air
WISER Trade Foreign Database	U.S. state	6 digit, HS, SITC	1999–2015	Month	Ton, Value	N	N	None
PIERS Global Intelligence Solutions	U.S. port, city, county, metropolitan area, state,	10 digit, HS	1992-	Day	Ton, Value, TEU	N	N	Highway, Rail, Water, Air
Freight Analysis Framework (FAF)	U.S. state, metropolitan area, port district, world region	2 digit, SCTG	1998–2045	Year	Ton, Value	Y	Y	Highway, Rail, Water, Air
Commodity Flow Survey (CFS)	U.S. state, Metropolitan area	5 digit, STCC, SCTG	1993-	Every 5 years	Ton, Value	N	Y	Highway, Rail, Water, Air
North American Transportation Atlas Data	U.S. state, Canada, Mexico	None	1998–2015	Year	None	Y	Y	Highway, Rail, Water, Air
Foreign Trade Statistics	Port, state, district, foreign country	6 digit, End Use	1960–2015	Year	Ton, Value	N	Y	Waterway,Air
U.S. International Trade Commission	U.S. state, region, Foreign country	4-10 digit, HTS, SITC	1989–2015	Month, Year	Ton, Value	N	Y	None
TradeStats Express™	U.S. state, region, Foreign country	3 digit, HS, SITC	1999–2015	Year	Value	N	Y	None

N.B. STCC: Standard Classification of Transported Goods; SCTG: Standard Classification of Transported Goods; HS: Harmonized System Codes; SITC: Standard International Trade Classification; LPMS: Lock Performance Monitoring System; BEA: Bureau of Economic Analysis

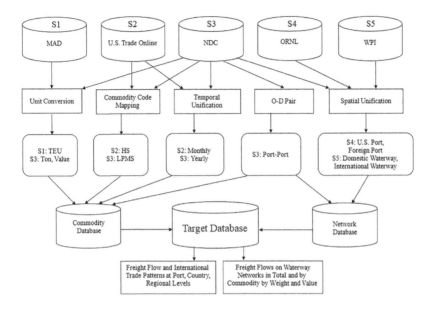

Figure 10.1 Maritime freight database integration

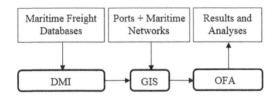

Figure 10.2 The modeling framework

process is needed and is used together with OFA and GIS. The details of the DMI operational process is illustrated in Figure 10.3.

The DMI has three main phases: filtration, integration, and interaction (Hand et al., 2001). The data filtration step involves selecting a valid set of data sources from all available sources. The data integration step is to implement specific techniques to build the target database for a specific purpose. At the data interaction step, the target database is used to provide data analyses, including modeling and reporting.

In the three-step DMI process, the integration step is the key, since it has to deal with various data issues. First, the source databases are at different scales (e.g., ODs at regional, country, or state, metro, port, or port-district levels). This issue can be addressed by aggregating or disaggregating OD matrices for the target database. Second, there are different commodity code systems (e.g., SCTG, SITC, LPMS, or HS). Table 10.2 illustrates an example of code mapping for cereal grains between codes. Third, three units are commonly used in maritime freight, namely value ($), tonnage (TON), and number of containers (TEU). Fourth, the missing or mismatched data is another important issue for database integration (Levine

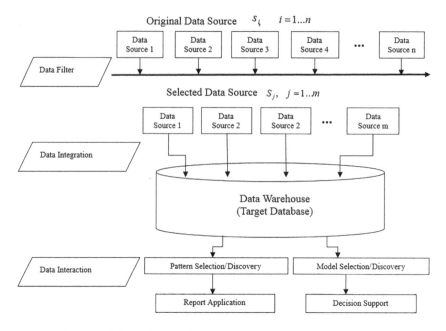

Figure 10.3 Data mining and integration process

Table 10.2 Code mapping example

		SCTG		LPMS			HS	
		2100	Wheat	62	Wheat		1001	Wheat and Maslin
		2200	Corn (except sweet)	63	Corn		1002	Rye in the grain
		2901	Rye				1003	Barley
		2902	Barley				1004	Oats
2	Cereal Grain	2903	Oats		Barley,	10	Cereals	1005	Corn (maize)
		2904	Grain Sorghum		rye, oats,		1006	Rice
			Other cereal grain, including	64	rice and sorghum		1007	Grain sorghum
		2909	rice (excludes soy beans, and other oil seeds)		grains		1008	Buck wheat millet & canary seed

et al., 2009; Shen and Aydin, 2014). Finally, in order to visualize in GIS and perform assignments in OFA, it is necessary to integrate port (as node) and waterway (as link) databases in ArcGISTM and TransCADTM.

Optimal Flow Assignment (OFA)

The OFA is based on the well-known Wardrop's second principle, which states that individual shippers cooperate in order to minimize the total system-wide freight movement cost or travel time. This traffic assignment is behaviorally unrealistic, but it is useful in studying the collaborative behavior that minimizes total freight movement costs in order to achieve an equilibrium of social optimum (Sheffi, 1985). However, since no link or route capacity is considered here, the OFA is essentially an all-or-nothing assignment, which assigns the flows between an OD to its shortest path.

Geographical Information System (GIS)

Various freight databases are processed for the target database in ArcGISTM, which provides various functions for data join, query, edit, and visualization and in TransCADTM, whose assignment module is used to produce OFA flows. The results are visualized in 2D in GIS and in 3D in Google EarthTM.

Results and highlights of US international freight flows

World regional highlights

Figure 10.4 shows the total average import and export flows between the Unites States and the eight world regions in 1997–2012. While Asia, Europe, North America, and South America had similar total imports and exports with the US, their aggregated shipping distances, costs, and modes are quite different. The trade-offs between longer distances but relatively cheaper labor in Asia with respect to closer

Figure 10.4 US total average international trade by world regions, 1997–2012

proximity but higher labor costs in Canada and Mexico can be inferred here. Similar inferences can be made for trade with South America and Africa. However, similar total US trade volumes and aggregated distances from Asia and Europe implied that the comparative advantages of specializations and costs are all-important.

World country highlights

Figure 10.5 portrays the total US maritime freight flows in tonnage by import, export and transition, respectively, for 1997–2012. It is clear that the US trade deficit was widening almost consistently during this period primarily due to the faster increase of imports and flat exports and relatively small and stable transition freight. Trade deficits were mainly with China, Mexico, Japan, Germany, Ireland, and Canada for general commodities and with Venezuela, Nigeria, and Saudi Arabia for oil products. The US trade deficit with China amounted to $273 billion in 2010, or about 40% of the total US trade deficit. US trade with Hong Kong, the Netherlands, Australia, and the United Arab Emirates showed surpluses.

Figure 10.6 shows the top 25 trade countries with the US in Asia, with China, Japan, South Korea, and Taiwan ranked in the top four. Canada and Mexico were the top two in North America. In Europe, Germany, United Kingdom, Belgium, and France were major traders. In South America, Venezuela, Columbia, and Brazil topped the list. Finally, in the Middle East, Saudi Arabia and the United Arab Emirates led the way.

US seaport highlights

Table 10.3 provides the top 25 US maritime seaports ranked by 2012 TEU volume. LA, LB, NY, Savannah, and GA ranked as the top four for both imports and exports.

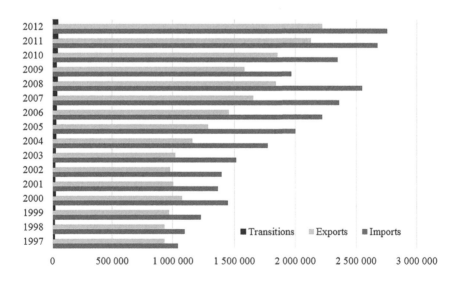

Figure 10.5 US maritime export, import, and transition flows in millions of tons, 1997–2012

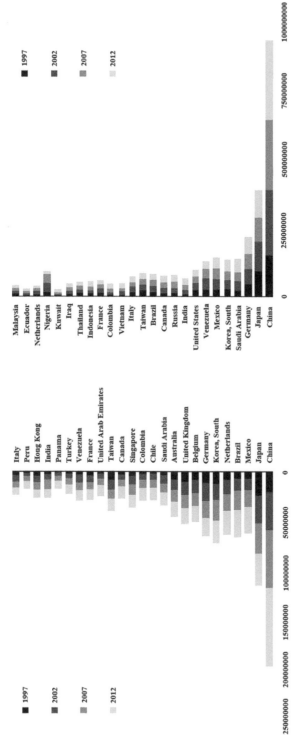

Figure 10.6 Top 25 world trade partners with US by value, 1997–2012

Table 10.3 Top 25 US maritime import and export ports by TEU (in 1000s), 2007–2012

Ports	Imports						Ports	Exports					
	2007	2008	2009	2010	2011	2012		2007	2008	2009	2010	2011	2012
Los Angeles, CA	4,327	4,048	3,507	3,881	4,057	4,068	Los Angeles, CA	1,427	1,633	1,517	1,681	1,954	1,870
Long Beach, CA	3,672	3,132	2,500	3,051	3,024	3,046	New York, NY	1,302	1,435	1,246	1,420	1,542	1,469
New York, NY	2,642	2,567	2,288	2,624	2,723	2,777	Long Beach, CA	1,314	1,453	1,233	1,385	1,294	1,284
Savannah, GA	1,079	1,088	913	1,055	1,073	1,076	Savannah, GA	970	1,032	1,001	1,115	1,212	1,212
Norfolk, VA	858	811	678	721	727	817	Houston, TX	800	800	773	827	859	876
Oakland, CA	797	726	641	739	740	749	Norfolk, VA	728	783	698	714	756	829
Seattle, WA	785	659	622	888	773	726	Oakland, CA	642	656	740	766	799	793
Charleston, SC	769	694	500	548	602	649	Charleston, SC	641	640	455	521	545	567
Tacoma, WA	722	651	458	496	520	649	Seattle, WA	505	425	451	529	591	514
Houston, TX	616	574	482	519	559	619	Tacoma, WA	425	476	413	340	366	443
Miami, FL	345	313	287	308	346	355	Port Everglades, FL	369	390	314	331	363	379
Baltimore, MD	254	262	229	280	305	320	Miami, FL	337	358	339	374	388	366
Port Everglades, FL	306	282	220	242	254	266	New Orleans, LA	179	159	156	203	220	220
Philadelphia, PA	162	160	144	144	157	186	Baltimore, MD	175	175	177	168	168	196
Wilmington, DE	142	134	129	132	141	160	Jacksonville, FL	97	97	107	146	160	154
San Juan, PR	148	156	153	153	156	160	Mobile, AL	33	37	53	47	53	92
Jacksonville, FL	41	50	76	93	117	127	Wilmington, NC	66	59	88	91	108	92
Wilmington, NC	85	89	97	115	120	111	West Palm Beach, FL	106	100	84	87	81	91
Gulfport, MS	104	107	100	105	108	103	Portland, OR	103	102	86	61	80	90
Boston, MA	94	93	84	80	97	95	Gulfport, MS	68	66	58	76	75	95
New Orleans, LA	79	83	75	78	87	80	Boston, MA	64	56	64	44	52	73
Portland, OR	106	97	69	69	74	63	Philadelphia, PA	36	60	36	42	46	58
Mobile, AL	35	38	35	35	55	60	Chester, PA	51	52	29	37	35	47
San Diego, CA	48	46	48	50	50	52	Anchorage, AK	28	25	25	27	38	38
Top 25 Share (%)	98.46	98.48	98.57	98.68	98.75	98.71	Top 25 Share (%)	97.57	97.68	97.92	98.15	98.61	98.75

Most seaports that ranked in the top 25 imports also ranked in the top 25 exports, with their actual ranking only slightly changed over the years, while some seaports were not in either ranking (e.g., San Diego, CA; Anchorage, AK). In terms of overall US import vs. export volumes, almost all these top 25 seaports had larger imports than exports, indicating trade deficit at the seaports. Finally, the top 25 ports consistently shared over 97% of US imports and exports between 1997 and 2012.

Foreign seaport highlights

Table 10.4 lists the top 10 foreign seaports for US imports and exports by weight in 1997, 2007, and 2012, respectively. For imports from the US at foreign seaports, Ras Tanura in Saudi Arabiawas in first place in 1997, but Cayo Arcos Terminal became the top seaport in 2012. Tokyo had been the top seaport for exports during the period. Wei Hai of China made it to the top 10 seaports in 2007. Other well-known world seaports, such as Pusan, Shanghai, Singapore, Hong Kong in Asia, Antwerp and Rotterdam in Europe, and some in South America and the Middle East were also ranked in Table 10.4.

Commodity highlights

Maritime freight flows provide us with different aspects of US international trade with the world. First, Table 10.5 shows the imports and exports between

Table 10.4 Top 10 foreign ports* for US imports and exports by weight for 1997, 2005, and 2012

Year	Im/Ex	Top 1	Top 2	Top 3	Top 4	Top 5	Top 6	Top 7	Top 8	Top 9	Top 10
1997	Import	51727	30771	20152	99930	20184	20154	30100	30753	30704	30763
	Export	58886	42157	58309	58840	42305	58023	6645	58029	58201	20199
2005	Import	20152	30700	99930	51727	30771	23645	20154	72105	14065	30140
	Export	58886	58309	6645	57000	58201	42157	58000	58023	20199	42305
2012	Import	20152	51727	30700	99900	99930	30771	72105	57035	14065	75300
	Export	58886	58309	42157	57000	6645	42305	72900	20199	58029	58201

* Ports are listed by port code and grouped by country with port code in () after each port

Venezuela: All Other Venezuela Ports (30700), Bahia De Amuay (30704), La Salina (30753), Puerto Miranda (30763), Puerto La Cruz (30771); Mexico: Altata (20100), Cayo Arcos Terminal (20152), Dos Bocas (20154), Pajaritos (20184), Tuxpan (20197), Veracruz (20199); Bahamas: South Riding Point (23645); Trinidad: Point Fortin (27420); Canada: Nanticoke (06645), Algoma, Ont (08525), Point Tupper, CBI (14065), Whiffen Head, NF (15230); Colombia: All Other Colombian Caribbean Region Ports (30100), Covenas (30110), Santa Marta (30140); Norway: Mongstad (40373); Netherlands: Rotterdam(42157); Belgium: Antwerp (42305); Iraq: Al Bakir (50505), Al Basrah (50525); Singapore: Singapore (55976); China: Weihai (5700), Shanghai (57035); South Korea: Cheju (58000), Pusan (58023), Jinsen (58029); Egypt: All Other Egypt Mediterranean Region Ports (72900); Hong Kong: Hong Kong (58201); Taiwan: Kaohsiung (58309); Japan: Itozaki (58800), Kobe (58840), Tokyo (58886); Nigeria: Akassa (75300), Kwaibo Terminal (75389); Saudi Arabia: Al Juaymah (51723), Ras Tanura (51727); Neth Antille: St. Eustatius (27730); Algeria: Arzew (72105); Unknown: High Seas (99900), High Seas, Gulf of Mexico (99930)

Table 10.5 Top imported or exported goods by countries with US, 1997–2012 (million tons)

China Import LPMS	China Import TON	China Export LPMS	China Export TON	Japan Import LPMS	Japan Import TON	Japan Export LPMS	Japan Export TON	Canada Import LPMS	Canada Import TON	Canada Export LPMS	Canada Export TON	Mexico Import LPMS	Mexico Import TON	Mexico Export LPMS	Mexico Export TON	Venezuela Import LPMS	Venezuela Import TON	Venezuela Export LPMS	Venezuela Export TON
70	29,48	65	12,28	70	8,30	63	16,08	21	26,32	10	14,39	21	82,13	22	5,09	21	81,99	32	2,15
52	7,84	42	8,06	53	1,64	41	4,20	43	21,00	44	8,35	43	10,90	63	4,57	22	5,55	62	0,92
54	5,56	32	3,86	32	0,92	24	3,93	22	8,99	43	3,55	22	2,74	32	4,16	10	4,07	70	0,65
53	4,56	68	2,32	23	0,85	65	3,77	23	8,27	24	2,64	53	1,53	24	3,73	23	2,72	63	0,50
49	2,89	54	1,61	48	0,84	62	3,49	44	6,16	23	1,81	23	1,44	65	1,65	24	1,33	23	0,41
32	2,62	70	1,32	10	0,77	67	2,33	47	4,45	22	1,58	47	1,43	23	1,45	32	1,20	24	0,20
99	1,70	41	0,89	22	0,68	32	2,08	52	4,01	62	1,09	68	1,06	64	1,14	44	0,98	68	0,11
68	1,27	47	0,84	54	0,37	68	1,96	32	1,74	32	1,08	32	0,73	62	1,11	31	0,48	99	0,09
10	1,14	51	0,80	99	0,30	64	1,27	41	1,72	63	0,75	24	0,48	31	0,75	53	0,46	53	0,07
51	1,00	46	0,69	51	0,18	29	1,20	24	1,58	41	0,60	70	0,44	54	0,49	29	0,41	66	0,07
31	0,69	31	0,52	68	0,14	31	0,93	10	1,50	46	0,59	52	0,28	10	0,36	70	0,27	42	0,06
55	0,67	66	0,37	21	0,11	70	0,75	48	1,46	47	0,48	49	0,23	29	0,33	47	0,27	44	0,06
41	0,59	67	0,33	24	0,10	51	0,71	51	0,73	65	0,28	41	0,14	70	0,32	52	0,27	31	0,06
47	0,57	24	0,29	52	0,07	47	0,67	53	0,34	54	0,21	54	0,12	67	0,27	46	0,24	65	0,05
21	0,46	99	0,28	46	0,04	66	0,66	31	0,33	70	0,15	51	0,12	68	0,25	68	0,15	51	0,05
66	0,44	61	0,26	66	0,03	42	0,57	46	0,28	48	0,13	55	0,10	42	0,20	54	0,09	67	0,04
46	0,38	10	0,25	61	0,02	54	0,40	54	0,27	52	0,13	66	0,08	44	0,18	41	0,04	54	0,04
61	0,36	44	0,25	55	0,02	23	0,31	66	0,19	66	0,07	99	0,07	51	0,14	67	0,04	47	0,03
43	0,32	23	0,23	67	0,01	61	0,29	70	0,14	31	0,06	61	0,05	66	0,08	43	0,03	22	0,02
24	0,20	63	0,19	41	0,01	22	0,24	64	0,14	42	0,06	44	0,05	47	0,07	49	0,01	52	0,01
64	0,13	62	0,14	31	0,01	99	0,16	62	0,11	53	0,06	29	0,04	99	0,03	99	0,01	41	0,01

67	0,09	53	0,13	43	0,01	46	0,14	42	0,10	66	0,03	31	0,03	41	0,03	61	0,01	61	0,00
22	0,07	52	0,08	47	0,01	52	0,09	49	0,07	99	0,03	46	0,02	53	0,03	65	0,01	64	0,00
65	0,06	43	0,04	65	0,01	44	0,08	68	0,07	51	0,02	67	0,02	46	0,02	51	0,00	43	0,00
48	0,02	55	0,03	49	0,00	49	0,02	61	0,05	64	0,02	42	0,01	52	0,02	55	0,00	29	0,00
42	0,01	49	0,02	44	0,00	43	0,02	55	0,04	61	0,01	62	0,00	49	0,02	66	0,00	46	0,00
23	0,01	64	0,01	64	0,00	53	0,02	29	0,04	67	0,01	65	0,00	55	0,01	64	0,00	49	0,00
44	0,00	22	0,00	42	0,00	55	0,01	67	0,02	49	0,00	64	0,00	61	0,01			10	
63	0,00	29	0,00	62	0,00	10	0,01	99	0,02	55	0,00	45	0,00	43	0,00			55	
45	0,00	45	0,00	45	0,00	45	0,00	63	0,01		63	0,00	45	0,00					
29	0,00		29		0,00			65	0,00		10			0,00					
62	0,00		63		0,00														
Total	63,13		36,10		15,42		46,43		90,16		38,17		104,24		26,51		100,63		5,61

other countries and the US in 2007. Canada led the way, followed by Mexico, Venezuela, China, and Japan. Interestingly, the US had trade deficits with all these countries except Japan. Second, the importation of certain types of goods into the US does not rule out the same goods types also being exported from the US (e.g., lopsided with China on LPMS = 70 or more balanced with Mexico on LPMS = 23). Third, the same commodity can be imported from and exported to multiple countries with different or similar volumes (e.g., imports from China are similar to exports to Japan on LPMS = 68, while the US imported 23 times the LPMS = 22 from Mexico over exports to Venezuela). Finally, each trading partner seemed to specialize in a handful of commodities, as evidenced by the dominantly large volumes of these commodities in total traded flows (e.g., with China on LPMS = 70, 52, 65, and 42 and with Canada on LPMS = 21, 43, 10, or 4).

Table 10.6 lists total US imports, exports, and differences (import – export) by 2-digit LPMS codes for 1997, 2002, and 2007. First, the total US imports increased more than exports fluctuated, leading to an increased trade deficit of 147 million tons of imported goods. Second, some imported and exported goods were consistently dominant over the years (e.g., LPMS = 21, 23, 53, or 70 as imports and LPMS = 10, 24, 32, 62, or 63 as exports in 1997, 2002, and 2007). Third, some goods contributed substantially to the US trade deficit (e.g., LPMS = 21, 23, 52, 53, or 70), while other goods balanced the trade deficit (e.g., LPMS = 10, 62, 63, or 65). Finally, some imported and exported goods added to the US international trade volume significantly (e.g., LPMS = 10, 21, 23, 68, or 70), while others only marginally (e.g., LPMS = 31, 41, 45, 48, 61, 66, 67, or 99).

US international maritime freight flow movement

Total US maritime flows and key routes

Figures 10.7 and 10.8 provide 2D snapshots of seaport-to-seaport freight flows between the US and foreign seaports in 2012 at world, country, and commodity levels. The figures clearly show that the Panama Canal is the most important canal for US maritime shipments, especially for the US East Coast ports. To a lesser extent, the Suez Canal handles heavy freight flows between Europe and countries around the Indian and western Pacific oceans.

Specifically, Figures 10.7a and 10.7b show total imported and exported US goods and their maritime flows on the global ocean network. Figure 10.7a also contains a close-up view of waterway freight flows to and from the US maritime ports. Figures 10.8a and 10.8b present two extreme cases – most and least imported commodities. Clearly, the freight ODs were at quite different foreign seaports and connected by various short routes to US seaports in the global maritime network.

Table 10.6 Total US imports/exports and deficits/surpluses by commodity (million tons), 1997, 2002, and 2007

Commodity category	LPMS	EX98	IM97	EX02	IM02	EX07	IM07	I-E97	I-E02	I-E07
Cereals	10	78.4	10.2	43.3	16.7	55.7	37.5	−68.2	−26.6	−18.2
Misc. edible preparations	21	3.6	425.8	1.2	479.2	0.1	521.5	422.1	478.0	521.4
Beverages, spirits, and vinegar	22	7.1	24.3	7.8	34.3	13.1	61.4	17.2	26.5	48.3
Residues from food industries, animal feed	23	15.1	56.0	19.3	64.0	33.3	66.7	40.9	44.7	33.4
Tobacco and manuf. tobacco substitutes	24	27.9	18.5	28.9	24.1	33.6	11.5	−9.4	−4.8	−22.1
Organic chemicals	29	2.2	4.3	2.8	7.7	2.1	18.2	2.1	4.9	16.1
Fertilizers	31	15.6	4.3	13.2	6.1	11.0	10.0	−11.3	−7.1	−1.0
Tanning or dyeing extracts, dyes, pigments, etc.	32	34.3	19.9	41.7	33.4	49.2	36.6	−14.3	−8.3	−12.6
Raw hides and skins and leather	41	20.0	3.8	8.9	7.0	9.2	7.6	−16.2	−1.8	−1.5
Articles of leather, saddlery and harness, etc.	42	10.5	1.1	12.7	1.2	17.6	2.0	−9.4	−11.4	−15.6
Furskins and artificial fur, manufactures	43	5.7	25.1	3.7	33.7	4.1	42.0	19.4	30.0	37.8
Wood and articles of wood, wood charcoal	44	14.4	21.8	11.8	15.5	19.0	12.3	7.4	3.7	−6.7
Cork and articles of cork	45	0.0	0.0	0.0	0.0	0.0	0.0	0.0	0.0	0.0
Manu. of straw, esparto, or other plaiting materials, etc.	46	3.4	19.6	2.2	15.5	2.7	18.3	16.2	13.3	15.6
Pulp of wood, waste, and scrap of paper	47	5.9	12.0	5.3	12.1	5.2	11.3	6.1	6.8	6.1
Paper and paperboard, articles of paper pulp	48	0.0	0.9	0.0	1.9	0.1	3.1	0.9	1.9	3.0
Printed books, newspapers, pictures, manuscripts, etc.	49	0.6	7.0	0.5	5.3	0.4	4.4	6.4	4.8	4.1
Wool and fine or coarse animal hair, etc.	51	9.1	3.8	6.0	4.8	8.0	6.7	−5.3	−1.2	−1.3
Cotton, inc. yarns and woven fabrics thereof	52	2.1	20.5	1.2	31.0	1.6	29.8	18.4	29.8	28.3
Veg. textile fibers nesoi, yarns, and woven, etc.	53	1.7	31.0	1.0	30.8	2.7	32.1	29.3	29.8	29.4
Man-made filaments, inc. yarns and woven, etc.	54	1.8	6.0	6.0	14.6	9.5	16.0	4.2	8.7	6.5
Man-made staple fibers, inc. yarns, etc.	55	1.2	1.6	0.3	2.7	0.4	2.9	0.4	2.4	2.5
Articles of apparel and clothing accessories-knitted, etc.	61	0.8	1.1	1.2	1.4	1.2	1.8	0.3	0.3	0.6

(Continued)

Table 10.6 (Continued)

Commodity category	LPMS	EX98	IM97	EX02	IM02	EX07	IM07	I-E97	I-E02	I-E07
Articles of apparel and clothing accessories-not knitted, etc.	62	27.9	0.3	26.1	0.2	32.9	0.1	−27.7	−25.8	−32.7
Made-up textile articles nesoi, needlecraft sets, etc.	63	43.9	0.1	47.9	0.1	54.8	0.1	−43.8	−47.8	−54.7
Footwear, gaiters, and the like	64	8.4	1.4	8.3	1.3	7.7	0.8	−7.0	−7.0	−6.9
Headgear and other parts	65	27.1	0.5	33.9	0.6	33.6	0.3	−26.6	−33.3	−33.3
Umbrellas, sun umbrellas, walking-sticks, whips, etc.	66	4.6	2.7	3.9	3.4	3.9	4.9	−1.8	−0.6	1.0
Prepared feathers, human hair and articles thereof, etc.	67	21.0	1.0	13.3	0.9	11.5	0.7	−20.0	−12.5	−10.7
Articles of stone, plaster, cement, asbestos, mica, etc.	68	15.2	21.6	15.7	24.2	18.2	28.1	6.4	8.5	10.0
Glass and glassware	70	13.6	32.8	12.4	54.9	20.3	74.3	19.2	42.4	54.0
Business services, health, financial/insur, real estate, etc.	99	0.4	0.5	4.0	6.2	3.7	5.9	0.1	2.3	2.2
All commodities		423.2	778.9	380.4	928.6	462.5	1063.2	355.8	548.2	600.7

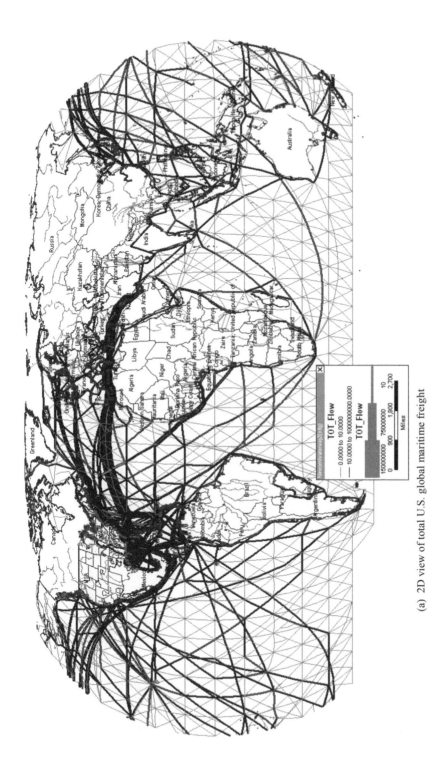

Figure 10.7 International freight of total commodity imports and exports with the US 2012

(a) 2D view of total U.S. global maritime freight

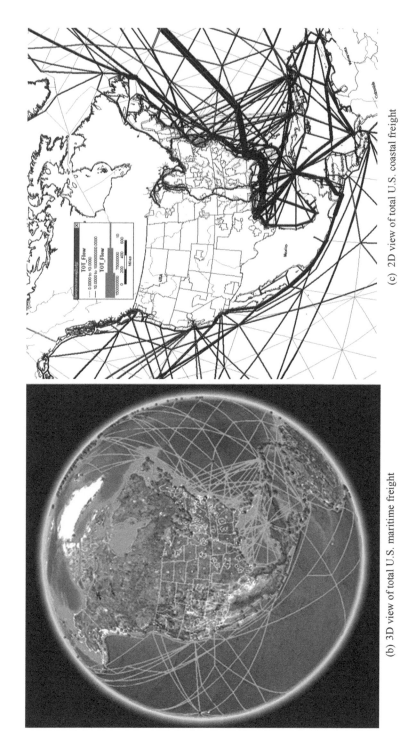

(c) 2D view of total U.S. coastal freight

(b) 3D view of total U.S. maritime freight

Figure 10.7 (Continued)

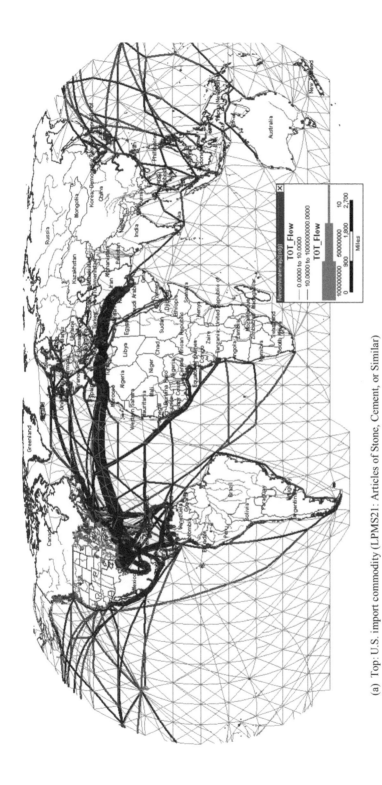

(a) Top: U.S. import commodity (LPMS21: Articles of Stone, Cement, or Similar)

Figure 10.8 US global freight flows for most and least tonnage commodities in 2012

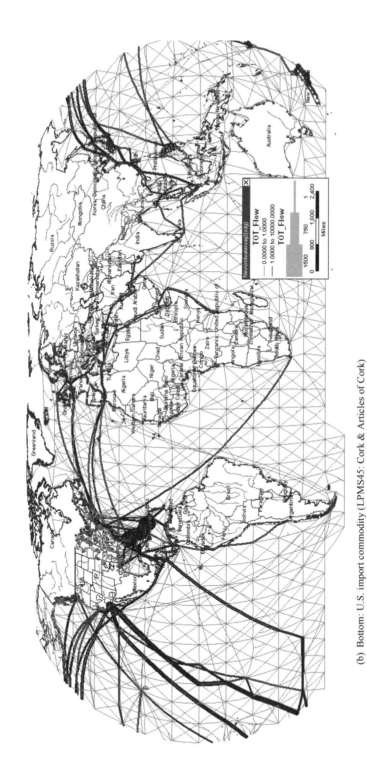

(b) Bottom: U.S. import commodity (LPMS45: Cork & Articles of Cork)

Figure 10.8 (Continued)

Total US maritime flows with China

Figure 10.9 portrays the maritime freight flows between China and the US in 2007. More specifically, Figure 10.9 (a) shows the total US imports from China's east coast five seaport clusters – Bohai Rim (e.g., Tianjin, Qingdao), the Yangtze River delta (e.g., Shanghai, Ningbo), the Pearl River delta (e.g., Hong Kong, Shenzhen), the southwest Coast (e.g., Zhanjiang, Fangcheng, and Haikou), and the southeast Coast (e.g., Fuzhou, Quanzhou, Putian and Zhangzhou). The first three seaport clusters are also the cores for the top three megacity regions in China – the Bohai, Yangtze River, and Pearl River megacity regions. In 2007, these three regions generated about 72% of total international trade and 80% of the total seaport cargo throughput in China. Together, they contributed over 87% of China-US maritime trade flows.

3D visualizations of global freight flows of US international trade were implemented in Google EarthTM. The total assigned maritime flows and routes between the US and the rest of the world in 2007 are shown in Figure 10.10, together with the total Sino-US maritime imports and exports.

Conclusion

This research reviewed various databases to build a target maritime freight database and develop an integrative framework with DMI, OFA, and GIS to highlight the US global maritime freight flows at global, regional, country, port, and commodity levels. Extensive 2D/3D visualization of optimal maritime freight movement for all and specific commodities was provided.

The results show that US imports outpaced exports in the period. North America (Canada and Mexico), Asia, Europe, and South America were among the top world regions exchanging commodities with the US. China, Japan, Canada, Mexico, and Venezuela were the top countries shipping goods to the US. At the port level, the ports of Long Beach and Los Angeles were the most important, followed by New York City Port, Houston, New Orleans, San Francisco, etc. Top world ports, such as Hong Kong, Shanghai, Singapore, and Pusan, were the most interactive foreign seaports with US ports. Panama and Suez were important canals in ocean freight flows to and from the US, respectively. Finally, China, a top trade partner with the US, exported and imported most of its goods to the US through its five east port clusters, whose cores are the Bohai, Yangtze River, and Pearl River megaregions.

Variations of maritime freight flows with the US at global, regional, country, and commodity levels may well be related to regional and country competitive advantages in manufacturing, productivity, proximity, and labor costs related to international trade. Throughput ranking shifts at seaport level may be largely due to port specialization, accessibility, and country supply/demand fluctuation. Optimal route choices for maritime freight flows in this research were determined by the shortest port-to-port paths, but also by many other physical and

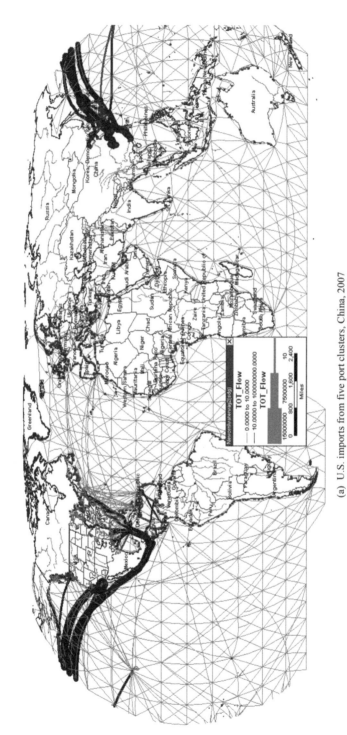

(a) U.S. imports from five port clusters, China, 2007

Figure 10.9 US global freight flow from China and Yangtze River Delta megacity region, 2007

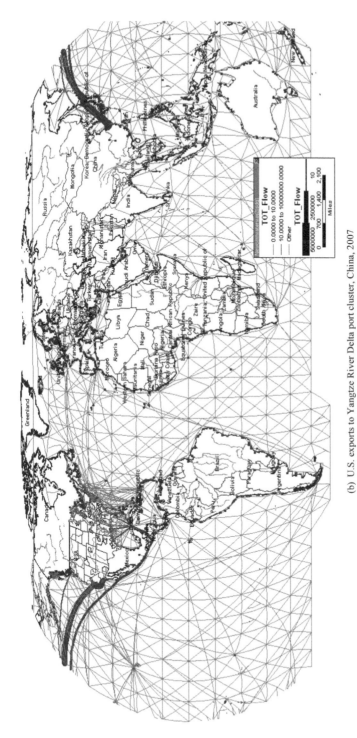

(b) U.S. exports to Yangtze River Delta port cluster, China, 2007

Figure 10.9 (Continued)

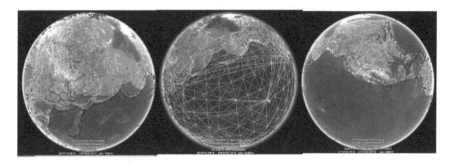

Figure 10.10 Google Earth 3D visualization of U.S.-China trade, 2007

socio-economic factors. All these underlying forces or factors call for further research beyond the highlighting and visualization of historical US maritime goods flows.

Consequently, this research could be improved in many ways. In the first instance, the freight flows were analyzed yearly; however, seasonal, monthly, or weekly trends could be employed for a better understanding of US maritime imports and exports dynamics. This would require extensive data collection and processing. Second, the international freight flows are very complex in the real world, calling for more detailed country-country and port-port commodity-level socio-economic and spatial-temporal studies. Third, the mapping of countries, ports, and the maritime network is mostly 2D, while 3D dynamic and real-time visualization is definitely better in displaying and analyzing freight flows. Fourth, since the US maritime import and export flows are shipped and produced on demand and supply points within the US, the linkage of international maritime port-to-port flows to their demand and supply points through US intermodal networks, (e.g., highway, railway, airway, and waterway), certainly warrants further research. Finally, it would be interesting to see simulations of this modeling framework for various policies and What-If scenarios concerning global maritime transportation and trade.

References

Bureau of Transportation Statistics. (2009) *America's Container Ports: Freight Hubs That Connect Our Nation to Global Markets*. Washington, DC: Research and Innovative Technology Administration, U.S. Department of Transportation.

Cullinane, K. (2005) The container shipping industry and the impact of China's Accession to the WTO. *Research in Transportation Economics*, 12: 221–245.

de Jong, G., Gunn, H., Walker, W. (2004) National and international freight transport models: An overview and ideas for future development. *Transport Reviews*, 20(1): 103–124.

Ducruet, C., Lee, S.W., Ng, A.K.Y. (2010) Centrality and vulnerability in liner shipping networks: Revisiting the Northeast Asian port hierarchy. *Maritime Policy and Management*, 37(1): 17–36.

Federal Highway Administration. (2012) *Freight Analysis Framework (FAF)*. Available at: http://ops.fhwa.dot.gov/freight/freight_analysis/faf/index.htm

Frémont, A. (2007) Global maritime networks: The case of Maersk. *Journal of Transport Geography*, 15(6): 431–442.

Frémont, A. (2009) Shipping lines and logistics. *Transport Reviews*, 29(4): 537–554.

Grobar, L.M. (2008) The economic status of areas surrounding major US container ports: Evidence and policy issues. *Growth and Change*, 39(3): 497–516.

Guerrero, D., Rodrigue, J.P. (2014) The waves of containerization: Shifts in global maritime transportation. *Journal of Transport Geography*, 34: 151–164.

Han J. and Kamber M. (2006) *Data Mining: Concepts and Techniques*. The Morgan Kaufmann Series in Data Management Systems. Burlington, MA: Morgan Kaufmann Publishers.

Hand, D.J., Mannila, H., Smyth, P. (2001) *Principles of Data Mining*. Cambridge, MA: MIT Press.

Harker, P.T. (1985) The state of the art in the predictive analysis of freight transport systems. *Transport Reviews*, 5(2): 143–164.

Kite-Powell, H.L. (2001) Shipping and ports. In: Steele J.H. (Ed.), *Encyclopedia of Ocean Sciences*, London: Academic Press, pp. 2768–2776.

Koncz, N.A., Adams, T.M. (2002) A data model for multi-dimensional transportation applications. *International Journal of Geographical Information Science*, 16(6): 551–569.

Landfall Navigation. (2005) *World Port Index*. Pub 150. Available at: www.landfallnavigation.com/-pd150.html

Levine, B., Nozick, L., Jones, D. (2009) Estimating an origin-destination table for US exports of waterborne containerised freight. *Maritime Economics and Logistics*, 11(2): 137–155.

Limão, N., Venables, A.J. (2001) Infrastructure, geographical disadvantage, transport costs, and trade. *The World Bank Economic Review*, 15(3): 451–479.

Longley, P.A., Goodchild, M.F., Maguire, D.J., Rhind, D.W. (2001) *Geographic Information Systems and Science*. New York: John Wiley & Sons Ltd.

Lyk-Jensen, S.V. (2011) Forecasting freight flows. *Transport Reviews*, 31(5): 603–624.

Mapa, S.M.S., da Silva Lima, R. (2014) Combining geographic information systems for transportation and mixed integer linear programming in facility location-allocation problems. *Journal of Software Engineering and Applications*, 7(10): 844–858.

Maritime Administration. (2012) *Maritime Statistics*. Available at:www.marad.dot.gov/

Miller, H.J., Shaw, S.L. (2001) *Geographic Information Systems for Transportation: Principles and Applications*. Oxford: Oxford University Press.

Oak Ridge National Laboratory. (2009) *CTA Transportation Networks*. Available at:http://cta.ornl.gov/transnet/

Pais Montes, C., Freire Seoane, M.J., Gonzalez Laxe, F. (2012) General cargo and containership emergent routes: A complex networks description. *Transport Policy*, 24: 126–140.

Robinson, R. (2002) Ports as elements in value-driven chain systems: The new paradigm. *Maritime Policy and Management*, 29(3): 241–255.

Rodrigue, J.P. (2013) Ports and maritime trade. In: Warf, B. (Ed.), *Oxford Bibliographies in Geography*. New York: Oxford University Press.

Sheffi, Y. (1985) *Urban Transportation Networks: Equilibrium Analysis With Mathematical Programming Methods*. Englewood Cliffs, NJ: Prentice-Hall, Inc.

Shen, G., Aydin, S.G. (2014) Origin–destination missing data estimation for freight transportation planning: A gravity model-based regression approach. *Transportation Planning and Technology*, 37(6): 505–524.

Statistics Canada. (2017) *Standard Classification of Transported Goods*. Available at: www.statcan.gc.ca/subjects-sujets/standard-norme/sctg-ctbt/sctgintro-ctbtintro-eng.htm

United Nations Statistics Division. (2008) *Detailed Structure and Explanatory Notes, Standard International Trade Classification*. Rev.3. Available at: http://unstats.un.org/unsd/default.htm

US Army Corps of Engineers. (2012) *Navigation Data Center, United States Waterway Data*. Available at: www.navigationdatacenter.us/data/data1.htm

USA Trade Online. (2012) *The Official Source for U.S. Merchandise Trade Data*. Available at: http://usatrade.census.gov/

World Customs Organization. (2012) *Harmonized Commodity Description and Coding System*. Available at: www.wcoomd.org/en/topics/nomenclature/instrument-and-tools/hs-online.aspx

Xu, J., Hancock, K., Southworth, F. (2003) Simulation of regional freight movement with trade and transportation multinetworks. *Transportation Research Record*, 1854: 152–161.

Yip, T.L. (2012) Seaborne trade between developed and developing countries. *The Asian Journal of Shipping and Logistics*, 28(3): 369–389.

11 Vessel tracking data usage to map Mediterranean flows

Alfredo Alessandrini, Virginia Fernandez Arguedas and Michele Vespe

The knowledge of maritime activities is fundamental for the optimization of customs operations and situational awareness at sea and for the development and implementation of several policy areas, including fisheries, safety, security, environment, tourism, energy and transport.

The characterization, analysis and modeling of maritime networks are mostly based on ship arrival and departure time notifications (Ducruet, 2013). This information is collected by port authorities, private companies and independent organizations. Maritime network literature is primarily focused on the analysis of commercial flows-container ships, tankers or bulk carriers (Kaluza et al., 2010; Ducruet and Notteboom, 2012). Only a few studies include details and descriptive analyses of the other ship types (passenger, sailing, fishing and others) using historical AIS data. Data-driven approaches permit the automatic extraction of knowledge relating to maritime networks, with the additional advantage of being quasi real-time, thus allowing the quantitative measurement of trends or recording of changes in maritime activities.

This chapter introduces a methodology for characterizing port anchorage areas, analyzing their relevant activities and building maritime traffic networks through the analysis of vessel tracking data from the Automatic Identification System (AIS) in the Mediterranean Sea (see Chapters 13 and 15 for other analyses of AIS data).

The remainder of this chapter comprises five main sections. Section II gives an overview of the data used. The novel methodological approach is detailed in Section III, while Sections IV and V present the main results areas -the vessel mooring area shapefile and network analysis. Finally, the last section is dedicated to conclusions and possible future research directions.

Data sources and datasets

Today, moving objects, such as ships, cars and people, are tracked using GPS devices. As a result, a huge amount of positioning data is generated and available, providing insights into trends and behaviors associated with moving objects. More specifically, GPS data can be processed to obtain information on the trajectories of moving objects. Such information allows us to monitor and analyze moving objects in a specific context. However, the extraction of knowledge from collective movements and trajectory-related datasets requires ad-hoc applications.

In the maritime domain, the AIS is the most extensively used positioning system to monitor vessel movements. The AIS was originally developed for collision avoidance and is currently widely deployed as a mandatory requirement for ships of 300 GT and upwards in international waters, 500 GT and upwards for cargoes not in international waters and passenger vessels (SOLAS, 2000). In Europe, fishing vessels of more than 15 m in length are also required to be fitted with AIS (EC Directive, 2002). The AIS system is based on VHF communications and relies on GPS positioning on board the vessel. AIS equipment transmits the vessel position at a variable rate, depending on the vessel speed, varying from a few seconds (fast moving or maneuvering dynamics) to a few minutes (stationary positions). A network of AIS receivers both along the coasts and on satellite constellations log AIS messages worldwide, contributing to a global awareness of vessel positions at sea.

AIS transponders transmit regulated messages composed of a set of data. Besides dynamic information, such as position, time, speed and direction, AIS also transmits vessel identification information and other static data including vessel flag, size and ship typology (ship type). However, AIS's greatest contribution is the wealth of spatio-temporal information that can be extracted from the vessel movements provided. Such information has pushed forward the use of AIS so that it is now widely employed not only for collision avoidance and traffic monitoring but also by the scientific community. An increasing community of data scientists is nowadays exploiting AIS-based spatio-temporal information for a wide range of applications such as detecting behavioral anomalies (Pallotta et al., 2013), better understanding fishing patterns (Mazzarella et al., 2014), estimating fishing pressure (Natale et al., 2015) and shipping emissions or to map activities in remote areas such as the Arctic (Vespe et al., 2015).

In the field of traffic network analysis, Lloyd's dataset (www.lloydslistintelligence.com/) is the most widely used source of information reporting the time of arrival and departure for each port. Literature reveals relatively few studies using AIS data as a source of information to model vessel behavior and port traffic.

Considering that the field of traffic network analysis is a developing research area and the wide range of opportunities offered by AIS data, in this study we propose to exploit the synergies between these fields. More specifically, in this study, we have defined a methodology to automatically detect port areas, to monitor port activities and to build a maritime network where the nodes represent the automatically detected ports. Our study is based on the analysis and modeling of AIS vessel-positioning data to automatically extract vessel trajectories and behavior models, the spatio-temporal information that serves as a foundation for our proposed methodology.

The data used in this work was collected in the framework of the Blue Hub (BH) project (Blue Hub, 2016). The BH data platform collects data from different sources, both from self-reported data (AIS, Long Range Identification and Tracking – LRIT, Vessel Monitoring Systems-VMS), or observed data (Earth Observation satellite, airborne or coastal radar) (Alessandrini et al., 2014). Optical and radar sensors, such as earth observation satellites, coastal radars or airborne radar systems can also be used to improve the understanding of vessel activities at sea. However, AIS data offers a good balance between coverage, refresh rate performance and data processing needs in recording port activities and maritime networks.

The analysis reported here is focused on the geographical area of the Mediterranean Basin and the analysis was limited to one month of data (1 October–31 October 2015). The Mediterranean Basin was selected as our area of interest due to its shape and closed-in aspect, being locked by the Strait of Gibraltar, the Suez Canal and the Bosporus Strait. The Mediterranean Basin thus represents a perfect scenario for the analysis of maritime traffic. Moreover, the whole region can be thought of as a network, where any possible vessel trajectory can be associated to one of its edges and ports representing its nodes. Finally, the Strait of Gibraltar, the Suez Canal and the Bosporus Strait can be modeled as nodes additional to ports.

The spatio-temporal data extracted from the dataset contains a selection of the available vessel track information, including the sequence of vessel positions, the MMSI identification number and the time referred to the position. Additional information on the ship type was used to better characterize port activities and the relevant network connections between ports or transit areas.

Trajectory modeling

Trajectories can be thought of as footprints left by moving objects such as ships, cars or people in a geographical space during a given time interval (see Figure 11.1). Defined as a spatio-temporal object, the trajectory has three main

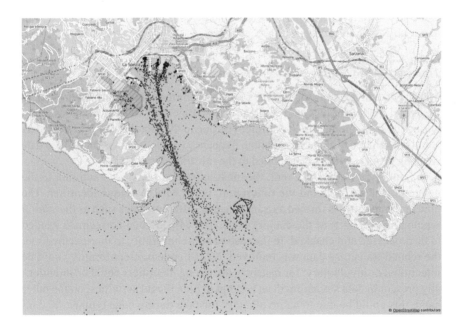

Figure 11.1 Vessel trajectories around the area of La Spezia (AIS data)

attributes: its geographical position, its time reference and its object identifier (in our case, the MMSI number of the vessel). Raw trajectory data is the starting point for further analysis in the current research, namely the detection of mooring areas and the network analysis.

Trajectory modeling is a necessary step to enable the automatic extraction of knowledge from a time series of positions, which identify the behavior of single entities. The trajectory modeling procedure permits the conversion of raw positioning data into a semantically enriched trajectory that can be used by a specific application and in a given context. The trajectory modelling procedure could be summarized in three main steps. During a pre-processing step, anomalies and inconsistencies are removed from the raw trajectory data following a data-cleaning procedure. Afterwards, in the segmentation phase, unique trajectory events are built based on a verification process that analyses the unique vessel identifier (MMSI) and the time stamp reference period. Finally, during the last step, a clustering approach methodology applied to trajectory events is used to identify collective "stop" and "move" points. This sequential methodology allows for an incremental extraction of the trajectory knowledge, which is fundamental to building ad-hoc applications such as traffic flow analysis, port activity statistics etc. (Alessandrini et al., 2016).

In the pre-processing phase, a geographical area is selected (Mediterranean Basin), identifying the region of interest where the trajectory samples are extracted. Moreover, assuming that the port anchorage areas are close to the coastline, only trajectories no further than 1 km from the coastline were included. Our approach has the drawback of excluding the anchorage area at oil rigs. However, the traffic associated with this particular activity could be considered negligible and distant to our objective, the analysis of port activities.

Trajectory data cleaning and segmentation

Missing data in the trajectory event or non-conforming static information (such as the vessel identification code) could affect the trajectory reliability and usability during the data mining process. Moreover, due to the fact that the trajectory data could be gathered at an inconstant time frequency (over- or under-sampled), a data cleaning process needs to be applied to the raw trajectory data.

In building a trajectory event, the most important feature, in addition to the geographical position and the timestamp, is the MMSI unique identifier. The nine digit identifier is formed as a sequence of different codes such as the station typology (first digit) or the country code. The MMSI code correctness needed to be processed and checked. In the case of non-conformity to the specification, the related trajectory data was removed. MMSI code non-conformity could be intentional or involuntary; for instance, the wrong identifiers could be intentionally present in data streaming in an attempt to hide illegal activities; on the other hand, this could be due to an involuntary mistake during code typing.

The presence of gaps in the trajectory data event has two main origins: a voluntary (illegal) AIS device manipulation (AIS off-switching or spoofing) or a gap in the AIS data streaming. Voluntary manipulations could occur with vessels engaged in illegal activities (illegal fishing or smuggling) (Alessandrini et al., 2016). Considering the potential data gaps in the vessel trajectory history, a time threshold was applied to split the main trajectory into sub-trajectories. If the gap between two consecutive positions exceeded 15 minutes, the trajectory was split into multiple trajectory events.

A gap in AIS data streaming could affect the temporal and spatial coverage and could seriously affect the usability of the data. For this reason, a coverage map was produced to validate the data. Moreover, the coverage map was used as a foundation for the proposed applications including the analysis of port activities and the monitoring of fishing activities.

Finally, a non-uniform temporal frequency resolution could be present in the AIS data. Despite vessels sending their messages every three to five minutes (depending on the vessel speed), some factors could impact the temporal frequency, such as a data provider streaming subsampling or a weak area coverage. Due to the above-mentioned reasons, and also to reduce the computation effort (in the case of oversampled data), all the trajectory events were resampled at a time frequency of five minutes.

Stop and moves detection

The stops and moves detection methodology aims to extract from the trajectory the sections where the ship is reducing speed or is stopping for a variable amount of time. Considering typical vessel behaviors, these trajectory sections represent the anchorage areas. The detection of these areas is essential to automatically produce a port traffic analysis and to build a maritime traffic network from an AIS dataset. Our aim was to give a complete picture of the Mediterranean traffic network; thus, this study considered all the anchoring areas and not only the main ports. There are several algorithms used to extract interesting sections from the trajectory data (Alvares et al., 2007; Palma et al., 2008).

We applied the methodology suggested by Palma et al. (2008), the CB-SMoT algorithm, largely aimed at detecting the vessel stay points in each anchorage area. The CB-SMoT algorithm is mainly a clustering algorithm that identifies the trajectory segments where the vessel is stopping or reducing speed for a certain amount of time. Palma used that methodology to find interesting places in the trajectories (stops), based on the vessel speed. The CB-SMoT is a variation of the clustering algorithm DBSCAN; the main difference consists in using the vessel speed and the Euclidean distance position to determine the cluster. Further details can be found in Palma et al. (2008). In Figure 11.2, the trajectory stop sections are visible around the main port areas and are identified using a ring.

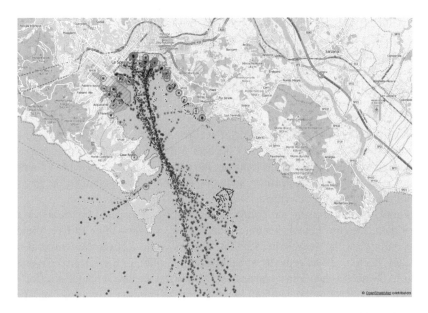

Figure 11.2 Trajectories and stop areas identified using the CB-SMoT algorithm (circles)

Permanent mooring area detection

To build a maritime traffic network using an AIS dataset, it is essential to have a reliable polygon layers of the ports. Such information is not easily obtainable. Moreover, our challenge was to automatically extract not only the main ports but all the permanent mooring areas that could provide a complete picture of the maritime traffic network. To extract the permanent mooring areas from the AIS dataset, we present a method consisting in three steps, trajectory stop-move detection, stopping points clustering and semantic annotation. The last two steps are illustrated in the following paragraphs. The trajectory stop-move detection methodology is described in the next paragraphs.

Spatial clustering

Once the staying points are detected using the CB-SMoT algorithm, it is essential to define the different groups of "stop points" that could represent possible anchorage areas (see Figure 11.3). For this procedure, the DBSCAN clustering algorithm was used. This well-known clustering methodology is the optimal solution for our data because it does not define an a priori number of clusters but detects the number of clusters based on the data structure. It permits the detection of the different clusters of "stop points", each of which can potentially represent a port or a temporary anchorage area. In Figure 11.3, the stopping points are clearly visible (each color represents a different cluster). The stop points that are far apart from the coastline and could represent off-shore anchorage areas have been removed.

Figure 11.3 Anchorages areas are clustered using the DBSCAN algorithm. The points not far from the coastline are removed

Figure 11.4 Port anchorages areas are identified using a concave hull approach

An additional procedure was needed to derive the potential anchorage areas from the group of points belonging to the same cluster. That polygon area was extracted using a concave hull grouping the stay points of the same cluster (refer to Figure 11.4). At that level, we had a series of polygons depicting the potential anchorage needed to analyze the maritime traffic network. However, relying only on that level of information, it is not possible to build a real maritime network because a chunk of semantic information is missing. For this reason, a specific procedure was applied to define a semantic definition for each port polygon.

Trajectory semantic annotation

The processing of trajectory stops-moves allows us to extract a detailed picture of the staying areas but does not give any semantic information of the permanent ports or temporary anchorage areas.

To enrich the usability of the port polygon areas, a semantic annotation, reporting at least the port name, is needed. That approach is essential to enhance the usability of the port network traffic analysis. Moreover, additional semantic information is essential to build specific applications in a given context, such as port in/out analysis and Estimated Time of Arrival (ETA) estimation.

A semantic annotation approach is based on two main components, a detected area context and a series of geographical information layers. The semantic annotation methodology is mainly based on the extraction of the features from the geographical layer having a spatial overlap with the trajectory staying areas (port polygons).

In the existing literature, several semantic annotation approaches are referred to, with different application contexts. In our approach, two geographical information layers were used: the World Port Index (WPI) dataset and the OpenStreetMap (OSM) vector features. The WPI dataset is collected from the National Geospatial Intelligence Agency and contains the geographical position and additional information of about 3,700 ports across the world (https://msi.nga.mil/NGAPortal/MSI. portal). The OSM project is a volunteering mapping project, where users across the world are mapping the geographical data. Within the same project, the OSM initiative is collecting maritime data to provide a free nautical database and navigational chart (http://wiki.openstreetmap.org/wiki/OpenSeaMap).

The semantic annotation was performed by extracting all the geographical features included inside a distance from the port polygon centroid. An empirical approach was used to define the threshold distance, relying also on the feature classification. As an example for the OSM features, in selecting the geographical urban feature points, such as village, town or city, an increasing distance threshold was used. The features extracted were ranked based on different weights. At the end of the process, the feature with the highest rank was selected.

The semantic annotation methodology can be considered only as a preliminary prototyping requiring a validation phase. However, the semantic annotation used in combination with the OSM vector features is an excellent procedure that can be widely used to enhance knowledge in trajectory analysis related to a specific context.

As a final product, we were able to provide a complete picture of the Mediterranean staying areas, taking into account not only the main ports but all the anchorage area. The improvement with respect to the existing port polygon dataset is remarkable. In the future, it could be useful to compare the different port polygons to understand the reliability of the proposed method. Finally, the distance selection threshold and the ranking procedure need to be improved by taking into consideration the vector feature typology and validated using an accurate port polygon.

Mediterranean maritime flow network analysis

Network analysis

The Mediterranean port anchorage areas obtained by means of the trajectory modelling procedure provided the starting point to build the maritime traffic network. We built the classical network representation by means of nodes and edges. The nodes are represented from the port anchorage areas, and the traffic activities and the "node to node" connections were extracted from the AIS vessel positioning data. One month of AIS data (October 2015) was collected and a spatial query was applied, selecting only the vessel positions within the anchorage areas polygons. With the anchorage areas as nodes of the network, we built the network connections (edges) by means of the vessel journey between two nodes. We validated the vessel journey only if the time travelled between two anchorage areas was compatible with the travelled distance node to node; otherwise, we removed that information. That simple network modeling allows us to obtain a complete and accurate maritime network, with which we derive some standard network characterization statistics of the main network and the ship types' sub-networks (Table 11.1).

Overall, the total number of different ships is 18,244, with the cargo vessels representing the largest group (3,707 ships). The network has 950 nodes and 9,090 edges. Cargo ships, in spite of being the bigger group, tend to have a lower number of visited ports (331 nodes) and a less dense network (2,639 edges), especially in comparison to passenger ships, totaling just one third of their number (1,318 ships), but with a greater number of visited ports. The fact that cargo vessels tend to have the same scheduled itinerary and a lower number of visited ports and edges is already reported in the cargo network analysis of Kaluza et al. (2010). The network asymmetry (Table 11.1) represents the ratio of single connection edges

Table 11.1 Maritime network characterization

	No. ships	No. nodes	No. edges	Network asymmetry	Mean degree	Clustering coefficient	Average shortest path length	Average no. journeys per link
All	18,244	950	9,090	0.60	19.14	0.24	3.60	11.20
Cargo	3,707	331	2,639	0.72	15.95	0.27	3.27	3.03
Sailing	2,579	481	2,014	0.73	8.37	0.22	4.68	1.61
Passenger	1,318	458	1,857	0.45	8.11	0.28	4.31	31.87
Tanker	1,174	221	900	0.67	8.14	0.24	3.76	3.15

(one-way direction) with respect to the total number of edges. The asymmetry tends to be close to zero if there are a great number of port-to-port connections in both directions. As expected, the passenger ship sub-network tends to be the least asymmetric network, having the majority of connections in both directions. The cargo sub-network has the highest mean degree value in respect to the other ship types, representing a network with fewer nodes but a greater number of connections per node. A notable variability across the different sub-networks is shown in the mean journeys per link (J) value that has the highest values for passenger vessels and the lowest values for sailing vessels.

Regarding the port ranking in the Mediterranean maritime network, Table 11.2 shows the ranking based on total port calls. The highest value is represented from the ports of Piraeus, Eskihisar and Messina. Table 11.3 shows the ranking of the ten most central ports, and the relative node degree values. The highest value is represented by the Maltese port of Valletta having a double value in respect to the second port, Piraeus. The centrality of the Valletta port is clearly visible in Figure 11.5, where we also notice the geographical centrality.

Table 11.2 Most important ports in the maritime network

Port	No. ship calls
Piraeus	8,972
Eskihisar	5,964
Messina	5,884
Topçular	5,740
Villa San Giovanni	5,114
Paloukia	4,961
Ibiza	4,597
Naples	3,950
Rio	3,180
Antirrio	3,173

Table 11.3 Most central ports in the maritime network

Port	Degree	Betweenness
Valletta	196	107,259
Piraeus	155	53,272
Kusadasi	69	42,633
Barcelona	219	37,588
Palma de Mallorca	180	37,500
Split	79	35,458
Ceuta	132	34,331
Brindisi	83	28,917
Koper	100	25,762
Salerno	108	25,247

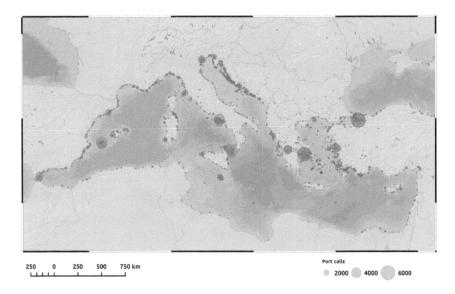

Figure 11.5 Port calls for all the vessels

Network visualization

The maritime network derived from the AIS dataset can give an accurate picture of the maritime traffic network in the Mediterranean basin. In Figure 11.6, all the anchorage areas derived from the vessel trajectory analysis are presented together with the port calls (using a circle proportional to the vessel traffic). The figure clearly shows not only the main ports with the greater traffic intensity, but also a multitude of small anchorage areas with only a few monthly connections. In particular, the east side of the Adriatic Sea has a high density of small anchorage areas. Except for the North Africa anchorage areas that are less represented, the entire basin is very well depicted. On the map, some high traffic intensity spots are clearly visible, in particular the sea channels, such as the Bosphorus, the strait of Messina or the Corinth Canal.

Using the ship type classification transmitted in the AIS message, it is possible to originate a specific maritime network representing a subset of the main network. An example of this is the cargo network reported in Figure 11.7. As for the previous map, some high density spots are clearly visible relating to Mediterranean ports with heavy cargo vessel traffic. In respect to the previous figure, the number of anchorage areas has reduced considerably.

Port activity statistics

The methodology applied in our work could be used not only to analyze maritime traffic by means of the network. In addition, for each port it is possible to

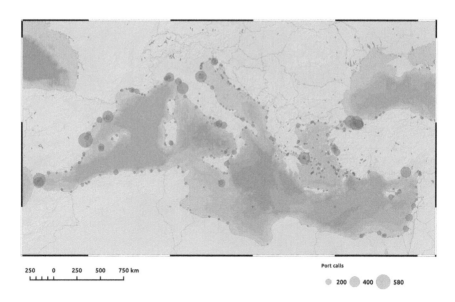

Figure 11.6 Port calls for the cargo vessels

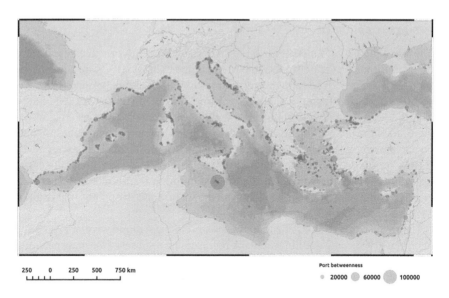

Figure 11.7 Port betweenness

derive accurate traffic statistics such as in/out daily, weekly or seasonal ship-ping activities and Average Turnaround Time (ATT). An accurate detection of the in/out shipping traffic is possible using the port anchorage areas as refer-ence: every ship boundary crossing is detected, thus permitting the computation

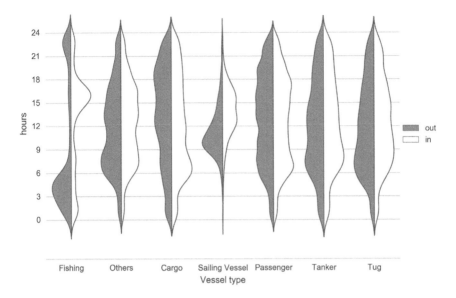

Figure 11.8 Port activities for the port of Genova

of flows statistics. As an example, the daily traffic computed for the port of Genova following the aforementioned methodology is reported in Figure 11.8. The daily traffic analysis is a useful instrument for highlighting interesting patterns. Some ship typologies, for instance, have a symmetrical in/out distribution such as passenger vessels, tankers and tugs, which record a higher activity during the morning that tends to decrease in the afternoon. Interesting patterns are also visible in the case of the fishing, cargo and sailing vessels. Fishing vessels have the highest frequency of outgoing traffic in the early morning and late evening, while the incoming traffic tends to concentrate in a short time interval between 15:00 and 17:00.

Cargo vessels have the most asymmetrical time distribution, with their incoming activities concentrated in the morning, while outgoing activities increase throughout the day. Finally, sailing vessels tend to have an activity distribution concentrated in the morning for port outbound flows and during the evening for the return. ATT *"corresponds to the average difference between date of departure and date of arrival among all container vessels calling at a port (or country) within one month of navigation"* (Ducruet and Merk, 2013). ATT plays a key role in analyzing port efficiency or increasing the energy efficiency of the sea shipping route (Johnson and Styhre, 2015). Using in/out detection methodology it is possible to analyze the ATT statistics for each port. By way of example, in Figure 11.9, it is possible to evaluate the mean ATT (days) according to ship typology.

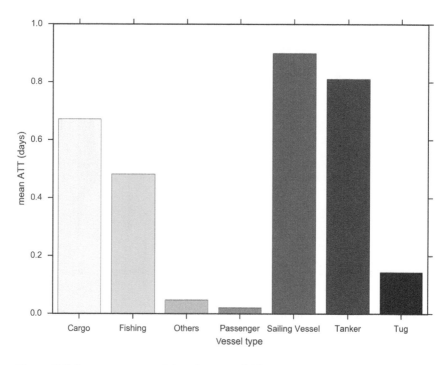

Figure 11.9 Average turnaround times by type of ship

Conclusion

In this chapter, we have presented a new methodology to characterize, analyze and model maritime networks based on location data reported within AIS messages. The methodology presented here makes use of AIS data to automatically extract port information in terms of geographic extent and activities. Such an extraction method is based on clustering the stop points detected by CB-SMoT algorithm, followed by a semantic knowledge extraction process. The second method proposed in this paper consisted in the automatic construction of a maritime network based on the connections between automatically detected port areas. The results reveal that the network descriptive statistics and topology are shaped by ship types and that such patterns can be explained by geographical, trade and geopolitical factors.

Acknowledgements

The U.S. Navy and the Volpe Center of the U.S. Department of Transport are acknowledged for the MSSIS data.

Bibliography

Alessandrini, A., Alvarez, M.A., Greidanus, H., Gammieri, V., Fernandez Arguedas, V., Mazzarella, F., Satnamaria, C., Stasolla, M., Tarchi, D., Vespe, M. (2016) Mining vessel tracking data for maritime domain applications. In: *2016 IEEE 16th International Conference on Data Mining Workshops (ICDMW)*.

Alessandrini, A., Argentieri, P., Alvarez, M.A., Barbas, T., Delaney, C., Fernandez Arguedas, V., Gammieri, V., Greidanus, H., Mazzarella, F., Vespe, M., Ziemba, L. (2014) Data driven contextual knowledge from and for maritime situational awareness. In: Huang, H., Hahn, J., Claramunt, C., Reichenbacher, T. (Eds.), *Proceedings of the International Workshop on Context-Awareness in Geographic Information Services (CAGIS 2014)*, Vienna, Austria, pp. 39–49.

Alvares, L.O., Bogorny, V., Kuijpers, B., Fernandes de Macedo, J.A., Moelans, B., Vaisman, A. (2007) A model for enriching trajectories with semantic geographical information. In: *Proceedings of the 15th annual ACM International Symposium on Advances in Geographic Information Systems (GIS '07)*, ACM, New York, NY, USA, Article 22, 8 pages. doi:10.1145/1341012.1341041

Blue Hub. (2016) Available at: https://bluehub.jrc.ec.europa.eu/research_areas_maritime/

Directive 2002/59/EC of the European Parliament and of the Council establishing a Community vessel traffic monitoring system, as amended by Directive 2009/17/EC. (2015) *Recommendation ITU-R M.585-7 (03/2015): Assignment and Use of Identities in the Maritime Mobile Service*. Geneva, Switzerland: ITU. March 2015.

Ducruet, C. (2013) Network diversity and maritime flows. *Journal of Transport Geography*, 30: 77–88.

Ducruet, C., Merk, O. (2013) Examining container vessel turnaround times across the world. *Port Technology International*, 59: 18–20.

Ducruet, C., Notteboom, T.E. (2012) The worldwide maritime network of container shipping: Spatial structure and regional dynamics. *Global Networks*, 12(3): 395–423.

Johnson, H., Styhre, L. (2015) Increased energy efficiency in short sea shipping through decreased time in port. *Transportation Research Part A*, 71: 167–178.

Kaluza, P., Kölzsch, A., Gastner, M.T., Blasius, B. (2010) The complex network of global cargo ship movements. *Journal of the Royal Society Interface*, 7(48): 1093–1103.

Mazzarella, F., Vespe, M., Damalas, D., Osio, G. (2014) Discovering vessel activities at sea using AIS data: Mapping of fishing footprints. In: Paper presented at the 17th *International Conference on Information Fusion*, Salamanca, July 7–10.

Natale, F., Gibin, M., Alessandrini, A., Vespe, M., Paulrud, A. (2015) Mapping fishing effort through AIS data. *PLoS ONE*, 10(6). doi:10.1371/journal.pone.0130746

Pallotta, G., Vespe, M., Bryan, K. (2013) Vessel pattern knowledge discovery from AIS data: A framework for anomaly detection and route prediction. *Entropy*, 15(6): 2218–2245.

Palma, A.T., Bogorny, V., Kuijpers, B., Alvares, L.O. (2008) A clustering-based approach for discovering interesting places in trajectories. In: *Proceedings of the 2008 ACM Symposium on Applied Computing (SAC '08)*, New York, NY, USA, pp. 863–868.

SOLAS. (2000) *Safety of Life at Sea Convention*. Chapter V, Regulation 19.

Vespe, M., Greidanus, H., Santamaria, C., Barbas, T. (2015) Knowledge discovery of human activities at sea in the Arctic using remote sensing and vessel tracking systems. In: Paper presented at the *ShipArc 2015 International Conference*, Malmö, Sweden, August 25–27.

12   Geovisualizing the sail-to-steam transition through vessel movement data

Mattia Bunel, Françoise Bahoken, César Ducruet, Claire Lagesse, Bruno Marnot, Eric Mermet and Séléna Petit

Despite the crucial importance of maritime transport for world trade and economic development, dedicated tools to map the evolution of vessel movements remain lacking. Such movements, especially those recorded by the maritime insurance company *Lloyd's List*, represent the only available information documenting the changing spatial distribution of the world's shipping routes in the last century or so. This chapter tackles the lacuna head on by discussing how this particular type of shipping data can be accurately represented on a map (see Chapter 1 for a review of the field). Such an exercise poses specific issues in terms of geovisualization, as it necessitates, among other developments, the creation of a virtual maritime grid to which port nodes and their mutual vessel flows are assigned. Beyond geomatics, this research is also an opportunity to shed new light on a vibrant research question in maritime history, namely how steam has replaced sail shipping in space and time. We extracted snapshots of global maritime flows every five years from the *Lloyd's Shipping Index* between 1890 and 1925 in order to test the capacity of the geoportal to visualize such flows, and at the same time verify the spatio-temporal evolution of a bi-layered maritime network. The remainder of this chapter is organized as follows: the next section discusses the scarcity of maritime data cartography until recent years in the light of general knowledge on flow mapping in geography and elsewhere. It is followed by a description of how vessel movement data had been incorporated into a dedicated visualization system. Lastly, it provides the first-ever cartographies of such movements while discussing the gaps between our results and the existing literature on the transition from sail to steam shipping. Conclusions point to a number of ways how the visualization system may be improved in the future and how it can contribute toward addressing numerous other issues in global transport studies in general.

The cartography of spatial maritime flows

Theoretical issues

Flow mapping consists in representing over a given space, often geographic (i.e. generally based on a continuous vision of proximities between places, such as kilometers), a link-node diagram where the nodes are the origin and destination places and the link their (weighted) relation. In other words, flow mapping is a form of graph spatialization across a geometric space (x,y) where the positions of nodes are constrained by a force-directed function. Thus, the choice of the quasimetric is not of first importance because i) spatial considerations are often ignored in Social Network Analyses and theory; and ii) the aim of the figure is to focus more on the easier perception of the relationships (weighted or not) between nodes than their position. In doing that, the method aims to reduce links' cross effects and repositioning nodes, the latter being often shifted to deliver an aesthetical figure of the whole system.

Therefore, in opposition to flow mapping, spatial movements necessitate a broader reflection on the cartographic process of the so-called flow maps. Spatial transfers – generally called movements, currents or flows – correspond to a changing position in a spatiotemporal framework, a shift between two places represented on the map by a direct link. Weighted links characterize flows designed by lines, directed or not. Such links belong to a (spatial) planar graph, when the transport infrastructure that supports movement is well known, for a specific mode like roads, but then it does not translate a flow per se. Otherwise, it is non-planar. Whatever the nature of the graph, the semiotic approach of flow mapping consists in a variation of the width of the line as underlined by earlier engineers such as Harness (1837), Minard (1845) and then Bertin (1967), with reference to basic principles of graphical semiology (especially the visual variable of size). Mapping a movement instead of a flow leads then to a similar approach, but fundamentally differs in terms of semantics (Bahoken, 2016a). The main difference between the two approaches is the greater importance given to spatial interaction in the first case in terms of both the analysis and the interpretation of the map. Such issues have great implications in terms of semantics, database construction and flow measurement, especially in terms of the importance given to the cartographic background (Goodchild et al., 2007). The length of the link itself is an essential component of its understanding in addition to its volume, in other words, the traveled cartographic distance (Bahoken, 2016a). Length and width are thus two essential components of the cartography of any transfer across space. However, while Bahoken (2016a) introduced the cartographic distance in flow and movements mapping, the perspective emerged in the early 1970s with pioneering discussions on the concept of graphic distance (Tobler, 1979; Müller, 1979), later followed by L'Hostis (1997) for the construction of network maps. Such advances were a response to previous theoretical research on transport development and the revolution of speed (Bretagnolle, 2009). An increasing number of maps were produced by modifying the position of places rather than the statistical information behind the flows. Examples include vector anamorphic maps (unipolar and multipolar) allowing the use of real instead of Euclidean metrics; they are also known as isochronic maps, where the ". . . symbolic representation expresses the time factor, through the overlap of lines sharing equal transport time, speed, or accessibility" (Bretagnolle, 2005: 56).

In such a context, the French geographer Bertin (1973: 345) provided an example that justifies the decomposition of the numeric information before mapping.

As underlined by the author: "it is not sufficient to trace the real itineraries to represent a system of relations. A map of shipping lanes, even weighted, does not show the commercial function of activity centers. It shows the density of ships on the sea. The diversity, weight, and directionality of commercial maritime relations between European and Mediterranean cities only appear when each relation, albeit maritime, is represented by a straight line" (Bertin, 1973: 344). Despite the impossibility of answering such questions directly, what becomes clear is the complementarity (Bahoken, 2016a: 172–173) between their movement mapping (top) and flow mapping (bottom), taking into account that topographic constraint leads to map movement and not just simple flows or relations. Here, the territorial space is not a simple layout for aesthetical aims; it has a strong influence on the graphic aspects of the design of such flows, but also on their semantic aspects in a theoretical framework, in that it considers the role of distance frictions and spatial detours in the mapping process (L'Hostis, 2014), in addition to the numerical modeling.

The specifics of maritime flows

While the cartography of shipping data evolved considerably over the last century (see Chapter 1), subsequent cartographies grew scarce and tended to ignoring space and the connected territories in their focus on graph topology. From the early 2000s, maritime flow maps were characterized by various levels of data aggregation, from the space-time trajectory of individual vessels (Buard et al., 2015; Etienne et al., 2015) to the network of inter-port linkages and the intercontinental trunk lines, often resulting in density maps (or heatmaps) using various techniques of which spatial interpolation or grid mapping. Most of the time, such works represent straight O-D lines without paying much attention to weight, space, distance and detours. The geographic background often remains a simple support eluding the numerous topographical constraints mentioned above, especially on a world scale. Because maritime flows occur across the sea or ocean space, namely, a continuous surface limited by coastlines, and remain bound to ports situated at the sea-land interface, their visualization remains somewhat fuzzy (Rodrigue et al., 2017), and it is particularly difficult to avoid crossing continents (Grataloup, 2011). In addition, "*the straight line between two points across the ocean is rarely [never?] the fastest route for commercial vessels*" (Galton, cited in Bretagnolle, 2005).

Whatever their resolution and scale, maritime flows are necessarily situated on the ocean space – namely, a continuous area limited by coastlines and directed towards the ports. This constraint is specific to maritime flows, being a non-planar network constrained by physical space much more than airlines, for instance. Not taking into account such a geographic dimension thus leads to unrealistic maps (Bahoken et al., 2016a). The Euclidian logic of classic flow mapping inevitably makes maritime flows cross continents by means of more or less curved, directed or weighted lines. In other transport sectors, flows are attributed to physical infrastructures (road, railway, river . . .) or cross continents without causing major distortions of reality (airlines, telecommunications). In addition, maritime flows overcome additional constraints such as the location of ports, the natural conditions for navigation (straits, ice), and other economic or political barriers. Throughout the last decade however, data-related solutions for visualization have grown apace in relation to shipping. As described and explained in Chapter 1 by Ducruet about existing geovisualization portals from the private or academic world, such solutions often remain limited when it comes to data sources, analytical tools and time coverage.

Lloyd's List as a source to measure global sail and steam traffic

Throughout the history of literature on global shipping, a vast majority of works had documented the emergence of steam navigation from its early days (i.e. 1820s), due to the enormous consequences of such a technological innovation for world trade (Buxton, 2010; Stott, 2017). Yet, there remains considerable debate among scholars about the pace and the geography of the transition from sail to steam. In their synthetic work, Williams and Armstrong (2012) underline another transition, namely, from the subjective self-confidence of early historians, who took for granted the rapid and overwhelming domination of steam over sail, to the more objective and critical contributions of other scholars from the 1950s onwards, which moderated the manner in which the technological transition truly occurred. In addition and based on a largely untapped data source on shipping movements at British ports between 1853 and 1910, Williams and Armstrong (2012) proposed a quantitative analysis to tackle this debate. One of the ambitions of this chapter is to go one step further by placing the latter study in the light of a new spatio-temporal perspective. In fact, the results of Williams and Armstrong (2012), which will be discussed below in more detail, only reflect British port traffic, thereby causing a bias in their effort to extrapolate the observed trends to the rest of the world. What remains lacking is a global approach that would take into account all world ports and further insist on the local and regional differences of this technological transition (Ducruet and Marnot, 2016).

Despite its episodic recognition by scholars throughout maritime studies as a whole, the *Lloyd's List* corpus – and in particular, the Shipping Index – is the only source capable of documenting the movements of merchant vessels globally and back in time (see Ducruet et al., 2015 for a detailed description of this corpus). We extracted vessel movement data every five years between 1890 and 1925, the period that marks the demise of sail shipping. The year 1890 was chosen because that is when the Shipping Index starts to cover not only British but all vessels. It also marks the decisive progress of propulsion machines from the 1880s, thanks to the spread of the so-called compound machines, i.e. alternative machines with triple expansion. Such a technical innovation gave a decisive boost to the deep-sea transport of goods by steam vessels. Table 12.1 serves as a first step that compares our results with those of Williams and Armstrong (2012), together with

Table 12.1 Share of steamer fleet and traffic by data source, 1855–1925

Year	British ports*		World ports**	
	Entrances with cargo and in ballast (% tonnage)	Entrances with cargo and in ballast (% vessels)	Number of vessels (% vessels)	Number of calls (% calls)
1855	15.8	12.4	–	–
1860	20.9	15.5	–	–
1870	33.8	22.8	–	–
1880	63.0	47.0	–	–
1890	82.8	69.8	34.7	38.2
1900	91.8	81.4	57.7	61.6
1910	97.1	90.5	80.8	84.6
1920	–	–	88.2	90.4
1925	–	–	96.5	98.3

Source: Adapted from Williams and Armstrong (2012)* and *Lloyd's List* data**

Figure 12.1. Unfortunately, the tonnage capacity of vessels was not reported in the *Shipping Index* for sailing vessels, and for other years, such information had not been kept due to OCR imperfections. One important difference is the measurement unit (tonnage vs. number of calls and vessels). While both time series end up with approximately the same steam dominance (around 97%), this was already the case as early as 1910 for British ports; however, it was not until 1925 when the majority of other ports and regions in the world embraced the change in terms of technological innovation from sail to steam.

Our results thus imply strong regional inequalities in relation to this transition, as confirmed by Figure 12.2. Europe as a whole largely surpasses the world average and is very close to the results of Williams and Armstrong (2012), with 93.2% of steam vessel calls in 1910. Our calculation for British ports even returned a result of 100% for the same year. The rest of the figure reveals drastic differences among world regions. Asia largely dominates with its much earlier and higher switch to steam over sail during the period 1890–1925, closely followed by Europe and Africa, together constituting a distinct group made up of the "metropolis" and the main "colonial empires". The other group is made up of the Americas and Oceania, which started at much lower levels and went through a much more gradual and slower transition than the previous group, although by 1925, steam shipping was dominant in all regions. The resilience of sail shipping in the second group is explained by the continued economic profitability of specific trade routes and niche markets, such as Australian wheat carried by the so-called "windjammers", nickel and chrome exports from New Caledonia, nitrates from Chile, copper from California as well as grain and lumber from North America's West Coast. Favorable winds also to a large extent explain such a regional divergence. Conversely, the state of technological steam in 1890 does not permit shipping with profitability in the South Seas, due to the absence of coal bunkering ports.

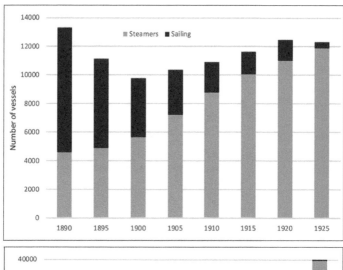

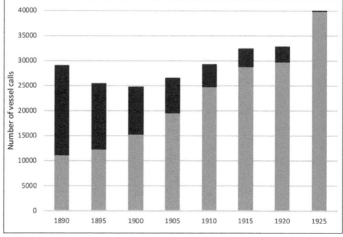

Figure 12.1 Evolution of sail and steam fleet and traffic size, 1890–1925

The same analysis is proposed at port level (Figure 12.3) based on the share of sailing vessel traffic in total port traffic, making it possible to confirm the aforementioned trends but at the same time to detect interesting main nodes as well as outliers to such trends. The map for 1890 reveals the high level of steam traffic on the Far East-Europe route via the Suez Canal as well as in the Black Sea, which is one of the first seas where steam power was used at the beginning of the 19th century. As for the Mediterranean and Baltic, the Black Sea is a closed sea which can be easily served by several coal bunkering ports. The significance of the Black Sea steam traffic can be illustrated by the role of Russian steam merchant and military fleets in the ports of Odessa and Sebastopol. In fact, the very low attendance of sailing ships on the Suez Canal route is almost a remarkable exception before 1900. By

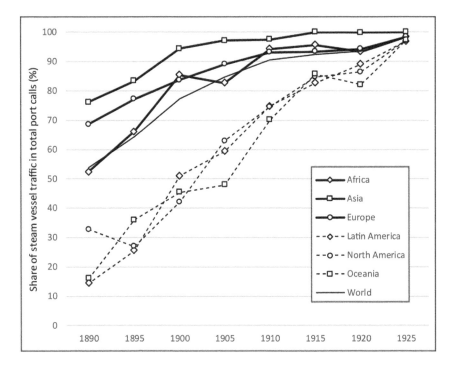

Figure 12.2 Sail to steam traffic evolution by world region, 1890–1925

contrast, as explained above, sail shipping traffic is always significant along the South American coast and on the South Seas routes which are crossed by very fast windjammers. In 1900 and 1905, sail shipping traffic lost ground everywhere except for the American West Coast and Oceanian ports like Australia. The singular situation of Cape Town in 1900, as demonstrated by its exceptional traffic growth, is explained by the Boer War (1899–1900), as the port was used by the British government for debarking troops and as a logistic base for the task force.

The share of sailing traffic decreased quickly after the First World War. A first explanation can be provided by the opening of the Panama Canal in July 1914. This effect may be compared with that of the Suez Canal after 1869 for the Europe-Asia route. With the new Panama Canal, which quickly linked America's West and East coasts, ships could avoid the long and dangerous detour around Cape Horn. Although Buenos Aires was still considered a very important world port at the time, its share of sail shipping traffic remained below 20% of its total traffic, like most of the other large ports worldwide. Such a global trend is directly attributable to technological progress in relation to engines in the Interwar Period. Indeed, advances in oil-heating technology meant that it was progressively replacing coal as an energy resource for merchant steam vessels. By contrast, the use of diesel technology remained rare in the early 1920s, but witnessed a continuous development during the Interwar Period. Thus, although sail shipping remained very

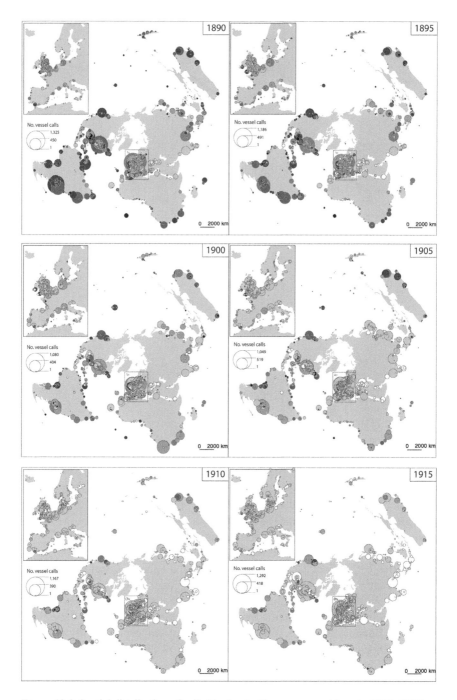

Figure 12.3 Spatial distribution of sail shipping traffic among world ports, 1890–1925

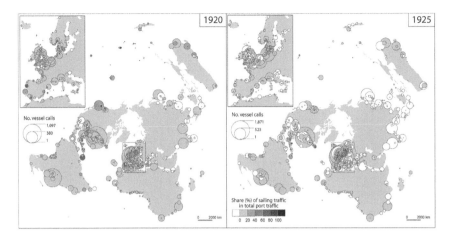

Figure 12.3 (Continued)

residual in the late period, this analysis shows that it had not yet entirely disappeared in 1925. Such evidence confirms the quality of Lloyd's data and motivates us to visualize in more detail the observed patterns and evolutions by means of more advanced tools.

Towards a geovisualization of the sail to steam transition

Constructing a dedicated geovisualization system

Visualizing Lloyd's data on the map necessitated the development of a dedicated cartographic website, namely GeoSeastems. Such a tool is currently under development aimed at allowing users to navigate through a cartographic interface, visualize and analyze the database. Yet, such a project relies on a very robust structure. A number of issues had to be overcome during this development, based on the steps described in Figure 12.4.

Vessel movement data (among ports of the world) do not reveal the exact circulation path of ships (see Chapter 10 for a visualization of US seaborne trade data based on a worldwide grid). A grid was therefore constructed to provide an approximation of such paths to map maritime movements while respecting the geographic constraints of territories (Bahoken, 2016b). Three approaches were envisaged, depending on the importance given to graphical aspects: the graphical fusion of nodes or linkages (cf. *edge bundling*), the statistical modeling of maritime trade exchanges or the cartographic modeling of movements. In theory, this leads us to define how to segment and partition the continuous ocean space where ships circulate. Lloyd's database provides the frequency of vessel calls at and between ports, which had to be assigned to a virtual grid in order to be visualized.

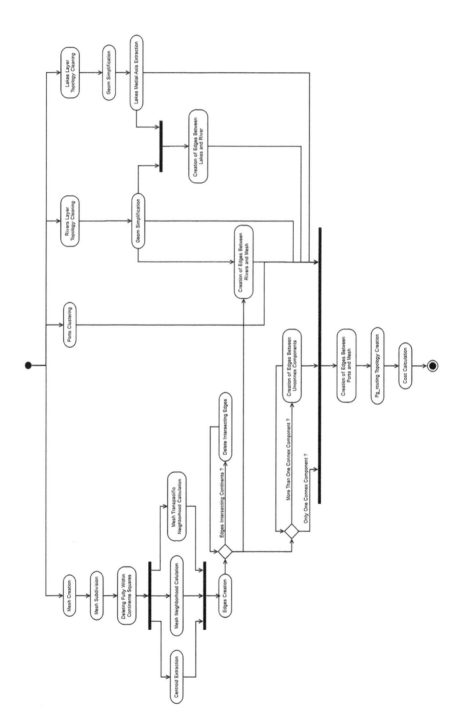

Figure 12.4 Data conceptual model

Extracted data from Lloyd's records were stored in a PostGreSQL/PostGIS database. This database is requested by Django, a Python web framework. The Python choice as the principal language of development on the server side (i.e. for the calculation done on the database side) allows the use of numerous libraries specialized in scientific calculation (Numpy) or graph treatment (NetworkX). By opting for this choice, the user is able to visualize different types of statistical or graph-theory based indicators on chosen data. On the client side (i.e. on the web browser), the results are mapped with OpenLayers and Cesium JavaScript libraries, completed by graphs done with D3.js.

In the first place, ship movements were represented as straight lines, linking the port of departure to port of destination. However, this approach was too schematic to be relevant. The use of a virtual grid was selected, as used in Chapter 10, for instance, and in the Orbis project (Scheidel, 2013), although with a slightly different objective than simply increasing the readability of a statistical flow mapping for the first and displaying dynamics on a website for the second. Specific constraints led us towards another kind of methodology to avoid handmade corrections following the automated operation and to increase the generic dimension of our method. Handmade operations remain a possible option only if the studied area and the expected precision do not imply the creation (or deletion) of too many edges. In the specific case of Lloyd's data, the huge number of port nodes (about 9,000) motivated us to fully automatize a process building and control.

Based on "keep it simple" (KISS) methodology, and after the generation of a regular meshing, a network was built using Delaunay triangulation. This first approach was not satisfactory due to the emergence of castellated trajectories on the map and other technical reasons, such as the necessity to increase significantly the number of links near the coastline. This led to an increase in computing time, incompatible with the real-time calculation of trajectories.

The regular meshing was thus improved, by first removing the random component. The idea of a grid with a mixed density of links was kept; but the building itself, with a heterogeneous densification of a simple grid, is fundamentally different. A worldwide meshing was built, composed of eight squares of 90° side (Figure 12.5). From this starting element, the meshing was refined with an iterative process. Each square intersecting a continent was subdivided into four same sized squares; those fully included in a continent or an ocean were not divided. Thus, at each iterative step, the number of squares is potentially multiplied by four, as their area is potentially divided by four. This process leads to a refined meshing near coastlines. After several tries, the number of iterations is fixed to seven (this number of iterations having the best ratio between complexity and accuracy). The final meshing is composed of 23,000 squares with areas between 6.10^3 km² and 6.10^6 km². These are the basis of the grid calculation. A trajectory is considered to be a list of adjacent squares. As the database software used to compute the shortest ways (pgRouting) only works on segments, the list of squares is turned into line strings by linking their respective centroids, using the Moore neighborhood.

The created grid allowed a fluid mapping of trajectories on seas and oceans but did not include river traffic. Thus, it was completed by new links based on Natural

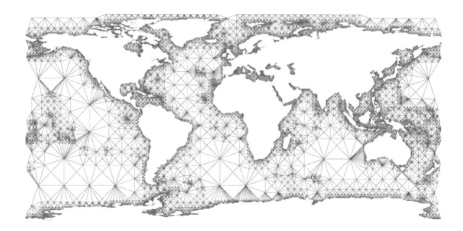

Figure 12.5 The world maritime grid

Earth physical data. Polygons and lines of lakes and rivers were simplified, to avoid the creation of too many links. River links were then added to the ones previously generated, while the integration of lakes needed an additional step: their median axes were extracted to transform polygons in a set of links.

Once rivers and lakes links were connected to the grid, the final procedure was the creation of links between the grid and the actual position of ports. The first attempt was the linking of each port to the closest node of the grid. However, this solution was not exploitable: the created links were intersecting continents. Closest ports were thus grouped into clusters, and those cluster centroids were linked to the grid. Finally, the links were weighted according to the distance between their two extremities.

Geovisualization results

The new maps can be considered as the first-ever visualizations of world maritime trade flows in the late 19th and early 20th centuries (Figures 12.6 to 12.9). Although they confirm a number of trends already observed in previous figures, they also show more clearly a number of elements, as explained in the following, based on one map every ten years since 1890. In that year, the Europe-Mediterranean-Far East route appears already dominated by steam shipping. As expressed by Fletcher (1958), "*the Suez Canal became, nearly without exception, the route of all-steaming*". The main advantage offered by the canal resided logically in the reduced deviation distance for ships. The voyage between Liverpool and Bombay was reduced by 42% and to Singapore by 30%. Moreover, the multiplicity of coal stations on the way permitted an increased loading capacity for freight. Up to 1910, the Indian Ocean-Australia line still exhibited the relative importance of sail shipping, as was the case with the Atlantic-to-Pacific route around Latin America.

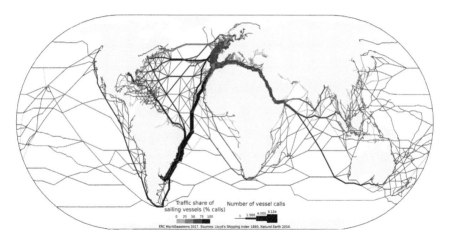

Figure 12.6 World maritime flows, 1890

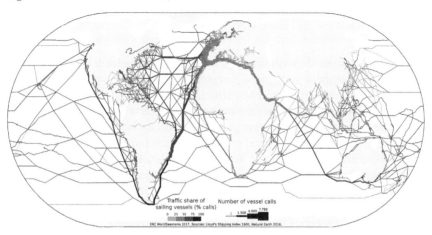

Figure 12.7 World maritime flows, 1900

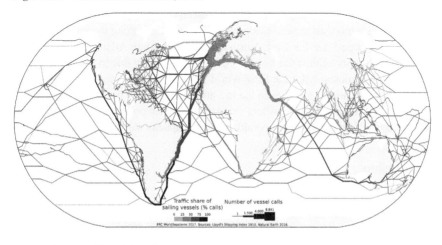

Figure 12.8 World maritime flows, 1910

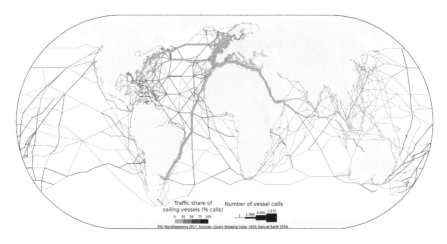

Figure 12.9 World maritime flows, 1920

Lines still dominated by sail shipping, in particular the routes of the southern seas sailed by windjammers, were global circumnavigation routes connecting the three main capes of the southern hemisphere (Horn, Good Hope and Leeuwin). Elsewhere, certain routes were peripheral on the map but carried vital raw materials for the world economy. This was the case, for instance, of the coal exchange from Europe to the Antipodes, which, in turn, exported ores and minerals (nitrate, nickel, copper etc.). A mixed-use area was the Atlantic itself. In particular, the Europe-Argentina route was characterized by the lack of coal stations and the profitability for certain types of cargo carried by steam ships. The same applied to the Europe-Caribbean route. However, such a result is particularly surprising for the North Atlantic routes between Europe and North America. In 1890, liners transporting migrants and travelers were all using steam. The relatively important presence of sail shipping can thus be explained by cargo shipping, here also for profitability reasons.

Between 1900 and 1920, from a European-centered core (Atlantic and Mediterranean), steam navigation becomes gradually hegemonic along the world's busiest sea lanes: Europe-Suez-Far East, North Atlantic and South Atlantic. The center of the Atlantic resists against the invasion of steam, certainly due to the lesser profitability of such routes. After the First World War, the southern seas and the Pacific, sailed by secondary routes, remain the last areas still reached by sail merchant shipping. In the case of Australian wheat exports, Australian ports remain poorly accessible and less than financially favorable to large capacity steamers (Lenhof, 2005).

Conclusion

This chapter is innovational at several levels. Here, for the first time, global vessel movement data is condensed, distinguishing sail from steam shipping in order to broach one of the most important debates in maritime and economic history on technological transitions. Secondly, and in order to reach such a goal, it mobilized a full circle of cartographical and geomatics competencies and knowledge, giving birth to a new geovisualization tool dedicated to mapping vessel movement data. Thirdly, via these two elements our research managed to produce the first-ever maps of global maritime trade in the 1890–1925 period. Such advances contribute both to economic history and cartographic science. Our main results confirmed a considerable amount of acquired knowledge on the evolution of world shipping, but also delivered novel findings. Our quantification of sail versus steam importance, which was previously based on British port traffic only, contributed toward questioning the rapidity of this technological transition. In addition, it provided the much-overlooked geographic dimension of technological change, at the level of continents, routes, and ports.

Further research shall be led in several ways. The refinement of cartography first should concentrate on refining the mesh refining during the maritime grid development, such as by taking into account, during the mesh subdivision step, not only continents but also the situation of ports. Such a procedure would allow reducing the number of edges in low-frequency coastal areas. In addition, the aggregation of nodes at the level of larger spatial units such as maritime ranges would improve the readability of the maps, by avoiding the multiplication of low-capacity linkages across the ocean-space. The use of color and other aesthetical features, with the ultimate goal to provide an open source and open access online webmapping tool, will offer more possibilities. Another research pathway is the additional extraction of Shipping Index items to obtain a fuller time-series database that would be more representative of yearly trends, from 1880 onwards. Such a database could be extended to later years in order to map and analyze other technological transitions, such as from steam to combustion (diesel engines), vessel specialization, of which the container revolution, up to the current era of mega-ships. This would help us to compare the spatial dynamics of each transition, in terms of geographic distribution and pace, given that earlier works found noticeable resemblance between past and current mechanisms of port competition in times of technological progress (Marnot, 2005). We also should better understand the emergence and diffusion of containerization, a wide research area where quantitative investigations remained bound to country-level data (Bernhofen et al., 2013) or container port throughout data (Guerrero and Rodrigue, 2014), thus missing the relational and multi-commodity perspectives offered by Lloyd's shipping flows. Beyond the description of technological change, such efforts shall lean towards a confrontation to classic models about the spatial diffusion of innovations (Hägerstrand, 1952) but also to wider models of diffusion and propagation in networks (Valente, 1996).

Acknowledgements

The research leading to these results has received funding from the European Research Council under the European Union's Seventh Framework Programme (FP/2007–2013) / ERC Grant Agreement n. [313847] "World Seastems".

References

Bahoken, F. (2016) *Contribution à la Cartographie d'une Matrice de Flux*. PhD Dissertation in Geography, University of Paris Diderot – Paris 7.

Bahoken, F., Grasland, C., Zanin, C. (2016a) D'une cartographie de flux à une cartographie du mouvement spatial, aspects sémiologiques. In: Paper presented at the *Colloque Temps, Art et Cartographie (TAC2016), Comité Français de Cartographie (CFC)*, Strasbourg, France, March 16–18.

Bahoken, F., Lagesse, C., Ducruet, C. (2016b) L'approche cartographique de la représentation du mouvement spatial. L'exemple des flux commerciaux maritimes euro-méditerranéens. In: *Proceedings of the SAGEO'2016 Conference*, Nice, December 6–9.

Bernhofen, D.M., El-Sahli, Z., Kneller, R. (2013) *Estimating the Effects of the Container Revolution on World Trade*. Lund University Working Paper 2013:4, Department of Economics, School of Economics and Management.

Bertin, J. (1973) *Sémiologie Graphique*. Paris: Mouton-Gauthier-Villars.

Bretagnolle, A. (2005) De la théorie à la carte: histoire des représentations géographiques de l'espace-temps. In: Volvey, A. (Ed.), *Echelles et Temporalités*. Paris: Atlande, pp. 55–60.

Bretagnolle, A. (2009) *Villes et Réseaux de Transport: des Interactions dans la Longue Durée (France, Europe, Etats-Unis)*. Habilitation à Diriger des Recherches, University of Paris 1 Panthéon-Sorbonne.

Buard, E., Devogele, T., Ducruet, C. (2015) Trajectoires des objets mobiles dans un espace support fixe. *Revue Internationale de Géomatique*, 25(3): 331–354.

Buxton, I. (2010) Enabling technology and the naval architect 1860–2010. *International Journal of Maritime Engineering*, 152: 51–60.

Ducruet C., Haule S., Ait-Mohand K., Marnot B., Kosowska-Stamirowska Z., Didier L., Coche M.A. (2015) Maritime shifts in the contemporary world economy: Evidence from the Lloyd's List corpus, 18–21 c., In: Ducruet C. (Ed.), *Maritime Networks: Spatial Structures and Time Dynamics*, Routledge Studies in Transport Analysis, London and New York: Routledge, pp. 134–160.

Ducruet, C., Marnot, B. (2016) Analyser les trafics portuaires mondiaux en 1890 et en 1925 à partir des registres du Lloyd's. In: GIS d'Histoire Maritime (Ed.), *La Maritimisation du Monde de la Préhistoire à nos Jours*. Paris: Presses Universitaires de Paris-Sorbonne, pp. 383–398.

Etienne, L., Alincourt, E., Devogele, T. (2015) Maritime network monitoring: From position sensors to shipping patterns. In: Ducruet, C. (Ed.), *Maritime Networks: Spatial Structures and Time Dynamics*. London and New York: Routledge Studies in Transport Analysis, pp. 190–209.

Fletcher, M.E. (1958) The Suez Canal and world shipping, 1869–1914. *The Journal of Economic History*, 28: 558.

Goodchild, M.F., Yuan, M., Covas, J.T. (2007) Towards a general theory of geographic representation in GIS. *International Journal of Geographic Information Science*, 21(3): 239–260.

Grataloup, C. (2011) *Représenter le Monde*. La Documentation Française, La Documentation photographique – Les dossiers, No. 8084.

Guerrero, D., Rodrigue, J.P. (2014) The waves of containerization: Shifts in global maritime transportation. *Journal of Transport Geography*, 34: 151–164.

Hägerstrand, T. (1952) *The Propagation of Innovation Waves*. Lund, Sweden: Royal University of Lund, Lund Studies in Geography.

Lenhof, J.L. (2005) *Les Hommes en Mer. De Trafalgar au Vendée Globe*. Paris: Armand Colin.

L'Hostis, A. (1997) *Représentation en relief des réseaux de transport de l'arc atlantique: déformations de l'espace-temps en "vallées" et "montagnes"*. Actes du colloque Theo-Quant, pp. 107–112.

L'Hostis, A. (2014) *Le Détour, la Pause et l'Optimalité. Essai sur la Distance et ses Apports au Transport et à l'Urbanisme*. Habilitation à Diriger des Recherches, Université Paris-Est-Marne-la-Vallée, LVMT, IFSTTAR.

Marnot, B. (2005) Interconnexion et reclassements: l'insertion des ports français dans la chaîne multimodale au XIXe siècle. *Flux*, 59(1): 10–21.

Müller, J.C. (1979) La cartographie d'une métrique non euclidienne: les distances-temps. *L'Espace Géographique*, 3: 215–227.

Rodrigue, J.P., Comtois, C., Slack, B. (2017) *The Geography of Transport Systems*. London and New York: Routledge.

Scheidel, W. (2013) *The Shape of the Roman World*. Working Paper, Stanford University.

Stott, P.W. (2017) Shipbuilding innovation: Enabling technologies and economic imperatives. *Journal of Ship Production and Design*, 33(3): 1–11.

Tobler, W.R. (1979) Estimations of attractivities from interactions. *Environment and Planning A*, 11: 121–127.

Valente, T.W. (1996) Social network thresholds in the diffusion of innovations. *Social Networks*, 18(1): 69–89.

Williams, D.M., Armstrong, J. (2012) An appraisal of the progress of the steamship in the nineteenth century. In: Harlaftis, G., Tenold, S., Valdaliso, J.M. (Eds.), *The World's Key Industry*. London, UK: Palgrave Macmillan, pp. 43–63.

13 Foreland mix and inland accessibility of European NUTS-3 regions

David Guerrero, Fernando I. González-Laxe,
María Jesús Freire-Seoane and Carlos Pais Montes

The heterogeneity of maritime transport supply in regions can be understood as the visible manifestation of two complementary dynamics. On the one hand, there are factors related to demand, such as the size of the local market, which is determined by economic activities and population. On the other hand, there are a series of dynamics resulting from strategies pursued by transport companies, which are obviously related to the former but to other factors as well. These two dimensions, which are necessary conditions for the success of (maritime) transport terminals, have been conceptualized as centrality and intermediacy. Both are necessary for the success of a transport hub, but their combination can vary considerably from one case to another Fleming and Hayuth (1994). Within the context of container-ized transport, pure hubs are characterized by a substantial share of transshipment, where intermediacy within the shipping network is the main advantage.

Conversely, gateway ports, where the transshipment rate is lower, tend to be characterized by their centrality, namely their proximity vis-à-vis inland markets. It should be noted, however, that gateways can hardly be "pure" since their large local markets greatly contribute toward enhancing their intermediacy both within inland and maritime networks, making them attractive locations for transshipment activities as well. In the academic literature of port studies, a similar debate took place in the aftermath of World War II on the relative importance of maritime and land-based factors on the success of ports. Amphoux (1949, 1951) and Weigend (1956) emphasized the prominence of maritime-related factors on the cargo-generating potentials of Le Havre and Hamburg. The success of both ports was not unrelated to the strength of their locally based shipping companies and, more broadly, to the trade policies implemented by France and Germany. By contrast, the fates of other ports within the Northern Range, like Antwerp and Rotterdam, seemed to be much more related to inland factors such as the historical know-how of their local merchants and traders and the high density of shippers in their hinterlands, spreading far beyond national borders (Boerman, 1951). This academic debate was later relativized by those who considered ports as broader systems in which inland, maritime and port-related elements were interrelated but not necessarily in the same proportions (Vigarié, 1964). In recent decades, the further integration of transport modes allowed by containerization has somewhat blurred the lines between land and sea related factors within the context of a global intermodal transport system. To secure good access to the hinterlands, containerized shipping lines have been increasingly involved in inland transport, often by investing in deep-sea terminals and sometimes by providing inland transport services (Franc and Van der Horst, 2010). Other intermediaries such as freight forwarders have supported this integration as well, by providing integrated door-to-door services (Ducruet and Van der Horst, 2009).

Few works have succeeded in empirically measuring the relationship between centrality and intermediacy, mainly because of the lack of data (Guerrero et al., 2015). One of them showed that the rate of transshipment of container ports in the Mediterranean mainly depends on the throughput and on the deviation from the main Europe-Asia maritime route (Zohil and Prijon, 1999). Today, when containerization seems to have reached a stage of maturity (Guerrero and Rodrigue, 2014) the main challenge for a container port is not just to cumulate high levels of centrality and intermediacy regarding inland markets and shipping networks, but also to maintain and improve its position within value chains (Robinson, 2002). To support the adherence of the local people and economic actors to port expansion projects, ports are also expected to attract activities and jobs related to the maritime flows within the context of international supply chains (Hall and Jacobs, 2010). The existence of frequent services with a wide range of ports in overseas regions could allow an efficient integration of its inland customers in global production systems. But port performance issues are rarely considered from the point of view of the shippers (inland customers) for whom the frequency of services and their geographical variety are central.

The purpose of this chapter is to help to fill this void with a systematic analysis of the contribution of inland potential demand to the concentration of container services in Europe, by taking into account the diversity of overseas regions involved in maritime trade. While we show that inland accessibility certainly reflects the concentration of services, we also identify other factors. Indeed, we attempt to understand why in some regions the maritime transport supply seems to be less well linked than we might expect from its inland market potential (see also Chapters 14 and 17 on the relationships between shipping, cities, and regional development, respectively). The segmentation of maritime transport supply by overseas regions could help to explain these deviations.

The rest of this chapter is structured as follows: next section presents the data and methodology applied in the subsequent section to describe and understand the relationship between maritime services and inland accessibility.

Data and method

Data: database on maritime transport supply

This research was carried out using a set of Automatic Information System (AIS) positions. The implementation of this new tracer technology on the bridge of ships begins with the IMO A.917 (22) resolution (Harati-Mokhtari et al., 2007), and it is currently compulsory for all vessels over 300 GT's to report call, departure and vessel data to the port authorities by means of this device. This database has been used by many authors to describe maritime transport trade networks for several different classes of vessel (Kaluza et al., 2010).

A sample of vessel paths was built with the following criteria: (a) not to consider containerships with less than 1,000 TEUs to eliminate short range navigation activity noise; (b) to consider vessels built before 2007, in order to obtain an equilibrated amount of AIS positions stored per ship; (c) to eliminate anchorage, strait or canal positions and (d) to prioritize for the final sample vessels that perform intercontinental activity. This selection procedure guarantees, as a corollary, that at least the most important ports (AIS call – berthing – positions) will be taken into account.

The analysis was conducted by splitting each vessel class sample into two years: 2009 and 2010 AIS positions. So for each year, the sequence of vessel calls defines subsequently another sequence of port of departure-port of arrival pairs. Hence, using a programming language with vector calculus features (postgreSQL), one can build a structure of nodes and edges that will allow us to perform a calculus of complex network parameters over this general cargo and AIS containership sets.

An additional layer of meaning was added to the entire set of worldwide call positions, in order to differentiate world trade areas. The division considered can be seen in Figure 13.1 and is roughly based on the geographical regions considered by containerized shipping companies. The final sample composition and its main network features can be seen in Table 13.1. According to total world fleet supply estimated by UNCTAD (Wilmsmeier and Hoffmann, 2008), our database covers approximately 80% of the existing containership fleet. One can observe a growth in vessels analyzed from 2009 to 2010, with the corresponding increases in total AIS positions.

A very important difference can be seen in the number of different ports considered for containerships. It decreases per containership sample (from 749 in 2009 to 527 in 2010). There are some quantitative approximations made using complex network-measuring methodologies (González-Laxe et al., 2012) explaining part of this behavior as an outcome of the demand crisis of 2008, which had a severe impact on the main containerized lines, affecting the mean connectivity of world gateways, and causing a conjunctural concentration during 2009–2010 of all the remaining active supply lines in fewer containerized terminals.

Figure 13.1 Foreland aggregates used in this study

Table 13.1 Sample composition

	Time scope sample	Containerships (supply in TEUs)	
		2009	2010
Number of vessels analyzed		2,032	2,144
Number of AIS positions analyzed		126,920	145,736
	Maximum	15,550	15,550
Vessel capacity	Minimum	450	1,057
	Average	4,533	4,730
Total fleet supply present in sample		9,211,236	10,142,327
Total world fleet supply estimated*		10,760,173	12,142,444
Number of different ports of call (world sample)		749	527
Number of different ports of call (Europe)		162	124

Source: Own calculations from AIS data from Lloyd's Registry Database (2010)

Data: NUTS-3 aggregation of maritime data

Starting from the 2010 version of NUTS-3[1] available at Eurostat, a bijective identification between administrative coastal units and ports has been performed in
order to proceed to the analysis: the maximum throughput of all the ports belonging to a NUTS-3 unit, has been considered as a proxy of the throughput of the
entire NUTS-3 region.[2] Figure 13.2 illustrates how the first step of this attempt to
identify ports with those geographical units was made. Using GIS software, the
superposition between ports and regions along the English Channel can be seen.
For example, in FR232, we can see the port complex of Le Havre (633), Antifer
(589) and Dieppe (5061). This suggests the following identification criteria: the
port with maximum throughput in the considered period is the representative of its
native NUTS-3, in the case of NUTS-3, the FR232 region, called Seine-Maritime,
will be identified with all network parameters of Le Havre. The size of NUTS-3
appears to be adequate to perform the identification between hinterland parameters
and port connectivity, as will be shown in this chapter.

Thus, with this method, each NUTS-3 coastal region is associated with a unique
value of throughput, degree and centrality for each time period. In a second stage
of postgreSQL programming tasks, the total throughput for each geographical unit
will be divided according to the share of TEUs moving towards (or coming from)
each world region. This last algorithm will allow an index of trade importance of
each world region to be obtained with each NUTS-3 unit.

Data: road accessibility to population

When studying the links between maritime activity and accessibility to inland
markets, the question of the delineation of the hinterlands of the ports is a difficult
issue. Even when taking into account large spatial units (i.e. countries, NUTS-2
regions), some large seaports obviously serve much wider territories. Unfortunately, many different parameters can influence the size and shape of hinterlands.

Figure 13.2 NUTS-3 regions and ports used in this study

Reviewing recent literature, Chapelon (2006) proposes a first measure of the economic potential of the port cities on the basis of the accessibility parameters, not
considering the activity of the ports but just the hinterland influence. Later, Guerrero (2014) and Notteboom (2010) show that the size of hinterlands varies a lot
from one port to another, particularly in relation to their size, the nature of cargo
handled and the distance from clients and competing ports.

Unfortunately, empirical evidence on the actual hinterlands is only available
through enquiries that do not exist on a comprehensive, Europe-wide basis. For
these reasons we have decided to use an indicator of accessibility to population;
knowing that it is an imperfect proxy of what is currently in practice, we used a
measure of accessibility implemented by S&W for the European Spatial Planning
Observatory Network (Spiekermann et al., 2007; Espon, 2009). This indicator is
based on two elements: (1) the population in NUTS-3 regions and (2) the effort in
time to reach them by road, which is the largely dominant mode of pre- and post-
maritime carriage. The accessibility model measures the minimum time between
all NUTS-3 regions by road. The potential accessibility of a NUTS-3 region is
calculated by adding up the population figures for all other European regions,
weighted by the transport time it takes to reach them (Figure 13.3). Compared to

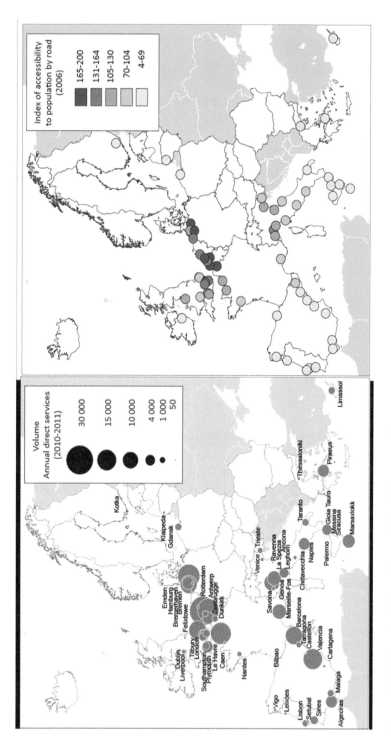

Figure 13.3 Volume and index of accessibility of the port-regions

the mere consideration of the potential of the region where the port is located, this method allows the potential of every region to be taken into account, in particular, those that are close to the port.

Results

Network vs hinterland differentiation

To evaluate the respective importance of the parameters of hinterland access and maritime connectivity, the variables road access and volume, which are highly correlated, have been converted by Principal Component Analysis into two uncorrelated variables (Figures 13.4 and 13.5). The first component, called hinterland, accounts for 68.5% of the total variance. The second component, explaining 31.5% of the variance, has been called "Network", since it differentiates the part of the port volume which is not related to the hinterland potential. Using the coordinates of the two factors, ports have been aggregated in clusters with Agglomerative Hierarchical Clustering. Five categories of ports can be distinguished on the basis of their "Hinterland" and "Network" dimensions. "Pure" Mediterranean hubs such as Algeciras, Gioia Tauro and Marxalkoxx, with large volumes and low or almost inexistent hinterland, are clustered in a same subgroup together with Piraeus and Limassol.

To provide a description of the foreland orientation of ports, a second Principal Component Analysis has been done on the table of percentages of ports with each

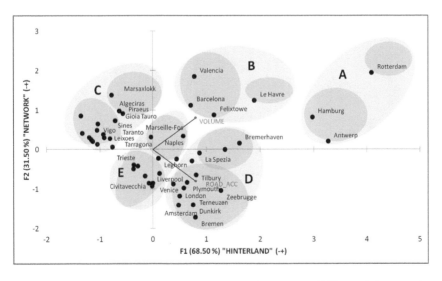

Figure 13.4 Principal Component Analysis (Volume*Road Accessibility) and cluster analysis (10 types)

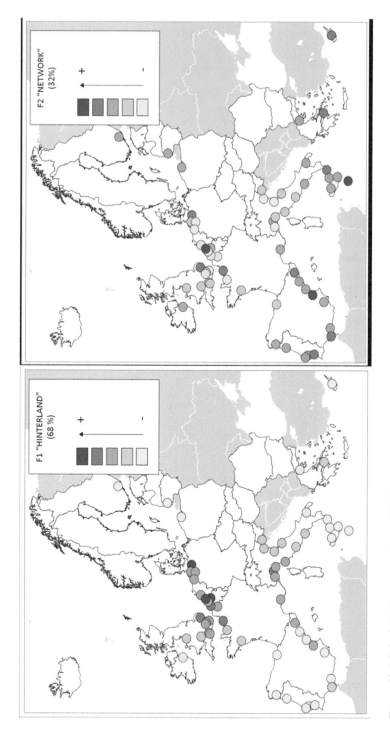

Figure 13.5 Principal Component Analysis (Volume*Road Accessibility)

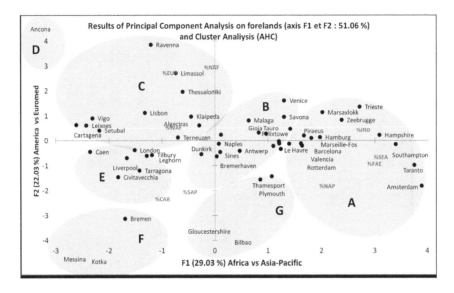

Figure 13.6 Principal Component Analysis diagram (share of different forelands on the total)

of the 12 overseas regions, weighted by the volume (Figures 13.6 and 13.7). The two main factors represent 51% of the foreland variability of ports. The first, explaining 29% of the variations, is strongly correlated to the shares of Asian and West African forelands which are generally opposed. The second factor, explaining 22% of the variability of foreland orientation of ports, is defined by the opposition between European and North African forelands versus American ones. Ports have been aggregated in seven categories. This time, an unequal orientation to African and Asian forelands spreads them over three different categories (see also Tables 13.2 and 13.3).

Does inland accessibility provide a good estimation of port volume?

To explain the geography of European container transport supply, we simply assessed the linear correlations between transport supply and road accessibility to population at the NUTS-3 level (Table 13.4). The correlation is significant ($R^2=.33$), which means that 33% of container supply differences between NUTS-3 regions are described by accessibility to population by road. This is partly due to the importance of the container supply of Northern Range ports that are close to the economic core of Europe, where most of the population and wealth is concentrated. However, several other factors, like the strategies of shipping lines (hub and spokes networks) and the proximity of certain European regions to main container routes also explain this geography. In order to distinguish the inland and maritime dimensions, a Principal Component Analysis has been applied to both variables.

According to the model, inland accessibility to a large extent explains the spatial variation in European shipping services. However, this type of analysis naturally

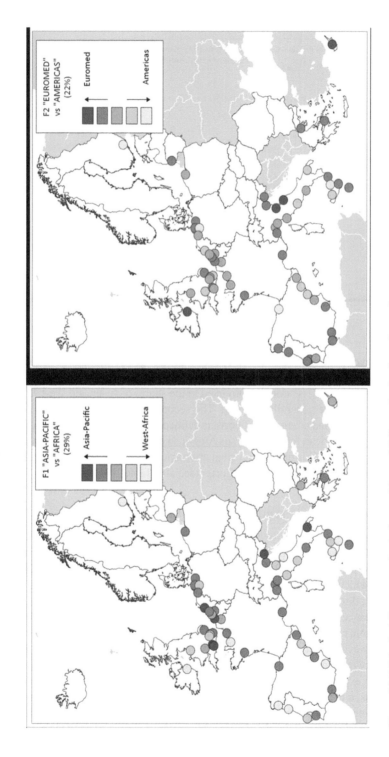

Figure 13.7 Principal Component Analysis map (share of different forelands on the total)

Table 13.2 Road accessibility of port regions by world area

Road accessibility index	Europe (EUR)	North Africa (NAF)	West Africa (WAF)	South America Atlantic (SAA)	North America Atlantic (NAA)	Caribbean (CAR)	Oceania (OCE)	North America Pacific (NAP)	South America Pacific (SAP)	Indian Ocean (IND)	South-East Asia (SEA)	Far East (FAE)	World
Core (>100)	36 415	18 852	4 880	3 684	9 184	11 190	1 461	4 867	2 713	14 312	28 072	14 362	85 666
Intermediate (50–100)	11 307	6 312	2 473	772	3 204	2 879	341	1 514	407	4 446	8 117	3 494	17 353
Peripheral (10–50)	7 309	4 127	1 744	598	1 821	1 596	158	1 089	280	3 322	5 639	2 417	1 704
Ultra-Peripheral (<10)	811	669	65	21	85	39	14	14	14	168	92	18	12 009
Med Hubs (transshipment>60%)	5 018	3 315	1 030	421	1 186	846	193	312	142	2 040	3 033	1 316	18 659
Total	60 860	33 275	10 192	5 496	15 480	16 550	2 167	7 796	3 556	24 288	44 953	21 607	244 053

Source: Own calculations from AIS data from Lloyd's Registry Database (2010)

Table 13.3 Maritime connectivity of port regions by world area

No. of connections	Europe (EUR)	North Africa (NAF)	West Africa (WAF)	South America Atlantic (SAA)	North America Atlantic (NAA)	Caribbean (CAR)	Oceania (OCE)	North America Pacific (NAP)	South America Pacific (SAP)	Indian Ocean (IND)	South-East Asia (SEA)	Far East (FAE)	World
XL (>25K)	33 043	10 263	5 107	3 086	8 652	9 174	1 049	4 434	2 045	13 678	25 572	12 741	128 844
L (>10K–25K)	15 421	5 137	2 370	913	3 229	2 769	506	1 812	491	6 881	13 244	6 107	58 880
M (>2K–10K)	10 896	680	2 124	1 393	3 361	4 014	578	1 456	776	3 539	5 875	2 609	37 301
S (>0.05K–2K)	1 407	17 139	575	88	214	512	26	89	191	155	222	133	20 751
Total	60 953	33 331	10 208	5 512	15 504	16 631	2 175	7 801	3 609	24 323	44 993	21 624	246 664

Source: Own calculations from AIS data from Lloyd's Registry Database (2010)

Table 13.4 Correlations between the main variables

Variables	ROAD_ACC	VOL (Log)	ISLAND-0	ISLAND-1	NR-0	NR-1	MED-0	MED-1	BRI-0	BRI-1	BALT-0	BALT-1	ATL-0	ATL-1	%EUR	%NAF	%WAF	%NAA	%SAA	%CAR	%OCE	%NAP	%SAP	%IND	%SEA
ROAD_ACC																									
VOL(Log)	0.33																								
ISLAND-0	0.12	0.04																							
ISLAND-1	-0.12	-0.04	-1.00																						
NR-0	-0.67	-0.25	-0.28	0.28																					
NR-1	0.67	0.25	0.28	-0.28	-1.00																				
MED-0	0.40	-0.01	-0.08	0.08	-0.44	0.44																			
MED-1	-0.40	-0.01	0.08	-0.08	0.44	-0.44	-1.00																		
BRI-0	-0.21	-0.02	-0.70	0.70	-0.22	0.22	-0.39	0.39																	
BRI-1	0.21	0.02	0.70	-0.70	0.22	-0.22	0.39	-0.39	-1.00																
BALT-0	0.24	0.21	-0.10	0.10	-0.09	0.09	-0.16	0.16	-0.08	0.08															
BALT-1	-0.24	-0.21	0.10	-0.10	0.09	-0.09	0.16	-0.16	0.08	-0.08	-1.00														
ATL-0	0.19	0.26	-0.20	0.20	-0.18	0.18	-0.32	0.32	-0.16	0.16	-0.07	0.07													
ATL-1	-0.19	-0.26	0.20	-0.20	0.18	-0.18	0.32	-0.32	0.16	-0.16	0.07	-0.07	-1.00												
%EUR	-0.22	-0.20	-0.08	0.08	0.22	-0.22	-0.30	0.30	0.10	-0.10	0.13	-0.13	-0.06	0.06											
%NAF	-0.13	-0.11	-0.12	0.12	0.13	-0.13	-0.40	0.40	0.13	-0.13	0.12	-0.12	0.17	-0.17	0.84										
%WAF	-0.33	-0.22	0.21	-0.21	0.21	-0.21	-0.06	0.06	0.16	-0.16	0.00	0.00	-0.59	0.59	0.16	-0.18									
%NAA	-0.17	0.00	0.12	-0.12	0.12	-0.12	-0.03	0.03	-0.07	0.07	-0.08	0.08	0.23	-0.23	0.09	-0.13	-0.10								
%SAA	-0.07	-0.16	0.22	-0.22	0.08	-0.08	0.13	-0.13	-0.31	0.31	0.07	-0.07	-0.02	0.02	-0.32	0.07	0.09	0.06							
%CAR	-0.04	-0.40	0.03	-0.03	0.04	-0.04	0.13	-0.13	-0.01	0.01	0.01	-0.01	-0.09	0.09	-0.17	-0.44	-0.02	0.37	-0.10						
%OCE	0.19	-0.08	0.11	-0.11	-0.12	0.12	0.07	-0.07	0.09	-0.09	-0.14	0.14	0.03	-0.03	-0.16	-0.10	-0.09	-0.22	0.10	-0.09					
%NAP	0.19	0.06	0.06	-0.06	-0.10	0.10	-0.02	0.02	-0.09	0.09	0.20	-0.20	0.16	-0.16	-0.39	-0.39	-0.28	-0.32	0.08	-0.21	-0.19				
%SAP	0.03	-0.35	0.08	-0.08	-0.04	0.04	0.25	-0.25	0.05	-0.05	-0.43	0.43	-0.09	0.09	-0.39	-0.39	-0.32	0.00	-0.11	-0.04	0.04	0.10			
%IND	0.16	0.53	0.04	-0.04	-0.20	0.20	0.00	0.00	0.05	-0.05	0.01	-0.01	-0.01	0.01	-0.29	-0.10	-0.08	-0.33	-0.31	-0.16	0.38	0.02	-0.24		
%SEA	0.32	0.61	0.02	-0.02	-0.22	0.22	-0.03	0.03	-0.05	0.05	0.19	-0.19	0.32	-0.32	-0.39	-0.08	-0.48	-0.31	-0.28	-0.54	-0.16	0.33	-0.31	0.74	
%FAE	0.39	0.44	0.01	-0.01	-0.30	0.30	0.08	-0.08	-0.11	0.11	0.22	-0.22	0.24	-0.24	-0.35	-0.09	-0.37	-0.29	-0.30	-0.44	-0.12	0.50	-0.25	0.36	0.82

Source: Own calculations from Lloyd's Registry Database (2010)

raises questions regarding the deviations from the predictions. The relationship is particularly strong with Asian forelands (Far East, South-East Asia) meaning that these regions are largely served by metropolitan ports located near large urban areas or heartland Europe. The relationship with West Africa is good as well, but in this case, it is negatively correlated to accessibility, meaning that peripheral regions are more specialized than central ones. This is partly due to niche markets (i.e. counter-season fruits, timber, agricultural raw materials), where peripheral ports far from the European core are also important. In the particular case of France, the strong ties between secondary ports and West Africa are partly inherited from the colonial period.

Results of the OLS regression

For each geographical aggregate, an approximation of the foreland dependence with respect to the NUTS-3 road accessibility parameter (ROAD_ACC) and the NUTS-3 hierarchy in terms of shared-with-foreland supply lines (LogVOL) is built using an OLS approximation.

In order to improve the accuracy of this approach, two kinds of models are computed for each foreland aggregate: one with just the two dependent variables (simple model); and another (extended model) trying to reflect the effects of the specific features that each European macro-region (Island, Northern Range, Mediterranean, British Islands, Baltic Sea areas and Atlantic Arc) is able to induce, by adding them as a dummy variable additional dependent regressor.

The results are expressed in Tables 13.5 and 13.6, in which several important outcomes can be highlighted. First, the 12 forelands are able to produce ten meaningful relations, sometimes with the ROAD_ACC parameter acting as the main controller (West Africa and Oceania); in other cases, with the LogVOL parameter as a key element in grasping the meaning of the relationship analyzed (Caribbean, South America Pacific, Indian Ocean, South-East Asia and Far East). In one case, for the simple model computed for the Far East foreland, the two dependent variables ROAD_ACC and LogVOL succeed in achieving joint significance (which should be the ideal model sought).

The relations in which ROAD_ACC is the significant regressor are elusive, but if they appear, they could allow for a highly suggestive set of possible interpretations:

*   For the influence of road access and volume of TEUs shared with West Africa, the extended model suggests that belonging to a peripheral EU region (coef=–0.001) improves the network influence with respect to this foreland aggregate. In other words: for each additional unit of ROAD_ACC gained, 0.1% of influence units with respect to the West Africa foreland could be lost. In this case, it must be noted the negative influence of the Atlantic Arc on the West Africa foreland (coef=–0.171), hence setting the European Mediterranean macro-region (West Med range) as the main service area for containerized trade with West Africa, with important global hubs such as

Table 13.5 Simple and extended model for foreland aggregates' influence (part 1)

		%EUR		%NAF		%WAF		%NAA		%SAA		%CAR	
		coef	p>|t|	coef	p>|t|	Coef	p>|t|	coef	p>|t|	coef	p>|t|	coef	p>|t|
	Constant	0.4726	0.0071	0.3237	0.0035	0.3992	0.0047	−0.2048	0.2353	0.1265	0.0254	0.3282	0.0016
	ROAD_ACC	0.0000		0.0005	0.2706	−0.0008	0.0158	−0.0002	0.3674	−0.0004	0.0918	0.0003	0.4027
	VOL(Log)	−0.0349	0.1855	−0.0323	0.2508	0.0000		0.0000		−0.0094	0.2696	−0.0539	0.0040
	ISLAND-0	−0.0618	0.3423	−0.1304	0.0812	0.0666	0.0575	0.0000		0.0179	0.4326	−0.0274	0.5651
	ISLAND-1	0.0000		0.0000		0.0000		0.0000		0.0000		0.0000	
	NR-0	0.0000		0.0000		−0.0686	0.1961	0.0690	0.1794	−0.0342	0.1631	0.0000	
	NR-1	0.0000		0.0000		0.0000		0.0000		0.0000		0.0000	
	MED-0	−0.0892	0.0713	−0.1351	0.0070	−0.0414	0.2557	0.0725	0.0704	0.0000		0.0174	0.5914
	MED-1	0.0000		0.0000		0.0000		0.0000		0.0000		0.0000	
	BRI-0	0.0371	0.6530	0.1071	0.2346	−0.0993	0.1033	0.0532	0.2484	−0.0717	0.0158	0.0308	0.5917
	BRI-1	0.0000		0.0000		0.0000		0.0000		0.0000		0.0000	
Extended model	BALT-0	0.0815	0.4703	0.0000		0.0000		0.0557	0.3437	0.0375	0.3014	−0.0931	0.2419
	BALT-1	0.0000		0.0000		0.0000		0.0000		0.0000		0.0000	
	ATL-0	−0.0577	0.4084	0.0000		−0.1706	0.0001	0.1175	0.0103	0.0000		0.0000	
	ATL-1	0.0000		0.0000		0.0000		0.0000		0.0000		0.0000	
	F	1.8140		3.1342		7.0258		1.6823		1.8722		2.2311	
	P>F	0.1140		0.0148		< 0.0001		0.1435		0.1029		0.0542	
	R2	0.1704		0.2249		0.4430		0.1600		0.1749		0.2016	
	Adj-R2	0.0765		0.1532		0.3800		0.0649		0.0815		0.1113	
	Model	0.2215	0.1704	0.3771	0.2249	0.1949	0.4430	0.0409	0.1600	0.0247	0.1749	0.1319	0.2016
	Residual	1.0784	0.8296	1.2995	0.7751	0.2450	0.5570	0.2145	0.8400	0.1166	0.8251	0.5224	0.7984
	rootMSE	0.1426		0.1551		0.0680		0.0636		0.0469		0.0993	

(Continued)

Table 13.5 (Continued)

		%EUR	%NAF		%WAF		%NAA		%SAA		%CAR	
	coef	p>|t|	coef	p>|t|	Coef	p>|t|	coef	p>|t|	coef	p>|t|	coef	p>|t|
Constant	0.4526	<0.0001	0.2621	0.0054	0.1589	0.0006	0.0781	0.0305	0.0608	0.0243	0.2713	<0.0001
ROAD_ACC	-0.0005	0.2089	-0.0003	0.4447	-0.0005	0.0309	-0.0002	0.1840	0.0000	0.8547	0.0002	0.4307
VOL(Log)	-0.0276	0.2896	-0.0165	0.5841	-0.0143	0.3284	0.0050	0.6686	-0.0093	0.2886	-0.0581	0.0014
F	2.0498		0.6590		4.0983		0.9046		0.7356		5.6985	
P>F	0.1381		0.5213		0.0217		0.4104		0.4837		0.0055	
R2	0.0671		0.0226		0.1257		0.0308		0.0252		0.1666	
Adj-R2	0.0344		-0.0117		0.0950		-0.0032		-0.0090		0.1374	
Model	0.0872		0.0379		0.0553		0.0079		0.0036		0.1090	
Model (%)	0.0671		0.0226		0.1257		0.0308		0.0252		0.1666	
Residual	1.2126		1.6387		0.3846		0.2475		0.1378		0.5453	
Residual (%)	0.9329		0.9774		0.8743		0.9692		0.9748		0.8334	
rootMSE	0.1459		0.1696		0.0821		0.0659		0.0492		0.0978	

Simple model

Source: Own calculations from Lloyd's Registry Database (2010)

Table 13.6 Simple and extended model for foreland aggregates' influence (part 2)

	%AUS		%NAP		%SAP		%IND		%SEA		%FAE	
	coef	p>|t|	coef	p>|t|	coef	p>|t|	coef	p>|t|	coef	p>|t|	coef	p>|t|
					EXTENDED MODEL							
Constant	0.0153	0.6438	−0.0177	0.5630	−0.1874	0.0559	0.0529	0.5475	−0.1874	0.0559	−0.0552	0.4389
ROAD_ACC	0.0003	0.0434	0.0000		0.0002	0.4551	0.0000		0.0002	0.4551	0.0002	0.3860
VOL(Log)	−0.0051	0.3124	−0.0026	0.6489	0.0695	< 0.0001	0.0417	< 0.0001	0.0695	< 0.0001	0.0254	0.0169
ISLAND-0	−0.0073	0.5884	0.0236	0.0964	0.0096	0.7306	−0.0099	0.6280	0.0096	0.7306	0.0000	0.0000
ISLAND-1	0.0000		0.0000		0.0000		0.0000		0.0000		0.0000	0.0000
NR-0	0.0126	0.3888	0.0000		0.0091	0.8110	−0.0245	0.3393	0.0091	0.8110	−0.0148	0.6053
NR-1	0.0000		0.0000		0.0000		0.0000		0.0000		0.0000	
MED-0	0.0000		0.0000		0.0000		−0.0149	0.4735	0.0000		0.0000	
MED-1	0.0000		0.0000		0.0000		0.0000		0.0000		0.0000	
BRI-0	0.0214	0.2180	−0.0219	0.1645	0.0000		0.0000		0.0000		−0.0101	0.6662
BRI-1	0.0000		0.0000		0.0000		0.0000		0.0000		0.0000	
BALT-0	−0.0307	0.1591	0.0423	0.0815	0.0382	0.5533	−0.0502	0.2572	0.0382	0.5533	0.0354	0.4086
BALT-1	0.0000		0.0000		0.0000		0.0000		0.0000		0.0000	
ATL-0	0.0000		0.0218	0.1181	0.0575	0.1233	−0.0137	0.6432	0.0575	0.1233	0.0207	0.3963
ATL-1	0.0000		0.0000		0.0000		0.0000		0.0000		0.0000	
F	1.1991		1.4760				3.8569		6.4132		3.5620	
P>F	0.3213		0.2129				0.0029		< 0.0001		0.0049	
R2	0.1195		0.1202				0.3039		0.4206		0.2874	
Adj-R2	0.0198		0.0388				0.2251		0.3550		0.2067	
Model	0.0057	0.1195	0.0074	0.1202			0.0646	0.3039	0.2647	0.4206	0.0664	0.2874
Residual	0.0417	0.8805	0.0544	0.8798			0.1480	0.6961	0.3645	0.5794	0.1646	0.7126
rootMSE	0.0280		0.0317				0.0528		0.0829		0.0557	

(Continued)

Table 13.6 (Continued)

	%AUS		%NAP		%SAP		%IND		%SEA		%FAE	
	coef	p>|t|	coef	p>|t|	coef	p>|t|	coef	p>|t|	coef	p>|t|	coef	p>|t|
					SIMPLE MODEL							
Constant	0.0210	0.1656	0.0240	0.0038	0.1246	0.0006	-0.0405	0.1437	-0.1074	0.0172	-0.0437	0.1396
ROAD_ACC	0.0001	0.0827	0.0001	0.1425	0.0002	0.2218	0.0000		0.0003	0.2503	0.0003	0.0272
VOL(Log)	-0.0059	0.2396	0.0000		-0.0352	0.0029	0.0408	<0.0001	0.0759	<0.0001	0.0285	0.0046
F	1.7661		2.2101		4.8688		22.6361		18.4101		10.2337	
P>F	0.1802		0.1425		0.0112		<0.0001		<0.0001		0.0002	
R2	0.0584		0.0367		0.1459		0.2807		0.3925		0.2642	
Adj-R2	0.0253		0.0201		0.1159		0.2683		0.3711		0.2384	
Model	0.0028		0.0023		0.0399		0.0597		0.2469		0.0610	
Model (%)	0.0584		0.0367		0.1459		0.2807		0.3925		0.2642	
Residual	0.0446		0.0596		0.2334		0.1529		0.3823		0.1699	
Residual (%)	0.9416		0.9633		0.8541		0.7193		0.6075		0.7358	
rootMSE	0.0280		0.0321		0.0640		0.0513		0.0819		0.0546	

Source: Own calculations from Lloyd's Registry Database (2010)

Lagos (Nigeria), Abidjan (Ivory Coast) or Dakar (Senegal). This coefficient also confirms that the remarkable box-transshipment activity of Sines (Portugal, Atlantic Arc) is still centered exclusively on the services to the East Asia-Northern Range lines;

- There's a slightly positive effect for the influence of the Australasia foreland with respect to its favorable location in terms of ROAD_ACC (coef=0.0002), which must be interpreted as a sign of the capacity for the best connected NUTS-3 regions to establish containerized relations even with the most distant forelands.

The relations in which LogVOL is the significant regressor appear more frequently:

- The Caribbean foreland prefers European small-sized containerized terminals to perform trade operations (coef=–0.054), (i.e., each additional TEU moved by a NUTS-3 region with some Caribbean node yields a penalty of e1 (–0.054)=-14.7% units of influence with the box trade on this area).
- The South American Pacific, Indian Ocean, South-East Asia and Far East still prefer the Northern Range European hubs to perform their containerized trade operations, with different significant intensities (coefficients of 0.069, 0.042, 0.069 and 0.025, respectively).

In the South American Atlantic model, there is evidence of high connectivity with respect to European Atlantic Arc hubs that can be seen in the significant 0.118 coefficient. The case of the simple model for the Far East positions, without including the modulation coming from European macro-regions dummy-variables, allows a richer interpretation than in the extended case (although less powerful in terms of ROAD_ACC influence): a joint positive effect both of road connectivity and throughput capacity of the NUTS-3 region can be detected by the common positive influence of the two regressors (0,0003 for ROAD_ACC and 0,028 for throughput). This should be interpreted in terms of the special requirements that the supply lines connecting Europe with China Bohai Bay-South Korea-Japan have: long-standing containerized trade operations in which efficiency in terms of cost effectiveness transcends the traditional regular service patterns.

   Figures 13.8 and 13.9 present the residuals of the simple model for South-East Asia. The main overestimations (negative residuals) can be founded mostly in the core European regions with high accessibility to markets but with a lower share of trade with South-East Asia, either because they are close powerful gateways (ex. Felixtowe in Southern England) or because their foreland mix is highly diversified. That is the case of the top-ranked Antwerp and Bremerhaven, where all forelands are well represented, particularly those of North America and the Caribbean. The underestimations of the model (positive residuals) follow a more complex pattern, partly resulting from historical ties of ports resulting from colonial relationships of the countries involved (i.e. Southampton, Amsterdam) or from hubbing strategies of shipping companies (ie. CMA at Marxalkoxx and Evergreen at Taranto).

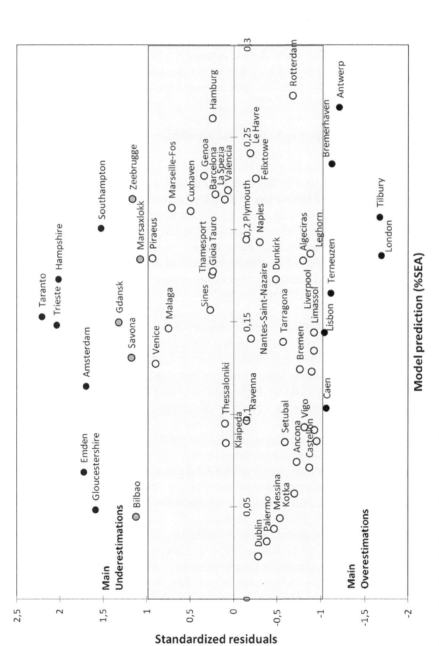

Figure 13.8 Standardized residuals of the Simple Model %SEA=F(Volume, Road Accessibility)

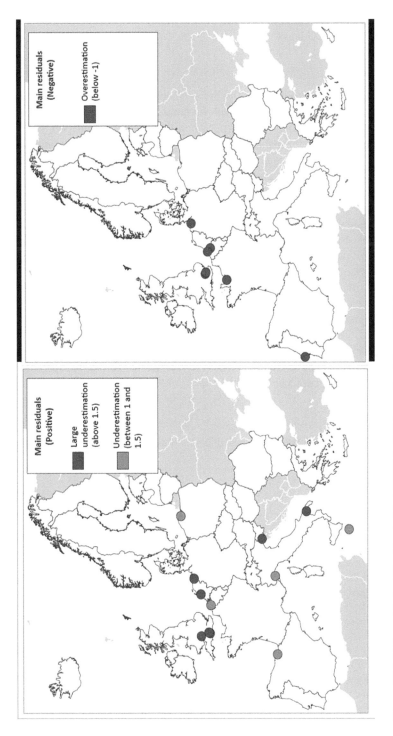

Figure 13.9 Main residuals of the Simple Model %SEA=F(Volume, Road Accessibility)

We also see, to a lesser extent, excess supply in highly industrial peripheral regions, such as Bilbao and Gdansk.

Conclusion

This chapter attempts to measure the linkage between maritime transport supply and inland accessibility in Europe, both for container and general cargo services. The results obtained support the expectation that maritime transport supply is strongly dependent on the demographic size and economic potential of hinterlands. More specifically, the findings here suggest that inland accessibility to population explains 33% of the geographic variations in maritime transport supply for containers. Beyond these global figures it should be noted that the relationship between accessibility and maritime transport supply varies considerably depending on the overseas market served. East and South-East Asia markets seem to be more linked to inland accessibility than the other forelands.

The work provides an accurate GIS methodology for correlating port activity with hinterland flows and opens up a wide field of study, which might be completed in further research, adding port specialization, foreland specific features and other hinterland parameters. It also raises questions about the opportunities for some peripheral regions directly connected to some specific forelands to take advantage of their situation, for example, by choosing suppliers in countries with cheap labor costs. At the same time, however, this option has inherent risks, since sudden changes in the strategies of shipping companies may have repercussions on the entire production network.

Notes

1 NUTS-3 was chosen given the unavailability of hinterland accessibility data at a higher spatial resolution.
2 Feasible due to the statistical properties of the maximum estimator.

References

Amphoux, M. (1949) Les fonctions portuaires. *Revue de La Porte Océane*, 5(54): 19–22.
Amphoux, M. (1951) Géographie portuaire et économie portuaire. *Revue de La Porte Océane*, 7(70): 5–8.
Boerman, W.E. (1951) The need for special examination of particular aspects of port geography. *Tijdschrift voor Economische en Sociale Geografie*, 42: 307–319.
Chapelon, L. (2006) L'accessibilité, marqueur des inégalités de rayonnement des villes portuaires en Europe. *Cybergeo: European Journal of Geography*, 345. Available at: http://cybergeo.revues.org/2463
Ducruet, C., Van Der Horst, M.R. (2009) Transport integration at European ports. *European Journal of Transport and Infrastructure Research*, 9(2): 121–142.
ESPON. (2009) *Territorial Dynamics in Europe: Trends in Accessibility*. Territorial Observation No. 2.
Fleming, D.K., Hayuth, Y. (1994) Spatial characteristics of transportation hubs: Centrality and intermediacy. *Journal of Transport Geography*, 2(1): 3–18.

Franc, P., Van der Horst, M.R. (2010) Understanding hinterland service integration by shipping lines and terminal operators: A theoretical and empirical analysis. *Journal of Transport Geography*, 18(4): 557–566.

González-Laxe, F., Freire Seoane, M.J., Pais Montes, C. (2012) Maritime degree, centrality and vulnerability: Port hierarchies and emerging areas in containerized transport (2008–2010). *Journal of Transport Geography*, 24: 33–44.

Guerrero, D. (2014) Deep-sea hinterlands: Some empirical evidence of the spatial impact of containerization. *Journal of Transport Geography*, 35: 84–94.

Guerrero, D., Laxe, F.G., Freire-Seoane, M.J., Pais Montes, C. (2015) A geographical analysis of the relationship between inland accessibility and maritime transport supply. *Région et Développement*, 41: 33–46.

Guerrero, D., Rodrigue, J.P. (2014) The waves of containerization: Shifts in global maritime transportation. *Journal of Transport Geography*, 34: 151–164.

Hall, P.V., Jacobs, W. (2010) Shifting proximities: The maritime ports sector in an era of global supply chains. *Regional Studies*, 44(9): 1103–1115.

Harati-Mokhtari, A., Wall, A., Brooks, P., Jin, W. (2007) Automatic identification system AIS: Data reliability and human error implications. *The Journal of Navigation*, 60: 373–389.

Kaluza, P., Kölzsch, A., Gastner, M.T., Blasius, B. (2010) The complex network of global cargo ship movements. *Journal of the Royal Society Interface*, 7(48): 1093–1103.

Notteboom, T.E. (2010) Concentration and the formation of multi-port gateway regions in the European container port system: An update. *Journal of Transport Geography*, 18(4): 567–583.

Robinson R. (2002) Ports as elements in value-driven chain systems: the new paradigm. *Maritime Policy and Management*, 29(3): 241–255.

Spiekermann, K., Schürmann, C., Brockmann, M., Heidenreich, C. (2007) *Update of Selected Potential Accessibility Indicators*. Final Report, European Spatial Planning Observatory Network.

Vigarié, A. (1964) *Les Grands Ports de Commerce de la Seine au Rhin: leur Evolution devant l'Industrialisation des Arrière-Pays*. Paris: Sabri.

Weigend, G.G. (1956) The problem of hinterland and foreland as illustrated by the port of Hamburg. *Economic Geography*, 32(1): 1–16.

Wilmsmeier, G., Hoffmann, J. (2008) Liner shipping connectivity and port infrastructure as determinants of freight rates in the Caribbean. *Maritime Economics and Logistics*, 10(1–2): 130–151.

Zohil, J., Prijon, M. (1999) The MED rule: The interdependence of container throughput and transhipment volumes in the Mediterranean ports. *Maritime Policy and Management*, 26(2): 175–193.

14 The local determinants of interregional shipping flows

César Ducruet, Claudio Ferrari,
Hidekazu Itoh and Alessio Tei

The analysis of the determinants of shipping flows includes a wide array of approaches, which is mainly the focus of transport and maritime economics as well as operations research. The majority of related studies take the firm as the core unit of analysis, trying to unravel the determinants of port selection and shipping network design from a company perspective (Tiwari et al., 2003; Tongzon, 2009), using either quantitative or qualitative methodologies. While "location" is often cited as one of the numerous determinants, space in itself is considered in very basic ways, such as Euclidian or nautical distance between ports as a complementary proxy for time and cost parameters in various models (Wilmsmeier, 2014). This, for example, is the case of numerous studies using the gravity model to explain the intensity and distribution of trade flows among countries and regions of the world, but often overlooking the maritime mode (Guerrero et al., 2015). Another focus on shipping flows mainly describes the topology of the network made of port nodes and their mutual linkages (Ducruet and Itoh, 2015), with reference to general models of networks (see Kaluza et al., 2010), as a means to detect industry-specific influences such as the emergence of hub-and-spokes systems and global transport players in various contexts (McCalla et al., 2004).

Overall, the local, socio-economic background of shipping flows is much neglected in contemporary literature. The role of the local economy in shaping flows has been investigated in the case of port cities and regions (Ducruet and Itoh, 2016), but without a relational or network perspective (see also Chapters 13 and 17 on the relationships between shipping, inland accessibility, and regional development, respectively). Most of the time, scholars preferably look at the economic impacts of ports on local economies (Ng et al., 2014; Bottasso et al., 2014). This chapter thus adopts a different perspective, by raising the question on how the intensity, distribution, specialization, and topology of shipping flows is determined not only by operational but also territorial factors. Its main objective is not to underestimate the role of supply chain actors and their main requirements (i.e. cost, time, performance, reliability, etc.) but to provide a more balanced view on the influence of demand factors on the pattern of global shipping networks. The relational or network perspective with regard to territorial factors implies that not only port nodes and their interlinkages are considered, but their surrounding socio-economic environment, which is barely mentioned in related studies, except for a few where roads networks (Tavasszy et al., 2011) or land use and other territorial features (Nelson, 2008) are added as complementary indicators. Strangely enough, this approach is new and necessitates a number of methodological choices in terms of database construction and variable selection.

First, a global matrix of inter-port vessel movements was constructed for the year 2008 by aggregating the daily flows of most of the world's merchant fleet, based on original shipping data provided by *Lloyd's List Intelligence* for the months of March, June, September, and December. Such vessels were classified under six main categories (i.e. containers, general cargo, liquid bulks, solid bulks, passengers, and vehicles), while their carrying capacity in deadweight tons (DWT) was attributed to every port of call and inter-port link, the total amount of traffic being a product of ship capacity and call frequency. Links between ports can be either direct calls through a one-stop voyage, or indirect calls with intermediary stops in between, along the whole and uninterrupted vessel voyage. In the meantime, port nodes were aggregated with each other at the level of subnational administrative regions in order to work on a broader unit of analysis (the port region). This allowed collecting supplementary data for the year 2008/2009 on socio-economic activities, population, productivity, etc. from various sources ranging from national accounts and transport ministries to broader online databases such as the OECD Territorial Database or Eurostat. Lastly, network-specific indicators were calculated using the TULIP software on port region centrality but also link centrality, as well as other classic indicators on traffic concentration and specialization. Most of the time, regional indicators such as those on employment and regional gross product (RGDP) were transformed into location quotients and the share of national total to take into account the national and global context and also to make local economies comparable using relative rather than absolute figures (see Appendix 14.1 for a full list and description of link variables).

The main novelty of the present analysis is thus to provide a joint analysis of regional and shipping indicators at global level for no less than nearly 300 port regions situated in about 40 developed and developing countries. In addition, and as seen in the following sections, it shifts the focus from node level (port region) to link level (inter-port region), creating new variables that translate similarities or gaps in terms of socio-economic and traffic structure by port region pairs. The remainder of this chapter are organized as follows: the second section deals with port regions as nodes in a global maritime network, where we investigate the degree of affinity between regional specialization and traffic specialization as a first step towards the understanding of the local determinants of shipping flows. The third section adopts a complementary perspective based on the concepts of homophily and assortativity in maritime networks (and, more specifically, in spatial networks), namely how port regions of similar or contrasted profiles connect through certain types of shipping flows. The fourth section gives more importance to the distance parameter, or friction of trades, by applying a gravity model to interregional (long-distance) shipping flows and contrasting the results with observed flows. In the conclusion we discuss the outcomes of this research and its contribution to existing regional and transport studies, while examining possible transfers in terms of decision-making support.

Traffic structure, regional specialization, and port region centrality

In this section we examine the interplay between the socio-economic and traffic variables that characterize network nodes, in our case subnational port regions. A Principal Component Analysis (PCA) was applied to two different global datasets, which mainly differ by number of employment categories; the first dataset comprises 273 regions based on three main economic sectors, while the second includes fewer regions (222), but it details seven economic sectors (agriculture, industry, construction, trade, finance, public, and other services). For each analysis, we retained only the four main load factors (or principal components), which concentrate 54.8% of total variance for the first sample with 25 variables; and 52.2% (as above) for the second sample with 28 variables. Such a result in itself suggests that the sample under study is characterized by heterogeneity; as traffic, network, and local economic indicators have complex relationships, and, accordingly, their explanation can be similarly complicated.

Yet, the analysis based on 273 port regions reveals a number of interesting trends that validate earlier works on port regions (see Ducruet and Itoh, 2016, for a review and empirical test based on port tonnage). As seen in Figure 14.1, the main trend

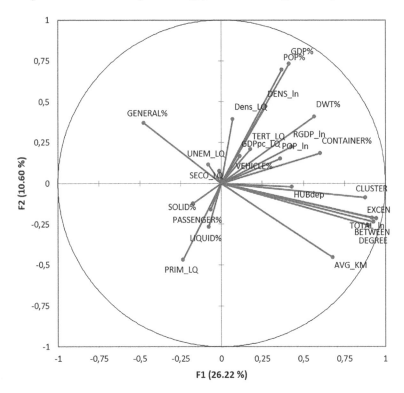

Figure 14.1 Principal Component Analysis of 273 port regions (top) and 222 port regions (bottom)

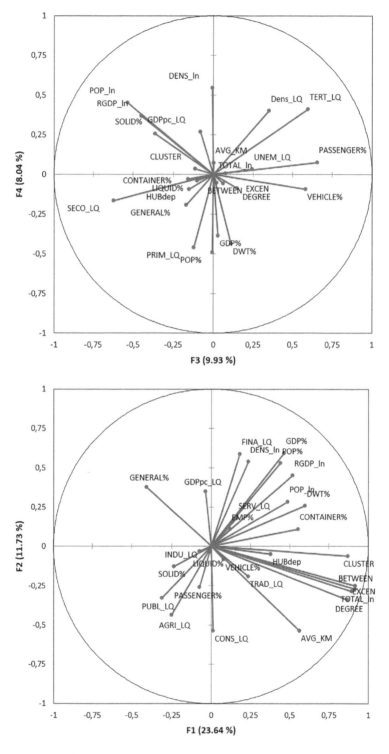

Figure 14.1 (Continued)

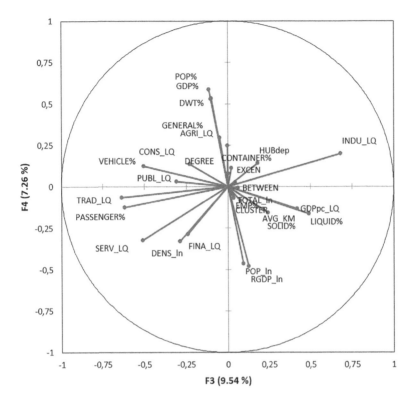

Figure 14.1 (Continued)

(F1) is an opposition between two different types of port regions. Positive scores underline a concomitant importance of traffic volume (DWT), concentration, network centrality, geographic reach, demographic and economic size and concentration, population density, RGDP per capita, with a specialization in the tertiary sector and in container as well as vehicle flows, the most valued commodities. This is the typical profile of bigger and richer port regions with a dominant position in the maritime network and concentrating the majority of maritime flows. Thus, this profile is a combination of mass or size effect (large urban nodes) and specialization effect (high-valued cargo, economic productivity, and prosperity). The opposite profile is characterized by a combined specialization in solid bulks, general cargoes in the primary sector and, to a lesser extent, in liquid bulks and passenger traffic in the secondary sector, with a slightly more pronounced unemployment rate compared with the national average. Such a profile corresponds to regions being more peripheral at national and global scale in terms of size and situation, based on more traditional or labor-intensive activities and less valued cargoes.

The second factor (F2) provides a complementary trend whereby regions specialized in the primary sector can also be very central in the network and have far-reaching spatial connectivity, especially because solid and liquid bulk traffics, unlike liner shipping, are often operated through direct origin-destination and long-distance flows. In turn, the opposite profile (positive F2 score) is specialized in more valuable traffics (general cargo, containers, vehicles) and tends to have a very crucial importance within its national territory in terms of population, productivity, and traffic concentration, with a more tertiary profile, but a lower centrality in the global shipping network and higher unemployment rate. Four types of port regions can thus be defined based on the crossing of the first two components: large urban regions specialized in services and containers/vehicles (top-right quadrant); larger and longer traffic nodes with a strong centrality in the shipping network (bottom right); primary sector regions specialized in bulk traffics (bottom left); and general cargo regions with higher unemployment rates and industrial specializations (top left).

Although it excludes numerous regions situated in developing countries where disaggregated data on employment categories is not available, the analysis of 222 port regions provides additional evidence on such trends. While the main oppositions are very similar to the former analysis, one can observe that the top-right quadrant remains defined by a profile of large urban regions concentrating economic wealth, population, and container traffic, but also and more specifically, financial and insurance activities as well as "other services". These core economic regions are thus also the most advanced in terms of shipping technology and capital-intensive activities. The same opposition occurs with the bottom-left quadrant with port regions specialized in agricultural activities, solid and liquid bulks and passengers, but also public services and manufacturing activities to a lesser extent. Interestingly, centrality indicators remain grouped in the bottom-right quadrant, but together with the specialization in "distributive trade, repairs, transport and accommodation" that concentrates most of the port, logistics and transport-related activities.

A complementary analysis is proposed based on six quantiles applied to selected key indicators to reveal how regional and shipping indicators, which are standardized by the average of each indicator for the comparison between indicators, statistically fit with each other (Figure 14.2). When taking demographic population as the dependent variable, we see that most of the shipping indicators increase in relation to the number of inhabitants from the lower to the higher quantile, especially betweenness centrality that exhibits the widest gaps among quantiles. Thus, again, here more populated regions tend to be more central in the network (betweenness centrality, degree centrality, clustering coefficient) and to exert longer-distance shipping linkages on average. Very similar results were obtained based on RGDP as dependent variable, with the exception of the average kilometric length of shipping linkages, which, albeit fuzzier than those based on population, still exhibit the highest value for richest regions. Overall, the same goes for population density and RGDP per capita taken as location quotients (no figures because of space constraint). This means that not only the port handling itself but its socio-economic and demographic performance regarding the rest of the host country has a clear and noticeable influence on traffic intensity, interaction range,

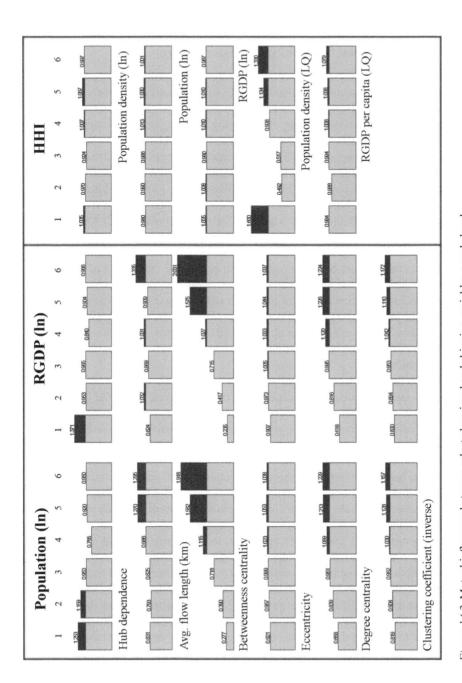

Figure 14.2 Mutual influences between selected regional and shipping variables a node level

and network centrality. In turn, port regions that are more specialized, based on the Herfindahl-Hirschman Index (HHI), or where traffic structure is more concentrated around fewer cargo types, tend to be more populated and richer.

Maritime linkages, homophily, and assortativity

This approach consisted in further understanding how maritime linkages are influenced by the socio-economic characteristics of the connected regions. However, since the unit of analysis becomes the inter-port link itself, it is difficult to conceptualize the territorial embedding of this link in two regions simultaneously. The chosen solution has been to reason in terms of homophily and assortativity, two relatively common approaches in network analysis, in particular social networks for the first and complex networks for the second. Homophily in social networks, notably those that are spatially embedded (Wong et al., 2006), is defined by stronger connectivity probability between nodes sharing certain common features than between contrasted nodes. Assortativity is a parent concept, with a noticeable difference that the same probability is based on the size of nodes. In other words, a network will exhibit assortative mixing when nodes of similar size (i.e. based on degree centrality) are better connected with each other than nodes of dissimilar size, in the latter case the network being more disassortative (Newman, 2002). Empirical studies showed, for instance, that airline networks get more disassortative as the network grows, due to deregulation fostering the emergence of hub-and-spokes configurations (Barrat et al., 2005). In this chapter, both concepts target a better understanding of maritime flows in relation to local socio-economic development.

While the empirical testing of such ideas in a maritime context does not yet exist, it faces a number of conceptual and methodological issues. At conceptual level, it is relatively straightforward to test assortativity since maritime transport, in particular container shipping, adopted similar configurations to airlines in the mid-1990s, namely the establishment of transshipment hub ports at strategic locations. Yet, the whole shipping industry does not follow this network design since it is also based on coastal and short-sea shipping, direct origin-destination flows, such as for bulk shipping, as well as itineraries, such as for cruise shipping, which do not depend on hubs. In terms of homophily, the extent to which similar port regions will be (a) more strongly connected and (b) connected by specific types of flows is not an easy question. In particular, maritime transport had increasingly become one element only of wider value chains (Robinson, 2002), which means that it does not constitute a complete system on its own, if land transport and logistics between the true origins and destinations of flows are not included. Maritime transport is thus a segment connecting regions scattered across the world at different phases of value creation, from raw materials to manufactured goods. This leads us to question the relevance of testing homophily on the sole basis of maritime flows (given that many port regions are transit nodes, not the production or consumption markets, e.g., Ducruet and Itoh, 2016). In addition, our maritime network based on vessel movements is an artifact from which it is difficult to assess whether port regions belonging to the same shipping route truly trade with each other.

Despite such issues, it has been possible to measure in relatively simple ways how homophily and assortativity determine (or not) the topological and spatial distribution of the global maritime network. First, each interregional shipping link is characterized by a number of variables describing its own profile, such as traffic volume, geographic length (orthodromic distance), number of handled commodity types, and HHI for their capacities and various centralities (betweenness, clustering, strength). Second, the territorial embedding of each link is measured by socio-economic differentials among region pairs. One group of such variables is a ratio (i.e. gap index, 1 being completely similar size and 0 being very dissimilar size) between the minimum and the maximum value (i.e. population, RGDP), and another looks at the correlation (Pearson) between the employment structure of the connected regions. Such gaps and correlations thus become attributes of the link itself and are compared with traffic/network variables. Two complementary analyses are proposed, namely a multivariate analysis of combined traffic and socio-economic indicators on links and descriptive statistics based on quantiles.

The PCA is a first approach to test the possibility for global maritime flows to exhibit homophily and assortativity (Figure 14.3). In other words, are similar port regions more connected with each other than dissimilar port regions and through similar or dissimilar types of shipping flows? Given the vast number of links under scrutiny (22,578), our PCA results provided a large number of principal components with an eigenvalue over 1, i.e. fourteen components for all 41 variables included (75.4% of cumulated variance), and eight components for 22 variables excluding certain redundant variables (69.5% of cumulated variance). Our discussion on such results will, however, mainly focus on the first four components, reaching about half of the total cumulated variance in both cases (42.1% for all variables and 47.1% for selected variables), to highlight the main groupings and oppositions at stake. In terms of traffic characteristics, we observed that shipping links carrying bigger traffic volumes (DWTs) are generally more diversified (number of cargo types), with a tendency to specialize in containers, but shorter in terms of kilometric length.

This is in line with former works showing that most of the world's container traffic concentrates over links of 500 kilometers or less (Ducruet and Notteboom, 2012), while container flows are specific in a sense that they present the greatest overlap with other traffic types in the global network, while most diversified links are also shorter (Ducruet, 2013). This explains why such bigger links are less international on average (i.e. more domestic). When it comes to region pairs in terms of traffic, there is a clear assortativity of the network since bigger links preferentially connect port regions of similar traffic weight, commodity diversity, network position (i.e. degree centrality, clustering coefficient on links), and geographic reach. In turn, links of smaller traffic volumes tend to connect more distant regions, to be more specialized (higher HHI), and to have a more crucial position in the network (strength links, betweenness centrality links), with a pronounced specialization in passengers, general cargo, and solid bulk. In terms of homophily

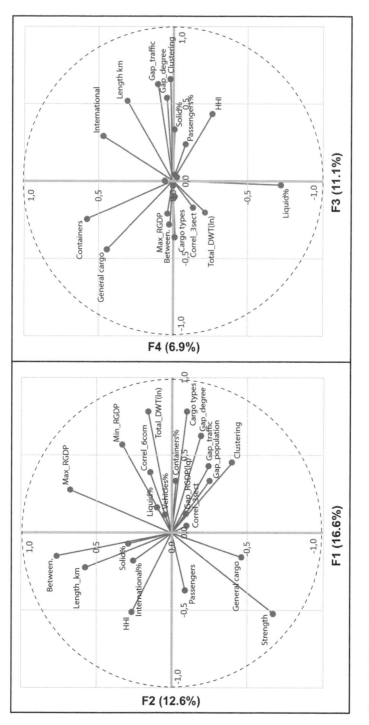

Figure 14.3 Principal Component Analysis of interregional shipping linkages

when focusing on the demographic and socio-economic similarity of connected regions, bigger links tend to concentrate in more productive regions (higher RGDP) as well as between regions of similar demographic size (higher gap index) and economic structure to a lesser extent. These results are meaningful in the sense that they empirically demonstrate that the spatial distribution of the global shipping network is far from being randomly organized. On the contrary, spatial structures greatly influence the intensity and profile of shipping flows, notwithstanding noticeable oppositions between bigger and smaller flows.

A complementary analysis consisted in classifying links according to six quantiles to check the mutual influences between territorial and logistical elements in the network (Figure 14.4, standardized by the average of each indicator for the comparison between indicators). Based on demographic (population) and economic productivity (RGDP) gaps among region pairs, it appeared that connected regions of similar weight share a similar network centrality, as mentioned above, while being connected through less crucial links (i.e. lower betweenness centrality links and strength index), and at the same time more densely connected with their neighbors (clustering coefficient). The gap of hub dependence (vulnerability) is narrower between regions of similar economic weight (RGDP), which is less apparent from a demographic perspective. This means that the economic productivity of connected regions is perhaps a better indicator than population to highlight similarities in network connectivity. Finally, results were compared based on the similarity (Pearson correlation coefficient) between the respective employment structure of port regions, for three and seven economic sectors. In the case of three sectors, connected regions with a similar employment structure (higher quantiles) tend to have a wider gap (lower gap index) in most centrality indicators (i.e. betweenness centrality gap, degree centrality gap, betweenness centrality links) and to be connected through more diversified traffic linkages (i.e. lower HHI). This means that economic differentiation, as a potential complementarity between connected regions, fosters similarity in terms of network performance and specialization in terms of commodity structure. Such results underline that socio-economic homophily is associated with centrality disassortativity, and vice versa. When it comes to seven sectors, results are similar only for the betweenness centrality links, since the opposite is shown for all other gaps and link characteristics. One likely reason is the restricted availability of seven-sector data for regions in developing countries: connected regions in more developed (OECD) countries show a slight tendency to share both homophily and assortativity. In other words, such connected regions are more similar and less complementary to each other. In addition, more specialized links (i.e. higher HHI) connect regions with wider socio-economic and demographic gaps (i.e. lower gap index). Thus, more diversified links (i.e. lower HHI) are found between regions of similar size and productivity (higher gap index). These trends confirm previous research showing that the most diversified maritime links actually concentrated between port cities with similar total port traffic size (Ducruet, 2013). In this analysis, diversified links are also seen to concentrate between demographically and economically similar regions.

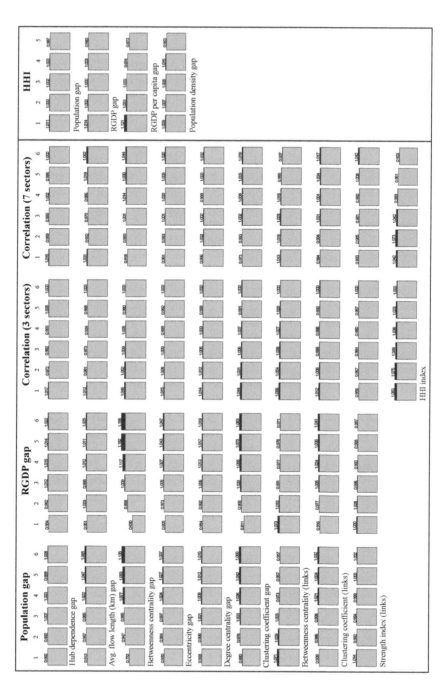

Figure 14.4 Mutual influences between selected regional and shipping variables at link level

Gravity model

Maritime networks are driven by forces related to connectivity between ports (i.e. the nodes). As noted by Lam and Yap (2011), shipping networks interconnect different kinds of ports, while the role of these ports within the network also affects their competitive position within global supply chains. On the other hand, maritime network development prioritizes main nodes, creating a hierarchy that influences port competitiveness and its role in respect of the main shipping routes, and additionally serving major hinterlands (e.g., Ducruet et al., 2010). This scenario is connected with the possibility of studying maritime flows as driven by the port traffic volume, in which main distribution nodes (i.e. hubs) can have an advantage in comparison with minor nodes (i.e. minor ports, or satellites on the network). Moreover, the presence of frictions (e.g., transport and logistics costs) that differ in relation to both "distance" and "specific route" issues is also a characteristic of the current maritime network. The spatial interaction –within a given network– between nodes that partially compete through their traffic volume and different costs depending on network design naturally calls for the use of a spatial interaction model, such as gravity.

Gravity models are a specific kind of spatial interaction analysis in which the flow between two "nodes" –and the related network– carries "hidden costs" (i.e. frictions) that affect flow distribution with respect to an ideal or optimal scenario. Gravity models are often used in regional economics (e.g., Karemera et al., 2010; Burger et al., 2009) and related disciplines (e.g., Khadarooa and Seetanah, 2008), with several applications in transportation science (e.g., Simini et al., 2012; Anas, 1983). Concerning maritime studies, gravity models were applied to hinterland flows connecting specific ports (e.g., Ferrari et al., 2011; Guerrero, 2014).

As suggested by Haynes and Fotheringham (1984), a general gravity model appears as:

$$T_{ij} = A_i \, O_i \, D_j \, B_j \, (d_{ij}) \tag{1}$$

in which T equals the "interactions (i.e., maritime traffic volume)" between regions i and j; O and D are the "production" and "destination" flows; while A and B are "balancing constraints" for the origin or the destination, respectively. If A and B are used simultaneously, the gravity model is called "doubly" constrained, while if only one of them is used the model can be "production" (in the case of A) or "destination" (in the case of B) constrained.

In general terms, where: $A_i = [\Sigma_j \, B_j \, D_j \, f(d_{ij})]^{-1}$ $\tag{2}$

$$B_i = [\Sigma_i \, A_i \, O_i \, f(d_{ij})]^{-1} \tag{3}$$

A and B should be solved interactively in order to identify the constraints related to the in- and out-flows of origin and destination. (d_{ij}) represents the effect of the physical distance between regions in the spatial interaction. Often $f(d_{ij}) = (d_{ij})^\beta$ where β shows the sensitivity to the distance of the studied variables and the effect of potential frictions. In our case, Euclidian distance has been used between port regions attracting different kind of cargoes. This choice is linked to the main differences in the organization of the shipping services that is actually affecting the shipping distance (e.g., transshipment, not direct call services).

In order to evaluate spatial interaction between the maritime regions, SIMODEL software has been used. This software allows the estimation of the gravity model, comparing the actual T_{ij} and the predicted T'_{ij}. As said, the application of either A or B (or both) changes the model; in particular, when both are applied, traffic between each node is kept constant, whereas if only one is applied, the traffic generated by each origin remains constant both in the observed (T_{ij}) and the predicted (T'_{ij}) matrix, while the traffic attracted by each destination is redistributed among them.

In order to solve the model, a hypothesis on the $f(d_{ij})$ is necessary; in accordance with main literature (e.g., Ferrari et al., 2011), we used a power function equal to (d_{ij}^{β}). In such a model, the parameter β represents the "probability" for the estimating values to be equal to the real value, therefore, representing the relation between the distance and the "generalised costs" (i.e. frictions that affect the model) that impact in the development of the network. Since distance should have a decay effect, the parameter β is expected to be negative. Moreover, $\beta < -1$ means costs have an effect more than proportional in respect to distance, while if $-1 < \beta < 0$ costs are less proportional than distance. When β is equal to zero there are no frictions and the distribution has no connections with the distance. Another interesting outcome is the standard deviation (e) that represents a goodness of fit in the model. Moreover, the standard deviation also provides information on the redistribution among the regions of total traffic and containers only (TEU).

The analysis targets the NUTS-2 regions belonging to our database, representing the maritime network. The main results provide a comparison of NUTS-2 interactions along three main shipping routes (e.g. Transpacific, Transatlantic, and Far East-Europe) for the discussion on long-distance trade excluding short-sea and coastal shipping. In fact, the gravity model only takes into account the regions belonging to the above listed route, as representative examples of the differences within the current maritime network. Table 14.1 shows the results of the analyses for the production model and the doubly constrained model.

Table 14.1 Gravity model results

Production constraints model			
TOTAL	EU-Far East	Transpacific	Transatlantic
B	−0.44	−0.36	−0.50
(e)	65%	58%	81%
Container (TEU)	EU-ASIA	ASIA-AM	EU-AM
B	−0.34	−0.30	−0.37
(e)	52%	52%	63%
Doubly constrained model			
TOTAL	EU-Far East	Transpacific	Transatlantic
B	−0.48	−0.39	−0.53
Container (TEU)	EU-ASIA	ASIA-AM	EU-AM
B	−0.40	−0.33	−0.40

The analysis underlines how "frictions" act differently among the main trade routes while distance impacts on the distribution of commercial flows. Moreover, the standard deviation (e) – that is, a proxy for the degree of redistribution– is higher in the transatlantic matrix in comparison with the other routes, demonstrating a difference between predicted and observed values. In particular, higher values of both β and e for the Europe-America routes can be explained by a different traffic organization (e.g., fewer main nodes and different use of transshipment) in respect to the other two main routes, or including Asian trade.

Moreover, the high value of the standard deviation highlights a great difference among predicted and observed values. This issue underlines how some regions are able to attract more than what they might be, generating agglomeration effects at port regions. In general, Asian and American regions seem to have a better distribution pattern than European ones. Figure 14.5, for instance, compares the results related to the trade routes of American and European regions. In the figure, the axes represent the difference between the expected and real values of the studied routes per region (i.e. the European graph represents the differences characterising the European-Asia routes and European-Americas route). The fact that the majority of the regions are more or less concentrated around the origin means that expected and actual values do not differ too much (even if differences can be underlined). Thus, outliers in both graphs have specific explanations depending on the quarter to which they belong. For instance, ES70 (i.e. Canary Islands) and ES61 (i.e. Andalusia), representing two outliers located on the first quarter of "Europe", demonstrate an unexpected flow from/

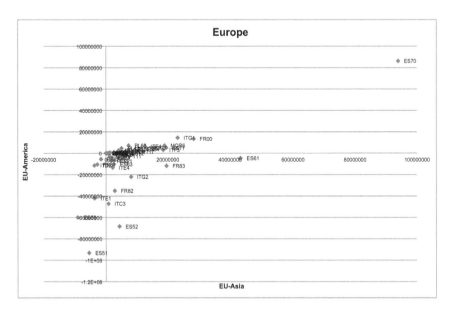

Figure 14.5 Position of port regions by observed/estimated traffic volume along selected major shipping routes

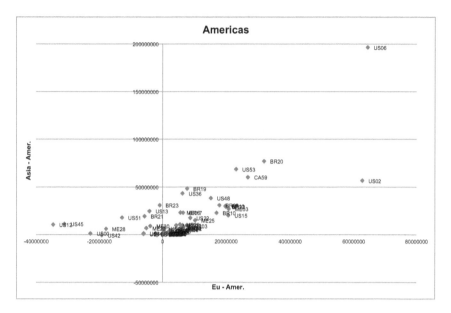

Figure 14.5 (Continued)

to these regions in both the EU-Asia and transatlantic routes. Similarly, there is an imbalance situation in the ES52 (i.e. the Community of Valencia) outlier belonging to the fourth quarter of the same graph, but only for the EU-Asia route, while it has a negative difference in the transatlantic route. These outliers are often related to big hub ports (e.g., Algeciras, Valencia) that provoke a distortion to the "estimated" connections, deviating flows that would otherwise be "naturally" and more directly reaching other regions. Similar cases occur in the "Americas" graph, with regions hosting port hubs (e.g., California, South Carolina, and Florida) that became regional pivotal nodes. Interestingly, among the outliers there are also some few regions that register either heavy underperforming (e.g., Balearic Islands) or over-performing values (e.g., Alaska), not for structural reasons but for demographical and market specialization (e.g., bulk and cruise) characteristics. Nevertheless, Figure 14.5 demonstrates how the shipping network reflects not only distance effects but also organizational effects (e.g., transshipment) that promote both scale and scope economies to overcome the distance factor.

Conclusion

This chapter underlines how contemporary maritime flows remain very much linked to the economic structure of the regions that they help to interconnect, contributing to existing literature on the impact of the local economy of port regions and maritime flows, an area so far insufficiently researched. Preliminary findings from current research underline how it is possible through the study of maritime networks to differentiate regions according to their role within the network and with their economic characteristics. The PCA – and related analyses – showed how regional centrality in respect to specific traffic flows (e.g., liquid bulk, container, general cargo) depends on the regional environment (e.g., population, sectoral specialization, economic productivity), demonstrating how the international transport network is still shaped by local strategies and policies. Moreover, links carrying bigger traffic volumes are generally more diversified (in terms of lower HHI), with a tendency to specialize in containerized cargo, but shorter in terms of kilometric length. On the other hand, the gravity model showed that the main commercial routes are differently affected by distance- and transport-related costs. These findings showed how the different organization on main routes is still affecting main trade volumes among different world regions. The differences between real and expected values estimated by the gravity model also underline an unbalanced situation among the flows that is not fully explained by distance and is principally due to specialization and agglomeration effects (especially in the container business) in the port regions and in their neighboring regions too.

Moreover, even if the assumption related to distance (i.e. Euclidian distance) seems quite reasonable considering the differences between various maritime transport sectors, further research could improve the overall findings of the gravity model. In fact, nautical distance is only partially representative for all those kinds of traffic that do not use direct calls (e.g., containers) or, generally speaking, do not load/unload completely at every port of call (e.g., general cargo, passengers). As a matter of fact, the complexity of the freight distribution – and the related network – leads to a low representation of the connectivity using simple nautical distance within the region, and for this reason, Euclidean distance has been chosen. Nevertheless, further investigations could try to overcome this issue, differentiating the distance used for different kinds of services (e.g., container, bulk).

Thus, even if further research needs to be done, the findings of this chapter shed new light on the understanding of maritime network development and characteristics. Eventually, as potential extensions of the current research, one could further differentiate the effects among different traffic categories in order to identify specific patterns that characterize the different shipping markets and their network development.

Acknowledgements

The authors would like to thank Ali El Hosni for his help with the database construction. The research leading to these results has received funding from the European Research Council under the European Union's Seventh Framework Programme (FP/2007–2013) / ERC Grant Agreement n. [313847] "World Seastems".

Appendix 14.1 List of indicators retained in this study

Variable type	Variable name	Definition
Node characteristics	POP_ln	Natural log of total port region population, gross domestic product, population density, and vessel traffic
	RGDP_ln	
	DENS_ln	
	LN_DWT	
	POP%	Share of port region's population, RGDP or vessel traffic in host country total
	RGDP%	
	DWT%	
	RGDP_pc_LQ	Location quotient of RGDP per capita, population density, unemployment, primary, secondary, and tertiary sectors
	DENS_LQ	
	UNEM_LQ	
	PRIM_LQ	
	SECO_LQ	
	TERT_LQ	
	Clustering	Clustering coefficient or "hub power"
	Eccentricity	Topological proximity to other nodes
	Hub dependence	Share of the largest flow link in total traffic
	Degree	Number of adjacent neighbor nodes
	Betweenness	Occurrences on shortest paths
	Avg_km	Average kilometric distance of shipping linkages
Link characteristics	INTERNATIONAL	Dummy for domestic (0) or international (1) links
	CONTAINER	% of this commodity in total link traffic (%dwt)
	GENERAL	
	LIQUID	
	PASSENGER	
	SOLID	
	VEHICLE	
	LN_DWT	Natural log of total link traffic
	LN_DIST	Natural log of link's kilometric distance
	NB_COM	No. commodity types carried
	CC	Clustering coefficient
	STRENGTH	Strengh index
Differentials among region pairs	COR_3SECT%	Correlation coefficient between respective employment shares (%), absolute scores (ABS) or location quotients (LQ) based on 3 or 7 economic sectors
	COR_3SECT_LQ	
	COR_7SECT_ABS	
	COR_7SECT_LQ	
	COR_6COM%	Correlation coefficient between respective traffic distribution (%) based on 6 commodity types
	GAP_POP	minimum score / maximum score among the 2 regions
	GAP_RGDP	
	GAP_DWT	
	GAP_HUBDEP	
	GAP_AVGKM	
	GAP_BETW	
	GAP_CC	
	GAP_EXCENT	
	GAP_DEGREE	

References

Anas, A. (1983) Discrete choice theory, information theory and the multinomial logit and gravity models. *Transportation Research Part B*, 17(1): 13–23.

Barrat, A., Barthélemy, M., Vespignani, A. (2005) The effects of spatial constraints on the evolution of weighted complex networks. *Journal of Statistical Mechanics*, 5: P05003.

Bottasso, A., Conti, M., Ferrari, C., Tei, A. (2014) Ports and regional development: A spatial analysis on a panel of European regions. *Transportation Research Part A*, 65: 44–55.

Burger, M., van Oort, F., Linders, G.J. (2009) On the specification of the gravity model of trade: Zeros, excess zeros and zero-inflated estimation. *Spatial Economic Analysis*, 4: 167–190.

Ducruet, C. (2013) Network diversity and maritime flows. *Journal of Transport Geography*, 30: 77–88.

Ducruet, C., Itoh, H. (2015) The mutual specialization of port regions connected by multiple commodity flows in a maritime network. In: Ducruet, C. (Ed.), *Maritime Networks: Spatial Structures and Time Dynamics*. London and New York: Routledge Studies in Transport Analysis, pp. 285–302.

Ducruet, C., Itoh, H. (2016) Regions and material flows: Investigating the regional branching and industry relatedness of port traffic in a global perspective. *Journal of Economic Geography*, 16(4): 805–830.

Ducruet, C., Lee, S.W., Ng, A.K.Y. (2010) Centrality and vulnerability in liner shipping networks: Revisiting the Northeast Asian port hierarchy. *Maritime Policy and Management*, 37(1): 17–36.

Ducruet, C., Notteboom, T.E. (2012) The worldwide maritime network of container shipping: Spatial structure and regional dynamics. *Global Networks*, 12(3): 395–423.

Ferrari, C., Parola, F., Gattorna, E. (2011) Measuring the quality of port hinterland accessibility: The Ligurian case. *Transport Policy*, 18: 382–391.

Guerrero, D. (2014) Deep-sea hinterlands: Some empirical evidence of the spatial impact of containerization. *Journal of Transport Geography*, 35: 84–94.

Guerrero, D., Grasland, C., Ducruet, C. (2015) Explaining international trade flows with shipping-based distances. In: Ducruet, C. (Ed.), *Maritime Networks: Spatial Structures and Time Dynamics*. London and New York: Routledge Studies in Transport Analysis, pp. 303–321.

Haynes, K.E., Fotheringham, A.S. (1984) *Gravity and Spatial Interaction Models*. Beverly Hills: Sage Publications.

Kaluza, P., Kölzsch, A., Gastner, M.T., Blasius, B. (2010) The complex network of global cargo ship movements. *Journal of the Royal Society Interface*, 7(48): 1093–1103.

Karemera, D., Oguledo, V.I., Davis, B. (2010) A gravity model analysis of international migration to North America. *Applied Economics*, 32: 1745–1755.

Khadarooa, J., Seetanah, B. (2008) The role of transport infrastructure in international tourism development: A gravity model approach. *Tourism Management*, 29: 831–840.

Lam, J.S.L., Yap, W.Y. (2011) Dynamics of liner shipping network and port connectivity in supply chain systems: Analysis on East Asia. *Journal of Transport Geography*, 19: 1272–1281.

McCalla, R.J., Slack, B., Comtois, C. (2004) The geographical hierarchy of container shipping networks in the Caribbean basin and Mediterranean Sea. In: Paper presented at the *10th World Conference on Transport Research (WCTR)*, Istanbul, July 4–8.

Nelson, A. (2008) *Travel Time to Major Cities: A Global Map of Accessibility*. Global Environment Monitoring Unit, Joint Research Centre of the European Commission, Ispra, Italy.

Newman, M.E.J. (2002) Assortative mixing in networks. *Physical Review Letters*, 89: 208701.

Ng, A.K.Y., Ducruet, C., Jacobs, W., Monios, J., Notteboom, T.E., Rodrigue, J.P., Slack, B., Tam, K.C., Wilmsmeier, G. (2014) Port geography at the crossroads with human geography: Between flows and spaces. *Journal of Transport Geography*, 41: 84–96.

Robinson, R. (2002) Ports as elements in value-driven chain systems: The new paradigm. *Maritime Policy and Management*, 29(3): 241–255.

Simini, F., González, M.C., Maritan, A., Barabási, A.L. (2012) A universal model for mobility and migration patterns. *Nature*, 484: 96–100.

Tavasszy, L.A., Minderhoud, M., Perrin, J.F., Notteboom, T.E. (2011) A strategic network choice model for global container flows: Specification estimation and application. *Journal of Transport Geography*, 19(6): 1163–1172.

Tiwari, P., Itoh, H., Doi, M. (2003) Shippers' port and carrier selection behaviour in China: A discrete choice analysis. *Maritime Economics and Logistics*, 5(1): 23–39.

Tongzon, J.L. (2009) Port choice and freight forwarders. *Transportation Research Part E*, 45: 186–195.

Wilmsmeier, G. (2014) *International Maritime Transport Costs: Market Structures and Network Configurations*. Aldershot: Ashgate.

Wong, L.H., Pattison, P., Robins, G. (2006) A spatial model for social networks. *Physica A*, 360: 99–120.

15 Identifying small-scale fishing zones in France using AIS data

Damien Le Guyader, Cyril Ray
and David Brosset

Estimates of the spatial distribution and intensity of fishing activities are necessary to provide relevant information for natural resources management, impact assessment and maritime spatial planning. However, there is a need for a multi-scale approach, and access to high-resolution information is challenging, especially for small-scale fisheries (Breen et al., 2015).

Since the European Union (EU) adopted the Vessel Monitoring Systems (VMS) to monitor fishing vessels, significant advances have been made in that domain (e.g., Russo et al., 2014; Hintzen et al., 2012). However, VMS data has some limitations. Small vessels (<12 m) are not included, and VMS data analyses are usually conducted at spatial resolutions ranging from 1–10 km because of the low reporting rate. In addition, due to confidentiality and commercial sensitivity, access to raw VMS data is restricted (Lee et al., 2010), which hampers the use of VMS data studies and publications (Hinz et al., 2013).

In recent years, the Automatic Identification System (AIS), which was initially intended to improve ship safety and transmits at high frequencies, has provided a valuable source of information for the analyses of the spatial and temporal distributions of human activities at multiple scales (Shelmerdine, 2015). The AIS has been mandated by the International Maritime Organization (IMO) through the Safety of Life at Sea Convention (SOLAS) since 2002. The archived AIS data are relatively easy to access, which, combined with the growing worldwide coverage, has recently opened up research opportunities for mapping fishing activities at global (Souza et al., 2016), European (Natale et al., 2015) and regional scales (McCauley et al., 2016). All these studies describe fishing activity by gear type (see also Chapter 11 on the use of AIS data for spatial analysis).

Regardless of the data sources system (VMS/AIS), estimates of the spatial distribution and intensity of commercial fishing generally follow four methodological steps: (i) they enrich data with qualitative information on the fishing activity (specifying gear type or métier); (ii) they infer whether a ship is engaged in fishing activity; (iii) they identify fishing grounds and (iv) they estimate the fishing intensity within those grounds.

Neither the AIS nor VMS data contained information on the types of fishing activities in which vessels are engaged; instead, gear type and métier identification for each fishing trip was determined by linking to logbook data using dates and vessel identifiers (Russo et al., 2011). Logbook records describe daily catch weight by species, gear type employed and effort. Catch locations are recorded in ICES statistical rectangles consisting of a grid of 0.5° latitude by 1° longitude.

Because positional reports are not explicitly associated with a specific activity pattern, the use of VMS or AIS data to identify fishing grounds and intensity depends on the ability to distinguish between fishing and non-fishing activities (e.g., steaming vs. stationary). A ship's speed is generally used to determine the fishing action (Mills et al., 2007). Other methods rely on multivariate analysis of speed, deviation angle, trajectory tortuosity (Enguehard et al., 2013) or on data mining and machine learning approaches (Gloaguen et al., 2015; Joo et al., 2013) to improve the detection of fishing positions.

According to Russo et al., (2013), the term "fishing ground" is widely used in literature, but no precise and commonly accepted definition exists for identifying these entities. In this article, we assume that fishing grounds correspond to the spatial extent of high ship density sub-trajectories when they are in a fishing state. Recently, Natale et al. (2015) used the notion of utility distribution based on kernel density estimators (Silverman, 1986), which place a decay probability function at each observed location and sum these up into a surface. However, one of the problems with standard kernel density estimators is that they rarely consider the temporal dimension and sequentiality of points in a trajectory (Demšar et al., 2015).

This research focuses on AIS data processing to estimate the spatial distribution and intensity of dredging métiers (i.e., the association of a fishing gear type with a target species) with high spatial resolution. In response to a request made by local fishermen, an experiment was conducted in the Bay of Brest. Located on the westernmost tip of Brittany, France (Figure 15.1), the Bay of Brest is a maritime basin of approximately 180 km2 where diverse human maritime activities occur (Gourmelon et al., 2014), including commercial fishing dredges. This fleet, composed of approximately 60 vessels, targets four main species: the great scallop (Pecten maximus), the warty venus (Venus verrucosa), the variegated scallop (Mimachlamys varia) and the flat oyster (Ostrea edulis). Commercial bivalve mollusc resources in the Bay of Brest are managed through specific spatial and temporal regulations, associated since 1983 with a program managed by the Tinduff hatchery together with a committee of local fishermen that produces juvenile crustaceans. Moreover, fishing vessels must own an annual fishing license for bivalve molluscs and must be equipped with an AIS transponder. In addition to resources management and optimization issues, knowledge of the spatial and temporal distribution of dredging activities is essential because of its potential impact on marine habitats of community interest (Directive 92/43/EEC) such as maerl beds.

The remainder of the chapter is organized as follows: the next section develops the material and methods, before presenting the main results of the data analyses applied to our case study. Finally, the last section discusses the main findings and limitations and outlines further work.

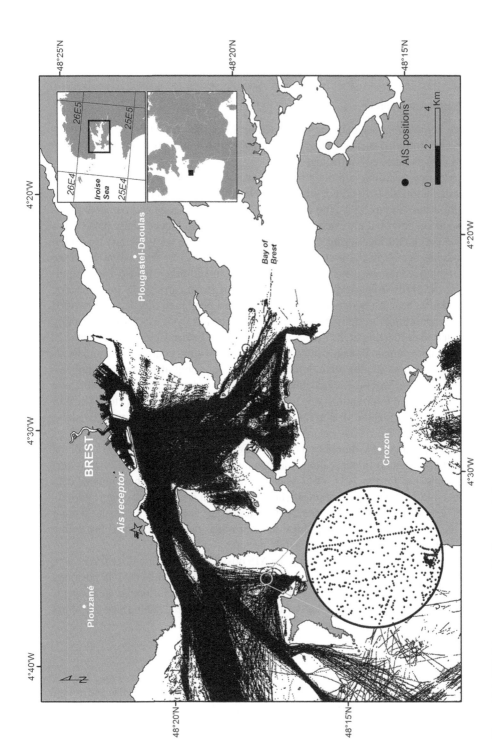

Figure 15.1 AIS data coverage used in the case study

Material and methods

In this section, we first present the datasets and then detail the three-step method used to map fishing grounds and evaluate fishing intensity.

Datasets description

Five complementary datasets were used in this study: raw AIS positions, commercial landings, auction prices and regulatory data concerning fishing calendars and vessels licensed for fishing.

AIS raw positions provided by the Naval Academy Research Institute were available for 2011–2012, but only those related to the location of the AIS receiver in Plouzané (Figure 15.1); therefore, the AIS spatial coverage was partial and corresponded only to the western part of the Bay of Brest. Indeed, these data limitations precluded identifying the fishing grounds for the warty venus, for which dredging occurs in the eastern part of the bay. However, this spatial coverage encompassed the great scallop fishing grounds. In addition, because it is compulsory, the entire dragged gear fleet in the Bay of Brest carries AIS transponders. Therefore, because both previous conditions had been met, this dataset provided a rare opportunity to study the potential of AIS data analysis as a proxy for fishing ground identification at the métier level for vessels below 12 meters in length.

AIS data contain dynamic information (ships position, course, speed and heading at each time stamp), static information (a unique ship identification number – the Maritime Mobile Service Identity (MMSI) – name, length, breadth) and voyage-related information (ship's status, estimated time of arrival etc.). The AIS positional data include all ship categories (cargo ships, tankers, passengers, fishing vessels and so on).

The Landings table describes the daily weights of nominal landings (in kg) of the four target species (great scallop, warty venus, variegated scallop and flat oyster) for each ship for the 2011–2012 season. The Auction prices table contains data concerning the daily auction prices (in €/kg) for each species for the same period.

The Fishing calendar provides the dates and hours authorized for dredge fishing in the Bay of Brest, while the Ships' table provides the name of each ship with a valid dredging license during the study period.

The first step involved scrubbing the AIS positional data using three filters. The AIS positions located on land were removed (spatial filter), while the AIS positions corresponding to fishing ships with a valid fishing license for dredge gear operations in the Bay of Brest (qualitative filter) during authorized fishing date and hours (temporal filter) were conserved.

Method

The method, conducted in three chronological steps, aims to: (i) identify and assign daily métiers for each fishing trip; (ii) differentiate between fishing and non-fishing activities and (iii) identify fishing grounds and estimate the fishing intensities.

The data were stored in a Postgres PostGIS database. The analyses were conducted with R software using three successive algorithms corresponding to each step.

The métier identification was based on the landings reported for each vessel and for each day. Unique-species landings represented more than 80% of the total landings. In such cases, the daily métier can be easily identified through the combination of dredge gear and the unique species. For multi-species landings, homogeneous classes of fishing trips are identified using an Agglomerative Hierarchical Clustering (AHC) and analysis was conducted using the species composition of the landings and auction prices. Assuming that fishermen aim to maximize revenue rather than landing volume, species composition was expressed as a percentage of the total monetary value of each landing based on auction prices. Due to wide variances in auction prices during a fishing season, daily auction prices were used instead of mean prices. First, we used logbook data that specify the weight landed (W) for each boat (value B_i, for i from 1 to 61); for each species (value S_j, for j from 1 to 4) and for each day of the fishing season (value D_k, for k from 1 to 84). Second, we used auction prices (value A) given the species (S_j) and the day (D_k). Then, the relative percentage of the total monetary value of each landing for one species (P_{B_i,S_j,D_k}) is given in Equation 1:

$$P_{B_i,S_j,D_k} = \frac{W_{B_i,S_j,D_k} \times A_{S_j,D_k}}{\sum_{k=1}^{n} W_{B_i,S_j,D_k} \times A_{S_j,D_k}} \times 100 \tag{1}$$

The dissimilarity matrix between landings was calculated given the Euclidean distance of P_{B_i,S_j,D_k}. The hierarchical classification of groups was based on Ward's method (1963). The number of classes is selected automatically to explain up to 95% of the total inertia. The resulting classes contain homogeneous but different values of P_{B_i,S_j,D_k}. Therefore, the mean value of P_{B_i,S_j,D_k} (value $\bar{P}_{B_i,S_j,D_k}$) was calculated for each class. To select unambiguous classes (classes containing a clear representation of a target species), we retained only those classes where $\bar{P}_{B_i,S_j,D_k} > 80\%$. Finally, the linkage between identified daily métier and AIS positions was carried out using the MMSI and Date fields as keys.

The differentiation between fishing and non-fishing activity was estimated from the distribution of a vessel's speeds. Previous analysis from trips with on-board observers (Mills et al., 2007) showed that the speed density profile for trawlers consists of a multi-modal composition that can be related to discrete behavioral states. The speed density profile can be decomposed into three modes (low-speed peak, medium-speed peak and high-speed peak) associated respectively, with near-stationary or embarking behaviors, fishing behaviors and steaming behaviors (Bastardie et al., 2010). Assuming that the relationship between the speed density profile and behavior (fishing/steaming) is similar for dredgers, the lower and upper bounds of fishing speed for each métier were identified using a density estimation and then classified via a finite mixture model (Fraley and Raftery, 2002). No assumption was made concerning the model and number of components that best fit the data. The "optimal" model was identified in order to maximize the Bayesian

Information Criterion (BIC) and the "optimal" number of components was selected based on maximizing the Normalized Difference in Entropy index (Baudry et al., 2010). Second, these parameters were used to decompose the speed profile with an EM initialized by hierarchical clustering for parameterized Gaussian mixture models. Third, the resulting mixture model was projected to the speed profile to identify the cluster that best fits with medium-speed peak values. Finally, as the lower and upper fishing speed bounds for each métier were known, the AIS positions were assigned using a supplementary variable notated as "fishing" and coded with Boolean attributes (0: likely steaming, 1: likely fishing).

The identification of fishing grounds from our data presupposes a spatial aggregation of likely fishing positions, using AIS positional data. First, the existence of spatial aggregates of fishing positions not resulting from a random distribution was tested using a spatial Kolmogorov-Smirnov test. Second, in the case of spatial aggregation, fishing segments corresponding to at least three time-consecutive fishing positions were computed. Third, assuming that fishing grounds correspond to a higher density of fishing activity, we computed the kernel density of fishing segments for different time windows (daily, monthly and seasonal). Here, the segment Kernel Density Estimation (KDE) was preferable because traditional point-based bivariate KDE does not take the temporal dimension or sequentiality of points in trajectories into account (Steiniger and Hunter, 2013) (Figure 15.2). Grid size (g) and the smoothing factor (h) were calculated using non-parametric estimates: (g) was determined by the 90*th* percentile of the distance between nearest-neighbor AIS positions ($k = 2$), and (h) was estimated using the Least-Square

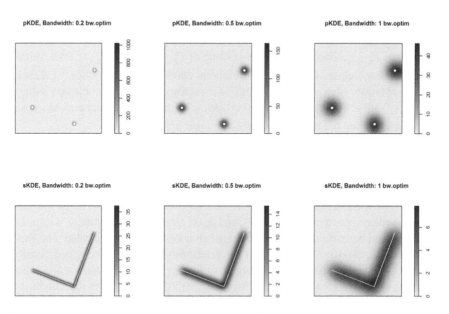

Figure 15.2 Differences between point Kernel Density Estimation (pKDE) and segment Kernel Density Estimation (sKDE) with varying bandwidths

Cross-Validation (LSCV) algorithm. Delimitation of the fishing grounds was performed by the extraction of the 95*th* percentile of the kernel density of fishing segments. This threshold, set *a priori*, is usually used to define the home range of mobile animals (Powell, 2000). Finally, we computed the fishing intensity expressed as the total fishing time spent per unit area per métier per time unit (a dredging season) (Lee et al., 2010).

Evaluation

The accuracy of differentiating fishing from non-fishing activity and error propagation through the methodological framework (estimates of fishing grounds and estimates of fishing intensity) were tested against known fishing positions.

Complementary data were gathered with on-board observers who collected GPS positions during two fishing trips: one for warty venus dredging and the other for variegated scallop dredging. Great scallop dredging has been prohibited since 2014 due to persistent blooms of Pseudo-nitzschia; therefore, observation data for this métier were not collected. The starting and ending time were reported for each fishing behavior ("fishing" and "steaming"). In total, 1,408 GPS positions were collected during warty venus dredging and 1,041 GPS positions were collected during variegated scallop dredging.

The comparison of known fishing positions with the estimated fishing positions resulting from the proposed method was performed using a confusion matrix. The overall accuracy (A) and the Kappa index (K) were calculated to evaluate the classification accuracy. Fishing grounds and fishing intensities were computed from known fishing positions and with estimated fishing positions. The results were compared using the I similarity statistic.

Results

Métier

Great scallop dredging (1,875 landings) represented up to 75% of the total landings. Warty venus dredging (821 landings, 20%) and variegated scallop dredging (161 landings, approximately 5%) comprised the remainder. Warty venus dredging with 310 landings represented the highest percentage of the total number of multispecies landings (74%), whereas great scallop and variegated scallop dredging occurred at the same proportion (approximately 13% each). The linkage between identified daily métier and AIS positions enabled the identification of 81,273 positions for great scallop, 2,394 for warty venus and 21 for variegated scallop dredging. Almost all the AIS positions (97%) involved great scallop dredging. This result is coherent with the limitations of the spatial coverage in the raw AIS database as explained in the datasets description. Nevertheless, although the AIS database contains 164 fishing trips for warty venus dredging, there is no assurance that all the positions during the fishing trip were recorded. Using these incomplete data in further steps of the analysis could lead to erroneous fishing ground estimates for warty venus dredging. Therefore, further analyses were performed only for great scallop dredging (951 fishing trips).

Fishing activity

The density estimation and classification for the great scallop dredging speed profile via a finite mixture model are shown in (Figure 15.3). Automatic parameter identification for classification selected the V model (variable variance) as the optimal model according to the BIC criterion. The speed density profile comprised four components according to the Normalized Difference in Entropy index. The results of the speed profile decomposition identified the first cluster as 0–0.79 ms^{-1}, the second cluster as 0.80–1.82 ms^{-1}, the third cluster as 1.83–2.90 ms^{-1} and the fourth as 2.91–6.09 ms^{-1}. The projection of the mixture model to the speed profile revealed that the second peak in the density of speed values that appear to be

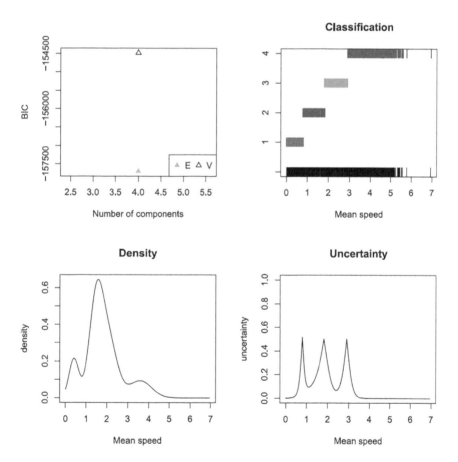

Figure 15.3 Density estimation and classification via a finite mixture model for the great scallop dredging speed profile

associated with fishing activity is composed by the second and third clusters. The lower and upper bounds of fishing speed for great scallops dredging were 0.8 and 2.9 ms^{-1}, respectively. Based on this criterion, 50,820 AIS positions (62.5% of the total positions for the great scallop dredging) were classified as likely fishing positions.

Fishing grounds and intensity

The great scallop dredging fishing grounds expressed as the 95*th* percentile of the kernel density of fishing segments for the 2011–2012 season are shown in Figure 15.4. The observed distribution of AIS positions for great scallop dredging differs significantly from a uniform distribution (two-sided spatial KS test of CSR, $D = 0.274$, $p < .001$). Therefore, the input parameters for the kernel density of fishing segments (the grid size (g) and the smoothing factor (h)) were estimated as $g = 25$ m and $h = 47$ m.

The 95*th* percentile of the kernel density delimits seven zones. The total fishing duration was estimated at 573 h for all fishing zones. Fishing duration was mainly concentrated in two zones lying in the center and in the south of the Bay of Brest (a total of 192 h). A third zone 3, in the east, represents about half this duration with 99.1 h, and finally the others with, respectively, 47.1 h, 35.6 h, 5.9 h and 1.6 h. The temporal distribution of fishing duration is concentrated during November and October 2011 (with 183 h each, representing 64% of the total duration). It is noteworthy that monthly fishing activity is unevenly distributed among the fishing zones; consequently, the spatial distribution of fishing intensity for the entire season reveals an intra-fishing-grounds variability as well as variability between

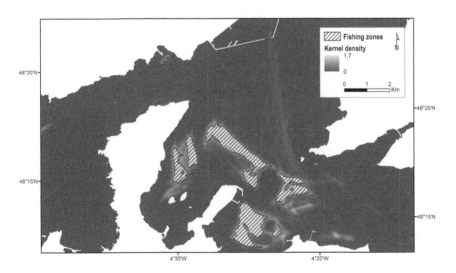

Figure 15.4 Spatial distribution of yearly kernel density of fishing segments for the great scallop dredging for 2011–2012

fishing grounds. The discrete fishing intensity in each zone (I_f) ranged from 121.1 h km^{-2} to 53.5 h km^{-2} ($I_f = 100.9$, $IQR = 37.4$).

Evaluation

The overall classification accuracy of the method for distinguishing fishing from non-fishing states is estimated to range from 91% ($K = 0.80$) to 87% ($K = 0.73$), respectively, for vessels (Wv) engaged in warty venus dredging and vessels (Vs) engaged in variegated scallop dredging. The misclassification rate is balanced between the two vessels métiers for steaming positions (5% and 3%), but it is higher (two and a half times higher) for fishing positions between Wv and vessels (4% and 10%). However, the detection method's errors propagation for fishing grounds identification and fishing intensity estimation is very low. Indeed, the estimated spatial distributions for both descriptors are extremely close to the observed distributions according to Warren's similarity index ($I_{Wv} = 0.95$, $I_{Vs} = 0.94$ for fishing grounds and $I_{Wv} = 0.96$, $I_{Vs} = 0.92$ for fishing intensity).

Conclusion

The goal of this study was to explore the feasibility of providing information on the intra-annual variability of spatio-temporal fishing for dredge métiers at a fine spatial scale using AIS data. To our knowledge, no previous study has used AIS data to assess the spatio-temporal distribution and intensity of fishing activity at the métier level.

Using complementary data (landings, auction prices, regulatory data and AIS) concerning fishing vessels of less than 12 meters for one dredge-fishing season (2011–2012) in the Bay of Brest, we followed global baselines proposed by previous studies based on VMS (Russo et al., 2014) or AIS (Natale et al., 2015) data, but included a number of adaptations related to local-context applications (the description of fishing activity at the métier level with a daily resolution, the fishing grounds identification based on segment KDE, the non-parametric estimations for fishing activity and for the kernel parameters, and the quantitative evaluation of the methods).

Our results are promising, but the method application depends on certain conditions and has limitations. Acceptance for the provision of landings data and acceptance of on-board observers depends on a strong collaboration with fishermen over time. In addition, the availability of AIS data is also a prerequisite for the analysis. Moreover, the analysis was conducted using a temporal period of only one fishing season, which does not allow for generalizations. The evaluation of the accuracy of this method of differentiation was estimated based on complementary datasets which cannot be considered as representative of the whole dredge fleet in the Bay of Brest (60 ships). Therefore, the total number of trips used for comparison should certainly be augmented in future studies. Further work might evaluate whether the ability to differentiate between fishing and non-fishing behaviors could be improved using methods from the field of behavioral ecology or machine learning (Souza et al., 2016). The limitations inherent to the nature of AIS data should also be considered. Indeed, although AIS regulations are certainly clear for the dredge fleet (vessels under 12 meters) in the Bay of Brest, not all fishing vessels have to carry AIS systems under UE regulations (see Section 1). Moreover, AIS data can be incomplete (Robards et al., 2016) or falsified, and AIS transmissions can be shut down.

Notwithstanding the caveats above, we believe that this approach is complementary to other sources of information such as VMS data or participatory mapping. In cases where data are scarce, this framework provides a potential solution for small-scale fisheries to estimate fishing grounds and fishing intensities at high resolution. The method was developed using free and open source software and is intended for dissemination within an R package. Further work might include data analysis over several years and with better spatial coverage to estimate the interannual variability of fishing grounds. This would also enable allocating dredging spatial catches (landings), spatial effort and seabed pressure (Eigaard et al., 2016). By adding additional layers of fishing intensity compliant with local scales, trade-offs could be evaluated between socio-economic and conservation objectives using spatial optimization tools such as Marxan.

Acknowledgements

This study was funded by the Fondation de France through the program "Coasts for tomorrow". It also benefited from a state subsidy managed by the Agence Nationale de la Recherche (ANR, National Agency for Research) within the framework of the "Investments for the Future" program, reference ANR-10-LABX-19-01. We would like to thank the committee of local fishermen for their willingness to share their knowledge.

References

Bastardie, F., Ramus Nielsen, J., Ulrich, C., Egekvist, J., Degel, H. (2010) Detailed mapping of fishing effort and landings by coupling fishing logbooks with satellite-recorded vessel geo-location. *Fisheries Research*, 106(1): 41–53.

Baudry, J.P., Raftery, A.E., Celeux, G., Lo, K., Gottardo, R. (2010) Combining mixture components for clustering. *Journal of Computational and Graphical Statistics*, 9(2): 332–353.

Breen, P., Vanstaen, K., Clark, R.W.E. (2015) Mapping inshore fishing activity using aerial, land, and vessel-based sighting information. *ICES Journal of Marine Science: Journal du Conseil*, 72(2): 467–479.

Demšar, U., Buchin, K., Cagnacci, F., Safi, K., Speckmann, B., Van de Weghe, N., Weiskopf, D., Weibel, R. (2015) Analysis and visualisation of movement: An interdisciplinary review. *Movement Ecology*, 3(1). doi:10.1186/s40462-015-0032-y

Eigaard, O.R., Bastardie, F., Breen, M., Dinesen, G.E., Hintzen, N.T., Laffargue, P., Nielsen, J.R., Nilsson, H., O'Neil, F., Polet, H., Reid, D.G., Sala, A., Sköld, M., Smith, C., Sørensen, T.K., Tully, O., Zengin, M., Rijnsdorp, A.D. (2016) Estimating seafloor pressure from demersal trawls, seines, and dredges based on gear design and dimensions. *ICES Journal of Marine Science*, 73(suppl. 1): i27–i43.

Enguehard, R.A., Hoeber, O., Devillers, R. (2013) Interactive exploration of movement data: A case study of geovisual analytics for fishing vessel analysis. *Information Visualization*, 12(1): 65–84.

Fraley, C., Raftery, A.E. (2002) Model-based clustering, discriminant analysis, and density estimation. *Journal of the American Statistical Association*, 97(458): 611–631.

Gloaguen, P., Mahévas, S., Rivot, E., Woillez, M., Guitton, J., Vermard, Y., Etienne, M.P. (2015) An autoregressive model to describe fishing vessel movement and activity. *Environmetrics*, 26(1): 17–28.

Gourmelon, F., Le Guyader, D., Fontenelle, G. (2014) A dynamic GIS as an efficient tool for integrated coastal zone management. *ISPRS International Journal of Geo-Information*, 3(2): 391–407.

Hintzen, N.T., Bastardie, F., Beare, D., Piet, G.J., Ulrich, C., Deporte, N., Egekvist, J., Degel, H. (2012) VMStools: Open-source software for the processing, analysis and visualisation of fisheries logbook and VMS data. *Fisheries Research*, 115–116: 31–43.

Hinz, H., Murray, L.G., Lambert, G.I., Hiddink, J.G., Kaiser, M.J. (2013) Confidentiality over fishing effort data threatens science and management progress. *Fish and Fisheries*, 14(1): 110–117.

Joo, R., Bertrand, S., Tam, J., Fablet, R. (2013) Hidden Markov Models: The best models for forager movements? *PLoS ONE*, 8(8): e71246.

Lee, J., South, A.B., Jennings, S. (2010) Developing reliable, repeatable, and accessible methods to provide high-resolution estimates of fishing-effort distributions from vessel monitoring system (VMS) data. *ICES Journal of Marine Science*, 67(6): 1260–1271.

McCauley, D.J., Woods, P., Sullivan, B., Bergman, B., Jablonicky, C., Roan, A., Hirshfield, M., Boerder, K., Worm, B. (2016) Ending hide and seek at sea. *Science*, 351(6278): 1148–1150.

Mills, C.M., Townsend, E., Jennings, S., Eastwood, P.D., Houghton, C.A. (2007) Estimating high resolution trawl fishing effort from satellite-based vessel monitoring system data. *ICES Journal of Marine Science*, 64(2): 248–255.

Natale, F., Gibin, M., Alessandrini, A., Vespe, M., Paulrud, A. (2015) Mapping fishing effort through AIS data. *PLoS ONE*, 10(6): e0130746.

Powell, R.A. (2000) Animal home ranges and territories and home range estimators. In: Pearl, M.C., Boitani, L., Fuller, T.K. (Eds.), *Research Techniques in Animal Ecology: Controversies and Consequences*. New York: Columbia University Press, pp. 65–110.

Robards, M., Silber, G.K., Adams, J.D., Arroyo, J. (2016) Conservation science and policy applications of the marine vessel Automatic Identification System (AIS) – A review. *Bulletin of Marine Science*, 92(1): 75–103.

Russo, T., D'Andrea, L., Parisi, A., Cataudella, S. (2014) VMSbase: An R-package for VMS and logbook data management and analysis in fisheries ecology. *PLoS ONE*, 9(6): e100195.

Russo, T., Parisi, A., Cataudella, S. (2011) New insights in interpolating fishing tracks from VMS data for different métiers. *Fisheries Research*, 108(1): 184–194.

Russo, T., Parisi, A., Cataudella, S. (2013) Spatial indicators of fishing pressure: Preliminary analyses and possible developments. *Ecological Indicators*, 26: 141–153.

Shelmerdine, R.L. (2015) Teasing out the detail: How our understanding of marine AIS data can better inform industries, developments, and planning. *Marine Policy*, 54: 17–25.

Silverman, B. (1986) *Density Estimation for Statistics and Data Analysis*. Monographs on Statistics and Applied Probability. London: Chapman & Hall.

Souza, E.N. de, Boerder, K., Matwin, S., Worm, B. (2016) Improving fishing pattern detection from satellite AIS using data mining and machine learning. *PLoS ONE*, 11(7): e0158248.

Steiniger, S., Hunter, A.J.S. (2013) A scaled line-based kernel density estimator for the retrieval of utilization distributions and home ranges from GPS movement tracks. *Ecological Informatics*, 13: 1–8.

16 Spatio-temporal data modeling of ship-to-ship interactions in mid-19th-century high seas

Amin Mobasheri, Alexander Zipf and César Ducruet

Since the late seventeenth century, the shipping newspaper *Lloyd's List* (Figure 16.1) and its direct successors have published weekly and subsequently daily information on global shipping. This information comes in tabular format in five separate categories: "Shipping Intelligence", "Speakings", "Foreign Mail", "Casualties", and "War". The "Speakings" category lists sightings of ships on the high seas and records both the sighted and the reporting ship with names and geographical coordinates. Thus, the "Speakings" data refer to interactions between two ships on the high seas. Such interaction could involve an exchange of goods, information, or people. So far, only very few researchers have recognized the analytical potential of the *Lloyd's Lists*. Yrjö Kaukiainen (2001) and, later, Roland Wenzlhuemer (2010) have looked at the shrinking of global communication times (first due to improved naval technology, later thanks to telegraphy) that become visible under "Shipping Intelligence". In a more recent study, Ducruet (2013) has employed data from the *Lloyd's Lists* in order to understand maritime flows. This study has shown the potential of this dataset for uncovering various uncertainties in maritime studies. The hypothesis of this research is that geo-processing the spatiotemporal *Lloyd's List* data on the movement of people, goods and information on board nineteenth-century ships vividly brings to life the migrational, commercial, and hence, the cultural circuits and networks that powered contemporary processes of globalization.

This article deals with addressing the question of how to model space-time information from *Lloyd's Lists* shipping records in order to prepare it for spatial statistical processing. The following sections provide information concerning related studies on spatio-temporal data modeling, followed by details about the model we have developed. Later, we will show how this model is used with an example of hotspot analysis of ship-to-ship "Speakings" information and discuss the results. Finally, the chapter ends with an outline of future work on this project.

Related study

Our research deals with two main subjects: spatio-temporal data modeling and spatio-temporal statistics. In the first case, several studies present methods for

LLOYD'S LIST.

No. 11,478.] LONDON, SATURDAY, JANUARY 4, 1851.

Subscription £2. per Annum, in London, paid in advance. A postage of 1d. each upon Lists sent into the Country

| Wind at Midnight,. SSE | | Bar. Therm. | Greatest pressure since yesterday at Noon..... 1½ h. p ft. | High Water at London Bridge { Morning 24 min. past 4 |
| Do. Noon...... SE | At Noon 29.93 49 | Least .. /. do ...... do....... do........} | on Monday { Afternoon 40 min. past 4 |

1	2	3	4
GRAVESEND .... *arrived from*	FALMOUTH [3, variable] *arrived from*	BEARHAVEN .... *arrived from*	REVAL.... [Dec. 24].... *arrived from*
29 John & Ann, —— Sunderland	2 Florence, Roberts Manfredonia	1 Ebenezer, Bell Leghorn	previous to Dec. 24.
with considerable damage, having	for Sligo—with sails split, and	for Tralee	Anna Berg, Moller Messina
been in contact 25th Dec. near	loss of galley	Commodore, Curb Vianna	Condor, Rasmussen dº
Lowestoffe, with the *Mary Ellie-*	LIVERPOOL [3. E. to SE] *arr. from*	for Limerick	Haken Adelsteen, Christensen dº
nor, of Sunderland.	2 Frances Barclay, Reed Valparaiso	BELFAST.... [2, W].... *arrived from*	LIBAU .... *arrived from*
2 King Alfred, Knill St. Michael's	Wm. Patten, Theobald New York	2 Killiow, Willis Naples	Dec. 3. Friedrich, de Boer Dundee
Thomas, Brown Rouen	3 Neptune, M'Donald Munsooreottah	Prudenter, Hansen Riga	11 Concordia, Christiansen Lisbon
3 Astarte, Roberts Canton	Wm. Penn, Mahony Philadelphia	FRASERBURGH .... *arr. from*	
Magellan, Sproule dº	Breadalbane, —— Wallace, N.S.	29 Matilda, Rea Newcastle	WARNEMUNDE........ *arrived from*
Forfarshire, Tudor dº	Surpass, Sherris Lisbon	for Belfast—with loss of an-	Dec. 26. Providentia, Beek Charleston
Steadfast, Spencer Calcutta	Aim, Roberts Dieppe	chor and chain.	27 Friedrika, Niemann London
Christabel, Harding Madras	.... *sailed for*	DUNDEE .... *arrived from*	Pauly Vietschow, Kerf dº
Devonshire, Stevens Singapore	3 Mary Ray, Ellwood Singapore	3: Zitella, Monkman Königsberg	Wolfgang, Voss Hull
Edgar, Gibbens Algoa Bay	SirHenryPottinger, Conway Calcutta	.... *sailed for*	Anna, Niemann Grangemouth
Henrietta, Butchard Callao	Ceres, Ashton Natal	31 Ellangowan, Will Havana	TRAVEMUNDE .... *arrived from*
	England, Cobban Valparaiso	KIRKCALDY .... *arrived from*	Dec.28. Arnold von Winkelried, Benfeld

Figure 16.1 Part of a page of *Lloyd's List* published on Jan 4th, 1851

recording information characterized by both spatial and temporal information. Each method has its own approach for dealing with spatio-temporal data and facing the challenges concerned with the integration of spatial and temporal concepts (Nikos et al., 2004). Hence, each method is useful for a specific application. This depends on the requirements of the application as well as the data characteristics. The main requirements that a space-time model should be able to address include four categories (Nikos et al., 2004):

- Spatial semantics: relating to the purely spatial aspects, such as structure of space, orientation/direction, measurement, and topology.
- Temporal semantics: dealing with the nature of time and the basic features used to describe it, such as granularity, time density, time order, transaction, etc.
- Spatio-temporal semantics: combining both spatial and temporal semantics. For example, it makes the data model capable of capturing changes in the shape and size of the object features.
- Query capabilities: this category deals with the classification of existing spatio-temporal data models based on their query capabilities. Examples are: queries about locations, spatial properties, and spatial relationships or queries about time, temporal properties, and temporal relationships and, finally, queries about spatio-temporal behaviors and relationships.

Several models exist for spatio-temporal data modeling. These models range from simple approaches such as the snapshot model (Langran and Chrisman, 1988), simple time-stamping (Hunter and Williamson, 1990) and space-time composite (STC) models (Tryfona and Jensen, 1999) to more sophisticated versions, such as the entity-relationship (STER) model (Tryfona and Jensen, 2000), and spatio-temporal object-oriented data models (Worboys et al., 1990; Wachowicz and Healey, 1994). For detailed information on each of these models, please refer to Mobasheri and Bakillah (2014). In the field of spatial-temporal statistics, there are numerous studies and methods available on hotspot spatial analysis. The numerical analysis of spatial point distributions has interested academics for a very long time. A very early work that resulted in the famous Moran's I statistic was done by Moran (1948). Berry and Marble (1968) present an early collection of work on general spatial analysis, and later books by Cliff and Ord (1973, 1981) illustrate the development of spatial point analysis theory.

Lloyds Lists data model

The spatio-temporal modeling of *Lloyd's* data is required in order to record the information in a coherent and flexible manner and allow analysis and querying of this information. The speakings information contains latitudes and longitudes recorded by a point feature as well as two timestamps: the date that the actual speaking occurred and the reporting date. When modeling *Lloyd's* data, some approaches cannot be used due to their specific characteristics. For example, the snapshot model is not appropriate as a means of describing changes in space through time. Each snapshot is relevant to a specific time, but in order to under-stand how Ti differs from Tj, two snapshots should be compared exhaustively. As an example of the disadvantages of the STC model, the fact that it is very difficult to define rules of internal logic and/or integrity constraints is a big problem (Mobasheri et al., 2015).

Among the existing approaches of spatio-temporal data modeling discussed in the previous section, we have selected object-oriented modeling because of its four main advantages in spatio-temporal modeling (Nikos et al., 2004; Worboys et al., 1990):

- A single object represents the whole history of an entity
- Efficient temporal data handling
- Uniform treatment of spatial and temporal data handling
- Simple queries due to its capacity for dealing with each single object of an entity

A large amount of published information for two specific time periods (1851 and 1871) of interest to historians were read and transferred into Excel spreadsheets. In the next step, in order to design a geo-database for the *Lloyd's* data, a geo-data modeling task using the object-oriented modeling was carried out. As an extra data source, we used the digitized maps of shipping routes downloaded from David Rumsey's map collection (2014) and the CLIWOC database (Wheeler et al., 2006), which provides weather data (e.g., wind speed and direction, air temperature, etc.). From all the necessary information that needed to be recorded, a total of nine classes (Figure 16.2) were designed, each with special attributes. The first four tables are normal tables containing several necessary items of information (e.g., ship name, captain name, event date, journal date, etc.); yet, the two last

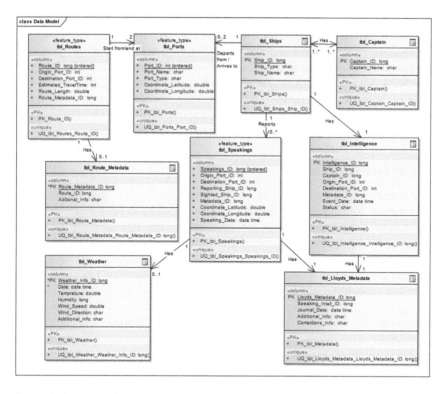

Figure 16.2 Extended version of the data model adapted from Mobasheri et al. (2015)

tables are considered as feature types since they have spatial components and can thus be treated as point features.

Tbl_Speakings is the table in this model that we are interested in because it contains coordinate values in forms of latitude and longitudes where the actual speaking happened (somewhere at sea), as well as information relating to the plan of the other ship (the sighted ship), such as its port of origin and destination.

Hotspot analysis

A geo-database with the introduced data model was designed and populated with the records of speakings information from the years 1851 and 1871. In order to prepare for the statistical analysis, an initial data investigation and cleaning was necessary, since we expected to encounter errors (caused by digitization mistakes) at the data entry stage. All the tasks relating to this section were carried out using R software.

Basic data exploration and organization

Here we checked for missing or mixed-up data to avoid including incorrect data into our analysis. The checks that we performed on the dataset included:

- Ensuring the location columns only contained numbers.
- Assessing how much data was available, and how much included both dates and locations (in order to exclude null data in our statistical analysis).
- Ensuring against unexpected figures in our date columns.
- Removing any points located on land; generating a spatial object using data point locations.

Basic visualization of speakings through time

Histograms depicted in Figure 16.3 shows how the speakings data of 1851 are distributed across months and weeks. Furthermore, in order to properly project the data into a planar projection system we chose the EPSG: 32663, an Equidistant Cylindrical projection that minimizes the distortion of distances, especially along a north/south line. Figure 16.4 depicts the basic visualization of 1851 speakings data around the globe.

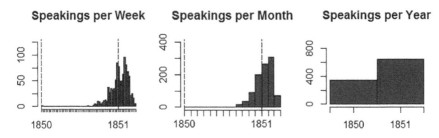

Figure 16.3 Temporal distribution of 1851 speakings data

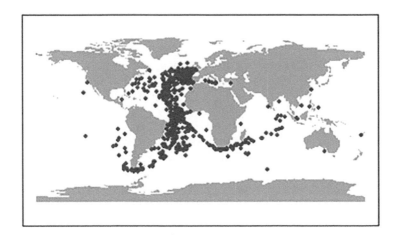

Figure 16.4 Spatial distribution of 1851 speakings data

Modeling the intensity of points across space

In order to perform a hotspot analysis of ship speakings information, we performed spatial analysis hypothesis tests, starting with a basic test for complete spatial randomness (CSR). We generated a new type of spatial object -a "point pattern". The test for CSR was done using the k-function (Dixon, 2002).

$$\hat{K}(r) = \frac{1}{\lambda^2 A} \sum_{i=1}^{n} \sum_{j \neq i}^{n} I_r(r_{ij}) \tag{1}$$

In the K function (Equation 1), A is the study area; λ is the intensity (or the number of speaking events divided by the area of our study); r is the distance from point i (j is all points other than i), and I_r is an indicator function that takes on a value of 0 if point j is not within distance r of i and a value of 1 otherwise. Essentially, we are tallying all points within incremental distances of i. When points are distributed randomly, the expected number of points in any given area is simply λ multiplied by the area in question. Strong departures from this pattern can indicate clustering of a point pattern (more neighbors than expected at given neighborhood sizes) or over-dispersion (fewer neighbors than expected at given neighborhood sizes).

The results of the test (Figure 16.5: for 1851 data) show that values are well outside the limits – much higher at (nearly) every value of r (r is in meters). The

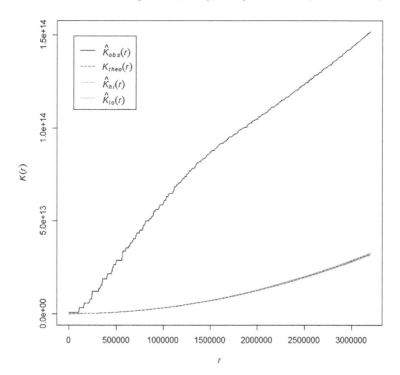

Figure 16.5 K test for complete spatial randomness (CSR) of 1851 speakings data

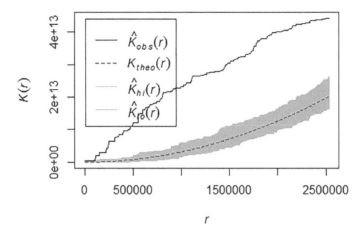

Figure 16.6 K test for complete spatial randomness (CSR) of 1871 speakings data

Point Intensity, 1850 to 1851

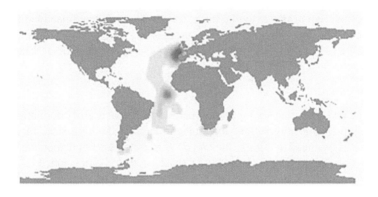

Figure 16.7 Speakings hotspots of the year 1851

rate of increase of our observed $K(r)$ does begin to slow down at very high values of r – around 15,000,000 meters. Figure 16.6 shows the result of the same test for the speakings data of year 1871.

Finally, we analyzed the degree of inhomogeneity in the dataset by estimating the (smoothed) intensity of points across space (Figures 16.7 and 16.8). We used the Kernel density method for this purpose. KDE (Peterson, 2004) is a non-parametric way to estimate the probability density function of a random variable. It makes no assumption about an underlying distribution. Instead, the underlying distribution is built from kernel functions centered at each data point. The density estimate is an aggregation of all kernel functions on our point pattern. A smoothing

Point Intensity, 1870 to 1871

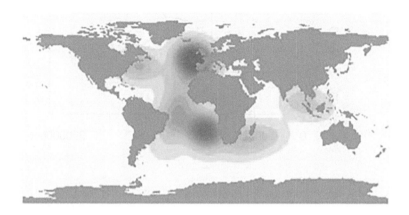

Figure 16.8 Speakings hotspots of the year 1871

parameter, or bandwidth, determines the width of the kernel functions and their degree of overlap in space. In this study, we computed a "fixed-bandwidth kernel estimate" of the intensity function of the process that generated our observed point pattern. We used a cross-validation method to determine our optimal bandwidth.

Conclusion

Modeling and analyzing ship speakings data could reveal useful information about where ship-to-ship interactions have taken place on the high seas. In order to achieve this, we need to digitize the *Lloyd's Lists* newspaper and populate the data into a proper geo-database. This geo-database needs to be developed based on a proper data model. We developed and presented a data model of *Lloyd's Lists* shipping information (Figure 16.2) and furthermore presented the initial results of spatio-temporal statistical analysis of this dataset. As an initial step, we tested the spatial randomness of speakings data, and the result of the test (Figure 16.5: for 1851 data) showed that values were well outside the limits – much higher at (nearly) every value of r. The rate of increase of our observed $K(r)$ does begin to slow down at very high values of r – around 15 million meters.

   Our analysis continued with performing hotspot detection on speakings data. The results of hotspot analysis (Figure 16.7: for year 1851) showed that there are some rather abrupt transitions from low-intensity to high-intensity and that there is no obvious higher-order distribution of these changes. Most of the world is low-density. A limitation of this study was related to the year 1871. Where our dataset from 1870 to 1871 contained far fewer points (n=50), this general pattern detected with density-based clustering was repeated with that set (Figure 16.8). The main reason that these two timeslots (e.g. ,1851 and 1871) were chosen is that we were interested to see how the generation and working of the Suez Canal may have affected shipping behavior and, more specifically, ship-to-ship interactions. The results of hotspot analysis show some changes in this regard. The main changes discovered were that more interactions between ships occurred in Southeast Asia as well as Southeast Africa in 1871, while there were very few speakings in these regions in 1851. Another important change is the hotspot located in Southwest Africa in 1871, where this did not exist earlier in 1851. Although these results indicate some changes in where shipping interactions occurred, nevertheless, in order to have a clear and solid conclusion on the issue we would need to continue further with this study. Therefore, in the next step of our study we would complete the data for the year 1871 (and possibly other years) and investigate this issue at a more complete and more detailed scale.

Acknowledgments

This study is funded by the Excellence Initiative of the German Research Foundation (DFG). The first author would like to thank Kilian Schultes (HGIS club, Heidelberg University) for his helpful feedback and discussions. The research leading to these results has received funding from the European Research Council under the European Union's Seventh Framework Programme (FP/2007–2013) / ERC Grant Agreement n. [313847] "World Seastems".

References

Berry, B.J., Marble, D. (1968) *Spatial Analysis*. Prentice Hall: Englewood Cliffs.

Cliff, A.D., Ord, J.K. (1973) *Spatial Autocorrelation*. London: Pion.

Cliff, A.D., Ord, J.K. (1981) *Spatial Processes: Models and Applications*. London: Pion.

David Rumsey Map Collection. Available at: www.davidrumsey.com/view. Accessed on May 2014.

Dixon, P.M. (2002) Ripley's K function. In: El-Shaarawi, A.H., Piegorsch, W.W. (Eds.), *Encyclopedia of Environmetrics*. New York: John Wiley & Sons, pp. 1796–1803.

Ducruet, C. (2013) Network diversity and maritime flows. *Journal of Transport Geography*, 30: 77–88.

Hunter, G.J., Williamson, I.P. (1990) The development of a historical digital cadastral database. *International Journal of Geographic Information Systems*, 4(2): 169–179.

Kaukiainen, Y. (2001) Shrinking the world: Improvements in the speed of information transmission, c. 1820–1870. *European Review of Economic History*, 5(1): 1–28.

Langran, G., Chrisman, N.R. (1988) A framework for temporal Geographic Information. *Cartographica*, 25(3): 1–14.

Mobasheri, A., Bakillah, M. (2014) Towards spatio-temporal data modeling of geo-tagged shipping information. In: Paper presented at the *17th AGILE Conference on Geographic Information Science*, Castellón, Spain, June 3–16.

Mobasheri, A., Bakillah, M., Zipf, A. (2015) Web mapping of geo-tagged shipping information. Case study: The LLOYDS Lists. In: Paper presented at the *27th International Cartographic Conference (ICC 2015)*, Rio de Janeiro, Brazil, August 23–28.

Moran, P.A.P. (1948) The interpretation of statistical maps. *Journal of Society Series B*, 10(2): 243–251.

Nikos, P., Theodoulidis, B., Kopanakis, I., Theodoridis, Y. (2004) Literature review of spatio-temporal database models. *The Knowledge Engineering Review*, 19(3): 235–274.

Peterson, L.E. (2004) *Kernel Density Estimation (KDE)*. Available at: https://pdfs. semanticscholar.org/6755/9e80bf45e5a47fefffccdbfc827bd401357c.pdf

Tryfona, N., Jensen, C.S. (1999) Conceptual data modeling for spatiotemporal applications. *GeoInformatica*, 3: 245–268.

Tryfona, N., Jensen, C.S. (2000) Using abstractions for spatio-temporal conceptual modeling. In: Carroll, J., Damiani, E., Haddad, H., Oppenheim, D. (Eds.), *Proceedings of the 2000 ACM Symposium on Applied Computing – Volume 1*. New York, NY: ACM, pp. 313–322.

Wachowicz, M., Healey, R.G. (1994) Towards temporality in GIS. In: Worboys, M.F. (Ed.), *Innovations in GIS*. London: Taylor & Francis, pp. 105–115.

Wenzlhuemer, R. (2010) *Transforming Global Spaces: The Telegraph, Communication and Globalization in the Nineteenth and Early Twentieth Century*. Habilitationsschrift einge- reicht an der Philosophischen, Fakultät der Universität Heidelberg.

Wheeler, D., Garcia-Herrera, R., Koek, F.B., Wilkinson, C., Können, G.P., Prieto, M.R., Jones, P.D., Casale, R. (2006) *CLIWOC, Climatological Database for the World's Oceans: 1750 to 1850*. Research Project EVK1-CT-2000-00090, European Commission, Brussels.

Worboys, M.F., Hearhshow, H.M., Maguire, D.J. (1990) Object-oriented modeling for spatial databases. *International Journal of Geographical Information Systems*, 4(4): 369–383.

17 World shipping flows across the global urban hierarchy

*César Ducruet, Sylvain Cuyala
and Ali El Hosni*

It is a fact that maritime transport has never been studied as an urban network in academic literature (Bretagnolle, 2015), although such networks existed throughout history, for example, the Hanseatic League (Lemarchand, 2000) and Italian or Asian city-states (Gipouloux, 2009). This is particularly surprising, given that even today maritime transport is responsible for no less than 90% of world trade volumes and about 40% of the world's urban population resides in coastal cities (Noin, 1999).

One of the main reasons for this is that the available theories supporting inter-urban relationships have all been developed in the context of continental (inland) settings (Beyers and Fowler, 2012; Peris, 2016). As a consequence, empirical analyses of urban networks mainly focused on land-based communication systems such as roads, railways and rivers, before extending their focus to airlines and multinational firms (Ducruet and Beauguitte, 2014), with a growing preference for immaterial rather than physical flows (Hall and Hesse, 2012). Geographers, though, recurrently proposed to include more maritime elements in existing urban theories (Rimmer, 1967; Vance, 1970; Bird, 1977; Brocard et al., 1995). The well-known work of Braudel (1979) on major (maritime) cities being centers of functional world regions supported the idea that seas and oceans facilitate rather than constrain human interaction (Lewis and Wigen, 1999). Critiques of the closed nature of urban theories are also found more recently, such as the central flow theory (Taylor et al., 2010) whereby long-distance horizontal relationships take over local vertical ones. However, although maritime flows were already mapped by famous geographers in the 1940s, such analyses occurred in isolation from network theory and urban theory (Ducruet, 2016). Maritime network analysis today remains highly static and largely ignores the local socio-economic features of the connected nodes (see also Chapters 13 and 14 on the relationships between shipping, inland accessibility and regional development). Whereas Jacobs et al. (2011) incorporated urban elements in their study of the locational determinants of maritime Advanced Producer Services (APS), such an approach is more popular in other transport sectors, such as airlines (Dobruszkes et al., 2011) and land-based networks (Guerrero and Proulhac, 2014). A rare few other studies do exist looking at global urban accessibility based on multiple indicators including maritime flows (Nelson, 2008), the multiplexity of maritime networks aggregating port nodes into urban areas (Ducruet, 2013), and the combined analysis of traffic and regional specialization in the Asia-Pacific maritime network (Ducruet and Itoh, 2015).

Another explanation for the rarity of such attempts is the trend towards port-city spatial and functional separation, well documented by several spatial models in geography (Bird, 1963; Hoyle, 1989; Norcliffe et al., 1996), in history (Murphey, 1989) and in regional science (Fujita and Mori, 1996). Increased vessel size and port competition in a context of growing global trade are often seen as the main technological and economic factors behind such a separation, notwithstanding urban growth and diversification. Changing trade patterns can also provoke the diversification of maritime activity despite the presence of modern cargo handling facilities (Thayer and Whelan, 1989; Vigarié, 1991). The traditional view of ports and cities as interdependent and mutually beneficial tended to lose ground as these models were validated throughout the world by numerous qualitative case studies and quantitative applications (Ducruet and Lee, 2006). In parallel, geographers shifted their focus to the more technical and operational aspects of shipping and ports (Ng and Ducruet, 2014). The rare quantitative analyses of port-city or port-region interdependencies (Ducruet and Itoh, 2016) rarely adopted a relational perspective.

More recently however, numerous scholars have supported the idea of maintained port-city interdependencies, arguing that port-city separation was not a universal process (Lee et al., 2008), while cities continued to bring valuable externalities to ports (Hall and Jacobs, 2012). Another supporting argument came from the observation that some major metropolises were actually developing new port facilities near the urban center (El Hosni, 2015), such as London and Taipei but also Jakarta. There is also a belief that while current maritime patterns are largely inherited from the past (Fleming and Hayuth, 1994; Marnot, 2005; Guerrero, 2014), cities continue to grow and concentrate global economic activity. How are cities and maritime flows mutually dependent? How did such interdependency evolve over time? What is the respective role of port and non-port cities?

The remainder of the chapter continues as follows. The next section introduces the data and methodology for an empirical analysis of this relationship over the last 120 years based on untapped historical records of worldwide vessel movements connecting ports. The core of the chapter lies in the third section, which presents the main results based on the application of several network analytical tools to the evolving matrix of interurban maritime flows. Concluding remarks serve as a discussion on the contribution of this research to both urban and network studies, while underlining potential lessons for practice and further research.

Data and methodology

The only possible way to map and analyze the long-term evolution of global maritime networks is by extracting vessel movement information from the *Lloyd's List* archives. The maritime insurance company has been the world's leading marine intelligence provider for decades and even centuries. Its first publication dates back to 1696 and still exists nowadays in digital format. *Lloyd's Shipping Index* provides

Figure 17.1 Sample data taken from the *Lloyd's Weekly Index*, 29 April 1915

a snapshot of global maritime flows published daily or weekly since 1880, with technical information on most of the world's merchant vessels and their latest inter-port movement.

Our methodology consisted in extracting one entire paper publication every five years or so between 1890 and 2008, with the support of Optical Character Recognition (OCR) software after digitization. Enormous efforts were then put into the harmonization and disambiguation of 11,797 place names for the entire period. The whole maritime database consisted in a global matrix of no less than 769,272 vessel movements creating about 200,000 possible linkages between nearly 9,000 ports of the world. Publications were selected around the month of April–May to ensure a year-on-year comparability of the results (Figure 17.1).

The next step was to assign every port or port terminal to a city. This constituted the main focus of this research, given that cities change over time, and may contain one or more ports depending on their spatial definition, while the same port may be attributed to several cities, depending on the case. The most relevant approach to urban development has been to adopt a morphological definition of cities to avoid issues arising from incomparable administrative definitions across countries and time periods. In addition, this morphological approach shifted the focus closer to the functional dimension of cities, i.e. their economic importance as reflected beyond the sole city center area, being more in accordance with the fact that port terminals often locate not inside but in the vicinity of Central Business Districts (Savy, 1991). Each port was retrieved on the world map and assigned to a city in two different ways (Figure 17.2), in all cases considering the spatial pattern of urbanization and communication networks at the present time and using documentation on past periods whenever necessary.

A first assignment was the host city, i.e. the local administrative unit to which the port belongs (level 1), this unit often being part of a larger urban area with one or multiple centers. Under this perspective, ports serve coastal cities. The highest number of ports within a coastal city was found to be six (Kitakyushu), followed by a number of cities in Asia and other emerging countries. It was then decided to extend the focus to the nearest large urban center, whether located on the coast or inland (level 2). Such "extended city-regions" are not necessarily port cities, but are most likely to be the traffic generation center of the region. The largest number of ports is

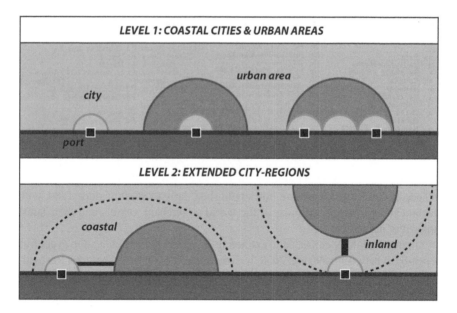

Figure 17.2 Methodology for port-city matching

contained by the London extended city-region (31), followed by a number of large Northern European, North American and Japanese cities. This operation was judged necessary for many ports, being obvious gateways for nearby cities located within a short distance, and for which the host city does not appear to be the relevant unit of analysis (Wackermann, 1998). This was also a way to shift the analysis of cities closer to the likely extent of port hinterlands, although it was in practice impossible to verify their true delineation over the last 120 years (see Appendix 17.1 for a cartography of the distribution of vessel calls across world cities for selected years).

Just as maritime traffic is measured in this chapter by the number of vessel calls, the dimension of urban development is measured by the number of inhabitants, which is also comparable over time and across space, and constitutes a good proxy of urban development (Pumain et al., 2009). Three main urban databases were combined to obtain time series of population data, all of which gave a separate number for administrative and morphological cities; namely Geopolis for the period 1950–1990 (Moriconi-Ebrard, 1994), Population Statistics for the period 1880–2005 (Lahmeyer, 2015) and World Gazetteer for the year 2010 (Helders, 2012). For many cities, the population data was carefully verified and corrected to avoid disruptions or abnormal fluctuations in time series. As a result, and based on Figure 17.3, the global database consisted in 2,853 coastal cities having at least one vessel call between 1890 and 2010 (level 1), 831 extended city-regions (level 2), giving a combined total of 3,081 urban areas (levels 1 and 2).

While the number of ports and vessel calls has continuously grown between 1890 and 2010, despite some fluctuations, global maritime activity has mainly

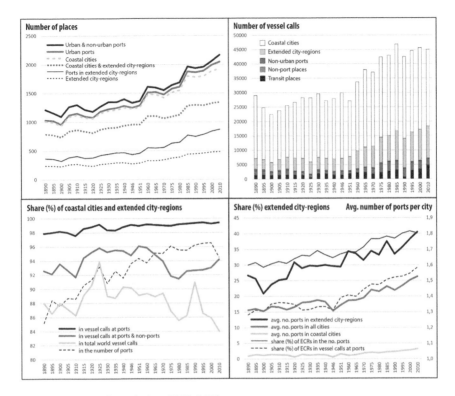

Figure 17.3 Sample evolution, 1890–2010

concentrated in coastal cities (level 1), but extended city-regions (level 2) have attracted a growing share of world maritime traffic, rising from 14% in 1890 to 29% in 2010 (see also Appendix 17.1). All these cities taken as a whole accounted for no less than 98–99% of all port traffic, and this share has even increased from 97.8% in 1890 to 99.4% in 2010. The importance of extended city-regions is exemplified by their higher average number of ports compared with coastal cities, from 1.5 in 1890 to 1.8 in 2010. Lastly, it was calculated that the port-city sample had concentrated a noticeable, but shrinking, proportion of world urban population, from 55.4% in 1890 to 38.9% in 2010, all cities included (levels 1 and 2).

In addition, cities were classified among six classes of demographic size (quantiles), and we calculated the orthodromic distance (kilometers) of interurban maritime linkages as well as a series of centrality measures, such as degree centrality (number of adjacent neighbors), betweenness centrality (number of occurrences on shortest paths), clustering coefficient (share of observed links in the maximum possible number of links) and excentricity (topological proximity to all other nodes). The situation of the city in the maritime network and its demographic size correspond to the concepts of intermediacy and centrality, respectively (Fleming and Hayuth, 1994), the first being a capacity to attract flows and the second a traffic generation power.

Main results

Traffic volume and urban hierarchy

The distribution of world vessel calls per city, size and class confirms the over-whelming dominance of the largest cities (Figure 17.4), which concentrated no less than 70% of world traffic on average over the period. The largest coastal cities

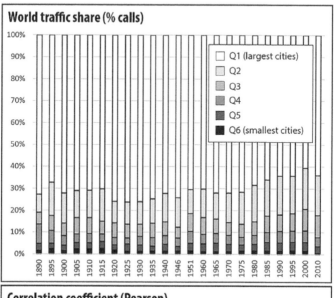

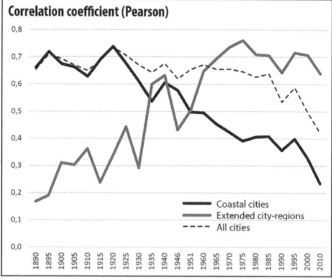

Figure 17.4 Traffic distribution and urban hierarchies, 1890–2010

(level 1), however, see their world share decreasing in recent years, especially from the 1980s onwards, from 69.7% in 1975 to 60.5% in 2010. In fact, traffic has become slightly more concentrated in other large cities (Q5 and Q4), at the expense of the smaller cities (Q1 to Q3). Such trends well reflect the growing difficulty for high-density urban locations to handle the bulk of global maritime trade. After a phase of continuous traffic concentration at the main coastal node (Taaffe et al., 1963), diseconomies of scale resulting from lack of space, congestion and land-use tensions between ports and their host cities motivated the "challenge of the periphery" (Hayuth, 1981), whereby traffic shifted to distant and secondary nodes. Extended city-regions (level 2) went through a somewhat different evolution, as the share of the largest of these tended to be greater to the one of coastal cities, from 1965 onwards, having started from much lower levels in the early period. Here also, one notices a redistribution of traffic from the largest to other large cities, at the expense of the smallest; another important difference with coastal cities being the much smaller share of Q1 cities. This is mainly due to the fact that on average extended city-regions are 1.8 times larger than coastal cities, a gap that has widened over time from 1.3 in 1890 to 2.7 in 2010.

The correlation between the amount of vessel calls and the number of inhabitants per city had already dropped dramatically for coastal cities (level 1) since the 1930s, which underlines profound changes in the spatial pattern of traffic distribution, falling from 0.66 in 1925 to 0.28 in 2010. Conversely, extended city-regions (level 2) witnessed a regular increase of this correlation over the same period, from 0.29 in 1925 to 0.63 in 2010. The same analysis including all cities exhibits a similar trend to coastal cities, but with a less pronounced fall-off, i.e. 0.40 in 2010. This contrasting evolution of coastal cities and extended city-regions means that maritime traffic is increasingly explained by distant rather than host cities. This evidence sheds new light on the growing importance of road transport in freight distribution across hinterlands. It is confirmed by the same correlation depending on the location of cities (Figure 17.5). At the level of coastal cities (level 1) and in accordance with James Bird's (1963) Anyport model (1963), upstream (river or delta) cities lost important traffic shares over the period, dropping from 22.6% in 1890 to 11.8% in 2010 and notably since the 1960s. This trend corresponds to the growing specialization and size of ships, as upstream cities often have a good urban centrality but limited maritime accessibility (Brocard, 1988) contrary to downstream cities; although in some cases the downstream city may be more developed than the inland cities thanks to water access to vast hinterlands (Zaremba, 1962). The share of downstream cities has also declined in similar ways, from 33.2% in 1890 to 22.2% in 2010, but this share remained quite stable between 1970 and 2010. The downstream shift of port terminals as in the model of Bird (1963) must have compensated for the decline. In fact, throughout the period, the dominant share has always been concentrated at coastal (maritime) cities with no river access, and it has regularly been growing, from 44.1% in 1890 to 66.0% in 2010. After a first phase of decline, those maritime cities concentrated a continuously growing proportion of world traffic from 1930 to the present day.

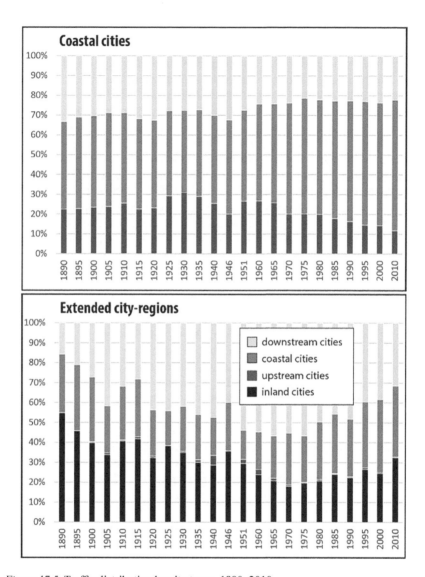

Figure 17.5 Traffic distribution by city types, 1890–2010

Several factors may explain this trend, such as nautical accessibility (e.g. penin-sula, deep-water bay) but also intermodal transport connections with the hinterland by rail and road. In extended city-regions (level 2), inland cities enjoyed the highest share in 1890 (54.8%), but recorded a rapid fall-off until 1970 (18.1%), before a second stage of growth until 2010 (32.5%). Coastal (maritime) cities followed a similar pattern with a relative decline up to 1951 and a regular growth since then. This is directly attributable to the regular relative growth of downstream cities, from

15.8% in 1890 to 56.7% in 1975, followed by a decline to 31.5% in 2010. In fact, downstream cities had been the most attractive nodes to ensure sea-land cargo transfers before the generalization of truck transport in the 1970s around the world, accelerated by the functional and spatial effects of containerization.

It is therefore meaningful to compare not only traffic distribution but also correlations based on the location of cities (Figure 17.6). For instance, the aforementioned correlation fall-off for coastal cities (level 1) is mainly explained by how upstream cities fared, declining from 0.78 in 1890 to 0.19 in 2010. As in the spatial model of port evolution "Anyport" (Bird, 1963), those cities gradually faced accessibility limitations hampering the possibility of welcoming increasingly larger vessels, while urban growth inevitably resulted in lack of space for port expansion and led to transport congestion in urbanized areas. A similar drop was registered in coastal cities located on islands, but from a much lower initial value, i.e. from 0.48 in 1890 to 0.18 in 2010. Other types of coastal cities have, by comparison, maintained a relatively stable correlation between traffic and population over the period. For extended city-regions (level 2), the driving force behind the increasing correlation comes from inland cities (from 0.11 in 1890 to 0.92 in 2010) as well as from downstream cities (from -0.12 in 1890 to 0.75 in 2010). All of this indicates that such cities benefited from the development of inland transport networks

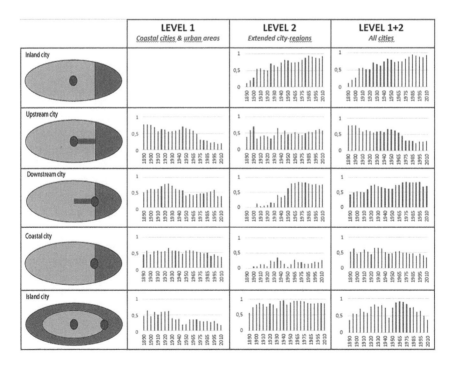

Figure 17.6 Correlation between vessel calls and urban population by city types, 1890–2010

enabling non-port cities to access maritime trade, and the development of satellite terminals at the mouth of rivers, deltas and estuaries relieving major sea-river gateways from congestion. In turn, these gateways benefited from the decline of upstream river port cities, notwithstanding certain notable counter-examples, such as Antwerp and Hamburg (Notteboom, 2016). The elevated, stable correlation for extended city-regions situated on islands underlines that vessel traffic may in fact serve distant cities not necessarily located on the coast, but in a way that keeps traffic and urban population more proportional (0.85 on average). All in all, the correlation between traffic and population has remained somewhat stable over time, from 0.63 in 2010 (coastal cities) to 0.60 in 2010 (extended city-regions), regardless of spatial change.

Traffic diversity and specialization

More detailed vessel information allowed for a disaggregated analysis based on vessel types at both ends of the study period. Relating traffic diversity to city size is motivated by earlier observations about the significant and positive effects of the latter on the former (Carter, 1962; Doumenge, 1965). Two types of vessels characterize the early period (1890–1925) based on their propulsion means: sail and steam. These two types share a common purpose of transporting all sorts of goods as well as passengers, but differ in terms of size, speed, sensitivity to natural conditions, service design and port handling facilities. Steamers represented the most modern means of transportation at the time. Vessel types in the late period were aggregated into six main categories, which reflected the type of cargo being transported.

As seen in Figure 17.7, a comparative analysis of sail and steam traffic is most relevant for coastal cities (level 1). Results for extended city-regions provided insignificant results due to the fact that in the early period most of the world's traffic concentrates in coastal cities. Sailing traffic dominates until 1900 and declines rapidly but gradually since then. The linear correlation with city size is very significant and much higher for steamer than for sailing traffic during the entire period (0.66 against 0.44 on average), which confirms that the larger the city, the more it concentrates innovative and advanced technologies. In addition, and throughout the whole period, the quantile of largest cities is specific as it handles the highest traffic mix. It means that larger cities are not only the most advanced in terms of shipping technologies, they also maintain a diversified portfolio. This reflects their longstanding role as key nodes in the shipping network as well as the diversity and path-dependency of their markets and equipment. In turn, smaller cities tend to be more specialized in either sailing or steamer traffic.

When it comes to the late period (Figure 17.8), we observe a similar trend whereby the largest cities always handle a more diversified cargo mix than smaller ones, which is valid for both coastal cities (level 1) and extended city-regions (level 2), albeit at varying degrees. The most employment-generative (general cargo), and valued (containers) traffic modes have the highest

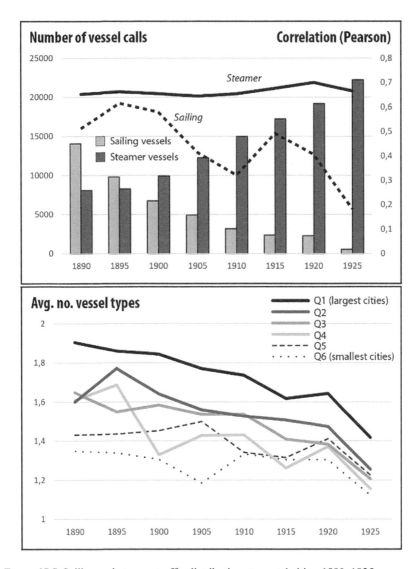

Figure 17.7 Sailing and steamer traffic distribution at coastal cities, 1890–1925

correlations with urban population, followed by vehicles and solid bulks. Correlations are much more significant for extended city-regions than for coastal cities (0.60 against 0.25 on average), meaning that such city-regions are the relevant spatial units that explain the distribution and specialization of traffic, especially solid bulks, which are closely related to the economy of large cities (i.e. construction and raw materials).

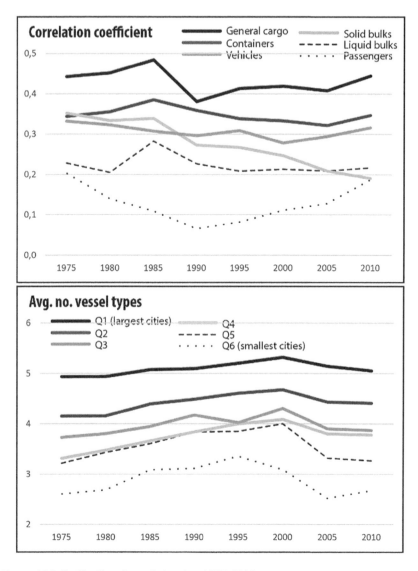

Figure 17.8 Traffic diversity and city size, 1975–2010

Interurban maritime flows

As in the case of spatial networks in general (Barthelemy, 2015), and as verified for airline networks (Guimera et al., 2005), we expect demographically larger cities to exert longer-distance interactions than smaller cities. In Figure 17.9, despite some fluctuations in the early period (1890–1900), we observe a clear dominance of the largest cities in terms of kilometric length and call-kilometers,

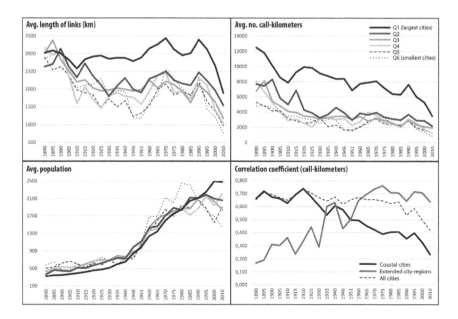

Figure 17.9 City size and scope of maritime interactions, 1890–2010

and for both samples (levels 1 and 2). It means that larger cities expand their forelands due to a more diverse and dynamic economic base than smaller cities, backed by a stronger cargo-handling capacity on site (level 1) or at some distance (level 2). Another important result obtained from the calculation of maritime distances is the fact that linear correlations between urban population and call-kilometers almost always surpassed the correlation with sole calls. This was verified for both levels 1 and 2 as well as for all cities taken as a whole. Therefore, the spatial extent of traffic is better explained by city size for the same reasons as cited above. In this respect, the maritime network linking cities of the world is not so different from theoretical models such as the central place theory, where larger cities attract goods, populations and activities from farther distances than smaller cities.

This leads us to analyze a complementary aspect of spatial networks, termed homophily, in social networks and assortativity in complex networks, which is the tendency for nodes of the same nature or size to be more connected with each other. In maritime networks, it is important and relevant to verify such a tendency as city size, in addition to the already confirmed effects, may lead to such effects. Just like in any other communication system, larger cities may dominate smaller cities while at the same time connect primarily with one another based on the idea that rich-club effects govern their relationships. For that reason, we applied the existing methodology to urban population as node weight instead of degree

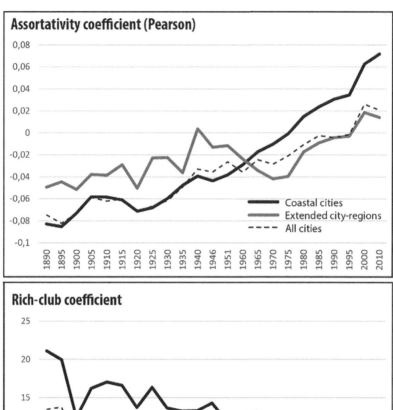

Figure 17.10 Assortativity and rich-club effects by city type, 1890–2010

centrality. As seen in Figure 17.10, the global maritime network tended to connect cities of dissimilar size in the first half of the period (negative coefficient). This structure has evolved towards zero correlation for extended city-regions and all cities, while for coastal cities (level 1) there has been a tendency towards assortativity. This means that city size differentials have given way to other factors in the distribution of maritime flows, mainly due to the fall-off in correlation between traffic and population.

The rich-club approach is based on the ratio between the gamma index of the whole network and the gamma index for the subnetwork of larger cities. Larger cities here are those within the sample with a population above world average. The gamma index is defined as the proportion of actual links within the maximum possible number of links, sometimes coined as density in literature. It is useful to check whether larger nodes are more densely connected with each other compared with the rest of the network. In the same figure, we see that the rich-club coefficient is always very high, but has regularly dropped over time. It is 1.5 times higher among coastal cities (level 1) than among extended city-regions (level 2) because the maritime network is more sparsely connected for the first than for the latter. Another interesting fact is that whereas the gamma index is on a downward trend in all cases, it declines more rapidly for the sub-networks of larger cities than for the whole network, especially since the 1930s. Comparatively speaking, the density of maritime flows among larger cities declined by 85% between 1890 and 2010, while the whole network declined by only 60%. It underlines that maritime flows became reorganized around certain intermediary hubs located outside large cities.

Cities' maritime centrality

Several complex network measures were computed to gain an understanding of their relationship with city size in the global maritime network (Figure 17.11). Overall, coastal cities (level 1) and all cities (level 1 and 2) witnessed very similar trends over time. Excentricity had the lowest correlation with city size in both cases, but nevertheless exhibited a very stable correlation, oscillating around 0.3. The three other measures have a much more significant correlation with city size, but declined drastically and regularly between 1890 and 2010. The number of calls, including extended city-regions (level 2) greatly improved the correlation and attenuated this decline. Yet, betweenness centrality, a global measure of accessibility, had the highest correlation with city size until the 1950s, reflecting on their role as hubs in a core-periphery system where interregional flows are routed through larger, primate cities. Since then, this relationship has become less significant than degree centrality. This implies that the number of direct linkages, a more local measure, is still significant in the post-1950 period, although it has also been declining. Larger cities still develop numerous linkages nowadays but their global hub function shifted to smaller cities with better infrastructure and/or accessibility. The last measure, clustering coefficient, went through a similar trend to degree centrality, but at lower levels. City size used to be a noticeably influential factor explaining hub functions in the past, but it also lost significance over time.

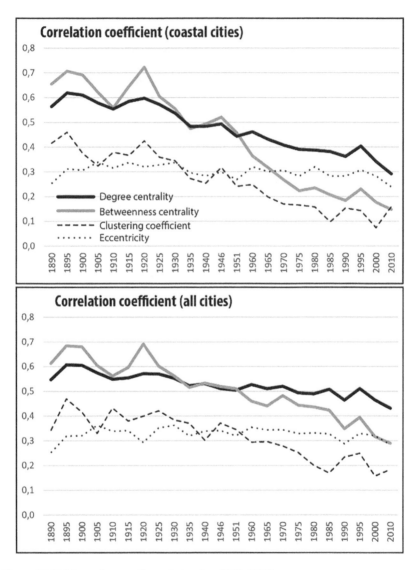

Figure 17.11 Network centrality and city size, 1890–2010

Average centrality scores by demographic size (Table 17.1) increase regularly from the smallest (Q1) to the largest cities (Q6), the latter class at a considerable distance from the others. Thus, despite the lowering correlations observed in the previous figure, larger cities persistently dominate the global maritime network.

Table 17.1 Average centrality by city size and type, 1890–2010

Class	Coastal cities				All cities			
	K	BC	CC	EX	K	BC	CC	EX
1	5	410	1.62	0.60	5	200	1.37	0.58
2	7	666	2.11	0.63	7	334	1.70	0.60
3	9	1,034	2.35	0.65	9	478	1.86	0.62
4	13	1,558	2.52	0.68	12	691	2.06	0.65
5	20	2,817	2.85	0.71	19	1,431	2.31	0.68
6	51	13,587	3.85	0.79	49	7,367	3.21	0.77

N.B. measures correspond to degree centrality (K), betweenness centrality (BC), clustering coefficient (CC) and eccentricity (EX)

One likely reason is that centrality shifts may have given advantage to a relatively small number of outliers, or less-urbanized nodes becoming more central.

Conclusion

The long-term analysis of world city networks through the lens of maritime flows confirms well-known facts such as the declining overlap between urban and port hierarchies over time. Nevertheless, demographically larger cities have maintained their prominence in the maritime network. They are more diversified in terms of cargo types, connect over longer distances, have denser connectivity with each other and remain to the present day more central than smaller cities on average. Variations of these trends according to the geographic situation of cities could also be highlighted. What could appear as a contradiction is explained by the fact that port terminals handling the bulk of global maritime trade have become more distant from main urban centers over time, whether coastal or inland. This trend reflects the growing importance of road transport in relation to the concentration of flows at such terminals where an increasing proportion of their activity is transshipment. But the scale of extended city-regions shows that such terminals remain in the vicinity of main urban centers and therefore the correlation between city size and maritime flows has been rather constant over time despite these spatial and functional changes.

Acknowledgements

The research leading to these results has received funding from the European Research Council under the European Union's Seventh Framework Programme (FP/2007–2013) / ERC Grant Agreement n. [313847] "World Seastems". The authors would also like to thank Mrs. Liliane Lizzi for her support on cartography.

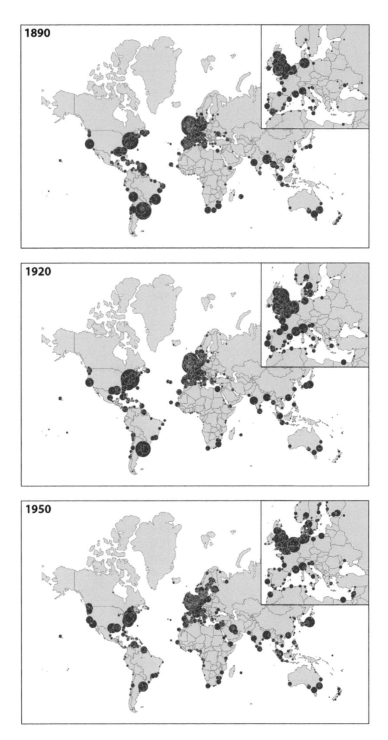

Appendix 17.1 Vessel traffic distribution by extended city-region at selected years, 1890–2010

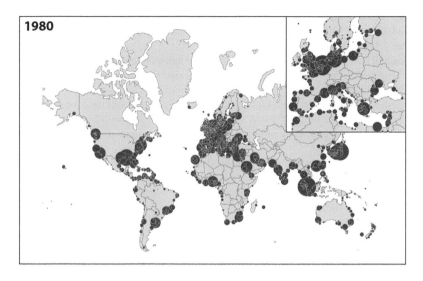

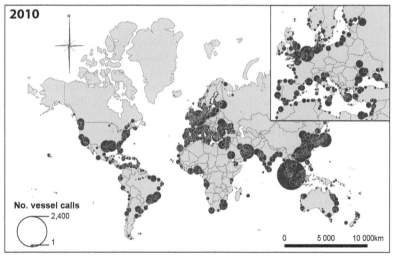

Appendix 17.1 (Continued)

References

Barthelemy M. (2015) Spatial networks: tools and perspectives. In: Ducruet C. (Ed.), *Maritime Networks: Spatial Structures and Time Dynamics*, Routledge Studies in Transport Analysis, London and New York: Routledge, pp. 50–60.

Beyers, W.B., Fowler, C.S. (2012) Economic structure, technological change and location theory: The evolution of models explaining the link between cities and flows. In: Hall, P.V., Hesse, M. (Eds.), *Cities, Regions and Flows*. London: Routledge, pp. 23–41.

Bird, J. (1963) *The Major Seaports of the United Kingdom*. London: Hutchinson.

Bird, J. (1977) *Centrality and Cities*. London: Routledge & Kegan Paul.

Braudel, F. (1979) *Civilisation matérielle, économie et capitalisme, XVe-XVIIIe siècle*. Paris: Armand Colin.

Bretagnolle, A. (2015) City systems and maritime transport in the long term. In: Ducruet, C. (Ed.), *Maritime Networks: Spatial Structures and Time Dynamics*. London and New York: Routledge Studies in Transport Analysis, pp. 27–36.

Brocard, M. (1988) Les relations fonctionnelles entre le port et la ville. In: Proceedings of the *First Annual Conference of the International Association Cities and Ports*, Le Havre, p. 69.

Brocard, M., Lecoquierre, B., Mallet, P. (1995) Le chorotype de l'estuaire européen. *Mappemonde*, 3: 6–7.

Carter, R.E. (1962) A comparative analysis of United States ports and their traffic characteristics. *Economic Geography*, 38: 162–175.

Dobruszkes, F., Lennert, M., Van Hamme, G. (2011) An analysis of the determinants of air traffic volume for European metropolitan areas. *Journal of Transport Geography*, 19(4): 755–762.

Doumenge, F. (1965) *Géographie des Mers*. Paris: Presses Universitaires de France.

Ducruet, C. (2013) Network diversity and maritime flows. *Journal of Transport Geography*, 30: 77–88.

Ducruet, C. (2016) *La spatialité des réseaux maritimes. Contributions maritimes à l'analyse des réseaux en géographie*. Mémoire d'Habilitation à Diriger des Recherches, University of Paris I Panthéon-Sorbonne.

Ducruet, C., Beauguitte, L. (2014) Spatial science and network science: Review and outcomes of a complex relationship. *Networks and Spatial Economics*, 14(3–4): 297–316.

Ducruet, C., Itoh, H. (2015) The mutual specialization of port regions connected by multiple commodity flows in a maritime network. In: Ducruet, C. (Ed.), *Maritime Networks: Spatial Structures and Time Dynamics*. London and New York: Routledge Studies in Transport Analysis, pp. 285–302.

Ducruet, C., Itoh, H. (2016) Regions and material flows: Investigating the regional branching and industry relatedness of port traffic in a global perspective. *Journal of Economic Geography*, 16(4): 805–830.

Ducruet, C., Lee, S.W. (2006) Frontline soldiers of globalisation: Port-city evolution and regional competition. *Geojournal*, 67(2): 107–122.

El Hosni, A. (2015) *Le Retour du Port dans la Ville*. Unpublished Master Dissertation in Geography, University of Paris 4 Sorbonne, Paris.

Fleming, D.K., Hayuth, Y. (1994) Spatial characteristics of transportation hubs: Centrality and intermediacy. *Journal of Transport Geography*, 2(1): 3–18.

Fujita, M., Mori, T. (1996) The role of ports in the making of major cities: Self-agglomeration and hub-effect. *Journal of Development Economics*, 49(1): 93–120.

Gipouloux, F. (2009) *La Méditerranée asiatique, villes portuaires et réseaux marchands en Chine, au Japon et en Asie du Sud-Est, XVIe-XXIe siècle*. Paris: CNRS Éditions.

Guerrero, D. (2014) Deep-sea hinterlands: Some empirical evidence of the spatial impact of containerization. *Journal of Transport Geography*, 35: 84–94.

Guerrero, D., Proulhac, L. (2014) Freight flows and urban hierarchy. *Research in Transportation Business and Management*, 11: 105–115.

Guimera R., Mossa S., Turtschi A., Amaral L.A. (2005) The worldwide air transportation network: Anomalous centrality, community structure, and cities' global roles. *Proceedings of the National Academy of Sciences USA*, 102(22): 7794–7799.

Hall, P.V., Hesse, M. (2012) *Cities, Regions and Flows*. London and New York: Routledge.

Hall, P.V., Jacobs, W. (2012) Why are maritime ports (still) urban, and why should policy makers care? *Maritime Policy and Management*, 39(2): 189–206.

Hayuth, Y. (1981) Containerization and the load center concept. *Economic Geography*, 57(2): 160–176.

Helders, S. (2012) *World Gazetteer*. Discontinued website.

Hoyle, B.S. (1989) The port-city interface: Trends, problems, and examples. *Geoforum*, 20(4): 429–435.

Jacobs, W., Koster, H.R.A., Hall, P.V. (2011) The location and global network structure of maritime advanced producer services. *Urban Studies*, 48(13): 2749–2769.

Lahmeyer, J. (2015) *Population Statistics. Growth of the Population Per Country in a Historical Perspective, Including their Administrative Divisions and Principal Towns*. Available at: www.populstat.info/

Lee, S.W., Song, D.W., Ducruet, C. (2008) A tale of Asia's world ports: The spatial evolution in global hub port cities. *Geoforum*, 39(1): 372–385.

Lemarchand, A. (2000) *La dynamique des ports: mesures de la valeur et des emplois, emplois et valeur des mesures*. Paris: DATAR.

Lewis, M.W., Wigen, K. (1999) A maritime response to the crisis in area studies. *Geographical Review*, 89(2): 161–168.

Marnot, B. (2005) Interconnexion et reclassements: l'insertion des ports français dans la chaîne multimodale au XIXe siècle. *Flux*, 59(1): 10–21.

Moriconi-Ebrard, F. (1994) *Geopolis: pour Comparer les Villes du Monde*. Paris: Economica.

Murphey, R. (1989) On the evolution of the port city. In: Broeze, F. (Ed.), *Brides of the Sea: Port Cities of Asia From the 16th–20th Centuries*. Honolulu: University of Hawaii Press, pp. 223–245.

Nelson, A. (2008) *Travel Time to Major Cities: A Global Map of Accessibility*. Global Environment Monitoring Unit, Joint Research Centre of the European Commission, Ispra, Italy.

Ng, A.K.Y., Ducruet, C. (2014) The changing tides of port geography (1950–2012). *Progress in Human Geography*, 38(6): 785–823.

Noin, D. (1999) La population des littoraux du monde. *L'Information Géographique*, 63(2): 65–73.

Norcliffe, G., Bassett, K., Hoare, T. (1996) The emergence of postmodernism on the urban waterfront: Geographical perspectives on changing relationships. *Journal of Transport Geography*, 4(2): 123–134.

Notteboom, T.E. (2016) The adaptive capacity of container ports in an era of mega vessels: The case of upstream seaports Antwerp and Hamburg. *Journal of Transport Geography*, 54: 295–309.

Peris, A. (2016) *Penser les villes en réseaux: une analyse des théories sur les liens interurbains*. Master Dissertation in Geography, University of Paris I Panthéon-Sorbonne.

Pumain, D., Paulus, F., Vacchiani-Marcuzzo, C. (2009) Innovation cycles and urban dynamics. In: Lane, D., van der Leeuw, S., Pumain, D., West, G. (Eds.), *Complexity Perspectives in Innovation and Social Change*. Springer Methodos Series 7, Basel, Switzerland: Springer, pp. 237–260.

Rimmer, P.J. (1967) The changing status of New Zealand seaports, 1853–1960. *Annals of the Association of American Geographers*, 57(1): 88–100.

Savy, M. (1991) Port, ville et territoire. In: Collin, M., Baudouin, T. (Eds.), *Villes Portuaires et Nouveaux Enjeux Internationaux*. Le Havre: International Association Cities and Ports, pp. 91–101.

Taaffe, E.J., Morrill, R.L., Gould, P.R. (1963) Transport expansion in underdevelopped countries: A comparative analysis. *Geographical Review*, 53: 503–529.

Taylor, P.J., Hoyler, M., Verbruggen, R. (2010) External urban relational process: Introducing central flow theory to complement central place theory. *Urban Studies*, 47(13): 2803–2818.

Thayer, R.E., Whelan, R.K. (1989) Port cities face complex challenges. In: Knight, R.V., Gappert, G. (Eds.), *Cities in a Global Society*. Urban Affairs Annual Review 35. London: Sage Publications, pp. 120–131.

Vance, J.E. (1970) *The Merchant's World: The Geography of Wholesaling*. Englewood Cliffs: Prentice-Hall.

Vigarié, A. (1991) Villes portuaires et changements économiques. In: Proceedings of the *3rd International Conference of the International Association Cities and Ports*, Genoa, November, 19–22, pp. 44–52.

Wackermann, G. (1998) *Façades Maritimes en Mutation: une Géographie Socioéconomique des Littoraux*. Paris: Ellipses.

Zaremba, P. (1962) *Les Principes du Développement des Villes Portuaires*. Paris: Académie Polonaise des Sciences.

Part III
Vulnerability analyses

18 Attacker-defender modelling of vulnerability in maritime logistics corridors

Pablo Achurra-Gonzalez, Panagiotis Angeloudis, Konstantinos Zavitsas, Ali Niknejad and Daniel J. Graham

Within maritime transport, container liner shipping has revolutionised the way products are transported between countries by increasing efficiency and reducing transportation costs. Containerisation and intermodal operations mean that all countries are potentially connected to each other despite not having direct shipment services between them. This connectivity allows exporters and importers from distant regions to trade with each other, even if their individual trade transactions would not economically justify chartering a ship to transport a few containers from country A to country B (Fugazza, 2015).

Like all transportation systems, liner shipping networks are exposed to disruptions that range in severity from minor operational incidents to large-scale natural disasters or terrorist attacks (Bell et al., 2008). These disruptive events impact the network ability to route cargo in ways that vary significantly based on the location and severity of the disruption. The measurement and understanding of the liner shipping network susceptibility to disruptions (transport vulnerability) is therefore of vital importance to public and private stakeholders responsible for ensuring operability and accessibility to the global network of liner shipping services.

While it may be unattainable to remove all vulnerability from a transport network (Achurra-Gonzalez et al., 2016), it is possible to undertake a series of interventions that would increase its overall robustness. The objective of this chapter is to develop a quantitative framework that can be used to design such interventions against a range of potential network disruptions.

Lhomme (2015) extends previous works on power grid systems (Ouyang et al., 2014) to classify two types of methodologies for the assessment of vulnerability in maritime networks. The first type is based on complex network topological models that measure indicators such as connectivity, betweenness and degree centrality of network components (Angeloudis et al., 2007; Ducruet et al., 2010; Ducruet, 2016). Nodes and links with the highest performance on these metrics are then assumed to be the most vulnerable in the network. The second type is based on real-flow models that use transport system constraints and operation costs to describe the performance of networks and flow redistribution in the aftermath of disruptions (Paul and Maloni, 2010).

Though complex-network topological models provide a sound approach to ranking vulnerable components, they fail to capture re-routing capabilities on secondary path alternatives with spare capacity and the financial gains (if any) from the prevention of disruptions. The latter is vital for decision-makers evaluating the feasibility of investment decisions aimed at increasing the robustness of the network.

In this chapter, we propose a real flow-based approach to capture redistributions of flows in container shipping networks under disruption and a game-theoretic approach for the quantitative measurement of transport vulnerabilities using an attacker-defender model (ADM). The ADM consists of a two-player, non-cooperative, mixed-strategy game between a malevolent agent (attacker) which tries to maximise disruption costs and a global network router (defender) seeking to minimise routing costs (Bell, 2000; Bencomo, 2009). The game is formulated as a maximin linear program (Hillier and Lieberman, 2005), where, at the mixed-strategy Nash equilibrium, the most vulnerable nodes and links are identified, and the minimum cost routes for given origin-destination (OD) pairs are found.

To deploy our ADM, we generate a payoff matrix for both players implementing a cost-based container assignment model (CBCAM) adapted for networks under disruption building upon previous work by Bell et al. (2013) and Achurra-Gonzalez et al. (2016). The CBCAM is formulated as an LP and is used to generate routing costs for the ocean carrier and disruption costs for the attacker on each of the scenarios evaluated in the payoff matrix. Contrary to traditional graph theory approaches, the joined CBCAM and ADM formulation is suitable for the context of our study because it illustrates the re-distribution of container flows aggregating cost dependencies such as container transport costs and penalty costs for cargo not routed. Furthermore, the CBCAM includes network component capacity constraints and a virtual task network approach (Jourquin et al., 2008), which accurately represent liner shipping operations where vessels can skip disrupted network components on pre-established port call sequences. The latter is a distinctive feature of maritime networks where, unlike road and rail transport, most edges connecting vertices are not dependent on physical infrastructure (except for canals or draft-restricted navigable areas) which allows for greater flexibility when re-routing vessels.

In this chapter, we improve previous formulations of the CBCAM for the analysis of liner shipping disruptions by introducing additional dependency parameters to the network links defined by Bell et al. (2011, 2013) and Angeloudis et al. (2016). The dependency assignment is done using a maritime pathfinder that automatically detects the use of physical maritime infrastructures such as canals, straits or access channels and provides the capability of modelling disruption scenarios on these critical network components. Our enhanced model includes additional capacity constraints that restrict or impede the flow of containers through physical maritime corridors in the aftermath of disruptions. The result is a methodology capable of modelling container routing paths and costs in scenarios of disruptions at ports, liner services and maritime logistics corridors defined by the user.

The LP formulations allow for extensions to large-scale liner shipping networks while still allowing the problem to be efficiently solvable with commercially available solvers (Achurra-Gonzalez et al., 2016; Bell et al., 2013). With this capability, we construct a numerical case study of a realistic global-scale network from a major ocean carrier where disruptions occur on main maritime logistic corridors identified by Rodrigue et al. (2017). The case study network encompasses eight main maritime logistics corridors, 88 distinct liner services, 230 active container ports and 6,311 OD flow pairs representing about 111,500 weekly FFE (containers of forty-foot equivalent units) to be routed in the network. To the best of our knowledge, this is the largest implementation of both the CBCAM and attacker-defender model in liner shipping networks to the date.

Results indicate higher vulnerability in the Malacca Strait, followed by the Suez Canal. Hypothetical scenarios of network interventions allow us to measure the financial gains from preventing disruptions on each of the main maritime logistics corridors identified and to quantitatively rank their importance in the network. The remainder of this chapter is organised as follows: the methodology section describes the two-player game and CBCAM and formulation to generate the pay-off matrix. The numerical case section describes the data sourcing process, calibration and input parameter selection for the model. The results sections highlight the main findings from the numerical case study network. The conclusion summarises the contributions achieved in this work and outlines future work.

Methodology

We define a two-player, non-cooperative, mixed-strategy game between a malevolent agent (attacker) and a global network operator (defender), where each player tries to optimise its utility. The objective of the game is to find the mixed-strategy Nash equilibrium and respective network disruption and routing costs for both players (Zavitsas, 2011).

In our formulation, the attacker is an abstract entity that encompasses all potential sources of disruption risks in liner shipping networks. These include, but are not limited to, accidents, labour strikes, equipment failure, natural disasters, political conflicts and terrorist attacks. For comprehensive reviews of disruption risks affecting maritime supply chains, we refer to Lam (2012) and Loh and Van Thai (2014). On the other hand, the defender is a typical global ocean carrier seeking to meet transport demands at the lowest possible routing cost while avoiding links or nodes disrupted by the attacker.

The defender's objective is to identify any critical component the attacker may disrupt so it can divert container flows through other network components to minimise routing costs. By contrast, the attacker's objective is to disrupt critical components, which the defender does not expect to be affected, in order to maximise disruption costs.

We implement a CBCAM adapted for the analysis of shipping networks under disruption to generate a payoff matrix of utilities for the two-player game. The payoff matrix is formed by routing costs for the ocean carrier and disruption costs for the network attacker. In the following subsections, we describe the assumptions and formulations of the CBCAM and two-player game.

Cost-Based Container Assignment Model

The following key network concepts and assumptions used in our CBCAM implementation are adopted from previous work by Bell et al. (2013) and Achurra-Gonzalez et al. (2016):

- *Liner services* are scheduled sequences of port calls operated by an ocean carrier or alliance.
- *Links* are physical connections between pairs of port calls served by a liner service.
- *Legs* are virtual transport tasks executed by a given liner service (formed by one or more links).
- *Paths* are chains of transport tasks or legs.
- A single container type is considered, with a fixed set of daily rent and handling costs, which enables the aggregation of data on container flows and liner service capacities. Repositioning of empty containers is not considered.
- An exogenous OD matrix is used as demand input for the model. The rate at which containers are shipped does not vary with time.
- Containers are transported by ocean carriers operating fixed liner service routes between ports. Liner services have fixed port call frequency, but the arrival at each port is uncoordinated between ships of different services. Hence, container dwell time at each port is assumed to be the inverse of the sum of the service frequencies at each port.
- Multiple legs connecting identical port pairs are possible, but their capacity cannot be aggregated due to distinct characteristics such as transit time, container handling costs and frequency.
- Cost components considered in our formulation are: container handling costs, container rental costs, cargo depreciation and penalty costs for containers not transported (5). Ship operating costs such as fuel and crew expenses are treated as fixed and vary according to vessel cargo carrying capacity (example shown in Table 18.3).

Previous formulations of frequency and cost-based container assignment models by Bell et al. (2011, 2013) provided the groundwork for the implementation of the transit assignment approach (Spiess and Florian, 1989), extensively used in urban transport, to the routing of full and empty containers in a given liner shipping network. The application of transit assignment in conjunction with a virtual task network approach (Jourquin et al., 2008) to include liner service capacity constraints provided an accurate representation of liner shipping operations where vessels within a liner service can skip disrupted ports in a pre-defined sequence of port calls. However, both applications of Bell et al. (2011, 2013) assumed sufficient transport capacity (in links and nodes) to meet transport demands between ports, which is not always the case in the aftermath of network disruptions.

Later implementations of the CBCAM by Achurra-Gonzalez et al. (2016) included additional decision variables that sought to identify the largest possible amount of containers to be routed and a penalty cost for each container not transported in scenarios of port disruptions. The latter implementation allowed feasible solutions when transport capacity fell below transport demand, but it was not sufficient to model disruptions on physical corridors such as canals, straits, access channels or other key maritime logistics corridors in the network, which are equally exposed to disruptions.

In this chapter, we improve previous formulations of the CBCAM for the analysis of liner shipping disruptions with the introduction of additional dimensions to the network links defined by Bell et al. (2011, 2013) to capture their dependency on maritime infrastructures, such as canals, straits or access channels. This improvement is done taking each port call sequence (liner service) from the network input and implementing a maritime pathfinder that identifies the shortest maritime corridor path (formed by links) connecting each port pair. Then, the generated path is checked against a set of predefined geographical lines for each of the corridors to see if they have been traversed. If there is an intersection, we assign 1 to Boolean parameter δ_{alk} to indicate link l used in transport task a traverses maritime corridor k and 0 otherwise. The assignment of maritime infrastructure corridors to each link allows the addition of capacity constraints that restrict or impede the flow of containers through these physical maritime corridors in the aftermath of disruptions.

Table 18.1 presents the model notation used in our implementation of the CBCAM and ADM. To simplify the formulation of the CBCAM, we adopt the custom notation introduced in [13], [16] where $+$ replaces the summation over $s \in D$ in x_{as}^f and $++$ replaces the summation over $r \in O, s \in D$ in w_{rs}^f as follows: $x_{a+}^f = \sum_{s \in D} x_{as}^f, w_{++}^f = \sum_{r \in O} \sum_{s \in D} w_{rs}^f$. The CBCAM is then formulated as the following LP:

Objective:

$$
\begin{aligned}
Min \, Uij = \sum_{n \in N} \sum_{a \in A} CHC_{an}^f x_{a+}^f + \left(\sum_{a \in A} x_{a+}^f C_a + w_{++}^f \right) \\
\left(CR + DV \right) + \sum_{r \in O} \sum_{s \in D} (TDF_{rs} - t_{rs}^f) PC
\end{aligned}
\tag{1}
$$

Subject to:

$$
\sum_{a \in A_k^+} x_{as}^f - \sum_{a \in A_k^-} x_{as}^f = B_k^f \quad \forall k \in K, s \in D
\tag{2}
$$

$$
B_k^f = \begin{cases} -\sum_{s \in D} t_{rs}^f & \text{if } k = r \in O \\ \sum_{r \in O} t_{rs}^f & \text{if } k = s \in D \\ 0 & \text{otherwise} \end{cases}
\tag{3}
$$

$$
x_{as}^f \le w_{ks}^f F_a \quad \forall a \in A_i^-, k \ne s \in K, s \in D
\tag{4}
$$

$$
LS_n \ge \sum_{a \in A} x_{a+}^f \delta_{aln} \quad \forall l \in L_n, n \in N
\tag{5}
$$

Table 18.1 CBCAM and ADM notations

Sets		Subsets		Indices	
A	Legs	A_k^+	Legs entering port k	a	For legs
K	All ports	A_k^-	Legs leaving port k	k	For ports
D	Destination ports	A_n	Legs on liner service n	y	For maritime corridors
O	Origin ports	L_y	Links on maritime corridor k	l	For links
Y	All maritime corridors	L_n	Links on liner service n	n	For liner services
L	All links			r	For origin ports
N	All liner services			s	For destination ports
J	Components the attacker can disrupt			j	For attacker components
I	Components the defender can divert flows from			i	For defender components

Parameters

B_k^f	Net flow of full containers at each port k
C_a	Sailing time on leg a, including loading and unloading times at ports
CHC_{an}^f	Container handling cost per full container on leg a using liner service n
C_R	Rental cost per unit time per container
TDF_{rs}	Total demand for full containers to be transported from origin r to destination s
SD_{rs}	Serviced demand from origin r to destination s
DV	Depreciation cost per unit time per full container (inventory cost)
δ_{aln}	1 if leg a uses link l on liner service n, and 0 otherwise
δ_{aly}	1 if leg a uses link l on maritime corridor k, and 0 otherwise
F_a	Frequency of sailing on leg a
PT_k	Maximum throughput capacity at port k
φ_k	0 if the attacker disrupts port k or the defender diverts flows from port k, and 1 otherwise
PC	Penalty cost for full containers not transported
LS_n	Capacity of liner service n
MC_y	Capacity of maritime corridor y
α_y	0 if the attacker disrupts maritime corridor y or the defender diverts flows from maritime corridor y, and 1 otherwise

Decision variables

t_{rs}^f	Flow of full containers transported from origin r to destination s
x_{as}^f	Flow of full containers on leg a en route to destination s
w_{ks}^f	Expected dwell time at port k for all full containers en route to destination s
p_i	Probability defender diverts flows from component i
q_j	Probability attacker disrupts component j
z	Value of the game for the attacker (disruption costs)
v	Value of the game for the defender (routing costs)

Source: Adapted from Achurra-Gonzalez et al. (2016)

$$\varphi_k PT_k \geq \sum_{a \in A_k^-} x_{a+}^f + \sum_{a \in A_k^+} x_{a+}^f \quad \forall k \in K \tag{6}$$

$$\varphi_k = \begin{cases} 0 \, if \, i \in K \\ 0 \, if \, j \in K \\ 1 \, otherwise \end{cases} \tag{7}$$

$$\alpha_y MC_y \geq \sum_{a \in A} x_{a+}^f \delta_{aly} \quad \forall \in L_y, y \in Y \tag{8}$$

$$\alpha_y = \begin{cases} 0 \, if \, i \in Y \\ 0 \, if \, j \in Y \\ 1 \, otherwise \end{cases} \tag{9}$$

$$x_{as}^f \geq 0 \quad \forall a \in A, s \in D \tag{10}$$

$$t_{rs}^f \leq TDF_{rs} \quad \forall r \in O, s \in D \tag{11}$$

Objective function (1) minimises total network costs U_{ij} when the attacker disrupts component j and the defender diverts cargo flow from component i. Total network costs are the sum of container handling, inventory and rental costs generated from the assignment of container flows to network legs and penalty costs for cargo not transported. Flow conservation is enforced in constraints (2) and (3). Constraint (4) ensures that container dwell time at ports k is at least as large as the inverse of combined liner service frequency of legs bound to destination s. Capacity constraints for liner services n are defined in (5). Port throughput capacities are defined in (6) where constraint (7) disables ports k disrupted by the attacker or avoided by the defender. Similarly, maritime corridor capacities in infrastructures such as canals, access channels and straits are defined in (8). Constraint (9) disables maritime corridor y disrupted by the attacker or avoided by the defender. Constraint (10) ensures non-negative flow assignments in the optimal solution. Lastly, constraint (11) sets the total number of containers routed to be less than or equal to original OD demand matrix TDF_{rs}. The latter allows for quantifying and penalising the amount of containers not routed in cases where transport demand falls below maximum transport capacity in the network.

Attacker-Defender Model

Assumptions of our implementation of the attacker-defender model include (Zavitsas, 2011):

- The attacker is capable of disrupting one network component (node or link) at a time;
- The defender is capable of routing cargo through any component of the network;
- The game is played simultaneously;
- Both players know the abilities of their opponent but have no knowledge of the strategy played by their opponent.

Following the notation presented in Table 18.1, given that the attacker disrupts a component j and the defender diverts cargo from a certain component i, the following two outcomes are possible for each U_{ij} scenario (Zavitsas, 2011):

1   $i = j$: The attacker disrupts component j, and the defender diverts cargo from component $i = j$. This results on $m - 1$ functional components in the network for the routing of cargo flows.
2   $i \neq j$: The attacker disrupts component j, and the defender diverts cargo from component $i \neq j$. This results on $m - 2$ functional components in the network for the routing of cargo flows.

Network costs for all possible U_{ij} scenarios are presented in the payoff matrix of the game. In our study, this matrix is square as $I = J$ and is constructed with the format shown on Table 18.2. We populate U_{ij} values of the matrix using iterations of the CBCAM. Given J^2 components and $U_{ij} = U_{ji}$, the minimum number of CBCAM iterations required to populate the payoff matrix of our attacker-defender model increases polynomially according to $J^2/2 - J$. The diagonal values represent scenarios where the defender predicts accurately the component disrupted by the attacker. Since $U_{ii} < U_{ij}$, the attacker never selects values in the diagonal (Zavitsas, 2011).

Our implementation of the attacker-defender model is then formulated as the following maximin problem building upon previous work by Bell (2000) and Zavitsas (2011):

Objective:

$$Max\left(Min \sum_i \sum_j p_i U_{ij} q_j \right) \tag{12}$$

Subject to:

$$\sum_j q_j = 1 \tag{13}$$

$$\sum_i p_i = 1 \tag{14}$$

$$q_j, P_i \geq 0 \; \forall i \in I, j \in J \tag{15}$$

Table 18.2 Payoff matrix format

Scenario i: Defender diverts flows from component i	Scenario j: Attacker disrupts component j				
	Components	1	2	...	n
	1	U_{11}	U_{12}	...	U_{1n}
	2	U_{21}	U_{22}	...	U_{2n}
	...	...	...	...	...
	m	U_{m1}	U_{m2}	...	U_{mn}

Source: Adapted from Zavitsas (2011)

The objective function (12) seeks component choice probabilities that maximise disruption costs for the attacker while simultaneously seeking component choice probabilities that minimise expected routing costs for the defender subject to constraints (13) and (14).

It is well known (Bell, 2000; Hillier and Lieberman, 2005) that maximin problems can be solved by transforming them to conventional LP problems. For the LP transformation of our maximin problem, we introduce decision variable z (network disruption costs) in objective function (16) as the value of the game for the attacker. As demonstrated in Hillier and Lieberman (2005), z is maximised setting it as the right-hand side of inequality (17) for expected payoffs of the attacker from all scenarios i. Constraint (18) ensures that the sum of probabilities q_j is equal to 1.

Objective:

$$Max\ z \tag{16}$$

Subject to:

$$\sum_j U_{ij} q_j \geq z \quad \forall i \in I \tag{17}$$

$$\sum_j q_j = 1 \tag{18}$$

$$q_j \geq 0 \ \forall j \in J \tag{19}$$

Similarly, we introduce decision variable v (network routing costs) in objective function (20) as the value of the game for the defender. Variable v is minimised setting it as the right-hand side of inequality (21) for the expected payoffs of the defender from all scenarios j. Constraint (22) ensures that the sum of probabilities p_i is equal to 1.

Objective:

$$Min\ v \tag{20}$$

Subject to:

$$\sum_i U_{ij} p_i \leq v \quad \forall j \in J \tag{21}$$

$$\sum_i p_i = 1 \tag{22}$$

$$p_i \geq 0 \ \forall i \in I \tag{23}$$

The LP formulation of the attacker is the dual of the defender's LP and viceversa (Bell, 2000; Hillier and Lieberman, 2005). Therefore, at optimum, $z = v$, which represents the mixed strategy Nash equilibrium of the game. For a more in-depth discussion of LP transformations and solutions for mixed-strategy games, we refer to Hillier and Lieberman (2005).

Kanturska and Angeloudis (2013) indicate that, at equilibrium, component-based probabilities for the attacker identify the worst case attack probabilities, assuming that these are what the defender is reacting to. Therefore, components with higher attack probability are the most vulnerable in the network. By contrast, component-based probabilities for the defender indicate the safest path choice frequency, which often involves using more than one path (crucial in maritime supply chain networks).

The optimal value of the game for the attacker ensures that a certain disruption cost can be expected irrespective of the routing paths selected by the defender. Therefore, the value of the game can be used as a quantitative measure of overall transport vulnerability (Kanturska and Angeloudis, 2013). On the other hand, the value of the game for the defender indicates the expected total routing cost in the worst-case scenario. The routing strategies selected by the defender guarantee that no matter the attacker's choices for component disruption, the experienced cost will be no higher than the value of the game (Kanturska and Angeloudis, 2013).

Case study outline

We applied the proposed methodology to a numerical case study network generated using publicly available data. The case study network encompasses 8 main maritime logistics corridors, 88 distinct liner services, 230 active container ports and 6,311 OD flow pairs representing 111,523 weekly FFE to be routed in the network. All parameters are adjusted to FFE or FFE/week using the conversion factor 1 *FFE* = 2 *TEU*. Table 18.3 provides a summary of the parameters used in the case study network.

The data for OD demand flows and container transport costs for different vessel types were obtained from the LINER-LIB-2012 dataset described in Brouer et al. (2014). This dataset is generated from past and public data from Maersk Line and industry publications from sources such as Drewry Shipping Consultants and Alphaliner. LINER-LIB-2012 was made available to the general public to benchmark algorithms that solve liner shipping network design problems (LSNDP) which require realistic data inputs often inaccessible to researchers due to industry confidentiality practices. LSNDP and the container routing problem addressed in our work share a common set of inputs (e.g., OD flows in terms of container units and container vessel costs) which make LINER-LIB-2012 equally suitable for our analysis.

Specific OD flows used in our network are from the *World Large* network instance in LINER-LIB-12. Container transport costs for each vessel class (shown in Table 18.3) are computed dividing time charter (TC) rates by the vessel's FFE carrying capacity. TC rates in our network are also obtained from LINER-LIB-12 and include operating expenses (OPEX), crew and maintenance costs (Brouer et al., 2014).

Liner shipping network data describing port call rotations, transit times, and nominal vessel cargo carrying capacity is also publicly available on most ocean carrier websites or through private industry data providers. For our case study network, the *Georgia Tech Panama Logistics Innovation & Center* provided us

Table 18.3 Summary case study network parameters

Transport cost per vessel class			
Vessel class	*Capacity (FFE)*	*Time charter rate (USD/day)*	*Handling cost (USD/FFE/day)*
Feeder_450	450	4,680	10.40
Feeder_800	800	7,966	9.96
Panamax_1200	1,200	11,683	9.74
Panamax_2400	2,400	21,774	9.07
Post_Panamax	4,200	33,922	8.08
Super_PostPanamax	7,500	48,750	6.50
Network particulars			
Cargo rate of depreciation for loaded containers	40 USD/FFE/day		
Maritime corridors	Panama Canal, Suez Canal, Strait of Gibraltar, Bab el-Mandab, Cape of Good Hope, Bosporus Strait, Strait of Hormuz, Strait of Malacca		
Number of distinct liner services	88		
OD flows	6,500 OD pairs; 111,523 FFE/week		
Penalty cost for containers not transported	25,000 USD/FFE		
Rental cost for loaded/empty containers	9 USD/FFE/day		

with a sample data set sufficient to model liner shipping network configurations of representative ocean carriers as of May 2014. This sample dataset was processed to remove errors such as double-counting of liner capacity in cases where two ocean carriers advertise the same liner service under different names (e.g., as a result of vessel sharing agreements). We filtered the Georgia Tech Panama dataset for Maersk Line services to correspond with the ocean carrier OD demand flows obtained from LINER-LIB-2012.

For liner service capacity inputs, we adopt the approach by Achurra-Gonzalez et al. (2016), where for services with weekly port call frequency, LS_n is equal to the average nominal container carrying capacity of vessels deployed. For liner services with port call frequencies not given in a weekly time-window, we standardise them using equation (21) below:

$$LS_n = \left(\frac{\sum_{p=1}^{V_n} NC_{pn}}{V_n} \right)\left(\frac{SMF}{F_n} \right) \tag{24}$$

Where

NC_{pn} Nominal FFE capacity of vessel p deployed in liner service n
V_n Total number of vessels deployed in liner service n

p Index of vessels ranging from 1 to V_n
SMF   Standardised model input frequency in which the capacity will be expressed
F_n Port call frequency of liner service n

The confidentiality of Maersk Line data is maintained in LINER-LIB-2012 applying a reasonable random perturbation described in Brouer et al. (2014). Similarly, container vessel particulars (e.g., nominal cargo carrying capacity) in our sample network data were adjusted to average vessel types in LINER-LIB-2012 and the names and specific port rotations in the network remain confidential. Despite these perturbations to the data, model inputs remain realistic and do not affect the analysis presented in this study. In practice, network configurations, vessel capacities, and demand flow data will vary by ocean carrier. The purpose of the data used in this study is to test the applicability of the quantitative framework proposed and not the evaluation of the network of a specific ocean carrier. Practitioners or researchers with access to real commercial data could replace the model input presented in this study with their specific data sets.

Rental and cargo depreciation costs used in the model are commensurate with the pricing structures employed in previous studies by Bell et al. (2011, 2013) as shown in Table 18.3. Penalty costs for containers not transported due to transport capacity limits are assumed to be USD 25,000 per FFE. This value is calibrated to be higher than any alternative routing costs in U_{ij} disruption scenarios to ensure that cargo flows are maximised when routing capacity is available (Achurra-Gonzalez et al., 2016).

Main maritime corridors in our network are the *primary passages* identified by Rodrigue et al. (2017). These corridors are critical locations in global trade and play a strategic role in maritime networks, as disruptions in any of them would significantly impair cost-effective shipping (Rodrigue et al., 2017). Maritime corridors in our case network (shown in Figure 18.1) are the Panama Canal, the Suez Canal, the Strait of Gibraltar, Bab el-Mandab, the Cape of Good Hope, the Bosporus Strait, the Strait of Hormuz and the Strait of Malacca.

Disruptions in our network are assumed to occur only in maritime corridors (set Y defined in the methodology section). For a link to be affected by such disruptions, it has to traverse the logistics corridor fully. For example, containers shipped from Tanjung Pelepas (Malaysia) to Algeciras (Spain) cross the Strait of Malacca, Bab el-Mandab and the Suez Canal (in this order). Even though the port of Algeciras is in direct proximity to the eastern side of the Strait of Gibraltar, any cargo coming from Tanjung Pelepas does not have to traverse Gibraltar fully to be unloaded in Algeciras. Hence, the container flows described in this example are not affected by possible disruptions in the Gibraltar corridor. Container flows are considered to traverse maritime corridors fully when transiting through the defined red lines shown in Figure 18.1 for each maritime corridor. The maritime path line intensity is based on the logarithm of the number of times each maritime path is used to connect port pairs in our case study network.

Port and maritime corridors are assumed to meet container transport demands. This assumption does not affect our analysis because the case study network

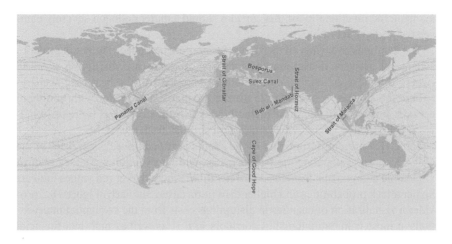

Figure 18.1 Global distribution of liner shipping services and main maritime logistics corridors in case study network

Source: Own elaboration based on Rodrigue et al. (2017)

captures liner services of only one representative ocean carrier. In practice, container ports and maritime corridors provide service to multiple ocean carriers. Therefore, when fully functional, these network components have sufficient capacity to route OD flows of the representative ocean carrier in our network.

Implementation and results

The LPs for the CBCAM and ADM were formulated in OPL (Optimization Programming Language) and the optimal solutions were found using the ILOG CPLEX optimization engine on a relatively modern workstation (6-Core Intel Xeon E5-1650 v2 3.50GHz processor with 64GB RAM). The average solution time for U_{ij} scenarios was 11:43 minutes. Since we had $J = 8$ disruptable maritime corridors, we ran the model 36 times (minimum number of required iterations defined as $J^2 / 2 - J$) to populate the payoff matrix.

Once a complete payoff matrix is available, the game of the attacker is solved to compute disruption costs $z*$ (in USD) as a global measure of transport vulnerability. Attack probabilities identify maritime corridors that would maximise disruption costs if disabled by the attacker and therefore are critical for the network under consideration. We include hypothetical scenarios of sequential intervention strategies where the most critical maritime corridor of each iteration $t - 1$ is defended against disruptions in iteration t.

Potential interventions to defend maritime corridors assume tackling distinct regional risks. For example, an intervention to defend the Bab el-Mandab corridor will consist of a political intervention to increase the presence of naval coalitions aimed at reducing piracy attacks. Similarly, the second set of locks in the Panama

Canal expansion project is considered an infrastructure intervention strategy to maintain the functionality of this corridor should a major collision severely damage the primary set of locks.

The iterations end when all maritime corridors are defended. The result provides a range of network disruption costs z^* from a worst-case disruption scenario (where the most vulnerable component is disrupted) to the best case scenario (where the attacker is only able to disrupt the maritime corridor with minimum network impact). This iterative method ranks maritime corridors by relative network vulnerability expressed as attack probabilities from the ADM.

Table 18.4 presents a summary of the results obtained from U_{ij} scenarios of the CBCAM used to populate the payoff matrix and intervention strategies at most vulnerable components from the ADM iterations where darker red values indicate higher attack probabilities and higher disruption costs. Similarly, Figure 18.2 provides a visualisation of changes in disruptions costs from the sequential interventions at most vulnerable logistics corridors in $t-1$ as well as marginal financial gains from such interventions.

As shown in Table 18.4 and Figure 18.2, at iteration $t = 0$, no maritime corridors are defended. The Malacca Strait is the most vulnerable component followed by the extended Suez Canal corridor with attack probabilities 0.982 (MAL) and 0.018 (GIB) respectively. The extended Suez Canal corridor is formed by Gibraltar, the Suez Canal and Bab el-Mandab. These maritime corridors were grouped due to their geographic locations and maritime traffic relationship, where disruptions in test iterations at any of these three corridors significantly hamper container flows through each other. Since *secondary passages* identified by Rodrigue et al. (2017) were not included at this stage of the study, disruptions in the Malacca Strait are assumed to be sufficiently large to impede flows through the alternative secondary maritime corridors such as Makassar, Sunda and Lombok.

Components of the extended Suez Canal corridor and the Strait of Hormuz rank as most vulnerable until iteration $t = 4$ in the following order: GIB, BEM, HOR and SUC. Subsequent iterations ($t = 4$ to $t = 7$) respectively rank the Bosporus Strait, Cape of Good Hope and the Panama Canal as the remaining maritime corridors in terms of network vulnerability.

Total disruption costs from the worst to best case scenarios range from USD 1.4 billion to USD 4.2 million. There is a dramatic decrease in disruption costs (-63%) from iteration $t = 0$ to $t = 1$ resulting in USD 873 million from defending the Strait of Malacca. This represents the largest gain from defending a network component. The second largest gain is achieved when completing the defense of components of the extended Suez Canal corridor: USD 301 million from iteration $t = 4$ to $t = 5$. These results consolidate the Malacca Strait as the most vulnerable maritime corridor in the network studied followed by the extended Suez Canal corridor.

Evaluating these results while disaggregating the extended Suez Canal components sheds light on the criticality of corridors such as Gibraltar and Bab el-Mandab in supporting flows in major trade lanes, such as Asia to Europe. For example, the importance of Gibraltar is demonstrated by its stand-alone ADM ranking (second

Table 18.4 Summary of results from CBCAM and ADM

CBCAM payoff matrix (USD)

Attacker: Scenarios j

Defender: Scenarios i	Network component	PAC	SUC	GIB	BEM	CGH	BOS	HOR	MAL
	PAC	4280275	5.19E+08	7.05E+08	5.38E+08	28506047	56809666	4.39E+08	1.57E+09
	SUC	5.19E+08	3.40E+08	1.02E+09	4.46E+08	2.01E+09	3.58E+08	6.93E+08	1.77E+09
	GIB	7.05E+08	1.02E+09	4.76E+08	1.10E+09	1.54E+09	5.28E+08	8.61E+08	1.76E+09
	BEM	5.38E+08	4.46E+08	1.10E+09	3.59E+08	2.00E+09	3.77E+08	7.16E+08	1.72E+09
	CGH	28506047	2.01E+09	1.54E+09	2.00E+09	24532313	77068575	4.55E+08	1.65E+09
	BOS	56809666	3.58E+08	5.28E+08	3.77E+08	77068575	52536261	4.81E+08	1.41E+09
	HOR	4.39E+08	6.93E+08	8.61E+08	7.16E+08	4.55E+08	4.81E+08	4.35E+08	1.68E+09
	MAL	1.57E+09	1.77E+09	1.76E+09	1.72E+09	1.65E+09	1.41E+09	1.68E+09	1.39E+09

Attacker-Defender Model (ADM)

t	Intervention strategy	Disruption costs z^* (USD)	Marginal financial gain (USD)	Attack probabilities							
				PAC	SUC	GIB	BEM	CGH	BOS	HOR	MAL
0	NONE	1.40E+09	-	0.000	0.000	0.018	0.000	0.000	0.000	0.000	0.982
1	MAL	5.22E+08	8.78E+08	0.000	0.000	0.881	0.000	0.000	0.000	0.119	0.000
2	GIB	4.59E+08	6.30E+07	0.000	0.000	0.000	0.207	0.000	0.000	0.793	0.000
3	HOR	3.74E+08	8.50E+07	0.000	0.000	0.000	0.991	0.009	0.000	0.000	0.000
4	BEM	3.56E+08	1.80E+07	0.000	0.991	0.000	0.000	0.009	0.000	0.000	0.000
5	SUC	5.45E+07	3.02E+08	0.000	0.000	0.000	0.000	0.081	0.919	0.000	0.000
6	BOS	2.51E+07	2.94E+07	0.141	0.000	0.000	0.000	0.859	0.000	0.000	0.000
7	CGH	4.28E+06	2.08E+07	1.000	0.000	0.000	0.000	0.000	0.000	0.000	0.000
8	PAC	0.00E+00	4.28E+06	0.000	0.000	0.000	0.000	0.000	0.000	0.000	0.000

N.B. PAC: Panama Canal, SUC: Suez Canal, GIB: Strait of Gibraltar, BEM: Bab el-Mandab, CGH: Cape of Good Hope, BOS: Bosporus Strait, HOR: Strait of Hormuz, MAL: Strait of Malacca

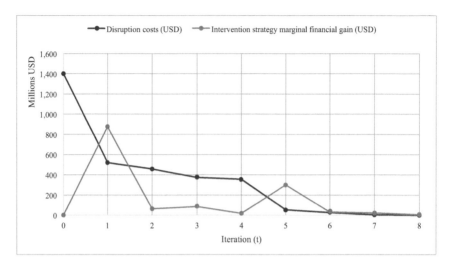

Figure 18.2 Disruption costs and marginal financial gains from iterative intervention scenarios

only to Malacca) where disruptions in this location simultaneously hamper Asia-to-Europe flows through Suez and trade from North America and West Africa to the Mediterranean. Therefore, defending each of the components of the group in the extended Suez Canal corridor is arguably of equal importance.

Our results are significantly influenced by the OD matrix input where most container flows are between Asia, Europe and the Middle East. Consequently, disruptions in maritime corridors such as the Panama Canal and the Bosporus, which mainly connect other regions such as the Americas and East Europe (Black Sea), have a lesser impact on total global routing costs. The configuration of the liner service network of the ocean carrier is another key factor in the results. However, complete networks of global ocean carriers, such as the one selected for our analysis, provide a good coverage of overall network flows and transport vulnerability.

Conclusion

The main contribution of this work is the development of a quantitative framework capable of identifying the most vulnerable components in liner shipping networks and measuring the extent to which disruptions hamper the ability of the network to re-route cargo flows. The proposed methodology applies a game-theoretic approach with a CBCAM, which provides a better representation of liner shipping network operations under disruption when compared to traditional graph theory methods.

The LP formulations of the ADM and CBCAM are capable of implementations on large realistic networks while still allow-ing the problem to be efficiently solved with commercially available solvers (Bell et al., 2013). We demonstrate this capability using ILOG CPLEX to find optimal solutions in the full-scale global network of a major ocean carrier constructed from publicly available data. The case study network encompasses eight main maritime logistics corridors, 88 distinct liner services, 230 active container ports and 6,311 OD pairs where 111,523 FFE containers must be routed weekly. At the mixed-strategy Nash equilibrium, the most vulnerable maritime corridors are identified and the minimum cost routes for OD pairs are found. To the best of our knowledge, this is the largest implementation of both the CBCA and attacker-defender model in liner shipping networks to date.

Results indicate a significant concentration of attack probabilities in few network components which suggest a high vulnerability state of the case study network. The Malacca Strait is identified as the most vulnerable maritime corridor followed by the extended Suez Canal corridor. Hypothetical scenarios of network interventions allow us to measure updated disruption costs where critical network components are sequentially defended. Financial gains from preventing disruptions on each of the maritime logistics corridors provide a quantitative rank of their relative transport vulnerability.

Disaggregating the extended Suez Canal components highlights the criticality of corridors such as Gibraltar and Bab el-Mandab in supporting flows in major trade lanes such as Asia to Europe. As such, defensive interventions on these supporting corridors are of equal importance in preventing disruptions on maritime corridors that have traditionally received more attention in previous works, such as the Suez Canal.

Networks of global ocean carriers, such as the one selected for our analysis, provide a good understanding of overall global liner shipping vulnerability but often do not capture intra-regional demands, which are necessary for localized analysis of critical components. Future improvements including extensions to subsets of intra-regional feeder carrier networks could highlight relevant component vulnerability not captured in this study. Similarly, the inclusion of disruption scenarios in secondary maritime passages (Rodrigue et al., 2017) (e.g., English Channel, Taiwan Strait) and main transshipment ports in the network (e.g., Rotterdam, Shanghai) could extend the vulnerability ranking generated in this study to additional critical network components.

Further improvements may include the application of a $N+M$ player game where, for example, two (or more) ocean carriers compete (or cooperate) to route cargo flows through components that reduce disruption costs. A fully developed methodology (e.g., including empty container repositioning or an efficient liner shipping network design algorithm) could improve the accuracy of vulnerability measures generated in this study and serve as a decision-support tool for public and private stakeholders to test the effectiveness of interventions intended to increase the overall robustness of liner shipping networks.

Acknowledgments

The authors extend their gratitude to the Georgia Tech Panama Logistics Innovation & Research Center for providing part of the data used in this chapter. We also thank anonymous reviewers from the Transportation Research Board Annual

Conference and colleagues at the Port Operations Research & Technology Centre (PORTeC) of Imperial College London for their feedback to earlier versions of this work. The corresponding author would like to thank the National Secretariat of Science Technology and Innovation of the Republic of Panama for the financial support received through research fellowship No. 2199-35-2012.

References

Achurra-Gonzalez, P.E., Novati, M., Foulser-Piggott, R., Graham, D.J., Bowman, G., Bell, M.G.H., Angeloudis, P. (2016) Modelling the impact of liner shipping network perturbations on container cargo routing: Southeast Asia to Europe application. *Accident Analysis & Prevention*. doi:10.1016/j.aap.2016.04.030

Angeloudis, P., Bichou, K., Bell, M.G.H., Fisk, D. (2007) Security and reliability of the liner container-shipping network: Analysis of robustness using a complex network framework. In: Bichou, K., Bell, M.G.H., Evans, A. (Eds.), *Risk Management in Port Operations, Logistics and Supply Chain Security*. London: Informa, pp. 95–106.

Angeloudis, P., Greco, L., Bell, M.G.H. (2016) Strategic maritime container service design in oligopolistic markets. *Transportation Research Part B*, 90: 22–37.

Bell, M.G.H. (2000) A game theory approach to measuring the performance reliability of transport networks. *Transportation Research Part B*, 34(6): 533–545.

Bell, M.G.H., Kanturska, U., Schmöcker, J.D., Fonzone, A. (2008) Attacker–defender models and road network vulnerability. *Philosophical Transactions of the Royal Society A*, 366(1872): 1893–1906.

Bell, M.G.H., Liu, X., Angeloudis, P. (2013) A cost-based maritime container assignment model. *Transportation Research Part B*, 58: 58–70.

Bell, M.G.H., Liu, X., Angeloudis, P., Fonzone, A., Hosseinloo, S.H. (2011) A frequency-based maritime container assignment model. *Transportation Research Part B*, 45(8): 1152–1161.

Bencomo, L.A. (2009) *Modeling the Effects of a Transportation Security Incident on the Commercial Transportation System*. Monterey, CA: Naval Postgraduate School.

Brouer, B.D., Alvarez, J.F., Plum, C.E.M., Pisinger, D., Sigurd, M.M. (2014) A base integer programming model and benchmark suite for liner-shipping network design. *Transportation Science*, 48(2): 281–312.

Ducruet, C. (2016) The polarization of global container flows by interoceanic canals: Geographic coverage and network vulnerability. *Maritime Policy and Management*, 43(2): 242–260.

Ducruet, C., Lee, S.W., Ng, A.K.Y. (2010) Centrality and vulnerability in liner shipping networks: Revisiting the Northeast Asian port hierarchy. *Maritime Policy and Management*, 37(1): 17–36.

Fugazza, M. (2015) *Maritime Connectivity and Trade*. Geneva: United Nations Conference on Trade and Development.

Hillier, F.S., Lieberman, G.J. (2005) *Introduction to Operations Research*. Boston: McGraw-Hill Higher Education.

Jourquin, B., Iassinovskaia, G., Lechien, J., Pinna, J. (2008) *Lines and Services in a Strategic Multi-modal Freight Network Model: Methodology and Application*. Association for European Transport.

Kanturska, U., Angeloudis, P. (2013) Introduction to network theory and game theory as frameworks for the analysis of critical infrastructure. In: The Institution of Engineering and Technology (Ed.), *Infrastructure Risk and Resilience: Transportation*, The Institution of Engineering and Technology, pp. 22–28.

Lam, J.S.L. (2012) Risk management in maritime logistics and supply chains. In: Song, D.W., Panayides, P.M. (Eds.), *Maritime Logistics: Contemporary Issues*. Bingley, UK : Emerald, pp. 117–131.

Lhomme, S. (2015) Vulnerability and resilience of ports and maritime networks to cascading failures and targetted attacks. In: Ducruet, C. (Ed.), *Maritime Networks: Spatial Structures and Time Dynamics*. London and New York: Routledge Series in Transport Analysis, pp. 229–241.

Loh, H.S., Van Thai, V. (2014) Managing port-related supply chain disruptions: A conceptual paper. *Asian Journal of Shipping and Logistics*, 30(1): 97–116.

Ouyang, M., Zhao, L., Pan, Z., Hong, L. (2014) Comparisons of complex network based models and direct current power flow model to analyze power grid vulnerability under intentional attacks. *Physica A*, 403: 45–53.

Paul, J.A., Maloni, M.J. (2010) Modeling the effects of port disasters. *Maritime Economics and Logistics*, 12(2): 127–146.

Rodrigue, J.P., Comtois, C., Slack, B. (2017) *The Geography of Transport Systems*. London and New York: Routledge.

Spiess, H., Florian, M. (1989) Optimal strategies: A new assignment model for transit networks. *Transportation Research Part B*, 23(2): 83–102.

Zavitsas, K. (2011) *The Vulnerability of the Petroleum Supply Chain*. London: Imperial College London.

19 Cluster dynamics in the collapsing Soviet shipping network

Rawya Zreik, César Ducruet,
Charles Bouveyron and Pierre Latouche

Port and shipping dynamics during the Soviet period is not a very popular topic for scholars. In their review of about 400 scientific articles on ports published in geography journals since 1950, Ng and Ducruet (2014) could only find two papers focusing on socialist ports, one on Odessa published in 1964, and another on Poland in 1986. Ports and shipping do not constitute a common field of interest for specialists on Russia and socialist economies either. Over the past decades, geographers such as Thorez (1998a, 1998b) devoted their attention to socialist shipping trends (Vigarié, 1995) documenting the changes affecting post-Soviet ports following the collapse of the Union of Soviet Socialist Republics (hereafter USSR). While ports in Eastern Europe (Ledger and Roe, 1993), and in the Baltic in particular (Serry, 2011; Thorez, 2011), as well as the special case of North Korea (Ducruet et al., 2009), received a lot of their attention, the bulk of research on ports and shipping concentrated on developed and developing countries in the capitalist world, one exception being China, given its rapid economic growth since the Open Door Policy (see Wang and Ducruet, 2013). Such works primarily insisted on the important changes and uneven adaptation of ports and shipping flows to the various influences of political transitions on trade activities (see Chapter 8 for an analysis of the Black Sea liner shipping network). Yet, a global approach to the way USSR ports and maritime networks experienced the collapse remains lacking today.

The aim of this chapter is to fill this gap and to place the topic within the broader, transdisciplinary field of network science. Network analysis has become a strong discipline, which is no longer limited to sociology as it applies to many areas, such as biology, geography or history (Zreik, 2016). The USSR provides great potential for such research since it presents us with the case of a major shock affecting a vast economy and the objective of testing its collapse on its internal and external maritime linkages. Many aspects that have become paramount in network analysis are, for instance, how spatial networks evolve in relation to distances and proximities of all kinds and how disruption affects connectivity. Another research pathway is to test such effects on the emergence of communities (or clusters) in a given network.

The most recent statistical methods for the modeling and processing of relational data are generally based on the stochastic block model (SBM) (Wang and

Wong, 1987; Nowicki and Snijders, 2001). The SBM model assumes that each vertex belongs to a latent group and that the probability of connection between a pair of vertices depends exclusively on that group. Among the recent extensions of the SBM model is the random subgraph model (RSM) proposed by Jernite et al. (2014), which aims at modeling categorical edges using prior knowledge of a partition of the network into subgraphs. The subgraphs are assumed to be made of latent clusters, which have to be inferred from the data in practice. The vertices are then connected with a probability depending only on the subgraphs, whereas the edge type is assumed to be sampled conditionally on the latent groups.

In this work, we consider the methodology introduced in Zreik et al. (2017) that permits the inference of a dynamic version of the RSM model on real data. Our approach allows us to analyze the evolution of USSR-related maritime flows between ports of the world over ten years (1987–1996) through the traffic of ships. Our main hypothesis is that the topology and spatial distribution of flows, the emergence of clusters and the impact of the collapse are determined by the political belonging of port nodes. This is questionable since shipping networks both reflect and transgress the border effects that characterize the markets that they help to connect.

The next section provides a review of port and shipping dynamics in Russian and Soviet ports based on the few available scholarly works on the subject. It also provides a methodological standpoint with preliminary analyses based on the definition of the USSR maritime ego network to identify main traffic trends. This is followed by the application of stochastic methods to reveal how the topology of this network has evolved according to the political belonging of port nodes before, during, and after the USSR collapse of the early 1990s. The conclusion discusses the contribution of this analysis to broader research on socialist economies, ports and shipping, and spatial network analysis in general.

Socialist ports and maritime transport: from bipolarization to globalization

General trends in USSR shipping

Traditionally, socialist economies are believed to develop through mainly continental relationships among preferential trade partners (Vigarié, 1995), thereby neglecting maritime transport as a growth engine. Such a conception inherited from the Marxist-Leninist economy theory rapidly lost ground from the 1960s onwards, given the necessity for socialist powers to expand their relationships internally and with the rest of the world, whether for commercial or military purposes, through a growing network of friendly partners in the extended socialist and developing world (e.g., Cuba, Vietnam and Africa). Thus, the Soviet Union gradually strengthened its global influence by competing with the capitalist world along all major maritime routes, as reflected in the continuous growth of its total port tonnage (Vigarié, 1995) in the 1970s–1980s, despite cumbersome customs regulations and deficient port infrastructures. Yet, in the early 1980s, a total 240 million tons of maritime trade remained coastal (16.5%), with socialist partners (32.1%), developing countries (6.1%) and capitalist countries (45.3%) (Thorez, 1998a).

The ambition of this chapter is to shed new light on the impact of a major geopolitical shock on the topology and spatial distribution of a spatial, -in our case, maritime-network. This shock is multifaceted. Its chronology is well known, with the dismantlement of the COMECON (Council for Mutual Economic Assistance) in June 1991, impacting strongly on Soviet foreign trade; the dissolution of the Warsaw Pact in July 1991, and the partition of the USSR itself in December 1991, immediately followed by the constitution of the Commonwealth of Independent States (CIS). Such events are both a cause and a consequence of the weakening Russian economy throughout the 1980s, leading to a sudden drop in trade exchanges, a disorganization of former relationships and a growing debt, all resulting in a reorganization of ports and maritime networks (Vigarié, 1995).

The aforementioned reorganization is well documented by the works of Thorez (1998a, 1998b) and can be synthesized as follows: prior to the disintegration of the USSR, ports and maritime transport were characterized by a spatial and functional division of labor centered upon and organized from Moscow. Soviet shipping companies were specialized in certain trades and routes, each having their base or hub port at locations around the block from the Baltic Sea to the Far East. Certain large ports were multifunctional, while others remained specialized in specific commodities, mainly raw materials and intermediate inputs, given the late adoption of containerization in the USSR. The 1991 collapse had been a "brutal thunderstruck" (Thorez, 1998a: 13) forcing port authorities and shipping companies to rethink their activity in terms of hinterland supply chains and management in a context of falling demand and traffic decline. Such a decline – the whole USSR area concentrated no more than 3.5% of world maritime trade in 1994 – was accentuated by the modal shift of traffic from sea to land (road, rail), especially towards West European transit hub ports, such as Antwerp, Rotterdam and Hamburg, thereby causing a severe decline at a number of post-Soviet ports. The shrinking of maritime trade had been severe internally (coastal shipping) while former Soviet ports, including those in Russia, strove to diversify their traffic to compensate the loss of their formerly vast hinterland.

The shock was felt differently among countries and ports depending on their capacity to adapt to a new competitive and global environment and the importance given to maritime trade for domestic demand or transshipment; although in relative terms, maritime traffic volumes declined less (-42%) than total transport traffic (-49.6%) between 1990 and 1995 (Thorez, 1998b). This is because certain ports recovered more quickly from the shock than others: positively in the Baltic and Far East regions, negatively in the Black Sea and in Russia itself. The process was characterized by many of the republics of the Soviet Union declaring their independence and being recognized as sovereign nation-states.

Constructing the Soviet ego network: preliminary results

Despite our current knowledge of the impact of the disintegration of the USSR on ports and maritime transport, to date the relational or network perspective had not been contemplated. Such a major event in economic and political terms provides fertile ground for the study of the changing topology and geography of a spatial network. For that purpose, we constructed the (maritime) ego network of the USSR defined by internal (intra-USSR vessel movements) and external (vessel movements between USSR ports and other ports, and between the latter ports) relationships, based on the *Lloyd's List* database over the period 1987–1996. This corresponds to the definition of the ego network in social network analysis (Wasserman and Faust, 1994). Such a network places the USSR at the core of the analysis, leaving aside the rest of the global maritime network, (i.e., vessel movements between ports not at all connected with the USSR). The choice of the period (ten consecutive years) is justified by the need to verify the true impact of the shock that lies in the middle of the period (1991). Yet, it is acknowledged that the economic downturn of Russia and the USSR already started long before the collapse itself, namely, already in the late 1980s. Overall, this methodology allows us to get closer to the shock and reduce the noise caused by unrelated factors. For each year under study, we compiled four complete months of vessel movements between such ports, taking into account not only adjacently connected ports but also intermediary stops along the whole voyage during the months of March, June, September and December, to avoid the effect of trade seasonality. As a result, the spatial pattern of aggregated USSR shipping traffic during the study period reveals its concentration in the vicinity, along Russian, Soviet shores, especially in the Baltic and Black Seas for the largest (volume) and most specialized (share) nodes (Figure 19.1). Elsewhere, high shares of USSR traffic in total port traffic are clearly visible in partner, or politically close, countries, despite the distance: Cuba, Algeria and Vietnam, but also in small groups of ports in Peru, India and Canada. Due to physical proximity and regardless of political affinities, certain nodes emerge on the world map, such as several specialized ports in Japan (Far East Russian trade), Helsinki and Hamburg, as the most specialized of the largest, non-Soviet nodes, as well as Rotterdam and Antwerp, which both act as multifunctional/transshipment ports as mentioned above.

We also measure traffic evolution per political group or subgraph: USSR, Eastern Block, other socialist ports, as well as non-aligned and capitalist ports (Figure 19.2).

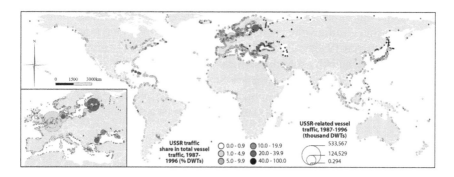

Figure 19.1 USSR-related traffic volume and share at world ports, 1987–1996

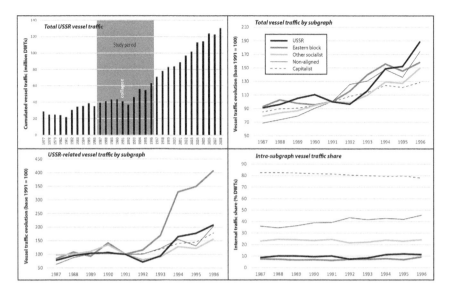

Figure 19.2 USSR-related traffic evolution, 1987–1996

The "other socialist" group is composed of ports in countries having had socialist elements in their political constitution at a given point in time of their contemporary history. Our results confirm the aforementioned trends in several ways, namely: (1) total traffic of USSR ports; (2) traffic of each subgraph relative to the year 1991; (3) traffic between USSR and each subgraph relative to the year 1991 and (4) internal traffic of each subgraph. As expected and coinciding with the collapse, USSR ports witnessed a sharp slowdown in the years 1991–1992 after a period of growth, followed by rapid recovery, as seen over the broader 1977–2008 period based on the same database. Each subgraph went through distinct evolutions, however. Relative to the year 1991, USSR ports are the ones handling the highest traffic prior to the collapse, while Eastern Block ports already faced decline in 1989–1990, but recovered more rapidly than the USSR. Ports of the "other socialist" subgraph went through a slowdown comparable to the USSR after 1991 and before recovery. Interestingly, ports in non-aligned and capitalist countries did not much suffer from the demise of the USSR, given the stability of their growth over the period. Traffic evolution between the USSR and other subgraphs reveals complementary trends. For instance, based on the year 1991, USSR traffic preferentially connected "brother" countries prior to its collapse, while such traffic became relatively more important with the Eastern Block afterwards and also internally (intra-USSR). Thus, the dissolution of the USSR affected long-distance relationships, such as those with "other socialist" countries to a greater extent and less so within its vicinity. The share of intra-group traffic shows that in this ego network flows among capitalist ports dominate around 80% on average despite a slight decline;

non-aligned ports increased a noticeable share of mutual linkages, from about 35% to nearly 50%; while all socialist ports in the three other subgraphs exhibit a very low internal share, given their reliance on external, non-socialist ports to connect with the rest of the world but also with each other. In fact, USSR traffic mainly connected capitalist ports (70% on average), followed by intra-Soviet traffic (10%), other socialist (8%), Eastern Block (6%) and non-aligned ports (6%), with little change over time.

The model of dynamic random subgraphs

The remainder of the analysis involves the application of the dynamic random subgraphs model (dRSM) (Zreik et al., 2017) on a slightly different network whereby USSR ports and Eastern Block ports are grouped into the same subgraph, given their geographic and political proximity and their relatively low number (Figure 19.3). In addition, network analysis only applies to ports connected every single year during the period, thereby leaving aside a number of fluctuating ports. Despite much discrepancy due to the overwhelming importance of capitalist ports, our port sample is as follows: 48 USSR ports, 17 Eastern Block ports (65 in total for both), 77 other socialist ports, 93 non-aligned ports and 584 capitalist ports. This sample consists of 819 ports within the 2,691 ports connecting the USSR during the period, which means about 30.4% of all ports, but mainly large traffic nodes.

In the following section, we describe the dynamic RSM (dRSM) model, as introduced in Zreik et al. (2017). Thus, we consider a set of T networks $\{G^{(t)}\}_{t=1}^{T}$, where $G^{(t)}$ is a directed graph observed at time t and for which a partition $P^{(t)}$ of S subgraphs is also known. Each $G^{(t)}$ is represented by its $N \times N$ adjacency matrix $X^{(t)}$ and N denoting is the number of nodes (assumed constant over time). No loops are considered. The edge $X_{ij}^{(t)}$, describing the relationship between nodes i and j is assumed to take its values in $\{0, \ldots C\}$ such that $X_{ij}^{(t)} = c$ means that nodes i and j are linked by a relationship type c at time t and $X_{ij}^{(t)} = 0$ indicates

Figure 19.3 World distribution of political ensembles (subgraphs) of ports

the absence of relationship. Our goal is to cluster at each time t the N nodes into K latent groups with homogeneous connection profiles, (*i.e.* find an estimate at each time t of the binary matrix Z, which is such that $Z_{ik}^{(t)} = 1$ if at time t, the node i belongs to the class k, and 0 otherwise). In our maritime application the $Z_{ik}^{(t)} = 1$ if at time t, the port i belongs to the class k and 0 otherwise; however, the type of connections between ports is binary in this application, so $X_{ij}^{(t)} = 1$ means that port i and j are linked by a one or several ships at time t and $X_{ij}^{(t)} = 0$ indicates the absence of relationship.

The dRSM model at each time t

The network is assumed to be generated at each time t as follows: each vertex i is first associated to a latent class k with a probability depending on the subgraph to which it belongs. So, we assume that for a number K of latent groups given, the variable $Z_i^{(t)}$ is drawn from a multinomial distribution of parameter $\alpha_{s_i}^{(t)}$:

$$Z_i^{(t)} \sim \mathcal{M}(1, \alpha_{s_i}^{(t)}),$$

where $\alpha_s^{(t)} = (\alpha_{s_1}^{(t)}, \ldots, \alpha_{s_K}^{(t)})$ is the vector of prior probabilities of the K latent groups in the subgraph s at time t and is such that $\sum_{k=1}^{K} \alpha_{s_k}^{(t)} = 1, \forall s \in 1, \ldots, S$. On the other hand, we assume that the type of link between nodes i and j is sampled from a multinomial distribution depending on the latent vectors $Z_i^{(t)}$ and $Z_j^{(t)}$,

$$X_{i,j}^{(t)} \mid Z_{ik}^{(t)} Z_{jl}^{(t)} = 1 \sim \mathcal{M}(1, \Pi_{kl}),$$

with $\Pi_{kl} \in [0,1]^{C+1}$ and $\sum_{c=0}^{C} \Pi_{klc} = 1$.

Modeling the evolution of random subgraphs

We present a hidden state, in the form of a state-space model to model the evolution of the subgraphs over time (Figure 19.4). So, we introduce a new latent variable $\gamma_s^{(t)}$, which is assumed to be distributed according to a normal distribution with mean $B\nu^{(t)}$ and covariance matrix Σ:

$$\gamma_s^{(t)} \sim \mathcal{N}(B\nu^{(t)}, \Sigma). \tag{1}$$

Note that this variable which was introduced in our model for characterizing temporal processes, could make the link between the proportions of subgraphs $\alpha_s^{(t)}$ at different times through a logistic transformation, in the form:

$$\alpha_{sk}^{(t)} = \exp\left(\gamma_{sk}^{(t)} - C\left(\gamma_s^{(t)}\right)\right), \forall k = 1, \ldots, K-1, \tag{2}$$

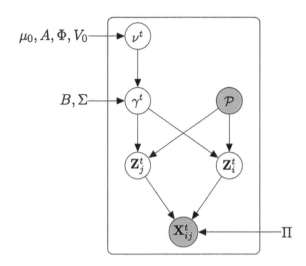

Figure 19.4 The graphical model for dRSM

where $C(\gamma_s^{(t)}) = \sum_{l=1}^{K-1} \exp(\gamma_{sl}^{(t)})$ and $\alpha_{sK}^{(t)} = 1 - \sum_{l=1}^{K-1} \exp(\alpha_{sl}^{(t)})$.

The variable $\alpha_s^{(t)}$ s is generated by sampling $(k-1)$ of the components of $\gamma_s^{(t)}$ according to normal distribution with mean $B\nu^{(t)}$ of dimension $(K-1)$ and a covariance matrix Σ of size $(K-1) \times (K-1)$. The last component of the vector $\gamma_s^{(t)}$ is arbitrarily set to zero. Due to that $\gamma_s^{(t)}$ has a $(K-1)$ degree of freedom. The rest of the modeling includes a classic state-space model for linear dynamic systems that evolves over time. The model is as follows:

$$\begin{cases} \nu^{(t)} = A\nu^{(t-1)} + \omega \\ \gamma_s^{(t)} = B\nu^{(t)} + \upsilon \\ \nu^{(1)} = \mu_0 + u, \end{cases}$$

where A and B are two transition matrices of size $(K-1) \times (K-1)$. The terms of noise ω, u and υ are supposed to be Gaussian such as $\omega \sim N(0; \Phi)$; $\upsilon \sim N(0; \Sigma)$; $u \sim N(0; V_0)$. Finally, our model has three latent variables (ν, γ, Z), and is parameterized by $\theta = (\mu_0, A, B, \Phi, V_0, \Sigma, \Pi)$. This model is called the dynamic random subgraph model (dRSM). Figure 19.4 presents the graphical model for dRSM. The inference of the model relies on variational EM bounds as an algorithm. The number of clusters is estimated using a BIC criteria. For more details, we refer to Zreik et al. (2017).

Main results

In this section, we apply the methodology associated with the dRSM model to the maritime flows data, which describes the varied traffic between 819 ports active in the world at each time t. Here, we concentrate on the period around the

Table 19.1 Terms Π_{kl1} of the matrix Π estimated using the variational EM algorithm to $K = 6$ clusters

	cluster 1	cluster 2	cluster 3	cluster 4	cluster 5	cluster 6
cluster 1	0.663	0.708	0.123	0.141	0.115	0.000
cluster 2	0.708	0.955	0.362	0.682	0.697	0.187
cluster 3	0.123	0.362	0.000	0.1408	0.109	0.000
cluster 4	0.141	0.682	0.140	0.431	0.474	0.000
cluster 5	0.115	0.697	0.109	0.474	0.930	0.639
cluster 6	0.000	0.187	0.000	0.000	0.639	0.500

occurrence of this event in 1991, studying it over ten consecutive years (1987–1996). As this event impacted Socialist countries more than others, we decided to analyze the aforementioned four subgraphs based on their political category. Therefore, the network is a directed network without loops and binary: $C = 1$ and $X_{ij}^{t} = 1$ if i and j exchanged at least one ship during the period t, 0 otherwise, with $t \in \{1, \ldots, 10\}$ and $S = 4$, we looked for $K = 6$ clusters in the data.

By construction, the matrix Π verifies $\Pi_{kl0} + \Pi_{kl1} = 1, \forall (k, l)$ therefore, only Π_{kl1} term, describing the connection probabilities given in Table 19.1.

Topological and functional trends

One first result is the identification of clusters composing the USSR ego network, based on their connection probabilities and intra vs. inter-class probabilities (Figures 19.5 and 19.6). This allows us to define clusters 1 and 3 as the "cores" of the network, as they connect all other clusters, connect each other and have a noticeable amount of internal connectivity. All other clusters connect these cores, but differ in terms of size (i.e. number of ports), while clusters 4 and 6 are the only ones among them to share a mutual connection. Clusters 2 and 5 have no mutual relationships, and cluster 2 has no internal connectivity. We can thus infer a strong opposition between the core and several peripheries that do not otherwise connect. The rest of the analysis will investigate whether such a core-periphery pattern reflects the bipolarization of the world, if it reflects other logics, what is the role of USSR ports in such a pattern and how the political transition affected the geographic distribution of clusters over time.

Our main results point to a body of evidence relating to the specific evolution of each cluster depending on each subgraph (Figure 19.7). Overall, the USSR collapse is largely responsible for the sudden growth or decline of group proportions, especially for the years 1991–1993. Core clusters 1 and 3 that dominate the entire network exhibit very different evolutions during this transition. Cluster 3, the most central cluster, lost significance for USSR and Eastern Bloc ports in 1991–1993 until a recovery in 1995–1996. By comparison, the same cluster gained ground for non-aligned ports and other socialist ports and underwent a slight decline for capitalist ports. Thus, the demise of the USSR had been most

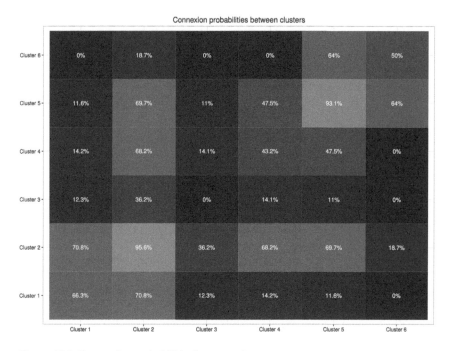

Figure 19.5 Connection probabilities between clusters

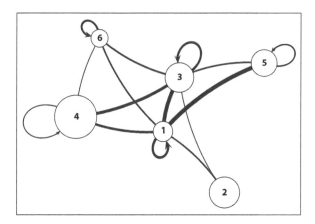

Figure 19.6 Inter- vs. intra-class probabilities among clusters

detrimental with a direct effect on communist ports and perhaps on capitalist ports well-connected to the USSR and Eastern Bloc. The other core cluster 1 reveals another similarity between USSR/Eastern Bloc and capitalist ports during the collapse, with a growth as opposed to a decline for other socialist and

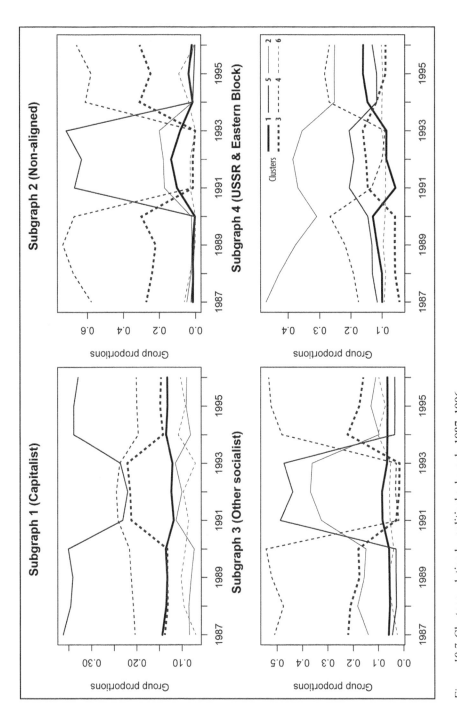

Figure 19.7 Cluster evolution by political subgraph, 1987–1996

non-aligned ports. In fact, the tight interdependence between communist and capitalist markets, despite their political opposition, led to similar effects during the shock in both blocks.

When it comes to peripheral clusters, some of them display drastically different behavior from one subgraph to the other. The largest of these in terms of number of ports, cluster 4, registered a considerable decline in importance in all subgraphs except for the capitalist one. The opposite trend occurred for cluster 5, bearing in mind that these two clusters only connect indirectly, through a different core cluster. The most peripheral cluster 2 increased its proportion in all subgraphs, while the smallest cluster, number 6, did not witness any particular trend over time. These evolutions shed new light on the topological and functional trends characterizing world ports and their connectivity during the disintegration of the USSR. In other words, the two cores of the network (clusters 1 and 3) have an opposite behavior during the collapse, with communist and capitalist ports losing importance in the main core (cluster 1) and gaining importance in the secondary core (cluster 3). The two large semi-peripheries (clusters 4 and 5) also show an opposition, but this time between capitalist ports and all other ports. Capitalist ports gain importance in the largest and best-connected cluster 4, while other socialist, non-aligned and USSR-Eastern Block ports gain importance in cluster 5, which strongly connects the main core cluster 1. The most peripheral cluster 2 increased its importance mainly for other socialist and USSR-Eastern Bloc ports, suggesting that becoming peripheral had been mainly the case of socialist/communist ports.

Spatial trends

Based on the aforementioned topological and functional trends that characterize the evolution of the USSR ego network and its components, it is crucial to investigate the changing spatial embeddedness of identified clusters on the world map (Figure 19.8). The core cluster 1 is principally composed of European ports, including most of the largest gateways and hubs along the so-called North European Range (e.g., Le Havre, Antwerp, Rotterdam and Hamburg) but also Felixstowe, Dunkirk, Liverpool, London, Bremerhaven and a number of meridional ports like Algeciras, Bilbao and Piraeus. These gateways and hubs are crucial for the USSR to connect to the rest of world although they belong to capitalist economies, because they act as modern transshipment nodes in the global shipping network not only for the USSR but also for an extended Europe as a whole. It is worth noting that many USSR and Eastern Bloc ports belong to the same cluster, featuring ports from Russia, Poland, East Germany and Baltic States and more on the Scandinavian shores of the communist maritime system.

With the demise of the USSR, several of the aforementioned ports remained in cluster 1, regardless of whether capitalist (e.g., Le Havre-Hamburg range) or communist (e.g., St. Petersburg), but the cluster took on a different geographic scope, with the addition of many more non-European ports (New York, Los Angeles, Hong Kong, Singapore, Japan, Brazil, Mediterranean ports) and a number of large

cluster 1

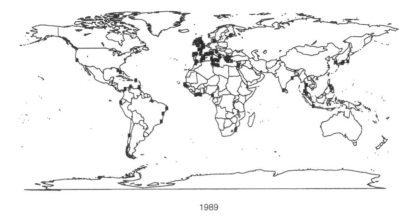

1989

cluster 1

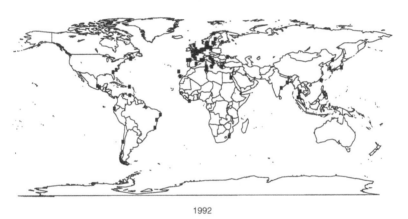

1992

cluster 1

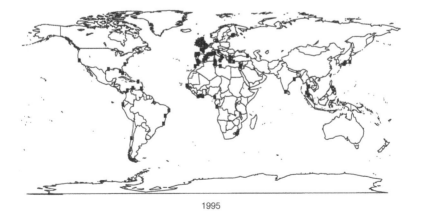

1995

Figure 19.8 Spatial distribution of clusters at selected years

cluster 2

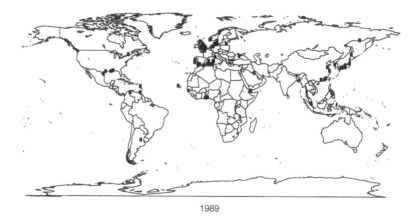

1989

cluster 2

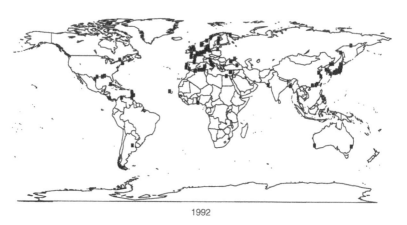

1992

cluster 2

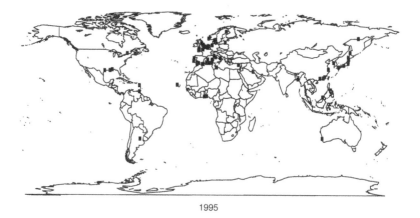

1995

Figure 19.8 (Continued)

cluster 3

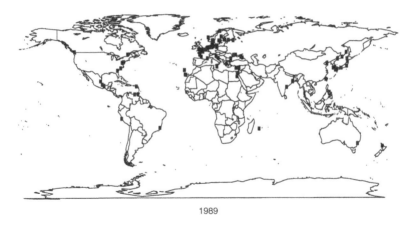

1989

cluster 3

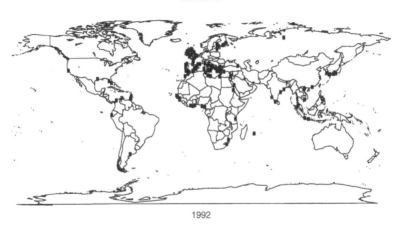

1992

cluster 3

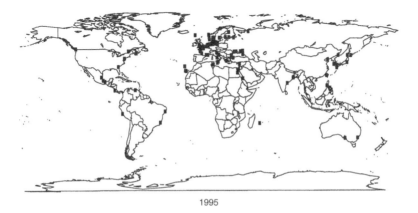

1995

Figure 19.8 (Continued)

cluster 4

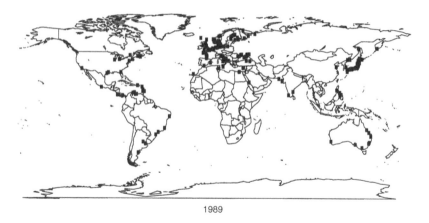

1989

cluster 4

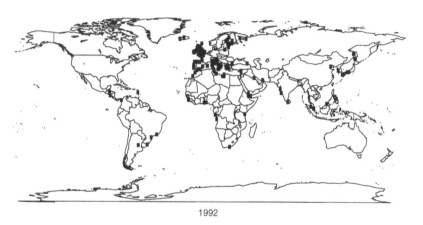

1992

cluster 4

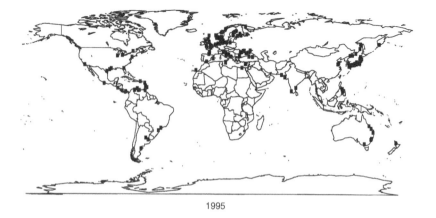

1995

Figure 19.8 (Continued)

cluster 5

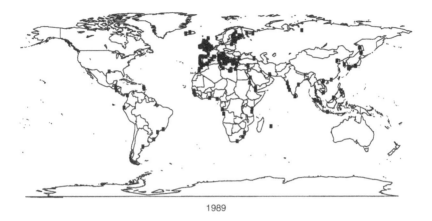

1989

cluster 5

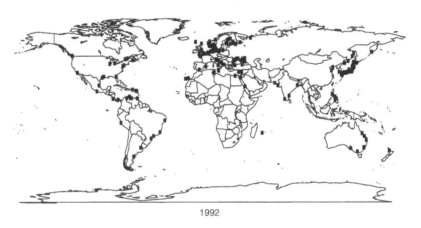

1992

cluster 5

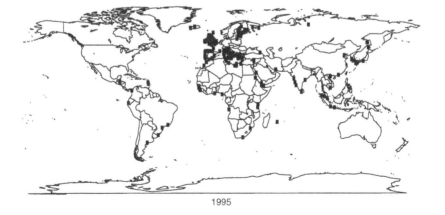

1995

Figure 19.8 (Continued)

cluster 6

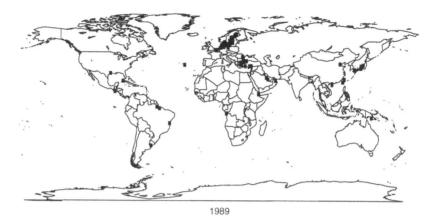

1989

cluster 6

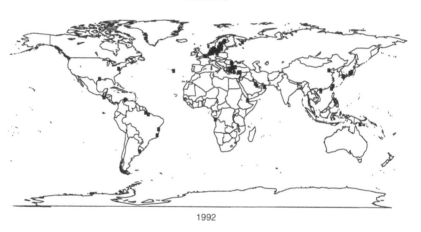

1992

cluster 6

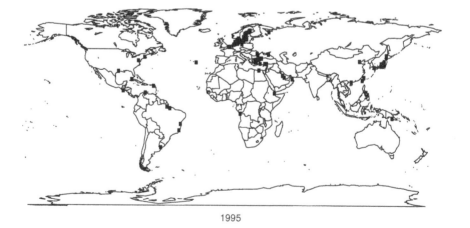

1995

Figure 19.8 (Continued)

communist ports (e.g. Odessa, Constantza). All other ports shifted to cluster 3, as mentioned above, composed mainly of small and medium-sized North European ports. One of the main effects of the USSR collapse on core clusters is thus the shift of a few large communist ports in the center of the system (cluster 1) together with the world's largest ports. The dislocation of the USSR thus provoked a displacement of the network's center of gravity towards the largest external hubs mainly, because of the loosening political significance of flows. All other communist ports shifted to other, more peripheral, clusters. Before looking at these clusters, it is interesting to note that cluster 6, which does not react to the collapse in any subgraph, is geographical by nature, (i.e. mainly composed of Asian and Oceanian ports). Certain Chinese and Vietnamese ports, which belonged to the "other socialist" subgraph and to the peripheral cluster 2 in the late 1980s, became fully part of cluster 6 after the collapse. Geographic proximity and regional integration effects thus gradually superseded former political factors influencing the fading pattern of Soviet trade between former brother countries.

The evolution of cluster 2, the most peripheral and extroverted cluster, is interesting as it shows a group of mainly small and medium-sized ports, with a sizeable proportion of communist ports (USSR and other socialist regions such as China, Vietnam and North Korea), absorbing many more ports on all continents during the collapse, but without losing its original composition. This means that the collapse created more peripheral ports due to trade reorientation, but these ports maintained their linkages with the core of the system (cluster 1). Geographically, cluster 2 expanded mainly towards the Americas and the Mediterranean/Black Sea, but also to South Asia (e.g., India). The case of Cuba's main port, Havana, is emblematic of such a trend, which suggests a shrinkage of port and maritime activity during the collapse. This also explains why clusters 1 and 2 share a common feature: the growth of their respective proportions mainly in the "other socialist" subgraph, (i.e. in partner countries of the USSR).

Lastly, in relation to the evolution of semi-peripheries, clusters 4 and 5 also exhibit interesting geographic patterns and shifts. The populous and well-connected cluster 4, before and after the USSR collapse, is mainly composed of a spatially continuous region including medium-sized Latin American, African and Mediterranean/West Asian ports. Cluster 5 comprises mostly minor North European and Scandinavian ports. The breakup of the USSR provoked an inversion of these clusters in the years 1991–1993, as they replaced each other on the map. This reinforces the idea of shrinkage and dilatation of Soviet influence during the shock. The likely reason is that cluster 5 is the best connected to the core (cluster 1), so that the shock provoked a connectivity shift from the Old World (Northern Europe) to the New World (Latin America/Africa/West Asia). The smaller Northern European ports, well connected to their large European neighbors before the shock at least partly through USSR shipping, became suddenly better connected with the "secondary core" (cluster 3), it too becoming more "European" and more "socialist" (cf. Figure 19.7). Overall, the USSR collapse created a lock-in of small and medium-sized capitalist European ports together with their socialist counterparts, based on geographic proximity and high-density linkages, while the rest of the world, outside Europe, became the new core of the system, notwithstanding the permanent presence of a few large socialist ports.

Conclusion

The analysis of the Soviet ego network evolution using a recent statistical model called dRSM to analyze a dynamic network with stochastic methods shows a new step towards a better understanding of the influence of political and spatial factors shaping transport and communication systems. Our main results convey the idea that the diminishing importance of political factors in times of crisis gives more importance to geographic proximity and node hierarchy, when a given transport system reorients its trade activities and becomes more embedded in the global maritime network. The crucial importance of geographic proximity had already been underlined in previous studies using various clustering methods on shipping network data (Kaluza et al., 2010; Sun et al., 2012; Ducruet and Zaidi, 2012; Bouveyron et al., 2015), but this is the first time that political factors are introduced as a complementary – and perhaps more fertile – dimension.

Yet, if the structure of the USSR ego network and the effect of its dissolution could be well described through such methods as a vital and advanced complement to more classic descriptive statistics, one question remains: why did the network go back to its initial pattern? The short-lasting impact of three consecutive years (1991–1993) is rather surprising, given the end of world bipolarization from those dates. Perhaps running the same analysis over a longer period would better high-light more profound and structural changes affecting shipping flows. As mentioned earlier, in the late 1980s, the USSR had already become a relatively open and highly maritime-oriented economy, compared with the early phases of its develop-ment, before and up to the 1960s–1970s. This explains why the observed changes are mainly conjectural, but they were profound. We could also learn from such a shock the relative influence of geography and politics on network structures and dynamics. Further research will refine the analysis by integrating links weights and perhaps focus on the diversity of cargo flows from bulks to containers, while enlarging the time span to better reveal such influences.

Acknowledgements

The research leading to these results has received funding from the European Research Council under the European Union's Seventh Framework Programme (FP/2007–2013) / ERC Grant Agreement n. [313847] "World Seastems".

References

Bouveyron, C., Latouche, P., Zreik, R., Ducruet, C. (2015) Cluster identification in mari-time flows with stochastic methods. In: Ducruet, C. (Ed.), *Maritime Networks: Spatial*

Structures and Time Dynamics. London and New York: Routledge Studies in Transport Analysis, pp. 210–228.

Ducruet, C., Roussin, S., Jo, J.C. (2009) Going West? Spatial polarization of the North Korean port system. *Journal of Transport Geography*, 17(5): 357–368.

Ducruet, C., Zaidi, F. (2012) Maritime constellations: A complex network approach to shipping and ports. *Maritime Policy and Management*, 39(2): 151–168.

Jernite, Y., Latouche, P., Bouveyron, C., Rivera, P., Jegou, L., Lamassé, S. (2014) The random subgraph model for the analysis of an ecclesiastical network in Merovingian Gaul. *Annals of Applied Statistics*, 8(1): 377–405.

Kaluza, P., Kölzsch, A., Gastner, M.T., Blasius, B. (2010) The complex network of global cargo ship movements. *Journal of the Royal Society Interface*, 7(48): 1093–1103.

Ledger, G.D., Roe, M.S. (1993) East European shipping and economic change: A conceptual model. *Maritime Policy and Management*, 20(3): 229–241.

Nowicki K., Snijders T.A.B. (2001) Estimation and prediction for stochastic blockstructures. *Journal of the American Statistical Association*, 96(455): 1077–1087.

Ng, A.K.Y., Ducruet, C. (2014) The changing tides of port geography (1950–2012). *Progress in Human Geography*, 38(6): 785–823.

Serry, A. (2011) Dynamiques du transport maritime en Baltique orientale. *Territoire en Mouvement*, 10: 36–48.

Sun, Z., Zheng, J., Hu, H. (2012) Finding community structure in spatial maritime shipping networks. *International Journal of Modern Physics C*, 23(6): 1250044.

Thorez, P. (1998a) La difficile mutation des transports maritimes dans la C.E.I. *Bulletin de l'Association des Géographes Français*, 75(1): 10–29.

Thorez, P. (1998b) Le transport maritime dans les pays issus de l'ex-URSS. *Le Courrier des Pays de L'Est*, 426: 18–52.

Thorez, P. (2011) Les enjeux portuaires de la Russie en mer Baltique. *Territoire en Mouvement*, 10: 49–59.

Vigarié, A. (1995) *La Mer et la Géostratégie des Nations*. Paris: Economica.

Wang, C., Ducruet, C. (2013) Regional resilience and spatial cycles: Long-term evolution of the Chinese port system (221BC-2010AD). *Tijdschrift voor Economische en Sociale Geografie*, 104(5): 521–538.

Wang, Y.J., Wong, G.Y. (1987) Stochastic blockmodels for directed graphs. *Journal of the American Statistical Association*, 82: 8–19.

Wasserman, S., Faust, K. (1994) *Social Network Analysis: Methods and Applications*. Cambridge, UK: Cambridge University Press.

Zreik, R. (2016) *Statistical Analysis of Networks and Applications in Social Sciences*. Doctoral dissertation, Université Paris 1 Panthéon Sorbonne.

Zreik, R., Latouche, P., Bouveyron, C. (2017) The dynamic random subgraph model for the clustering of evolving networks. *Computational Statistics*, 32(2): 501–5331.

20 Hub dependency and vulnerability of China's overseas connections

Mengqiao Xu and Haoxiang Xia

International freight transportation, the main element supporting the mobilization of global commodity, has always been an indispensable component of world economic development (Leinbach and Capineri, 2007). With a sophisticated network of regularly scheduled services that transport goods worldwide at lower cost and with greater energy efficiency than any other form of international transportation, liner shipping remains a highly important engine for the mobility of international freight flows. As indicated by the *World Shipping Council*,[1] liner shipping carries about 60 percent of the value of goods moved internationally by sea each year. International liner shipping flows, therefore, can be reasonably regarded as a practical looking-glass for global-local connectivity.

In transporting international container cargo, liner carriers mainly focus on a small number of hub ports in the world, as they widely adopt the hub-and-spoke structure in service network design in pursuit of economies of scale (Notteboom, 2004; Tongzon and Sawant, 2007). Thus, the development of hub ports, either as regional gateway hubs or transshipment hubs, has been a significant issue in regional and national development for regions and countries with coastal access. The issue of hub port development also attracts considerable research discussions on topics such as regional port system evolution (Wang and Slack, 2000; Notteboom, 2010; Wilmsmeier and Monios, 2016), port governance policies (Wang and Slack, 2004; Ng and Pallis, 2010; Lee and Flynn, 2011) and liner shipping service network design (Gelareh et al., 2010; Gelareh and Pisinger, 2011; Meng and Wang, 2011). The intrinsic property of hub port dependency in global liner shipping practice conditions a certain level of vulnerability in global-local liner shipping connections. This is worth analyzing, as such analysis can help us better understand the sustainable development of local regions within the context of the global liner shipping network. Unfortunately, current studies addressing hub port phenomena in global-local liner shipping connections rarely go further in assessing the vulnerability therein. But several of them should be specially mentioned, as they are very helpful in contributing to a better understanding of the addressed issue here. Ducruet (2008) proposed a methodology for measuring external-hub dependency of a given country, focusing on the maximum share and concentration level of traffic between the country's directly connected external ports. The proposed methodology was then applied to a case study of North Korea. Fleming and Hayuth (1994) initially qualitatively identified intermediacy as a crucial spatial factor defining the hub status of individual ports in transportation systems. Ducruet et al. (2010) further quantitatively investigated the hub status of regional ports within the liner shipping network of Northeast Asia, by applying a popular indicator of intermediacy from complex network analysis (i.e. node betweenness). They also gave a simple definition of port vulnerability: the share of the dominant flow connection within total port traffic.

To address the above research gap, we empirically investigated the hub dependency and vulnerability in China's (People's Republic of China, abbreviated to China) international liner shipping connections with various overseas regions (see also Chapter 5 for an analysis of cross-strait container flows). Driven by the rapid growth of its economy and international trade over the past decades, China has well established widescale liner shipping connections with most regions in the world and thus offers a good case for maritime research on the global-local connectivity (see Chapters 6, 10, and 21 on Portugal, USA, and North Korea for other analyses of external linkages of national port systems). The latest UNCTAD statistics[2] show that in 2014 port throughput of mainland China and Hong Kong reached 181.64 and 22.30 million TEUs, respectively, together accounting for about 30% of the world total container throughput; and the Chinese ports of Shanghai, Shenzhen, Hong Kong, Ningbo-Zhoushan, Qingdao, and Guangzhou ranked first, third, fourth, fifth, seventh, and eighth in the world, respectively, in terms of annual container throughput. Meanwhile, due to Chinese container ports' diverse strategies for geographical connectivity with international foreland markets (Wang and Ng, 2011), different patterns of China's connections with overseas regions exist today in terms of liner shipping services. This practical reality validates the necessity and effectiveness of a decomposition analysis of hub dependency and vulnerability in China's international liner shipping connections by overseas region. The objectives of the present study are as follows:

1   to propose systematic methodologies for a quantitative analysis of hub dependency and vulnerability in inter-regional liner shipping connections between a pair of regions;
2   in China's case, to identify the external and internal hub ports that are important for the fulfilment of China's international liner shipping connections with individual overseas regions, and to measure the levels of hub dependency and vulnerability therein.

The remainder of this chapter introduces data sources and methodology in the next section. It is followed by an analysis of traffic concentration of China's international container flows by overseas region and by the core analysis of hub dependency and vulnerability in the sub-distributions of China's international container flows with individual overseas regions. Our conclusions are presented in the last section.

Data and methodology

Data source and processing

So far, obtaining the exact data on inter-port container traffic at global level is almost impossible for any maritime shipping studies. One primary reason is that the current statistical data on container traffic among served ports of a liner company is considered to be a crucial commercial secret in terms of market competition. Therefore, shipping capacities, the theoretical maximum traffic volume, are commonly used by current studies to replace the actual traffic flows on the port pairs (e.g., Ducruet, 2008; Wang and Cullinane, 2014). In the present study, container capacity in TEU is used as a faithful representation of inter-port container traffic between China and overseas regions.

We collected the required data from the Alphaliner database (www.alphaliner.com) in April 2015. By aggregating the service data of the world's top 100 container lines that together account for more than 92% of the total global container capacity, this database provides detailed information on container capacity (in TEU) and the number of vessels deployed on the existing liner services worldwide. It updates with a monthly frequency. Compared with a data source of *Lloyd's List*, which is widely adopted by many studies (e.g., Ducruet et al., 2010; Ducruet and Zaidi, 2012), the present data has two merits. First, it provides detailed information on port rotation in each liner service, including ports of origin and destination as well as calling sequence. Second, it avoids taking account of any other calling activities unrelated with the service rotation (e.g., refueling and maintenance). But one major limitation of the data is the lack of information on the duration of some rotations, with the result that an analysis of daily or weekly container capacity for the ports is impossible. Still, it provides a good opportunity for the present research to empirically investigate China's international liner shipping connections.

The process to achieve inter-port container flows between China and overseas regions involved three steps. First, we extracted 468 liner services that contribute to China's international container connections, (i.e. services including at least one Chinese port and one overseas port in their port rotations). Note that Chinese ports here refer to the mainland ports and the port of Hong Kong, as they currently together serve China's international cargo transportation, inbound and outbound. Figure 20.1 presents the geographical distribution of the 33 studied Chinese ports. Second, each service constitutes a graph of all links (i.e. two arbitrary ports in the port rotation are linked by an edge), and container capacity deployed on the service is regarded as the edge weight. Ultimately, by merging all these individual services and combing the container capacities for the links for the same origin-destination pairs, all of China's international container flows, together with the traffic on them,

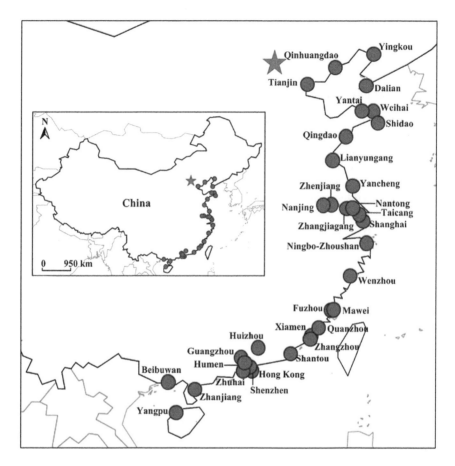

Figure 20.1 Geographical distribution of Chinese international container ports

are achieved (Figure 20.2). There are 1303 inbound flows, referring to 28 Chinese ports and 274 overseas ports; and 1480 outward flows, referring to 29 Chinese ports and 266 overseas ports. Figure 20.3 further presents the distribution of China's international container flows by overseas region; for the division of world shipping regions, see Xu et al. (2015).

Methodology

Based on the inter-port level of container flows, this chapter proposes a conceptual framework for the quantitative analysis of hub dependency and vulnerability in inter-regional liner shipping connections. Core ideas here are: significance (or salience) offering an intrinsic classification of a given set of inter-port container flows linking the two analyzed regions, either significant or non-significant, where a threshold for significance is determined. Significant inter-regional container

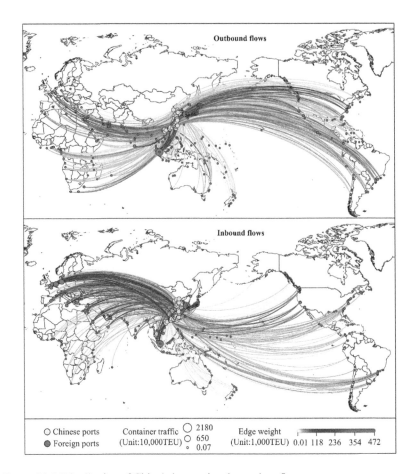

Figure 20.2 Distribution of China's international container flows

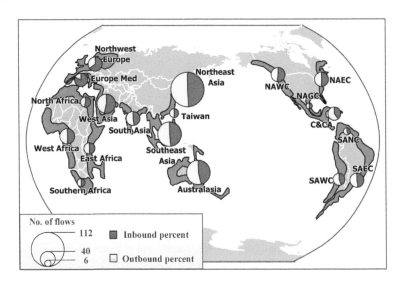

Figure 20.3 Distribution of China's international container flows by overseas region

flows, to a certain degree, help to reveal the skeleton structure supporting inter-regional liner shipping connections, and to uncover the competitive positions of regional ports with respect to each other.

Within the above context, the main concepts for analyzing inter-regional liner shipping connections in the present study are defined as follows. A port is identified as a hub port if it possesses significant inter-regional container flows linking its host region with another region; level of hub dependency on an identified hub port refers to the proportion of significant inter-regional traffic undertaken by this port in all inter-regional traffic; and level of vulnerability is the level of overall dependency of inter-regional liner shipping connections on all the identified hub ports in the region. The implementation of the proposed methodology for analyzing hub dependency and vulnerability in inter-regional liner shipping connections follows two steps, as illustrated in Figure 20.4.

By emphasizing traffic volume on spatial flows, Holmes and Haggett (1977) developed a mathematical method to identify significant flows from a whole set of flows of a given node. Modified from their method, an algorism for identifying significant inter-regional flows between two given regions is adopted here. First, all inter-regional flows should be ranked from the largest (w_1) to the smallest (w_k). w_i indicates the traffic volume of flow i, with $i \in K$ (the set of inter-regional flows between two analyzed regions). Then a set of expected flows $\{\hat{w}_i\}$ for each of a series of cycles 1, 2, 3, ..., k, is generated as follows:

$$\text{1st cycle, } \hat{w}_1 = \sum_{i=1}^{k} w_i, \ \hat{w}_2 = \hat{w}_3 = \cdots = \hat{w}_k = 0$$

$$\text{2nd cycle, } \hat{w}_1 = \frac{1}{2}\sum_{i=1}^{k} w_i, \ \hat{w}_3 = \hat{w}_4 = \cdots = \hat{w}_k = 0$$

$$j\text{th cycle } (j < k), \hat{w}_1 = \hat{w}_2 = \cdots = \hat{w}_j = \frac{1}{j}\sum_{i=1}^{k} w_i, \ \hat{w}_{j+1} = \hat{w}_{j+2} = \cdots = \hat{w}_k = 0$$

$$k^{\text{th}} \text{ cycle, } \hat{w}_1 = \hat{w}_2 = \cdots = \hat{w}_k = \frac{1}{k}\sum_{i=1}^{k} w_i$$

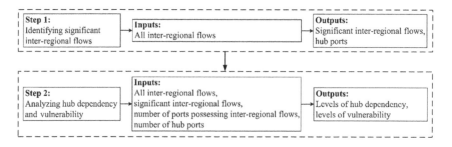

Figure 20.4 A diagram of analyzing hub dependency and vulnerability in inter-regional liner shipping connections

For each cycle, measure the goodness of fit between the set of observed inter-regional flows $\{w_i\}$ and the set of expected flows $\{\hat{w}_i\}$ by the coefficient of determination (r^2). If the maximum r^2 occurs in the jth cycle, then categorize all those flows with higher ranking (i.e. from w_1 to w_j), as significant inter-regional flows, and the rest with lower ranking (i.e. from w_{j+1} to w_k), as insignificant ones.

Figure 20.5 presents an example of the implementation of the above procedures. Assuming there exist four and seven ports in region A and B, respectively, i.e. $\{A\} = \{a_1, a_2, a_3, a_4\}$ and $\{B\} = \{b_1, b_2, b_3, b_4, b_5, b_6, b_7\}$; and ten container flows between them, i.e. $\{W\} = \{w_1, w_2, w_3, w_4, w_5, w_6, w_7, w_8, w_9, w_{10}\}$, with traffic volume of 131, 103, 89, 78, 71, 61, 50, 36 and 25 thousand TEUs respectively. In the fifth cycle, the coefficient of determination r^2 reaches the maximum value, thus inter-regional container flows w_1, w_2, w_3, w_4, w_5 are identified as significant, ports a_1 and a_3, and ports $b_1, b_2, b_3, b_4, b_5, b_6$, as regional hub ports in regions A and B, respectively.

Given that inter-regional liner shipping connections between two regions rely on hub ports on both sides, hub dependency phenomena in one given region's (say, region A) liner shipping connections with another (say, region B) not only exist internally (i.e. relying on the hub ports in region A itself), but also exist externally (i.e. relying on the hub ports in region B); and thus, vulnerability in region A's liner shipping connections with region B, contributed to by such internal and external hub dependency, should also be addressed from internal and external perspectives respectively.

The level of dependence of inter-regional liner shipping connections on an identified hub port m (p_m), D_{p_m}, in either region A or B, is the proportion of significant inter-regional traffic undertaken by this port in all inter-regional traffic. It is calculated as follows:

$$D_{p_m} = \frac{\sum_{i' \in p_m} w_{i'}}{\sum_{i=1}^{k} w_i} \tag{20.1}$$

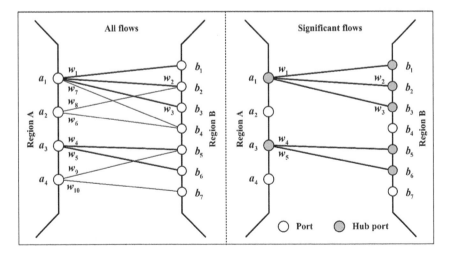

Figure 20.5 A diagram of identifying significant inter-regional container flows

where, w_i' indicates that inter-regional flow w_i is identified as significant; $i' \in p_m$ refers to those significant inter-regional flows undertaken by port m. The value of D_{p_m} ranges from 0 to 1, and the larger, the higher level of dependence on port m.

The level of vulnerability in region A's liner shipping connections with region B is mainly impacted by two factors. One is the proportion of significant inter-regional traffic in all inter-regional traffic (i.e. the combined level of dependence on all the individual hubs in the region). The other is the concentration level of significant inter-regional flows, by number, among regional ports. The more significant the inter-regional traffic undertaken by fewer ports, the higher the level of vulnerability in the inter-regional liner shipping connections. The formula is as follows:

$$V = \frac{\sum w_{i'}}{\sum_{i=1}^{k} w_i} \times \frac{1 - \frac{N_h}{N}}{1 - \frac{1}{N}} = \left(\sum_{m=1}^{N_h} D_{p_m} \right) \times \frac{1 - \frac{N_h}{N}}{1 - \frac{1}{N}}, \ N \geq 2, 1 \leq N_h \leq N \quad (20.2)$$

Where V is the vulnerability level of inter-regional liner shipping connections in one region side, either A (internal vulnerability) or B (external vulnerability). $\frac{\sum w_{i'}}{\sum_{i=1}^{k} w_i}$ is the traffic share of significant inter-regional flows in all inter-regional flows, with a value ranging between 0 and 1. N and N_h are the number of ports that undertake inter-regional flows and significant inter-regional flows, respectively, in the addressed region, and $(1 - \frac{N_h}{N})$ indicates the concentration level of significant inter-regional flows among relevant ports in the region. For any given region, this concentration level reaches the maximum value in a situation where significant inter-regional flows are undertaken by only one port in the region (i.e. $N_h = 1$). It is normalized into $\frac{1 - \frac{N_h}{N}}{1 - \frac{1}{N}}$ for better comparing regions of varying numbers of ports, generating a value ranging from 0 to 1.

Analysis of China's international liner shipping connections

Through segmenting China's international liner shipping connections by overseas region, this study provides empirical investigations into the spatial distribution of China's international container flows with individual overseas regions. Firstly, we analyzed the traffic concentration in the distribution of China's international container flows, externally (i.e. in each overseas region) and internally (i.e. in China itself), by using the Herfindahl-Hirschman Index (abbreviated to HHI)[3] because traffic concentration could condition the emergence of hub dependency and thus vulnerability. We then made detailed analyses of hub dependency and vulnerability in China's international liner shipping connections with each overseas region.

Traffic concentration

China's international container traffic is divided into 19 overseas regions, and the concentration level of its sub-distribution among ports in each overseas region is measured (Figure 20.6). First, the overall distribution of China's international container traffic among overseas regions is quite unequal. For instance, its inbound traffic mainly originates from Northwest Europe, Mediterranean Europe, Southeast Asia, and Northeast Asia (i.e. individual traffic shares reach 24.24%, 15.02%, 14.61%, and 14.34%, respectively). Such unequal traffic distribution reflects the different realities of China's international trade connections with these regions.

Secondly, sub-distributions of China's international container traffic among ports in most overseas regions show certain levels of concentration. Taking China's inbound container traffic, for instance, the overseas regions of the South American north coast, Taiwan, the North American Gulf Coast, South Asia, and North Africa are of very high concentration levels, as their HHI values reach 9,974, 6,018, 4,822, 4,428, and 4,078, respectively. In the case of the South American North Coast, the port of Buenaventura carries almost all container flows originating from this region to China. And in the case of Taiwan, the port of Kaohsiung accounts for 76% of the total containers transported from Taiwan to the mainland. It is worth noting that for the regions of Mediterranean Europe and Australasia, although their HHI values are below 1,000, it does not mean equal traffic distributions among their ports. Rather, it indicates that several ports are of similar importance to inter-regional liner shipping connections between the host region and China, (e.g., the European Mediterranean ports of Marsaxlokk, Valencia, Barcelona, Genova, Fos, Piraeus, and La Spezia accounting for 75.6% of total container traffic transported from this region to China).

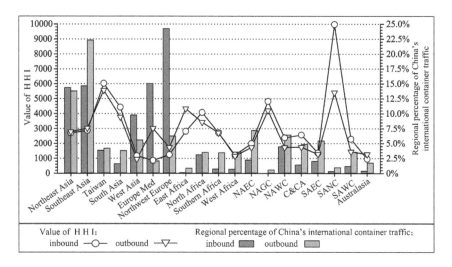

Figure 20.6 Concentration levels of China's international container traffic among ports in overseas regions

Table 20.1 Statistics on Chinese top ports' overseas liner shipping connections

Ports	Inbound		Outbound	
	No. of connections	*Traffic share (%)*	*No. of connections*	*Traffic share (%)*
Shanghai	212	23.36	236	21.60
Hong Kong	157	14.51	169	16.32
Tianjin	142	4.21	133	3.35
Ningbo-Zhoushan	134	17.53	191	18.29
Shenzhen	131	19.15	160	20.72
Qingdao	125	7.91	154	7.49
Dalian	103	2.67	112	2.43
Xiamen	80	6.59	95	4.97
Guangzhou	73	3.62	68	4.19

Source: Calculated by authors based on Alphaliner data

Generally, the ports of Shanghai, Hong Kong, Ningbo-Zhoushan, Shenzhen, Tianjin, Qingdao, Dalian, Xiamen, and Guangzhou are the most outstanding gateways that facilitate China's liner shipping connections with the outside world. As indicated in Table 20.1, the ports of Shanghai, Hong Kong, Ningbo-Zhoushan, and Shenzhen account for 74.55% and 76.94% of China's inbound and outbound international container traffic, respectively, and each port of Tianjin, Qingdao, Dalian, Xiamen, and Guangzhou takes up a traffic share between 1% and 10%, while each of the remaining Chinese ports only has a traffic share of less than 1%.

Internal distributions of China's international container traffic with most overseas regions obviously concentrate on a few Chinese ports themselves, as they are of HHI values higher than 1,000 (Figure 20.7). Looking closely at some highly-concentrated sub-distributions (e.g., sub-distributions of China's inbound container traffic from the North American Gulf Coast, the South American East Coast, West Africa, Southern Africa), it is interesting to observe that the respective Chinese ports on which this inter-regional traffic concentrates vary considerably. For instance, China's inbound traffic from the South American East Coast is mainly undertaken by the ports of Hong Kong and Shanghai, as indicated by their respective traffic shares of 57.4% and 33.8%. China's inbound traffic from the North American West Coast is mainly undertaken by the ports of Shanghai, Shenzhen, Ningbo-Zhoushan, and Hong Kong, with a combined traffic share of 74.19%. Such observations imply that one port is not necessarily of the same significance to its host region's liner shipping connections with various overseas regions. Therefore, further investigations into the hub dependency and vulnerability in China's international liner shipping connections should be carried out decompositionally (i.e. segmenting them by overseas region).

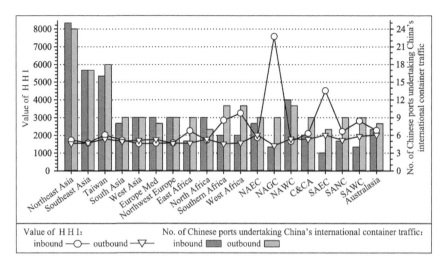

Figure 20.7 Concentration levels of China's international container traffic among Chinese ports by overseas region

Hub dependency and vulnerability

By identifying significant inter-regional flows between China and each overseas region, the external hub ports and internal hub ports for China's international liner shipping connections are revealed (Figure 20.8). Although abundant inter-port level of container flow connections linking China and the outside world have been established by world liner carriers, only about 14% of these connections are significant, in terms of traffic volume.

Externally, China's significant international liner shipping connections concentrate on a small number of overseas ports, (i.e. 67 and 57 for inbound and outbound, respectively). Individual dependence levels on these identified external hubs are also shown in Figure 20.8. Notably, the ports of Buenaventura, Kaohsiung, Colombo, Houston, Said, Singapore, and Busan are especially crucial to China's international liner shipping connections with their respective host regions, as indicated by the relatively high dependence levels. Such high-level hub dependency is very likely to result in high-level vulnerability in the inter-regional liner shipping connections between China and the corresponding overseas regions. Note that the prominent importance of a few ports (e.g., Buenaventura) may be caused by the artificial effect of world region division. But their superior roles in the liner shipping connections between their host regions and China should be reasonable, as such results can also be generally achieved by applying some common indicators, such as traffic share, to the original service data.

Internally, China's significant international liner shipping connections involve only nine ports, i.e. Shanghai, Ningbo-Zhoushan, Shenzhen, Hong Kong,

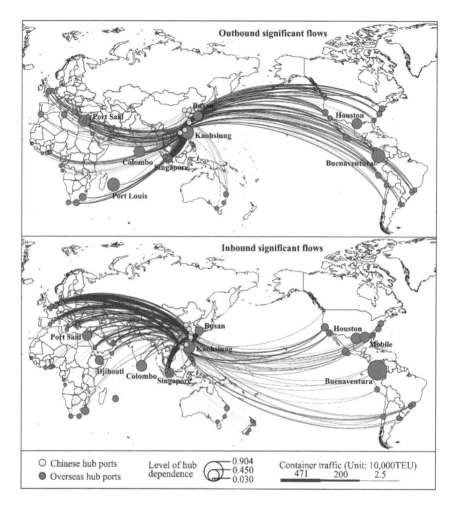

Figure 20.8 Distribution of China's significant international container flows and the related hub ports, by overseas region

Guangzhou, Xiamen, Qingdao, Tianjin, and Dalian. Figure 20.9 shows to what degree China's international liner shipping connections depend on each of them, by overseas region. On the one hand, the competitive positions of these hub ports vary considerably in terms of China's liner shipping connections with different overseas regions. On the other hand, the ports of Shanghai, Ningbo-Zhoushan, Hong Kong, and Shenzhen generally hold superior positions to their other five counterparts, in that they serve as primary and secondary hubs, respectively, for China's international liner shipping connections. The gateway roles of the ports of Guangzhou, Xiamen, Qingdao, Tianjin, and Dalian in serving China's international liner shipping connections are quite limited to a few foreland markets, if we

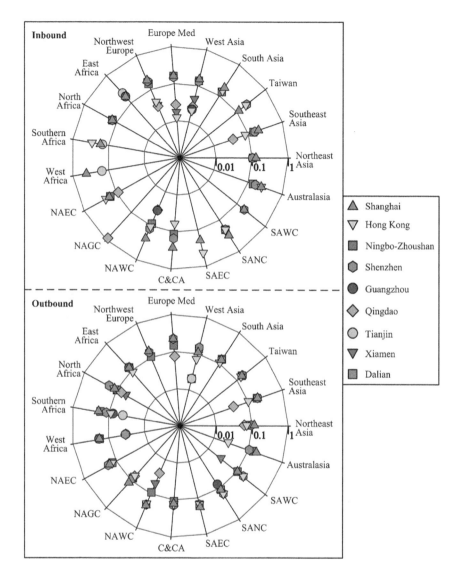

Figure 20.9 Levels of dependency of China's international liner shipping connections on Chinese hub ports, by overseas region

consider the significance of overseas liner shipping connections. Taking China's inbound significant flows, for example, the port of Qingdao only has flows from seven overseas regions, and the port of Guangzhou only from the overseas regions of West Asia, East Africa, and the North American West Coast.

Following the above analysis of hub dependency, we further measured the vulnerability levels of China's international liner shipping connections with individual overseas regions, externally and internally. The results are presented in Figure 20.10, including values of vulnerability levels, and also the two contributing factors (i.e. combined level of hub dependency and concentration level of significant inter-regional flows).

Firstly, looking externally, the vulnerability levels of China's international liner shipping connections with individual overseas regions vary a lot. This is understandable, given the diversity between overseas regions in the development of port systems, economy and international trade. An extremely vulnerable external sub-distribution of China's international container flows lies in China's inbound flows from the South American North Coast. These significant container flows originating from this region to China take up a very large share of the total inter-regional

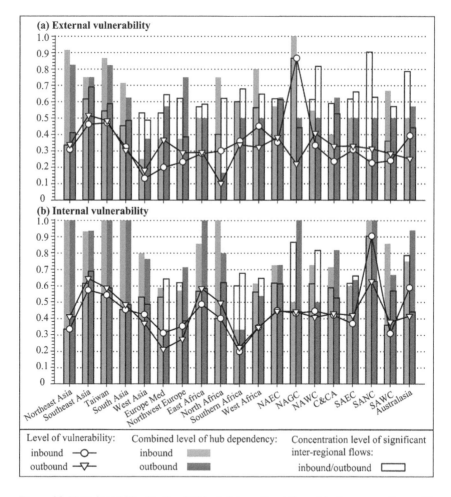

Figure 20.10 Vulnerability levels of China's international liner shipping connections with overseas regions

container traffic between the two regions, but they are totally monopolized by the port of Buenaventura.

Meanwhile, some relatively robust external distributions of China's international container flows lie in regions of Southern and West Africa, Mediterranean Europe, Northwest Europe, the South American West and East coasts, and Northeast Asia. In the case of Northeast Asia, although the port of Busan undertakes all the significant inter-regional container flows between the region and China, traffic on those significant flows only takes up 33.67% of the total inter-regional traffic. Driven by close trade connections and geographical adjacency between South Korea, Japan and China, many small carriers have long been actively participating in this inter-regional shipping market, by providing direct services between Chinese ports and other main Northeast Asian container ports like Inchon, Nagoya, Tokyo, Yokohama, Kobe, and Osaka.

Secondly, vulnerability levels in the distribution of China's international liner shipping connections among Chinese ports themselves, by overseas region, are also presented in Figure 20.10. Looking at China's international liner shipping connections with most overseas regions, it is generally less vulnerable on the Chinese side than overseas. The reason for this is: despite the fact that China's significant container flows with most overseas regions are undertaken by no other Chinese ports than the nine identified hubs (i.e. the ports of Shanghai, Hong Kong, Ningbo-Zhoushan, Shenzhen, Guangzhou, Qingdao, Tianjin, Xiamen, and Dalian), they rarely concentrate on only one or two hubs thanks to the diverse port selections of global carriers. For instance, China's inbound container flows from West Asia are dispersed among nine Chinese ports, and those significant flows are undertaken by seven of these ports.

Note that the results of two particular cases should be reviewed with caution. One is the existence of a huge difference in vulnerability levels between China's inbound and outbound liner shipping connections with the North American Gulf Coast. Such strange results may be caused by the limited data period considered in the present study whereas port rotations in the service networks of world liner carriers are generally stable in normal situations. The other is that the results of China's liner shipping connections with Taiwan are achieved under an ideal status of liner shipping across Taiwan Strait. So far, there still exist strict regulations (e.g., foreign vessels may not carry any cargo from Taiwan that is destined for the mainland, or vice versa). But this matter is beyond the consideration of this study, due to a lack of such information in data sources available to the authors.

Conclusion

To understand hub dependency and vulnerability in global-local liner shipping connections carried out by the service networks of world carriers, this study proposed a practical framework for identifying hub ports and measuring levels of hub dependency and vulnerability, in the spatial distribution of a given region's international liner shipping connections with overseas markets, externally and internally. An empirical investigation into China's international liner shipping connections demonstrates the validity of the proposed methodology. The main findings are twofold.

1　Externally, China's significant international container flows with most overseas regions, to a large degree rely on a few hub ports in those overseas regions; although there are a large number of well-established container flow connections between a wide range of overseas ports and Chinese ports, carried out by regular liner shipping services, thanks to the rapid growth of China's economy and international trade over the last two decades.

2　Internally, nine Chinese ports (i.e. Shanghai, Ningbo-Zhoushan, Shenzhen, Hong Kong, Dalian, Qingdao, Tianjin, Guangzhou, and Xiamen) are identified as hubs facilitating China's international liner shipping connections with the outside world by undertaking significant overseas container flows. However, specific Chinese hubs, levels of hub dependency, and levels of vulnerability in the sub-distributions of China's international liner shipping connections with individual overseas regions vary quite substantially.

In summary, the present method is exploratory, as it only focuses on traffic volume in evaluating the significance (or salience) of inter-regional liner shipping connections. Besides, a further interpretation of driving factors behind such hub-dependency phenomena is also beyond the current method. Nevertheless, it can help to achieve some in-depth understanding on how the global-local liner shipping connections are carried out for a given region, through decomposition analyses that segment the region's international container flows into various overseas regions. Some remaining research questions are open to future studies; for instance, to analyze the impact of technical improvement (e.g., increasing vessel capacity), shipping route development (e.g., canal expansion), and competition among carriers (e.g., merger and alliance) on hub dependency and vulnerability in connections between local regions and the global liner shipping network.

Notes

1　www.worldshipping.org/
2　http://unctadstat.unctad.org/wds/TableViewer/tableView.aspx
3　The Herfindahl-Hirschman Index is a commonly accepted measure of market concentration, calculated by squaring the market share of each firm competing in the market and then summing the resulting numbers. The U.S. Department of Justice provides broad divisions of market concentration as measured by the HHI: unconcentrated (HHI below 1000), moderately concentrated (HHI between 1000 and 1800), and highly concentrated (HHI above 1800). These widely accepted standards are used here for analyzing container traffic concentration among regional ports.

References

Ducruet, C. (2008) Hub dependence in constrained economies: The case of North Korea. *Maritime Policy and Management*, 35(4): 374–388.

Ducruet, C., Lee, S.W., Ng, A.K.Y. (2010) Centrality and vulnerability in liner shipping networks: Revisiting the Northeast Asian port hierarchy. *Maritime Policy and Management*, 37(1): 17–36.

Ducruet, C., Zaidi, F. (2012) Maritime constellations: A complex network approach to shipping and ports. *Maritime Policy and Management*, 39(2): 151–168.

Fleming, D.K., Hayuth, Y. (1994) Spatial characteristics of transportation hubs: Centrality and intermediacy. *Journal of Transport Geography*, 2(1): 3–18.

Gelareh, S., Nickel, S., Pisinger, D. (2010) Liner shipping hub network design in a competitive environment. *Transportation Research Part E*, 46(6): 991–1004.

Gelareh, S., Pisinger, D. (2011) Fleet deployment, network design and hub location of liner shipping companies. *Transportation Research Part E*, 47(6): 947–964.

Holmes, J.H., Haggett, P. (1977) Graph theory interpretation of flow matrices: A note on maximization procedures for identifying significant links. *Geographical Analysis*, 9(4): 388–399.

Lee, T.W., Flynn, M. (2011) Charting a new paradigm of container hub port development policy: The Asian doctrine. *Transport Reviews*, 31(6): 791–806.

Leinbach, T.R., Capineri, C. (2007) The global economy and freight transport flows. In: Leinbach, T.R., Capineri, C. (Eds.), *Globalized Freight Transport: Intermodality, E-Commerce, Logistics and Sustainability*. Cheltenham, UK: Edward Elgar Publishing, pp. 1–14.

Meng, Q., Wang, S. (2011) Liner shipping service network design with empty container repositioning. *Transportation Research Part E*, 47(5): 695–708.

Ng, A.K.Y., Pallis, A.A. (2010) Port governance reforms in diversified institutional frameworks: Generic solutions, implementation asymmetries. *Environment and Planning A*, 42(9): 2147–2167.

Notteboom, T.E. (2004) Container shipping and ports: An overview. *Review of Network Economics*, 3(2): 86–106.

Notteboom, T.E. (2010) Concentration and the formation of multi-port gateway regions in the European container port system: An update. *Journal of Transport Geography*, 18(4): 567–583.

Tongzon, J.L., Sawant, L. (2007) Port choice in a competitive environment: From the shipping lines' perspective. *Applied Economics*, 39(4): 477–492.

Wang, J.J., Ng, A.K.Y. (2011) The geographical connectedness of Chinese seaports with foreland markets: A new trend? *Tijdschrift voor Economische en Sociale Geografie*, 102(2): 188–204.

Wang, J.J., Slack, B. (2000) The evolution of a regional container port system: The Pearl River Delta. *Journal of Transport Geography*, 8(4): 263–275.

Wang, J.J., Slack, B. (2004) Regional governance of port development in China: A case study of Shanghai International Shipping Center. *Maritime Policy and Management*, 31(4): 357–373.

Wang, Y.H., Cullinane, K. (2014) Traffic consolidation in East Asian container ports: A network flow analysis. *Transportation Research Part A*, 61: 152–163.

Wilmsmeier, G., Monios, J. (2016) Institutional structure and agency in the governance of spatial diversification of port system evolution in Latin America. *Journal of Transport Geography*, 51: 294–307.

Xu, M., Li, Z., Shi, Y., Zhang, X., Jiang, S. (2015) Evolution of regional inequality in the global shipping network. *Journal of Transport Geography*, 44: 1–12.

21 Geopolitical and logistical factors in the evolution of North Korea's shipping flows

César Ducruet, Sung-Woo Lee and Stanislas Roussin

Traditionally in socialist economies, maritime transport has been considered costly and useless, its role being often limited to coastal shipping within the socialist block (Vigarié, 1995). Nevertheless, North Korea possesses and operates eight international trading ports located along two maritime façades, which directly connect its major cities with international trade. North Korean ports are the potential gateways for a Eurasian land bridge (Choi et al., 2003; Rozman, 2004). Internally, coastal shipping may remedy the growing logistical difficulties caused by a prolonged economic crisis. Maritime transport remains the principal vector of inter-Korean economic exchange with 90% of commercial relationships ensured by sea (Kim, 2001; Olsen et al., 2003). Studying North Korea's shipping flows thus presents numerous challenges for academic research in both conceptual and empirical terms. How does a major and deepening economic and geopolitical crisis impact the pattern and evolution of shipping flows? What are the respective roles of internal and external factors? (see Chapters 6, 10, and 20 on Portugal, USA, and China for other analyses of external linkages of national port systems, and Chapters 8 and 19 on the link between shipping flows and socialist economies).

The fact that even an ostensibly closed country like North Korea is fully part of a global system for recording vessel movement means that such questions do not go unanswered. The majority of North Korean vessels are insured in London by *Lloyd's Register* (Smith, 2009); thus, vessel movement at North Korean ports has been surveyed for decades, although it is only recently that such information has served economic and geographic analyses and offset the lacks and deficiencies of data on North Korea as a whole (Noland, 2000; Nanto and Chanlett-Avery, 2005) by looking at the changing distribution and concentration of maritime flows internally and with the rest of the world (Ducruet et al., 2009).

This chapter proposes to update and extend previous analyses by expanding the time period, from the early twentieth century to the year 2015, for which shipping data has recently become available. Vessel calls at North Korean ports were measured across different units and time periods, either through a simple count based on the Shipping Index (1905–2008) or on their tonnage weight and spatial distribution (1977–2015) using digital information from *Lloyd's List Intelligence*. We systematically confront traffic trends with general (and often limited) knowledge of transport and trade characteristics gathered from field observation and official, second-hand information sources. This will help us to better understand the origin and ultimate development of maritime transport in the North Korean economy, through the successive phases of Korean unity, Japanese colonization, war and partition, Cold War growth and Soviet support, isolation, decline, and Chinese influence.

The second section of the chapter provides a historical background on ports, transport, and economic development in the light of contemporary political changes. It also presents new results on traffic evolution at North Korean ports from various angles, such as fleet nationality and performance. The third section investigates the importance of maritime transport in the North Korean economy. Lastly, we analyze the changing distribution of overseas linkages, with a specific focus on shipping flows between the Koreas and with China.

The North Korean port system

There is evidence that ports in North Korea have been operating since the Three Kingdoms and Goryeo era (37 BC–1392 AD). In particular, during the Balhae Kingdom (698–934), shipping routes existed between Seoanpyeong (Amnok River) and the Shandong Peninsula in China and between Yeomju (current Russia) and Namgyeong with Japan. Under the Goyeo period, Seogyeong (currently Pyongyang) was well connected with China. Later on, the Korean fleet became the most important on the Yellow Sea, frequently trading with Arab merchants along the Yaeseong River near the then capital city, Gaeseong. Before the Manchu invasions, sea transport was promoted by the government, which even planned to build a national fleet around 1402, before letting private interests do so after 1529, due to the related cost and labor issues. In that period, ports in North Korea remain less connected to main trade routes, except from Wonsan, which connects the East coast with southern Siberia. The Choseon era (1392–1910) is mainly character- ized by the decline of maritime trade, due to Manchu invasions, China's confu- cianist preference for landward development and growing Japanese pressure on the construction and modernization of North Korean ports before the 1910 inva- sion and colonial rule. Investments particularly concentrated at Nampo, Haeju, Yongampo-Sinuiju, Wonsan (with the British) but also Incheon and Busan in the South, while the Japanese created the rail link Seoul-Wonsan in 1904, buying the rights from the British but also from the French (Seoul-Sinuiju). After the Japa- nese and Manchu invasions, several ports kept a domectic role only, such as Hwangju (south of Pyongyang), Wonsan, Yongampo (Amnok River), and Cheon- gjin. While shipping activity in North Korea (and Korea as a whole) does not appear in *Lloyd's Shipping Index* before 1905, it provides us with a long-term view over the last century (Figure 21.1).

Under Japanese rule (1910–1945), the northern part of the Korean Peninsula became the prime focus of Japan's strategy to conquer Manchuria, with invest- ments in railways, mining (purchasing rights from the US or UK), ports, and factories. During the Korean War (1950–1953), many port sites were heavily dam- aged if not entirely destroyed. While North Korea managed to overcome such a

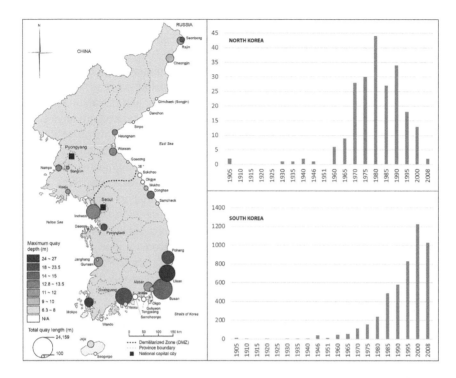

Figure 21.1 Infrastructures (2005) and vessel calls (1905–2008) at Korean ports

disaster and become East Asia's second most industrialized nation in the 1960s after Japan, its dynamism faltered in the 1970s and started to collapse in the 1980s. The 1961 seven-year Development Plan with its strong focus on maritime transport and foreign trade had somewhat limited effects (Ahn, 2003) due to the reliance, during the Cold War, on Soviet and Chinese support (Cotton, 1996). Ports received little investment apart from the creation of Rajin port in 1974 and some oil berths and storage facilities. A move towards openness started in 1984, with the opening of the Rajin-Seonbong (Raseon) free-trade zone in 1991 (Jo and Ducruet, 2007). However, the collapse of the Soviet Union (1989–1993) and the Socialist Block immediately resulted in the loss of North Korea's main trading partners and the lack of capital to purchase hydrocarbons on international markets, resulting in traffic decline.

Subsequently, factories ceased to operate, mines were flooded, transport became paralyzed, and agricultural productivity declined without sufficient fertilizers and mechanization, aggravated by natural disasters (1994–1995) and the three-year vacancy at the head of the State after the death of President Kim Il-Seong (1994). US-North Korean tensions rose over Pyongyang's nuclear program, leading to an internal policy more and more centred on the Army as a reaction against the Wassenaar Agreement (1996), restraining exports and controlling the importation of technological goods. Limited foreign trade and the deterioration of infrastructure and capital stock (Yoon and Babson, 2002) persisted until the agricultural reforms of 1998, the June 2000 inter-Korean summit, and the July 2002 reforms, which conferred certain autonomy to businesses, and led to improved labor welfare, and commercial distribution (e.g., Pyeonghwa Automobiles), and the development of factories, farms, and private businesses. One important factor had also been to become able to purchase oil, giving a small boost to the economy. Despite the failure of the Special Administrative Region (SAR) of Sinuiju in 2002, a number of economic development projects grew rapidly, such as the International Tourism Zone of Mount Geumgang (1999), and the Gaeseong Industrial Complex (2004) financed by South Korea. Such initiatives, in addition to the development by the army of hydro power plants, housing, and highways, helped compensate for the decline of the industrial sector (Ahn, 2003), However, despite its numerous advantages over China in terms of labor force and natural resources (Roussin, 2015), North Korea's appeal for the international business community continuously decreased (Lee, 2005). The devastation in the manufacturing and transport sector was such that only 20% of factories remained operational, with energy production meeting only 30–50% of the country's needs, and companies spending about 40% of their manufacturing costs on logistics (Forster-Carter, 2001). The priority given to railways and heavy industries, combined with poor technical standards and cumbersome customs regulations, resulted in prolonged shipping time (Ahn, 2002), a lack of modern cargo-handling facilities (Kim, 2001), exorbitant port-entry fees and 45% of containers returning empty (Forster-Carter, 2001). Certain containers even disappear or are changed into hangars or lodging boxes. Port modernization mainly occurred thanks to Chinese and Russian support, such as in Nampo and Rajin (Jo and Ducruet, 2006), leading to greater accessibility and a boost to transit trade, but for the external interests of Russia and China.

Traffic dynamics of North Korean ports

Domestic versus foreign fleet traffic

As referred to by Smith (2009) based on Lloyd's Register 2008 data, the vast majority of North Korean vessels are general cargo ships (53%) and fishing vessels (24%), followed by some oil tankers and bulk carriers. The same report also underlined its aging and limited capacity, the fragmentation of ownership, and the majority of vessels being flagged at home. It was possible to verify a number of traffic dynamics based on daily vessel movement data. Based on Figure 21.2, one can observe significant traffic fluctuations over the period, with a noticeable decline from the 1980s to the 2000s until a recent but timid recovery. Following regular traffic growth until 1987, the economy started to falter before the Soviet Union collapsed. Certain exceptions can be observed, such as the effects of the Rajin-Seonbong free-trade zone (1991–1992), humanitarian aid, economic reforms, the

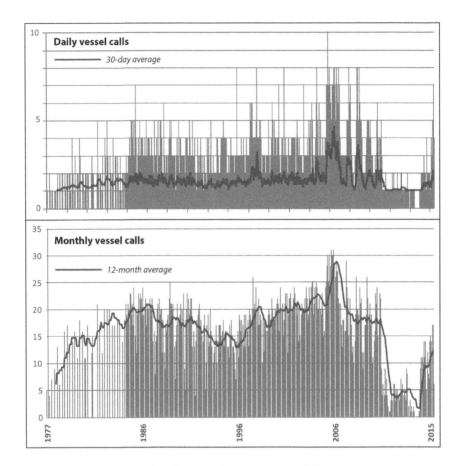

Figure 21.2 Monthly vessel traffic at North Korean ports, 1977–2015

KEDO project, and inter-Korean cooperation (1999–2002), the inter-Korean maritime agreement (2004–2005), and growing trade with China (2014–2015).

Disaggregating traffic figures according to vessel flags – North Korean or foreign – allows us to further understand the technical evolution of the domestic fleet as well as North Korea's level of reliance upon other fleets (Figure 21.3). As such, foreign traffic concentrated more than 70% of the total traffic on average, but with different phases: 85% in 1977–1984; 70% in 1985–1992; 57% between 1993–2002 (under 50% in 1996–1998); and 80% in 2003–2015. Yet in absolute terms, foreign traffic has registered a constant decline since the mid-1980s. By comparison, traffic under the North Korean flag remained somewhat stable between 1984 and 2002. This may be explained by the use of naval ships for commercial purposes in emergencies. Trains that were responsible for most landward communications got paralyzed by the lack of electricity, most of the railway network being electrified.

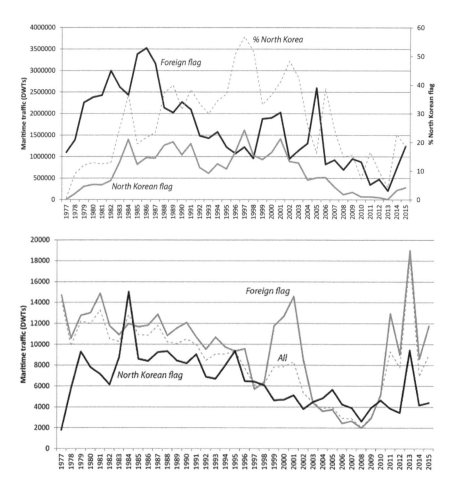

Figure 21.3 Total and average vessel traffic, North Korean and foreign flags (1977–2015)

In terms of average vessel size, foreign traffic largely dominated, except in 1984, 1997, and 2004–2009, while both foreign and domestic vessels have regularly reduced over time, due to falling demand, accessibility issues, and a deterioration in cargo-handling equipment. In addition, larger ships that are costlier to repair and operate tend to disappear over time, as North Korea lacks sufficient capital or shipbuilding facilities to maintain and modernize its fleet. The exception of 1999–2002 for foreign vessels relates to humanitarian support. Vessel sizes also reflect wider issues, such as the missile crisis with Japan (1998) and the levy of sanctions by Washington in 1999. The sudden decline in 2002 marks an end to oil shipments from the United States, Japan, and the European Union due to Pyongyang's suspected uranium enrichment program. The upward turn in 2005 could reflect the impact of the inter-Korean agreement that liberalized the movement of vessels between North and South. From 2008–2009, the average vessel size for both fleets grew once again, despite low cargo volumes.

The analysis of turnaround times (Figure 21.4) by fleet, excluding a few exceptional stays lasting more than one year, is based on the average time difference between arrival date and sailing date for each call at North Korean ports. Without exception, North Korean ships stayed longer in ports than foreign ships, partly due to the "home effect". Maritime transport by sea often constituted a secondary option compared with overland (cross-border). Despite inspection and bureaucratic procedures affecting foreign ships, the latter witnessed a growing turnaround

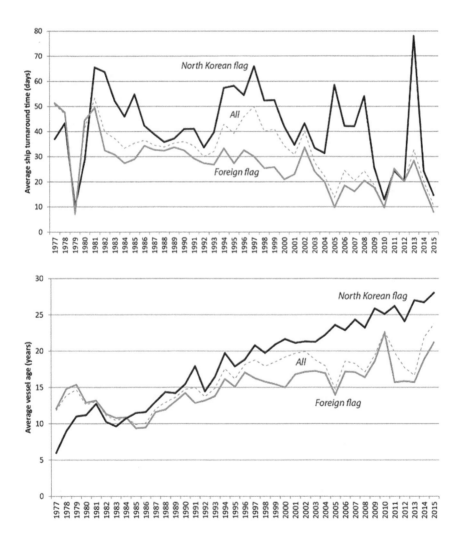

Figure 21.4 Average turnaround time and fleet age, North Korean and foreign flags (1977–2015)

time gap compared with the domestic fleet from the 1990s onwards. The reduction and disappearance of former trade routes deprived North Korean ships of their activity, which was aggravated by the lack of fuel supplies. Thus, the majority remained anchored at their home terminals, until the situation improved from 2000 onwards, although important delays at North Korean ports were regularly reported in the press, most cargoes being handled by hand. The peak of 2005 marks North Korea's very unstable attitude in relation to humanitarian organizations and nuclear talks with other nations. Nevertheless, a decrease in turnaround times for foreign ships also suggests greater flexibility in the management of North Korean ports through less cumbersome regulations.

In terms of fleet age, North Korean vessels have always been older than foreign vessels except in the period 1977–1984. From 1985 onwards, domestic and foreign fleets followed a similar trend, but from 1997 North Korean vessels aged more rapidly and foreign vessels stabilized. The average age of foreign ships was 15 years, compared with 18 for the North Korean fleet, while the average age per ship for fleets from developing countries was around 14 years (see UNCTAD, 2000). Due to the crisis in the North Korean shipbuilding sector since the mid-1980s most of the currently operated vessels were constructed before 1984. Again, the impact of the mid-1990s crisis is clearly visible, North Korea being forced to push the fleet to its limits to palliate deficiencies in the wider transport system. As a result, Japanese authorities banned North Korean ships from their ports on the grounds of technical and hygiene issues. Thus, while North Korean vessels were aged 14 years on average between 1977 and 1996, this had increased to 23 between 1997 and 2015, compared with 13 and 17 years for foreign vessels for the respective periods.

Shipping and trade

Traditionally in North Korea, inland transportation has dominated the modal split, as a long-term effect of Japanese occupation (1910–1945) and of the priority given to railways as in Russia. The modal split in North Korea is as follows: railways (70%), roads (17%), sea (10%), and air (3%) (Roussin, 2015). However, railways were particularly affected by the economic crisis (Oh, 2001); the high electrification rate became a constraint in a context of energy scarcity, while only 7% of roads were paved (Bang, 2004). The road network, costlier to maintain and less well adapted to the transport of raw materials (80% of transported products according to Tsuji, 2005), remains strictly controlled by the government through inspection tolls between main cities and provinces. Train and truck accidents were frequently reported (Cotton, 1996), aggravated by the rarity of signals, gas stations, and the poor condition of tracks and roads. The deepening crisis reinforced the influence of elevation and climate (Roussin, 2015), harming smooth domestic transport connectivity and concentrating traffic within Pyongan province, while 80% of North Korea's exports passed through Sinuiju at the Chinese border (Tsuji, 2005). Eastern regions, by contrast, declined rapidly (Pons, 2004).

The respective evolution of North Korea's international trade and maritime traffic, however, exhibit a widening gap (Figure 21.5), mainly due to increased cross-border trade with China, which occurred inland. According to the Korea International Trade Association (KITA), nearly 91% of North Korea's products were exported to China in 2013, compared with 51% in 2003, while Chinese investments in North Korea expanded from US$1.12 million to US$86.2 million between 2003 and 2013. Some experts reported a steady increase of trade between North Korea and Dandong between 2000 and 2008 (Lee, 2009), as Dandong's exports to North Korea tripled and its imports from North Korea increased tenfold.

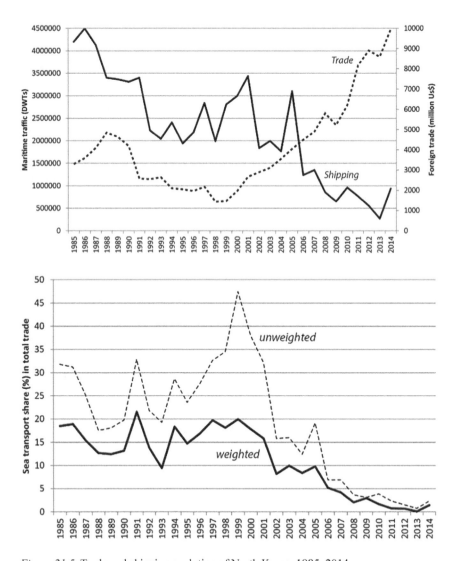

Figure 21.5 Trade and shipping evolution of North Korea, 1985–2014

Overall, border trade with China represented about one-third (32%) on average of North Korea's total trade with China, and 9% on average of North Korea's total foreign trade in 1997–2005 (Kim, 2001). In 2011, coal was being shipped from North to South China through the port of Rajin, while in the late 2000s the Chinese government announced the restart of the Changchun-Jilin-Tumen project as a pilot economic zone and obtained a 50-year concession for operating a port terminal in Rajin in 2010, the two other terminals being operated by Russia and North Korea, respectively. Cross-border trade thus experienced steady growth, especially with Shandong, Hebei, and Jiangsu provinces, which altogether reached 50% of the total (Kim, 2014). In 2012, just over 87% of both North Korea's exports and imports were with China, which is indicative of its growing dependency. Nearly 90% of trade between China and North Korea was with the six provinces, of which 42.7% with Liaoning and 32.3% for Shandong, Hebei, and Jiangsu. The Jilin province witnessed a Gross Regional Domestic Product (GRDP) growth rate of 13.4% in 2012, more than China's own GDP growth rate (Kim, 2014).

Another approach has been to estimate the importance of maritime transport in total foreign trade. We estimated the value of maritime flows by converting dead-weight tons (dwt) into dollars based on US$250 per ton (Ducruet and Jo, 2008), which was the average dwt-dollar ratio for Japanese and South Korean trade with North Korea in the 2000s. Results were compared with a weighted figure based on the estimation of value differentials among traffic types. As a result, the two ratios give a very different importance to maritime trade, with average shares of 19.2% for unweighted traffic and 11.1% for weighted traffic during the period. In fact, unweighted figures overestimate the importance of maritime transport mainly due to the high volume and low value of bulks. The observed evolutions show that North Korean trade was much less dependent on maritime flows in the recent period (2002–2014), with 4.3% on average compared with 16.3% for 1985–2001. 1991 registered an exceptional peak that can only be explained by the Rajin-Seonbong initiative, which mainly used the port during the construction and starting phases of the economic zone project (Jo and Ducruet, 2007). Another factor was the dramatic decline of shipping with Japan since 2002 (e.g., the Wonsan-Niigata ferry link). Lastly, maritime transport was mainly being used to carry lower-valued (but highly strategic) goods, such as oil or humanitarian aid, so that even in times of shipping growth in the recent period, the net value of shipping could not be reflected on account of its overall shrinking volume.

Overseas maritime connectivity

General trends

North Korea's foreign trade used to be dominated by the Soviet Union, whose share surpassed 50% in 1960, dropped to 25% in 1977, and reverted to 50% around 1986, while China's share gradually declined from 32% to 11% in the same period (Choi, 1992). Available statistics for trade with its main economic partners provided complementary results for the 1989–2014 period (Figure 21.6).

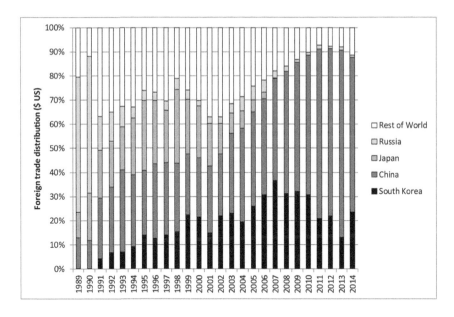

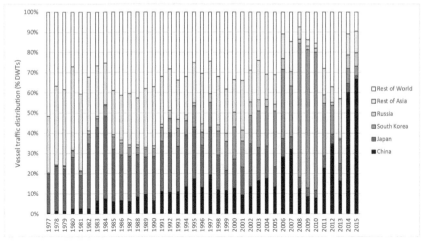

Figure 21.6 North Korea's overseas linkages in total foreign trade (top) and maritime traffic (bottom)

Soviet Russia still occupied about 60% of total foreign trade in 1989–1990 and nearly disappeared in subsequent years (1% in 2014), superseded by Japan and China. The "rest of the world", namely countries outside Northeast Asia, accounted for around 30% of total trade on average from the early 1990s to the early 2000s, but went through a drastic drop since then, reaching only 11% in

2014. This evolution confirms the shrinking of North Korea's long-distance economic ties, and greater concentration on its proximity, a key factor being the lack of oil to feed the economy. Japan officially ceased all trade with North Korea from 2009, after oscillating around 20% in the first half of the period. Conversely, South Korea's share rose rapidly since the 2000s due to the thaw in inter-Korean ties. In general, North Korean imports and exports were based on humanitarian shipments, non-commercial exports (i.e. cooperation projects), material aid, but also commercial exports (e.g., machinery and transport equipment, textile and chemicals, electric and electronic products (80% to 90%), while its exports to South Korea increased regularly after 2002 – mainly textiles, metals, agricultural, and fish products. However, an escalation of tensions from both sides caused the reduction of South Korea's share to the advantage of China, mainly based on inland border trade, as discussed above.

A similar but fuller picture is provided by vessel movement data. A major factor has been the drastic decline of Japan's share, from about 80% to negligible amounts in recent years (despite its official trade interruption with North Korea). A similar decline occurred for Hong Kong, despite a slight recovery to roughly 15% in 2011–2012. As for trade values, major changes concern South Korea and China. The latter had even become dominant in the last two years under study, culminating in around 73–78% of total traffic, reflecting its role as North Korea's dominant trading partner. While the respective shares of China and South Korea had been relatively even in the early period, China's share was superior to South Korea's share between 1986 and 1998, namely before North Korea's reforms. From 1999–2000 South Korea became North Korea's largest maritime partner for eight consecutive years (2003–2010), reaching peaks of 74%, 80%, and 81% in 2008–2010. This is somewhat counterintuitive, given the worsening of North-South political relationships from 2007 onwards and reinforced tensions around the Northern Limit Line (Gelézeau, 2007). Growing trade with China and uneven North-South relationships caused a rapid decline of South Korea's share, which fell to 20–30% in 2011–2013 and to only 9% and 6% in 2014 and 2015, respectively, i.e. the same share as in the late 1970s. Lastly, an interesting element is the share of domestic shipping, which fell from an average of 12% in the period 1985–1995 to 9% in 1996–2007 and only slightly more than 1% in the rest of the period. This indicates that domestic (or coastal) shipping was not used to palliate the deficiencies of the land-based transport system and logistics. Because coastal shipping is more likely to occur between East coast ports, its decline might also relate to the deliquescence of such cities, which are mostly connected by long-distance shipping bringing external aid.

Inter-Korean maritime flows

Official statistics provided by the Ministry of Unification in South Korea (2015) do not detail the modal split of inter-Korean trade and exchanges. Older statistics had underlined that inter-Korean maritime trade reached 15.7 million tons in

2006, a 240% growth rate compared with 2005, while the amount of vessels crossing the Korean border doubled between 2004 and 2005, following the 2004 inter-Korean maritime agreement, but this number has greatly reduced since then. Thus, the precise geographic distribution of inter-Korean maritime flows remains unknown. Absolute tonnage between North and South has been somewhat irregular: almost non-existent until the mid-1980s, moderate between 1989 and 1998, relatively strong between 1999 and 2010 (with a peak in 2005), and returning to low values since 2011. South Korea's share eventually reached 68% in 2008, after regular growth since 1996, echoing earlier works that described this process as North Korea's growing "hub dependence" on South Korea (Ducruet, 2008).

Mapping shipping flows across the Korean peninsula provides a clear picture of such an evolution (Figure 21.7). In the early phase of the period under study, inter-Korean flows shifted from almost non-existent to a concentration along the East coast between Wonsan and Ulsan principally (followed by Busan), all of which specialized in liquid bulks (oil and chemicals). Growing traffic became visible at Heungnam and Cheongjin to connect Busan, while Nampo and Incheon were also increasingly connected. We also see that East and West coasts were mainly connected through Busan and Incheon. That was followed by a multiplication of North-South linkages, with a marked increase in the number of connected ports.

Traffic had concentrated mainly along the West coast, with a shift from the Nampo-Busan line to the Nampo-Incheon line, followed in 2004–2006 by Haeju and Pyeongtaek, to absorb the growing traffic near the two country's capital cities. Shipping a container between Incheon and Nampo once cost as much as US$1,000 for 24h and a distance of only 100 kilometers, as much as the cost to reach Europe (Ahn, 2001). Later, operated by South Korean companies such as Hansung Shipping (90% of inter-Korean maritime flows), which exported South Korean textiles and imported North Korean raw materials for Samsung, LG, and Daewoo (Kim, 2004). Kook Yang Shipping was also involved on the Incheon-Nampo line to support further container traffic and weekly ferry shuttles, which would reduce the cost to US$750 (Korea Times, 2001; Ahn, 2002). In the more recent period, the Nampo-Incheon line maintained its importance, notwithstanding a drastic decline of all traffic (2010–2012).

On the East coast, Cheongjin and Heungnam remained the central nodes, connected primarily with Ulsan and Busan, while Wonsan began to lose ground gradually. In the last phase, the Incheon-Nampo linkage had nearly disappeared, replaced by new lines between secondary ports, such as Rajin, Daesan, Pyeongtaek, Boryoung, Donghae, and Pyongyang. Overall, North-South maritime dynamics were quite irregular, not only in traffic volumes, but also in terms of spatial distribution, with important shifts from one coast to the other, and between large and small ports. Recent figures corroborate certain press releases about plans to use Rajin as an inter-Korean hub, echoing earlier plans for Heungnam (Joongang Daily, 2006).

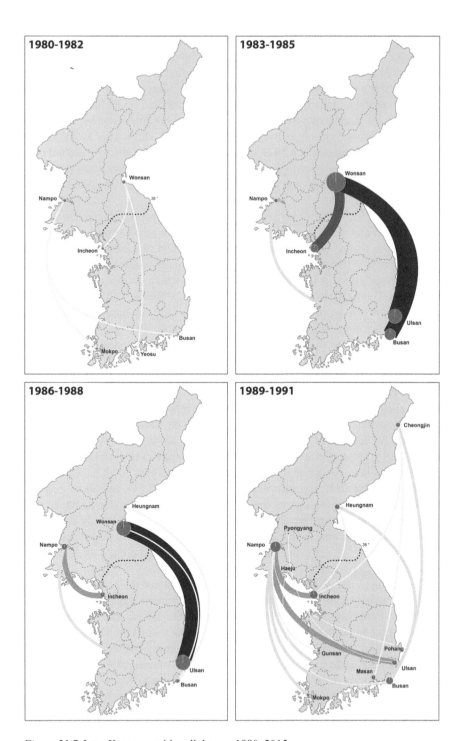

Figure 21.7 Inter-Korean maritime linkages, 1980–2015

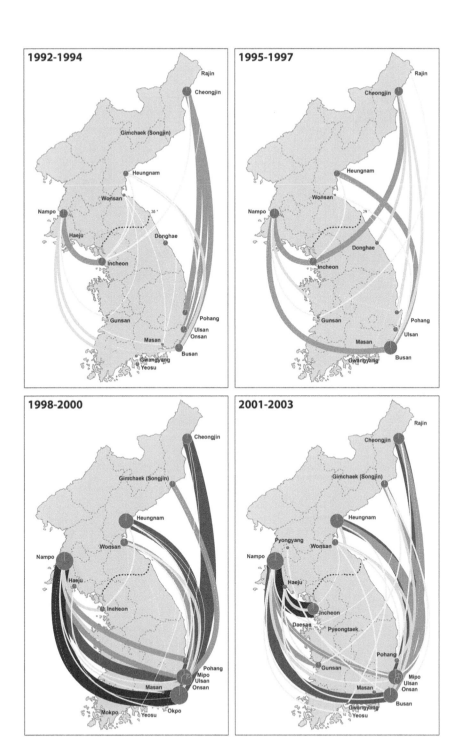

Figure 21.7 (Continued)

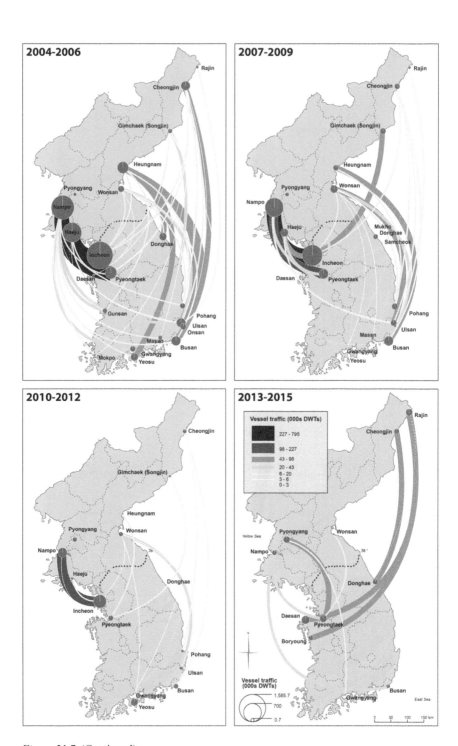

Figure 21.7 (Continued)

North Korea-China maritime flows

The overwhelming importance of China in North Korea's recent foreign trade is worth analyzing on a longer-term basis, notably for a comparison with inter-Korean shipping dynamics. Although most of the border trade of any value between China and North Korea occurs by land, on average 85% of its tonnage was transported by sea in the recent decade (Table 21.1). While the number of vessel crossings quadrupled between 2001 and 2013 and tonnage nearly doubled, it is only from 2009 that China has surpassed South Korea in this area.

Maritime linkages have experienced very distinct patterns over time since the early 1980s (Figure 21.8). One recurrent configuration is North Korea's reliance on the Hong Kong hub, a good indicator of long-distance shipping connecting regions such as the Black Sea and Europe. However, this link had become secondary in the late 1990s and has nearly disappeared since the 2000s, in line with South Korea's emerging role as North Korea's main transit hub. One exception is 2010–2012, when Hong Kong remained the only major link, just before South Korea lost its prominence in this network. Another stable feature has been the overarching importance of Nampo for shipping to and from China, mainly due to its geographic proximity (Yellow Sea) and gateway function for Pyongyang. Mainland Chinese connections have shifted hugely over time and space. Dalian is one of the major Chinese hubs, especially in the early period, mainly for containers. Other hubs have emerged, such as Rizhao and Dandong, to receive iron ore and coal from North Korea. The fact that bulk products are the main flow largely explains why

Table 21.1 Cross-border traffic between North Korea, China, and South Korea (2001–2013)

Year	China	South Korea	
	Share in total cross-border flows (% tons)	No. vessel crossings	
2013	82.7	4,457	31
2012	86.7	3,496	228
2011	82.7	4,916	142
2010	86.9	4,399	1,432
2009	87.1	2,664	2,577
2008	87.6	3,774	7,435
2007	91.5	3,383	11,891
2006	87.7	2,531	8,401
2005	87.6	2,613	4,497
2004	86.4	2,127	2,124
2003	74.7	1,383	2,022
2002	78.0	1,166	1,827
2001	88.8	1,032	1,686

Source: Own elaboration based on Ministry of Unification in South Korea and China Statistical Yearbooks

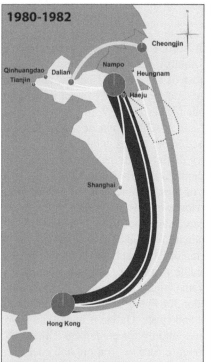
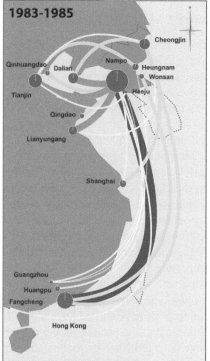
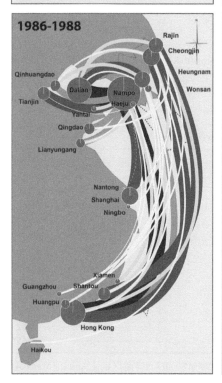
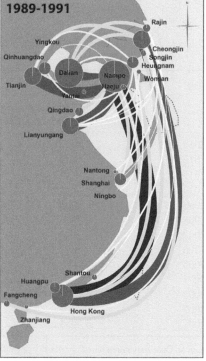

Figure 21.8 China-North Korea maritime linkages, 1980–2015

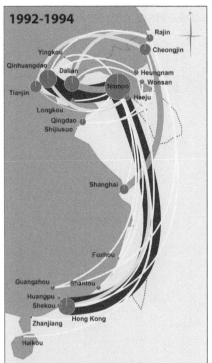

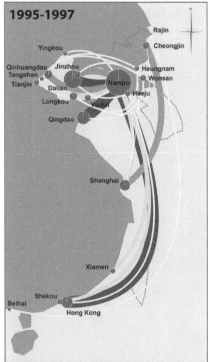

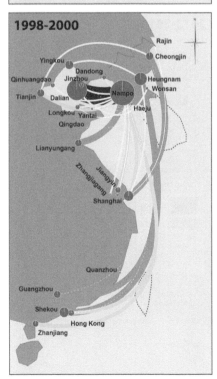

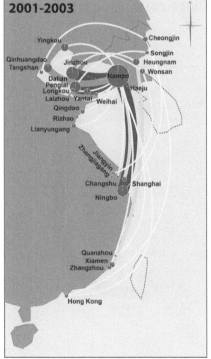

Figure 21.8 (Continued)

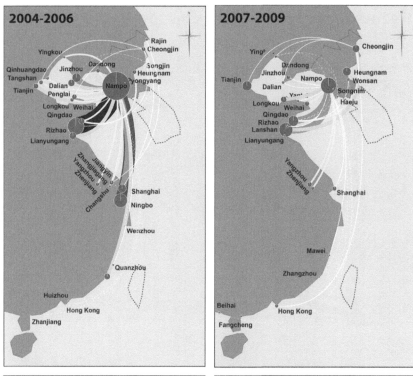

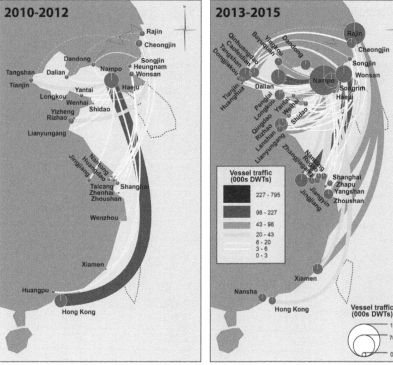

Figure 21.8 (Continued)

Shanghai and Shenzhen, China's main container ports, are underrepresented in the figure.

In the late period, a major driving force for reinforced shipping flows is the rapid increase of North Korea's coal exports to China (Vitelli, 2015), thereby becoming the latter's primary supplier after Australia and Indonesia. Although it was recently reported that the Russian port of Zarubino was preferred to Rajin for developing further Chinese (but also Russian and Mongolian) transit trade with the Pacific (Asia Cargo News, 2014), Rajin appears as a very central hub in the latest period, developing strong links with the coal-dependent region of Southern China (Wang and Ducruet, 2014). One favourable factor is Rajin's wide and standard railway gauge, offering easy and cheap access of Russian coal to the port, making it more attractive than Zarubino (Hong et al., 2014). The Russian railway company RDZ even sold part of Rajin port's concession rights on the third pier to a South Korean consortium (POSCO, Hyundai Merchant Marine, and Korea Railway) for shipping coal to Pohang, Gandjin, and Gwangyang (2013–2015), but nuclear tests in early 2016 interrupted the process.

Conclusion

Overall, this research has shed new light on the maritime dynamics of one of the most unknown countries in the world. In turn, the analysis of maritime traffic evolution over 39 years reveals interesting features that help to document and understand the economic and political issues at stake in North Korea. Accessing such untapped and first-hand statistics has been the only way to palliate the inadequate, approximate and outdated nature of other data on transport, logistics, and shipping in North Korea.

This analysis of data provided many clues about the long-term and short-term maritime dynamics affecting North Korean ports and their linkages with the outside world. On a daily, monthly or yearly basis, North Korea's maritime activity had been growing until the 1980s and has been on the decline since then, except for certain peaks largely attributable to humanitarian aid, at least for the early 2000s. This decline was at variance with growing foreign trade, leading to a high dependency on land-based freight flows (road, rail) with China. A rapid shrinkage of North Korea's forelands occurred in parallel with an ageing, considerably smaller and increasingly immobile North Korean fleet. Foreign vessels remained dominant to ensure the future of North Korean shipping and raising questions regarding the isolated reputation of a country which could not rely on its own ships. Drastic traffic shifts occurred within Northeast Asia, from Japan to South Korea and then China, reflecting wider trade patterns, i.e. from who are North Korea's oil and food needs fulfilled.

This research can be considered as an introduction to the potential offered by shipping data for the investigation of North Korea's changing economic and trading dynamics and linkages. This has enormous implications in terms of security and cargo tracking for organizations concerned with under-embargo trade. Further research will consider carrying out a survey of ship operators visiting North

Korean ports, based on the identity of ship operators. For academic research, this chapter may well contribute to a better understanding of how a major crisis affects shipping network design and spatial distribution.

Acknowledgements

The authors would like to thank Dr. Sungjun Park, Korea Maritime Institute, for his useful comments, and Dr. Chengjin Wang, Chinese Academy of Sciences, for sharing Chinese cross-border data. The research leading to these results has received funding from the European Research Council under the European Union's Seventh Framework Programme (FP/2007–2013) / ERC Grant Agreement n. [313847] "World Seastems".

References

Ahn, C.Y. (2003) *North Korea Development Report 2002/3*. Seoul: Korea Institute for Economic Policy.

Ahn, M.B. (2002) Restoration of the Seoul-Sinuiju line: Review and outlook. *East Asian Review*, 14(1): 107–119.

Ahn, M.Y. (2001) Slow boat to North Korea. *Cargo News Asia*, May 7.

Bang, H.K. (2004) Research notes: Towards an integrated logistics system in Northeast Asia. *East Asian Review*, 16(2): 111–121.

Choi, E.K., Kim, E.H., Merill, Y.S. (2003) *North Korea in the World Economy*. London and New York: Routledge.

Choi, S.Y. (1992) *Foreign Trade of North Korea: 1946–1988*. Unpublished PhD dissertation, Northern University.

Cotton, J. (1996) China and Tumen river cooperation: Jilin's coastal development strategy. *Asian Survey*, 36: 1086–1101.

Ducruet, C. (2008) Hub dependence in constrained economies: The case of North Korea. *Maritime Policy and Management*, 35(4): 374–388.

Ducruet, C., Jo, J.C. (2008) Coastal cities, port activities and logistics constraints in a socialist developing country: The case of North Korea. *Transport Reviews*, 28(1): 1–25.

Ducruet, C., Roussin, S., Jo, J.C. (2009) Political and economic factors in the evolution of North Korea's maritime connections. *Journal of International Logistics and Trade*, 7(1): 1–23.

Forster-Carter, A. (2001) The shipping forecast: Choppy waters. *Asia Times*, February 15.

Gelézeau, V. (2007) An island as interface: critical position of paengnyŏn-do in the Korean border region. In: *Association for Korean Studies in Europe, Conference Proceedings*, Dourdan, April 16–21.

Hong, S.G., Lee, S.W., Park, S.J. (2014) International cooperation and the logistics market in Northeast Asia: Problems and prospects for North Korea. *North Korean Review*, 10: 39–55.

Jo, J.C., Ducruet, C. (2006) Maritime trade and port evolution in a socialist developing country: Nampo, gateway of North Korea. *The Korea Spatial Planning Review*, 51: 3–24.

Jo, J.C., Ducruet, C. (2007) Rajin-Seonbong, new gateway of Northeast Asia. *Annals of Regional Science*, 41(4): 927–950.

Joongang Daily. (2006) *North Eyes Inter-Korean Port in the East*, June 14.

Kim, C.W. (2014) *Open North Korea: Economic Benefits to China From the Distance Effect in Trade*. Issue Brief, ASAN Institute for Policy Studies.

Kim, I.S. (2001) The Rajin-Sonbong Economic and Trade Zone (RSETZ): The sources of difficulties and lessons for the future. In: Yoon, C.H., Lau, L.J. (Eds.), *North Korea in Transition*. Cheltenham and Northampton: Edward Elgar, pp. 301–333.

Kim, S. (2004) *Inter-Korean Relations: Problems and Prospects*. Basingstoke: Palgrave Macmillan.

Korea Times. (2001) *Inter-Korean Processing Trade Set to Resume*, February 20.

Lee, C.J. (2005) *Trade and Investment in North Korea*. Seoul: Korea Institute for International Economic Policy.

Lee, J.U. (2009) Analysis of Chinese companies' border trade with North Korea. *World Economy*, 9(26): Korea Institute for International Economic Policy.

Nanto, D.K., Chanlett-Avery, E. (2005) *The North Korean Economy: Background and Policy Analysis*. Report for Congress, Congressional Research Service, February 9.

Noland, M. (2000) *Avoiding the Apocalypse: The Future of the Two Koreas*. Washington: Institute for International Economics.

Oh, J.H. (2001) Strategies for developing transport infrastructure in North Korea. In: Yoon, C.H., Lau, L.J. (Eds.), *North Korea in Transition*. Cheltenham and Northampton: Edward Elgar, pp. 215–236.

Olsen, J., Vannoni, M., Koelm, J. (2003) *Maritime Cooperation for the Koreas*. Sandia Working Paper n° 1843p, Cooperative Monitoring Center, Albuquerque.

Pons, P. (2004) Fragile dégel en Corée du Nord. *Le Monde*, December 16.

Roussin, S. (2015) *A Brief Journey in DPRK. A Geo-Economic Approach*. Seminar Presentation, June 23.

Rozman, G. (2004) *Northeast Asia's Stunted Regionalism: Bilateral Distrust in the Shadow of Globalization*. Cambridge: Cambridge University Press.

Smith, H. (2009) *North Korean Shipping: A Potential for WMD Proliferation?* East-West Center, Asia Pacific Issues No. 87.

Tsuji, H. (2005) *The Transport Infrastructure of the DPRK*. Niigata: Economic Research Institute for Northeast Asia.

UNCTAD. (2000) *World Seaborne Trade Continues Growth in 1999*. Available at: www.unctad.org

Vigarié, A. (1995) *La Mer et la Géostratégie des Nations*. Paris: Economica.

Vitelli, A. (2015) North Korea gains in China coal exports as Vietnam bows out. *Bloomberg*, July 20.

Wang, C., Ducruet, C. (2014) Transport corridors and regional balance in China: The case of coal trade and logistics. *Journal of Transport Geography*, 40: 3–16.

Yoon, D.R., Babson, B.O. (2002) Understanding North Korea's economic crisis. *Asian Economic Papers*, 1: 69–89.

22 Vessel navigation constraints in Canadian Arctic waters

Laurent Etienne, Mélanie Fournier, Leah Beveridge, Mark Stoddard and Ronald Pelot

Models and satellite-based observations show that sea ice is melting at an unprecedented rate (NASA, 2016). According to several models, though, the Northwest Passage will remain ice-covered and difficult to navigate for the foreseeable future (CASA, 2007; AMSA, 2009; SWIPA, 2011; Williams et al., 2011; ARCUS, 2008 to 2013). Since 2008, the Sea Ice Outlook (SIO) has gathered work from the research community on several domains and synthesizes their estimates into reports. They use a wide range of methods: heuristic forecasts, statistical and/or dynamical models, ice-ocean coupled models, ice-ocean-atmospheric models etc. (SIPN, 2014). Nevertheless, debates have arisen from the changing environment, particularly over the past 15 years, about the opening of the NWP and the future of maritime activities in the Canadian Arctic (AMSA, 2009). Important aspects of these discussions revolve around the interest of shipping companies entering or expanding operations in the region, and their interpretation of changing ice conditions: for example, "ice-free" waters are not synonymous with the absence of navigational risk (Marr, 2001; Kean, 2014). Freely floating ice, such as growlers and icebergs, are still hazardous for navigation, and vessels typically plan routes to avoid such conditions using sea ice charts provided by ice and meteorological services, such as the Canadian Ice Service (CIS) in Canada,[1] the Meteorological Institute in Finland or the National Snow and Ice Data Center (NSIDC) in the United States.[2] In this sense, ice coverage and conditions can dictate vessel behavior (see also Chapter 9 on Arctic shipping).

Ice conditions have a considerable temporal impact on maritime traffic in the Arctic. The navigation conditions including ice coverage, ice classification, motion and concentration, and meteorology are extensively monitored by satellite and forecasted since the 1970s (Johannessen et al., 1996; Pichel and Clemente-Colón, 2000; Comiso, 2010). Sea ice charts available since that date are derived from satellite-based monitoring (mostly from Synthetic Aperture Radar or SAR). NASA, Space Agencies (JAXA EORC, 2016), NGOs such as the WWF, universities and media publish and republish on a regular basis interactive maps and/or interactive graphs (Schultz, 2012) showing the decrease of the ice coverage, setting up the frequent records of ice minimum. But these are a global overview. What is crucial for navigation, from the perspective of risk assessment, is to understand

and to visualize how these changing ice conditions translate into changing risk conditions for ship operators.

Dynamic visualizations of the changes in sea ice conditions are a common sight today, but the global nature of these interactive maps do not necessarily reflect the operational conditions witnessed by ships navigating in specific areas. Previous work has established methods and products for visualizing the geospatial distribution of navigational risks from sea ice in the Canadian Arctic (Stoddard et al., 2016; Etienne, 2015), but no single visualization has adequately displayed the complexities and uncertainties of operating there. As such, the goal here is to develop the means for identifying areas with greater variability in ice conditions from year to year, and thus greater uncertainty in the level of operational risk. We began with matrices showing the distribution of changes in risk levels from ice over time, as a means for identifying those zones with the greatest interannual variability. We chose this approach because it provides a more focused analysis on the spatial distribution of risk levels and uncertainty at the level of risk that can be anticipated.

Navigating in ice

Navigating ice requires the consideration of ice regime conditions and the ice classification of the ship wishing to navigate therein. The ice classification of a ship is the categorization of the vessel according to its ability to navigate in ice conditions based on the strength of its hull. In the 1970s, the Canadian government developed a framework for assessing the risks to various classes of ships from ice regime conditions: the Zone/Date System (Z/DS). Pursuant to the Arctic Waters Pollution Prevention Act (AWPPA), the Shipping Safety Control Zones Order divides Canada's arctic waters into 16 zones. Within each of these, the Z/DS, implemented by the Arctic Shipping Pollution Prevention Regulations provides opening and closing dates for different classes of ships based on the expected ice conditions; these dates were determined based on an analysis of historical ice data.

Over time, it was found that the rigid open and closing dates of the Z/DS did not always align with the in situ ice conditions. To give more flexibility, the Arctic Ice Regime Shipping System (AIRSS) was introduced, which provides a means for assessing the risk from ice to a ship based on a calculation accounting for the class of ship and the in situ ice regime conditions. A third system, though not yet prescribed in Canadian law, was developed by the International Association of Classification Societies (IACS) – the Polar Operational Limits Assessment Risk Indexing System (POLARIS) – to advance the AIRSS system. In particular, it accounts for the speed of the vessel, icebreaker assistance and the effect of ice decay on the risk posed by different ice regimes, which were included as a result of feedback provided by operators who found that the results of AIRSS did not always reflect actual navigational conditions.

Methods

Sea ice

In selecting the years on which to focus our analyses, we turned to the Arctic Research Consortium of the United States (ARCUS), which has a program dedicated solely to analyzing Arctic sea ice data, including changes to extent in the short-term (one year) and the long-term (up to 2100). We also looked to Sea Ice Outlook, which is a forum for researchers that summarizes annual simulations, analyses and implications of the changes identified by ARCUS, with a particular eye to dramatic changes. Based on the reports generated from these two sources, we chose to focus on the period 2007–2014 because they have shown the eighth-lowest minimums in sea ice extent since the drastic decrease reported from 2006 to 2007 (ARCUS, 2014). Globally, the trend shows a growth in the time period that is ice-free, or with low concentrations of ice. This trend can also be seen within the Canadian Arctic specifically; there are years within the time period that have proven more difficult for navigation (ARCUS, 2007–2014). For example, in some years, the freeze-up has occurred earlier. To explore this contradiction between the extent of sea ice and reported conditions for navigation, we have chosen to highlight the years 2010 and 2012 here. The third lowest minimum after 2007 and 2008 was documented for 2010, and yet our results indicate it was a difficult season for navigation, while 2012 had the lowest minimum sea ice extent since 2007.

ARCUS and the Sea Ice Outlook offer data and information on the scale of the entire Arctic, but we wanted to look specifically at the Canadian Arctic, so we looked at the trends reported by the NSIDC only for Canada. In particular, we chose to incorporate the Multisensor Analyzed Sea Ice Extent (MASIE), which was provided on a 4 km x 4 km grid. For the purposes of this study, we combined the data for the Beaufort, Baffin and Gulf of St. Lawrence, Canadian archipelago, Hudson Bay and Central Arctic areas for the years 2007–2014 (Figure 22.1).

Although the ARCUS, Sea Ice Outlook and MASIE datasets aided in selecting the time period we would investigate, we used ice charts from the CIS to conduct our analyses. These charts are collected and stored by the NSIDC in a historical data repository in SIGRID-3 format, and include information such as the concentration, stage of development and type of ice across the Canadian Arctic (WMO-IOC, 2004; Canadian Ice Service, 2009).

Risk analysis

Although there are three systems through which the navigational safety of a ship through ice can be assessed (Z/DS, AIRSS, POLARIS), we also chose to focus our analyses on POLARIS because it is the most advanced of the three; it allows for the consideration of speed, icebreaker escort and the effect of ice decay on the risk posed by ice, whereas the others do not. This is done through a calculation of the

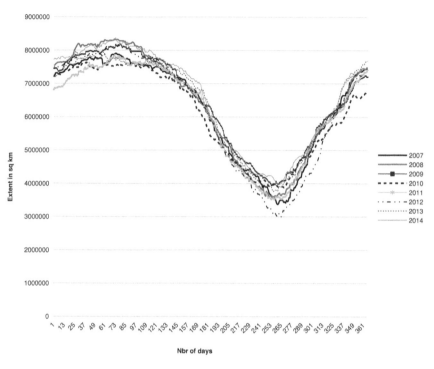

Figure 22.1 Trends in sea-ice extent for the Beaufort, Baffin and Gulf of St Lawrence, Canadian archipelago, Hudson Bay and Central Arctic areas combined

ice concentration (derived from the sea ice charts) and the risk value (found in Table 22.1):

$$RIO = \sum_{i=1}^{n} (IC_i \times RV_i)$$

where RIO = risk index outcome
IC   = ice concentration
RV   = risk value

Through the POLARIS calculation, a risk index outcome (RIO) is generated, and indicates the safe operational limits (SOL)[3] of the vessel through the given area: operations are permitted; proceed at low speed; proceed with an icebreaker escort; proceed at low speed with an icebreaker escort or operations are not permitted. The color code used in the following figures of this chapter is presented in Table 22.1 ranging from light gray (operation permitted) to black (operation not permitted).

For the purpose of this chapter, we decided to highlight zone 13 (see Figure 22.2) because it is the eastern "entrance" to all routes. Furthermore, we chose to focus on

Table 22.1 Risk value of different ship ice class depending on ice thickness and WMO ice regime[4]

Category	Ice Class	Ice Free	New Ice	Grey Ice	Grey White Ice	Thin First Year Ice, 1st	Thin First Year ice, 2nd	Medium First Year Ice	Medium First Year Ice 2nd	Thick First Year Ice	Second Year Ice	Light Multi Year Ice	Heavy Multi Year Ice
A	PC1	3	3	3	3	2	2	2	2	2	2	1	1
	PC2	3	3	3	3	2	2	2	2	2	1	1	0
	PC3	3	3	3	3	2	2	2	2	2	1	0	−1
	PC4	3	3	3	3	2	2	2	2	1	0	−1	−2
	PC5	3	3	3	3	2	2	2	2	1	−1	−2	−2
B	PC6	3	2	2	2	2	1	2	1	0	−2	−3	−3
	PC7	3	2	2	2	2	1	1	0	−1	−3	−3	−3
C	IA Super	3	2	2	2	2	1	1	0	−1	−3	−4	−4
	IA	3	2	2	2	1	0	0	−1	−2	−4	−4	−4
	IB	3	2	2	1	0	−1	−1	−1	−2	−4	−5	−5
	IC	3	2	1	0	−1	−2	−1	−2	−3	−4	−5	−6
	Not IS	3	1	0	−1	−2	−2	−2	−2	−3	−5	−6	−6

Legend: Operation permitted | Low speed | Ice breaker escort | Ice breaker escort at low speed | Operation not permitted

N.B. A positive RV indicates that a ship can operate safely in the given ice regime, whereas a negative RV means it cannot

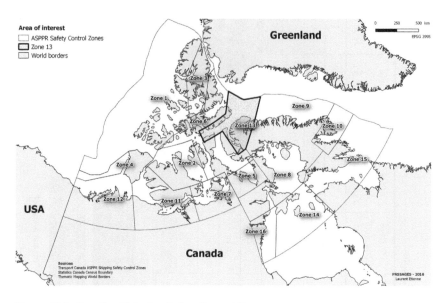

Figure 22.2 Canadian Shipping Safety Control Zones

two contrasting classes of ship: IA and nonice strengthened. The former was chosen because, according to data from Automatic Identification Systems (AIS) it is the most common class of ship found in zone 13; and the latter was chosen because they are not structurally capable of navigating through ice and as such are seen as a great concern.

Matrices

POLARIS, Canadian Ice charts, and ice class

The weekly SIGRID-3 Canadian Ice Services Sea Ice Charts (WMO-IOC, 2004; Canadian Ice Service, 2009) was downloaded on the National Snow and Ice Data Center website (2007 to 2014). The corresponding POLARIS RIO was computed for every ship ice class (using Table 22.1 risk values). Ice polygons having the same safe operational limit were merged together. Finally, the surface ratio of each safe operational limit per Canadian Shipping Safety Control Zone was computed. The zone surface percentage of each SOL can be visualized as a weekly bar graph depicting the operation limitations over time in the zone. An example of the SOL bar graph matrix is presented in Figure 22.3 for non ice strengthened vessels navigating in zone 13. The gray shade legend of this bar graph corresponds to the Table 22.1 SOL categories. As indicated on the National Snow and Ice Data Center website, the temporal coverage and resolution of the SIGRID-3 Canadian Ice Services Sea Ice Charts is limited to a weekly (summer) and bi-weekly (winter)

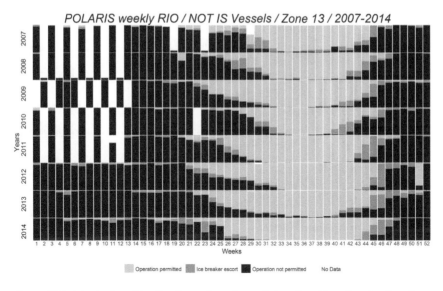

Figure 22.3 Matrix for a Non Ice Strengthened vessel, based on Canadian Sea Ice charts from 2007–2014

production for northern Canadian waters and a weekly winter-only production for southern Canadian waters. This explains the bi-weekly white bars (no data) included in the visualization matrix from 2007 to 2011. Moreover, the Canadian Ice Services take input from various sources such as satellites, aerial reconnaissance and ship reports based on data availability. These different data sources are analyzed and fused to create the regional ice charts based on MANICE procedures (Environment Canada, 2005). Low availability or manual processing of the data may also introduce errors in the evaluation of the ice thickness or concentration. Ice polygons having unknown thickness or concentration were classified as no data (white bars) in our POLARIS calculations.

Comparison IA and Non-IS vessel for the Zone 13, between 2007 and 2014

Figures 22.3 and 22.4 show the weekly evolution matrix of the five different POLARIS SOL surface ratios from 2007 to 2014 for different vessel ice classes. Each row shows the yearly evolution of the POLARIS surface ratio for one zone and one ship ice class. In our case study we chose to compare the evolution for an IA type and a Non-IS in Zone 13. The superposition of years points to the difficult and less difficult years, meaning the extension in time of the navigation season or an earlier freeze-up, for example.

We focused on two years: 2010 and 2012. 2010 was a difficult year. Based on the Sea Extent Outlook and the NSIDC reports, 2009 and 2014 should have been

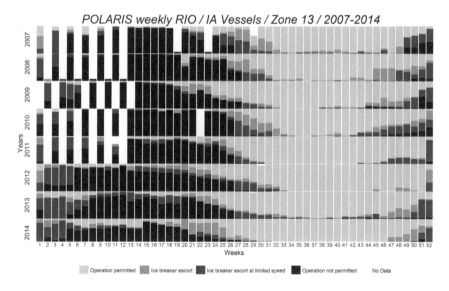

Figure 22.4 Matrix for a IA vessel, based on Canadian Sea Ice charts from 2007–2014

more difficult for navigation as 2009 had the highest minimum extent of the eight years; and the 2014 extent is even higher. In 2009 and 2014, the computation of POLARIS, for a Non-IS vessel (Figure 22.3), shows a high percentage of the zone 13 open for operations around weeks 24 and 25; whereas 2010 shows a difficult start to the opening season around Weeks 29 to 31. For an IA type vessel (Figure 22.4), 2010 would have been also a difficult year, the opening of the zone starting very slowly, and requiring an icebreaker escort for Weeks 26 to 29, a small percentage of the zone being open to operations. For the same period (Weeks 26 to 29) in 2009 and 2014, the navigation under POLARIS would have been already possible. A large percentage of the zone under POLARIS was already open to operations even though 2009 and 2014 ice extent was higher than 2010. However, it should be noted that the NWP was open for navigation, even the northern route, in 2010.

The year 2012 was an extremely low year. As we saw in the results of NSIDC, 2012 was the lowest of the eight years we chose (Figure 22.2). The matrices show a soft slope in the opening of the season. The navigation for a Not IS vessel, based on the POLARIS computation, would have been possible with an icebreaker escort around Weeks 22–23. A large percentage of zone 13 was open to operations during Week 24 in 2012, which does not happen before Weeks 31 and 32 in 2010. In 2012, operations could have been extended, as Week 45 still presented a large percentage of the area open with or without an icebreaker escort. However, the freeze-up came abruptly in Week 46 and navigation would have required an escort. For an IA-type vessel, zone 13 in 2012 was completely open, with a low requirement of an escort for Weeks 48 and 49. The year 2012 clearly shows an extension of the permitted operations season.

However, one limitation remains in our dataset, and this is due to the lack of satellite data between 2007 and 2011 consistently between Weeks 1 and 12 or 1 and 13 for the year 2009. Satellite data are also available only sporadically in 2007, 2010 and 2012. They are represented by the white bars in Figures 22.3 and 22.4 below. This lack of data has an impact on the next visualization (box plots) and will display variations or perturbations especially for Week 6, for which we have, consistently, four years without data. It should be noted that satellite measurements have confirmed that the NWP was open for navigation during five consecutive years, from 2007 until 2011.

Boxplots

The bar graph matrix depicts the natural spatiotemporal variation in sea ice conditions. The global trend in sea ice extent, illustrated in Figure 22.1, is also visualized in the POLARIS matrix for both IA and Not IS vessel classes (Figures 22.3 and 22.4). In the matrix, light-gray bars (operation permitted) cover most of the zone surface in summer and gradually shrink down to zero during winter. However, as discussed in the previous section, the freezing and melting of sea ice can be shifted, shrunk or spread out in time each year, depending on the meteorological conditions. This inter-annual variability poses a significant challenge to effective route planning and evaluation in Arctic waters. The variability can be analyzed using boxplot statistical visualization (Tukey, 1977), which is the representation of the main five order statistics (minimum, first quartile, median, third quartile, maximum) of a numerical dataset. The boxplot is an effective way to understand the statistical distribution of the dataset as the width of the inner box indicates the spreading (variation) of the numerical values around the median. The weekly values of the POLARIS RIO surface ratio matrix of zone 13 (Figure 22.3 and 22.4) were aggregated into 52 boxplots for Not IS vessels (Figure 22.5) and IA vessels (Figure 22.6). Cubic smoothing spline lines were added on top of the boxplots to depict the median (black line), quartiles (black dashed line) and extremum (gray dotted line) zone 13 surface percentage.

This boxplot visualization is efficient in summarizing the POLARIS safe operational limits for each vessel ice class in every zone of the Canadian Arctic. The median spline shows the natural spatiotemporal variation curve in sea ice conditions between winter and summer. The width of the boxplots indicates the variability observed in a zone for a given type of vessel over seven years. As expected, the boxes are bigger during the melting and freezing period, indicating a higher uncertainty. The biggest uncertainty corresponds to the center of the freezing/melting curve, gradually shrinking when the observed ice regime is stable. For Non-IS vessels, during winter the boxes are very thin showing that 100% of zone 13 does not permit operations. A comparison of Figures 22.5 and 22.6 shows a longer operating period for IA vessels in summer and the possibility of extending this

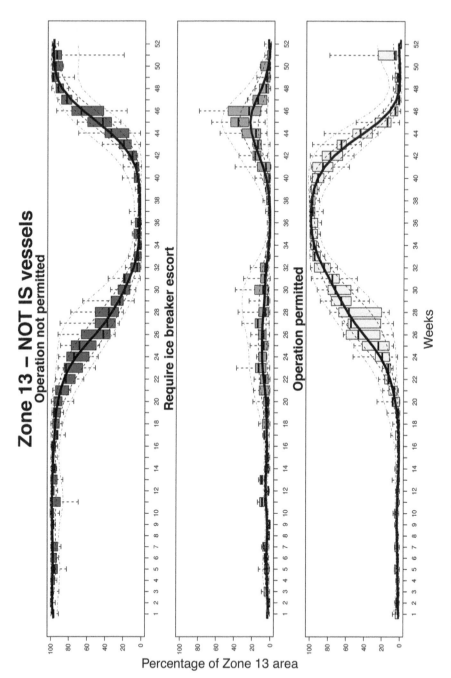

Figure 22.5 Zone 13 Not IS vessels

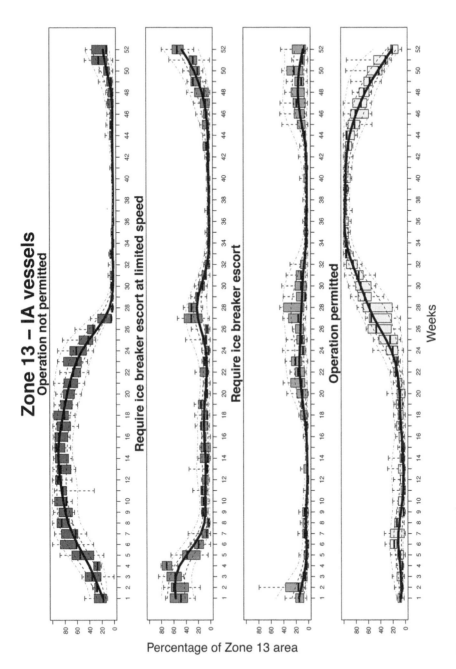

Figure 22.6 Zone 13 IA vessels

operating period using an icebreaker escort. IA vessels also have a higher degree of uncertainty about the "operation not permitted" areas during winter compared to Not IS vessels. This greater uncertainty can be explained by the icebreaker operations that might be allowed but with considerable uncertainty during the winter season.

The boxplot visualization gives an interesting feedback about the weekly evolution of the POLARIS risk index within a full zone of the Canadian Arctic. However, the ASPPR zones are wide and the boxplot cannot picture the exact location of the risky area within the zones. The next section extends the boxplot methodology to create spatial POLARIS risk maps.

Risk maps

In order to assess more precisely the location of the sea ice risk, the ASPPR zones were divided into a 1km² grid which correspond to approximatively 3 million grid cells (excluding landmass). The POLARIS risk index were calculated for each available CIS weekly sea ice charts (2006 to 2014). For each 1km² grid cell, the POLARIS values were aggregated by week number and ship ice class to produce the boxplot presented in previous section. The grid cells boxplot quartiles (25%, 50%, 75%) were used to create maps depicting the location of the risky area using POLARIS safe operational limits. The lower quartile map (25%) presents the worst case scenario (strongest ice conditions) observed over the time period (2006 to 2014) in each grid cell for a chosen week. Respectively, the median map (50%) presents the most likely scenario and the upper quartile map (75%) the best case scenario (weakest ice conditions). The Figure 22.7 map matrix compares the different POLARIS risk map scenario of two vessels ice class (IA vs Not Ice Strengthened). Week 28 was selected on purpose to depict a time period having high ice condition variation over years. Week 28 is located in the middle of the unfreeze slope of the boxplot for zone 13 (Figures 22.5 and 22.6). This week let us visualize important spatial variation between the best case and worst case POLARIS map scenario. The comparison of Figure 22.7a and 22.7c shows a significant increase of the POLARIS safe operation surface (light gray) for not ice-strengthened vessels. Figures 22.7d and 22.7f also depict a decrease of the surface where icebreaker escort is required (medium gray). Some zones, such as zone 1, have no POLARIS SOL surface variation between best case and worst-case scenario. Figures 22.7a, 22.7b and 22.7c indicate that not ice strengthened vessels cannot operate anywhere in that zone and highlights a stable POLARIS condition over years (2006–2014) for the selected week. Finally, this POLARIS map visualization is useful to compare ship ice class operational limits at a specific week. A comparison of Figures 22.7b and 22.7e indicates that a non-ice-strengthened vessel should not be able to operate in zone 9 during week 28, while an IA vessel should be able to operate under an ice breaker escort.

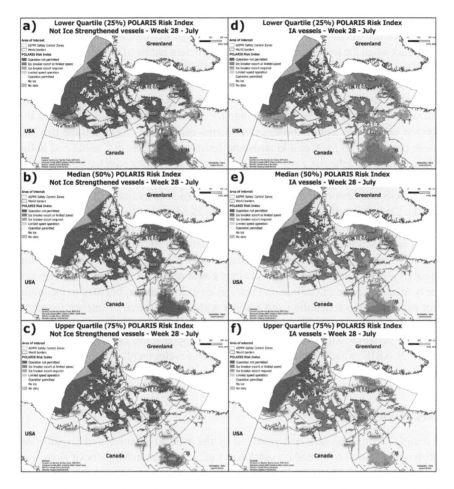

Figure 22.7 Not Ice Strengthened vs IA vessels POLARIS comparison map matrix for week 28

Conclusion

The previous sections illustrated how POLARIS and CIS SIGRID-3 ice information can be used to assess ship operational limitations over a large area (AIRSS Zone 13) over time (2007 until 2014) and depending on the ship classification.

We chose two polar ship classifications (IA and Not IS) in order to show how this can significantly influence the operational limitations of a ship throughout a given geographical area. These results could be used by decision makers to examine the selection of a particular polar classification for a planned route, or the feasibility of operations in a particular region of the Canadian Arctic during a specific time of the year (cruise ships, for example). In Figures 22.3 and 22.4, we compared the situation in terms of operations for difficult years, such as 2010, and for years when the lowest minimum of sea ice extent has been reported, as in 2012.

POLARIS can be used to make a full spatial analysis represented by thematic maps, to visualize operational limitations over a defined area of interest or over a scheduled route (Stoddard et al., 2016). It could have been interesting to use visualization on the Crystal Serenity voyage for example. The Crystal Serenity is the largest cruise ship sailing through the Northwest Passage. Although the trip had been planned with the Coast Guards and federal authorities in Canada and in the United States and the risks assessed, sailing in the NWP for a Non Ice Strengthened ship is still considered as "navigating in uncharted territory" (Nunez, 2016). POLARIS and historical data could have been used to evaluate the route chosen by the Crystal Serenity in terms of risks (Stoddard et al., 2016).

Our chapter shows that POLARIS provides an excellent risk assessment framework for assessing and visualizing ship operational limits over large areas. The several visualizations proposed (matrices, box plots and maps) as well as the underlying data presented in this chapter could be used by decision makers not only to assess polar classification issues as described above, but also to examine, for example, ship scheduling and routing within a large area of interest based on historical data, allowing the user to understand how ice may influence a particular vessel's behavior. The work presented in this chapter relies on the first version of the POLARIS, which was a framework under development. An updated version has been published by the IMO on the 26th of June 2016.

Acknowledgements

Funding for this research was provided by the Natural Sciences and Engineering Research Council of Canada, exactEarth Ltd., the German Ministry of Economy and Technology and Airbus Defense & Space.

Notes

1 www.ec.gc.ca/glaces-ice/default.asp?lang=En
2 http://nsidc.org/
3 www.arctis-search.com/tiki-index.php?page=Technical+Requirements+for+Navigation +on+NWP#386
4 It corresponds to the five different levels ranging from operation permitted to not permitted.

References

Arctic Council. (2009) *Arctic Marine Shipping Assessment (AMSA) Report*. Retrieved from https://pame.is/images/03_Projects/AMSA/AMSA_2009_report/AMSA_2009_ Report_2nd_print.pdf

Arctic Council. (2011) *Arctic Climate Issues 2011: Changes in Arctic Snow, Water, Ice and Permafrost*. SWIPA 2011 Overview Report.

Canadian Ice Service. (2009) *Canadian Ice Service Arctic Regional Sea Ice Charts in SIG-RID-3 Format, Version 1*. Boulder, CO: NSIDC: National Snow and Ice Data Center.

Comiso, J. (2010) *Polar Oceans From Space*. Atmospheric and Oceanographic Sciences Library 41, Springer.

Environment Canada. (2005) *Manual of Standard Procedures for Observing and Reporting Ice Conditions (MANICE)*. Meteorological Service of Canada. Available at: www.ec.gc.ca/glaces-ice/default.asp?lang=En&n=08D7D137–1

Etienne, L. (2015) *Ice Statistical Computation*. PASSAGES Project. Available at: http://passages.ie.dal.ca/Risks_analysis.html

IMO, International Code for Ships Operating in Polar Waters (POLAR CODE). Available at: www.imo.org/en/MediaCentre/HotTopics/polar/Documents/POLAR%20CODE%20TEXT%20AS%20ADOPTED.pdf

JAXA EORC. (2016) *Sea Ice Extent Trends*. Available at: http://kuroshio.eorc.jaxa.jp/JASMES/climate/index.html

Johannessen, O.M., Sandven, S., Melenteyev, V.V. (1996) Towards operational sea ice monitoring by satellite SAR data in the Northern Sea route. In: Paper presented at the *Oceanology International Conference*, Brighton.

Kean, T. (2014) *Personal Communication*.

The Mariport Group Ltd. (2007) *Canadian Arctic Shipping Assessment (CASA)*. Main Report. Prepared for Transport Canada, June 2007.

Marr, J. (2001) Impact of climate change in the Arctic on ship operations and support systems: A mariners perspective. In: Paper presented at the *Canadian Maritime Law Association*, 50th AGM, Montreal, June 15–16.

NASA Earth Observation. (2016) Available at: http://earthobservatory.nasa.gov/IOTD/view.php?id=89223

National Ice Center (NIC) and NSIDC. (2010) *Multisensor Analyzed Sea Ice Extent – Northern Hemisphere, 4km Grid*. Developed by F. Fetterer, M. Savoie, S. Helfrich, and P. Clemente-Colón. Boulder, CO, USA: National Snow and Ice Data Center. doi:10.7265/N5GT5K3K

Nunez, C. (2016) A luxury cruise liner is about to sail the Arctic's Northwest Passage. *National Geographic*. Available at: http://news.nationalgeographic.com/2016/08/crystal-serenity-luxury-cruise-arctic-northwest-passage/

Pichel, W.G., Clemente-Colón, P. (2000) NOAA Coast Watch SAR applications and demonstration: Status and plans. *APL Technical Digest*, 21(1): 49–57.

Schultz, C. (2012) What you need to know about Arctic sea ice melt in one 10 seconds animated gif. *Smithsonian.com*, August 6. Available at: www.smithsonianmag.com/smart-news/everything-you-need-to-know-about-arctic-sea-ice-melt-in-one-10-second-animated-gif-13895202/

Sea Ice Prediction Network. (2014) *Sea Ice Outlook*. Report. Available at: www.arcus.org/sipn/sea-ice-outlook/2014/post-season-highlights

ARCUS (2008) Search Sea Ice Outlook. Available at: www.arcus.org/search-program/seaiceoutlook/2008/summary

ARCUS (2009) Search Sea Ice Outlook. Available at: www.arcus.org/search-program/seaiceoutlook/2009/summary

ARCUS (2010) Search Sea Ice Outlook. Available at: www.arcus.org/search-program/seaiceoutlook/2010/summary

ARCUS (2011) Search Sea Ice Outlook. Available at: www.arcus.org/search-program/seaiceoutlook/2011/summary

ARCUS (2012) Search Sea Ice Outlook. Available at: www.arcus.org/search-program/seaiceoutlook/2012/summary

ARCUS (2013) Search Sea Ice Outlook. Available at: www.arcus.org/search-program/seaiceoutlook/2013/summary

Stoddard, M., Etienne, L., Fournier, M., Pelot, R., Beveridge, L. (2016) Making sense of Arctic maritime traffic using the Polar Operational Limits Assessment Risk Indexing System (POLARIS). In: *International Society for Digital Earth, 9th Symposium Proceedings*, Halifax, Nova Scotia, Canada, October 2015. Available at: http://passages. ie.dal.ca/Generic_documents/EES_34_1_012034.pdf

Tukey, J.W. (1977) *Exploratory Data Analysis*. Boston MA, USA: Addison-Wesley.

Williams, A., Aisling O'Sullivan, D., Wilkinson, A. (2011) *The Future of Arctic Enterprise: Long-term Outlook and Implications*. Smith School of Enterprise and the Environment, University of Oxford.

WMO-IOC. (2004) *SIGRID-3: A Vector Archive Format for Sea Ice Charts: Developed by the International Ice Charting Working Group's Ad Hoc Format Team for the WMO Global Digital Sea Ice Data Bank Project*. Retrieved from http://www.jcomm.info/index.php?option=com_oe&task=viewDocumentRecord&docID=4439

WWF. (2014) *Mapping the Changing Arctic Landscape*. Available at: wwfarcticmaps.org/

23 Northwest Africa from colonial to global shipping

Daniel Castillo and César Ducruet

Despite the importance of ports and seaborne trade for the African economies, literature on the evolution of African port systems is not in the front line of research (Debrie, 2012; Dickson, 1965; Hoyle, 1967; Mohamed-Chérif and Ducruet, 2016). Considering port geography as a whole, the proportion of articles written about Africa had dramatically decreased from about 20% in the 1950s to less than 5% in the 2000s, but had witnessed an increasing trend in the early 2010s (Ng and Ducruet, 2014). However, a number of scholars promoted historical approaches to port studies from an individual case perspective (Castillo Hidalgo, 2014; Olukoju, 2004; Peterec, 1967). A key issue is to explore the degree of stability of port hierarchies and maritime networks over time, namely from the colonial age up to the first stage of global container shipping. It could be argued that colonial dynamics and path-creation processes reinforced permanent effects on seaborne flows for the African ports, as underlined in early spatial models of port system evolution based on the cases of Ghana and Nigeria (Taaffe et al., 1963), although such models focused more on coastal and inland dynamics than on seaborne flows.

Thus, the main port functions and regional economic specialization promoted the emergence and consolidation of self-reinforcement effects (Martin and Sunley, 2010) on African ports, which were tied to inland transport infrastructures created to support economic extraction processes. Hence, the dynamics of seaborne trade remained almost unchanged from the late nineteenth century up to the last third of the twentieth century (UNCTAD, various issues).

This chapter deals with an analysis of the evolution of ports and port systems in Northwest Africa from 1880 to 1972. The chronological period studied runs from the first international shipping revolution (steamship navigation) to the first global wave of containerization (Guerrero and Rodrigue, 2014). We shall demonstrate how regional seaborne flows over time and how port hierarchies changed or remained unchanged in a historical perspective. It is important to note the role played by the African ports in the overall process of port reform that began in the second half of the nineteenth century (Kaukianen, 2012). The nature and evolution of regional economic structures – mainly south of the Sahara – delayed the modernization of ports, and it was a decisive obstacle to economic development in terms of decreasing transaction and transport costs. In this chapter, we will expose the main arguments that explain how this technical gap was motivated by the weakness of local capitals and the colonial policies developed by the imperial nations.

In this study, we have used the United Nations' geographical delimitation of territories to define the explored area of northwest Africa (for other analyses of transnational port systems, see Chapters 5, 8, 9, 11, 19, 23, and 24 on Taiwan Strait, Black Sea, Arctic, Mediterranean, USSR, and Indian subcontinent areas). Thus, we have collected data from all countries (former colonies) and territories (i.e. Spanish possessions) running from Tunisia to Angola. The first issue to bear in mind is the existence of historical port hierarchies where a central seaport concentrated most of the cargo handled and on the other hand, the number of vessels calling the country. As will be demonstrated later, these central ports were complemented by secondary ports. Most of them functioned similarly to Hoyle's description (1967: 65) of the East African ports:

> The smaller ports, where the tonnages of oil products imported are much smaller and where exports outweigh imports by a wide margin. This pattern reflects the fact that the primary function of both these ports is the export of a single primary product from the immediate hinterland, an area which does not constitute in either case a very important market for imported goods.

Under this scheme, from the 1970s cargo handled at regional ports (both central and secondary) featured a massive predominance in cash-crop exports (peanuts, palm-oil, vegetables, wheat, wax, rubber, coffee, cocoa, timber), mining commodities (phosphates, iron ores, copper), and oil products (crude oil and derivates). By contrast, imports were usually less important in volume but not in value: industrial manufactures, machinery, clothes, building materials, staples, etc. In the case of imported goods, a number of great seaports absorbed most of them and we provide compelling evidence on the lack of port development south of the Sahara during the first half of the twentieth century that contributed to economic stagnation in these regions. Otherwise, great seaports concentrated seaborne trade and promoted urban growth through the consolidation of a primate city, which hampered regional integration (Seck, 1970; see also the mercantile model of Vance, 1970).

In this chapter, we have collected data from *Lloyd's List* to rebuild shipping patterns across Northwest Africa between 1900 and 1970. This chronology is representative for the whole covered period and it permits a comparison between different primary sources. In particular, the Shipping Index provides a snapshot of global and regional maritime activity based on the last inter-port movement of every registered vessel. We then compiled port throughput data from a number of archival sources in France, United Kingdom, Senegal, Spain, Portugal, and other African countries between 1913 and 1972. Further efforts are being made to palliate the lack of information for all the region's ports and countries.[1] Using multiple shipping data sources also represents a challenge in terms of potential gaps and overlaps which may be caused by different measurement units and methods.

The waves of port modernization in Northwest Africa

The first consideration of note is the clear difference between the African Mediterranean ports and the Atlantic ports south of the Sahara. If we compare both regions, in terms of volume of cargoes, maritime connectivity and historical development, the Maghreb ports were well integrated into the Mediterranean maritime network during the late nineteenth century. Nevertheless, most colonial seaports in the West African colonies were poorly equipped in terms of modern infrastructures: berth posts, jetties, warehouses, bunkering facilities, intermodal connections, etc. If we observe the charts (see Tables 23.1 and 23.2) denoting port activity before 1950, we could argue that these point to an evident lack of port development. Comparing these charts with port throughput figures confirms the deficiency of port development in these regions. Yet, a number of large seaports constitute interesting exceptions, at least for the first half of the century, such as Dakar, Lagos, Accra, and Matadi. These ports retained important commercial functions and they operated as regional gateways for their hinterlands. They basically contributed to the cash-crop revolution in the late nineteenth century (Austin, 2015), which triggered the expansion of external trade and the construction of inland transport infrastructures, mainly colonial railways (Chaves et al., 2015). Hence, key to the understanding of the evolution of regional seaborne flows is the evolution of regional exports that marked the configuration of trade. The colonial economic extroverted system promoted this trend and how transport infrastructures were to evolve in a linear way (Mohamed-Chérif and Ducruet, 2016).

Table 23.1 summarizes the main driving factors that affected port evolution in general terms. We have included a number of elements that helped to explain how endogenous and exogenous events transformed the port systems in our study area. The first stage (1880–1913) is marked by the consolidation of colonial rule and the expansion of international steam navigation. During this period, port infrastructures were scarcely developed in most countries. On the eve of the Great War, ports and railways began to expand (i.e. Dakar, Conakry, Accra) and the main direct consequence was the rise of external trade and the consolidation of colonial economic and political institutions.

The second period is characterized by interwar instability. Improvements in shipping (transition from coal to fuel) required further changes in port infrastructures, which were hampered by international crises. The most important issue was the emergence of Casablanca as the world's main phosphate export port in the early 1920s. As we showed below, Casablanca represented an interesting example of mega-concentration in terms of volume and value of seaborne trade in Africa. On the other hand, before World War II, most regional ports expanded (i.e. Lomé, Douala, Cotonou, Matadi) as a consequence of the growth of export sectors.

From 1946 to 1960, an important phase of port expansion (throughput, connectivity) takes place throughout the African continent. Several major events such as the first Suez crisis, the independence processes, and a conjuncture of regional instability characterized this transitional stage. In the case of the Suez crises (1956–1975), the deviation of the new generation super-tankers from the Persian Gulf routes to the Atlantic stopover ports such as Cape Town, Dakar, and Las

Table 23.1 Historical driving factors of port evolution in Northwest Africa, 1880–1972

Period	World Shipping Industry	African Port Development	Inland Transport Infrastructures	Regional Economic Factors	Regional Institutional Factors
1880–1913	Last transition from sail to steam. British merchant fleet hegemony. Increased tonnages. Maritime industry changes.	Scarcely developed. Wharfs and low-developed infrastructures (WA). Higher port performance in Northern Africa.	Scarcely developed. Railway systems (sea-producer regions). Poor road systems. Non-competitive waterways.	Expansion of cash-crop productions and mining sectors. Growth of external sectors (trade) and GDP *per capita*.	Scramble of Africa. Colonial occupation. Border's configuration.
1914–1945	Oil tankers. Introduction of liquid fuels. Increased drafts.	Expansion of port infrastructures. Improved facilities (export cash-crops and ores). Slow mechanization.	Railway growth (until 1930s). Road transport concurrence (wagons) (late 1930s).	Cash-crop prices crisis. Urban growth and regional metropolization of imperial port-cities. Drop of GDP *per capita*.	Development of colonial institutional model. Definitive occupation and control of the inner-lands (WA). Introduction of modern port management models.
1946–1960	Post-war shipping boom. Increased tonnages and drafts. Scale economies and Super-Tankers (late 1950s). Beginnings of containerization.	New port functions. Port expansion (WA) (Suez crisis).	Decline of railways. Increased importance of road transports. Expansion of the paved roads.	Post-war inflation. Stagnation of cash-crop productions. Transfer of transport-economic infrastructures. Relative weak growth of GDP *per capita*.	Socio-economic instability and decline of colonial rule. North African revolutions. New management models in port infrastructures.
1960–1972	First wave of containerization. Expansion of bulk trade (crude oil and oil products). Free registry countries.	Relative stagnation of old colonial ports. Emergence of "new ports" and functions. Weak introduction of container technologies. *Technical gap* and lack of investments.	Financial troubles and weak investments on roads. Crisis of railway systems. Limited inland integration.	Massive public investments and nationalization of productive sectors. Increased international concurrence on raw materials. Slow growth of GDP *per capita*.	New pro-socialist States. Nationalism and regional rivalries. Political instability and financial crisis. Postcolonial affairs.

Source: Own elaboration from series of GDP obtained from Maddison Project

N.B. NA (North Africa); WA (West Africa)

Palmas challenged the efficiency of port infrastructures and the organizational capacity of other port communities. Further consequences of the Egyptian crises permanently affected regional bunkering ports which retained a part of these traffics in a context of enlarged vessels and the entrepreneurial policies of scale economies (Kaukianen, 2012: 67–68). The institutional flexibility of port institutions, the state of infrastructures and the quality of port services were key factors which help to explain the retention of these stopover traffic at these ports.

On the other hand, the French FIDES plan launched after 1947, which massively invested in infrastructure modernization in French West Africa (FWA), resulted in the improvement of Dakar's port infrastructures and the construction of Abidjan port. Both ports absorbed almost 60 percent of global investments in port infrastructures for the whole federation between 1947 and 1957.

The last period analyzed (1960–72) coincides with the onset of the second global shipping revolution whereby African ports faced important obstacles in terms of financial capacity. The first containerized cargo in Africa was handled in 1972, reinforcing established port hierarchies and shipping patterns based on bulks and non-containerized cargoes. The global dynamics of progressive decline of seaborne freights analyzed by Ekberg et al. (2012) did not reach most African countries due to trade tax restrictions, the state of regional infrastructures, the structure of seaborne trade and the entrepreneurial policies developed by the global shipping liners. These conditioning elements and mainly the latter aggravated during the 1980 decade. By 1990, UNCTAD states:

> There is considerable evidence that this "escalating" structure of freight rates is due to the arbitrary pricing policies of liner shipping cartels that charge what the traffic will bear. Nonetheless, their effect is to create a bias against further commodity processing in developing countries [. . .] The deterioration of ports and related infrastructures also plays a key role.
>
> (UNCTAD, 1990: 52)

Nevertheless, during this last period, new commercial ports like Abidjan emerged and other specialized ports, such as Bonny, Escravos (both in Nigeria) Ghazaouet, Arzew, Port Gentil, Cabinda, Kenitra, or Bedjaia, notably expanded. These ports were devoted to crude oil and refinery activities and their throughput increased at the same pace as that of global demand up to the 1973 crisis. The massive exportation of crude oil during the early 1970s from emergent ports in the Gulf of Guinea represents a new phase of regional evolution.

Furthermore, the analysis of port indicators reveals the configuration of port hierarchies which experienced self-reinforcement effects due to the centrality and predominance of great imperial seaports, at least for general cargo. Dobusch and Kapeller (2013: 298–300) have proposed a number of elements that help to explain how major ports retained their key functions over time. Mainly, based on their approach we argue that the learning and expectation effects (memory effects, habits, routines, historical trends, etc.) in imperial seaports such as Dakar, Algiers, Casablanca, or Lagos encouraged port activity, their regional centrality and the economic clustering processes that occurred during the colonial period and this trend strongly remained during the Postcolonial Age. Moreover, the institutional choice made by the colonial powers promoted the consolidation of port hierarchies but lock-in processes too. A relevant example could be found in Senegal (and subsequently the FWA) and French Morocco. In both cases, colonial institutions promoted the creation of an imperial seaport to provide support for colonization and then the effective exploitation of human and natural resources from the hinterland. The establishment of the first port of Dakar during the 1860s promoted its regional importance (Ba et al., 2013). The port articulated the inland transport network from the whole FWA, and as a consequence, seaports in Guinea, Benin (formerly Dahomey), and the Ivory Coast, were not developed. The lion's share of investments occurred in Dakar during the first decades of colonial occupation and then, in the aftermath of World War II massive investments were made in other infrastructures like in Abidjan. The case of Casablanca is the most impressive as we shall see. From the establishment of the French Protectorate in Morocco in 1912, the port of Casablanca began to increase its influence. After the Great War, the phosphate revolution in Morocco changed the maritime façade of the country and the concentration process began. By 1929, the port of Casablanca handled nearly 80 percent of Moroccan external trade in volume and value (Suárez and Maziane, 2014). Such a concentration of port activity was mainly a consequence of political conjunctures, in addition to other factors such as natural conditions or the financial capability of each government. In the next section, we will provide an analysis of port traffics and the configuration of historical hierarchies.

The historical evolution of port traffic in Northwest Africa

Port hierarchies

Based on a historical database of port throughput volumes by maritime façade between 1913 and 1972, we analyze cargo distribution as well as port specialization. Although the completion of this database is still underway, especially to include better coverage of the former British colonies, this analysis reports on four selected years (1913, 1938, 1955, and 1972), each of them corresponding to a relatively stable conjuncture from the eve of the Great War to the first decade of political independence in most countries included in the study. Then, referring to Castillo Hidalgo and Valdaliso (2017), we propose a taxonomy of ports based on their throughput volume and evolution:

- Leading ports: ranking among the top five in the early periods analyzed and remaining on top throughout.
- Declining ports: initially high-ranking but lost ground and became secondary.
- Emergent ports: did not exist in the early years but climbed to relevant positions.
- Secondary ports: played an ancillary role during the entire period under analysis.

Table 23.2 presents the top 20 ports ranked by throughput for the selected years. The first column (1913), with the notable absence of Lagos, Freetown and Accra,

Table 23.2 Top 20 rank of port throughput in Northwest Africa for 1913, 1938, 1955, and 1972 (in harbor tons)

	1913		1938		1955		1972	
	Port	Throughput	Port	Throughput	Port	Throughput	Port	Throughput
1	Algiers	3,500,000	Oran	4,487,000	Casablanca	7,850,000	Santa Cruz de TF	15,526,534
2	Tunis-Goulette	1,757,257	Algiers	3,459,000	Algiers	4,374,539	Casablanca	15,092,504
3	Oran	1,436,255	Annaba (Bône)	2,646,000	Annaba (Bône)	3,938,000	Bedjaia	12,560,000
4	Sfax	1,356,288	Casablanca	2,511,000	Santa Cruz de TF	3,754,301	Monrovia	10,893,000
5	Las Palmas	1,157,925	Dakar	2,390,238	Dakar	3,556,480	Skikda (Philippeville)	6,904,000
6	Santa Cruz de TF	850,152	Tunis-Goulette	1,823,000	Las Palmas	2,374,000	Cabinda	6,621,000
7	Dakar	712,471	Sfax	1,445,000	Tunis-Goulette	2,372,000	Namimba (Moçamedes)	6,045,000
8	Mindelo	670,000	Melilla	901,472	Sfax	2,145,000	Abidjan	5,925,015
9	Annaba (Bône)	516,179	Las Palmas	860,687	Oran	2,121,000	Dakar	5,015,000
10	Melilla	348,152	Santa Cruz de TF	767,000	Melilla	1,700,000	Las Palmas	4,985,492
11	Sousse	282,950	Matadi	530,567	Conakry	1,601,390	Port Gentil	4,811,215
12	Casablanca	270,000	Sousse	411,000	Matadi	1,492,000	Algiers	4,546,000
13	Skikda (Philippeville)	257,208	Saffi	388,561	Ceuta	1,038,918	Annaba (Bône)	4,154,000
14	Bizerte	250,051	Ceuta	328,762	Lobito	971,600	Sfax	3,437,000
15	Rufisque	102,665	Kaolack	284,225	Abidjan	947,015	Point Noire	3,217,990
16	Douala	100,000	Bizerte	273,000	Kenitra (Port Liautey)	612,000	Lagos	2,891,000
17	Accra	85,000	Kenitra (Port Liautey)	268,726	Libreville-Owendo	575,000	Freetown	2,891,000
18	Foundiougne	83,100	Conakry	217,056	Point-Noire	456,000	Tema	2,859,000
19	Matadi	79,000	Lobito	209,700	Bizerte	359,000	Oran	2,719,000
20	Rabat	67,484	Douala	198,884	Douala	300,000	Bizerte	2,593,000

Source: Own elaboration from African Ports Historical Database (forthcoming)

N.B. Figures for Nigeria, Gold Coast and Sierra Leone for early periods before 1972 are not yet completed. The same goes for Conakry by 1972. So, this rank must be considered as provisional and relatively representative. Sample of ports for: 1913 n=32; 1938 n=37; 1955 n= 29; 1972 n=51.

represented an overall economic expansion on the eve of the Great War. Bearing in mind that figures collected from archival sources could be not entirely accurate (lack of figures for a number of ports), there is little doubt that the predominance of Algiers is confirmed. Located in North Africa, the top five operated as commercial gateways, coaling stations (mainly Oran) or phosphate export centers (e.g. Sfax). The main Canary Island ports – Las Palmas and Santa Cruz de Tenerife – enjoyed important positions thanks to their logistical functions as coal suppliers (Suárez, 2004). It must be noted that Saint Vincent (Mindelo) had lost importance as stopover port and by 1913 the port began to compete with the recently inaugurated commercial port of Dakar (1910). This was triggered by the replacement of Mindelo as a port of call for the Italian shipping lines to Brazil and Argentina and the rerouting of this traffic to the port of Dakar, where Italian coaling companies were also established. A number of smaller ports deserve attention as well, such as Matadi and Douala (the main port of the former German colony of Cameroon), specialized in palm oil, palm kernels, and timber. External trade value at Ghanaian ports for instance grew impressively before the Great War from £4,434,535 in 1907 to £9,908,613 in 1913. Complementary figures on port calls confirm such a trend for Ghana during the same period, while the gross tonnage of vessels calling at Gold Coast ports increased from 560,578 tons (1896) to 1,526,048 tons (1913), representing an average growth of 62.3 percent (Colonial Reports of the Gold Coast, Colonial Office, various issues). Olukoju (2014: 125) found compelling evidence of a sustained growth of throughput in the wharves (Iddo, Ijora, Apapa) of Lagos during the period 1919–29, but overall figures must be tested through the analysis of the Blue Books of the Colonies or similar sources.

Figures for 1938 represent interesting changes in port hierarchy. The emergence of Oran, Annaba (Bône), Casablanca, and Dakar and the stagnation of Algiers are some of the main developments. Phosphate exports expanded in Algeria and Morocco, while the fall of the Canary Island ports is directly attributable to the outbreak of the Spanish Civil war and the deviation of vessels to Dakar for bunkering activities. Previously regional secondary ports (but leading ports for the colony), such as Matadi, exhibited rapid growth (i.e. over half a million tons). By 1955, port hierarchies remained relatively stable and Casablanca reached the first rank. The mid-1950s were characterized by an overall growth of port throughput (Table 23.3). An example of this is the impressive growth of Conakry that began in 1953 with massive iron-ore and bauxite exports (80–85 percent of the country's entire exports during that decade). Other key aspects include the aforementioned emergence of Abidjan, partly to exploit the economic resources of the Gulf of Guinea (Rougerie, 1950: 753). The opening of the Vridi Canal in early 1951 and other works boosted throughput from 215,256 tons in 1938 to 692,673 tons in 1951. Abidjan thus superseded the old wharfs of Grand Bassam and Port Bouët which had been the main commercial ports of the colony until the late 1930s (Direction du Port d'Abidjan, 1955). Another important event that marked the further evolution of the regional port system was the modification of Dakar's hinterland. In 1934, the Ivorian railway reached Bobodioulasso (Burkina, former Upper Volta); by 1956 it extended to Ouagadougou and to Niger in 1958. Thus,

Abidjan became a vital gateway for land-locked territories during the second half of the 1950s, causing important changes to historical trade patterns in the context of the balkanization of the FWA. Meanwhile, Santa Cruz de Tenerife's throughput expansion related to the growth of world oil markets due to the existence of a refinery close to the port that was inaugurated in November 1930.

The last column introduces interesting shifts within the port hierarchy. This was the most complete year, with 67 ports. New ports had emerged to occupy some of the top ten positions and other formerly leading ports had dropped. The key factor was the introduction and expansion of oil activities at these ports. The Nigerian port of Bonny climbed to the top thanks to the discovery of oil deposits in the Niger's Delta. The next four places were occupied by oil-related ports, with the emergence of Arzew (Algeria) and La Skhira (Tunisia). Only Casablanca retained its position. A number of bulk export ports such as Bedjaia (oil refinery), Monrovia and Buchanan (iron ores and timber), and Cabinda (crude oil) reached the top 10 for the first time. Abidjan superseded Dakar due to its faster growth in comparative terms. The drop of historical ports in relative terms (they remained to hold onto the general cargo trade) is important. Moreover, the main ports of the wealthiest former colonies of the Gold Coast and Nigeria remained below three million tons (relative higher value of exported cargoes, e.g., cocoa), but greatly expanded during the 1980s due to the expansion of oil market in the region, as Nigerian figures stated. Figures for 1972 are in line with the global expansion of bulk trade (liquid and solid), which at the global scale increased from 540 million tons in 1960 to 1,654 million tons in 1972. The same goes for dry bulk commodities, which passed from 233 million tons to 505 million tons in the same period (UNCTAD, various issues). Major port reforms across the African continent began in the second half of the 1970s and funds were granted by international institutions (World Bank, International Monetary Fund, European Development Bank) or global investors from the Western, Soviet, and Arab countries.

We have summarized some key figures on the evolution of port activity for the same test years in Table 23.3. This confirms the clear difference between North and West African ports in aggregated terms. By 1913, North Africa as a whole surpassed West Africa tenfold, even including Lagos, which was excluded due to lack of data. In 1938, differences were narrower due to the important growth, consolidation, and first phase of port sub-Saharan port reform, as seen with West Africa's 149.84% growth rate compared with 68.59% for North Africa. In 1955, the throughput ratio between North and West Africa declined to 3:1, as only Dakar reached a level comparable to that of North Africa's largest ports. In 1972, there was impressive growth in both regions, although it radically more accelerated in West Africa (1,103.49 percent) than North Africa (240.70 percent). This growth was directly tied to the expansion of oil activities, as explained. Individual case studies of port evolution in a number of West African ports need to be explored from a holistic perspective in order to analyze how internal evolution and the emergence of new ports modified the regional maritime networks.

Following on from this taxonomy, we could argue that historical port hierarchies marked the broader economic and institutional evolution of the analyzed regions.

Table 23.3 Throughput analysis in North and West Africa (1913, 1938, 1955, and 1972)

North Africa

	1913	1938	1955	1972
Ports analyzed (n)	20	19	16	24
Total Throughput	12.358.490	20.835.989	34.529.994	84.459.463
Growth rate	n/a	68.59 (1913–38)	65.72 (1938–55)	144.59 (1938–55)
Throughput avg.	617.925	1.096.631	2.158.125	3.519.144
Throughput median.	263.604	411.000	1.910.500	2.936.570
Ports (threshold 1)	Ports > 1.000.000 tons: 5	Ports > 2.000.000 tons: 4	Ports > 3.000.000 tons: 4	Ports > 10.000.000 tons: 3
Ports (threshold 2)	Ports > 500.000 tons: 7	Ports > 1.000.000 tons: 6	Ports > 2.000.000 tons: 8	Ports > 4.000.000 tons: 7

West Africa

	1913	1938	1955	1972
Ports analyzed (n)	12	18	13	27
Total Throughput	1.970.138	4.922.200	10.676.585	64.498.507
Growth rate	n/a	149.84 (1913–38)	116.90 (1938–55)	504.11 (1938–55)
Throughput avg.	164.178	273.456	821.276	2.388.834
Throughput median.	81.050	130.850	456.000	1.966.268 (top.20)
Ports (threshold 1)	Ports > 1.000.000 tons: 0	Ports > 2.000.000 tons: 1	Ports > 3.000.000 tons: 1	Ports > 10.000.000 tons: 1
Ports (threshold 2)	Ports > 500.000 tons: 2	Ports > 1.000.000 tons: 1	Ports > 2.000.000 tons: 1	Ports > 4.000.000 tons: 6

Sources: Own elaboration from African Ports Historical Database (forthcoming)

Yet, two distinct periods can be distinguished. Before 1955, historical port hierarchies remained unchanged and were tied to the colonization process and the continuation of long term trajectories (i.e., Algiers, Tunis-Goulette, Bône, and Dakar). In the second half of the twentieth century, new ports with new functions emerged and throughput expanded, following the global trends of seaborne trade. New specialized ports (oil ports) tied to export activities emerged and altered the regional port hierarchy, but former leading ports retained their influence as political and economic centers. Despite their relative decline, these port-cities retained their influence and urban hierarchy in terms of population, industrial clusters (e.g., Dakar), or regional redistribution of general cargoes.

Secondary ports managed to grow despite the persistent predominance of great imperial ports, notably due to their articulation of coastal shipping networks at various scales and their specific functions as micro-local hubs exporting commodities. The Moroccan port system provides an interesting example where the dominance of Casablanca was challenged by emerging ports.

As seen in Figure 23.1, the market shares of Moroccan ports between 1911 and 1972, despite missing data from 1955 to 1966, reveals an important trend of cargo concentration in Casablanca. Indeed, Casablanca itself concentrated about 80 percent of Moroccan seaborne trade by 1930 and more than 70 percent by 1972, despite the emergence of phosphate exports and fishing activities in the port of Saffi during the 1950s. Casablanca's hinterland permitted the evacuation of cash-crop productions (wheat, vegetables, and livestock) from the rich agricultural regions of Tadla and Chaouia (Suárez and Maziane, 2014: 78). Until the inauguration of the container terminal of Tangiers-Med in the late 1990s, most of Moroccan external trade concentrated in Casablanca. Such a concentration is typical of most national port systems in Africa, backed by the institutional choice made by the French governors during the Protectorate. In particular, the Marèchal Liautey administration decided to create an imperial port capable of confronting the British coaling station of Gibraltar.

The progress of shipping activities supported by the institutional environment in Casablanca contrasted with the stagnation of the "international" port of Tangiers. This port had been one of the most active port-cities on the Moroccan coast since the seventeenth century but since the signature of the Treaty of Fes (1912), it was transformed in a sort of no man´s land where international interests were represented. The self-reinforcement effects of Casablanca promoted by institutional decisions and commercial expectation dynamics strengthened its predominant position. Such an artificial lock-in process causing the stagnation of Tangiers as a regional hub for northern Morocco could have been verified based on French diplomatic archives. By 1946, the French consular agent in Tangiers officially stood against further investment in the local port to avoid competition with Casablanca, as the international administration of the port of Tangiers was seen as a threat to the imperial private interests around general cargo redistribution in Morocco.[2] A closer look at inter-port shipping patterns is provided in the next section to complement our understanding of port system evolution, port hierarchies, and specialization in Northwest Africa.

Shipping patterns and connectivity

Vessel movement data extracted from *Lloyd's List* archives were first compared with previous section figures based on tonnage in order to test their comparability.

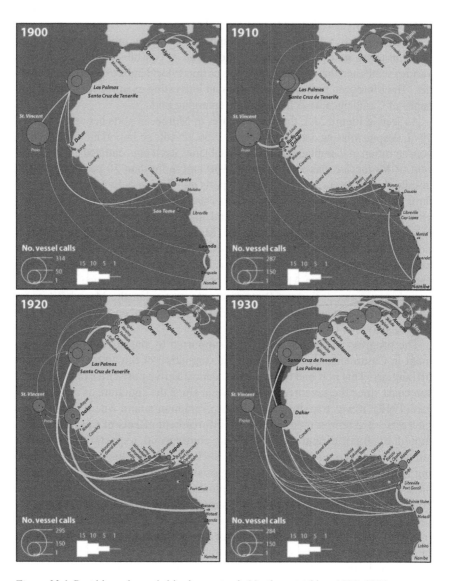

Figure 23.1 Port hierarchy and shipping routes in Northwest Africa, 1900–1970

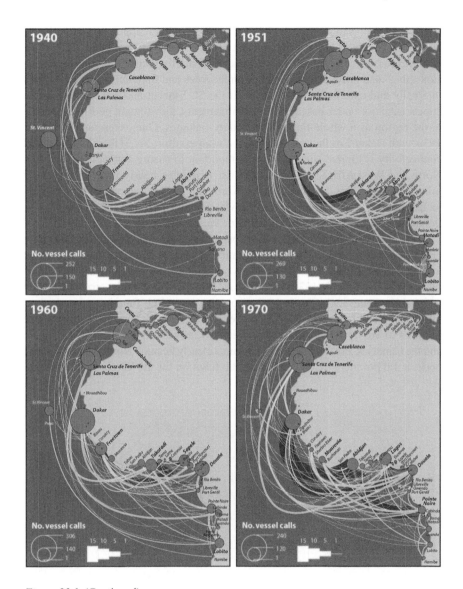

Figure 23.1 (Continued)

Results are relatively significant, based on a Pearson correlation coefficient (between the number of vessel calls and port throughput volume) of 0.63, 0.75, 0.83, and 0.15 for the years 1910/1913, 1935/1938, 1951/1955, and 1970/1972. The sudden decline in statistical significance in 1970/1972 is directly attributable to the emergence of new bulk ports as mentioned above, with a gap between low connectivity and high volume. Less significant results were obtained when replacing vessel calls by degree centrality (i.e. the number of flows of each port with other ports). The main objective of using Lloyd's shipping data in addition to throughput data is to provide a relational perspective by mapping the evolution of Northwest Africa's maritime network between 1910 and 1970 (Figure 23.2). If the main results in terms of port hierarchies subtsnatially confirm the above discussions, they also provide new evidence on the roles and functions of regional ports internally and externally. For instance, if the St. Vincent and Canary ports often appear as major nodes based on vessel movements, they remain poorly connected to the region as a whole through secondary linkages. One exception is the year 1930, with Dakar/Las Palmas as the region's largest flow. Yet, if their intra-regional connectivity is limited, such nodes are important to ensure connectivity between North and West Africa, which would otherwise have nearly inexistent, or very minor linkages. This division between North and West was already made evident in Table 23.3 in terms of throughput growth dynamics. In fact, the region's major linkages remain internal to either North or West Africa.

Another interesting affirmation is the parallel stability and shift among the major nodes of the network over time. For instance, Algiers in North Africa had been the leading node before the 1930s and was surpassed from then onwards by Casablanca (but also Oran in 1930 and 1940). As for other larger nodes, size is reflected in local connectivity, as such ports also carry out a hub function towards their immediate neighbors. However, there are sometimes huge gaps also between size (number of vessel calls) and local connectivity, as seen in the case of St. Vincent and the Canaries. For instance, if Casablanca clearly became North Africa's largest node, it did not increase an equivalent hub function for the Maghreb. This means

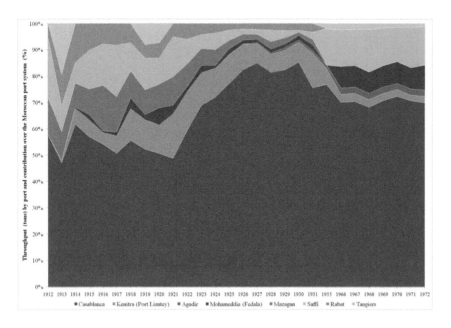

Figure 23.2 Market share evolution of Moroccan ports between 1911 and 1972

that such large ports are mainly extraverted, their activity being mainly linked to external regions such as Western Europe and North America, for instance.

A very distinct pattern emerged over time in West Africa, where Dakar had become the main pivotal hub for the whole sub-region, starting with a few minor linkages in 1900–1910 and gradually becoming connected to most of its neighbors in subsequent years, in a multilayered fashion (i.e. trunk lines and small linkages). We also observe that despite the predominance of Dakar, West Africa is quite polycentric, but with important shifts among the other hubs, such as Sapele (1920, 1960), Abo (1940, 1950), Douala (continuous), Takoradi (up to 1960), Freetown (1940 and 1960), Abidjan and Pointe-Noire (since the 1950s mainly), and Lagos (1970). In comparison, the limited intra-regional maritime connectivity of the Maghreb is rather specific compared with West Africa (Mohamed-Chérif and Ducruet, 2016). Some factors, such as the relatively "institutional" homogeneity among the northern territories under French colonial rule, could explain this specificity. On the other hand, institutional policies developed in the rest of territories promoted the direct linkages with overseas forelands (Debrie, 2012). This trend aggravated during the decolonization processes where countries competed against each other in the international markets.

Conclusion

This chapter has proposed a first approach to the evolution of port networks in Northwest Africa in a historical perspective. We have shown how the resilience of great imperial ports promoted the concentration processes, which were tied to the evolution of extroverted economic structures. We found compelling evidence of a delayed port modernization process in West Africa that affected the evolution of port indicators (both throughput and connectivity). In terms of port hierarchies in the long run, we have observed how they were almost unchanged until the decade of 1950. In a context of political independences, new ports with new functions emerged but the key feature is that these ports were specialized in the export of cash-crops, mining-ores or crude oil and oil products. These ports were built to enlarge the capacity of their respective countries in terms of external trade, but in general terms the structure did not change, except with the emergence of oil ports such as Bonny or Arzew. A process of divergence between North and West Africa can be observed on the basis of both tonnage and vessel movement data, defined by increasing gaps in terms of traffic growth and intra-regional shipping connectivity. Except for this divergence, the overall evolution remained relatively similar during the first decades of political independences (at least on a country-level analysis), while port hierarchies tended to persist over time. Individual studies by countries must be developed in order to detect the permanent self-reinforcement effects which could help to obtain valid explanations. The unbalanced structure of trade with high value imports hampered the economic performance of these countries. In the beginning of the 1970s, the first wave of containerization reached Africa but this market did not expand as a result of technical, political and financial obstacles. Therefore, further studies must be made regarding the fully long-term evolution of African maritime façades in order to observe the adaptation of African ports to global shifts in shipping and in particular the containerized general cargo revolution. Further research can also complement the current databases and expand the analysis by providing additional metrics in terms of centrality indicators and foreland traffic distribution.

Acknowledgements

This chapter benefited from the R&D project HAR2015-64044-R and ULPGC-2014-01. The research leading to these results has received funding from the European Research Council under the European Union's Seventh Framework Programme (FP/2007–2013) / ERC Grant Agreement n. [313847] "World Seastems".

Notes

1 A complete free access online database for African ports from 1880 up to 2016 is being completed. We expect that it will be available in its provisional first version by November 2017.
2 CADN. Tanger, 675POE, Carton 24. Protectorat de la RF au Maroc. Direction des Travaux Publics. Note pour le Secrétaire Générale du Protectorat, 2 September 1946.

References

Austin, G. (2015) Explaining and evaluating the cash-crop revolution in the 'Peasant' colonies of tropical Africa, ca.1890-ca.1930: Beyond 'Vent for Surplus'. In: Akyeampong, E., Bates, R.H., Nunn, N., Robinson, J.A. (Eds.), *Africa's Development in Historical Perspective*. New York: Cambridge University Press, pp. 295–320.

Ba, D., Diaw, A.T., Leclerc, G., Mering, C. (2013) Analyse de la dynamique spatiale du port de Dakar de 1900 à 2009: enjeux multi-scalaires et aménagements. *Cybergeo: European Journal of Geography*, 635. Available at: https://cybergeo.revues.org/25773

Castillo Hidalgo, D. (2014) The port of Dakar: Technological evolution, management and commercial activity (1857–1929). In: Suárez Bosa, M. (Ed.), *Atlantic Ports and the First Globalisation, c.1850–1930*. London: Palgrave MacMillan, pp. 90–111.

Castillo Hidalgo, D., Valdaliso, J.M. (2017) Path dependence and change in the Spanish port system in the long run (1880–2014): A historical perspective. *International Journal of Maritime History*, 29(3): 569–596..

Chaves, I.N., Engerman, S., Robinson, J.A. (2015) Reinventing the wheel: The economic benefits of wheeled transportation in early colonial British West Africa. In: Akyeampong, E., Bates, R.H., Nunn, N., Robinson, J.A. (Eds.), *Africa's Development in Historical Perspective*. New York: Cambridge University Press, pp. 321–365.

Debrie, J. (2012) The West African port system: Global insertion and regional particularities. *Echogéo*, 20. Available at: https://echogeo.revues.org/13070

Dickson, K.B. (1965) Evolution of seaports in Ghana: 1880–1928. *Annals of the Association of American Geographers*, 55: 98–111.

Direction du Port d'Abidjan. (1955) *Le Port d'Abidjan*. Abidjan: Imprimerie de la Côte d'Ivoire.

Dobusch, L., Kapeller, J. (2013) Breaking new paths: Theory and method in path dependence research. *Schmalenbach Business Review*, 65: 288–311.

Ekberg, E., Lange, E., Merok, E. (2012) Building the networks of trade: Perspectives in twentieth century maritime history. In: Harlaftis, G., Tenold, S., Valdaliso, J.M. (Eds.), *The World's Key Industry*. London: Palgrave Macmillan, pp. 88–105.

Guerrero, D., Rodrigue, J.P. (2014) The waves of containerization: Shifts in global maritime transportation. *Journal of Transport Geography*, 34: 151–164.

Hoyle, B.S. (1967) *The Seaports of East Africa: A Geographical Study*. Nairobi: Makerere Institute of Social Research.

Kaukianen, Y. (2012) The advantages of water carriage: Scale economies and shipping, c.1870–2000. In: Harlaftis, G., Tenold, S., Valdaliso, J.M. (Eds.), *The World's Key Industry*. London: Palgrave Macmillan, pp. 64–87.

Martin, R., Sunley, P. (2010) The place of path dependence in an evolutionary perspective on the economic landscape. In: Boschma, R.A., Martin, R. (Eds.), *Handbook for Evolutionary Economic Geography*. Chichester: Edward Elgar, pp. 62–92.

Mohamed-Chérif, F.Z., Ducruet, C. (2016) Regional integration and maritime connectivity across the Maghreb seaport system. *Journal of Transport Geography*, 51: 280–293.

Ng, A.K.Y., Ducruet, C. (2014) The changing tides of port geography (1950–2012). *Progress in Human Geography*, 38(6): 785–823.

Olukoju, A. (2004) *The Liverpool of West Africa: The Dynamics and Impact of Maritime Trade in Lagos, 1900–1950*. Trenton, NJ, USA: Africa World Press.

Olukoju, A. (2014) The port of lagos, 1850–1929: The rise of West Africa's leading port. In: Suárez Bosa, M. (Ed.), *Atlantic Ports and the First Globalisation, c.1850–1930*. London: Palgrave Macmillan, pp. 112–129.

Peterec, R.J. (1967) *Dakar and West African Economic Development*. New York: Columbia University Press.

Rougerie, G. (1950) Le port d'Abidjan. Le problème des débouchés maritimes de la Côte d'Ivoire. Sa solution lagunaire. *Bulletin de l'IFAN*, 12: 751–837.

Seck, A. (1970) *Dakar, Métropole Ouest-Africaine*. Dakar: Mémoires de l'IFAN.

Suárez Bosa, M. (2004) The role of the Canary Islands in the Atlantic coal route from the end of the nineteenth century to the beginning of the twentieth century: Corporate strategies. *International Journal of Maritime History*, 16(1): 95–124.

Suárez Bosa, M., Maziane, L. (2014) The port of Casablanca in the first stage of the protectorate. In: Suárez Bosa, M. (Ed.), *Atlantic Ports and the First Globalisation, c.1850–1930*. London: Palgrave Macmillan, pp. 70–89.

Taaffe, E.J., Morrill, R.L., Gould, P.R. (1963) Transport expansion in underdevelopped countries: A comparative analysis. *Geographical Review*, 53: 503–529.

UNCTAD (1990) *Review of Maritime Transport*. Geneva: United Nations Conference on Trade and Development.

Vance, J.E. (1970) *The Merchant's World: The Geography of Wholesaling*. Englewood Cliffs: Prentice-Hall.

24 Partition, independence and maritime networks in South Asia

*Kenmei Tsubota, Atiya Habeeb Kidwai
and César Ducruet*

British rule had been fully entrenched in most parts of South and Southeast Asia by the late nineteenth century. The countries in these regions had been converted into colonies, and, along with other British colonies elsewhere in the world, they were well connected to the United Kingdom, as stated as early as 1776 by Adam Smith: "What goods could bear the expense of land-carriage between London and Calcutta? . . . Those two cities, however, at present carry on a very considerable commerce with each other, and by mutually affording a market, give a good deal of encouragement to each other's industry" (Smith, 1776). This statement, however contentious from the point of view of the growth of industries in the colonies, was true in terms of the benefits accruing to the British Empire. Direct control subjugated these colonies through administrative, commercial, judicial and other controlling systems. By the late eighteenth century, Britain had become a nation that was "sending out its ships to explore every distant sea; its factors to open up commercial intercourse with every affluent coast" (Wilson Anti-Slavery Collection, 1840). The greater part of Asia's littoral and islands, of which the British Empire was a component, was integrated into the world economy during the first sixty years or so of the nineteenth century. The indigenous shipping industries became confronted with European maritime, technological, economic and political expansion that together formed the main dynamics of the ensuing age of Western domination.

Overseas trade and Indian shipping were greatly disadvantaged even before this integration was well established because of technological backwardness. Steam shipping from the beginning was dominated by Western ship owners until the Asian colonies achieved full political independence after 1945. Since the late 1960s, South Asia has witnessed – or, rather, created – a dramatic resurgence of its involvement in shipping. The main objective of this chapter is to examine how the end of the British Empire, by bringing independence to the colonies, restructured their trade patterns and shipping networks (Broeze, 1987, 1996; Bracken, 2015). By contrast with economic history and international economics, this chapter uses data on vessel movements instead of trade data over the period 1890–2000, i.e. during the heydays of colonialism and after the independences. The advantages of using vessel movement data published in the *Lloyd's Shipping Index* are numerous: vessels carry mostly commodities; the data cover a long period, are disaggregated at the port level and are relatively neutral, as they are collected due to the non-governmental nature of the organization, i.e. unaffected by interruptions caused by political changes.

Our geographical coverage is primarily focused on former British India, while "South Asia" includes Pakistan, India, Myanmar (Burma), Sri Lanka and the Maldives. This chapter contributes to the literature in the economic history of international trade in South Asia by providing a detailed analysis of historical shipping data. It questions whether and how political and economic evolutions affected the pattern of maritime networks in this area. Such an approach takes its inspiration from relatively few earlier studies of the kind. Todd and Zhang (1993) and Wang and Ducruet (2013) studied the impact of political or economic change on port activities in China, while Iheduru (1996) analyzed the effects of dismantled Apartheid on South Africa (for other analyses of transnational port systems, see Chapters 5, 8, 9, 11, 19 and 23 on Taiwan Strait, Black Sea, Arctic, Mediterranean, USSR and Northwest Africa).

Data and methodology

In order to measure and map shipping flows connecting South Asia inwards and outwards at various levels, we extracted vessel movement data from the *Lloyd's List* corpus (see Ducruet et al., 2015 for a detailed description). The information contained in the *Lloyd's Shipping Index* documents vessel characteristics, ports of origin and destination as well as the latest ship voyage on the date of the publication. We do not exlude a bias in our methodology, since the analysis focuses on the months of April or May every five years, due to the seasonality of trading flows. In South Asia, interrelated seasonality includes both weather and production factors, such as the rainy season marked by cyclones, which in turn affects the agricultural production (i.e. early harvesting period) of jute, which takes place after the rainy season. Seasonality may exclude certain ports from the sample if the specific commodity they trade relates to another season than spring. In turn, this possible drawback is compensated by an extraction at the same period for comparability and consistency. Secondly, data mainly documents oceanic or deep-sea voyages, leaving aside domestic fleet performing local trades (i.e. coastal shipping), as the Lloyd's principal purpose was the insurance of international trading vessels. Despite their smaller size, such domestic vessels may have an important role for cargo redistribution between global and local trade routes, such as junk vessels in China (Wang and Ducruet, 2013).

Thirdly, the number of ships and ship calls, which are the traffic measurement units retained in this study, do not account for the true freight volume (or value) of flows. Yet, the retained unit has the advantage to be comparable overtime. Fourthly, the actual routes of ships are in reality more complex than direct single port-to-port lines, thus missing successive and intermediary stops. Each segment between two ports is part of a longer voyage between origin and destination ports, regions, and continents, making it impossible to differentiate between intra- and extraregional flows. In terms of timeline, 1890 coincides with the middle of the

"British Raj" (1858–1947), with a steady demographic growth and a rapid development of India's private industries accompanied by heavy investments in physical infrastructures such as railways, canals, roads and ports up to the globalization era (Ghosh and De, 2001).

Following a steady work to disambiguate country and port names based on current names, we define routes as links between port pairs created by the movement of at least one ship. The number of vessel calls is measured at the level of ports, countries or regions as well as by interport link. Domestic routes are within the territory of a current country, while regional routes are within South Asia and international routes connect South Asia with the rest of the world.

Vessel movement distribution in South Asia

The direct or indirect British rule was gradually established in most of the regions in South Asia from 1757 after the Battle of Plassey. By 1890, the starting date of our dataset, the British governed almost the entire region.[1] For Myanmar (Burma), Lower Burma came under British control from 1826 and was annexed in 1853, whereas Upper Burma was annexed in 1886. The British also directly governed the Maldives from 1887, Sri Lanka (Ceylon) from 1815 and ceded around a third of Nepal's territory in 1816.

World War II resulted in both political as well as economic disruption in the region. The Japanese invaded and controlled Burma between 1942 and 1945, and also attacked the Indo-Burma border in 1944. The end of the war brought momentous changes in the form of freedom from colonialism in most of South Asia. After the long struggle for its independence, British India got separated into two nations, Pakistan and India in 1947.[2] Pakistan had two territories in the East and West of India. In East Pakistan, conflicts built around the issue of language and suppression of election results triggered the war of independence. Consequently, East Pakistan became independent as Bangladesh in 1971.

Burma had been separately administered since 1937 and became independent in 1948. As the socialist movements advanced, a coup d'etat occurred, and a military government has claimed the Burmese socialistic state since 1962. These changes disconnected economic relations with Western countries.[3] Ceylon was granted independence in 1948 and was given a Dominion status within the British Commonwealth, which was retained for the next 24 years until May 22, 1972, when it became a republic and was named the Republic of Sri Lanka. Independence for all these countries meant a complete overhauling of the international trade networks. In the following sections, we discuss our data at three levels of aggregation, from South Asia to the present-day countries and their port cities.

South Asia

The evolution of ship calls within South Asia (Figure 24.1) starts with 1,060 movements in 1890, covering 330 inter-port linkages among the 23 ports appearing in the database. International calls were already about 77% of total flows. From 1890

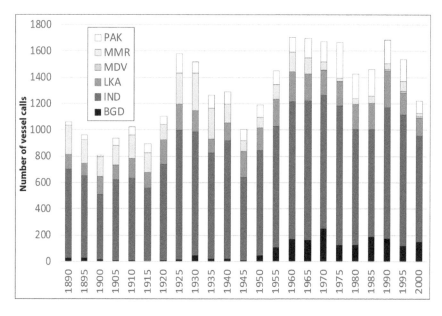

Figure 24.1 Shipping traffic distribution of Indian subcontinent ports by country,
1890–2000

onwards, the number of calls witnessed certain fluctuations such as a rapid but
temporary decline during the independence of the Indian subcontinent, and a rapid
growth afterwards.

Intra-regional flows oscillated around 30% of total flows throughout the period
(Figure 24.2). Prominent declines are observed for extra-regional flows, such as
with the United Kingdom from 33% in 1890 to 24% in 1935, around 8% in 1965
and only 1% in 2000. Flows with the Middle East increased from around 3–5%
before 1945 to around 12% in the 1980s and the 1990s. Routes with East Asia and
Southeast Asia also increased. East Asian routes increased from around 3% in 1890
to 10% in 1935 and remained so after 1945. For Southeast Asian routes, the share
was around 3–5% in the 1900s but increased after 1945 to 17% in 1980 and 35%
in 2000. These trends clearly show the unchanged importance of intra-regional
routes and the shifts from European routes to East and Southeast Asian routes after
1945. These trends both reflect trade and logistical changes. For the latter, operational and technological evolution of the port and maritime industries moved from
direct port-to-port shipping to pendulum services and hub-and-spokes configurations along the Europe-Asia route, with intermediary stops, especially with the
advent of containerization. This can accentuate the gap or uneven overlap between
shipping patterns and trade patterns as discussed earlier.

The cartographic representation of South Asian maritime networks only retains
the most voluminous flow link for each port node decade wise (Figure 24.3).
Although such an operation obliterates a vast quantity of information, it also

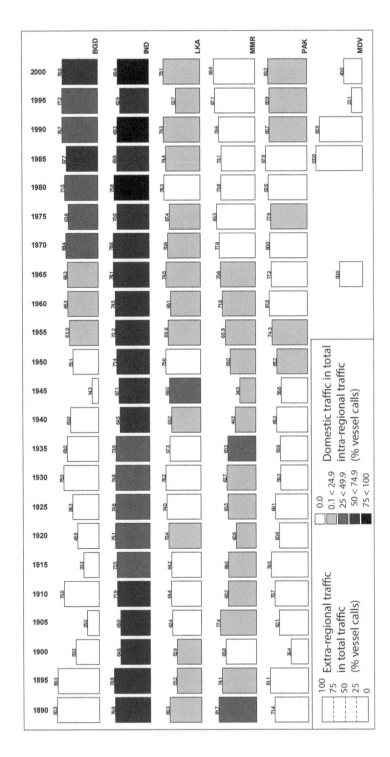

Figure 24.2 Distribution and connectivity of Indian subcontinent shipping flows, 1890–2000

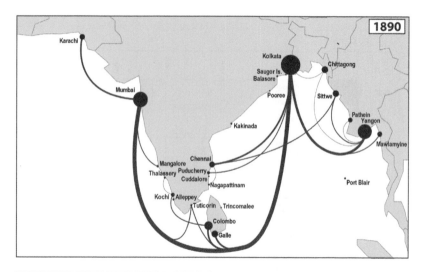

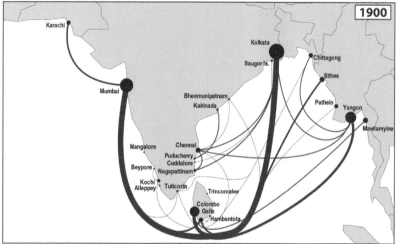

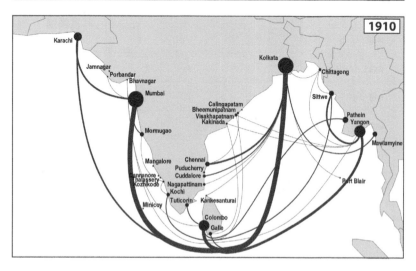

Figure 24.3 Spatial distribution of major Indian subcontinent shipping flows, 1890–2000

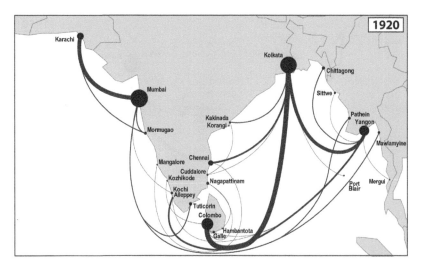

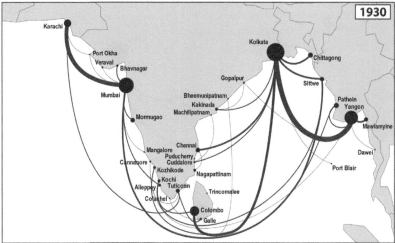

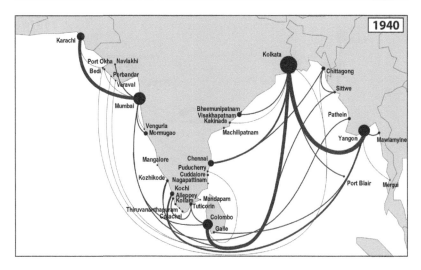

Figure 24.3 (Continued)

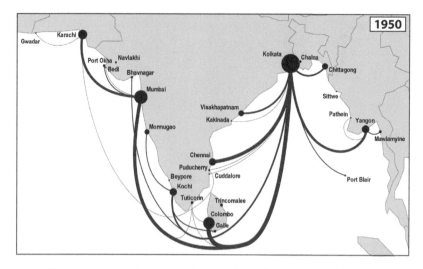

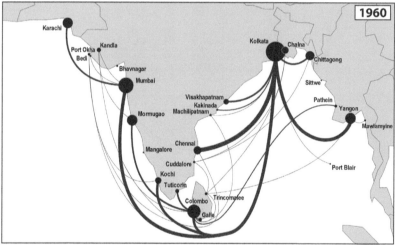

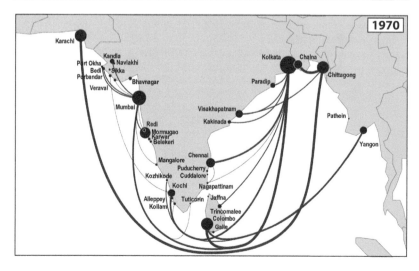

Figure 24.3 (Continued)

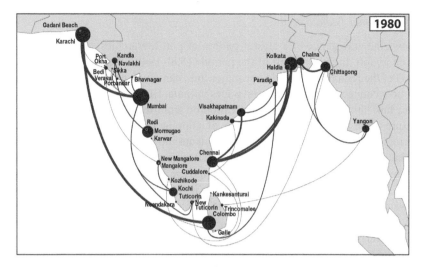

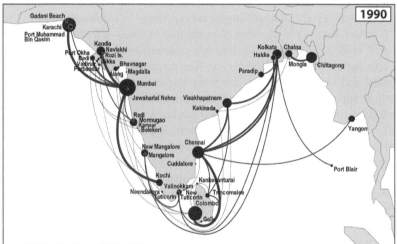

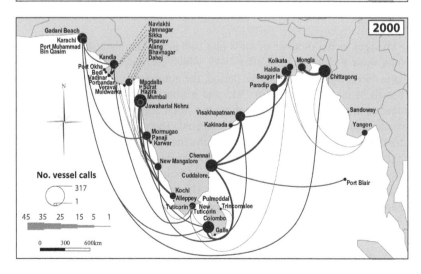

Figure 24.3 (Continued)

allows the emergence of a clearer pattern of port hierarchies and corridors in a given region. In the first half of the period (1890–1940), the eastern and western parts of the region connect via one major link, namely Kolkata-Mumbai, the largest flow connecting the two largest nodes in India. However, Kolkata's main shipping link shifted from Mumbai to Colombo from the 1920s onwards. Another feature is the much denser distribution of shipping linkages in the eastern part of the region, or the Bay of Bengal, where Kolkata and Yangon act as the most powerful hubs with the largest connecting flows. It means that many second-order nodes depend on them to ship their goods through the network. Mumbai, on the other hand, has a large size but its role as a hub is far less significant. From the 1950s onwards, Mumbai took over as the major port in India, while Kolkata started loosing its significance due to natural causes of siltation and inability to handle bigger ships (Murphey, 1964; Kidwai, 1992).

In the second half of the period (1950–2000), the major Mumbai-Kolkata link resumes temporarily (1950–1960). Kolkata remains the regions' largest node (in terms of total vessel calls) and largest hub (in terms of maritime centrality) until 1970. Afterwards, while Mumbai takes the lead in terms of traffic size, the whole network tends to split among several low-connected subsystems, the eastern and western parts losing interdependency. New second-order hubs emerge, such as Chennai and Visakhapatnam, while some formerly major nodes such as Yangon nearly disappear from the map. The figures until 2000 confirm that successive independencies (in addition to other factors) gradually resulted in the split of the networks' backbone into several disjointed parts. In parallel, the amount of maritime activity and the density of shipping linkages are more evenly distributed between east and west parts in the recent decades. One influencing factor is the emergence of new ports outside traditional port cities that distort inherited shipping patterns (Kidwai, 1989; Eliot, 2003). In the following section, we examine the data at country level and port level in each country.[4] A comparison of the dynamics of individual countries is provided in Figure 24.4 based on their foreland distribution.

Bangladesh

The changes in the number of calls and routes for Bangladesh are significant. Results show a clear increase after 1945, which corresponded to the partition of India in 1947. During the colonial period, the number of calls was on an average 18.8 with its minimum at six in 1915 and maximum at 44 in 1930. The average number of routes was 10.7. Throughout the colonial period, only Chittagong was connected, so that no domestic route appeared. The composition of international routes fluctuated significantly throughout the twentieth century. Since jute was the primary export item from Bangladesh in the nineteenth and early twentieth centuries, the routes to the United Kingdom were mainly to Dundee, Glasgow, Liverpool and London. Other than these Aden, Hamburg and some East African ports also appeared.[5] It was in 1950 that another port, Khulna (Chalna), appeared in the list,[6] followed by Mongla in 1990. The number of calls per route after 1950 was only one to three, and the destinations were diversified.

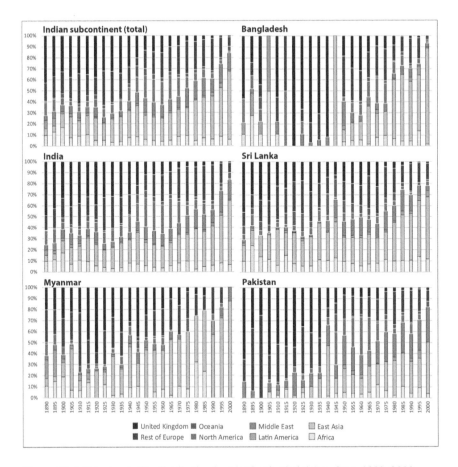

Figure 24.4 Shipping traffic distribution by (destination/origin) regions, 1890–2000

Singapore appears as an important port after 1950. The number of calls increased from three in 1951 to 32 in 1980 and to 71 in 2000. For the regional trade during the colonial period, the trading ports were Kolkata and Tuticorin in India and Sittwe and Yangon in Myanmar. It should be noted that Dhaka appears in the list only once; as an upstream port, its depth is not sufficient for international vessels.

As mentioned earlier, the region of current Bangladesh had been East Pakistan prior to 1971. As the trade between West and East Pakistan became important, vessel movements begin to appear in the data. There were five voyages between East and West Pakistan for the first time in 1950, three in 1960, 12 in 1965 and 16 in 1970.[7] After the independence of Bangladesh, this trend changed but did not vanish. There were six voyages in 1975 and between three and six from 1980 to 2000. On the other hand, regional routes with India increased once Bangladesh became independent. Between 1950 and 1985, the average number of calls between

India and Bangladesh reached 21, whereas they were only 4.2 during the colonial period. The peak was reached in 1960. After 1985, the number of calls decreased to around eight. Domestic routes were only four in 1960 and increased to 34 in 1985. It decreased in the 1990s but increased to 24 in 2000.

India

India's location in the middle of Indian subcontinents gives it a long coastline, and it has the historical advantage of having the main ports in the subcontinent from the colonial times. Thus, the number of vessel calls from here had always been the highest in the region. In 1890, there were 672 calls, 163 routes and 15 ports in India. International calls were 76.8% and regional calls 8.9%. From 1915 to 1925, there was a substantial growth in terms of calls from 552 to 985, with some decline until 1940. The number of routes clearly increased in 1925 but not in 1915 and 1920, which does not correspond with the increase in the number of calls. The major ports were Kolkata and Mumbai before the independence. In 1890, the share of these two ports was 87.8% and 69% at the lowest in 1940. When we compare the ship call data with the cargo handled data, we find a comparable picture which corroborates the pre-eminence of these ports in the port hierarchy (Kidwai, 1992). Between 1880 and 1950, Kolkata and Mumbai have been the first two top ranking ports in India in terms of the cargo handled (Kidwai, 1992). Port primacy had shifted from Chennai to Kolkata after its establishment in the late seventeenth century and remained with it well until the end of the nineteenth century. The primacy shifted between Kolkata and Mumbai between 1900 and 1950 and as a deviation of Kolkata's main shipping link from Mumbai to Colombo from the 1920s onwards, while loosing some of its traffic and rank to Mumbai.

After 1945, the trend reversed and substantial growth occurred, from 632 calls in 1945 to 1,059 in 1965. A noticeable decline again is observed in the 1980s followed by an increase in 1990 at around 1,000 calls. Kolkata and Mumbai continued to remain the main ports after India became independent but the share of these two ports steadily decreased down to 19.6% in 2000. This was mainly caused by the emergence of other ports in the country such as Chennai, Kandla, Mormugao and Visakhapatnam.

After 1945, the number of routes and ports in India continuously increased until 1975 and remained stable. The average share of international calls remained around 71% before and after 1945. In terms of regional trade, India had frequent connections with Sri Lanka (30 calls on average) and Myanmar (40 calls on average) during the colonial period. After 1945, the routes with Sri Lanka continued but the ones with Myanmar decreased to less than ten calls 1970 onwards. Routes with Pakistan were slightly more frequent during the colonial period with an average of 22.2, which reduced to 20 after the partition of the countries.

Myanmar

Across the Bay of Bengal, Myanmar has historically traded with Indian ports. However, the number of calls decreased after the independence of the country and after the establishment of the Socialist regime.

In 1890, the 218 calls and 97 routes of Myanmar witnessed important fluctuations until 1945.[8] In the post-colonial period, a growth is observed from 1950 onwards with a peak in 1960 followed by a decline until 1975.[9] This decline continued thereafter at a faster rate. On average, there were 176 calls during colonial period which decreased to 68 after the independence and 44 after 1970. Similar trends are found for the number of routes as well. Domestic calls are recorded until 1965 but disappear after 1970. The share of regional calls had two spikes in 1920 and 1945. Both corresponded to the timing of the local lows in the trends, which indicates a decrease in international calls and a less significant fluctuation in regional calls. After 1970, there was a clear expansion in the share of international calls to Southeast Asia, with Singapore as the main destination.

Yangon was the major port in Myanmar and Sittwe, Mawlamyine and Pathein were secondary ports that had more than ten calls at least once in the sample years in our data.

Pakistan

The data on Pakistan shows a gradual increase during the colonial period and from 1950 after independence. The growth after 1950 was led by the expansion of international routes and calls. The first spike is downwards in 1900 and shows a sharp decline in international calls, which became about one sixth of 1895. The second spike is upwards in in 1925 and was led by the expansion of international calls to UK and Europe. The third spike in 1975 was driven by the expansion of calls to almost all of the regions, as in 1965.[10] The major port in Pakistan was Karachi throughout the century.[11] From 1985, Port Muhammad Bin Qasim appears as its secondary port. Gadani Beach and Gwadar also appeared in our data only four times with less than five calls and twice with only one call.

The domestic calls do not appear consistently and their number was as low as six or less. The regional calls with India, on the other hand, appeared constantly for the entire period. The destinations in India were mainly Mumbai and Kolkata. Colombo a also consistently appeared from 1945. As discussed in the section on Bangladesh, the geographical separation of East and Western Pakistan resulted in domestic trade being carried only by maritime shipments. This route had appeared after the partition of the countries and decreased in frequency after the independence of Bangladesh. The share of regional calls was more than 20% until 1970 but remained under 15% until 1995.

During the colonial period, the United Kingdom had a high share in Pakistan's international trade, with an average of 42%, like the rest of Europe (31%). The opposite trend occurred with the Middle East and Southeast Asia, with their respective shares increasing from 10% and 2% during the colonial period to 27% and 20% after 1985. It is interesting to note that while the routes to the Middle East are evenly distributed among different countries, the routes to Southeast Asia are mostly to Singapore.

Sri Lanka

The traffic evolution of Sri Lanka drastically differs from the rest of the region, with less differentiation between colonial and post-colonial periods. While certain fluctuations are observed, most of the variables in our data are stable within certain ranges. For example, the number of calls started at 114 in 1890 with a minimum at 94 in 1895 and a maximum at 275 in 1990. The major port was Colombo and the secondary ports were Galle and Trincomalee.[12] The other ports had a minor role with less than ten calls on average, such as Point Pedro, Jaffna, Pulmoddai, Hambantota and Kankesanturai.

The destinations became more international as the average share of international calls was 65.5% in the colonial and 72.0% in the post-colonial periods. The average share of regional calls was 32.1% in the colonial and 25.4% in the post-colonial periods. One noticeable change in the trends is the increase in the share of international calls to Southeast Asia from an average of 7% during colonial period to 22% after 1985.

Conclusion

With the newly available data of vessel movements, we have examined the historical evolution of maritime networks in South Asia and its component countries and ports. One main result is to show that such networks were reconfigured after these countries achieved their independence from the colonial rule. These changes were very pronounced in Bangladesh, Pakistan and Myanmar and changed their politico-economic relations, such as the increased significance of Bangladesh and Pakistan. As it served as the hinterland of Kolkata, Bangladesh's disconnection with Kolkata after the partition led the substantial growth of Chittagong. The number of calls were nearly ten times more than the level during colonial period. Myanmar is a contrasting example. Its good connection to international markets through rice exports was impacted by the independence, especially due to the insular policies of the Socialistic military government. Within India, the pattern of port hierarchies remained somewhat stable overtime, notwithstanding the emergence of secondary hubs and a reorientation from British dominance to a polarization upon Southeast Asia and the Singapore hub.

There are, at least, two points to discuss from these contrasts, institutional changes and regional structures. Institutional changes are critical for the stable trade relations. As Myanmar took the radical step for socialism, the trade relation dramatically disappeared. Such changes were clearly shown from the vessel movements. Second is the regional structure. As each port represents its hinterland, the trade linkage on the land is also reflected on its rise and fall, i.e. the rise of Chittagong reflects its disconnection from Kolkata. Similar cases can be found in Punjab and Karachi. Further research shall refine the analysis of the impacts of specific events and concentrate on hinterland dynamics in response to the rise and fall of port cities.

No consistent pattern has been followed by the Indian ports in terms of their growth in shipping and their ranks in the port hierarchy. However, the general trend in the colonial period was that the colonial ports showed positive growth whereas the pre-colonial and intermediate and minor ports remained stagnant or indicated insignificant growth. This pattern changed in the post independence period and then again in the post-Reform period after 1991. The primate ports now show a relative loss of cargo handled and hence shipping in comparison to the intermediate and minor ports. In the post Reform period the Indian port system is no more path-dependent and is responding to the contingencies surfacing from the globalization and containerization process in the country (Kidwai, 2013).

Further research shall investigate how vessel movement data can reflect the two port policies of India and China, which are the big economic and strategic players in the Indian Ocean region. Under its "String of Pearls" strategy, China has set up ports in strategic maritime countries such as Myanmar and Pakistan. It also proposes to set up ports in Bangladesh, Sri Lanka, and the Maldives. These countries will attract Chinese shipping hubs to their own ports on foreign soils. India too has created a "Sagarmala" (Garland of the Oceans) port project under which six new major ports will be set up. India also has an "Act East" policy. Consequently, the newer state-owned and captive private ports on the east coast, which have been geared to the demands and specifications of international trade, especially with China and their Asian trade block, are increasing their share of cargo and are growing very fast.

Acknowledgements

We gratefully acknowledge financial support from the Institute of Developing Economies, JETRO. The research leading to these results has received funding from the European Research Council under the European Union's Seventh Framework Programme (FP/2007–2013) / ERC Grant Agreement n. [313847] "World Seastems".

Notes

1 Some parts of India were governed indirectly as princely states. Details of historical accounts of various British colonies can be found, for example, in Carrington (1950).
2 Princely states later joined either Pakistan or India.
3 Under the one-party system, due to the failure in economic policies, high inflation was severe and democratization movements advanced in 1988. The military government had kept their power by declaring martial law and suppressing free election in 1990. See, for example, Topich and Leitich (2013) in detail.
4 We omit the results for Maldives since it has low frequency in our data. In brief, there were 18 calls and four international routes throughout the period, with a first appearance in 1965 that became continuous only after 1985.
5 Exports of jute were predominantly dispatched from Kolkata. Chittagong served as a minor port. The export quantity of jute in million maunds was, for example in 1894–95, 12 from Kolkata and 0.4 from Chittagong (Ahmad, 1958: 258).
6 Khulna port opened in 1951. In the second half of the first year, the total trade amounted at 16.5 million rupees, 98% being Pakistani merchandise. On the other hand, cargo trade for import was not only with Pakistan and for export it was totally with other foreign countries (Ahmad, 1958: 264–271).

7 The capacity of Chittagong port had substantially increased. The number of handled cargo increased around 15 times from 1945 to 1955 (Ahmad, 1958: 270).

8 Despite the Depression of the 1930s, the number of calls peaked in this period. This corresponded to the trends in export volumes from chief Burma ports for the same period shown in Table 30 (Andrus, 1948: 216). On the comparative number of calls, in 1940, there were 1,377 steamers entering Yangon (Rangoon) whose traffic, exclusive of Burmese coastal traffic, was at least 828 (Andrus, 1948: 214–215).

9 The recovery to the pre-war level was not easy because the disruptions during war period were devastating (Andrus, 1948: 202–211).

10 On the capacity of the port, "Since Partition, the storage capacity has been increased substantially" and "ambitious" expansion had been installed by 1961. "In 1947 two shipping companies registered in Pakistan" and "by 1956, the seven shipping companies registered" for 20 merchant ships (Andrus and Mohammed, 1958: 244–249).

11 In 1843, "Karachi was a fishing village and small port with a population of only 14,000" (Andrus and Mohammed, 1958: 243).

12 Until the 1870s, the total shipping tonnages of Galle was larger than the one of Colombo. After the intensive investments in Colombo port in the 1880s, Colombo reached 80% of Sri Lankan trade value (Dharmasena, 1985).

References

Ahmad, N. (1958) *An Economic Geography of East Pakistan*. London: Oxford University Press.

Andrus, J.R. (1948) *Burmese Economic Life*. Stanford: Stanford University Press.

Andrus, J.R., Mohammed, A.F. (1958) *The Economy of Pakistan*. Oxford: Oxford University Press.

Bracken, G. (2015) *Asian Cities: From Colonial to Global*. Amsterdam, The Netherlands: University of Amsterdam Press.

Broeze, F. (1987) From imperialism to independence: The decline and re-emergence of Asian shipping. *The Great Circle*, 9(2): 73–95.

Broeze, F. (1996) The ports and port system of the Asian seas: An overview with historical perspective from c. 1750. *The Great Circle*, 18(2): 73–96.

Carrington, C. (1950) *The British Overseas: Exploits of a Nation of Shopkeepers*. London: Cambridge University Press.

Dharmasena, K. (1985) The port and dock workers of Colombo 1860–1960. *The Great Circle*, 7(2): 100–115.

Ducruet, C., Haule, S., Ait-Mohand, K., Marnot, B., Kosowska-Stamirowska, Z., Didier, L., Coche, M.A. (2015) Maritime shifts in the contemporary world economy: Evidence from the Lloyd's List corpus, 18–21 c. In: Ducruet, C. (Ed.), *Maritime Networks: Spatial Structures and Time Dynamics*. London and New York: Routledge Studies in Transport Analysis, pp. 134–160.

Eliot, E. (2003) Chorotype de la métropole portuaire d'Asie du Sud. *Mappemonde*, 69: 7–10.

Ghosh, P., De, P. (2001) Indian ports and globalisation: Grounding economics in geography. *Economic and Political Weekly*, 36(34): 3271–3283.

Iheduru, O.C. (1996) Post-Apartheid South Africa and its neighbours: A maritime transport perspective. *The Journal of Modern African Studies*, 34(1): 1–26.

Kidwai, A.H. (1989) Port cities in a national system of ports and cities: a geographical analysis of India in the 20th century. In: Broeze, F. (Ed.), *Brides of the Sea: Port Cities of Asia From the 16th–20th Centuries*. Honolulu: University of Hawaii Press, pp. 207–222.

Kidwai, A.H. (1992) Conceptual and methodological issues: Ports, port cities and port hinterlands. In: Banga, I. (Ed.), *Ports and their Hinterlands in India, 1700–1950*. New Delhi: Manohar Publications.

Kidwai, A.H. (2013) *Ports as Infrastructure, Ports as Cities: The Indian Port System From Colonialism to Globalization*. Project Report, Indian Council for Social Science Research, India.

Murphey, R. (1964) The city in the swamp: Aspects of the site and early growth of Calcutta. *The Geographical Journal*, 130(2): 241–256.

Smith, A. (1776) *An Inquiry Into the Nature and Causes of the Wealth of Nations*. London: Methuen & Co., Ltd.

Todd, D., Zhang, L. (1993) Political and technical factors impinging on port operations: The case of Manchuria. *Geojournal*, 30(4): 441–454.

Topich, W.J., Leitich, K.A. (2013) *The History of Myanmar*. Santa Barbara, CL: Greenwood.

Wang, C., Ducruet, C. (2013) Regional resilience and spatial cycles: Long-term evolution of the Chinese port system (221BC-2010AD). *Tijdschrift voor Economische en Sociale Geografie*, 104(5): 521–538.

Wilson Anti-Slavery Collection. (1840) *Present Condition of British India, 1840*. The University of Manchester, John Rylands University Library.

Afterword

Jan Hoffmann

Globalized trade and production depend on shipping connectivity, i.e. the possibilities for people, companies and countries to trade with each-other through their seaports and maritime transport networks. Most trade is seaborne – and if we include the raw materials and inputs, there is practically nothing you can buy that does not have some component that has crossed an ocean on a ship.

Analysing the economics of port and shipping services makes use of all kinds of tools and approaches available to economists, including finance, game theory, econometrics and the like. One area of research that has gained importance in recent years is networks analysis, benefiting from a growing pool of available data and modelling tools. The book *Advances in Shipping Data Analysis and Modeling* makes a timely and outstanding contribution in this regards.

As Ducruet points out, the book aims at, first, building bridges between different works on shipping; second, mainstream the research; and third, raise awareness about its importance to a wider audience. It is published at a moment where several international organizations have embarked on initiatives to better understand and promote transport connectivity. UNCTAD's Review of Maritime Transport 2017 has a special focus on shipping connectivity; the G20 initiated the Global Infrastructure Connectivity Alliance (GICA); and the WTO 2017 Aid-for-Trade Review focuses on Promoting Trade, Inclusiveness and Connectivity for Sustainable Development.

Most manufactured goods are transported by containerized liner shipping services. Containerships have a fixed schedule and call at several ports during the journey. Containers with goods belonging to different shippers are loaded, transhipped or unloaded in each port. This type of service is comparable to a city's metro network, where metro stations are connected to one or more lines. A passenger will look at the timetables and options to change from one line to another to arrive at his or her final destination.

For liner shipping services, we compare the "connectivity" of different countries by looking at the ships' schedules and the options importers and exporters have to connect to overseas markets through the liner shipping network. In this context, and building upon our UNCTAD Review of Maritime Transport 2017,[1] the following lessons learned and considerations for future research and policy options may be worth highlighting as an afterword to *Advances in Shipping Data Analysis and Modeling*.

The research agenda

Improved port services and shipping connectivity can help reduce trade costs and have a direct positive bearing on trade volumes. Low transport connectivity remains an important hurdle for many developing countries to connect to global markets. Especially land-locked countries and small islands are confronted with major challenges, as they have access to fewer, often less reliable and costlier transport connections. As maritime transport continues to be the main mode of transport for most developing countries' imports and exports, it is important to identify policies that help improve maritime transport connectivity. When negotiating trade deals, preparing trade policies or planning transport infrastructure investments, the research and forecasts can be significantly improved if data on maritime transport networks is included.

Further research needs to be done on specific components of shipping connectivity, as well as linkages to other dimensions of transport and trade connectivity. E-Commerce, global value chains and technological advances trigger demand for better digital and other forms of connectivity. There are opportunities from modern network technologies such as cargo and vessel tracking and numerous other digital developments that can help enhance maritime connectivity. Researchers and policy makers need to consider maritime connectivity as a component of broader dimensions of connectivity.

The future of shipping networks

Ships continue to get bigger on all markets, thanks to cascading and an order-book with larger ships than the existing fleet. The difference in size between the largest and the smallest ships will also increase, making it more economical to transship containers, to benefit from the optimum vessel size for different legs of the total route. Not making use of potential cost savings will be ever more difficult to justify. There is an increased awareness and mainstreaming of sustainability criteria in public policies; the promotion of short sea shipping is one way to reduce CO_2 emissions, as shipping is more energy efficient than any other mode of transport.

Shipping networks will also be affected by the continued trend of mergers and alliances. While today, freight rates are still very low, it is not a question of if but when markets will rebound, and a more concentrated market, with fewer carriers and alliances, will pose serious threats to competition authorities that aim at avoiding oligopolistic or even monopolistic markets. The challenge is not only for shippers to have a choice between service providers, but also for the partners in the supply chain, notably the seaports, who will come under growing pressure to give in to the demands of shipping lines.

One specific policy recommendation concerns cabotage. Limitations to national or regional cabotage markets can lead to unnecessary inefficiencies and loss of maritime connectivity. Allowing international lines to carry domestic trade and feedering cargo can enhance both, the competitiveness of the nation's seaports, and the access of importers and exporters to international shipping services.

Challenges for seaports and the hinterland

Important determinants of a country's maritime connectivity are beyond the control of policy makers. Notably, the geographic position and the country's own trade volumes are difficult to change. It is in the national seaports that investments can make a difference. These investments may take the form of PPPs, as most common user ports such as container terminals have in recent decades been concessioned or involved the private sector in some other form.

For ports along the same route, it makes sense to plan port investments jointly to accommodate the vessels that are expected to serve this route in future. Regional organizations and international development partners can play an important role when planning the port investments in countries within the same region.

Most seaports serve more than one country, be it through in-land connections or via transshipment operations and not every country can be host to the region's main hub port. Inter-port competition will encourage port operators to maximise their efficiency and pass on those efficiency gains to their clients, the shippers and shipping lines. Inter-port competition should not be limited to national seaports, but also to neighboring countries' ports. Efficient trucking markets, rail and road infrastructure, as well as transit regimes, are all important instruments to enhance inter-port competition.

Pressure from shipping lines to invest in seaports to accommodate ever larger ships, especially for transshipment operations, may not be worth the extra cost. Without additional volumes, increasing just the ship size will reduce the effective capacity of the seaport, as it would require larger yards to handle the same total volume.

Facilitating trade and its transport

Maritime connectivity benefits from a larger hinterland for the seaports to capture additional cargo from neighbouring countries. Transit can be facilitated in line with international standards and recommendations, including those of the United Nations, the WCO and the WTO. Regional and sub-regional transit regimes may also help and in fact are often more ambitious than the minimum requirements of the multilateral regimes.

Many international agreements are already in place to support trade and transport facilitation. They include the Revised Kyoto Convention of the World Customs Organization (WCO) and the UN transport facilitation conventions managed inter alia by the UN Economic Commission for Europe (UNECE), such as the TIR Convention, as well as the FAL convention of the International Maritime Organization (IMO). In addition, many international standards and guidelines cover international trade procedures, such as the UNECE and UN-CEFACT

Recommendations. These Conventions and standards all contribute in one way or another to facilitating elements of the trade transaction chain.

Outlook

Preparing for future research on seaports and maritime networks, identifying options for policy makers and helping ministries of transport and trade to plan their investments all benefit from the analysis of shipping data analysis and modelling. The book makes a substantial contribution, and in view of the growing relevance of the topic, its authors will certainly have more than enough questions and data to continue their research for years to come.

Note

1 UNCTAD: Review of Maritime Transport 2017, Geneva. http://unctad.org/RMT

Epilogue

Brian Slack

It was André Vigarié (1979) who coined the term *Port Trytique,* referring to the port as a spatial and functional entity that is fundamentally shaped by its connections with a hinterland and a foreland. Two parts of the *Tryptique*, the port itself and the hinterland, have historically been at the heart of maritime studies. Bird's 'Anyport'(1963) model of internal port morphology and the model of hinterland network development of Taaffe et al. (1963) served as catalysts for academic network research from the 1960s up to the present. The foreland of ports was much slower to receive attention, and it wasn't until the expansion of containerisation that linkages between ports began to generate wide academic interest. Here, the work of Fleming and Hayuth (1994) on the concept of centrality and intermediacy was important. Today, shipping networks and inter-port linkages have become the foci of research in a wide range of disciplines and have certainly redressed the former imbalance in the *Tryptique*. The chapters in this book have captured some of the scope, range and significance of recent academic research on shipping networks. These networks are analysed over different time dimensions, over a range of geographic scales and from a wide set of disciplinary perspectives.

What can be learned from this diversity?

1   As suggested in Chapter 1 this type of research is strongly shaped by data. The field of shipping networks has begun to 'take off' by accessing new and different data sources. Some of the more traditional sources were port lists of vessel arrivals and departures, and carrier data on their service networks and timetables, as for example Chapters 6 and 18. Vessel log books have been found to be useful in reconstructing shipping services in the past, and in Chapter 4, they are used to provide information on past climate changes. Commercial intelligence on shipping as obtained from Lloyds List form the basis of historical network analyses carried out in many chapters: 12, 16, 17, 19, 21, 23 and 24. Undoubtedly, the availability of Automatic Identification of Shipping (AIS) has provided a boon to academic research, providing a means of updating the network structures derived from Lloyds, but also forming the network data source employed in Chapters 11and 15. AIS was also used innovatively in Chapter 15 to map fishing zones. Chapter 10 employed flow data to convert into spatial structures.

Each of these data sources possesses advantages and constraints. Ship logs are uneven, both in terms of the quality of the information recorded, and by the fact that observations may be recording winds, sea conditions and visibility on the day of passage, but the next day, after the ship has moved on from that location, the weather may have changed. Shipping schedules may not in fact be followed, as lateness may result in a vessel call being skipped; ports may be by-passed because of lack of cargo, and,ships may be switched to another service. *Lloyd's List* relies on agency information that inevitably does not cover all ports in all trades. AIS data may be a panacea, but to convert the raw data is exceedingly complex and tiresome, in particular the problem of assigning non-movements to ports, as is recognised in Chapter 11. The latter problem may be overcome as in Chapter 12 and several others by purchasing data from a propriety filter, such as Lloyd's Maritime Intelligence Unit that does identify ports, but the data is very costly. AIS-based data is also somewhat imprecise, since there is no indication of what is actually taking place at each port call: cargo transfer, bunkering, ship supplies or repair? Interregional flow data have many limitations, particularly in determining actual paths. Thus, in Chapter 10, flows from Asia to the US East Coast ports are shown to be via Panama, whereas the majority of this trade is shipped overland from US West Coast ports or follows the longer Suez route.

Chapters 9 and 22 provide different perspectives on shipping and networks. In Chapter 9, many of the routes through the North West Passage displayed in maps of the future ice free Arctic are shown to be unreal, and the actual services today are limited and spatially constrained. This is emphasised in Chapter 22, where risk maps based on ice conditions and vessel type indicate that large parts of the North West Passage are restricted to narrow windows of a week or two for non-ice reinforced vessels.

2   The chapters provide insights into the many factors that shape shipping and port networks. Of course, port conditions and port hinterland productivity are important considerations and are investigated in many chapters, especially Chapter 13, thus confirming the *Tryptique* concept. Technology, too, is demonstrated to have given rise to significant adjustments in shipping networks (Chapter 12). However, it is noteworthy that many chapters examined political changes, including political independence, embargoes etc, (chapters 5, 8, 19, 21 and 24). Political and governance issues have been largely ignored up to this point in shipping network research, but it is evident that in a large number of regional cases these factors have played a determining role. With the present global threats of embargoes and protectionism these are clearly factors that have a powerful effect on network structure.

3   There is an overwhelming reference to container shipping in the chapters that focus on recent and contemporary shipping activity. Yet other trades, including cruise, short sea shipping and bulk, possess very different service network characteristics, and they account for an important percentage of all vessel movements and cargoes handled. Only Chapter 7 provides a case study of coastal shipping. Even here bulk and general cargoes are lumped

together despite their internal differentiation. It must be stated however that with the possible recent exception of cruise shipping these other trades have received far less attention than the container business in the wider academic literature.

Where do we go from here?

Given the importance of data to shipping network research as shown in this book, it is likely that data will continue to be an important issue in the future. There remain challenges in how existing types of data sources are used, and I am convinced that further methodological innovations of the types employed in several of the chapters here will continue. A major future challenge is big data and data mining. Chapter 10 in this book uses a wide range of commodity flow data along with GIS to demonstrate US seaborne trade data. The challenges are formidable since much of the data is not spatially specified. Thus while US-Canada and US-Mexico trade flows are among the most important overall, a significant proportion of these flows involve rail and road shipments. and as noted above flows from East Asia to the US East Coast do not all use the Panama Canal. The non-spatial character of most data sets represents a challenge to the use of data mining in network analysis.

As our present understanding of the relationships between container shipping networks widens, with recognition of network evolution over time, and assessments of relationships between port city and hinterland economies, inland connections, technology and political factors, it is time to consider other issues. Container shipping is becoming increasingly differentiated by vessel size. How do the vessel size networks differ? Larger ships may be expected to be deployed on the longer routes, but to what extent is this true? As mentioned above, it is important to differentiate networks by the types of trade, and bulk shipments in particular remain under-studied at present.

A topic that has important network implications is that of resilience. Container and cruise shipping in particular require service reliability. Customers expect the vessels will arrive and depart on time (Slack et al., forthcoming). Yet there are many factors that can disrupt a service, including weather, accidents, breakdowns, strikes, delays in earlier ports of call and attacks. This is beginning to receive attention in the Operations Research literature (Brouer et al., 2013; Reinhardt et al., 2016), where the problems of delays along a service string are modelled and solved. In this book, Chapter 18 explores the vulnerabilities of shipping routes to disruptions and attacks using game theory to identify the relative danger at key 'choke points' where ships are concentrated. The question of network and service resilience is a key question for ship service providers, supply chains and governments and network characteristics have an important role to play in measuring resilience and in providing solutions.

A corner has been turned! Shipping networks are becoming ever more integrated into maritime studies. I believe this book will make a contribution to furthering the trend.

References

Bird, J.H. (1963) *The Major Seaports of the United Kingdom*. London: Hutchison.

Brouer, B.D., Dirksen, J., Pisinger, D., Plum, C.E.M., Vaaben, B. (2013) The vessel schedule recovery problem (VSRP) – A MIP model for handling disruptions in liner shipping. *European Journal of Operation Research*, 224(2): 362–374.

Fleming, D.K., Hayuth, Y. (1994) Spatial characteristics of transportation hubs: Centrality and intermediacy. *Journal of Transport Geography*, 2(1): 3–18.

Reinhardt, L.B., Plum, C.E.M., Pisinger, D., Sigurd, M.M., Vial, G.T.P. (2016) The liner shipping berth scheduling problem with transit times. *Transportation Research Part E*, 86(2): 116–128.

Slack B., Comtois C., Wiegmans B., Witte P. (forthcoming) Ships time in port. *International Journal of Shipping and Transport Logistics*.

Taaffe, E.J., Morrill, R.L., Gould, P.R. (1963) Transport expansion in underdeveloped countries: A comparative analysis. *Geographical Review*, 53: 503–529.

Vigarié, A. (1979) *Ports de commerce et vie littorale*. Paris: Hachette.

Index